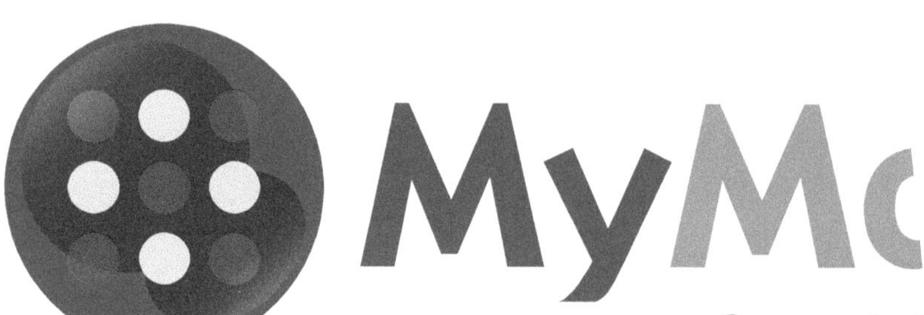

for Key Stage 3

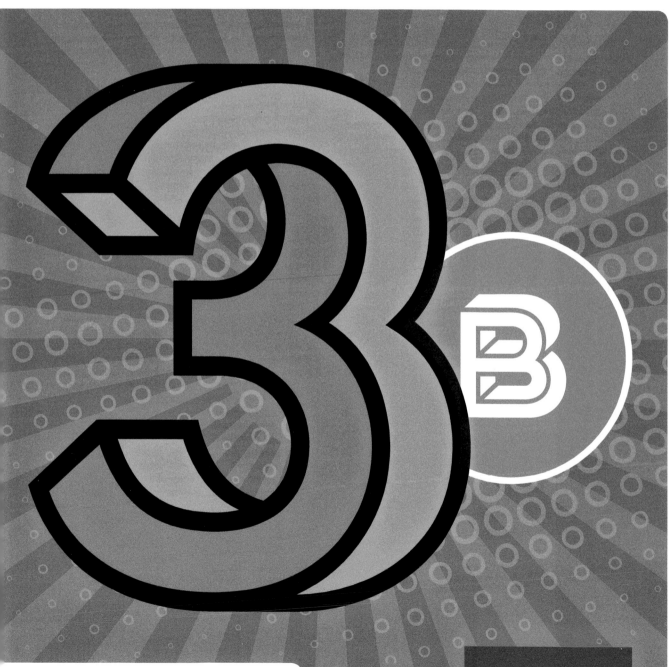

3B

owered by MyMaths.co.uk

OXFORD
UNIVERSITY PRESS

OXFORD
UNIVERSITY PRESS

Great Clarendon Street, Oxford, OX2 6DP, United Kingdom

Oxford University Press is a department of the University of Oxford. It furthers the University's objective of excellence in research, scholarship, and education by publishing worldwide. Oxford is a registered trade mark of Oxford University Press in the UK and in certain other countries

First published in 2014

British Library Cataloguing in Publication Data
Data available

978-0-19-830466-1

12

Paper used in the production of this book is a natural, recyclable product made from wood grown in sustainable forests. The manufacturing process conforms to the environmental regulations of the country of origin.

Printed and bound by CPI Group (UK) Ltd, Croydon, CR0 4YY

Acknowledgements

Although we have made every effort to trace and contact copyright holders before publication this has not been possible in all cases. If notified, the publisher will rectify any errors or omissions at the earliest opportunity.

p2–3: James Steidl/Shutterstock; **p16–17:** Gong Bing/xh/Xinhua Press/Corbis; **p20:** Quayside/Dreamstime; **p21:** Naiyyer/Dreamstime; **p34–35:** Science & Society Picture Library/Getty Images; **p52–53:** The Hound/Bigstock; **p67:** Speedo101/Dreamstime; **p74–75:** Rui Ferreira/Shutterstock; **p80:** Pipa100/Dreamstime; **p82:** Kated/Dreamsitme; **p90–91:** Monty Rakusen/Cultura/Corbis; **p106:** vovan/shutterstock; **p132–133:** Vasily Smirnov/Dreamstime; **p139:** Gaby Kooijman/Shutterstock; **p142:** Denis Rozhnovsky/Shutterstock; **p145:** Lee Martin/Alamy; **p162–163:** Ken Gillespie/All Canada Photos/Corbis; **p180–181:** Superstock/Glow Images; **p183:** De Agostini/Getty Images; **p189:** Boris Mrdja/Shutterstock; **p196–197:** Photodisc/OUP; **p205:** Jibmeyer/Dreamstime; **p212–213:** Corbis/Digital Stock/OUP; **p219:** Allan Bell/Alamy; **p232–233:** Fyletto/Istockphoto; **p242:** Clearviewstock/Dreamstime; **p243:** Flynt/Dreamstime; **p248–249:** P.Burghardt/Shutterstock; **p266–267:** PetrePlesea/Istockphoto; **p280:** Mquirk/Dreamstime; Lawrence Willard/Dreamstime; **p281:** Denis Rozhnovsky/shutterstock; **p286–287:** Pavel L Photo and Video/Shutterstock; **p288:** Corepics VOF/Shutterstock; Fuzzbones/Dreamstime.

Case Studies:
Scol/Dreamstime; Stefan Klein/iStockphoto; Mary Evans/iStockphoto; Mikhail Kokhanchikov/iStockphoto; Kmitu/iStockphoto; Juri Samsonov/Dreamstime; Terraxplorer/iStockphoto; Timothy Large/iStockphoto; Martin Applegate/iStockphoto; Lisa F Young/Dreamstime; Blackred/iStockphoto; Robert Mizerek/Dreamstime; Jf123/Dreamstime; Andy Brown/Dreamstime; Online Creative Media/iStockphoto; OUP/Corel; Dean Turner/iStockphoto; Heather Down/iStockphoto; Hulton Archive/iStockphoto; James Davidson/Dreamstime; Brianna May/iStockphoto; Stefanie Leuker/Dreamstime; Viktor Pravdica/Dreamstime; Karam Miri/iStockphoto; Giorgio Fochesato/iStockphoto; Greenwales/Alamy; Mehmet Salih Guler/iStockphoto; Mediagfx/Dreamstime; Dusan Zidar/Dreamstime; Dmitry Kovyazin/Dreamstime; Rixie/Dreamstime; Feng Yu/Dreamstime; Valentin Garcia/Dreamstime; John Archer/iStockphoto; Christophe Test/Dreamstime; Achim Prill/iStockphoto; Lucian Coman/iStockphoto; Sierpniowka/Dreamstime; Felinda/iStockphoto; Robyn Mackenzie/Dreamstime; Elena Elisseeva/Dreamstime; TT/iStockphoto; Fernando Soares/Dreamstime; Jan Rihak/iStockphoto; Gerald Hng/Dreamstime; Hanquan Chen/iStockphoto; Yakobchuk/Dreamstime.

Artwork by: Phil Hackett, Giulia Rivolta, Katri Valkamo & QBS.

Contents

About this book

MyMaths for Key Stage 3 is an exciting new series designed for schools following the new National Curriculum for mathematics. This book has been written to help you to grow your mathematical knowledge and skills during Key Stage 3.

Each topic starts with an Introduction that shows why it is relevant to real life and includes a short *Check in* exercise to see if you are ready to start the topic.

Inside each chapter, you will find lots of worked examples and questions for you to try along with interesting facts. There's basic practice to build your confidence, as well as problem solving. You might also notice the **4-digit codes** at the bottom of the page, which you can type into the search bar on the *MyMaths* site to take you straight to the relevant *MyMaths* lesson for more help in understanding and extra practice.

At the end of each chapter you will find *My Summary*, which tests what you've learned and suggests what you could try next to improve your skills even further. The *What next?* box details further resources available in the supporting online products.

Maths is a vitally important subject, not just for you while you are at school but also for when you grow up. We hope that this book will lead to a greater enjoyment of the subject and that it will help you to realise how useful maths is to your everyday life.

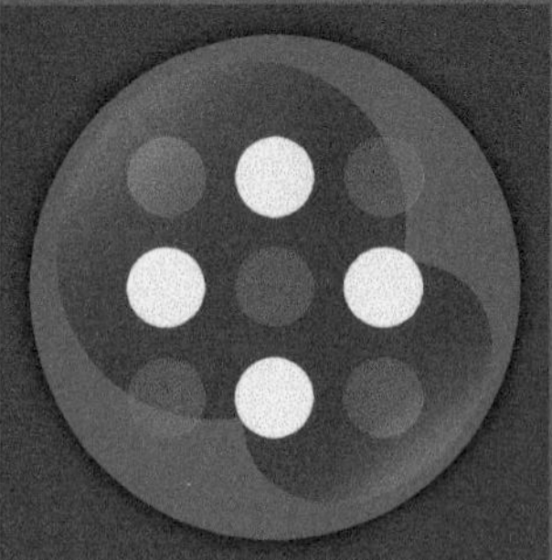

1 Whole numbers and decimals

Introduction

On the 3rd January 2004 the Mars Exploration Rover landed on the Martian surface within 200 m of its target. Navigators used radio signals sent by three antennae spread around the Earth's surface, to control the flight of the spacecraft. An error in their distance calculations of even 5 cm on Earth would have led to an error on Mars of over 400 m.

In a journey of 300 million miles the navigators and scientists needed to work to incredibly high levels of accuracy.

What's the point?

Scientists, engineers and nurses need to know how accurate their measurements must be, otherwise there could be disastrous consequences. An understanding of rounding is vital in all walks of life.

Objectives

By the end of this chapter, you will have learned how to ...

- Multiply and divide numbers by powers of 10.
- Multiply and divide numbers written in index form.
- Round whole numbers to a given power of 10.
- Round decimals to 2 decimal places.
- Round numbers to 1 significant figure.
- Use rounding to make estimates.
- Use factors, multiples and primes.

Check in

1 Work out

a 2×10 **b** 4×10^0 **c** $70 \div 10$ **d** $750 \div 100$

2 Put these decimal numbers in order.

3.825, 3.83, 3.085, 3.8, 3.9

Starter problem

If you fire a projectile such as rocket or a missile at an angle, you can calculate how far it will travel.

You call this distance its range.

$$\text{Range} = \frac{2v^2(\sin\alpha)(\cos\alpha)}{g}$$

α = angle at which you fire your rocket

v = starting speed (velocity) of your projectile

$g = 9.8\,\text{m/s}^2$

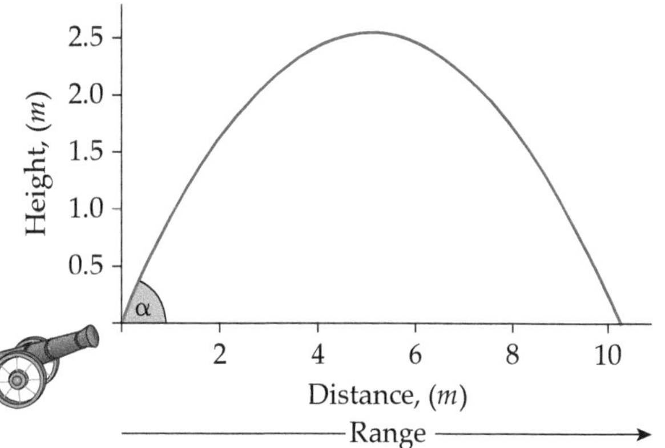

At what speed and angle should you fire a projectile so that it travels an exact distance of 100 km?

1a Powers of 10

- You can write all **powers** of 10 using **index notation**.
- The power is also called the **index**. It tells you how many times 10 is multiplied by itself.

1 thousand (kilo)	= 1000	= 10 × 10 × 10	$= 10^3$
1 hundred	= 100	= 10 × 10	$= 10^2$
1 ten	= 10		$= 10^1$
1 unit	= 1		$= 10^0$
1 tenth	$= \frac{1}{10}$	$= \frac{1}{10^1}$	$= 10^{-1}$
1 hundredth (centi)	$= \frac{1}{100}$	$= \frac{1}{10^2}$	$= 10^{-2}$
1 thousandth (milli)	$= \frac{1}{1000}$	$= \frac{1}{10^3}$	$= 10^{-3}$

Any number to the power of zero is 1.

- You can multiply and divide by powers of 10 by moving digits.

Example

Calculate

a 2.5×10^3 **b** $0.27 \div 0.1$ **c** 2.6×0.01

Rewrite the calculations.

a 2.5×10^3
$= 2.5 \times 1000$

b $0.27 \div 0.1$
$= 0.27 \div \frac{1}{10}$

c 2.6×0.01
$= 2.6 \times \frac{1}{100}$

Simplify.

a $= 2500$

b $= 0.27 \times 10$
$= 2.7$

c $= 2.6 \div 100$
$= 0.026$

Dividing by $\frac{1}{10}$ is the same as multiplying by 10.

Multiplying by $\frac{1}{100}$ is the same dividing by 100

- You can multiply and divide numbers written in **index form** using these rules:
  - the indices are added when multiplying
    $10^6 \times 10^4 = 10^{6+4} = 10^{10}$
  - the indices are subtracted when dividing
    $10^8 \div 10^2 = 10^{8-2} = 10^6$

Example

Calculate

a $10^3 \times 10^2$ **b** $10^4 \div 10^1$

a $10^3 \times 10^2 = 10^{3+2} = 10^5$ $(10 \times 10 \times 10) \times (10 \times 10) = 10^5$

b $10^4 \div 10^1 = 10^{4-1} = 10^3$ $\frac{10 \times 10 \times 10 \times 10}{10} = 10 \times 10 \times 10 = 10^3$

Exercise 1a

1 Calculate

a 3×100 **b** $16 \div 10$ **c** 1.2×10000 **d** $3.7 \div 100$

e $180 \div 10$ **f** 13.2×100 **g** $75 \div 100$ **h** 0.93×1000

2 Calculate

a 37×0.1 **b** $78 \div 0.01$ **c** 5.1×0.1 **d** $9.3 \div 0.1$

e $8.3 \div 0.01$ **f** $0.48 \div 0.1$ **g** 0.54×0.01 **h** 483×0.01

3 Here are six number cards. Copy these statements and fill in the missing numbers using the cards.

10	100	1000	0.1	0.01	0.001

a $3 \times \square = 300$ **b** $0.43 \div \square = 43$ **c** $78 \div \square = 7.8$ **d** $2.1 \div \square = 21$

e $3 \times \square = 0.03$ **f** $0.02 \div \square = 20$ **g** $570 \times \square = 57$ **h** $3200 \div \square = 3.2$

4 2.5×10^3 is written in **standard form**.
Each of these numbers has been written in standard form. p.202 ›
Work out the size of each number.

a 2.7×10^3 **b** 5.6×10^4 **c** 1.3×10^5

d 6.2×10^4 **e** 4.1×10^6 **f** 2.7×10^2

g 3.6×10^3 **h** 1.4×10^4 **i** 1.7×10^5

5 Simplify these leaving your answer as a single power of the number.

a $10^2 \times 10^2$ **b** $10^4 \div 10^2$ **c** $10^3 \times 10^4$

d $10^5 \div 10^2$ **e** $10^3 \times 10^2$ **f** $10^5 \div 10^2$

g $10^7 \div 10^3$ **h** $10^5 \times 10$ **i** $10^6 \div 10^2$

Problem solving

6 Jenny works out $3.4 \times 23.4 = 79.56$ on her calculator.

a Use this information to work out these multiplications without using your calculator.

i 34×23.4 **ii** 3.4×2.34 **iii** 0.34×234

b What other multiplications can you work out using Jenny's calculation?

7 Hannah says that to multiply by a power of 10 you just look at the power and move the digits that number of places to the left.

a Investigate Hannah's method for multiplying by 10^2 and 10^3.

b Does Hannah's method work for dividing by powers of 10?

c Does Hannah's method work for negative powers of 10?

Did you know?

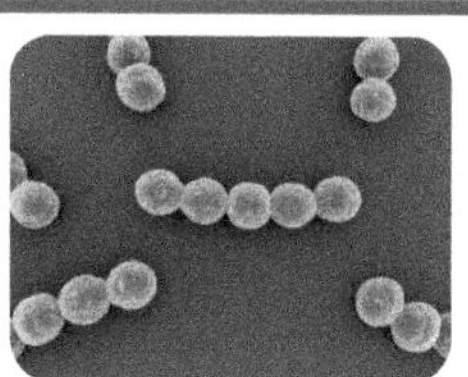

A micrometre μm (or micron) is a millionth of a metre. Bacteria are a few micrometres in size.

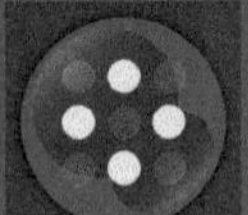

1b Rounding

- When you **round** a number, look at the next digit to see whether to round up or down.
- If the next digit is 5 or more, the number is rounded up.
- If it is less than 5, the number is rounded down.

6 ↑ 5.6 5.4 ↓ 5

Example

A young elephant has a mass of 229.476 kg.
What is the mass of the elephant to

a the nearest 100 kg
b the nearest 1 kg
c 2 decimal places (dp)?

In each case look at the next digit.

a The tens digit is 2, which rounds down: 229.476 kg
= 200 kg to the nearest 100 kg

b The tenths digit is 4, which rounds down: 229.476 kg
= 229 kg to the nearest 1 kg

c The thousandths digit is 6, which rounds up: 229.476 kg
= 229.48 kg to 2 dp

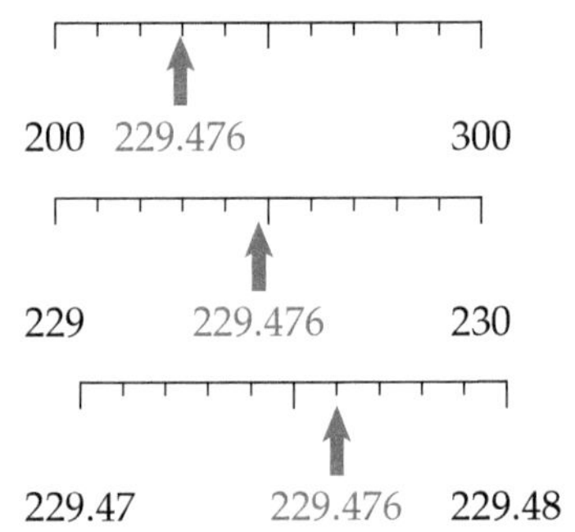

- You use **rounding** to make **estimates** in real-life examples.

Example

The weight of a blue whale is 181 tonnes (181 000 kg).
Jin wants to know if the weight of all the students in his school is more or less than that of the blue whale.
His school has 927 students and the mean weight of a student is 56.34 kg.

927 ≈ 900 Round 927 to the nearest 100.
56.34 ≈ 60 Round 56.34 kg to the nearest 10 kg.
p.94 ›
The total weight of the students ≈ 900 × 60 kg ≈ 54 000 kg ≈ 54 tonnes
So the combined students at Jin's school weigh a lot less than the blue whale.

Exercise 1b

1 Round each of these numbers to the nearest

i	1000	**ii**	100	**iii**	10		
a	3108	**b**	5677	**c**	9843	**d**	3992
e	13 175	**f**	26 394	**g**	3587.6	**h**	1965.384

2 Round each of these numbers to the nearest

i	whole number	**ii**	1 dp	**iii**	2 dp		
a	4.356	**b**	6.283	**c**	7.418	**d**	9.027
e	3.4035	**f**	17.6362	**g**	128.4347	**h**	0.7085

3 Use a calculator to do each of these calculations.
Write the answers to 2 dp.

a	1 ÷ 3	**b**	5 ÷ 16	**c**	13 ÷ 7	**d**	3 ÷ 11
e	7 ÷ 8	**f**	4896 ÷ 1000	**g**	8 ÷ 13	**h**	17 ÷ 12

4 Round each of these numbers to

i the nearest 100 **ii** the nearest whole number **iii** 1 dp

a	325.16	**b**	845.36	**c**	138.73	**d**	624.51
e	974.08	**f**	652.01	**g**	149.99	**h**	999.99

Problem solving

5 Solve each of these problems using rounding to estimate the answer.
Do not use a calculator.

a Which is heavier:
a group of 29 women with an average weight of 58.3 kg or
a group of 21 men with an average weight of 78.6 kg?
Explain and justify your answer.

b Heather weighs 48.6 kg.
Each day she eats a chocolate bar with a mass of 225 g.
In about how many days will Heather eat her own weight in chocolate bars?

6 Each of these measurements has already been rounded.
Write the greatest and smallest value each measurement could be.

a A giraffe is 6 m tall (to the nearest metre).

b A man is 1.8 m tall (to 1 dp)

c A VW Golf car weighs 1200 kg (to the nearest 100 kg)

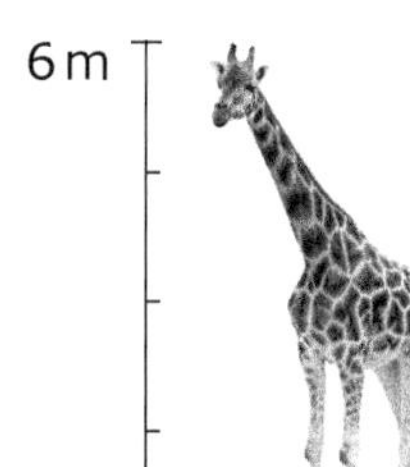

7 A swimming club decides to raise money for charity by swimming the equivalent distance from London to Newcastle, 457.4 km.
The length of the swimming pool is 24.8 m.
The average time to swim one length is 63 seconds.

a Estimate the number of lengths equivalent to the distance from London to Newcastle.

b Estimate the total time it takes to swim this equivalent distance.

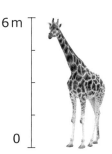

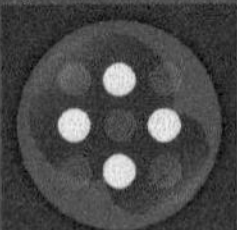

1c Factors, multiples and primes

- Any whole number can be written as the **product** of two **factors**.

The **factor pairs** of 12 are 1 × 12, 2 × 6, 3 × 4. So the factors of 12 are 1, 2, 3, 4, 6 and 12.

- The highest common factor (**HCF**) of two numbers is the largest number that will divide into both of them.

You could find the HCF of 12 and 20 by listing all their factors.
4 is the biggest number that appears in both lists.
So HCF = 4.

Number	Factors
12	1, 2, 3, 4, 6, 12
20	1, 2, 4, 5, 10, 20

- The lowest common multiple (**LCM**) of two numbers is the smallest **multiple** from their 'times tables'.

You could find the LCM of 12 and 20 by listing their multiples.
60 is the smallest number that appears in both lists.
LCM = 60.

Number	Multiples
12	12, 24, 36, 48, 60, ...
20	20, 40, 60, 80, ...

- A **prime** number only has two factors, 1 and itself.
  The first six prime numbers are 2, 3, 5, 7, 11, 13, ...

You can use a **factor tree** to find the **prime factors** of a number.

$360 = 2 \times 2 \times 2 \times 3 \times 3 \times 5 = 2^3 \times 3^2 \times 5$

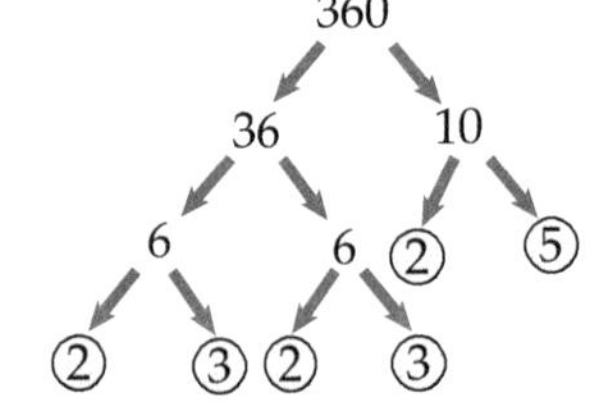

Example

Use factor trees to find the highest common factor and lowest common multiple of 126 and 105.

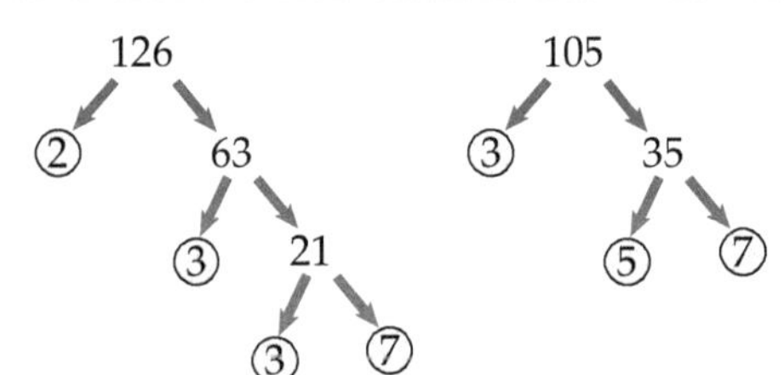

$126 = 2 \times 3 \times 3 \times 7$ $\quad 105 = 3 \times 5 \times 7$

126 and 105 have the prime factors 3 and 7 in common.

The HCF of 126 and 105 is $3 \times 7 = 21$.

The shortest list you can have that includes all the prime factors of 126 and 105 is $2 \times 3 \times 3 \times 5 \times 7$.

The LCM of 126 and 105 is $2 \times 3 \times 3 \times 5 \times 7 = 630$.

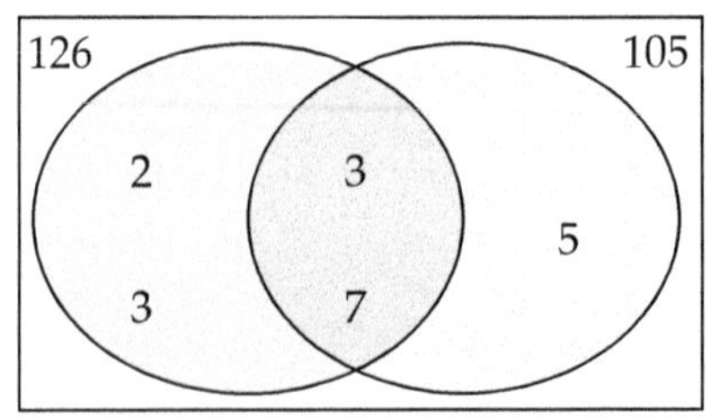

Exercise 1c

1 Find all the factor pairs for these numbers.
Then list all the factors for each number.

a 15 **b** 20 **c** 24 **d** 25
e 30 **f** 36 **g** 60 **h** 100

2 **a** Use this table to find the highest common factor of 16 and 24.
b Use the same method to find the highest common factor of these pairs of numbers.
i 12 and 28 **ii** 16 and 36 **iii** 32 and 40

Number	Factors
16	
24	

3 **a** Use this table to find the lowest common multiple of 12 and 15.
b Use the same method to find the lowest common multiple of these pairs of numbers.
i 8 and 10 **ii** 9 and 15 **iii** 6 and 14

Number	Multiples
12	
15	

4 **a** Write the next **three** prime numbers after these:
2, 3, 5, 7, ...
b Use factor trees to write these numbers as the product of their prime factors.
Give your answers using indices.

i 120 **ii** 48 **iii** 72 **iv** 200
v 300 **vi** 144 **vii** 1000 **viii** 720
ix 216 **x** 1080

120
12 10

5 **a** For each pair of numbers A and B, copy this Venn diagram and write in all the prime factors of the two numbers.
i A = 40, B = 110 **ii** A = 70, B = 42
iii A = 30, B = 54 **iv** A = 60, B = 210
v A = 150, B = 350 **vi** A = 90, B = 84
b Use your Venn diagrams to find the highest common factor and lowest common multiple of each pair of numbers.

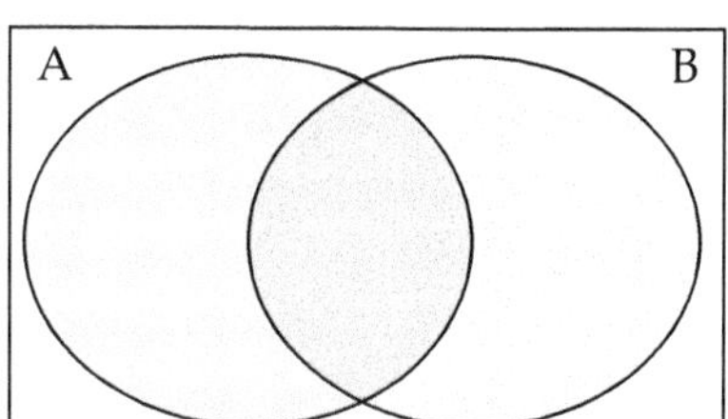

Problem solving

6 The HCF of 30 and the number N is $3 \times 5 = 15$. The LCM is 210. Find N.

30 N
2 3 5

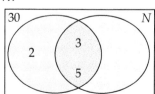

7 **a** Find all the positive integers less than 50 which have only three factors.
What do these numbers have in common?
b Find all the factors of 60. There are twelve of them.
Find another integer less than 100 which also has exactly twelve factors.

1d Estimating and approximating

To **round** a number to 1 **significant figure** (1 sf), you look at the value of the first non-zero digit in the number.

Example

Round each of these numbers to 1 sf.

a 2456 **b** 38 **c** 0.673

a The first digit is in the thousands column **2**456
so look at the hundreds digit: 2**4**56.
Round down to nearest 1000.
$2456 \approx 2000$ (1 sf)

b The first digit is in the tens column **3**8
so look at the units digit: 3**8**.
Round up to nearest 10.
$38 \approx 40$ (1 sf)

c The first non-zero digit is in the first decimal place 0.**6**73
so look at the second decimal place: 0.6**7**3.
Round up to 1 dp.
$0.673 \approx 0.7$ (1 sf)

Don't make this common mistake: $2456 \approx 2$ (1 sf). Common sense shows that this is wrong!

You can use rounding to make **estimates** in real-life situations.

Example

Siobhan buys and sells cheese.
In October she buys 5252 cheeses at a price of £3.29 a cheese.
Estimate the amount of money Siobhan spends on cheese each day.

Write the problem as a calculation.

$= \dfrac{5252 \times 3.29}{31}$

There are 31 days in October.

Round each number to 1 sf.

$\approx \dfrac{5000 \times 3}{30}$

≈ 500

Siobhan spends roughly £500 per day on cheese.

Exercise 1d

1 Round each of these numbers to 1 sf.

a 128 b 2437 c 94 d 18 372

e 4.56 f 0.379 g 138.7 h 17.363

2 Work out an estimate for each calculation.

a 237×29 b $29.8 \div 4.77$ c 2863×0.71

d 196×11.23 e $\frac{17.8 \times 235}{9.6}$ f $\frac{0.289 \times 978}{5.8}$

Start by rounding to 1 significant figure.

Problem solving

3 Work out an estimate for each of these problems.
Show all the numbers you have rounded and the calculations you have worked out.

a Nina spends £3511 on her food shopping each year.
Estimate her weekly shopping bill.

b At High Hill Language School the average height of a Year 9 boy is 1.64 m and the average height of a Year 9 girl is 1.49 m.
There are 68 boys and 79 girls in the school.
Estimate the total height of the students in Year 9.

Did you know?

The size of a dinosaur can be estimated from a single bone by assuming the ratio of bone length to total length is the same as for better-known dinosaurs in the same family.

4 The Run4Fun club want to raise money for Children in Need by organising a sponsored run.
Their target is to raise £44 444. There are 187 runners in the club.
The runners would like to run 874 miles between them.
Each runner can complete a mile in 6 minutes 45 seconds.

a About how far will each of the club members need to run?

b About how much money per mile will the runners need to raise?

c If the runners take turns, about how long will it take them to complete the sponsored run?

This is the distance from Land's End to John O' Groats.

5 Here are the daily, weekly, monthly and yearly costs of some household bills.
Use **estimation** to complete the table (do not work them out accurately).

Item	Daily cost	Weekly cost	Monthly cost	Yearly cost
TV licence				£139.50
Mobile phone			£24.99	
Food shopping		£88.95		
Newspaper	£0.85			
Total				

1 MySummary

Check out

You should now be able to ...

	Level	Test it ➡ Questions
✓ Multiply and divide numbers by powers of 10.	6	1
✓ Use index notation for integer powers.	6	2 – 3
✓ Round numbers to decimal places and significant figures.	6	4 – 5
✓ Use prime factors to find the HCF and LCM of pairs of numbers.	7	6 – 7
✓ Use rounding to make estimates.	7	8 – 9

Language	Meaning	Example
Index/indices	The index tells you how many times a number is multiplied by itself.	$5^3 = 5 \times 5 \times 5$
Significant figures (sf)	The first non-zero figures in a number.	The first two significant figures in 456.7 are 4 (400) and 5 (50).
Rounding	You can round numbers to a given number of sf.	456.7 rounded to 2 sf is 460
Estimate	Use rounding to approximate an answer.	$\frac{3.4 + 2.1}{1.9} \approx \frac{3 + 2}{2} = \frac{5}{2} = 2.5$
Factor	A number which divides exactly into another number.	1, 3, 9 and 27 are all factors of 27. $27 = 1 \times 27 = 3 \times 9$
Multiple	A multiple of a number appears in its times table.	6, 12, 18, 24... are all multiples of 6. $6 = 1 \times 6$, $12 = 2 \times 6$, $18 = 3 \times 6$, $24 = 4 \times 6$
Prime	A prime number has only two factors, the number itself and 1.	2, 3, 5, 7, 11, 13, 17... are all primes 1 is not a prime number
HCF (Highest common factor)	The highest number that is a factor of two or more numbers.	The HCF of 24 and 40 is 8.
LCM (Lowest common multiple)	The lowest number that is a multiple of two or more numbers.	The LCM of 24 and 40 is 120.

1 MyReview

1 Calculate

a 0.76×0.1 b $45.1 \div 0.01$
c 15.2×100 d 0.92×1000
e 216.8×0.01 f $0.36 \div 0.1$

2 Each of these numbers have been written in standard form. Work out the size of each number.

a 7.2×10^3 b 8.29×10^6
c 4.1×10^{-2} d 30.8×10^{-5}

3 Simplify leaving your answer as a single power of the number.

a $10^4 \times 10^3$ b $10^2 \times 10^5$
c $10^7 \times 10^9$ d $10^5 \div 10^4$
e $10^6 \div 10^3$ f $10^{10} \div 10^6$

4 Round 271.0985 to the nearest

a 100 b 10
c whole number d 1 dp
e 2 dp f 3 dp

5 Round each of these numbers to 1 sf.

a 462 b 25945
c 6.28 d 0.29
e 0.094 f 0.98

6 Write these numbers as products of their prime factors.

a 2376 b 546 c 680

7 a Complete the Venn diagram to show the prime factors of 180 and of 240.

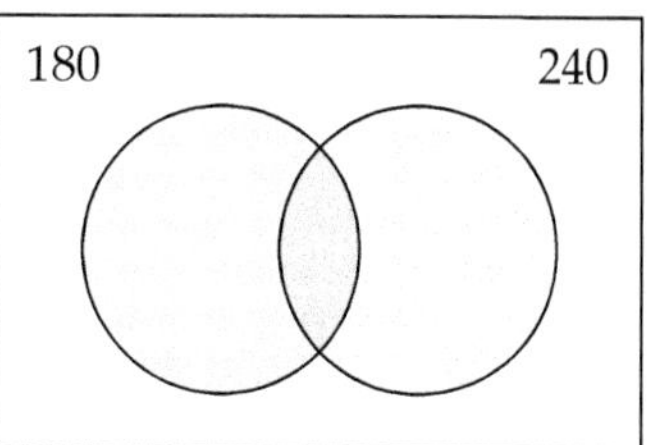

b Use your Venn diagram to find the HCF of 180 and 240.

c Use your Venn diagram to find the LCM of 180 and 240.

8 Estimate the answer to each calculation without using a calculator.

a 39×21
b $18.9 \div 5.1$
c $8870 \div 295$
d $413 \times (153 + 641)$
e $(0.473 + 0.509) \times 0.92$
f $\dfrac{0.708 \times 451}{4.71}$

9 One bottle of water costs £0.84, One bottle of cola costs £1.48.

a Estimate the cost of 19 bottles of water.

b Rita wants to buy 36 bottles of cola. She has £60 to spend. Use an estimate to decide if Rita can buy the cola.

What next?

Score	
0 – 4	Your knowledge of this topic is still developing. To improve look at Formative test: 3B-1; MyMaths: 1001, 1005, 1013, 1032, 1034, 1043 and 1044
5 – 7	You are gaining a secure knowledge of this topic. To improve look at InvisiPen: 112, 114, 135, 171, 172, 173 and 182
8 – 9	You have mastered this topic. Well done, you are ready to progress!

1 MyPractice

1a

1 Calculate

a $46 \div 10$ b 3.8×100 c $29.7 \div \frac{1}{10}$

d $0.16 \div 10$ e $13.02 \times \frac{1}{10}$ f 0.27×0.1

g 22.68×0.01 h $33.6 \div 0.1$ i $58.13 \div 0.01$

2 Each of these numbers have been written in standard form.

Work out the value of these numbers.

a 5×10^2 b 2.7×10^3 c 7.62×10^2

d 1.04×10^5 e 3.72×10^3 f 4.11×10^6

g 8.361×10^7

3 Calculate:

a 1.7×0.01 b 0.01×43 c 10000×1.2

d $8 \div \frac{1}{1000}$ e 9×0.001 f $23 \times \frac{1}{1000}$

g $3.7 \div 0.001$ h $0.025 \div 0.01$ i 0.07×0.01

1b

4 Round each number to the nearest

i 10 ii whole number iii to 1 dp iv to 2 dp

a 43.181 b 9.951 c 129.333 d 12.0999

e 98.985 f 26.007 g 144.236 h 11.777

i 101.101 j 12.6002 k 909.909 l 14.999

1c

5 a Use this table to find the HCF of 18 and 30.

b Find the HCF of 20 and 45.

c Find the HCF of 72 and 80.

Number	Factors
18	
30	

6 a Use this table to find the LCM of 8 and 10.

b Find the LCM of 6 and 9.

c Find the LCM of 15 and 25.

Number	Multiples
8	
10	

7 Use factor trees and prime factors to find

a the HCF of

i 60 and 260 ii 210 and 270

b the LCM of

i 12 and 20 ii 60 and 126

8 Round all of the numbers in each calculation to 1 or 2 significant figures.
Then work out an estimate for each calculation.

a 503×31

b $15.16 \div 2.97$

c 5673×0.388

d $\dfrac{19.3 \times 415}{11.4}$

e $\dfrac{0.482 \times 317}{4.9}$

f $\dfrac{38.2 \times 6.39}{0.783}$

9 Work out an estimate for this problem.
Show all the numbers you have rounded and the calculations you have worked out.

Debbie is trying to save money.
She spends £4.89 on a coffee and a sandwich each working day.
Her friend suggests that she could save some money by making a sandwich and bringing a flask of coffee from home.
Making her own sandwiches and flask of coffee costs £1.08 per day.
Debbie works 5 days a week for 46 weeks of the year. How much money could she save each year if she takes her friend's advice?

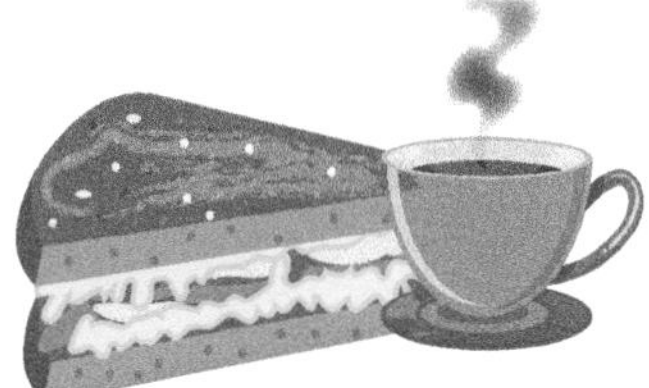

10 When a toilet flushes it use 9.24 litres of water.

a If a toilet is flushed 17 times a day, **approximately** how much water is used

- **i** per day
- **ii** per week
- **iii** per month
- **iv** per year
- **v** per lifetime of a person?

b The volume of water in Lake Windermere is about 330 000 000 m^3.
Approximately how long would it take to flush the volume of the lake down the toilet? ($1\,m^3 = 1000$ litres)

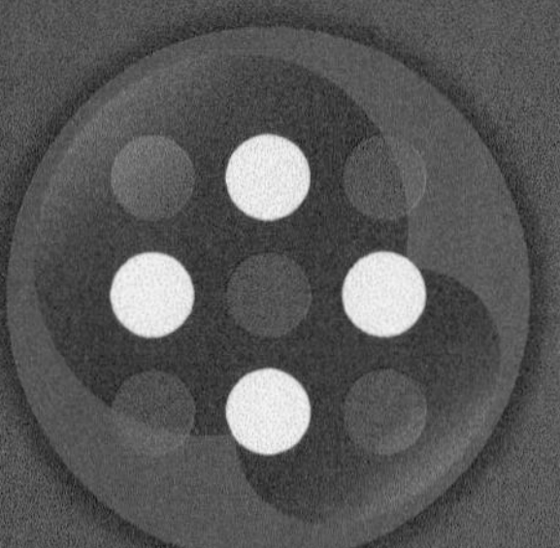

2 Measures, perimeter and area

Introduction

The fastest man in the world is Usain Bolt. In 2009 he ran 100 metres in 9.58 seconds. His average speed for the race was 10.44 m/s but his top speed during the race was 12.27 m/s.

However Usain would be chasing the tails of creatures such as greyhounds, antelopes, cheetahs and even the domesticated cat, which can all run faster.

What's the point?

Being able to measure distances and times accurately means that you can work out speed, which is highly useful in our increasingly fast-moving world!

Objectives

By the end of this chapter, you will have learned how to ...

- Convert between metric units.
- Convert between metric and imperial units.
- Work out the areas of rectangles, triangles, parallelograms and trapezia.
- Work out the circumferences and areas of circles.
- Recognise and use common compound measures.

Check in

1 Calculate the perimeter and area of each shape.

a

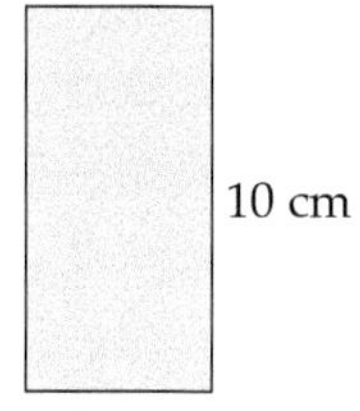

b

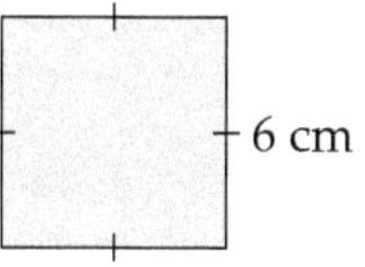

c

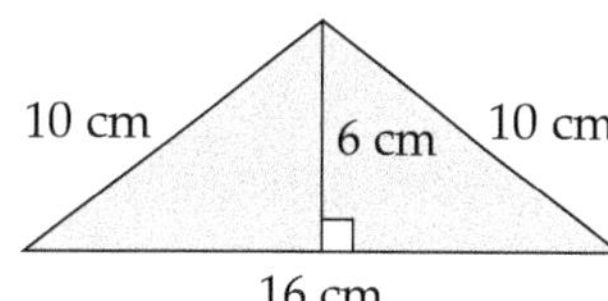

2 Calculate the volume of this cuboid.
Give the units of your answer.

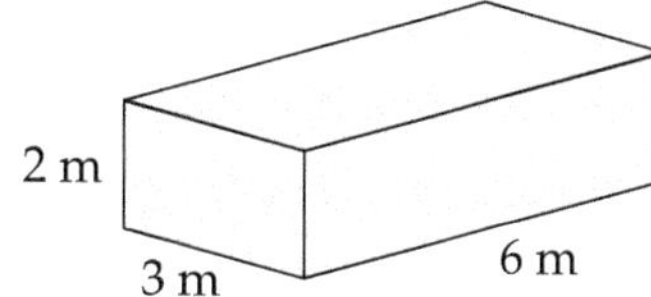

3 Calculate

a 5.5×1000 b $4000 \div 100$

Starter problem

A band is fastened around three identical circles with a radius of 10 cm.

Find the perimeter of the band and the area enclosed by the band.

Investigate.

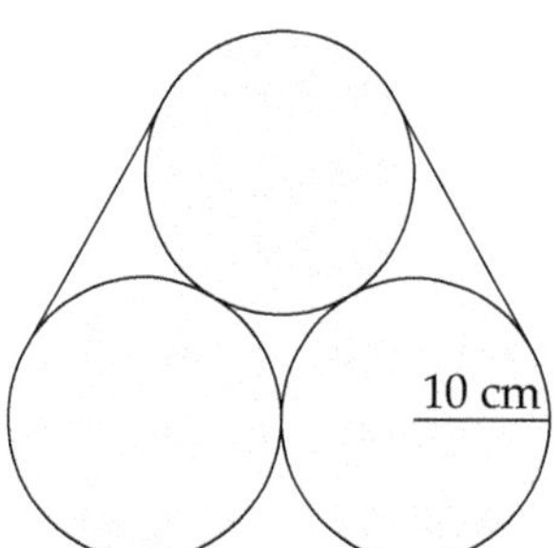

2a Measures 1

To look after a giraffe at a zoo you would need to know lots of **measurements**.
Different types of measurements use different **units**.

The height of a male giraffe is about 5 m.

The area of a giraffe's foot is about 700 cm^2.

- You can measure **length** using **metric** units.

millimetre (mm)
centimetre (cm)
metre (m)
kilometre (km)

1 cm = 10 mm
1 m = 100 cm
1 km = 1000 m

- **Area** is the amount of surface a shape covers.

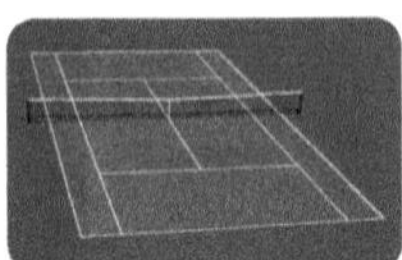

square centimetre (cm^2)
square metre (m^2)
hectare (ha)
square kilometre (km^2)

1 cm^2 = 100 mm^2
1 m^2 = 10 000 cm^2
1 ha = 10 000 m^2
1 km^2 = 1 000 000 m^2

- **Capacity** is the amount of liquid a container can hold.
- **Volume** is the amount of space a 3D shape occupies.

millilitre (ml)
centilitre (cl)
litre
cubic centimetre (cm^3)
cubic metre (m^3)

1 litre = 1000 ml = 100 cl
1 litre = 1000 cm^3
1 m^3 = 1000 litres
1 m^3 = 1 000 000 cm^3

- **Mass** is how heavy something is.

milligram (mg)
gram (g)
kilogram (kg)
tonne (t)

1 g = 1000 mg
1 kg = 1000 g
1 t = 1000 kg

A giraffe needs only 2 litres of water a day.

The mass of a male giraffe is about 1.3 tonnes.

Example

Convert
a 5.5 tonnes to kilograms **b** 60 000 cm^2 to square metres **c** 60 m^3 to litres.

a
1 t = 1000 kg (× 1000 → ; ← ÷ 1000)
5.5 t = 5.5 × 1000 kg
= 5500 kg

b
1 m^2 = 10 000 cm^2 (× 10 000 → ; ← ÷ 10 000)
60 000 cm^2 = 60 000 ÷ 10 000 m^2
= 6 m^2

c
1 m^3 = 1000 litres (× 1000 → ; ← ÷ 1000)
60 m^3 = 60 × 1000 litres
= 60 000 litres

Exercise 2a

1 Choose the most sensible estimate for

a the mass of an apple

10 g 100 g 1 kg

b the area of a table

1 cm^2 1 m^2 1 ha

c the diagonal length of a computer screen

50 mm 5 cm 50 cm

d the capacity of a can of drink

33 ml 33 cl 33 litres

e the distance from Madrid to Lisbon

600 cm 600 m 600 km

f the mass of a van

90 kg 900 kg 9 t

g the volume of a house brick.

140 cm^3 1400 cm^3 14 000 cm^3

2 Convert these metric measurements to the units in brackets.

a 480 cm (m) b 4.5 cm^2 (mm^2)
c 5000 m^2 (ha) d 4 000 000 cm^3 (m^3)
e 75 cl (litres) f 8 m^2 (cm^2)
g 0.75 kg (g) h 650 m (km)
i 0.5 m^3 (cm^3) j 750 kg (tonnes)

3 A rectangular football pitch measures 90 metres by 50 metres.
Calculate its area in

a square metres b hectares.

4 A trough is in the shape of a cuboid measuring 120 cm by 60 cm by 35 cm.

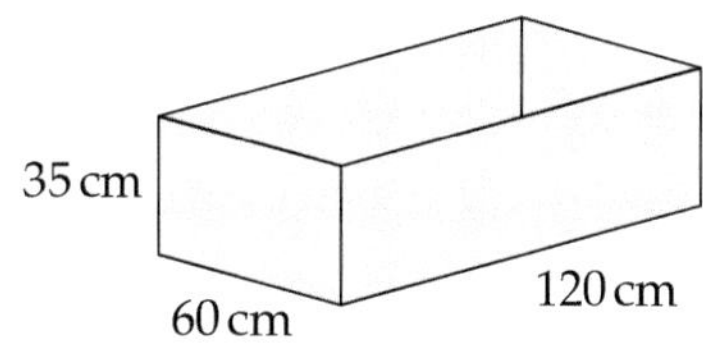

a Calculate its volume in cubic centimetres.

b How many litres of water will fill the trough?

Did you know?

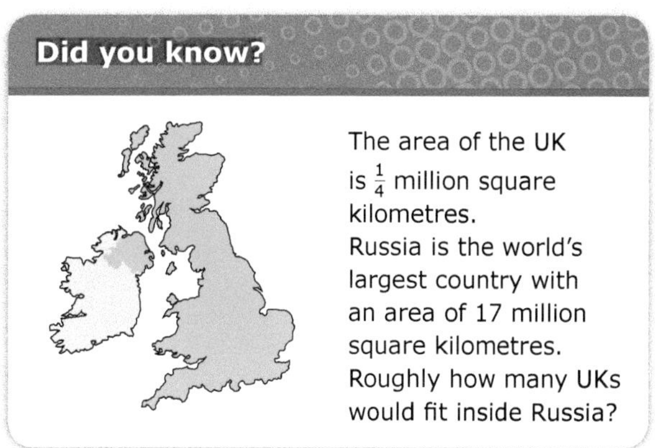

The area of the UK is $\frac{1}{4}$ million square kilometres.
Russia is the world's largest country with an area of 17 million square kilometres.
Roughly how many UKs would fit inside Russia?

Problem solving

5 Fold a sheet of A4 paper in half. This is now A5 paper.
Folding a sheet of A5 paper gives A6 size, and so on.

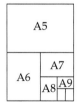

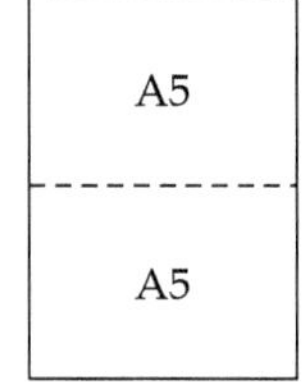

A sheet of A4 paper measures 297 mm by 210 mm.
Copy and complete the table with the length and width of the paper sizes A1 to A8, in millimetres.

Size	Measurements
A1	
A2	
A3	
A4	297 mm × 210 mm
A5	
A6	
A7	
A8	

2b Measures 2

You could give your height in **metric units** (metres and centimetres) or **imperial units** (feet and inches).

We still use some of the **imperial** units of **measurement**.

- You can measure **length** using

inch (in)	12 in = 1 ft
foot (ft)	3 ft = 1 yd
yard (yd)	1760 yd = 1 mile
mile	

1 inch ≈ 2.5 cm
1 yard ≈ 1 metre
5 miles ≈ 8 km

- You can measure **capacity** using

pint	8 pints = 1 gallon
gallon	

1 gallon ≈ 4.5 litres
1 pint ≈ 0.6 litre
1 pint ≈ 600 ml

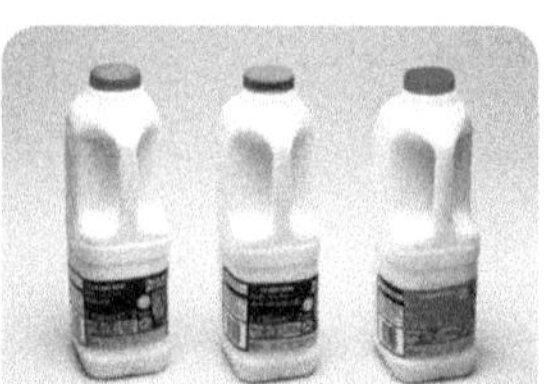

- You can measure **mass** using

ounce (oz)	16 oz = 1 lb
pound (lb)	

1 oz ≈ 30 g
1 kg ≈ 2.2 lb

The symbol ≈ means 'is approximately equal to'.

Example

Use approximations to convert

a 60 miles to kilometres b 240 ml to pints.

a
5 miles = 8 km
1 mile = 8 ÷ 5 km
60 miles = 60 × 8 ÷ 5 km
= 480 ÷ 5 km
= 96 km

b

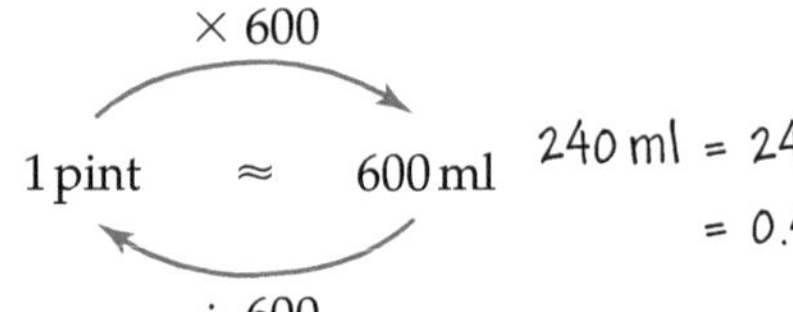

240 ml = 240 ÷ 600 pints
= 0.4 pints

None of these measurements are exact:

The population of Tahiti is 151 000.
The area of China is 36 000 km².
The length of the Humber Bridge is 2220 m.
The Loch Ness Monster is worth £5 000 000 a year to tourism in Scotland.

- When you measure a quantity, the measurement can never be exact. You give the measurement to the appropriate **degree of accuracy**.

10 20 30 kg

This measurement can be given as 20 kg.

Exercise 2b

Use approximations to answer these questions.

1 Which measurement is larger?
Explain your reasoning.

- **a** 1 mile or 1 kilometre
- **b** 1 pound (lb) or 1 kilogram
- **c** 1 inch or 1 centimetre
- **d** 1 pint or 1 litre
- **e** 1 ounce or 1 gram

2 Convert these imperial measurements to the **metric** units in brackets.

a	6 oz (g)	**b**	16 feet (m)
c	10 gallons (ml)	**d**	87.5 in (cm)
e	93.5 lb (kg)	**f**	36 in (m)
g	47 miles (km)	**h**	4.5 pints (ml)

Did you know?

A *chain* is an Imperial unit of measurement.
A chain is 22 yards and is the distance between the two wickets on a cricket pitch.

3 Convert these metric measurements to the imperial units in brackets.

a	450 g (oz)	**b**	10 cm (in)
c	9 litres (pints)	**d**	36 litres (gallons)
e	90 cm (feet)	**f**	1.7 m (in)
g	3.5 kg (lb)	**h**	150 ml (pints)

Problem solving

4 The distances, in kilometres, between four places in France are shown on the chart.

Calais			
461	Cherbourg		
859	922	Grenoble	
289	354	567	Paris

Convert the distances to miles.

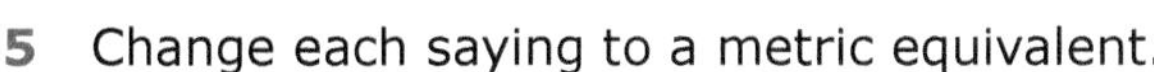

5 Change each saying to a metric equivalent.

- **a** *Give him an inch and he will take a yard.*
- **b** *You can't get a quart into a pint pot.*
- **c** *A miss is a good as a mile.*
- **d** *I wouldn't touch it with a ten-foot barge pole.*
- **e** *An ounce of prevention is worth a pound of cure.*

1 quart = 2 pints

Find some more sayings with imperial units and change them to their metric equivalents.

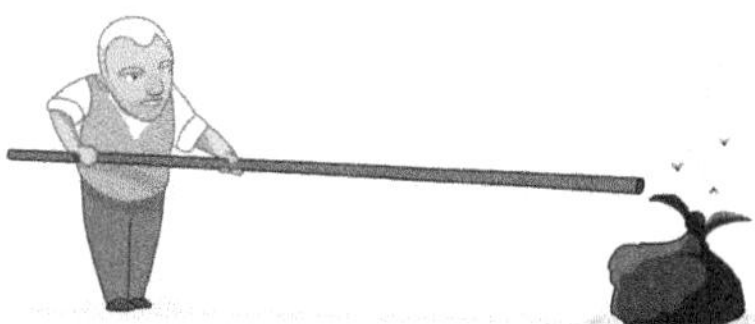

2c Area of a 2D shape

You can calculate the **area** of a rectangle and a **triangle**.

- Area of a rectangle
 $= l \times w$

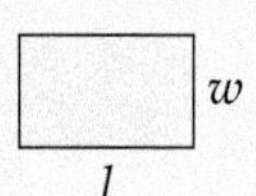

To use the **formulae**, all the lengths must have the same units.

- Area of a triangle
 $= \frac{1}{2} \times b \times h$

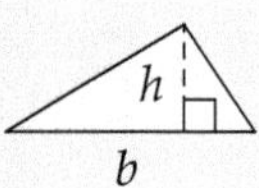

You can divide a **parallelogram** into two congruent triangles.

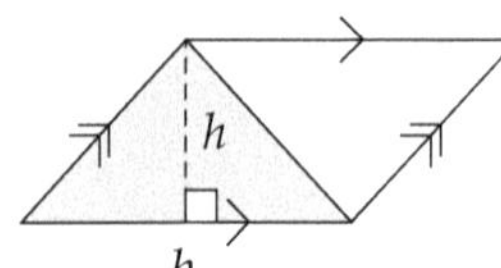

Area of the pink triangle $= \frac{1}{2} \times b \times h$

Area of both triangles $= 2 \times \frac{1}{2} \times b \times h = b \times h$

- Area of a parallelogram = **base** × **perpendicular height**

You can divide a **trapezium** into two triangles.

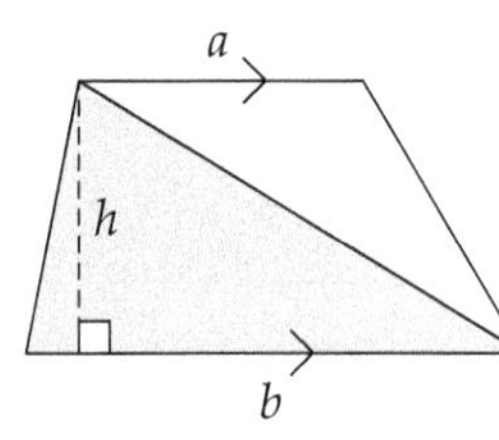

Area of the yellow triangle $= \frac{1}{2} \times a \times h$

Area of the pink triangle $= \frac{1}{2} \times b \times h$

Area of both triangles $= \frac{1}{2} \times a \times h + \frac{1}{2} \times b \times h$

$= \frac{1}{2} \times (a + b) \times h$

a and b are the lengths of the **parallel** sides. h is the perpendicular height.

- Area of a trapezium $= \frac{1}{2} \times (a + b) \times h$

Example

Calculate the areas of these shapes.

a

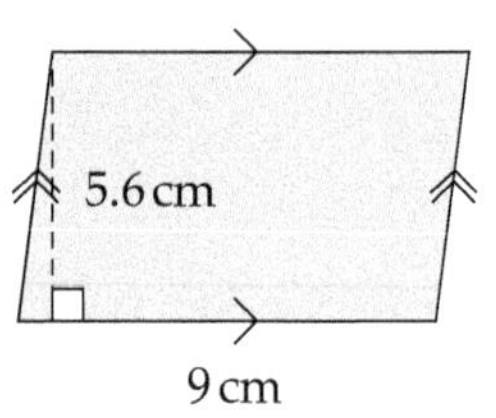

b

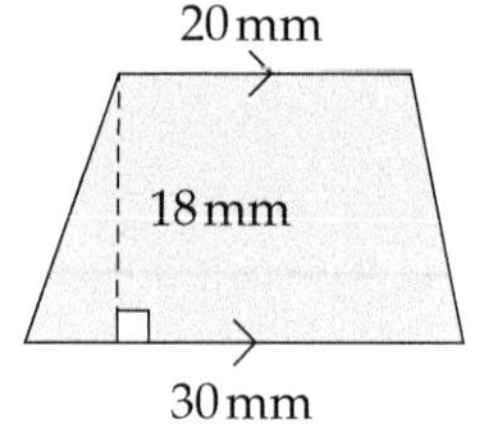

a Area of a parallelogram $= b \times h$

$= 9 \times 5.6$

$= 50.4\ \text{cm}^2$

b Area of a trapezium $= \frac{1}{2} \times (a + b) \times h$

$= \frac{1}{2} \times (20 + 30) \times 18$

$= 450\ \text{mm}^2$

Exercise 2c

1 Calculate the areas of these shapes made from squares, rectangles and triangles.

a

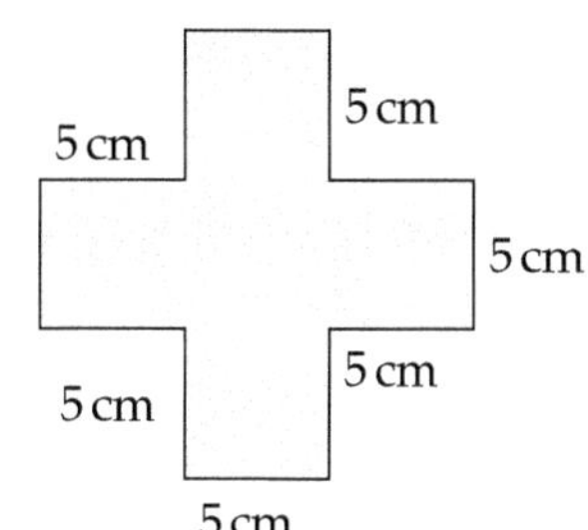

b

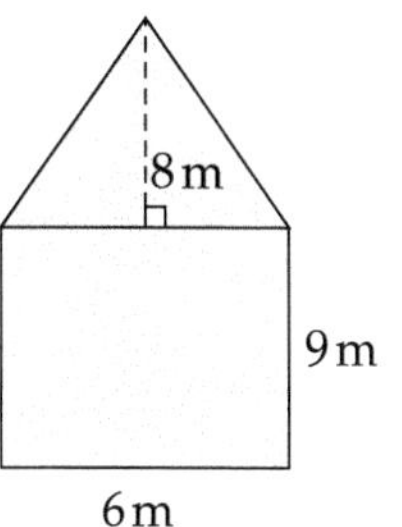

c

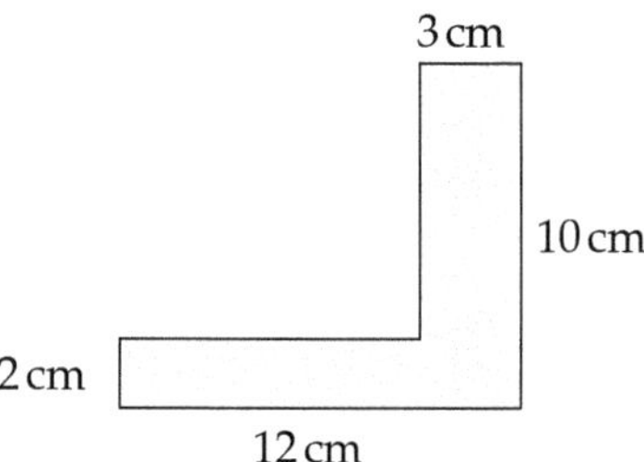

2 The length of a rectangle is 4 cm more than its width.
The area of the rectangle is 192 cm².

a Calculate the width of the rectangle.

b Calculate the perimeter of the rectangle.

3 The area of this triangle is 24 cm².

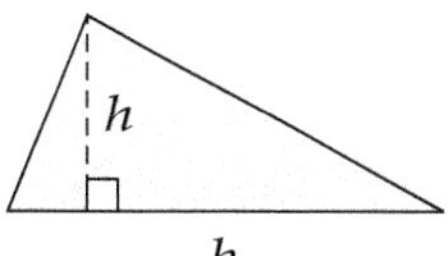

Calculate the value of b when

a $h = 12$ cm **b** $h = 8$ cm **c** $h = 5$ cm

4 Calculate the areas of these shapes.

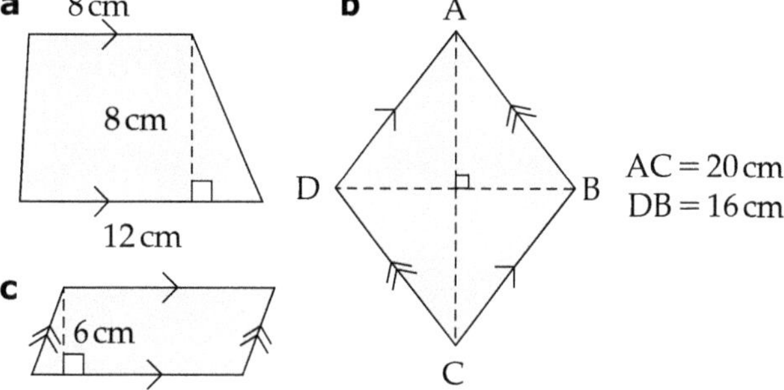

Problem solving

5 Boxes of biscuits measuring 4 cm by 5 cm by 6 cm are stacked on a tray measuring 20 cm by 24 cm. What is the greatest number of boxes that can be stacked in one layer on the tray?

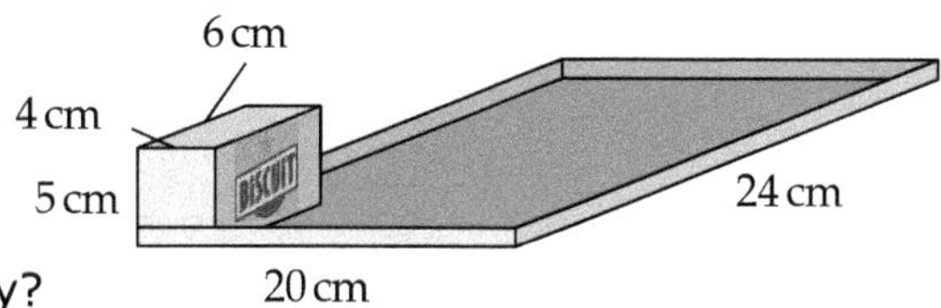

6 Two right-angled triangles and a square are arranged to make these shapes.

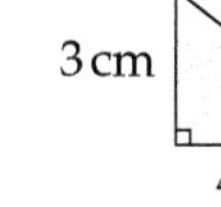

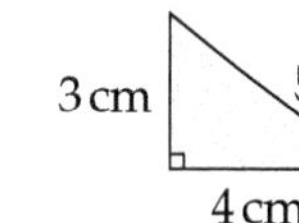

a

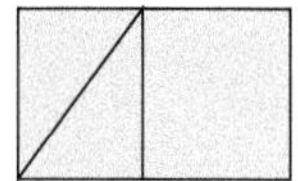

b

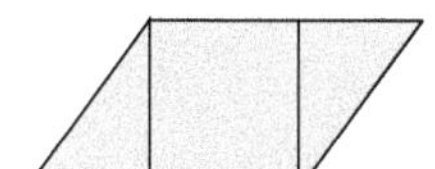

c

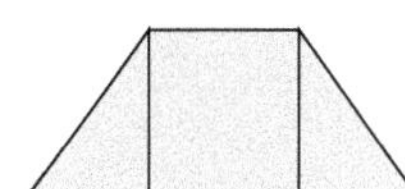

Calculate the perimeter and area of the triangle and square, and then of each shape **a**, **b**, and **c**.
Use the appropriate formula for each shape to check your area answers.

2d Circumference of a circle

- A **circle** is a set of points equidistant from a fixed point, its centre.

Equidistant means 'the same distance'.

The **circumference** (C) is the distance around the circle.

The **radius** (r) is the distance from the centre to the circumference.

Part of the circumference is called an **arc**.

The **diameter** (d) is the distance across the centre of the circle.

Circumferences are difficult to measure accurately because they are curved.

However, you can use the diameter to calculate the circumference.

The circumference of the circle is '3 and a bit' × the diameter.

You can use the symbol π (**pi**) for the exact value of '3 and a bit'.

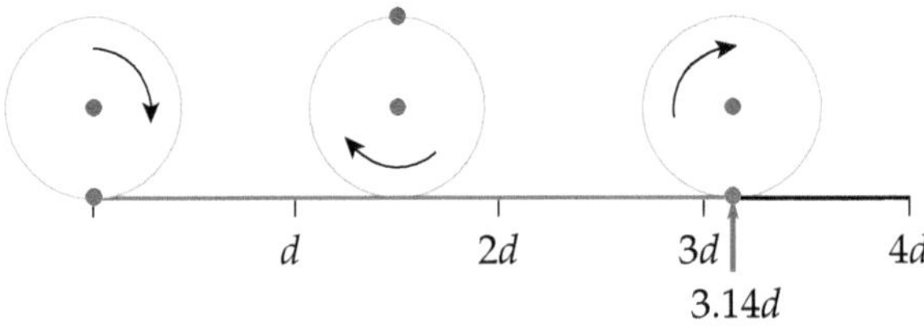

d
2d
3d
4d
3.14d

The exact value of π can never be written down – its decimal places go on forever without making a pattern.

- Circumference = $\pi \times$ diameter $\qquad C = \pi d$

- Circumference = $\pi \times 2 \times$ radius $\qquad C = 2\pi r$

You can use the π button on your calculator, or an estimate of the value of π such as 3.14 or $\frac{22}{7}$ to find the circumference.

Example

Calculate the circumference of each circle.

Take π to be 3.14.

a

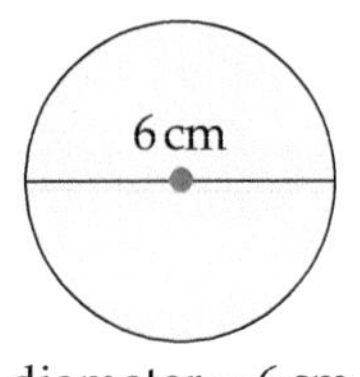

diameter = 6 cm

b

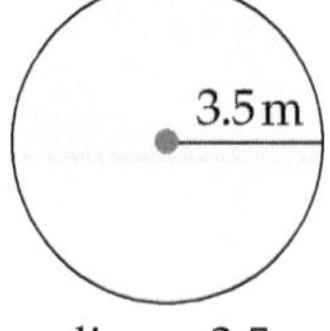

radius = 3.5 m

a $C = \pi d$

$= 3.14 \times 6$

$= 18.84$ cm

b $C = 2\pi r$

$= 2 \times 3.14 \times 3.5$

$= 21.98$ m

Circumference is a distance so is measured in units of length.

Exercise 2d

Use $\pi = 3.14$ for all the questions on this page.

d is the diameter.
r is the radius.

1 Calculate the circumference of these circles.

a $d = 8$ cm b $d = 20$ cm

c $r = 4.5$ cm d $r = 9$ m

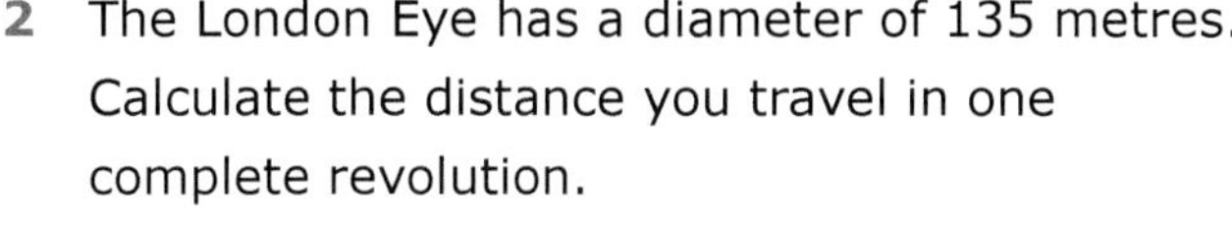

2 The London Eye has a diameter of 135 metres.
Calculate the distance you travel in one complete revolution.

3 The diameter of a bicycle wheel is 70 cm.

a Calculate the circumference.

b Work out the number of rotations of the wheel during a journey of one kilometre.

4 Calculate the perimeter of these shapes.

a

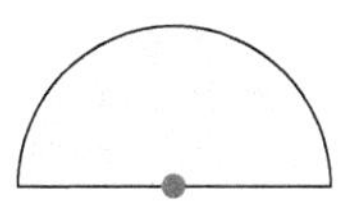

diameter = 4 cm

b

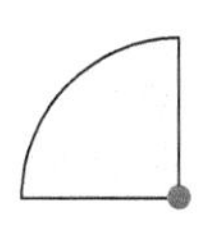

radius = 11 cm

c

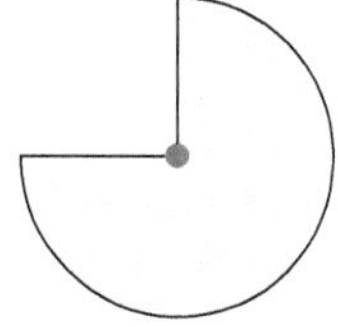

radius = 1.5 m

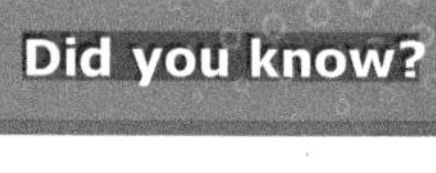

In 2002, scientists at the University of Tokyo calculated π to over one trillion (one million million) decimal places. The computer calculation took 25 days!

Problem solving

5 The circumference of a pie is 36 cm.
What is the diameter?

6 A regular hexagon fits inside a circle of radius 5 m.

a Calculate

i the perimeter of the hexagon

ii the circumference of the circle.

b Explain how you know that the perimeter of the hexagon is less than the circle's circumference.

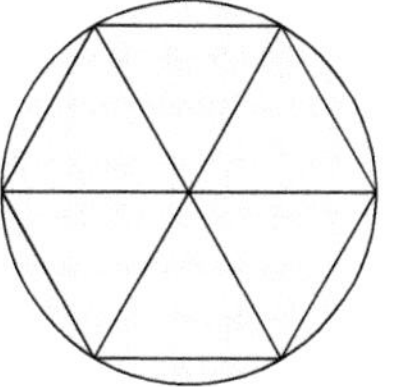

7 Make a collection of circular objects, for example, a coin or a plate.
Use a ruler and string to measure the diameter and circumference of your objects.
Copy and complete the table.

Object	Diameter	Circumference	π × diameter

You should find that the answers in the last two columns are approximately the same for each object.

You could work out the difference between the last two columns to see how accurate your measurements were.

2e Area of a circle

You should know the names of parts of a circle.

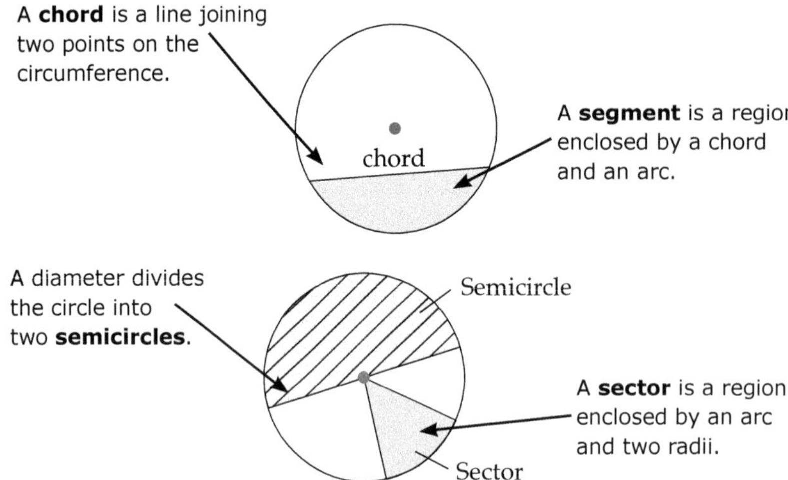

A **segment** is a region enclosed by a chord and an arc.

A **sector** is a region enclosed by an arc and two radii.

Radii is the plural of **radius**.

You can divide a circle into lots of tiny sectors and rearrange them into a rectangle.

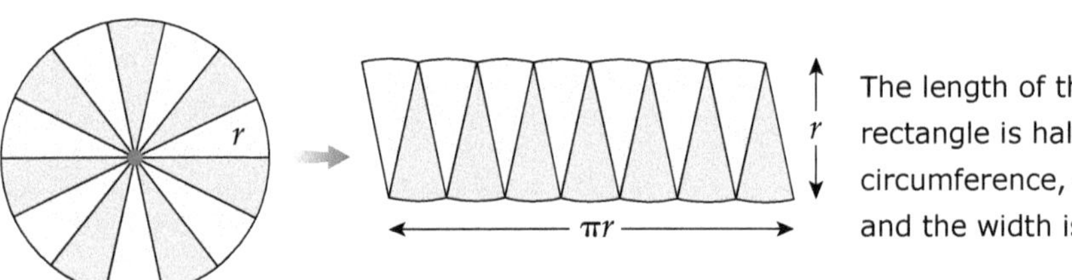

The length of the rectangle is half the circumference, πr, and the width is r.

The smaller you make the sectors, the closer the shape becomes to a rectangle.

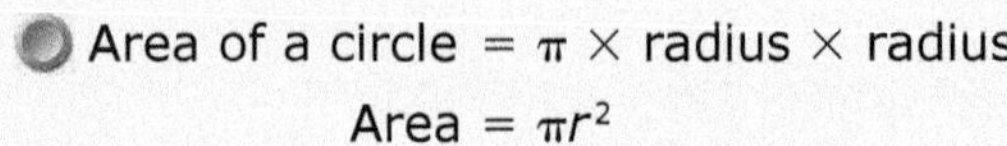

Area of a circle $= \pi \times$ radius $\times$ radius

Area $= \pi r^2$

You can use the π on your calculator or the approximation 3.14 to find the area.

Example

Calculate the area of each circle.

a

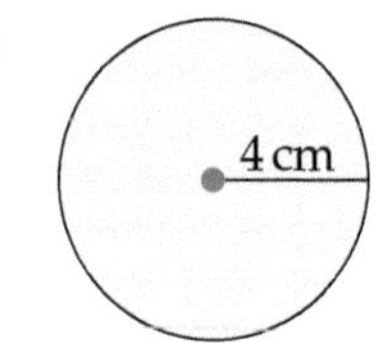

radius = 4 cm

b

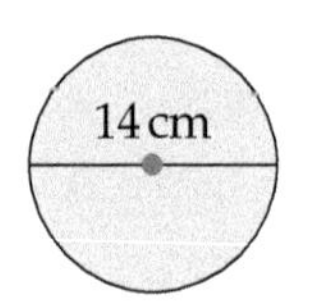

diameter = 14 cm

a Area $= \pi r^2$
$= 3.14 \times 4 \times 4$
$= 50.24\ \text{cm}^2$

b Radius $= 14 \div 2 = 7\ \text{cm}$
Area $= \pi r^2$
$= 3.14 \times 7 \times 7$
$= 153.86\ \text{cm}^2$

Area is measured in square units.

Exercise 2e

Use $\pi = 3.14$ for all the questions on this page.

r is the radius.

1 Calculate the area of these circles.

  a $r = 10\,\text{cm}$ **b** $r = 20\,\text{cm}$

  c $r = 9\,\text{cm}$ **d** $r = 2.5\,\text{m}$

2 A circular patio has a diameter of 3.5 metres.

  Calculate the area of the patio.

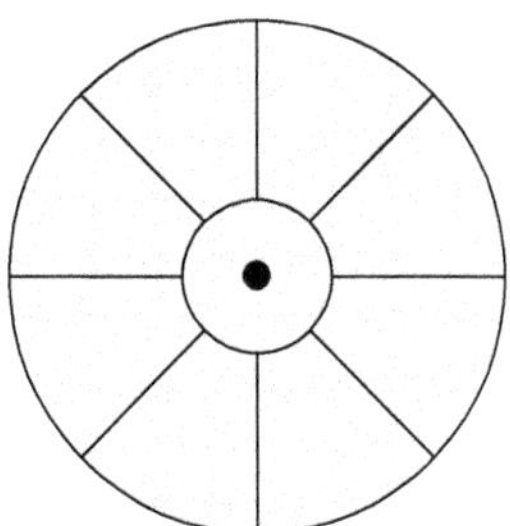

3 These shapes are based on a circle of radius 6 cm.

  Calculate the area of each shape.

  a

  b

  c

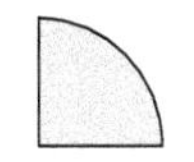

  d

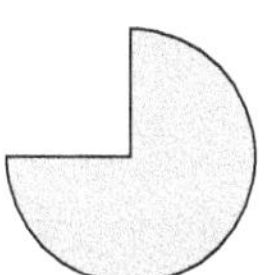

The shape in part **c** is called a quadrant.

4 The large circle has a radius of 8 cm.

  Calculate the blue area and the green area for each shape.

  Show your working out.

  a

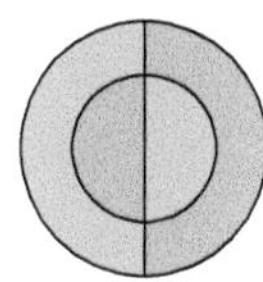

  b

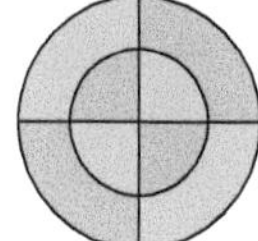

  c

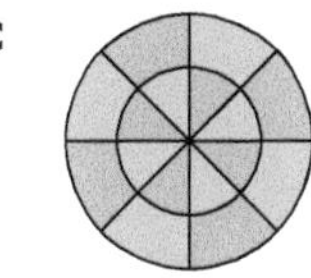

5 A **circumscribed** circle of radius 5 cm is drawn round a square.

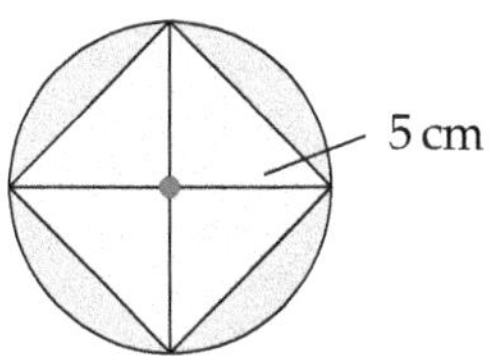

Circumscribed means it is drawn touching the corners of the shape.

  Calculate the area of

  a the square

  b the circle

  c the shaded region.

Problem solving

6 Calculate the area of the circle.

  Another circle has an area that is four times the area of this circle.

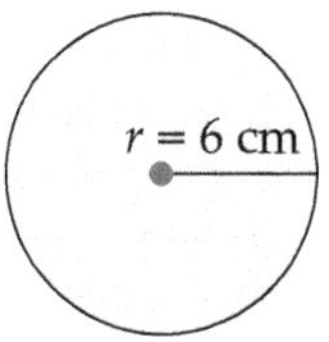

  What is the radius of the new circle?

  Check your answer.

7 A small pizza has a diameter of 22 cm.

  A large pizza has a diameter of 32 cm.

  a Find the area of the top of each pizza.

  b The small pizza costs £5, and the large pizza costs £9.
  Which is better value and why?

  c Choose a suitable size and price for a medium pizza. Explain your reasoning.

2f Compound measures

A **compound measure** uses a combination of measurements and units. For example, **speed** measures how fast something moves, or how quickly distance changes 'per unit time'.
If the speed is **constant**,

$$\text{Speed } (S) = \frac{\text{Distance travelled } (D)}{\text{Time taken } (T)}$$

Speed is measured in metres per second (m/s), miles per hour (mph) or kilometres per hour (km/h).

If the speed is changing, the same formula gives the **average speed**.

You can use a formula triangle to rearrange the formulae for speed, density and pressure.

Example

A cyclist travels 36 km in 1 hour 15 minutes.
Calculate the average speed in

a kilometres per hour
b metres per second.

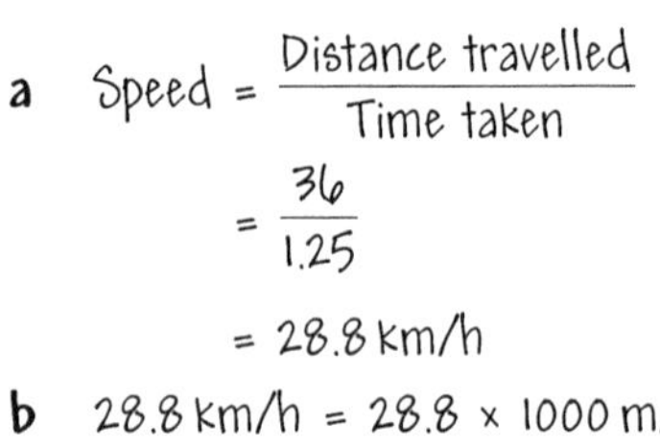

a $\text{Speed} = \frac{\text{Distance travelled}}{\text{Time taken}}$

$= \frac{36}{1.25}$ 15 minutes = 0.25 hours

$= 28.8$ km/h

b $28.8 \text{ km/h} = 28.8 \times 1000 \text{ m/h}$ 1 km = 1000 m

$= \frac{28800}{60}$ m/min 1 hour = 60 minutes

$= \frac{28800}{60 \times 60} = 8$ m/s 1 minute = 60 seconds

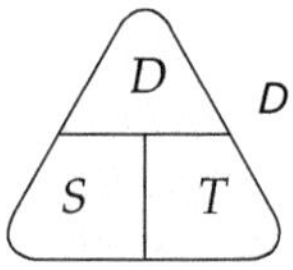

D triangle: D over S, T

$D = S \times T$

$S = \frac{D}{T}$ $T = \frac{D}{S}$

Density measures how heavy something is 'per unit volume'.

$$\text{Density } (D) = \frac{\text{Mass } (M)}{\text{Volume } (V)}$$

Density is measured in grams per cubic centimetre (g/cm^3) or kilograms per cubic metre (kg/m^3).

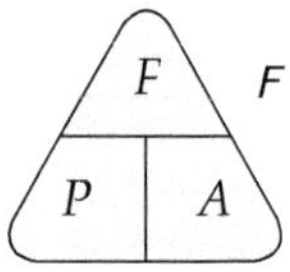

M triangle: M over D, V

$M = D \times V$

$D = \frac{M}{V}$ $V = \frac{M}{D}$

Pressure measures how force acts 'per unit area'.

$$\text{Pressure } (P) = \frac{\text{Force } (F)}{\text{Area } (A)}$$

A **newton** (N) is a unit of force. Pressure is measured in newtons per square metre (N/m^2).

F triangle: F over P, A

$F = P \times A$

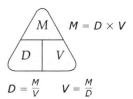

$P = \frac{F}{A}$ $A = \frac{F}{P}$

Exercise 2f

1 Calculate the speed when you travel

a 100 km in 2 hours **b** 350 km in 5 hours
c 80 miles in 2 hours **d** 30 km in 30 minutes
e 250 m in 5 s **f** 240 m in 3 minutes

Calculate the distance travelled when you travel at

g 25 km/h for 3 hours **h** 70 km/h for 2 hours
i 50 km/h for 3.5 h **j** 40 m/s for 15 seconds
k 55 m/s for 10 seconds **l** 30 m/s for 2 minutes

2 Kathy ran 100 metres in 25 seconds.
Jayne ran 400 metres in 125 seconds.

a Calculate their speeds in metres per second.
b Who ran faster, Kathy or Jayne?

Did you know?

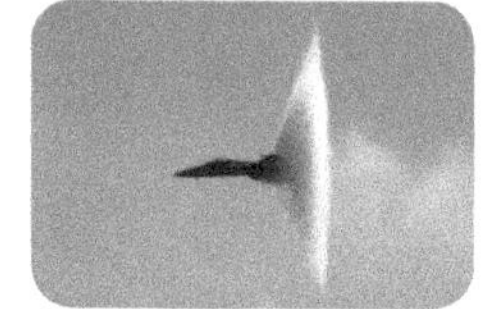

When an aircraft reaches the speed of sound, a conical pressure wave forms and there is a sonic boom.

Problem solving

3 The safety valve on a boiler releases the pressure if the pressure is greater than 4 million newtons per square metre.
If the force is 1 500 000 newtons and the area is 0.5 square metres, will the safety valve be activated?

4 In 2002, the fastest ever lap of a Formula One racing track was recorded at Monza in Italy. Juan Pablo Montoya completed one lap of 5783 metres in 80 seconds. Calculate his average speed in

a metres per second **b** kilometres per hour.

5 In 1997 Andy Green, an RAF fighter pilot, set the World Land Speed Record at Black Rock Desert in Nevada, USA, when he travelled at 768 mph in the ThrustSSC.

a Calculate his average speed in kilometres per hour.
At sea level the speed of sound is 1225 km/h.
b Did Andy Green travel faster than the speed of sound?

ThrustSSC

6 The density of cork is 0.25 g/cm^3 and the density of water is 1.0 g/cm^3. Calculate the mass of

a a 10 cm cube of cork **b** a litre of water.

7 Many singers use the words 'a million miles' in their lyrics.
'It feels like you're a million miles away.' (*Rihanna*)
'I can't stay a million miles away.' (*Offspring*)
'I'm still a million miles from you.' (*Bob Dylan*)
How many years would it take you to walk a million miles at a speed of 3 miles per hour?

2 MySummary

Check out

You should now be able to ...

	Test it ➡ Questions
✓ Convert between metric units.  	5 · 1
✓ Convert between metric and imperial units. 	5 · 2
✓ Calculate the area of a 2D shape.	6 · 3 – 5
✓ Calculate the circumference and area of a circle. 	6 · 6 – 7
✓ Recognise and use compound measures. 	7 · 8

Language	Meaning	Example
Metric unit	A unit of measurement from the metric system, which is based on powers of 10.	centimetres, metres, kilometres grams, kilograms, tonnes, are some examples of metric units
Imperial unit	A unit of measurement from the older imperial system.	inches, feet, yards, miles ounces, pounds, stone, tons are some examples of imperial units
Area	The space inside a 2D shape.	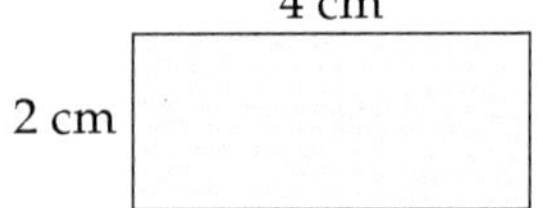 The area of the rectangle is 8 cm^2
Circumference	The distance around a circle.	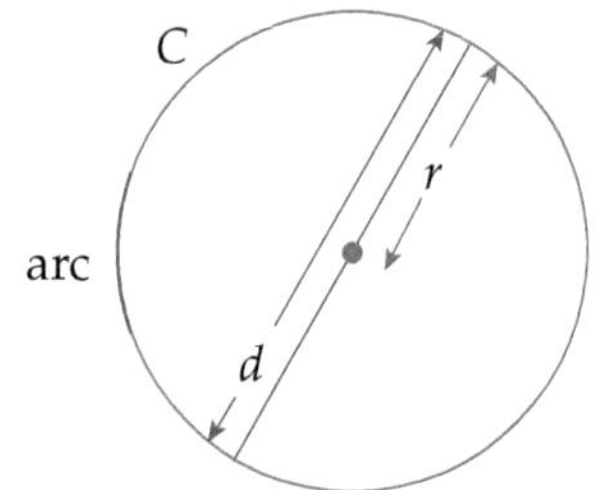
Diameter	The distance across a circle, through the centre.	
Radius	The distance from the centre of a circle to the circumference.	
Speed	A measure of the rate at which distance is covered.	The speed of sound travelling through air is roughly 343 metres per second.

2 MyReview

1 Convert between these metric measurements.

  a $4.9\,m$ to mm
  b $87\,cl$ to litres
  c $0.47\,kg$ to g
  d $0.9\,cm^2$ to mm^2
  e $3\,m^2$ to cm^2
  f $3\,l$ in cm^3

2 Convert these imperial measurements to metric.

  a 3 pints to litres
  b 24 lb to kg
  c 90 miles to km
  d 39 inches to m

3 Calculate the area of this shape. State the units of your answer.

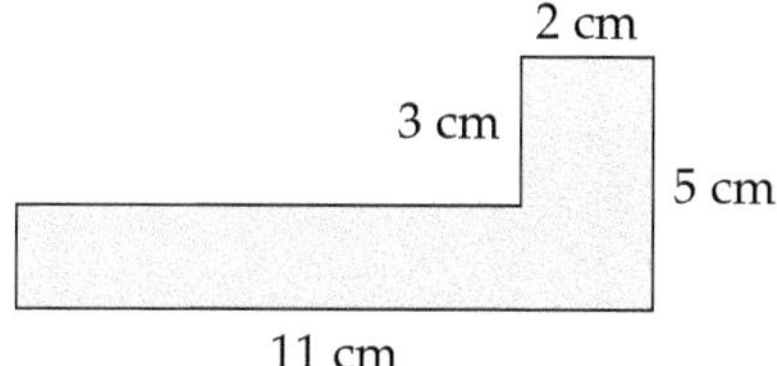

4 The area of a right-angled triangle is $16\,cm^2$. The base is 4 cm in length. What is the height of the triangle?

5

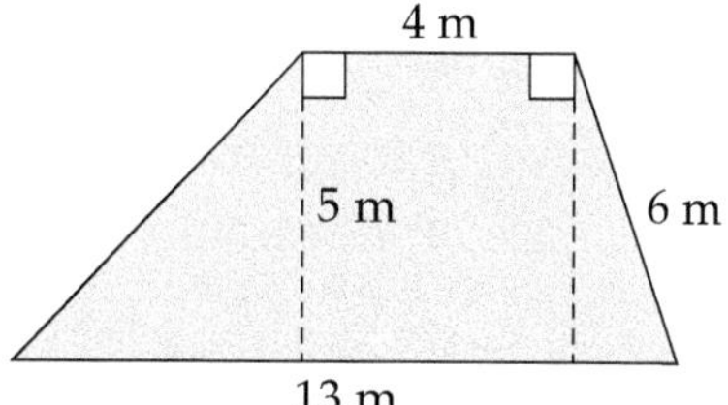

Calculate the area of the trapezium. State the units of your answer.

6 Calculate

  a the area
  b the circumference of the circle.

  Give your answers to 1 dp.

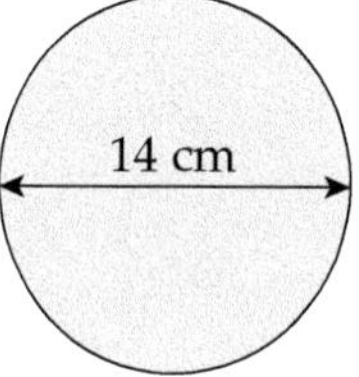

7 The diagram shows a quarter of a circle with radius 14 cm. Calculate

  a the area
  b the perimeter.

  Give your answers to 1 dp.

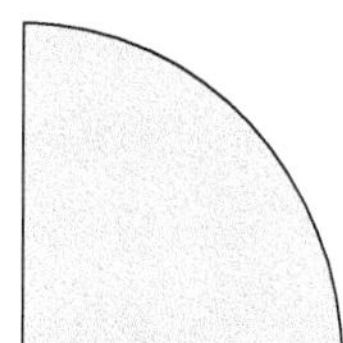

8 a A car travels 30 miles in 45 minutes. Calculate the car's average speed in miles per hour.

  b A 2 centimetre cube of lead has a mass of 90.7 grams. Calculate the density of lead in g/cm^3.

What next?

Score	
0 – 3	Your knowledge of this topic is still developing. To improve look at Formative test: 3B-2; MyMaths: 1061, 1083, 1088, 1091, 1108, 1121, 1128, 1191, 1246 and 1329
4 – 6	You are gaining a secure knowledge of this topic. To improve look at InvisiPen: 313, 314, 315, 316, 332, 333, 335, 351, 352 and 353
7, 8	You have mastered this topic. Well done, you are ready to progress!

2 MyPractice

1 Choose the most sensible estimate for these quantities.

a	the capacity of a medicine bottle	20 ml	200 ml	2 litres
b	the length of a badminton court	13.4 cm	13.4 m	13.4 km
c	the mass of a person	6 kg	60 kg	600 kg
d	the area of a window	1 mm^2	1 cm^2	1 m^2
e	the volume of a tennis ball	14 cm^3	140 cm^3	1400 cm^3

2 How many square millimetres are there in one square centimetre? Sketch a diagram to show your working.

3 Convert these metric measurements to the units in brackets.

a 67 mm (cm) **b** 850 g (kg)
c 8 m^3 (cm^3) **d** 1 km (mm)
e 400 g (kg) **f** 7.5 ha (m^2)
g 3.5 m (mm) **h** 75 000 cl (litres)
i 5 m^2 (cm^2) **j** 18 tonnes (kg)

4 Convert these imperial measurements to the metric units in brackets using approximations.

a 2.5 oz (g) **b** 7 pints (ml)
c 12 in (cm) **d** 40 in (cm)
e 154 lb (kg) **f** 35 miles (km)
g 8.5 pints (litres) **h** 2.5 gallons (ml)

5 Convert these metric measurements to the imperial units in brackets using approximations.

a 160 cm (in) **b** 3.9 litres (pints)
c 84 km (miles) **d** 48 kg (lb)
e 45 g (oz) **f** 49.5 litres (gallons)
g 8.4 m (feet) **h** 2100 ml (pints)

6 The area of the rectangle and the triangle are the same.
Calculate the value of *h*.

2c

7 Calculate the areas of these shapes.
State the units of your answers.

a

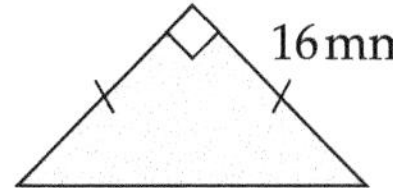

b

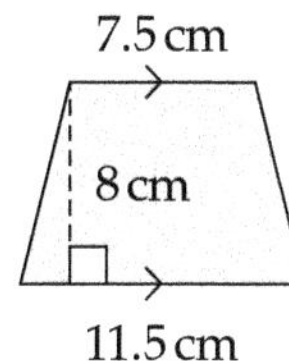

c

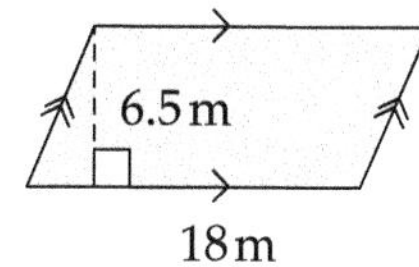

2d

8 Calculate the circumferences of these circles.
Use $\pi = 3.14$.

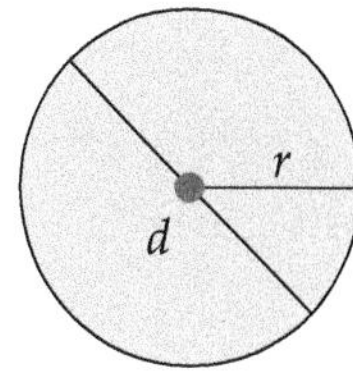

a $r = 6$ cm
b $r = 8.5$ m
c $d = 15$ cm
d $d = 11$ cm
e $r = 2.75$ cm

9 A coin with a diameter of 25 mm is rolled along a table.
Calculate

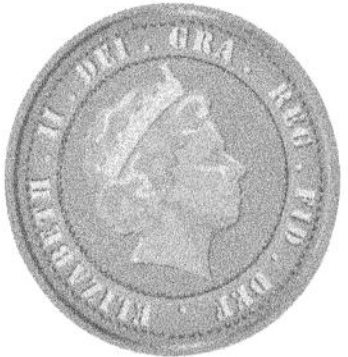

a the circumference
b the distance travelled in metres during 20 complete rotations.

Use $\pi = 3.14$.

2e

10 Calculate the areas of these circles.
Use $\pi = 3.14$.

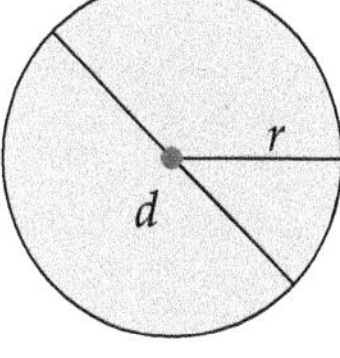

a $r = 7$ cm
b $r = 3.5$ m
c $r = 9.5$ cm
d $d = 11$ cm
e $d = 25$ cm

11 A circumcircle is drawn round a regular hexagon.
The hexagon has a perimeter of 36 cm.
Calculate the area of the circle.
Use $\pi = 3.14$.

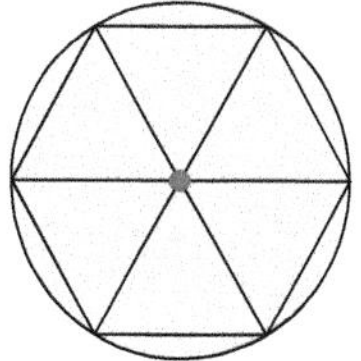

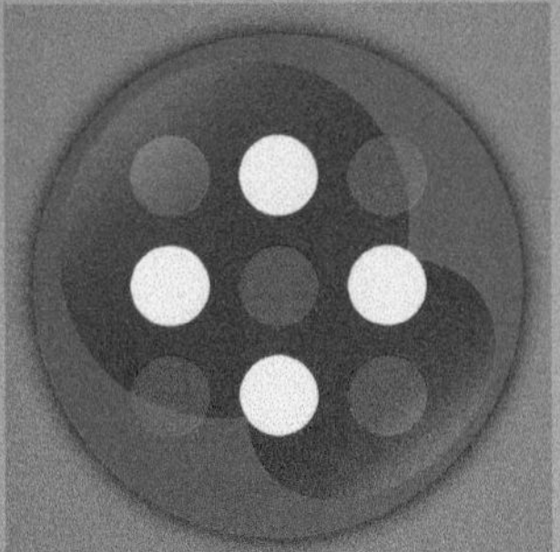

3 Expressions and formulae

Introduction

The most famous scientists have used mathematical formulae to describe their ideas. When an apple famously dropped on his head, Sir Isaac Newton used the formula

$$F = \frac{Gm_1m_2}{r^2}$$

to describe what he called gravity.

When Albert Einstein said that you could convert between mass and energy he changed the world and used the formula

$$E = mc^2$$

to show how it could be calculated.

What's the point?

A formula shows how one quantity is linked to another. Using formulae helps us to understand how our world is connected.

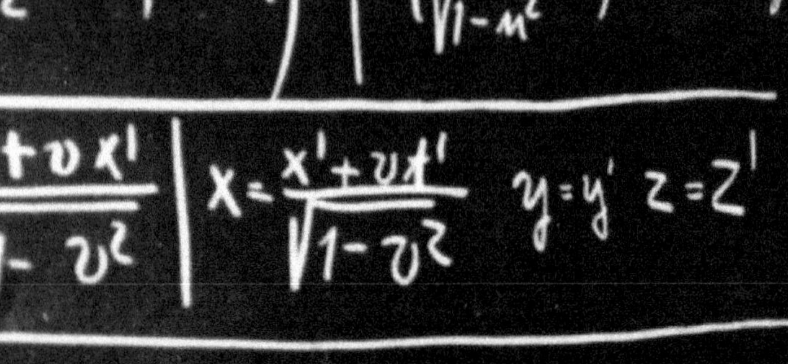

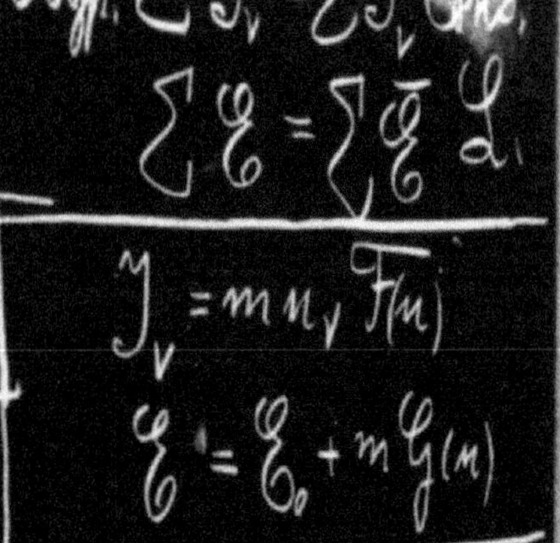

Objectives

By the end of this chapter, you will have learned how to …

- Know that factorising an algebraic expression is the inverse of expanding brackets.
- Find equivalent algebraic fractions.
- Add and subtract algebraic fractions.
- Substitute into formulae in different contexts.
- Change the subject of a formula.
- Derive formulae in practical situations.
- Draw graphs based on formulae.

Check in

1 **a** You think of a number n, treble it, and then add 4.

Treble means multiply by 3.

i Write an expression in terms of n for your final answer.

ii What is your final answer if n is 6?

b You think of a number, add 4, and then treble the result.

i Write an expression in terms of n for your final answer.

ii What is your final answer if n is 6?

2 **a** Find the value of $5(6 - 2) + 3(5 - 1)$.

b Expand the brackets in this expression and collect like terms.

$5(2x + 2) + 3(x - 1)$.

Starter problem

This L shape is drawn on a 10×10 grid numbered from 1 to 100. It has five numbers inside it.

We can call it L_{35} because the largest number inside it is 35.

The total of the numbers inside L_{35} is 138.

Pretend you are a famous scientist and see if you can find a connection between the L number and the total of the numbers inside the L shape.

Try and write your connection as a formula.

1	2	3	4	5	6	7	8	9	10
11	12	13	14	15	16	17	18	19	20
21	22	23	24	25	26	27	28	29	30
31	32	33	34	35	36	37	38	39	40
41	42	43	44	45	46	47	48	49	50
51	52	53	54	55	56	57	58	59	60
61	62	63	64	65	66	67	68	69	70
71	72	73	74	75	76	77	78	79	80
81	82	83	84	85	86	87	88	89	90
91	92	93	94	95	96	97	98	99	100

3a Factors in algebra

Algebraic expressions can have factors.

The factors of $3x$ are 3 and x, because $3 \times x = 3x$.

The factors of $2x + 14$ are 2 and $x + 7$, because $2(x + 7) = 2x + 14$

Here are two identical rectangles. Their areas are equal.

$x + 2$; 3 ; $3(x + 2)$ $\quad$ x ; 2 ; 3 ; $3x$; 6

expanding

$3(x + 2) = 3x + 6$

factorising

Factorising is the inverse of expanding brackets.

Example

Factorise **a** $10x + 15$ **b** $x^2 + 7x$

a 5 is a factor common to both $10x$ and 15.
Write the common factor 5 outside a bracket.
$5(\quad)$
Now find the factors which need to go inside the bracket.
$10x + 15 = 5(2x + 3)$

b x is a factor common to both x^2 and $7x$.
Write the common factor x outside a bracket.
$x^2 + 7x = x(x + 7)$

Check your answer by expanding the brackets.
5(2x + 3) = 10x + 15 ✓

You can have more than one common factor.

Example

Factorise $6x^2 - 9xy$.

$6x^2$ and $9xy$ have two common factors.
3 is common to 6 and 9. x is common to x^2 and xy.
Write the common factor $3x$ outside a bracket.
Complete the inside of the bracket using the other factors.
$6x^2 - 9xy = 3x(2x - 3y)$

Check your answer by expanding the brackets.
3x(2x - 3y) = 6x² - 9xy ✓

Exercise 3a

1 Write the factor which is common to the two terms in each of these expressions.

a $2x + 6$ b $3x + 6$
c $5z - 20$ d $4p + 16$
e $6q + 8$ f $9r - 6$
g $8x + 6$ h $15x - 20$

2 Factorise these expressions.

a $2x - 8$ b $3y + 9$
c $4x - 12$ d $5m + 30$
e $9n + 6$ f $6x - 10$
g $15y + 25$ h $8z - 10$
i $6 - 9x$ j $18 + 4x$
k $25 - 10x$ l $12 - 4x$
m $12x - 8$ n $10x + 5$
o $6x + 3$ p $7x - 14$

3 Factorise these expressions.

a $x^2 + 5x$ b $y^2 + 7y$
c $z^2 - 3z$ d $4p + p^2$
e $x^2 + 5xy$ f $a^2 - 2ab$

3 g $t^2 + 3st$ h $6yz - z^2$
i $8y + y^2$ j $8xy + y^2$
k $3z^2 + z$ l $5x^2 - x$
m $x^3 + 5x$ n $x^3 - 2x^2$
o $z^3 - z^2 + 3z$ p $2y + y^2 - y^3$

4 Factorise these expressions.
Look for two common factors.

a $2x^2 + 6xy$ b $9x^2 + 3xy$
c $2y^2 - 8yz$ d $6p^2 + 3pq$
e $4q^2 - 8pq$ f $6z^2 + 8yz$
g $9xy + 6yz$ h $4ab - 6bc$
i $6mn + 8np$ j $4x^2 - 6x$
k $6x^2 - 4x$ l $6x^2 - 2x$
m $9x^2 + 3xy$ n $12z + 8z^2$
o $9z^2 - 3z$ p $2y^3 + 4y$

5 Factorise these expressions.

a $8z^3 - 6z$ b $8z^3 - 6z^2$
c $8z^3 + 4z$ d $8z^3 + 4z^2$

Problem solving

6 The area of a rectangle is $3x^2 + 6x$.

a Factorise this expression in several different ways.

b Find at least three possible pairs of values for its length and width.

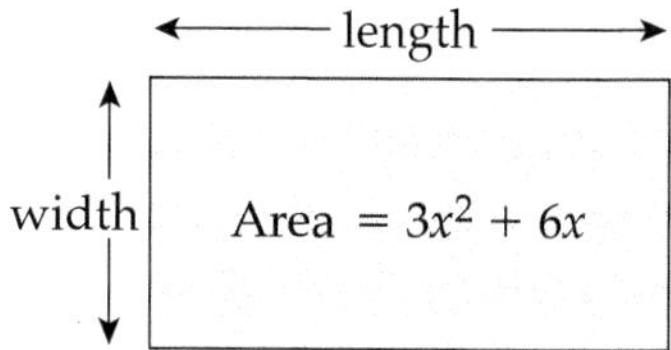

7 a The number x is an integer.
Write the next two integers greater than x.

b Write an expression for the total, T, when you add together x and the next two integers.

c **Prove** that T is always a multiple of 3.

8 A whole number x is added to its square to give a total, T.

a Prove that T is always equal to the product of two consecutive numbers.

b Find expressions for these consecutive numbers.

3b Algebraic fractions

You can find equivalent fractions by cancelling.

$$\frac{12}{18} \overset{\div 6}{=} \frac{2}{3} \quad \text{or} \quad \frac{\overset{2}{\cancel{12}}}{\underset{3}{\cancel{18}}} = \frac{2}{3}$$

You can do the same to **algebraic fractions**.

Example

Simplify

a $\frac{6x}{9xy}$

b $\frac{4a^2b}{6ac}$

a $\frac{6x}{9xy} = \frac{\overset{2}{\cancel{6}} \times \cancel{x}}{{}_3\cancel{9} \times \cancel{x} \times y} = \frac{2}{3y}$

b $\frac{4a^2b}{6ac} = \frac{\overset{2}{\cancel{4}} \times \cancel{a} \times a \times b}{{}_3\cancel{6} \times \cancel{a} \times c} = \frac{2ab}{3c}$

In part a: cancel 3 into 9 and 6, then cancel x.
In part b: cancel 2 into 4 and 6, then cancel a.

You can add and subtract fractions which have the same denominator.

In arithmetic,

$$\frac{2}{5} + \frac{1}{5} = \frac{3}{5}$$

In algebra,

$$\frac{2x}{5} + \frac{x}{5} = \frac{2x + x}{5} = \frac{3x}{5}$$

If the denominators are different, find equivalent fractions with the same denominator.

In arithmetic,

$$\frac{3}{8} + \frac{1}{4} = \frac{3}{8} + \frac{2}{8} = \frac{5}{8}$$

In algebra,

$$\frac{3x}{8} + \frac{y}{4} = \frac{3x}{8} + \frac{2y}{8} = \frac{3x + 2y}{8}$$

Example

Simplify $\frac{2a}{3} + \frac{3b}{4}$.

The lowest common multiple of 3 and 4 is 12 so change to equivalent fractions with a denominator of 12.

$$\frac{2a}{3} + \frac{3b}{4} = \frac{2a \times 4}{3 \times 4} + \frac{3b \times 3}{4 \times 3}$$

$$= \frac{8a}{12} + \frac{9b}{12} = \frac{8a + 9b}{12}$$

8a and 9b are not like terms and so you cannot simplify the numerator.

Exercise 3b

1 Find equivalent fractions by cancelling.

a $\frac{2x}{6}$ b $\frac{3y}{9}$

c $\frac{6z}{8}$ d $\frac{ab}{5a}$

e $\frac{uv}{4u}$ f $\frac{3pq}{p^2}$

g $\frac{2mn}{n^2}$ h $\frac{4x}{5xy}$

2 Simplify each fraction by cancelling as much as possible.

a $\frac{2xy}{8x}$ b $\frac{3mn}{9m}$

c $\frac{8ab}{100}$ d $\frac{6yz}{9xz}$

e $\frac{5pq}{10qr}$ f $\frac{8st}{4s}$

g $\frac{x^2}{xy}$ h $\frac{a^2}{abc}$

i $\frac{m^2n}{2mn}$ j $\frac{6yz}{9y^2}$

k $\frac{4h^2k}{6h}$ l $\frac{9xyz}{6xz^2}$

3 Add or subtract these fractions.

a $\frac{3x}{7} + \frac{2x}{7}$ b $\frac{3x}{7} + \frac{2y}{7}$

c $\frac{4a}{9} + \frac{a}{9}$ d $\frac{4a}{9} + \frac{b}{9}$

e $\frac{4s}{5} - \frac{3s}{5}$ f $\frac{4s}{5} - \frac{3t}{5}$

g $\frac{9y}{11} - \frac{3y}{11}$ h $\frac{9y}{11} - \frac{3z}{11}$

4 Add or subtract these fractions.
Your first step will be to find a common denominator.

a $\frac{x}{2} + \frac{x}{3}$ b $\frac{y}{5} + \frac{y}{3}$

c $\frac{3z}{2} - \frac{z}{5}$ d $\frac{x}{3} + \frac{2x}{5}$

e $\frac{3a}{7} + \frac{2a}{3}$ f $\frac{3c}{5} - \frac{c}{2}$

g $\frac{4m}{3} + \frac{3m}{8}$ h $\frac{3x}{8} + \frac{x}{4}$

i $\frac{11y}{12} - \frac{y}{3}$ j $\frac{5p}{6} - \frac{3p}{4}$

k $\frac{7q}{10} + \frac{3q}{4}$ l $\frac{3s}{8} - \frac{s}{6}$

5 Add or subtract these fractions.

a $\frac{2x}{3} + \frac{y}{4}$ b $\frac{5c}{2} - \frac{3d}{5}$

c $\frac{2e}{7} + \frac{f}{2}$ d $\frac{2x}{5} + \frac{x}{2}$

e $\frac{3p}{5} - \frac{3q}{4}$ f $\frac{5y}{4} + \frac{3z}{5}$

g $\frac{3z}{4} - \frac{z}{2}$ h $\frac{x}{8} - \frac{3y}{4}$

i $\frac{5y}{6} + \frac{z}{4}$ j $\frac{8a}{9} - \frac{5}{6}$

k $\frac{3p}{10} + \frac{1}{2}$ l $\frac{2x}{3} - \frac{1}{4}$

Problem solving

6 A student wrote these two calculations.
They are both wrong.
Explain the mistakes and find the correct answers.

a. $\frac{1}{2} + \frac{1}{3} = \frac{1+1}{2+3} = \frac{2}{5}$ ✗

b. $\frac{x}{2} + \frac{y}{3} = \frac{x+y}{2+3} = \frac{x+y}{5}$ ✗

3c Formulae in context

Formulae are used in science, engineering, business and medicine.
A formula is a statement in algebra that links two or more **variables**.

- A **variable** is a quantity which can change its **value**.

You use a **formula** to calculate a value for one variable.

Example

In science, the energy E needed to send a current I through a light bulb with resistance R is given by the formula $E = RI^2$.

Find the value of E when $R = 16$ and $I = 5$.

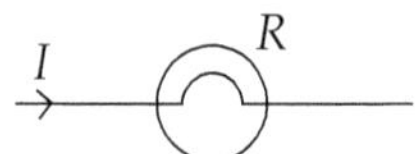

Substitute the values of R and I into the formula.

$E = RI^2$
$= 16 \times 5^2$
$= 16 \times 25$
$= 400$

- The **subject** of a formula is the variable by itself on the left-hand side of the formula.

E is the subject of the formula $E = mc^2$.

Example

When a car accelerates from an initial speed u for a time t with an acceleration a, its final speed v is given by this formula.

$v = u + at$

a Find the value of u when $v = 20$, $a = 4$ and $t = 3$.

b Find the value of t when $v = 40$, $u = 10$ and $a = 5$.

a Substitute the values you know into the formula.

$v = u + at$
$20 = u + 4 \times 3$

This is an equation. $20 = u + 12$
Subtract 12 from both sides. $8 = u$

The car's initial speed u is 8.

b Substitute the values you know into the formula.

$v = u + at$
$40 = 10 + 5 \times t$

This is an equation. $40 = 10 + 5t$
Subtract 10 from both sides. $30 = 5t$
Divide both sides by 5. $6 = t$

The car accelerates over a time $t = 6$.

If the variable that you are trying to find is not the subject, then you can think of the formula as an equation.

Exercise 3c

1 You have a savings account. The interest I that you earn on P pounds at a rate $R\%$ over T years is given by $I = \frac{PRT}{100}$. Find I when

a $P = 100$, $R = 5$ and $T = 2$. b $P = 500$, $R = 4$, $T = 3$.

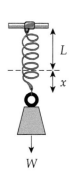

2 When an elastic string of strength λ and length L is stretched a distance x, the weight W on its end is given by $W = \frac{\lambda x}{L}$.

a Find W when $\lambda = 10$, $x = 2$ and $L = 5$.

b Find W when $\lambda = 50$, $x = 4$ and $L = 10$.

3 The voltage drop V in this electrical circuit is given by $V = E + RI$.

a Find V when $E = 10$, $R = 5$ and $I = 4$.

b Find V when $E = 22$, $R = 6$ and $I = 3$.

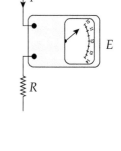

4 When drawing a pie chart, the angle θ for n items out of a total T is given by $\theta = \frac{360 \times n}{T}$.

a Find θ when $n = 20$ and $T = 60$.

b Find θ when $n = 30$ and $T = 40$.

5 The energy E of a car of mass m when it travels at a speed v is given by $E = \frac{1}{2}mv^2$.

a Find E when $m = 10$ and $v = 3$.

b Find E when $m = 40$ and $v = 4$.

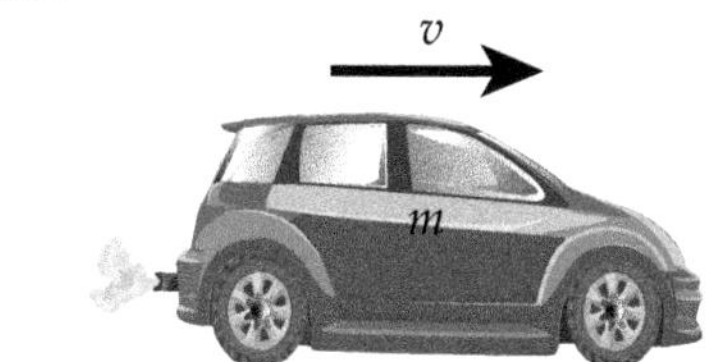

In these next questions, think of the formulae as equations.

6 If $V = E + RI$, find

a E when $V = 40$, $R = 8$ and $I = 2$ b I when $V = 100$, $E = 40$ and $R = 5$.

7 If $W = \frac{\lambda x}{L}$, find

a x when $W = 10$, $L = 4$ and $\lambda = 5$ b λ when $W = 15$, $L = 6$ and $x = 3$.

8 If $E = \frac{1}{2}mv^2$, find

a m when $E = 75$ and $v = 5$ b v when $E = 64$ and $m = 8$.

Problem solving

9 The body-mass index (BMI) for an adult of height h metres and mass m kg is given by $\text{BMI} = \frac{m}{h^2}$.
Use a spreadsheet to calculate the BMI for different adults you know. Research BMI on the Internet to find how the index is used to monitor a healthy body weight.

3d Rearranging formulae

The **subject** of a **formula** is the letter on its own on the left-hand side.
V is the subject of the formula $V = E + IR$.

You can **rearrange** a formula to find one of the other **variables**.
Think of the formula as an **equation** and use **inverse operations**.
When $V = E + IR$, you can make E the subject of the formula by

- subtracting $\boldsymbol{IR}$ from both sides
- changing sides to get $\boldsymbol{E}$ on the left.

$$V = E + IR$$
$$V - IR = E$$
$$E = V - IR$$

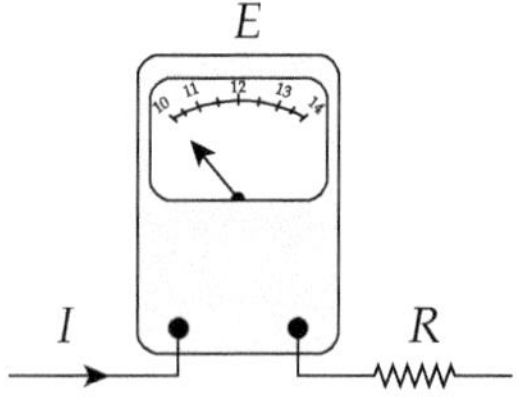

Example

Make I the subject of the formula $V = E + IR$.

You need to get I by itself. First remove E from the right-hand side and then remove R.

$V = E + IR$

Subtract E from both sides. $V - E = IR$

Divide both sides by R. $\dfrac{V - E}{R} = I$ so $I = \dfrac{V - E}{R}$

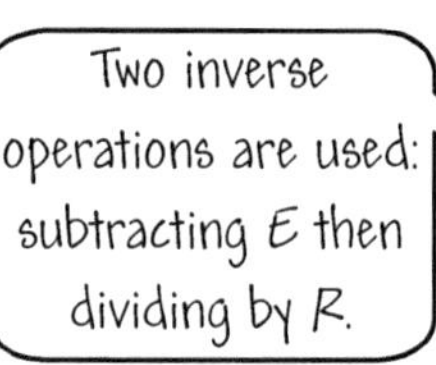

Two inverse operations are used: subtracting E then dividing by R.

Changing the subject of a formula allows you to work out different variables more easily.

Example

The area A of a triangle with height h and base b is given by the formula $A = \dfrac{bh}{2}$.

a Make h the subject of the formula.

b Find h when $A = 24\,\text{cm}^2$ and $b = 8\,\text{cm}$.

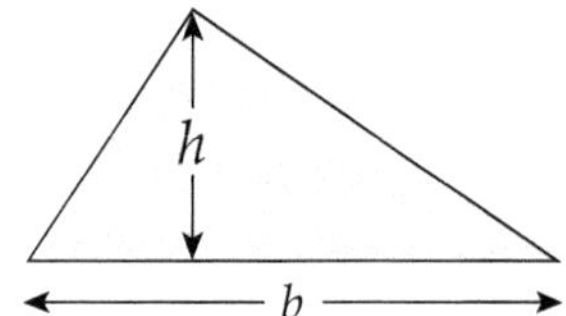

a Get h by itself by removing the 2 from the right-hand side and then removing b.

$A = \dfrac{bh}{2}$

Multiply by 2 $\quad 2 \times A = b \times h$

Divide by b $\quad \dfrac{2 \times A}{b} = h$

Change sides $\quad h = \dfrac{2A}{b}$

b Substitute $A = 24$ and $b = 8$.

$h = \dfrac{2A}{2}$

$= \dfrac{2 \times 24}{8}$

$= \dfrac{48}{8}$

$= 6\,\text{cm}$

Exercise 3d

These are the formulae used in this exercise. They come from different areas of the curriculum.

For moving vehicles	From science	For shapes	From medicine
$s = vt$	$V = RI$	$V = \frac{lbh}{3}$	$D = kW$
$v = u + at$	$V = E + RI$	$C = \pi d$	$\text{BMI} = \frac{m}{h^2}$
$E = \frac{mv^2}{2}$	$P = RI^2t$	$A = \pi r^2$	
		$V = \pi r^2 h$	

1 **a** Make t the subject of $s = vt$. **b** Find t when $s = 30$ and $v = 6$.

2 **a** Make R the subject of $V = RI$. **b** Find R when $V = 42$ and $I = 7$.

3 **a** Make W the subject of $D = kW$. **b** Find W when $D = 18$ and $k = 3$.

4 **a** Make u the subject of $v = u + at$. **b** Find u when $v = 42$, $a = 2$ and $t = 9$.

5 **a** Make E the subject of $V = E + RI$. **b** Find E when $V = 32$, $R = 12$ and $I = 2$.

6 **a** Make I the subject of $V = E + RI$. **b** Find I when $E = 52$, $V = 28$ and $R = 4$.

7 **a** Make m the subject of $\text{BMI} = \frac{m}{h^2}$ **b** Find m when $\text{BMI} = 24$ and $h = 10$.

8 **a** Make m the subject of $E = \frac{mv^2}{2}$. **b** Find m when $E = 48$ and $v = 4$.

9 **a** Make h the subject of $V = \frac{lbh}{3}$. **b** Find h when $V = 24$, $l = 6$ and $b = 2$.

10 **a** Make R the subject of $P = RI^2t$. **b** Find R when $P = 150$, $I = 5$ and $t = 2$.

11 The energy absorbed by a resistor in an electrical circuit is given by the formula $E = RI^2$. Make I the subject of the formula.

12 A rectangle has a perimeter given by the formula $P = 2l + 2w$. Make l the subject of the formula.

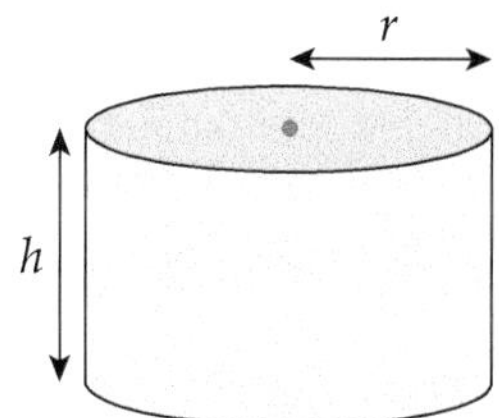

13 The volume V of a cylinder is given by the formula $V = \pi r^2 h$. Make r the subject of this formula.

Problem solving

14 Isaac Newton, born in 1643 in Lincolnshire, is one of the most influential men in human history. Use the Internet to find out about his contributions to mathematics and science. Can you find any formulae associated with Newton?

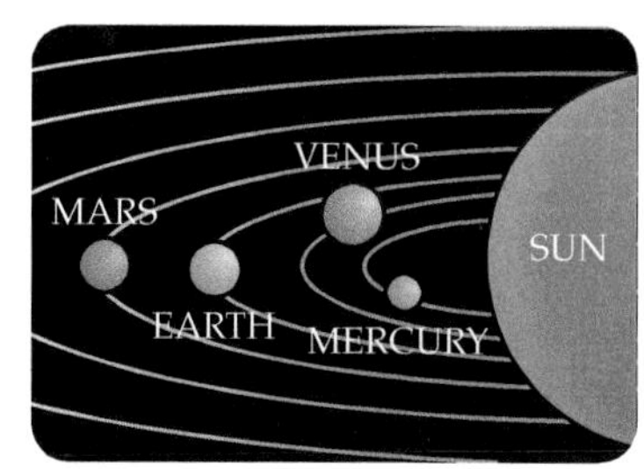

3e Deriving and graphing formulae

- You can write your own **formula** for a situation.

If you cut a hole (radius r) in a metal disc (radius R), you make a metal washer.

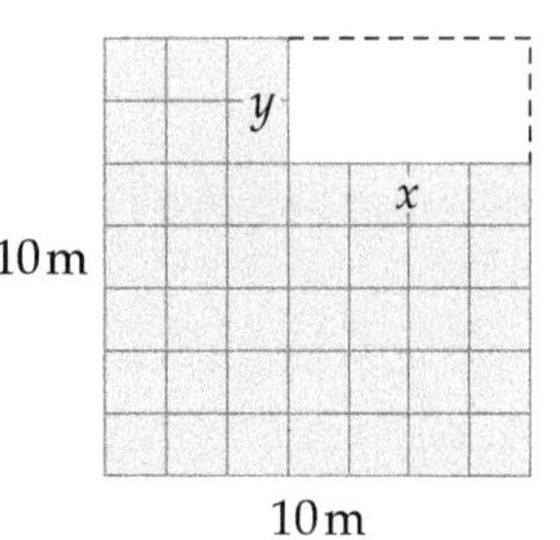

Area of washer = Area of disc − Area of hole
$= \pi R^2 - \pi r^2$
$= \pi(R^2 - r^2)$

The formula for the area of the washer is $A = \pi(R^2 - r^2)$.

π is a common factor.

Example

A patio is made by paving all of a 10-metre square except for a rectangular corner x metres by y metres.
Derive a formula for the paved area.

The 10-metre square has an area, in m², of $10 \times 10 = 100$.
The area, in m², not covered by paving is $x \times y = xy$.
So the formula for the paved area, in m², is
$100 - xy$.

10m, 10m, x, y

- You can draw a graph from the results given by a formula.

Example

The cost £C of hiring a car for x days is £20 plus an extra £10 for each day that you hire the car.

a Derive a formula for the total cost £C in terms of x.
b Draw a graph of C against x for up to 10 days of hire.

a £10 per day for x days gives a cost of £$10x$.
The £20 charge is then added on.
So the total cost £C is given by the formula
$C = 10x + 20$.

b Make a table of values by substituting values of x.
When $x = 2$, $C = 10 \times 2 + 20 = 40$
When $x = 4$, $C = 60$
When $x = 6$, $C = 80$ …

x (days)	2	4	6	8	10
C (£)	40	60	80	100	120

This table gives the coordinates of the points you plot to give the graph of C against x.

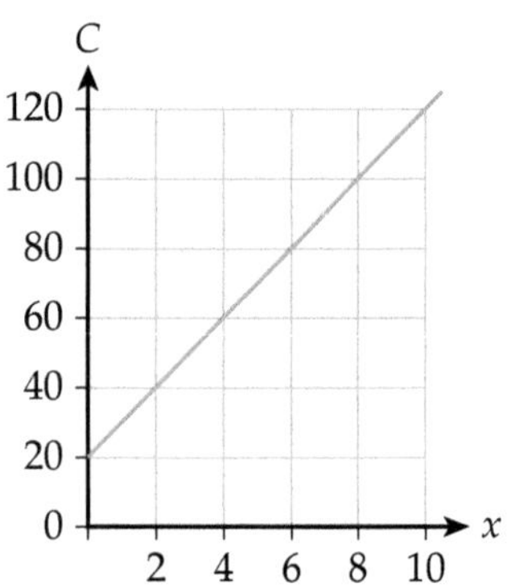

Exercise 3e

1 Derive formulae for the shaded area A in each of these diagrams.
All lengths are in centimetres.

a

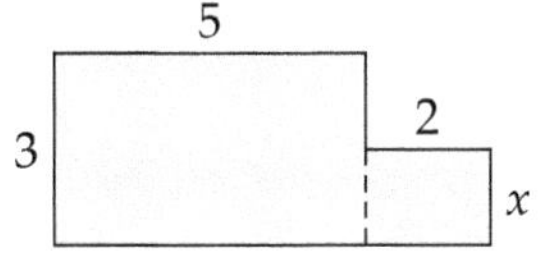

b

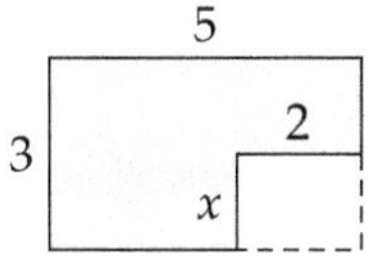

c

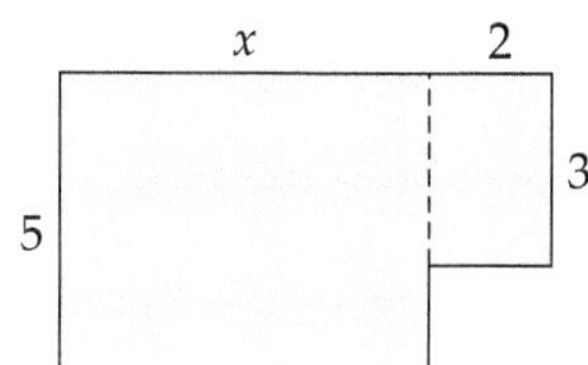

d

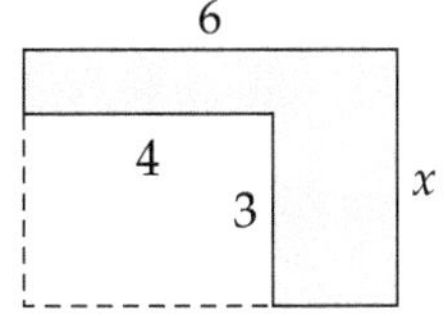

e

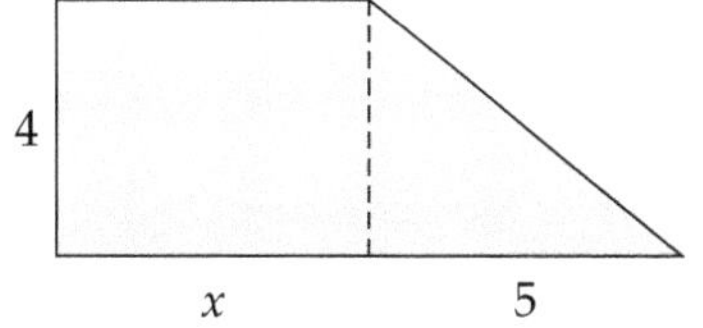

f

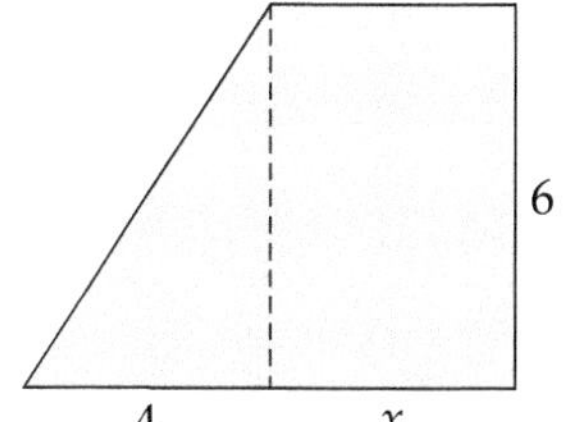

2 **a** Find a formula in terms of x for the area A of this shape.

b Copy and complete this table of values.

x (cm)	2	4	6	8	10
A (cm^2)					

c Draw a graph of A against x.

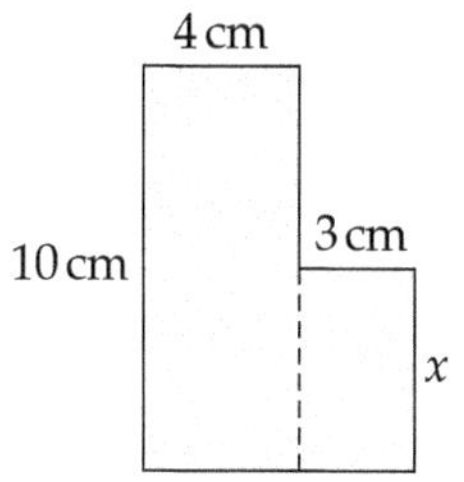

Problem solving

3 To cook a chicken, takes 50 minutes per kilogram (kg) and then an extra 20 minutes.

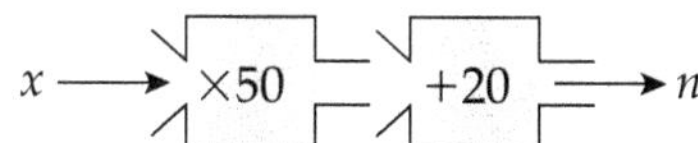

a Write a formula for the number of minutes, n, to cook a chicken with a mass of x kg. This flow diagram might help you.

b Find the cooking time n for $x = 6, 8, 10, 12$.
Construct a table of values and draw a graph of n against x.

4 **a** The average life expectancy in the UK is 80 years.
If a person is x years old now, write a formula for the number of years, n, they might still be expected to live.

b Find n for values of x from 10 to 70 and draw a graph of n against x.

Did you know?

Life expectancies estimated in 2008 range from 84.33 years in Macau to 31.99 years in Swaziland.

5 The formula $F = \frac{9 \times C}{5} + 32$ changes temperatures in degrees Celsius to temperatures in degrees Fahrenheit.
Construct a table of values for F with C = 60, 30, 0, -30 and -60.
Draw a graph of your results.
How cold has it to be for the temperature to have the same value in degrees Fahrenheit and in degrees Celsius?

3 MySummary

Check out

You should now be able to ...

Test it ➡

Questions

You should now be able to ...	Grade	Questions
✓ Factorise algebraic expressions.	7	1 – 2
✓ Simplify algebraic expressions.	7	3 – 4
✓ Substitute values in formulae to find unknown variables.	7	5
✓ Change the subject of a formula.	7	6 – 7
✓ Derive and graph formulae.	6	8 – 9

Language	Meaning	Example
Algebraic fractions	Fractions containing algebraic expressions.	$\frac{5x + 2y}{xy}$, $\frac{2z}{5}$ and $\frac{3}{a + b}$ are all algebraic fractions
Change the subject	Rearrange a formula so that a different variable is 'on its own'.	$v = \frac{b^2}{k}$ rearranged to make b the subject gives $b = \sqrt{vk}$
Derive	Construct a formula from information given.	The cost C pence of n chocolate bars each costing 35p is $C = 35n$
Expand	Multiply a bracket out.	$3(2x + 4y) = 6x + 12y$
Factorise	The reverse of expanding a bracket by taking out common factors.	$6x + 12y = 6(x + 2y)$
Formula (plural formulae)	A rule linking two or more variables.	The formula for finding the circumference of a circle is $A = \pi d$
Substitute	Replace variables with numerical values.	Substitute $a = 4$ in $a^2 - 2a$ gives $16 - 8 = 8$

3 MyReview

1 Factorise these expressions.

a $15x - 3$ b $8a + 24b$

c $24pq + 48p$ d $21 - 28v$

2 Factorise these expressions.

a $x^2 + 8x$ b $3x^2 + 9xy$

c $z^3 + 3z^2 - z$ d $16y^3 - 12y^2$

3 Simplify

a $\frac{6rs}{3s}$ b $\frac{pq^2}{5q}$

c $\frac{12a^2b}{4a}$ d $\frac{33x^2y}{44xy^2z}$

4 Add or subtract these fractions.

a $\frac{x}{6} + \frac{2x}{6}$ b $\frac{3a}{14} - \frac{a}{7}$

c $\frac{2y}{3} + \frac{y}{8}$ d $\frac{5b}{6} - \frac{3b}{8}$

5 A formula for distance travelled is given by

$s = ut + \frac{1}{2}at^2$

Use this formula to find the value of s when

$u = 30$, $a = -4$, $t = 3$

6 Make x the subject of each formula.

a $x - 3b = 2a$

b $8 + 2x = y - 7$

c $3x^2 + 4y = 5z$

7 a Make v the subject of $E = \frac{mv^2}{2}$

b Find v when $m = 7$, $E = 200$

c Find m when $E = 100$ and $v = -3$

8 a Derive a formula for the area, A, of this trapezium.

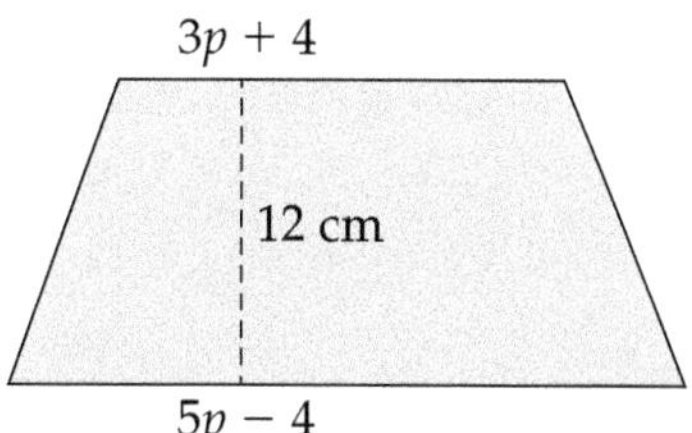

b If the area of the trapezium is 288 cm², what is the value of p?

9 a Find a formula for the shaded area, A, of this shape.

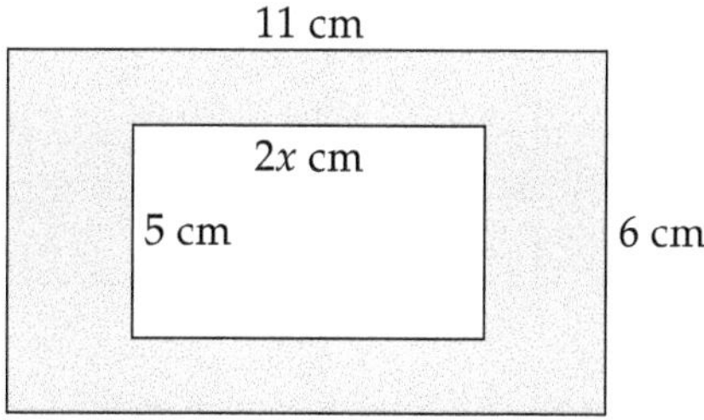

b Copy and complete the table of values.

x(cm)	1	2	3	4	5	6
A(cm²)						

c Draw a graph of A against x.

What next?

Score	
0 – 4	Your knowledge of this topic is still developing. To improve look at Formative test: 3B-3; MyMaths: 1155, 1171, 1178 and 1186
5 – 7	You are gaining a secure knowledge of this topic. To improve look at InvisiPen: 215, 223, 241, 252, 254, 255, 256 and 273
8, 9	You have mastered this topic. Well done, you are ready to progress!

3 MyPractice

3a

1 Factorise these expressions.

a $4x - 20$ b $5y + 15$ c $6b + 18$
d $7m - 35$ e $4 - 6z$ f $8p - 6$
g $12b + 16$ h $20 - 15q$ i $x^2 + 6x$
j $3y + y^2$ k $u^2 - 4u$ l $9f - f^2$

2 Factorise these expressions. Look for two common factors.

a $3xy + 6xz$ b $9pq + 3pr$ c $6x^2 - 4x$
d $8y^2 + 2yz$ e $6ab - 3a^2$ f $5xy + x^2y$
g $4g^2 - 18fg$ h $2m^2n - 11mn$ i $8r^2s - 13rs^2$

3b

3 Find equivalent fractions by cancelling.

a $\frac{3x}{6}$ b $\frac{2y}{8}$ c $\frac{4t}{16}$
d $\frac{9m}{18}$ e $\frac{6z}{10}$ f $\frac{mn}{3n}$
g $\frac{15r}{20}$ h $\frac{5ab}{6b}$ i $\frac{3xy}{6y}$
j $\frac{2yz}{8z}$ k $\frac{16pq}{20p}$ l $\frac{15mn}{24n}$
m $\frac{4a^2}{8a}$ n $\frac{4b^3}{6b}$ o $\frac{10x^2}{12x}$
p $\frac{24p^3}{32p}$ q $\frac{s^2t^3}{s^3t}$ r $\frac{x^3y}{x^2y}$
s $\frac{9ab^2}{6b}$ t $\frac{3y^2z}{6y^2z^2}$ u $\frac{20m^2n}{28m^2n^2}$

4 Add or subtract these fractions.

a $\frac{x}{5} + \frac{2x}{5}$ b $\frac{2y}{7} + \frac{3y}{7}$ c $\frac{5a}{9} + \frac{2a}{9}$
d $\frac{2x}{3} + \frac{y}{3}$ e $\frac{7v}{9} - \frac{5v}{9}$ f $\frac{3m}{10} - \frac{n}{10}$
g $\frac{z}{2} + \frac{z}{4}$ h $\frac{3a}{8} + \frac{a}{4}$ i $\frac{4t}{5} + \frac{s}{10}$
j $\frac{5c}{9} - \frac{c}{3}$ k $\frac{9x}{10} - \frac{3x}{5}$ l $\frac{11a}{12} - \frac{5b}{6}$
m $\frac{z}{2} + \frac{3z}{3}$ n $\frac{2a}{3} + \frac{a}{5}$ o $\frac{3p}{8} + \frac{p}{6}$
p $\frac{4x}{5} - \frac{3x}{4}$ q $\frac{2y}{5} - \frac{3y}{10}$ r $\frac{7a}{8} - \frac{5a}{6}$

3c

5 I cycle for x hours and walk for y hours.
The total distance travelled, D miles, is given by the formula $D = 12x + 2y$.

a Find D when $x = 4$ and $y = 3$.

b Find x when $D = 46$ and $y = 2$.

6 The speed, S, of water pouring from a tank is given by
$S = \frac{rt}{2h}$.

a Find S when $r = 10$, $t = 6$ and $h = 15$.

b Find t when $S = 24$, $r = 36$ and $h = 3$.

3d

7 **a** Make t the subject of the formula $v = u + at$.

b Find t when $v = 30$, $u = 18$ and $a = 2$.

8 **a** Make w the subject of the formula $P = 2l + 2w$.

b Find w when $P = 50$ and $l = 6$.

9 **a** Make n the subject of the formula $C = \frac{2n}{3}$.

b Find n when $C = 30$.

3e

10 I buy one packet of nails for 30 pence and x boxes of screws at 50 pence per box.

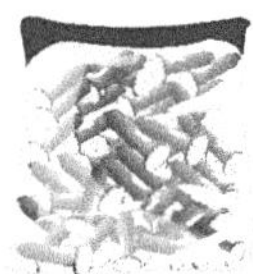

1 packet x boxes

a Write a formula for the total cost, C, of the nails and screws.

b Find the value of C when $x = 2, 4, 6, 8$ and 10 and draw a graph of C against x.

c Find the value of x when $C = 680$.

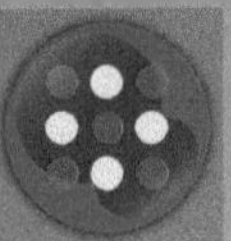

Case study 1: Why do bikes have gears?

Bikes are ingeniously simple structures which are very efficient at getting us around quickly and cheaply. This case study shows how bikes have developed over the years into the sophisticated machines they are today.

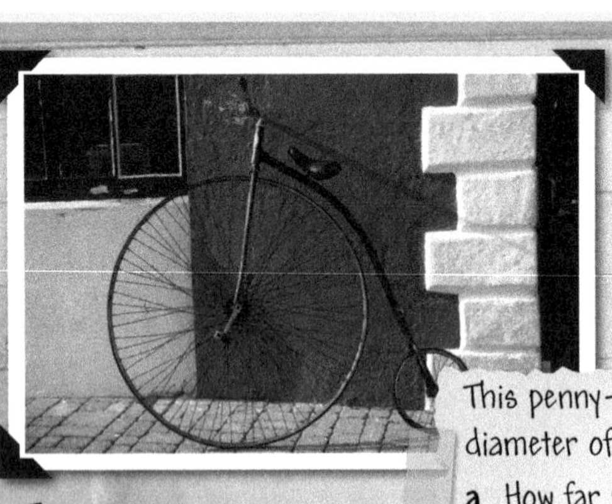

Task 1

The pedals of a penny-farthing bicycle were fixed directly to the front wheel so the wheel turned once for every turn of the pedals. The larger the wheel, the further the bike travelled for each turn.

This penny-farthing has a wheel diameter of 1.5 m.

a How far would the bike travel for one turn of the pedals? Remember: $C = \pi d$

b How many turns of the pedals would be needed to travel 1 km?

Task 2

If you remember riding a tricycle like this, you will know that you had to pedal quite quickly even at low speeds!

a With a 30 cm diameter front wheel, how many turns of the pedals would be needed to travel 500 m?

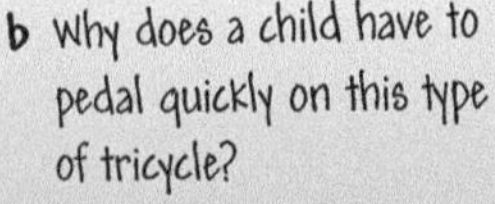

b Why does a child have to pedal quickly on this type of tricycle?

Task 3

As bikes developed, their wheels became smaller and a crank and chain drive was used. The larger front sprocket means that the wheel turns several times for each turn of the pedals.

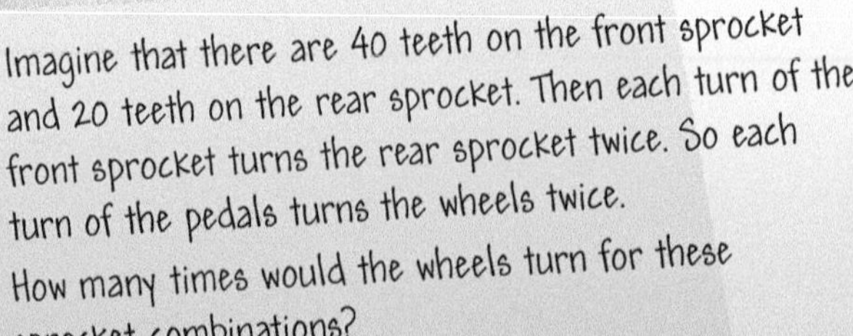

Imagine that there are 40 teeth on the front sprocket and 20 teeth on the rear sprocket. Then each turn of the front sprocket turns the rear sprocket twice. So each turn of the pedals turns the wheels twice.

How many times would the wheels turn for these sprocket combinations?

a 36 teeth front, 12 teeth rear

b 42 teeth front, 28 teeth rear

ust 280g, they're
ross, yet they still
e abuse.
edal designs – the
and Mag Lite.
igh in at 385g and
e, red, black, gold,
They contain two
; and a bush, and
service with a 5m
t.
similar but with a
and bolts that are
of the pedal instead
from the front. RRP
n gunmetal, gold or

the Mag Lites are
eeping the weight
ey have a slightly
other two models
black.
ble for bringing the
Even without this
the lightest flat
s. We've got a pair
how how they fare.

Task 4

Most bikes now have several gears which select different numbers of teeth on the front and rear sprockets.

This allows you to alter the number of turns of the wheels for each turn of the pedals.

a A 7-speed touring bike has wheel diameter 700 mm.
Find the distance travelled for each turn of the wheel, giving your answer to 2 d.p.

b Copy and complete this table, which shows different gear selections for the bike.
Give your answers to 2 d.p. where appropriate.

number of teeth front sprocket	number of teeth rear sprocket	number of turns of the wheel per turn of the pedals	distance travelled per turn of the pedals (m)
48	12	4	
48	14		
48	16		6.60
48	18		
48	20		
48	24		
48	28		

c With these gear selections, what is the fewest number of turns of the pedal that would be needed to travel 1 km?

Task 5

When riding comfortably, a cyclist makes between 40 and 90 turns of the pedals per minute.

Look again at the table in task 4.

What range of speeds will a cyclist travel at in each gear? Give your answers in kilometers per hour.

a Describe the amount of overlap between the speed ranges in different gears.

b Why would this be a good thing?

c What would the speed ranges be in miles per hour?
$1\text{ km} \approx \frac{5}{8}$ mile

d What would the speed ranges be if the cyclist were using their 32 teeth front sprocket?

Extension

If you have a bike, estimate how quickly you turn the pedals and work out the speed ranges for your gears.

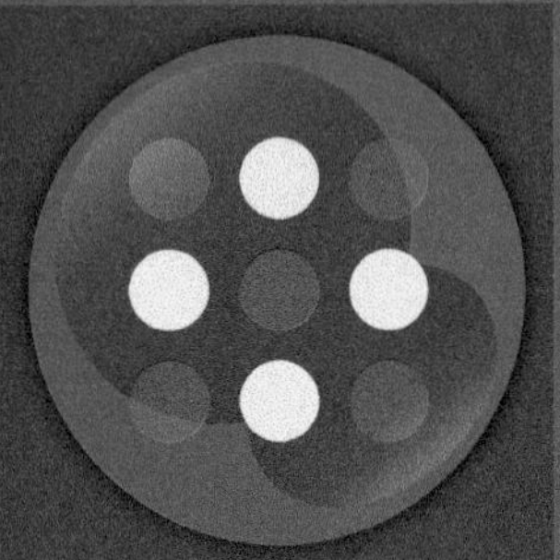

4 Fractions, decimals and percentages

Introduction

Fractals are at the cutting edge of modern mathematics, but are based on the simple idea of fractions. A fractal is a picture that, as you zoom in to any part of it, looks like the original picture! If the picture is infinitely detailed, then you should be able to zoom in for ever and you will end up with what you started with.

What's the point?

Fractals are vitally important in biology and medicine for understanding the organs of the human body at microscopic level; they are also useful for describing complex and irregular real world objects such as clouds, coastlines and trees. They are frequently used in computer games to generate 'real-life' environments.

Objectives

By the end of this chapter, you will have learned how to ...

- Add and subtract fractions.
- Multiply and divide fractions.
- Convert between decimals and fractions.
- Calculate percentage changes.

Check in

1 Copy and complete these equivalent fractions.

a $\frac{3}{10} = \frac{\square}{40}$ b $\frac{7}{8} = \frac{\square}{40}$ c $\frac{15}{25} = \frac{3}{\square}$

2 Calculate these using a suitable method.

a 15% of £30   b 55% of 40 km   c 18% of £128

3 Copy and complete this table, using a calculator where appropriate.

Fraction	Decimal	Percentage
$\frac{13}{20}$		
	0.625	
		8%

4 Work out the lowest common multiple (LCM) of

a 5 and 7   b 6 and 8

c 15 and 30   d 12 and 16

5 Work out the highest common factor (HCF) of

a 45 and 50   b 28 and 42   c 252 and 378

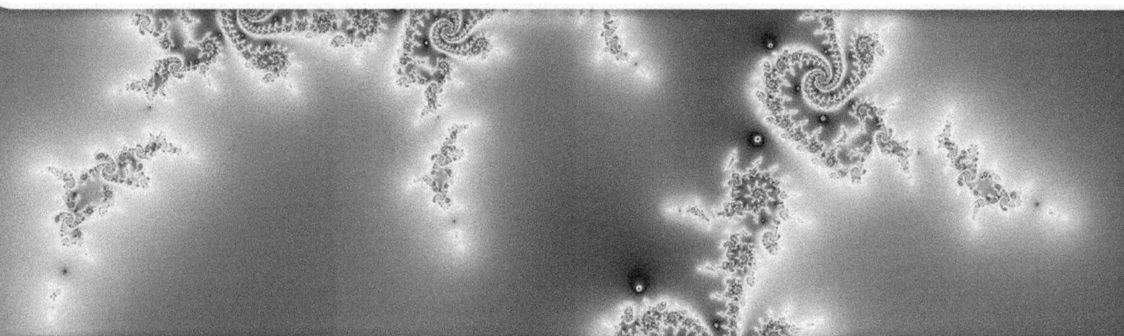

Starter problem

Look at this sequence

Describe a rule for making the next pattern in the sequence.

Draw the next pattern in the sequence

What additional fraction of the new square is now shaded?

Stage 0

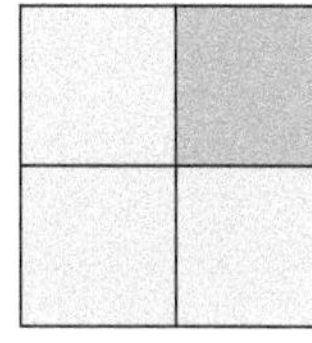

Stage 1

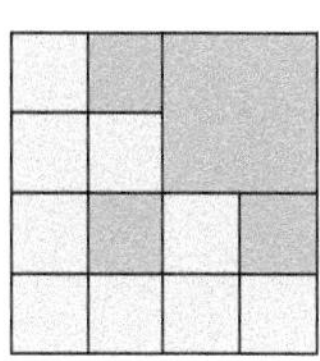

Stage 2

What is the total fraction of your new square that is now shaded?

Investigate this sequence.

4a Adding and subtracting fractions

- You can add or subtract **fractions** with different **denominators** by first writing them as **equivalent fractions** with the same denominator.

Example

Calculate

a $\frac{3}{5} + \frac{1}{4}$ **b** $\frac{7}{9} - \frac{5}{12}$

Rewrite as equivalent fractions with the same denominator.

a

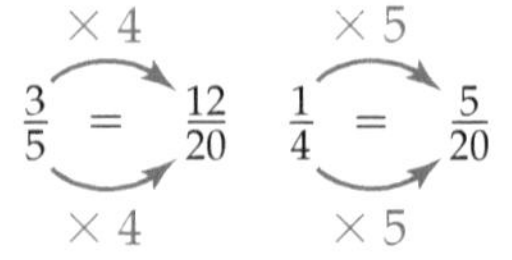

b

$\frac{7}{9} \xrightarrow{\times 4} \frac{28}{36}$ $\frac{5}{12} \xrightarrow{\times 3} \frac{15}{36}$

Add the numerators.

$\frac{12}{20} + \frac{5}{20} = \frac{12 + 5}{20} = \frac{17}{20}$

Subtract the numerators.

$\frac{28}{36} - \frac{15}{36} = \frac{28 - 15}{36} = \frac{13}{36}$

In part b, the LCM of 9 and 12 is 36.

- You can add or subtract **mixed numbers** by changing them into **improper fractions**.

You change a mixed number into an improper fraction using multiplication.

$4\frac{2}{7} = \frac{4 \times 7 + 2}{7} = \frac{28 + 2}{7} = \frac{30}{7}$

Improper fractions have larger numerators than denominators.

Example

Calculate $1\frac{3}{8} - \frac{5}{6}$.

Rewrite as an improper fraction.

$1\frac{3}{8} = \frac{1 \times 8 + 3}{8}$

$= \frac{11}{8}$

Rewrite as equivalent fractions with the same denominator.

$\frac{11}{8} \xrightarrow{\times 3} \frac{33}{24}$ $\frac{5}{6} \xrightarrow{\times 4} \frac{20}{24}$

Subtract the numerators.

$\frac{33}{24} - \frac{20}{24} = \frac{33 - 20}{24}$

$= \frac{13}{24}$

The LCM of 8 and 6 is 24, so this is the common denominator.

Exercise 4a

1 Find the missing number in each of these pairs of equivalent fractions.

a $\frac{1}{4} = \frac{\square}{20}$ **b** $\frac{5}{6} = \frac{\square}{24}$

c $\frac{3}{7} = \frac{12}{\square}$ **d** $\frac{7}{9} = \frac{\square}{54}$

2 Calculate these.
Give your answer as a fraction in its simplest form.

a $\frac{3}{5} + \frac{1}{5}$ **b** $\frac{7}{12} - \frac{3}{12}$

c $\frac{20}{13} - \frac{3}{13}$ **d** $\frac{4}{5} + \frac{4}{5}$

e $\frac{1}{5} + \frac{1}{2}$ **f** $\frac{2}{3} + \frac{1}{4}$

g $\frac{3}{8} - \frac{1}{3}$ **h** $\frac{3}{7} + \frac{1}{3}$

3 Work out these.
Give your answer as a fraction in its simplest form.

a $\frac{2}{5} + \frac{5}{10}$ **b** $\frac{5}{6} - \frac{3}{4}$ **c** $\frac{5}{6} - \frac{7}{12}$

d $\frac{5}{8} + \frac{7}{12}$ **e** $\frac{5}{18} + \frac{5}{24}$ **f** $\frac{7}{15} + \frac{3}{20}$

g $\frac{11}{16} - \frac{5}{8}$ **h** $\frac{17}{24} + \frac{3}{16}$

4 Work out these.
Give your answer as a fraction in its simplest form.

a $1\frac{3}{4} + 1\frac{1}{2}$ **b** $1\frac{1}{4} - \frac{5}{8}$ **c** $1\frac{2}{3} + 1\frac{2}{5}$

d $2\frac{3}{5} - 1\frac{4}{5}$ **e** $2\frac{3}{5} + 1\frac{5}{6}$ **f** $2\frac{3}{4} + 1\frac{2}{5}$

g $1\frac{5}{8} - \frac{3}{5}$ **h** $1\frac{3}{7} + \frac{2}{3}$

Problem solving

5 a Jacques needs $\frac{5}{8}$kg of flour to make a loaf of bread.
He tips $\frac{2}{5}$kg of white flour onto a weighing scale.
How much more flour does he need to add?

b Kalid runs $\frac{3}{7}$ of a race in pair of trainers.
For the next $\frac{8}{15}$ of the race he runs in bare feet.
Has Kalid completed the race?
Explain your answer.

6 A rectangular mobile phone has a length of $5\frac{3}{4}$cm and a width of $2\frac{2}{5}$cm.
Calculate the perimeter of the phone.

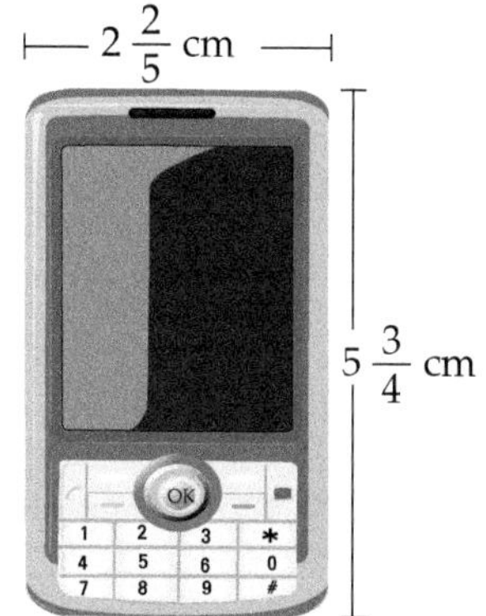

7 Ancient Egyptians only used fractions which had 1 as the numerator (unit fractions). Fractions were written as sums of unit fractions.
They would write $\frac{3}{4}$ as $\frac{1}{2} + \frac{1}{4}$ and $\frac{5}{12}$ as $\frac{1}{3} + \frac{1}{12}$.

a Write these fractions in the Egyptian way.
$\frac{5}{8}$ $\frac{7}{10}$ $\frac{7}{12}$

b Find more fractions that can be made by adding pairs of different unit fractions.

c Investigate adding three or more unit fractions.

Did you know?

$= \frac{1}{3}$ | $= \frac{1}{10}$

The Ancient Egyptians used to write fractions in hieroglyphics.

4b Multiplying fractions

- You can find a **fraction** of an amount by multiplying.

Example

Find $\frac{3}{5}$ of 14 km.

Using a written method	Using a calculator
$\frac{3}{5}$ of $14 = \frac{3}{5} \times \frac{14}{1}$	$\frac{3}{5}$ of $14 = \frac{3}{5} \times 14$
$= \frac{42}{5} = 8\frac{2}{5}$ km	$= 0.6 \times 14$
	$= 8.4$ km

$\frac{3}{5}$

14 km

Change the fraction into a decimal using division. $\frac{3}{5} = 3 \div 5 = 0.6$.

- You can find a fraction of a fraction by multiplying.

Example

Zak is given $\frac{2}{3}$ of half a pizza.
What fraction of the pizza does Zak get?

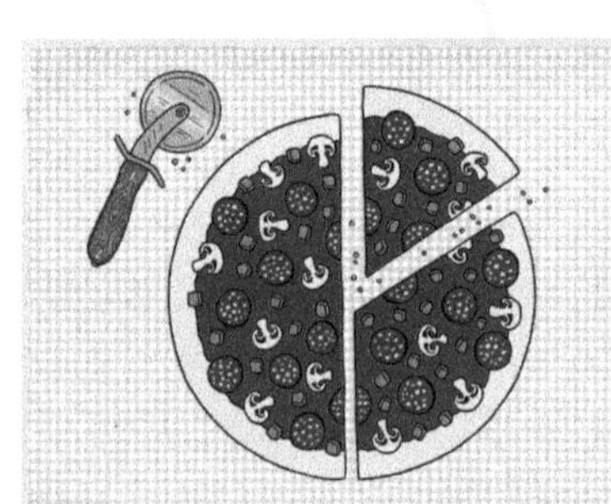

$\frac{2}{3}$ of half $= \frac{2}{3}$ of $\frac{1}{2} = \frac{2}{3} \times \frac{1}{2}$

$= \frac{2}{6} = \frac{1}{3}$

Zak gets $\frac{1}{3}$ of the pizza.

- You can multiply a pair of fractions and use cancelling to simplify your answer.

Example

Calculate $\frac{4}{9} \times \frac{3}{8}$

Method 1

Multiply the fractions

$\frac{4}{9} \times \frac{3}{8} = \frac{4 \times 3}{9 \times 8} = \frac{12}{72}$

Cancel any common factors

$\frac{12}{72} = \frac{1}{6}$ (÷ 12 top and bottom)

Method 2

Cancel common factors

$\frac{\cancel{4}^1}{\cancel{9}_3} \times \frac{\cancel{3}^1}{\cancel{8}_2} = \frac{1}{3} \times \frac{1}{2}$

Multiply the fractions

$\frac{1}{3} \times \frac{1}{2} = \frac{1 \times 1}{3 \times 2} = \frac{1}{6}$

A **product** is the result of a multiplication.

Exercise 4b

1 Calculate these. Give your answer in its simplest form and as a mixed number where appropriate.

a $3 \times \frac{1}{7}$ b $3 \times \frac{2}{7}$

c $4 \times \frac{3}{13}$ d $\frac{3}{5} \times 12$

e $\frac{2}{3} \times 16$ f $\frac{5}{8} \times 20$

g $\frac{3}{4} \times 28$ h $\frac{5}{7} \times 12$

2 Calculate these. Give your answer in its simplest form and as a mixed number where appropriate.

a $\frac{4}{5}$ of 8 cm b $\frac{3}{7}$ of 19 kg

c $\frac{3}{4}$ of 24 m d $\frac{4}{9}$ of 30 mins

e $\frac{7}{10}$ of 50 kg f $\frac{5}{12}$ of 7 feet

g $\frac{4}{11}$ of 28 tonnes h $\frac{5}{8}$ of 36 km

3 Copy and complete these equivalents.

a $\frac{3}{4}$ of 60 $= \frac{1}{2}$ of $\square$

b $\frac{1}{8}$ of 40 $= \frac{1}{4}$ of $\square$

c $\frac{3}{5}$ of 40 $= \frac{\square}{4}$ of 32

d $\frac{4}{7}$ of 28 $= \frac{2}{\square}$ of 24

Remember sometimes you can cancel common factors first to make the calculation easier.

4 Use an appropriate method to calculate these amounts.
Where necessary give your answer to 2 dp.

a $\frac{2}{5}$ of 134 km b $\frac{7}{12}$ of £400

c $\frac{4}{7}$ of 20 km d $\frac{3}{8}$ of 275 m

e $\frac{4}{13}$ of 50 kg f $\frac{5}{9}$ of 45 g

g $\frac{3}{11}$ of 1000 ml h $\frac{5}{16}$ of 180°

5 Calculate these products.

a $\frac{2}{3} \times \frac{4}{5}$ b $\frac{3}{4} \times \frac{5}{6}$

c $\frac{1}{8} \times \frac{4}{7}$ d $\frac{3}{5} \times \frac{5}{12}$

e $\frac{4}{7} \times \frac{5}{8}$ f $\frac{3}{10} \times \frac{5}{6}$

g $\frac{5}{8} \times \frac{4}{15}$ h $\frac{6}{13} \times \frac{5}{12}$

Problem solving

6 a A computer game normally costs £18.
In a sale all prices are reduced by $\frac{2}{5}$.
What is the sale price of the computer game?

b Astra buys a car for £22 500.
Two years later the car has gone down in value by $\frac{2}{7}$.
What is the new value of Astra's car?

7 Jack and Jermaine are trying to work out $\frac{3}{5}$ of $\frac{2}{3}$ of £60.
Jack says they should calculate $\frac{2}{3}$ of £60 and then calculate $\frac{3}{5}$ of their answer.

a Use Jack's method to work out $\frac{3}{5}$ of $\frac{2}{3}$ of £60.

b Jermaine says that he can improve Jack's method.
Investigate how to improve Jack's method.

c Work out i $\frac{3}{8}$ of $\frac{2}{5}$ of £40 ii $\frac{5}{7}$ of $\frac{2}{3}$ of 63 kg

4c Dividing by fractions

- You can divide an **integer** by any **unit fraction** by multiplying by the **inverse** of the unit fraction.

  $6 \div \frac{1}{4} = 6 \times 4 = 24$

Example

Sam cuts two cakes into thirds. How many slices are there?

$2 \div \frac{1}{3} = 2 \times 3 = 6$

There are six slices of cake.

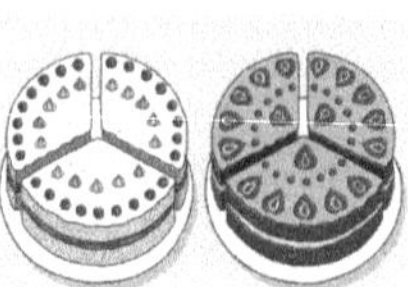

- You can divide an integer by any fraction by multiplying by the **inverted** fraction. The inverted fraction is sometimes called the **reciprocal**.

  $6 \div \frac{3}{4} = 6 \times \frac{4}{3} = \frac{24}{3} = 8$

Example

Calculate $6 \div \frac{2}{3}$.

Dividing by $\frac{2}{3}$ is the same as multiplying by $\frac{3}{2}$.

$6 \div \frac{2}{3} = 6 \times \frac{3}{2}$

$= \frac{18}{2} = 9$

You could cancel first.
$\overset{3}{\cancel{6}} \times \frac{3}{\underset{1}{\cancel{2}}} = \frac{9}{1} = 9$

- You can divide a fraction by another fraction by
  - changing the division into a multiplication
  - inverting the dividing fraction

$\frac{3}{4} \div \frac{5}{6}$

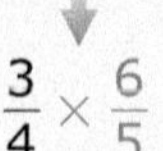

$\frac{3}{4} \times \frac{6}{5}$

Example

Calculate $\frac{2}{3} \div \frac{4}{5}$.

Dividing by $\frac{4}{5}$ is the same as multiplying by $\frac{5}{4}$.

$\frac{2}{3} \div \frac{4}{5} = \frac{2}{3} \times \frac{5}{4} = \frac{2 \times 5}{3 \times 4}$

$= \frac{10}{12} = \frac{5}{6}$

Exercise 4c

1 **a** How many fifths are there in 2?
b How many quarters are there in 3?
c How many eighths are there in 4?
d How many eighths are there in one quarter?
e How many sixths are there in one half?
f How many fifths are there in one half?

2 Calculate these divisions.

a $2 \div \frac{1}{4}$ **b** $5 \div \frac{1}{2}$ **c** $4 \div \frac{1}{3}$
d $3 \div \frac{1}{5}$ **e** $5 \div \frac{1}{4}$ **f** $6 \div \frac{1}{10}$
g $8 \div \frac{1}{7}$ **h** $7 \div \frac{1}{3}$

3 Calculate these divisions.
Give your answer in its simplest form.

a $3 \div \frac{3}{4}$ **b** $4 \div \frac{2}{3}$ **c** $4 \div \frac{2}{5}$
d $6 \div \frac{3}{8}$ **e** $10 \div \frac{5}{6}$ **f** $6 \div \frac{3}{5}$
g $12 \div \frac{4}{7}$ **h** $15 \div \frac{5}{8}$

4 Calculate these divisions.
Give your answer as a mixed number in its simplest form.

a $5 \div \frac{3}{4}$ **b** $7 \div \frac{4}{5}$
c $5 \div \frac{2}{3}$ **d** $8 \div \frac{3}{7}$
e $2 \div \frac{7}{9}$ **f** $5 \div \frac{4}{7}$
g $10 \div \frac{3}{8}$ **h** $9 \div \frac{7}{11}$

5 Calculate these divisions.

a $\frac{3}{4} \div \frac{2}{3}$ **b** $\frac{2}{3} \div \frac{4}{5}$
c $\frac{3}{7} \div \frac{3}{5}$ **d** $\frac{5}{6} \div \frac{1}{3}$
e $\frac{3}{7} \div \frac{2}{9}$ **f** $\frac{4}{9} \div \frac{2}{3}$
g $\frac{3}{12} \div \frac{5}{8}$ **h** $\frac{3}{4} \div \frac{15}{16}$

6 Calculate these divisions.
Give your answer in its simplest form.

a $1\frac{1}{2} \div \frac{3}{4}$ **b** $3\frac{1}{3} \div \frac{5}{6}$
c $2\frac{2}{5} \div \frac{3}{5}$ **d** $1\frac{1}{4} \div \frac{2}{5}$

Did you know?

Some people use fractions all the time in their jobs. Chefs must make different quantities of food, so they have to reduce or increase all the ingredients by the same fraction.

Problem solving

7 **a** Harriet makes 5 kg of jam. She puts the jam into jars.
Each jar can hold $\frac{3}{8}$ kg. How many jars does she need?
b To make one giant muffin Andreas needs $\frac{4}{25}$ kg of flour.
How many muffins can he make with 2 kg of flour?

8 Copy and complete the next three lines of each of these fraction division patterns.

a **i**
$1 \div \frac{1}{3} = 3$
$2 \div \frac{1}{3} = 6$
$3 \div \frac{1}{3} = 9$
...

ii
$1 \div \frac{1}{4} = 4$
$2 \div \frac{1}{4} = 8$
$3 \div \frac{1}{4} = 12$
...

iii
$1 \div \frac{1}{5} = 5$
$2 \div \frac{1}{5} = 10$
$3 \div \frac{1}{5} = 15$
...

b Describe a quick way of dividing an integer by a unit fraction.
c Investigate dividing by $\frac{2}{3}, \frac{2}{4}, \frac{2}{5}, \ldots$.

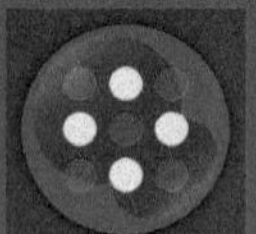

4d Decimals and fractions

- A **terminating decimal** has an exact number of decimal places. $\frac{1}{4} = 0.25$

1 dp = tenths
2 dp = hundredths
3 dp = thousandths

Example

Convert these decimals into fractions in their simplest form.

a 0.4 **b** 0.65 **c** 0.375

a $0.4 = \frac{4}{10}$

$\frac{4}{10} \overset{\div 2}{=} \frac{2}{5}$

b $0.65 = \frac{65}{100}$

$\frac{65}{100} \overset{\div 5}{=} \frac{13}{20}$

c $0.375 = \frac{375}{1000}$

$\frac{375}{1000} \overset{\div 125}{=} \frac{3}{8}$

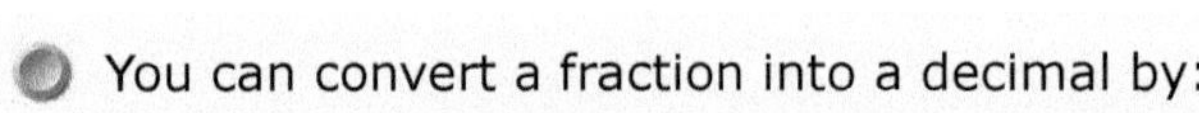

- You can convert a fraction into a decimal by:
  - rewriting the fraction as an equivalent fraction with denominator 10, 100, 1000, ...
  - dividing the numerator by the denominator.

$$\frac{3}{4} = \frac{75}{100} = 0.75$$

Example

Convert these fractions to decimals.

a $\frac{9}{20}$ **b** $\frac{5}{9}$

a $\frac{9}{20} \overset{\times 5}{=} \frac{45}{100} = 0.45$

b $\frac{5}{9} = 5 \div 9$

$= 0.555... = 0.\dot{5}$

You use dots to show which digits repeat.
$0.555... = 0.\dot{5}$ and
$0.616161... = 0.\dot{6}\dot{1}$

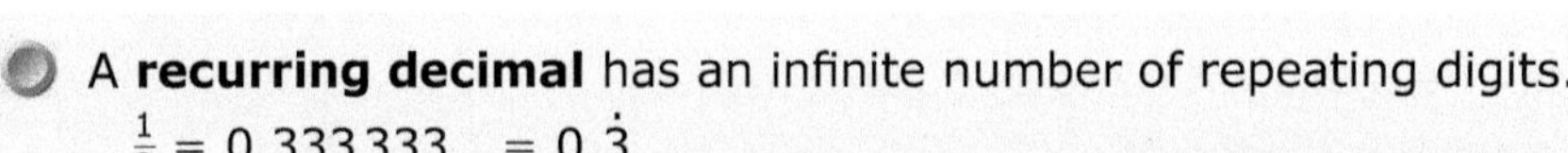

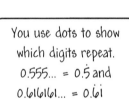

- A **recurring decimal** has an infinite number of repeating digits.
$\frac{1}{3} = 0.333333... = 0.\dot{3}$

Example

Put these fractions and decimals in order, lowest first.

$\frac{5}{11}$ $\frac{2}{5}$ 0.44

$\frac{5}{11} = 5 \div 11$

$= 0.454545... = 0.\dot{4}\dot{5}$

$\frac{2}{5} = 2 \div 5$

$= 0.4$

Put the decimals in order

$0.4, 0.44, 0.\dot{4}\dot{5}$

Put the decimals and fractions in order.

$\frac{2}{5}, 0.44, \frac{5}{11}$

Exercise 4d

1 Write these decimals as fractions in their simplest form.

a 0.6 **b** 0.48 **c** 0.25 **d** 0.74
e 0.125 **f** 0.585 **g** 1.5 **h** 1.05
i 2.25 **j** 1.56

2 Write these fractions as decimals without using a calculator.

a $\frac{7}{10}$ **b** $\frac{13}{20}$ **c** $\frac{11}{25}$ **d** $\frac{23}{50}$
e $\frac{31}{25}$ **f** $\frac{6}{5}$ **g** $\frac{27}{20}$ **h** $\frac{17}{40}$
i $\frac{12}{16}$ **j** $\frac{64}{80}$

3 Change these fractions into decimals using an appropriate method.
Give your answers to 2 decimal places where appropriate.

a $\frac{11}{16}$ **b** $\frac{7}{32}$ **c** $\frac{3}{11}$ **d** $\frac{6}{7}$
e $\frac{7}{6}$ **f** $\frac{11}{19}$ **g** $\frac{9}{7}$ **h** $\frac{11}{15}$
i $\frac{8}{13}$ **j** $\frac{23}{21}$

4 Copy these pairs of numbers.
Place $<$ or $>$ between the numbers to show which number is larger.

a 0.6 □ $\frac{5}{7}$ **b** $\frac{5}{12}$ □ $\frac{4}{7}$
c $\frac{6}{7}$ □ 0.83 **d** 0.19 □ $\frac{3}{16}$
e $\frac{2}{9}$ □ 0.25 **f** 0.55 □ $\frac{7}{13}$
g $\frac{1}{9}$ □ 0.12 **h** 0.165 □ $\frac{3}{19}$

5 Put these fractions and decimals in order from lowest to highest.

a $\frac{2}{7}$ 0.4 $\frac{4}{11}$ 0.33
b $\frac{1}{5}$ $\frac{3}{11}$ 0.3 0.2929...
c $\frac{6}{7}$ $\frac{9}{10}$ $\frac{8}{9}$ $\frac{7}{8}$

Problem solving

6 Which of these fractions are smaller than $\frac{1}{12}$?
Do not use a calculator. Explain and justify your answers.

a $\frac{1}{16}$ **b** $\frac{1}{8}$ **c** $\frac{3}{24}$ **d** $\frac{1}{4}$ **e** $\frac{4}{50}$

7 **a** Hannah has £0.45. Jameela has $\frac{6}{8}$ of £1. Who has more money? Explain and justify your answer.
b To make a cake Gary uses 1.6 kg of flour. To make a different cake Farah uses $1\frac{4}{5}$ kg of flour. Who uses more flour?

8 Write three decimal numbers, each with 1 decimal place, between $\frac{3}{7}$ and $\frac{3}{4}$.

9 Ryan changes a fraction into a decimal using his calculator.
The answer on his calculator is 0.6470588....
Both the numbers in his fraction are less than 20.
What fraction did Ryan type into his calculator?

4e Percentage change

- You can calculate a **percentage** of an amount using a mental, written or calculator method.

Example

A pair of jeans costs £50. In a sale the price is reduced by 15%.
What is the sale price of the pair of jeans?

£50 TOP–JEANS

15% Off !

First find the reduction in price.

Using a mental method

15% of £50 10% of £50 = £5.00
+ 5% of £50 = £2.50
15% of £50 = £7.50

To find 5% you find half of 10%.
To find 10% you divide the amount by 10.

Using an equivalent fraction

$$15\% \text{ of } £50 = \frac{15}{100} \text{ of } 50 = \frac{15 \times 50}{100} = \frac{750}{100} = £7.50$$

Using the decimal equivalent

$$15\% \text{ of } 50 = \frac{15}{100} \text{ of } 50 = 0.15 \times 50 = £7.50$$

The sale price of the jeans is £50 − £7.50 = £42.50.

- You can calculate a **percentage increase** or **decrease** in a single calculation using an **equivalent** decimal.

You need to remember how to convert from a percentage to a decimal.

$$80\% = \frac{80}{100} = 0.8 \qquad 120\% = \frac{120}{100} = 1.2$$

Example

a Increase £50 by 15%. **b** Decrease £50 by 15%.

a New price = (100 + 15)% of the old price
= 115% of £50
= 1.15 × £50
= £57.50

b New price = (100 − 15)% of the old price
= 85% of £50
= 0.85 × £50
= £42.50

Check that the answer to part a is greater than £50 and the answer to part b is less than £50.

Exercise 4e

1 Calculate these using a suitable method.

- a 15% of £80
- b 45% of 350 kg
- c 11% of 65 m
- d 36% of $12
- e 19% of 625 cm
- f 17% of £145
- g 6% of 128 MB
- h 99% of 33 kg

2

- a Increase £80 by 15%.
- b Decrease £80 by 15%.
- c Increase 22 km by 11%.
- d Decrease 58 kg by 20%.
- e Increase 32 m by 5%.
- f Decrease 67 cm by 27%.
- g Increase £135 by 95%.
- h Decrease 364 kJ by 8%.
- i Increase 32 kB by 6.5%.
- j Decrease £3250 by 1.8%.

Problem solving

3 a A shirt usually costs £35.
In a sale the price is reduced by 15%.
What is the sale price of the shirt?

b Last year Gina was paid £28 a week for her paper round.
At the start of this year, the newsagent increased Gina's wage by 12%.
What is Gina's new wage?

c A bar of chocolate usually weighs 240 g and costs 85 p.
The chocolate company decide to keep the price the same but reduce the weight of the chocolate bar by 20%.
What is the new weight of the chocolate bar?

d In January a litre of petrol cost £1.15.
By March the price had increased by 35%.
What was the cost of a litre of petrol in March?

4 Match each of these statements with the correct mathematical calculation.

- a Increase £40 by 30%.
- b 30% of £40.
- c Decrease £40 by 30%.
- d Increase £40 by 3%.
- e 3% of £40.
- f Decrease £40 by 3%.

0.03×40	1.03×40
0.3×40	1.3×40
0.97×40	0.7×40

5 a A computer game costs £20 in August.
In November it is increased in price by 10%.
In January the game is reduced in price by 10%.
Is the January sale price more, less or the same as the price in August?
Explain your answer.

b Investigate increasing and decreasing prices by other percentages.
Summarise what you notice and try to justify your answers.

4f Percentage problems

- You can represent a **proportion** as a fraction, decimal or **percentage**.

Example

Last year the Jones family earned £32 453 and spent £2543 on a holiday.

The Hussain family earned £25 000 and spent £2000 on a holiday.

Which family spent proportionately more on their holiday?

Calculator method

% spent on holiday

Jones Family

$= \frac{2543}{32453}$

$= 2543 \div 32453$

$= 0.078359...$

$= 7.8359\%$

$= 7.8\%$

Mental method

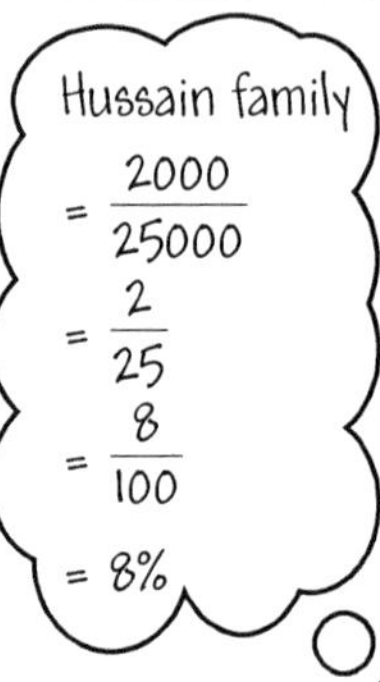

Write the answers as percentages so that they can easily be compared.

The Hussain family spent a greater percentage of their earnings on their holiday.

- You can calculate a percentage increase or decrease using a single multiplier.

Example

Talan receives a monthly allowance of £30.
His father increases Talan's allowance by 22%.
What is Talan's new allowance?

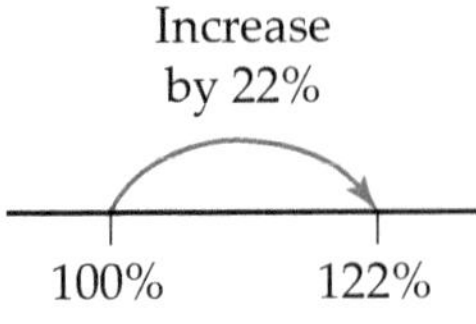

New allowance = (100 + 22)% of the old allowance

= 122% of £30

= 1.22 × £30

= £36.60

Convert the percentage into a decimal which you can then multiply using a calculator.

7

Exercise 4f

1 Here is some information about A levels. How many more students gained a grade A in Maths compared to English?

Subject	English	Maths
Number of students	75000	58000
% with a grade A	22%	36%

2 Last year the Kane family earned £46275 and spent £2962 on a holiday. The Walton family earned £20000 and spent £1700 on a holiday. Which family spent proportionately more on their holiday?

3 Jack invests £1200 in the National Bank for 1 year. At the end of the year he receives £78 in interest. Deidre invests £1650 in KRP bank for 1 year. At the end of the year she receives £99 in interest. Who had the better rate of interest, Jack or Deidre? Explain your answer.

4 To the right are two bags of sweets, A and B. Which bag of sweets is the better value for money? Explain your reasoning.

5 **a** A chocolate bar normally has a mass of 240 g. This week the mass of the bar is increased by 15%. What is the new mass of the chocolate bar?

b A shirt normally costs £30. In a sale all the prices are reduced by 18%. What is the sale price of the shirt?

6 When measuring distances, Jenny knows that her instruments have an error of ±5%. She measures the length of a room as 450 cm.

a What is the greatest possible length the room could be?

b What is the least possible length the room could be?

±5% means 'plus or minus 5%'

7 Jack buys a computer on the Internet. He has to pay an extra 15% of the price advertised in VAT. What percentage of the total price is the VAT?

Problem solving

8 In a sale all prices are reduced by 12%. A quick way of calculating the sale price is to multiply the original price by a single decimal number.

SALE! Prices ↓ 12%!

a What is the number?

b After three weeks the sale price is reduced by another 12%. Show that the original price has been reduced by 22.56%.

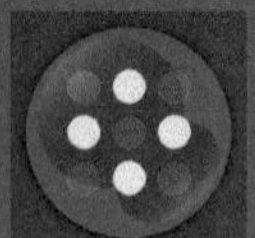

4g Financial maths 1: Repeated percentage change

p.64

When you borrow money it is important to know how much interest you will pay.

- You can calculate a **repeated percentage** increase using a **decimal multiplier**.

Example

Victor invests £3000 in a bank with an annual **interest** rate of 4%. How much money will he have after 3 years?

Each year the money grows by 4% — This is called compound interest

£3000 —(×1.04, Increase by 4%)→ £3120 —(×1.04, Increase by 4%)→ £3244.80 —(×1.04, Increase by 4%)→ £3374.592

After three years he will have £3374.59 (2 dp)

You can also perform the same calculation in one step

£3000 × $(1.04)^3$ = £3374.59 $\quad$ $1.04 \times 1.04 \times 1.04 = 1.04^3$

At the end of each year the bank works out 4% of the money in the account, called the interest, and adds this on.

- You can calculate a repeated percentage decrease using a decimal multiplier.

Example

Violet buys a new van for £20 000. Each year the value of the van depreciates by 12%. What will be the value of the van in two years' time?

Each year the value of the van decreases by 12%.

£20 000 —(×0.88, Decrease by 12%)→ £17 600 —(×0.88, Decrease by 12%)→ £15 488

At the end of each year the decrease is subtracted from the current value of the van.

After two years the van is worth £15 488.

You can also perform the same calculation in one step

£20 000 × $(0.88)^2$ = £15 488 $\quad$ $0.88 \times 0.88 = 0.88^2$

Most cars go down in value each year. This is called depreciation.

Exercise 4g

1 Write down the decimal multiplier for each of these changes.

   a Value increasing by 4% for one year
   b Value increasing by 4% for four years
   c Value increasing by 5% for five years
   d Value depreciating by 8% for six years
   e Value depreciating by 1% for 20 years
   f Value depreciating by 50% for 20 years.

Problem solving

2 a Ruby puts £8000 into a bank account. Each year the bank pays interest at 7%. Work out the amount of money in Ruby's bank account after two years.

   b Shahid buys a new car for £12 000. Each year his car depreciates in value by 15%. What will be the value of Shahid's car in three years' time?

3 Work out the value of each of these items after the number of years stated.

Item	Cost (£)	Time (years)	Percentage change each year
Car	24 500	3	Decrease 7%
House	125 000	2	Increase 8%
TV	250	5	Decrease 12.5%
Savings	15 000	4	Increase 3.29%

4 a Teresa invests £85 000 in a bank account. The bank pays 6% interest a year. How many years will it take for Teresa's money to be worth more than a million pounds?

   b Bertie owes £1800 on his credit card. Each month the credit card company adds 2.6% interest on his outstanding balance to his bill. Bertie manages to pay £80 a month to the credit card company. How long will it take him to pay off the whole bill?

Did you know?

If you invest your savings at 5% compound interest your money will double in just over 14 years.

5 Beatrice borrows £90 000 from a bank to buy a house. The bank charges 6% a year interest. She wants to know how much money she will have to pay back after 25 years. She uses a spreadsheet to help her investigate the problem.

   a Set up a spreadsheet to investigate the problem.
   b How much money will Beatrice owe in 25 years?
   c Plot a graph of time in years against the money owed. Write down what you notice.
   d Investigate changing the interest rate.
   e Investigate what happens if Beatrice starts to pay back some money at the end of each year. Find how much she has to pay back each year so that at the end of the 25 years she owes the bank no money?

	A	B	C	D
1	Year	Amount	Percentage change	New amount
2	1	90 000	1.06	95 400
3	2	95 400	1.06	101 124
4	3	101 124	1.06	107 191
5	4	107 191	1.06	113 623
6	5	113 623	1.06	120 440
7	6	120 440		

4 MySummary

Check out

You should now be able to ...		Test it ➡ Questions
✓ Add and subtract fractions.	6	1 – 2
✓ Multiply and divide fractions.	6	3 – 5
✓ Convert between decimals and fractions.	6	6
✓ Calculate percentage changes.	6	7 – 10
✓ Solve problems involving percentages.	7	11

Language	Meaning	Example
Numerator	The top number in a fraction.	In the fraction $\frac{4}{5}$, the numerator is 4.
Denominator	The bottom number in a fraction.	In the fraction $\frac{4}{5}$ the denominator is 5.
Simplify a fraction	Divide the numerator and denominator by common factors.	$\frac{30}{33}$ simplifies to $\frac{10}{11}$.
Mixed number	A number that is made of a whole number part and a fraction part.	$4\frac{2}{3}$ is a mixed number.
Proportion	A numerical comparison of the size of a part with the size of the whole.	If 4 out of 5 people in a room are girls, then the proportion that are girls is $\frac{4}{5}$.
Percentage	The numerator of a proportion out of 100.	$\frac{4}{5} = \frac{80}{100} = 80\%$
Recurring decimal	A decimal with an infinite number of repeating digits.	$\frac{1}{3} = 0.33333...$ $= 0.\dot{3}$
Terminating decimal	A decimal with a finite number of digits.	$\frac{3}{5} = 0.6$
Improper fraction	A fraction whose numerator is greater than its denominator.	$\frac{11}{8}$ is an improper fraction.

4 MyReview

1 Calculate these and give your answer as a fraction in its simplest form.

a $\frac{3}{8} + \frac{5}{32}$ b $\frac{9}{15} - \frac{3}{20}$

c $\frac{1}{4} + \frac{2}{7}$ d $\frac{19}{21} - \frac{5}{28}$

2 Calculate these, write your answers as improper fractions.

a $2\frac{3}{4} + 1\frac{1}{7}$ b $5\frac{1}{9} - 3\frac{5}{6}$

c $4\frac{1}{6} + 2\frac{1}{8}$ d $3\frac{3}{4} - 1\frac{5}{6}$

3 Calculate these, give your answer to 2 dp.

a $\frac{3}{11}$ of £60 b $\frac{4}{9}$ of 40 kg

c $1\frac{1}{3}$ of 11 m d $2\frac{2}{7}$ of 250 ml

4 Calculate these using a mental or written method, and simplify your answers.

a $12 \times \frac{3}{21}$ b $15 \times \frac{7}{20}$

c $\frac{2}{11} \times \frac{9}{20}$ d $\frac{9}{10} \times \frac{5}{21}$

5 Calculate and simplify your answers.

a $18 \div \frac{27}{28}$ b $\frac{2}{7} \div \frac{3}{14}$

6 Change these fractions into decimals without using a calculator.

a $\frac{3}{20}$ b $\frac{7}{35}$

c $\frac{11}{10}$ d $\frac{9}{40}$

7 Calculate these percentage changes.

a Increase 80 by 15%

b Decrease 240 by 38%

8 Jamie was paid £900 a month. His pay was increased by 3.2%. How much is he paid now?

9 An antique vase increases in value from £770 to £893.20. What is the percentage increase?

10 A laptop is reduced in price from £750 to £680. What is the percentage reduction?

11 The table shows the number of students in each class and what percentage passed their maths test.

Class	A	B	C
Students	24	20	28
% pass	54%	70%	43%

Which class had the most students passing the test?

What next?

Score

Score	
0 – 4	Your knowledge of this topic is still developing. To improve look at Formative test: 3B-4; MyMaths: 1016, 1017, 1040, 1046, 1047, 1060, 1063, 1073 and 1302
5 – 9	You are gaining a secure knowledge of this topic. To improve look at InvisiPen: 143, 144, 145, 152, 153, 155, 161 and 193
10, 11	You have mastered this topic. Well done, you are ready to progress!

4 MyPractice

4a

1 Work out these.

Give each answer as a fraction in its simplest form.

a $\frac{2}{7} + \frac{5}{14}$ b $\frac{1}{2} + \frac{1}{8}$ c $\frac{4}{9} - \frac{1}{3}$ d $\frac{5}{6} + \frac{3}{8}$

e $\frac{2}{12} + \frac{2}{5}$ f $\frac{7}{12} - \frac{1}{3}$ g $\frac{4}{21} + \frac{9}{14}$ h $\frac{11}{12} - \frac{3}{4}$

2 Work out these.

Give your answer as a fraction in its simplest form and as a mixed number where appropriate.

a $\frac{7}{12} + \frac{11}{18}$ b $\frac{2}{15} + \frac{7}{20}$ c $\frac{13}{15} - \frac{7}{10}$ d $\frac{1}{12} + \frac{5}{16}$

e $\frac{4}{21} + \frac{4}{15}$ f $\frac{13}{16} - \frac{3}{4}$ g $\frac{19}{30} + \frac{5}{18}$ h $\frac{17}{40} - \frac{3}{16}$

4b

3 Work out these.

Give each answer as a fraction in its simplest form and as a mixed number where appropriate.

a $\frac{3}{5}$ of 15 cm b $\frac{3}{8}$ of 13 kg c $\frac{2}{3}$ of £51 d $\frac{5}{12}$ of 40 sec

e $\frac{3}{10}$ of \$70 f $\frac{7}{12}$ of 15 m g $\frac{3}{5}$ of 240 ml h $\frac{3}{4}$ of 50 km

4 Work out these. Use cancelling to simplify your answers where possible.

a $\frac{3}{4} \times \frac{8}{9}$ b $\frac{2}{3} \times \frac{6}{7}$ c $\frac{5}{8} \times \frac{7}{10}$ d $\frac{2}{7} \times \frac{7}{12}$

e $\frac{3}{8} \times \frac{12}{21}$ f $\frac{9}{10} \times \frac{5}{6}$ g $\frac{3}{4} \times \frac{6}{7}$ h $\frac{8}{15} \times \frac{25}{32}$

4c

5 Work out these.

Give each answer as a mixed number in its simplest form.

a $3 \div \frac{2}{3}$ b $4 \div \frac{3}{5}$ c $8 \div \frac{3}{5}$ d $9 \div \frac{6}{7}$

e $4 \div \frac{8}{9}$ f $5 \div \frac{10}{11}$ g $12 \div \frac{3}{5}$ h $6 \div \frac{4}{11}$

6 Calculate these.

a $\frac{2}{5} \div \frac{3}{4}$ b $\frac{3}{4} \div \frac{5}{7}$ c $\frac{4}{9} \div \frac{2}{5}$ d $\frac{1}{6} \div \frac{1}{5}$

e $\frac{5}{8} \div \frac{3}{4}$ f $\frac{7}{9} \div \frac{5}{6}$ g $\frac{7}{12} \div \frac{3}{4}$ h $\frac{8}{15} \div \frac{16}{21}$

4d

7 Write these decimals as fractions in their simplest form.

a 0.8 b 0.76 c 0.75 d 0.77 e 0.875
f 0.325 g 1.4 h 1.35 i 3.75 j 2.16

8 Change these fractions into decimals using an appropriate method.
Give your answers to 2dp where appropriate.

a $\frac{13}{20}$ b $\frac{9}{16}$ c $\frac{5}{11}$ d $\frac{8}{15}$ e $\frac{7}{10}$
f $\frac{12}{15}$ g $\frac{17}{23}$ h $\frac{11}{22}$ i $\frac{14}{21}$ j $\frac{21}{30}$

4e

9 a A mobile phone normally costs £75.
In a sale the price is reduced by 20%. What is the sale price of the mobile?
b Last year Archie earned £240 a week.
At the start of this year, the manager increased Archie's wage by 18%.
What is Archie's new wage?

4f

10 Basil's salary last year was £32 600.
He had to pay £8234 in tax.
Mohinder's salary last year was £44 321.
He had to pay £12 765 in tax.
Who had to pay the higher percentage of their salary in tax?

11 Here are two offers.

Offer A 400 g pack of biscuits at 90p
Offer B 400 g pack + 15% extra at £1.02

Which offer is the better value for money?
Explain your reasoning.

12 a A bag of crisps normally weighs 150 g.
This week the weight of the bag is increased by 22%.
What is the new weight?
b A pair of trousers normally costs £76.
In a sale all the prices are reduced by 35%.
What is the sale price of the trousers?

MyAssessment 1

These questions will test you on your knowledge of the topics in chapters 1 to 4. They give you practice in the questions that you may see in your GCSE exams. There are 95 marks in total.

1 Calculate

a 3.4×10^3 (1 mark) **b** $0.34 \div 0.1$ (1 mark)

c 3.4×0.01 (1 mark) **d** $10^6 \times 10^4$ (1 mark)

e $10^6 \div 10^4$ (1 mark) **f** $10^2 \times 10^6 \div 10^4$ (1 mark)

2 Round each of these to the accuracy indicated in brackets.

a 5278 (nearest 10) (1 mark) **b** 0.8965 (2 dp) (1 mark)

c 1235.6 (nearest 100) (1 mark) **d** 4.6135 (1 dp) (1 mark)

e 86 422 (nearest 1000) (1 mark) **f** 0.873 (1 sf) (1 mark)

g 5278 (1 sf) (1 mark)

3 Find the HCF and LCM of 136 and 96 using a Venn diagram. (4 marks)

4 Work out an estimate for each calculation. Check your answer using a calculator. Giving your answers to 1 dp.

a $67.5 \div 3.72$ (2 marks) **b** 712×11.5 (2 marks)

c $\frac{13.9 \times 451}{7.3}$ (2 marks) **d** $\frac{0.837 \times 825}{9.4}$ (2 marks)

5 Convert these measurements into the units indicated in brackets. Give your answer to an appropriate degree of accuracy.

a 62 miles (km) (1 mark) **b** 428 ml (pints) (2 marks)

c 3000 m^2 (hectares) (1 mark) **d** 17 oz (grams) (1 mark)

6 A single sheet of A4 paper is 29.7 cm by 21.0 cm. A0 paper is 16 times larger. Work out the area of A0 paper and give your answer in square metres to 1 dp. (3 marks)

7 Atoms can be modelled as solid spheres and one of the simplest cell structures is shown.

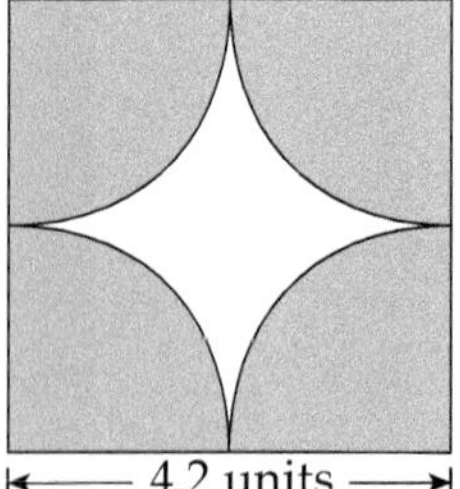

a Calculate the area of the square cell. (2 marks)

b Calculate the total area of the circular atoms inside the square. (3 marks)

c Hence determine the area of the free space inside the cell. (1 mark)

8 The diameter of a racing bicycle wheel is 70 cm. In a local cycle race distances of up to 40 miles are regularly run. Work out how many revolutions a bicycle wheel makes in order to complete the race. (4 marks)

9 The Devonshire Dome in Buxton is the second largest circular dome in the UK with a diameter of 44.2 m. Work out the circumference of this dome. (2 marks)

10 Factorise these expressions.

a $9x + 15$ (1 mark) **b** $y^2 - 4y$ (1 mark)

c $6m^2 + 3m$ (1 mark) **d** $4u^3 + 8u^2$ (2 marks)

11 Add or subtract these fractions and simplify where possible.

a $\frac{3x}{4} - \frac{2x}{3}$ (2 marks) **b** $\frac{4y}{7} + \frac{y}{3}$ (2 marks)

12 The energy E stored in a capacitor is given by $\frac{1}{2}CV^2$.

a Find E when $C = 3$ and $V = 20$. (2 marks)

b Find E when $C = 400$ and $V = 3$. (2 marks)

13 The force of an object that is moving in a circle is $F = \frac{mv^2}{r}$.

a Find F when $v = 12$, $r = 4$ and $m = 8$. (2 marks)

b Rearrange the formula to make v the subject. (3 marks)

c Find v when $F = 500$, $r = 2$ and $m = 5$. (2 marks)

14 Derive formulae for the shaded areas A in each of these diagrams.

a (2 marks)

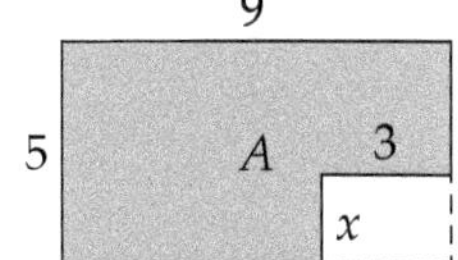

b (3 marks)

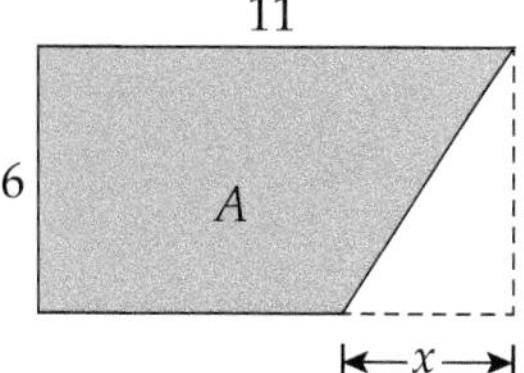

15 a A small passport-sized photograph measures $4\frac{3}{8}$cm by $2\frac{2}{3}$cm.

i What is the perimeter of the photograph? (3 marks)

ii What is the area of the photograph? (3 marks)

b It is being trimmed to size by cutting off $\frac{1}{2}$cm from the length and width.
What are the new dimensions of the photograph? (3 marks)

16 Calculate these divisions.

a $2\frac{3}{4} \div \frac{2}{3}$ (2 marks) **b** $5\frac{4}{7} \div \frac{3}{5}$ (2 marks)

17 In a recent test Sarah scored $\frac{26}{40}$ in Maths, $\frac{38}{50}$ in Biology and $\frac{45}{60}$ in Chemistry.

a Write these results in terms of decimals without using a calculator. (3 marks)

b Write these decimals as percentages. (1 mark)

18 a Increase 550 ml by 16%. (2 marks) **b** Decrease £28.50 by 8%. (2 marks)

19 a The number of people joining a gymnasium increased from 128 to 165.
What is the percentage increase? (2 marks)

b A house bought ten years ago for £275 000 has increased in value by 4%.
How much is the house currently worth? (2 marks)

5 Angles

Introduction

There are different units for measuring angles. The French tried to decimalise angles and invented a system where a right angle was equal to 100 grads. The most common measure is degrees (°), and there are 360° in a circle. However, mathematicians prefer a unit for measuring angles called the radian, and 1 radian = 57.2958°!

What's the point?

The ability to estimate, measure and describe angles is highly important to all of us, whether we are designing stage lighting, creating a pattern for a dress or lobbing a ball towards a goal.

Objectives

By the end of this chapter, you will have learned how to …

- Find missing angles in diagrams containing triangles and missing lines.
- Identify and use the properties of special quadrilaterals.
- Use the properties of regular polygons.
- Identify congruent shapes and use congruence.
- Solve angle problems that involve parallel lines.
- Apply facts about quadrilaterals to find missing angles.
- Calculate exterior and interior angles of polygons.
- Construct triangles and quadrilaterals accurately with a ruler and compasses.

Check in

1 Calculate the size of the angles marked with letters.

a

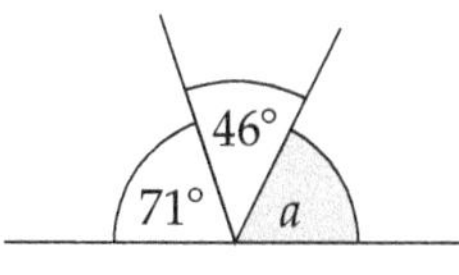

b

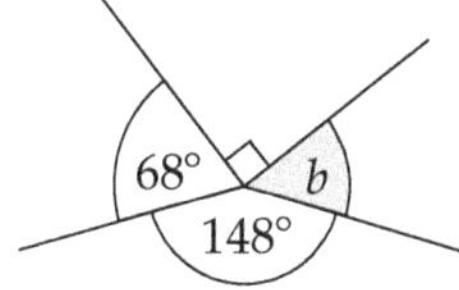

c

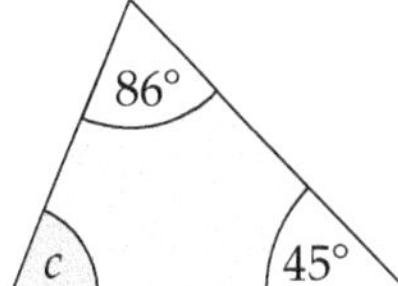

2 Match these quadrilaterals with their mathematical names.

square
rectangle
isosceles trapezium
parallelogram
kite
rhombus
arrowhead

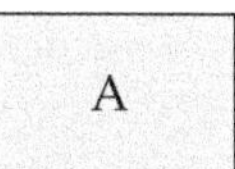

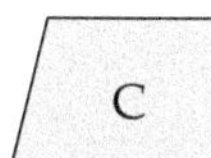

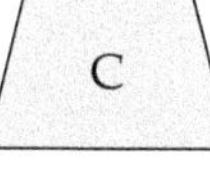

Starter problem

A tessellation is a tiling pattern with no gaps or overlaps.

Which regular polygons tessellate?

Which combinations of different regular polygons will tessellate?

5a Angle properties of a triangle

These angles are inside a shape.
They are called **interior** angles.

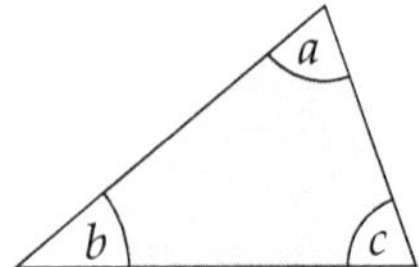

The interior angles of a triangle add to 180°.

$$a + b + c = 180°$$

Here are some useful facts about the angles made when lines cross.

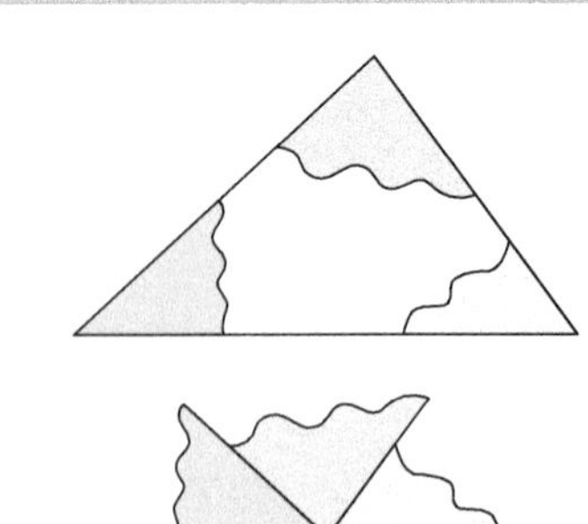

Try tearing off the corners of a triangle. They should fit together to make a straight line.

- When lines **intersect**
  - ▶ **vertically opposite** angles are equal.

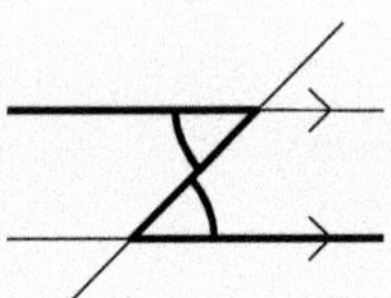

- When one line intersects two **parallel** lines
  - ▶ **alternate** angles are equal.

  - ▶ **corresponding** angles are equal.

Example

Calculate the values of

a p and q

b $p + q$.

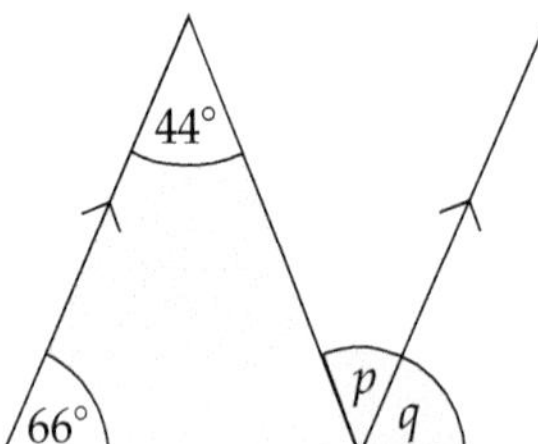

a $p = 44°$ Alternate angles

$q = 66°$ Corresponding angles

b $p + q = 44° + 66°$

$= 110°$

You make an **exterior** angle when you extend one side of a shape.

- The exterior angle of a triangle is equal to the sum of the two opposite interior angles.

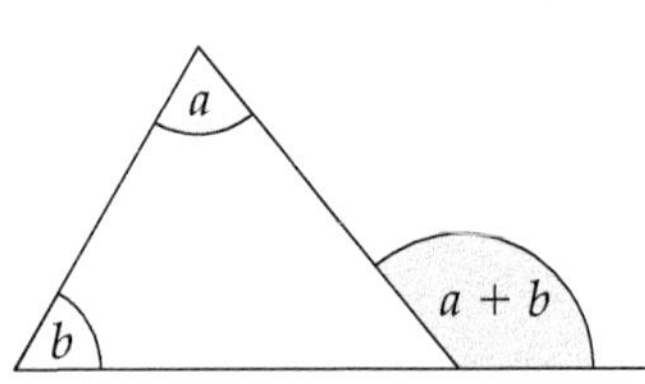

Exercise 5a

1 Calculate the third angle in each triangle. State if the triangle is right-angled, isosceles, scalene or equilateral.

a 43°, 47° **b** 32°, 116°

c 60°, 60° **d** 37°, 108°

e 45°, 45° **f** 18°, 144°

2 Calculate the angles marked with letters.

a

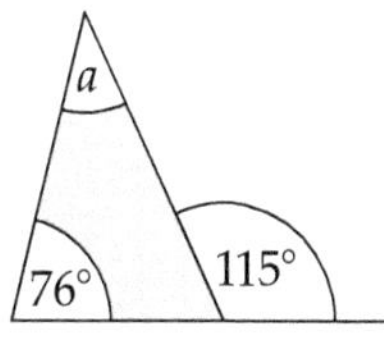

b

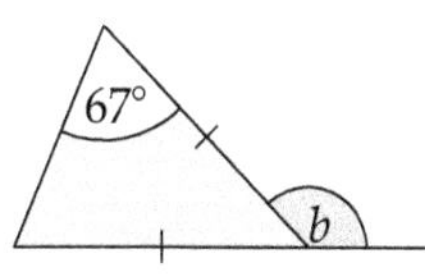

c

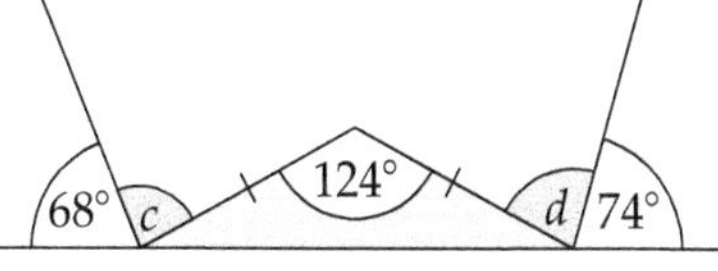

3 Calculate the angles marked with letters. Give a reason for your answers.

a

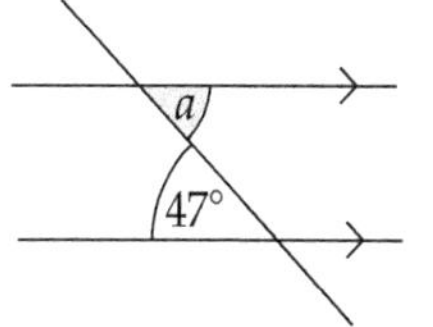

b

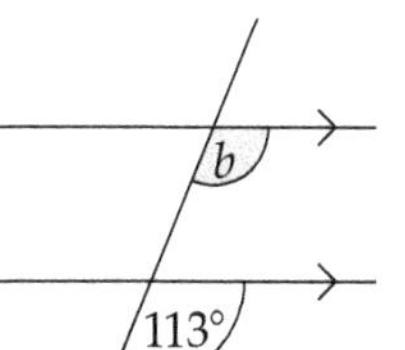

c

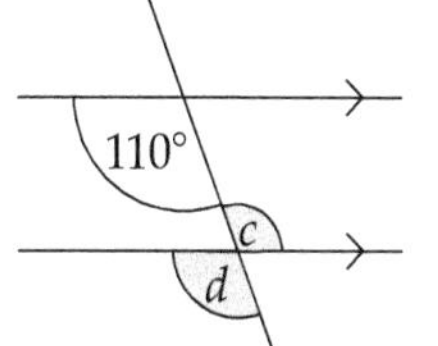

d

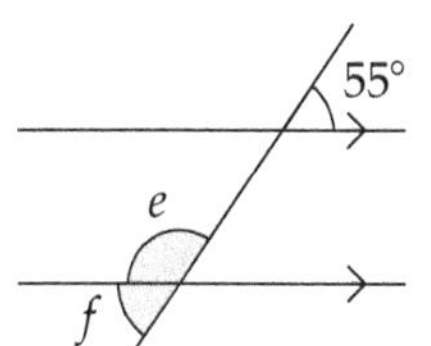

4 Calculate the angles marked with letters.

a

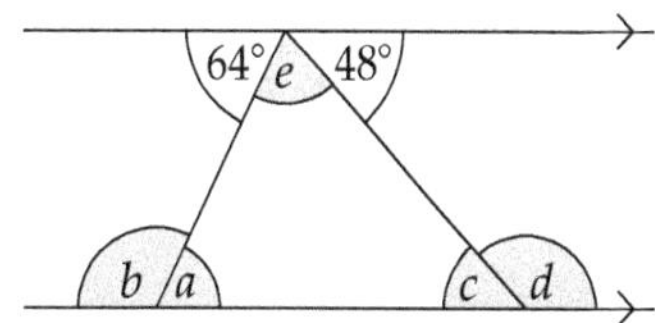

b

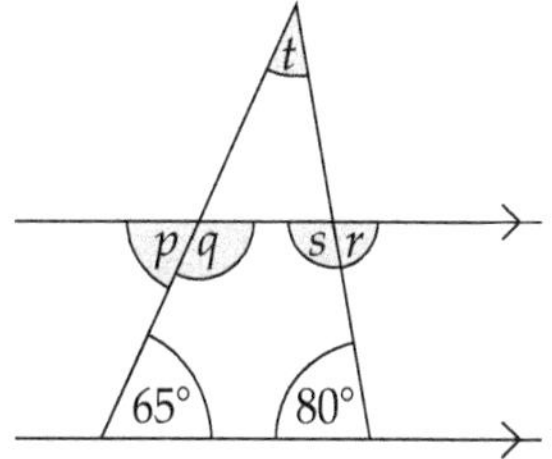

5 Find p and q in terms of a and b.

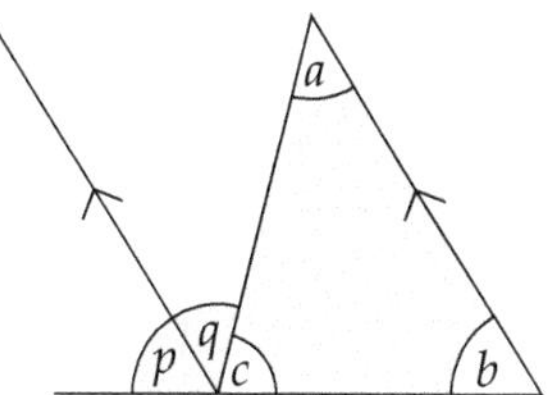

6 Ali says he can see why **Q5** proves that the sum of the angles in a triangle add up to 180°. Billie says, no, you have to use this diagram.

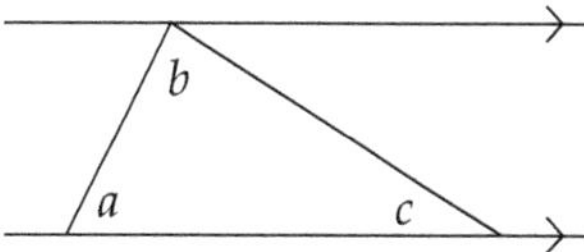

Explain how they can both be right.

Problem solving

7 Draw a triangle and colour the angles.

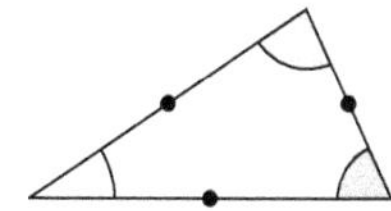

Rotate the triangle about the midpoint of each side to create a tessellation. Show examples of alternate and corresponding angles on your tessellation.

Did you know?

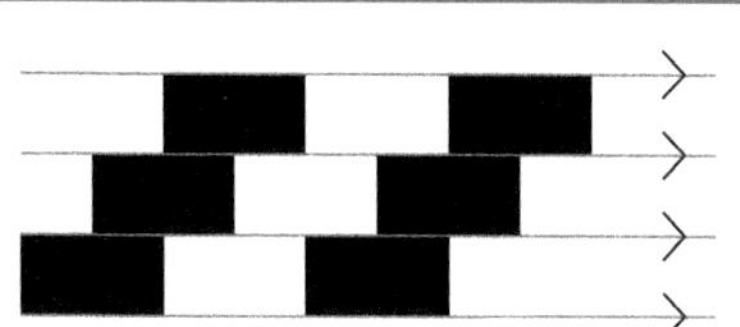

This is the café wall illusion: the lines are parallel but they don't look it. It was noticed in the pattern of tiles outside a café in Bristol.

5b Angle properties of a quadrilateral

Some **quadrilaterals** have special properties which you need to remember.

Square **Rectangle** **Rhombus** **Parallelogram**

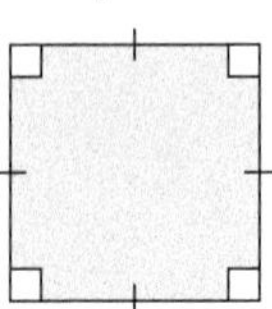

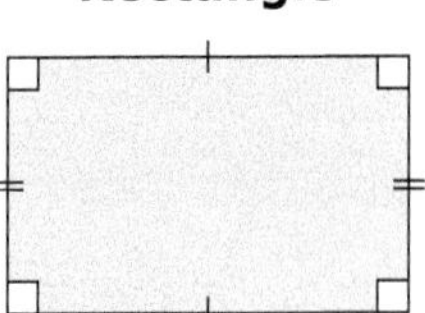

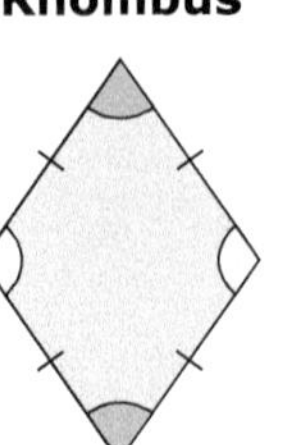

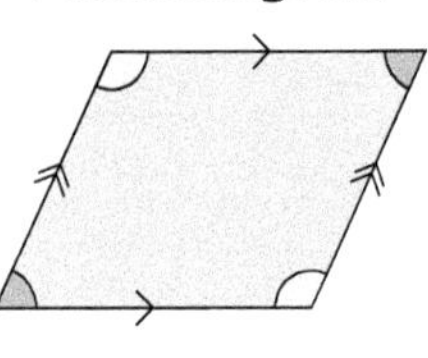

Trapezium **Isosceles trapezium** **Kite** **Arrowhead**

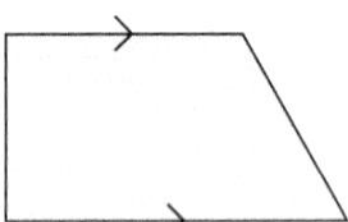

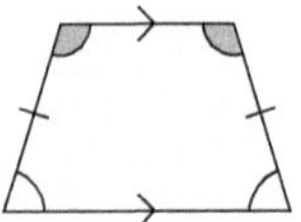

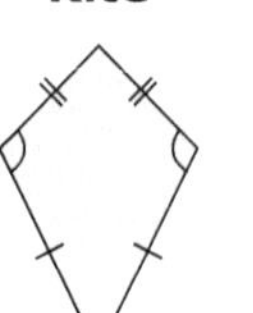

Some of these shapes have **symmetry**.

- A shape has **reflection symmetry** if you can divide it into two identical halves, each of which is the mirror image of the other.
- A shape has **rotational symmetry** if you can rotate it onto itself more than once in a complete turn.
- The number of times a shape rotates onto itself in one full turn is called its **order of rotational symmetry**.

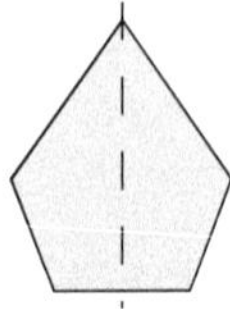

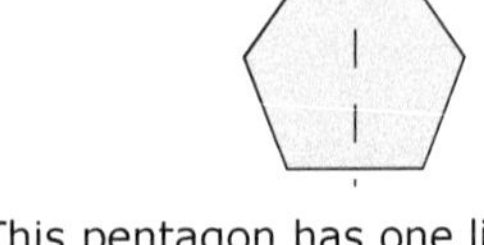

This pentagon has one line of reflection symmetry.

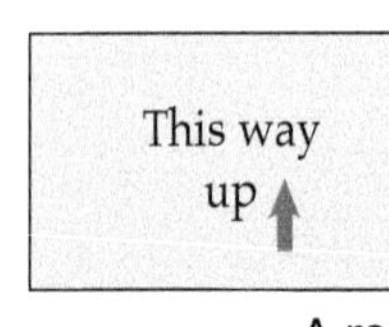

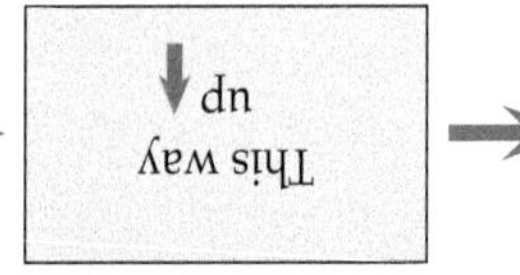

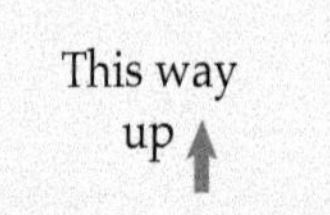

A rectangle has rotational symmetry of order 2.

The sum of the interior angles in any quadrilateral is 360°.
To see this, divide a quadrilateral into two triangles.

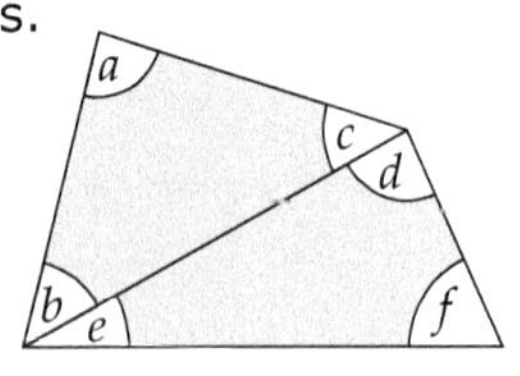

$a + b + c = 180°$ in one triangle
$d + e + f = 180°$ in the other triangle

So $a + b + c + d + e + f = 360°$

Example

Calculate the size of angle a.

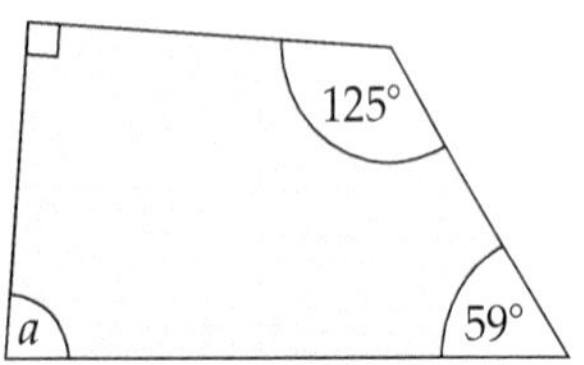

$a + 125° + 59° + 90° = 360°$
$a + 274° = 360°$
$a = 86°$

Exercise 5b

1 For each shape, name the type of quadrilateral and find the sizes of the labelled angles.

a

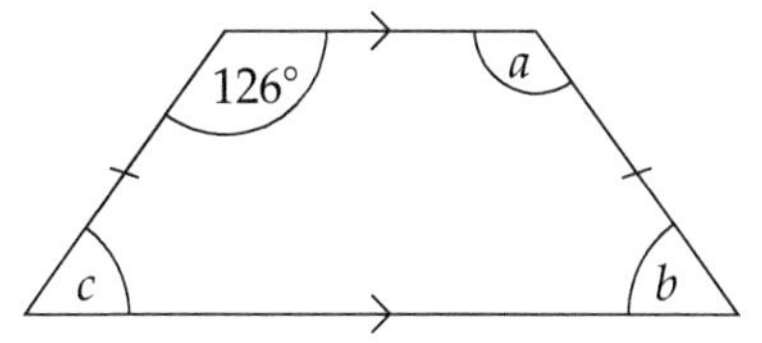

b **c**

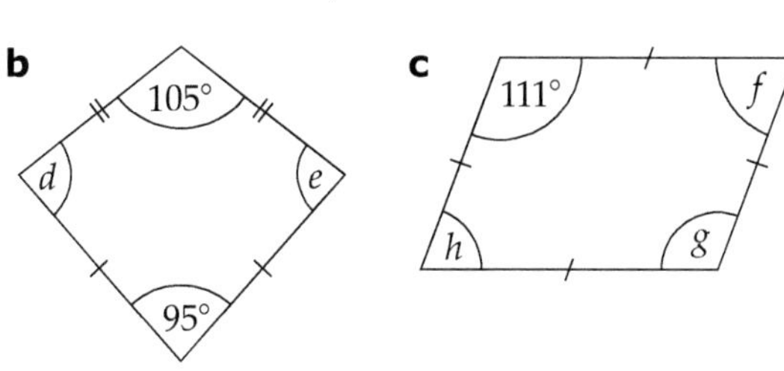

2 Copy this table and fill in the names of the eight quadrilaterals shown on page 76. The kite is done for you.

		Number of lines of symmetry				
		0	1	2	3	4
Order of rotation symmetry	1		kite			
	2					
	3					
	4					

3 Find the sizes of the labelled angles. ❮ p.76

a **b**

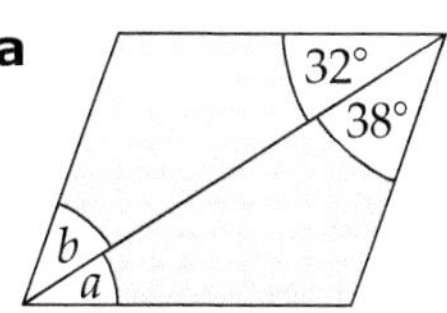

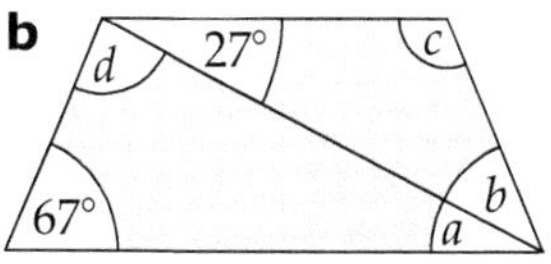

Parallelogram **Isosceles trapezium**

4 You have two congruent triangles which you can join by placing sides of equal length together. Draw the three possible shapes that you can make and name them. p.84 ❯

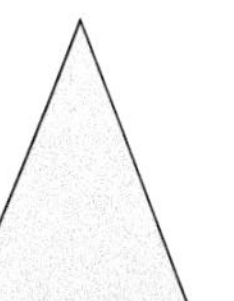

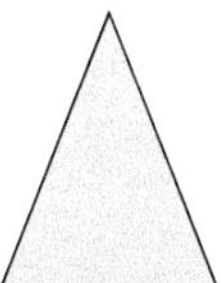

5

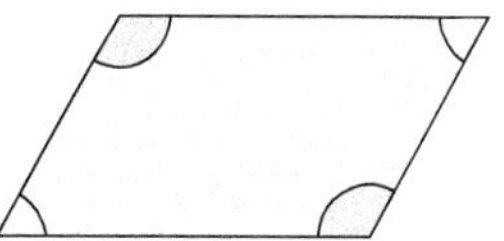

A parallelogram has rotation symmetry of order 2.
Explain why this shows that the opposite angles of a parallelogram are equal.

Problem solving

6 Fold a square piece of paper to form this quadrilateral.
State its mathematical name and calculate its interior angles.

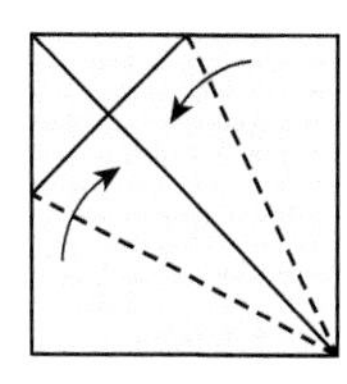

7 P is a point inside a quadrilateral joined to each of the vertices.
How could you use this diagram to show that the sum of the angles in the quadrilateral is 360°?
Can you use your argument to find the sum of the interior angles in a pentagon?

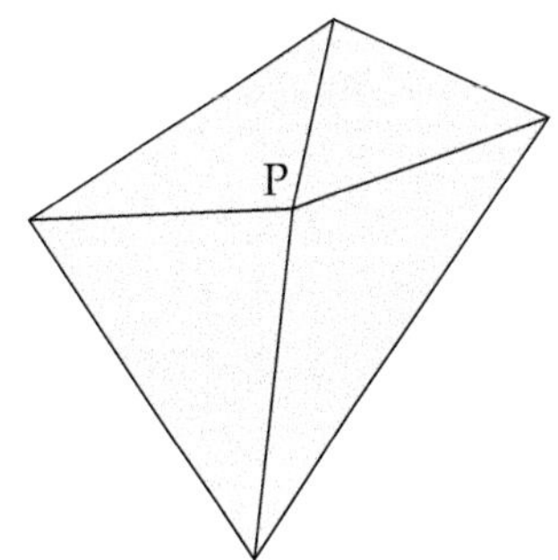

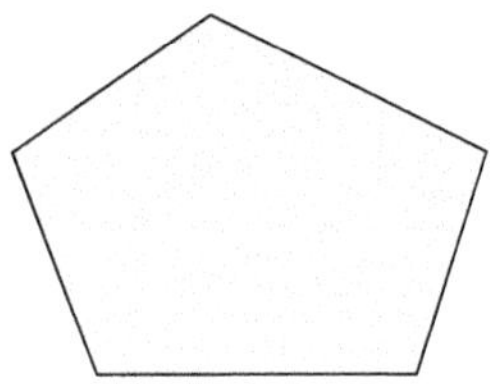

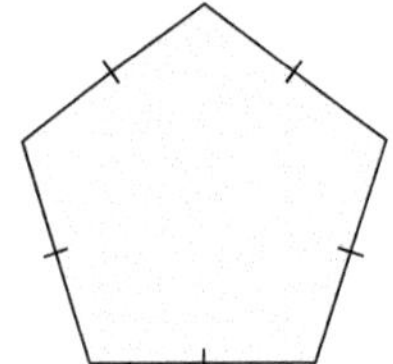

▲ Regular polygons are found in nature.

A shape with straight sides is called a **polygon**.
If its sides are the same *and* its angles are the same then it is called a **regular polygon**.

A regular polygon with n sides has n lines of reflection **symmetry** and **rotational symmetry** of order n.

To draw a regular polygon:

1 draw a circle
2 use a protractor to mark off equal angles from the centre
3 join up consecutive points around the edge of the circle.

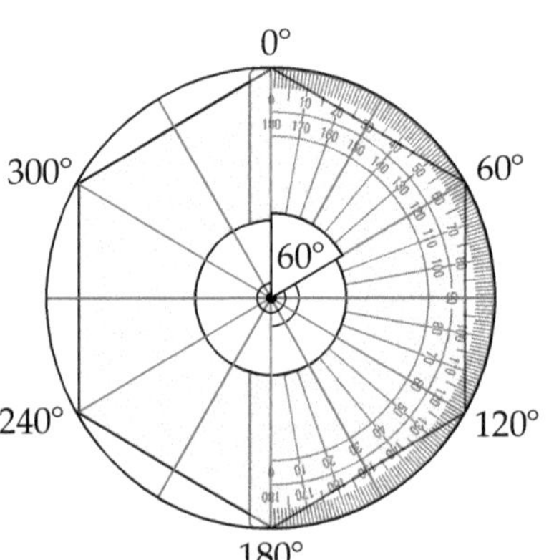

This regular hexagon has six lines of reflection symmetry and rotational symmetry order six.

The symmetries of a regular polygon help you to calculate its angles.

Example

For this regular pentagon, find

a the angles a, b, c, d
b the sum of the interior angles.

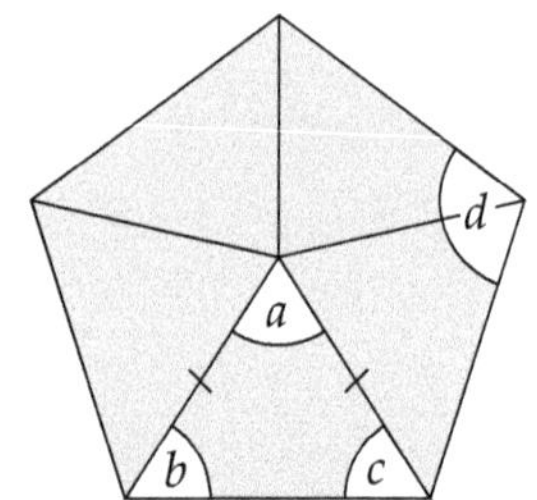

a There are 5 equal angles at the centre.
$360° \div 5 = 72°$ and so $a = 72°$
Angles in a triangle add up to 180°.
$180° - 72° = 108°$
b and c are angles in an isosceles triangle.
$108° \div 2 = 54°$
So $b = 54°$ and $c = 54°$
$d = 2 \times 54° = 108°$
b $5 \times 108° = 540°$

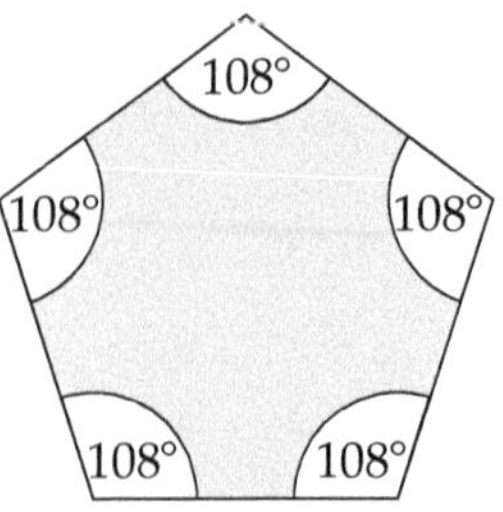

Make sure than you can justify each step in your reasoning.

Exercise 5c

1 **a** Draw these regular polygons and add the lines of reflection symmetry.

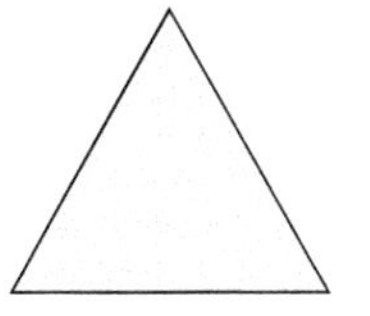

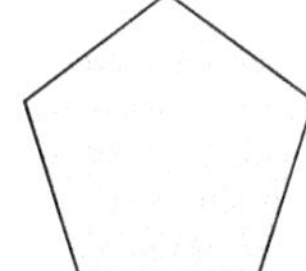
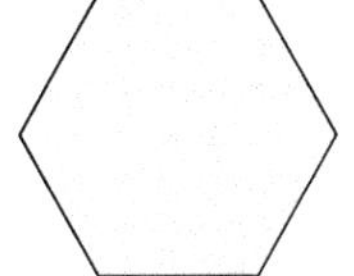
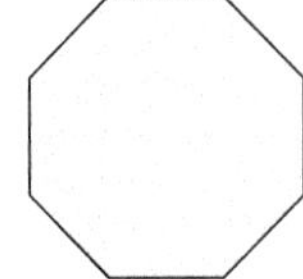

b State the order of rotational symmetry for each shape.

2 A regular hexagon is made from six equilateral triangles. Find

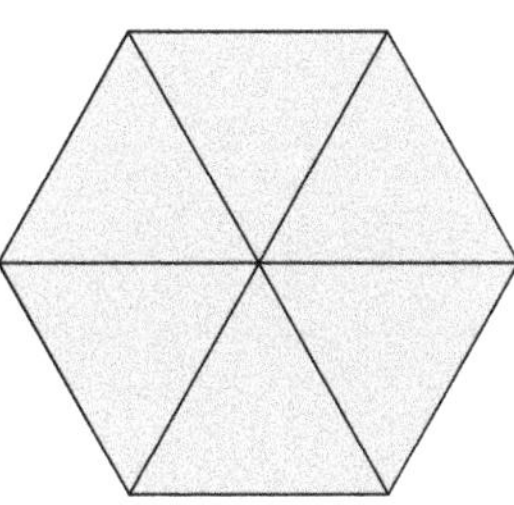

a the interior angle of an equilateral triangle

b the interior angle of a regular hexagon

c the sum of all the interior angles of a regular hexagon.

3 Calculate the angles *a*, *b*, *c*, *d* in each regular polygon.

a

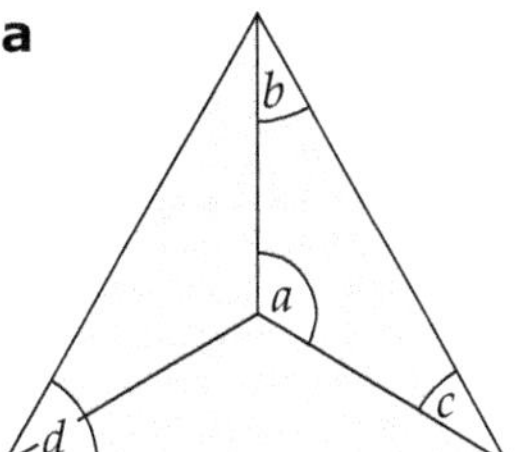

b

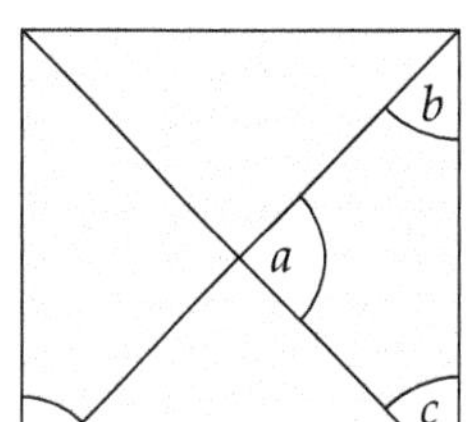

4 This is a regular decagon.

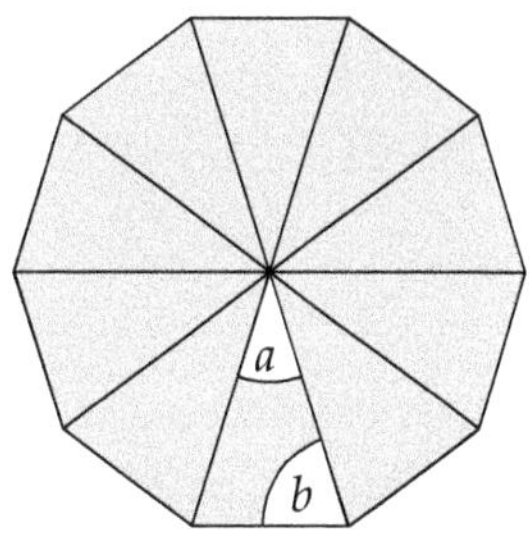

Find

a the angle at the centre, *a*

b the angle marked *b* in the isosceles triangle

c the interior angle of a regular decagon

d the sum of all the interior angles of a regular decagon.

Problem solving

5 **a** Construct an inscribed regular pentagon.

b Draw diagonals to form a smaller pentagon.

c Show that this smaller pentagon is regular.

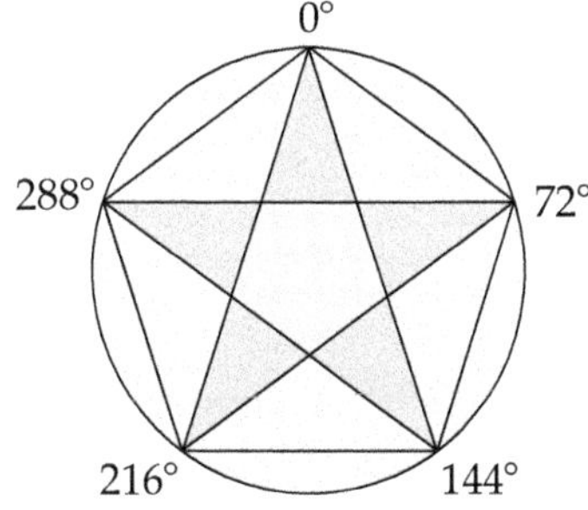

6 These two polygons are regular. Calculate the angle *y*.

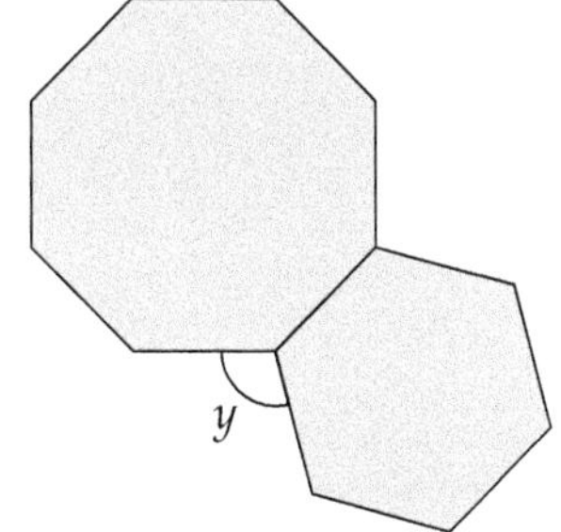

5d Angle properties of a polygon 2

The angles inside a shape are called **interior angles**.

If you extend a side of a polygon you create an **exterior angle**.

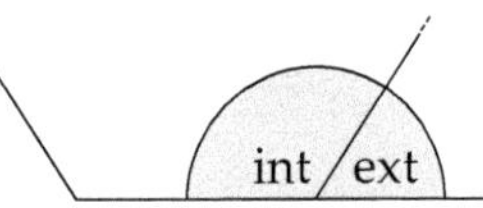

▲ Angles on a straight line add to 180°.

- At each **vertex** (corner) the exterior and the **interior** angles add to 180°.

Imagine an ant walking around the edges of a polygon. At each vertex the ant turns through the exterior angle at that vertex.

In total the ant turns through 360°.

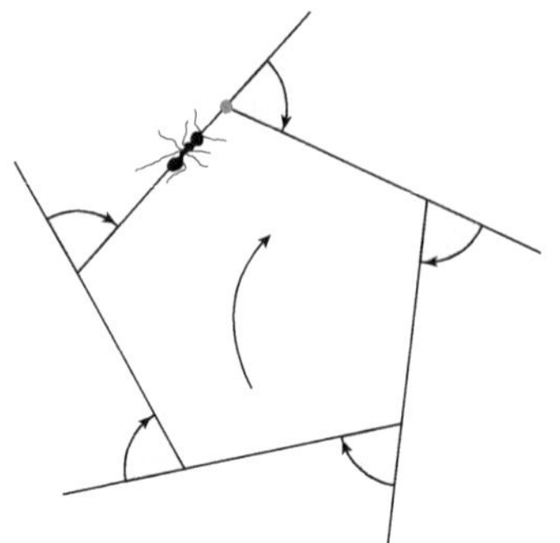

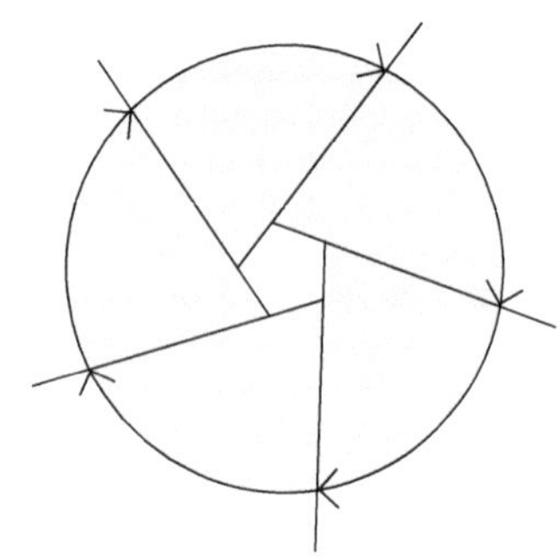

- The **exterior** angles of a **polygon** always add up to 360°.

- A **tessellation** is a tiling pattern with no gaps. You can rotate, translate or repeat shapes to make a tessellation.

You can use your knowledge of angles in polygons to decide if they will tessellate or not.

Example

a This shape is a regular octagon. Calculate the values of *a* and *b*.

b Explain why it is impossible to create a tessellation with just regular octagons.

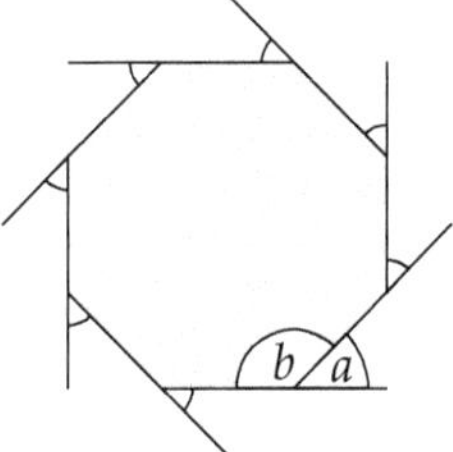

a The eight exterior angles add up to 360°.

360° ÷ 8 = 45°

So *a* = 45°

Angles on a straight line add up to 180°.

180° − 45° = 135°

So *b* = 135°

b 135° + 135° = 270°

Angles at a point add up to 360°.

360° − 270° = 90°

There is a 90° angle not filled.

Remember a tessellation pattern has to fit togther with no gaps or overlaps.

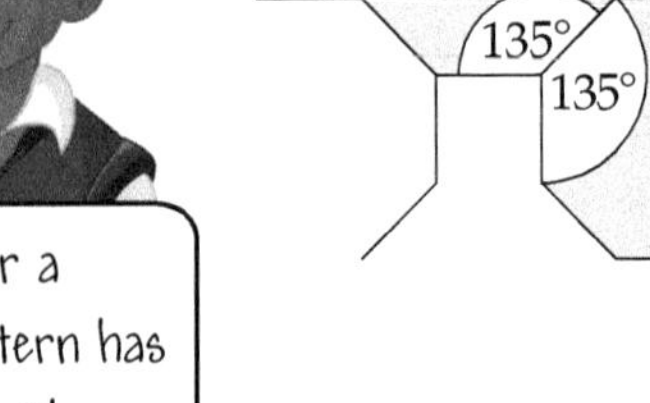

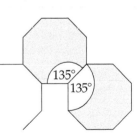

Exercise 5d

1 Copy these regular polygons.
Draw a set of exterior angles on each polygon.
Work out the value of one exterior angle for each polygon.

a

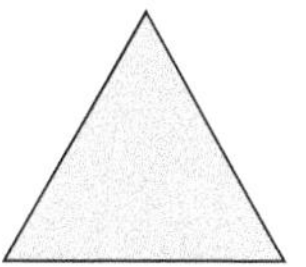

b

c

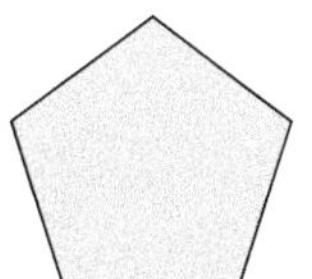

d

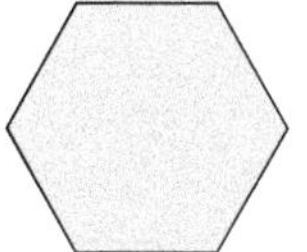

2 Copy and complete this table for regular polygons to 10 sides.
Use your answers to question **1** to help you.

Number of sides	Sum of the exterior angles	Each exterior angle	Each interior angle
3			
4			
.			
10			

3 Only three regular polygons tessellate.
Explain why it is possible to tessellate

a a regular hexagon
b a square
c an equilateral triangle.

4 Two diagonals of a regular pentagon are drawn to form three isosceles triangles.
Calculate the sizes of angles *a* to *i*.

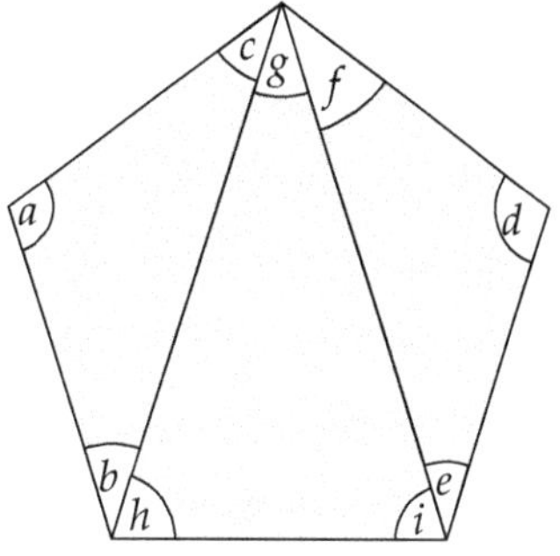

5 The exterior angle of a regular polygon is 24°.
How many sides does it have?

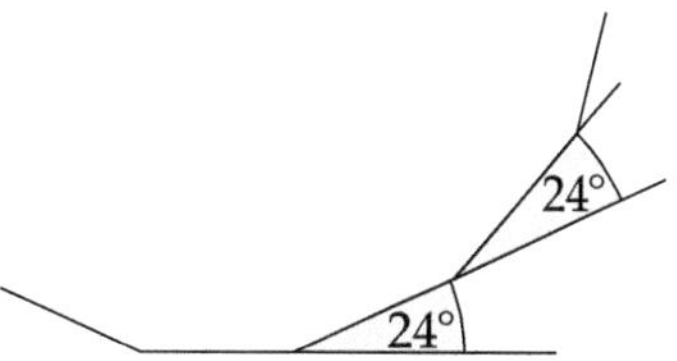

Problem solving

6 Show that the angle at the centre and the exterior angle of a regular polygon are equal.

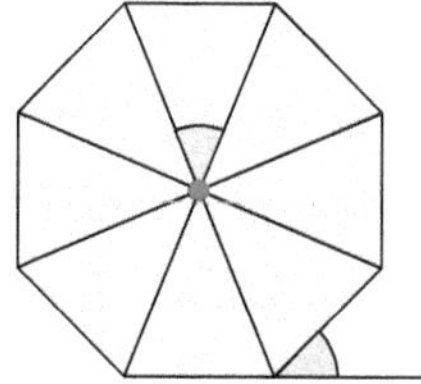

7 What is the maximum number of right angles you can have in an octagon?
What about other polygons?

Did you know?

The Giant's Causeway in Ireland contains about 40000 interlocking columns of volcanic basalt. Many are hexagonal and form a tessellating pattern.

5e Congruent shapes

If you reflect, rotate or translate a shape it keeps exactly the same shape and size: the two shapes are called **congruent**.

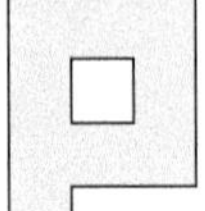 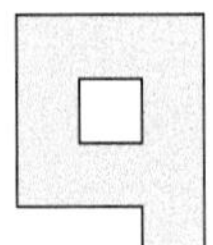 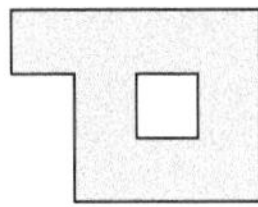 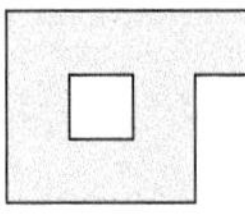

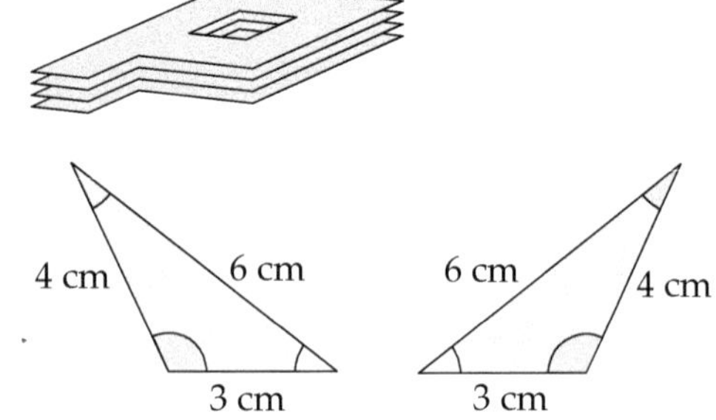

Each of these shapes can be reflected or rotated into the position of the first one.

- Two shapes are congruent if
  - **corresponding angles** are equal
  - **corresponding sides** are equal.

4 cm, 6 cm, 3 cm — 6 cm, 4 cm, 3 cm

Example

The green triangle and the yellow triangle are congruent. Calculate the size of the angles *a*, *b* and *c*, and state what type of triangle it is.

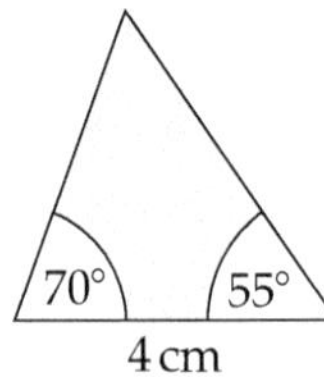

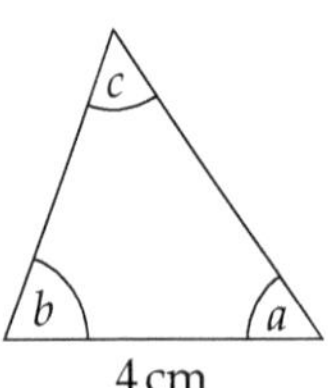

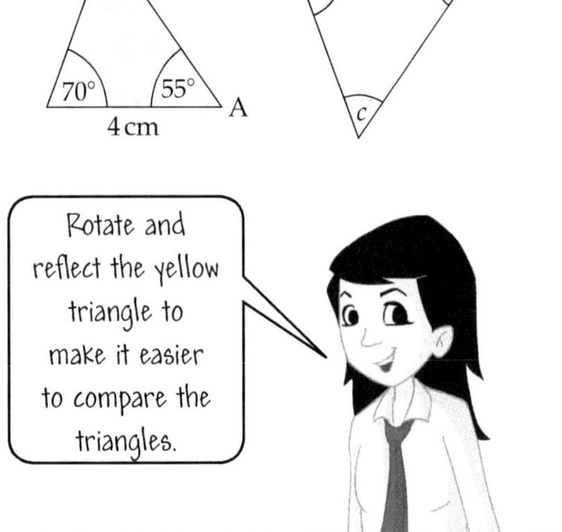

Angle $a = 55°$

Angle $b = 70°$

Angles in a triangle add up to 180°.

Angle $c = 180° - 125° = 55°$

So angle $c = 55°$ The triangle is isosceles.

Example

Explain how you can divide a regular hexagon into three congruent rhombuses.

The sides in each rhombus are all equal.

The angles in each rhombus are either equal to 60° or $2 \times 60 = 120°$.

Therefore, the three rhombuses are congruent.

A regular hexagon can be made from six equilateral triangles.

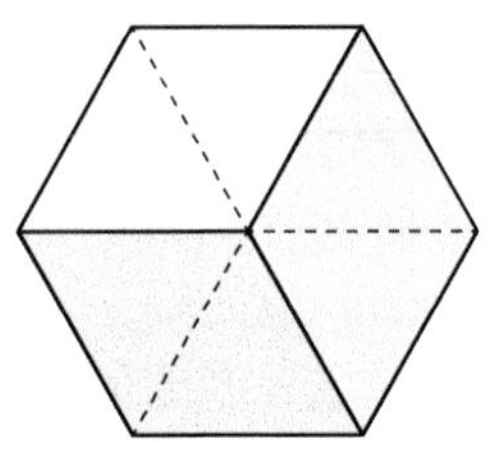

Exercise 5e

1 These isosceles triangles are congruent.

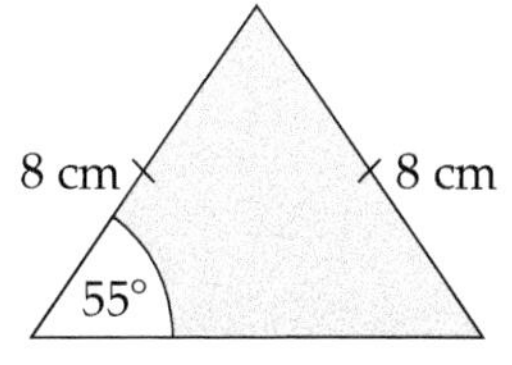

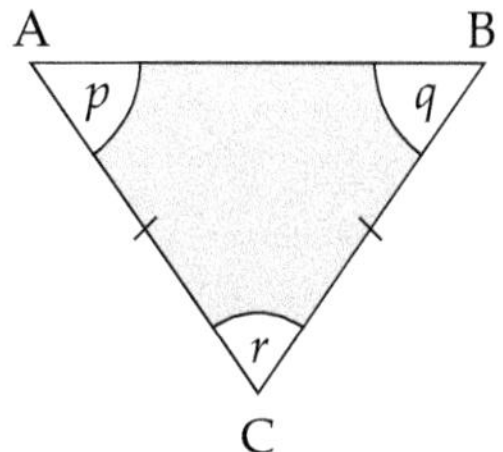

a Find the sizes of angles *p*, *q* and *r*.

b Find the lengths of sides AC and BC.

2 The green trapezium and the blue trapezium are congruent.
Find the sizes of angles *a*, *b*, *c* and *d*.

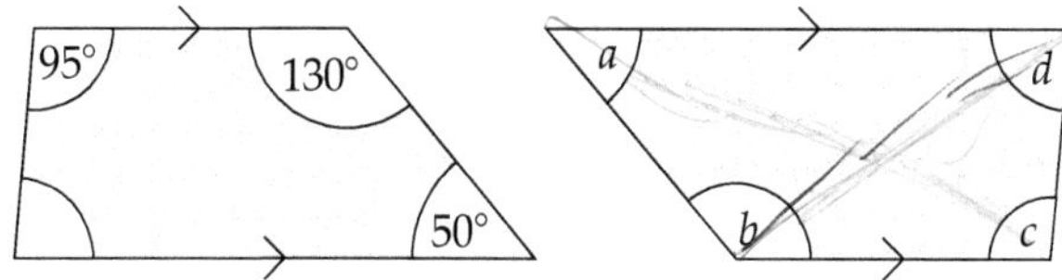

3 ABCD is an isosceles trapezium.
Which triangle is congruent to

a AXD

b ABD

c ACD?

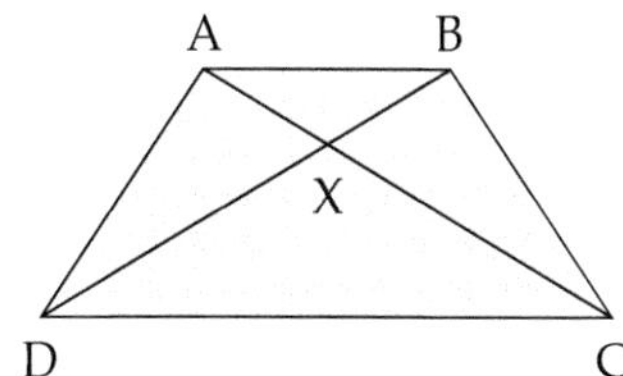

4 **a** Calculate the size of the lettered angle in each triangle.

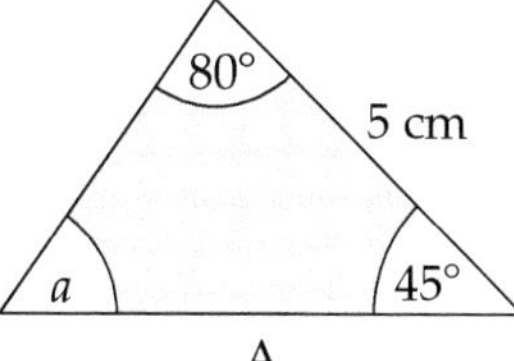

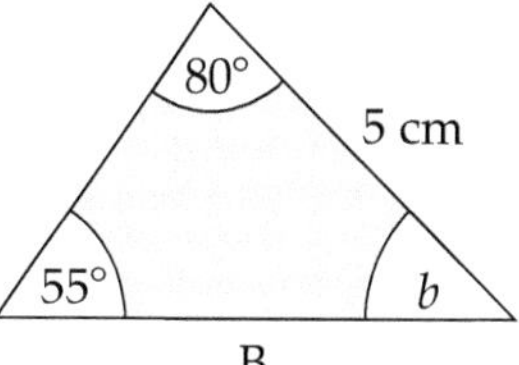

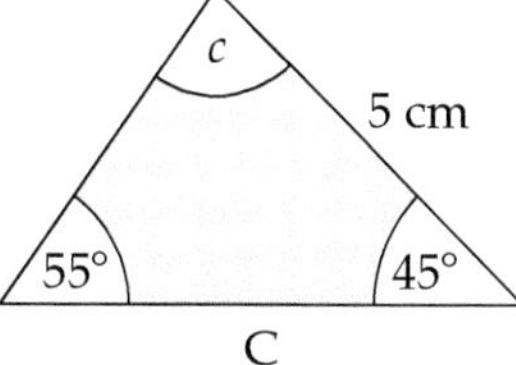

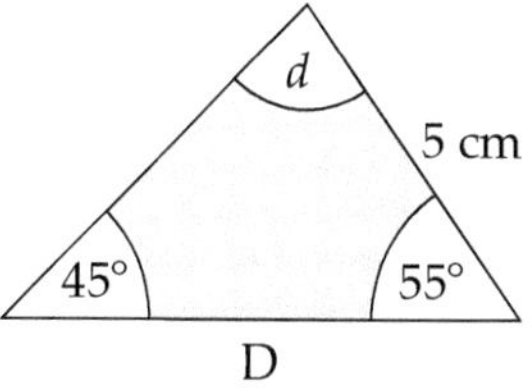

b Which triangles are congruent to triangle A?

5 One diagonal of a parallelogram is drawn to form two congruent triangles, ABC and CDA.

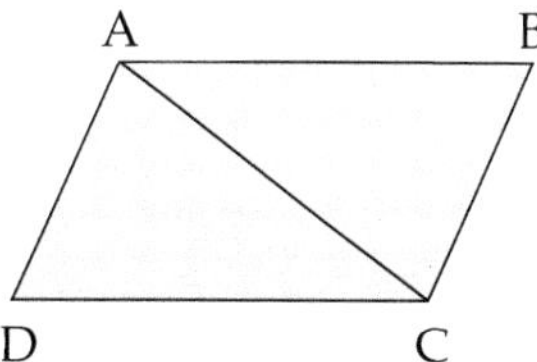

Copy the diagram and mark the equal angles and the equal sides in the congruent triangles.
Explain how you know which angles and which sides are equal.

Problem solving

6 Explain why these two triangles are congruent.
Hence find *x* and *y*.

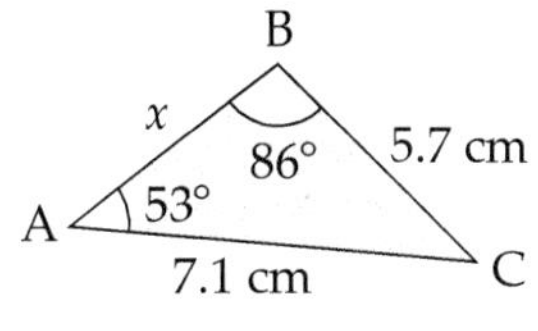

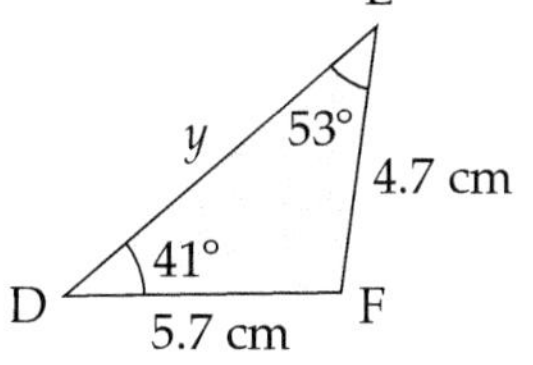

7 This decagon is drawn on isometric paper.

a Find one way to divide the decagon into four congruent pieces.

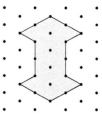

b Find 10 different ways to divide the decagon into two congruent pieces.

5 MySummary

Check out

You should now be able to ...

✓		**Test it ➡ Questions**
✓ Know and use angle facts for triangles and parallel lines.	6	1
✓ Know and use properties of quadrilaterals and regular polygons.	6	2
✓ Calculate interior and exterior angles of polygons.	6	3 – 4
✓ Use congruence.	7	5 – 6

Language	Meaning	Example
Alternate angles	When referring to parallel lines: 'Z shaped' pairs of angles.	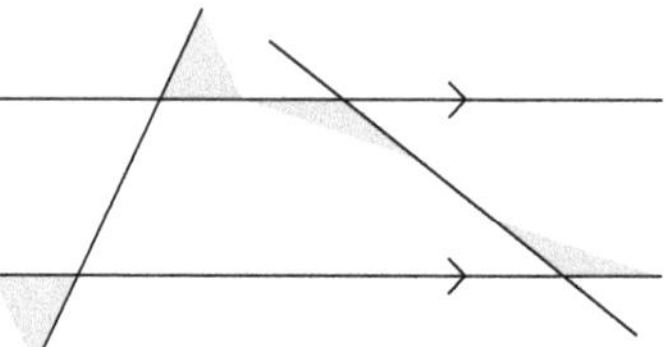
Congruent	Two shapes are congruent if they are exactly the same size and shape.	These triangles are all congruent. 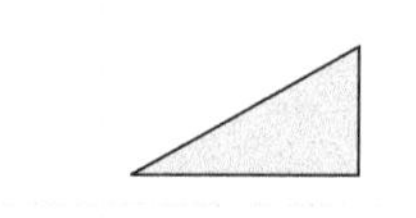 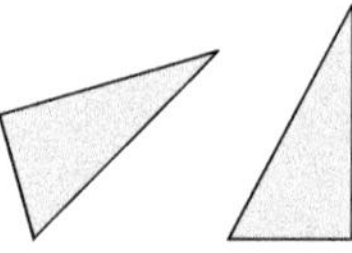
Corresponding angles	When referring to parallel lines: 'F–shaped' pairs of angles.	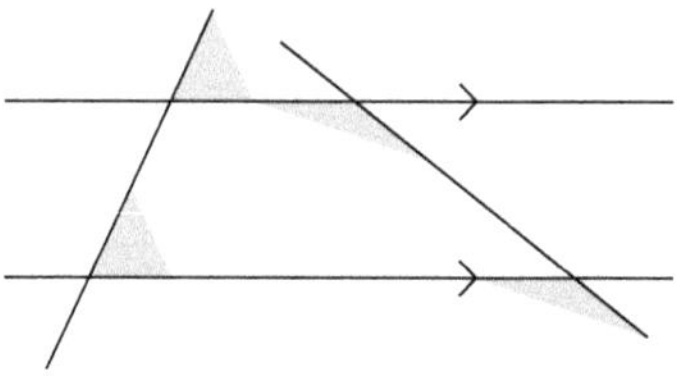
Polygon	A closed 2D shape. It is a **regular** polygon when all the sides and angles are equal.	A triangle is a type of polygon. An equilateral triangle is a regular polygon.
Interior angle	An angle inside a polygon.	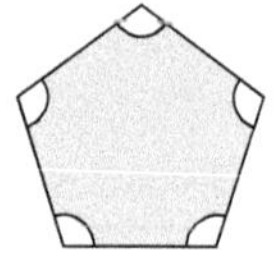
Exterior angle	The angle made between the side of a polygon and its extension.	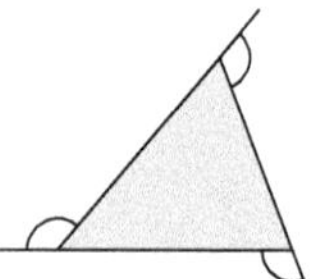

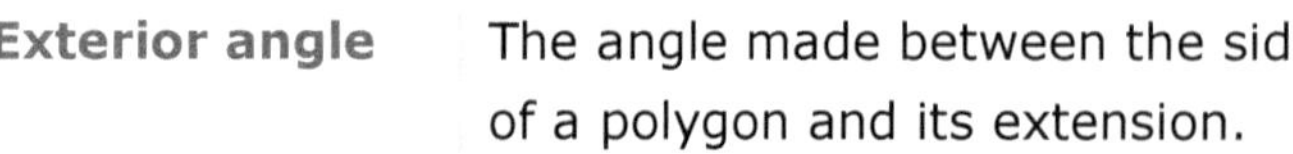

5 MyReview

1 Calculate the value of the letters. Explain which geometric facts you use in each case.

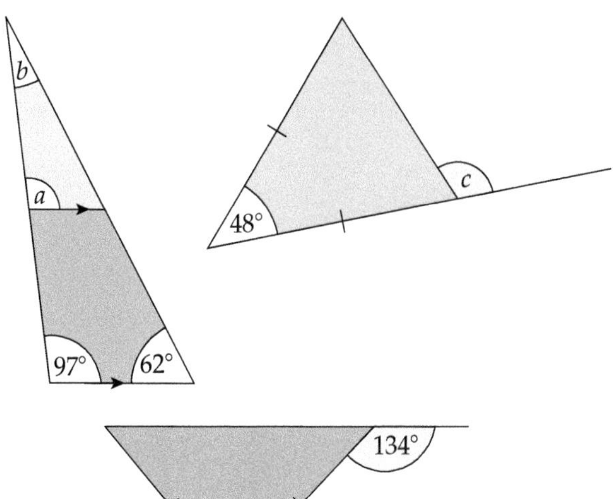

2 Calculate the value of the letters.

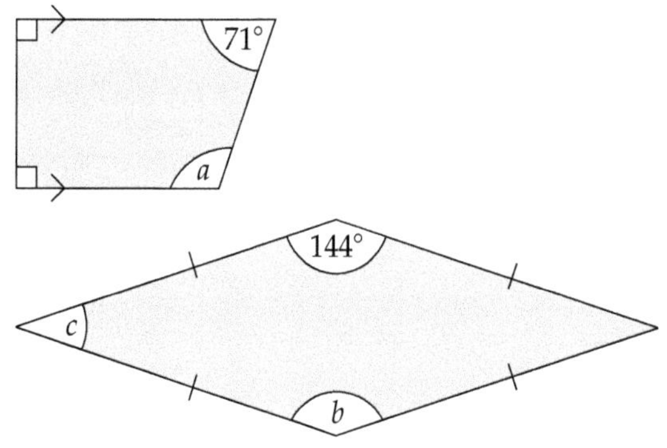

3 For a regular octagon, find

a the number of lines of symmetry

b the order of rotational symmetry

c the size of an interior angle

d the size of an exterior angle.

4 For each shape, decide whether or not it tessellates.

a an isosceles triangle

b a rectangle

c a regular pentagon

d a regular hexagon

5 These two parallelograms are congruent. State

a the length of AB

b the size of angle x

c the size of angle y.

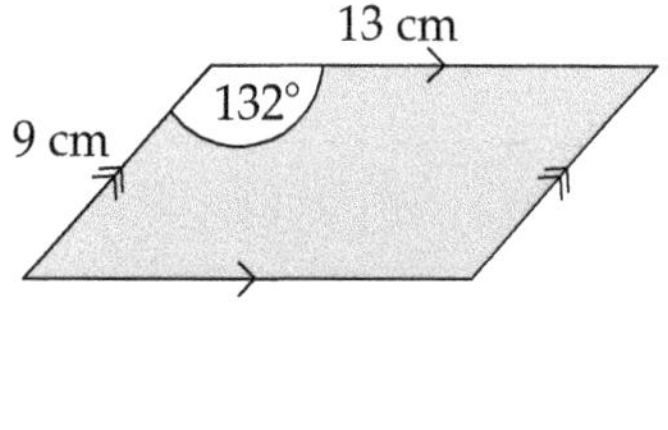

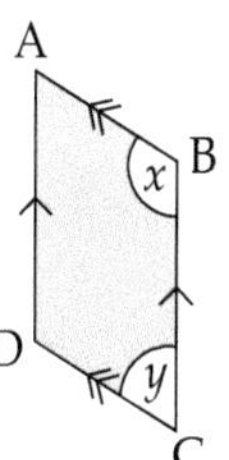

6 Show how you can divide a regular octagon into four congruent kites.

What next?

Score	
0 – 2	Your knowledge of this topic is still developing. To improve look at Formative test: 3B-5; MyMaths: 1080, 1082, 1100 and 1109
3 – 5	You are gaining a secure knowledge of this topic. To improve look at InvisiPen: 317, 342, 343, 344, 345 and 346
6	You have mastered this topic. Well done, you are ready to progress!

5 MyPractice

5a

1 Calculate the values of the unknown angles.

a

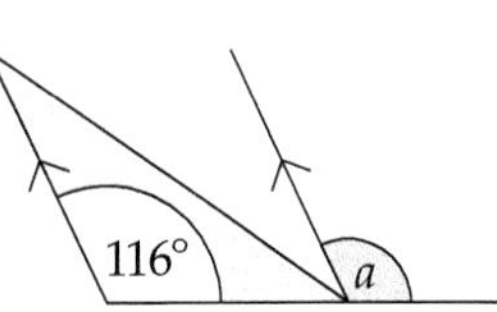

b

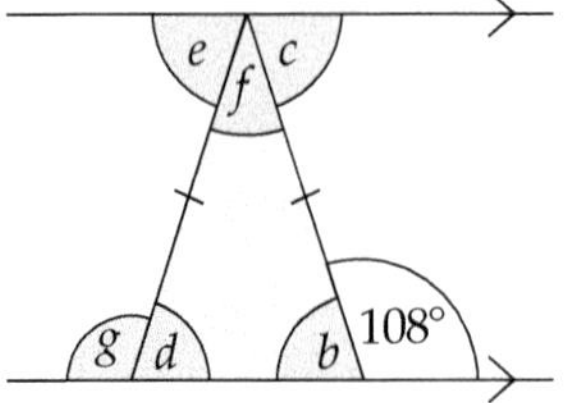

c

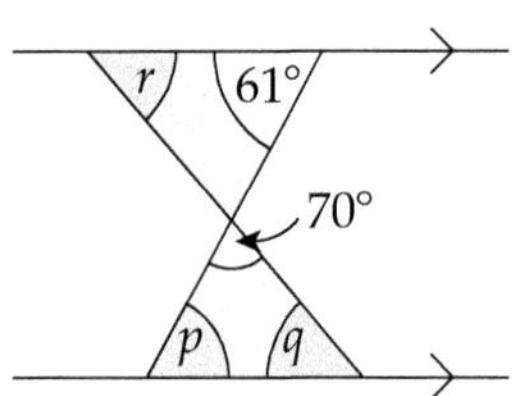

2 Calculate the angles marked with letters.

a

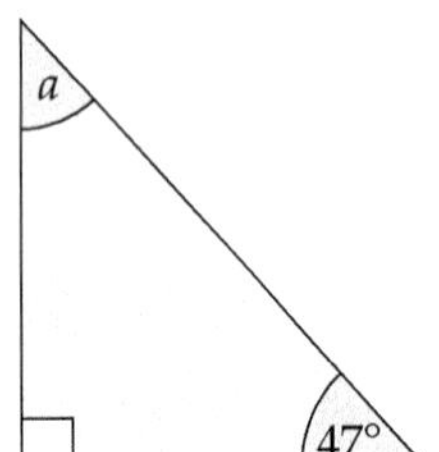

b

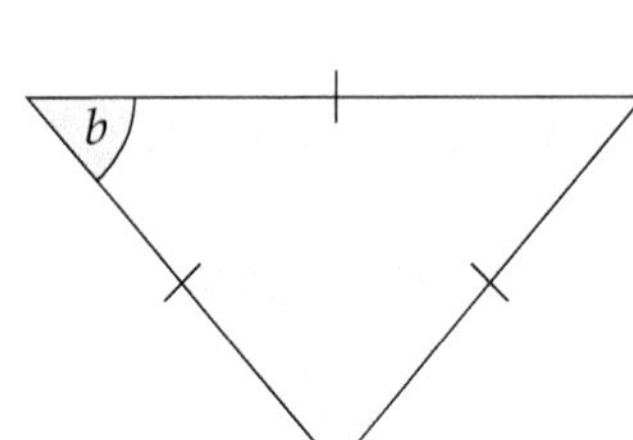

c

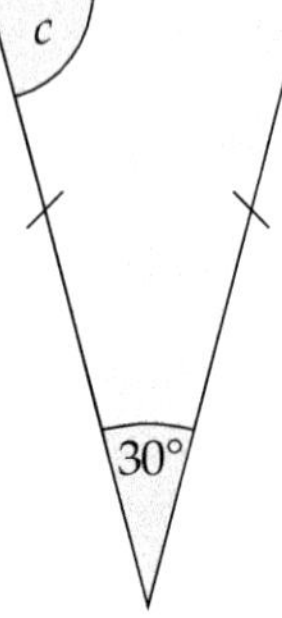

5b

3 Find the missing angles and give the mathematical name of each quadrilateral.

a

Angles 90°, 90°, □, □
Rotation symmetry of order 2

b

Angles 18°, 18°, 90°, □
1 line of reflection symmetry

c

Angles 45°, 135°, □, □
Rotation symmetry of order 2

d

Angles 36°, 36°, □, □
2 lines of reflection symmetry

4 Calculate the angles marked with letters.

a

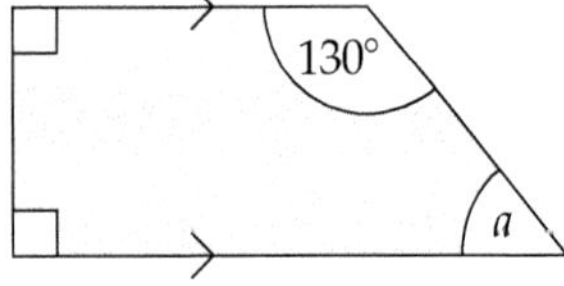

b

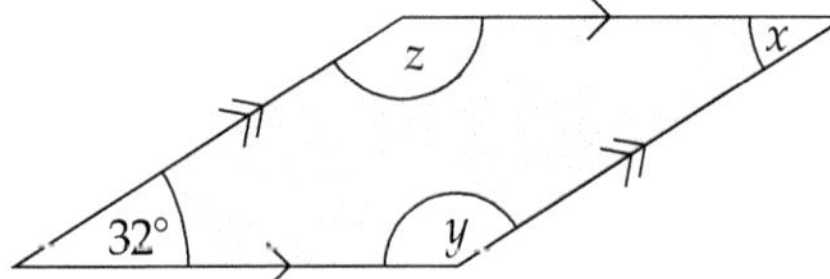

c

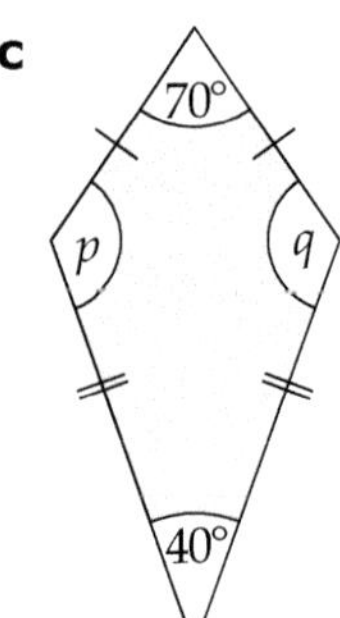

5c

5 The diagram shows a regular nonagon.

a Calculate the values of a, b and c.

b Hence find the interior angle of a regular nonagon.

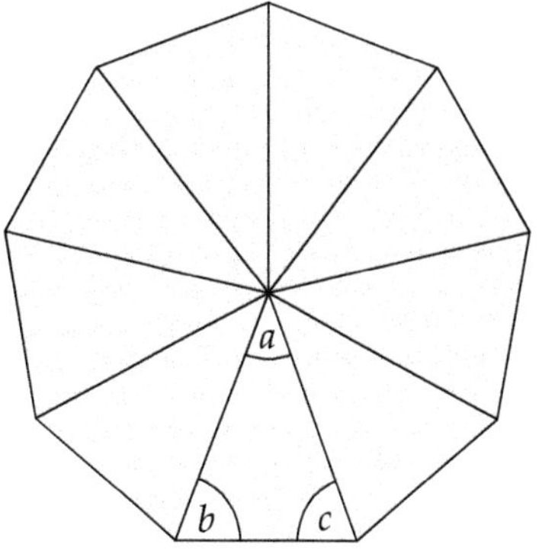

5d

6 An inscribed polygon is one whose vertices all lie on a circle.

a Draw a circle with radius 5 cm

b Construct the inscribed regular decagon.

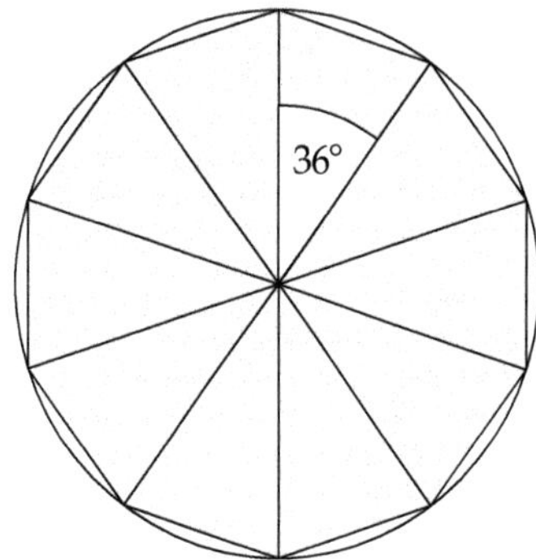

5e

7 ABCD is a kite.

Which triangle is congruent to

a ADX **b** ADC **c** DXC?

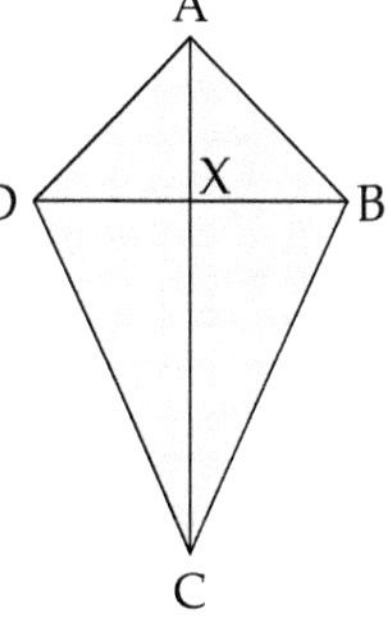

8 **a** Tessellate eight congruent trapezia on a copy of this grid.

b Draw the lines of reflection symmetry on your completed grid.

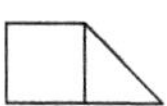

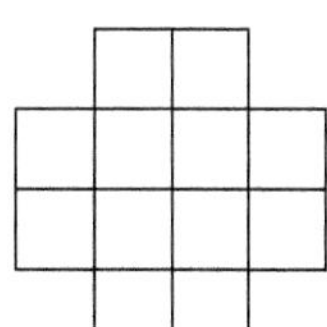

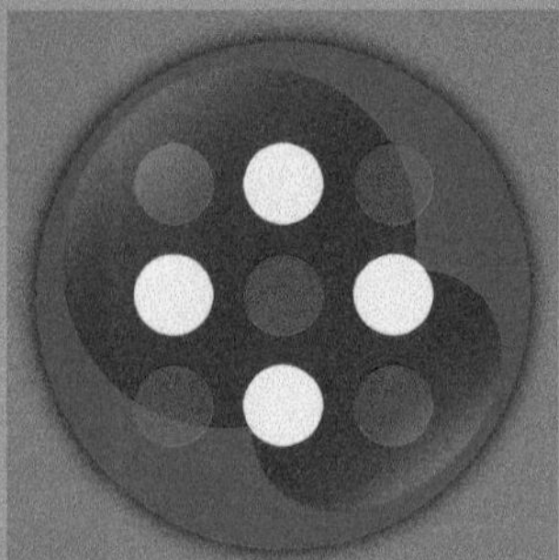

6 Graphs

Introduction

Maths is not all about numbers. Often the sheer volume of data that needs to be processed and understood is so vast that it only becomes clear when you draw a diagram. In business, people need to make the best decisions based on the data they are presented with. Graphs provide a clear visual picture that enables those decisions to be made.

What's the point?

There are lots of different types of graph, and they all serve different purposes, but they all have one thing in common – they help us to understand the patterns behind the numbers.

Objectives

By the end of this chapter, you will have learned how to …

- Use a table of values to draw a straight-line graph.
- Recognise the equations of simple straight-line graphs.
- Find the gradient of a line.
- Find the intercept of a line.
- Relate gradient and intercept to the general equation $y = mx + c$.
- Draw graphs from other forms of linear equations.
- Draw and interpret real-life graphs, including distance–time graphs.
- Draw and interpret time-series graphs.

Check in

1 Find the value of y in the equation $y = 6 - 2x$, when

a $x = 2$ **b** $x = 3$ **c** $x = -1$

2 **a** Draw and label both axes from -6 to 6.

Plot the points A(3, 4), B(-5, 4) and C(-5, -2).

b Find the coordinates of point D if the quadrilateral ABCD is a rectangle.

c Find the area of the rectangle ABCD.

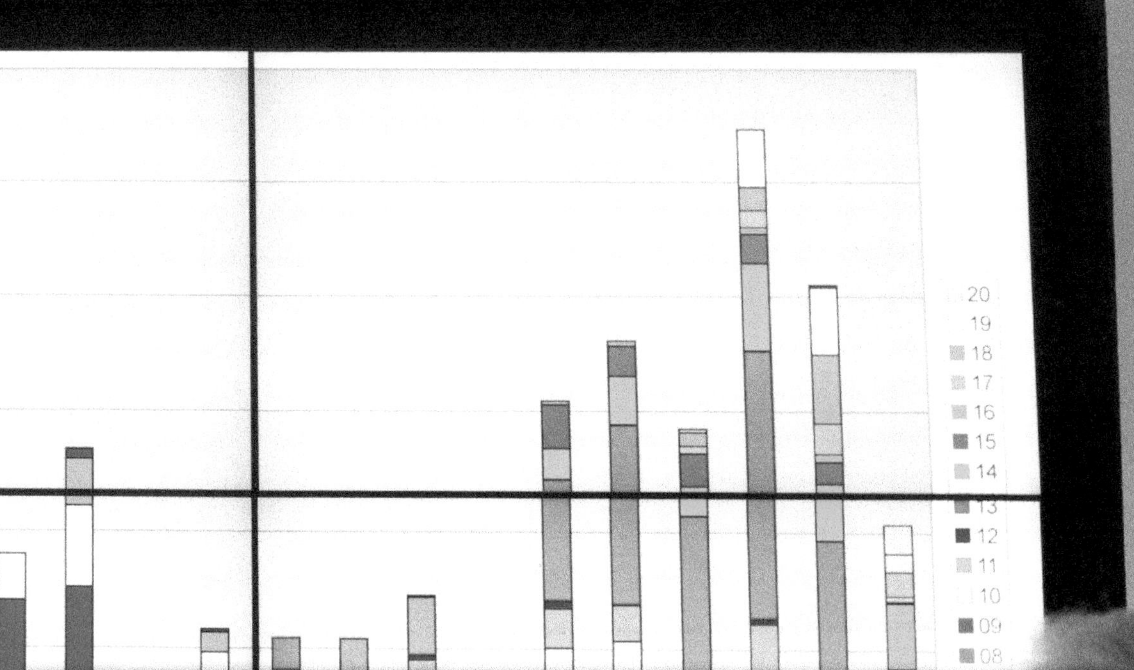

Starter problem

Here are some functions.

$y = 2x + 3$ $y = 2x - 3$ $y = x^2 + 2$

$y = -2x + 3$ $y = -2x - 3$ $y = -\frac{1}{2}x + 8$

Draw graphs of each function using x values from -4 to +4.

What is the same and what is different about these graphs?

6a Tables of values

When pairs of values are linked by a rule, you can create a **table of values**.

This **function** machine shows the rule *'double x and add 1'*.

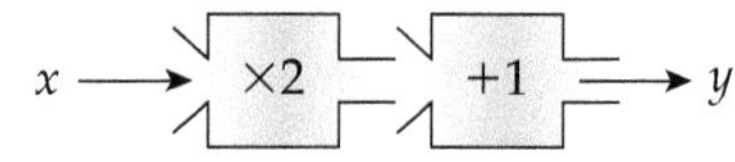

- You can write it as the **equation** $y = 2x + 1$.
- When $x = 0$, $y = 2 \times 0 + 1 = 0 + 1 = 1$
  $x = 1$, $y = 3$
  $x = 2$, $y = 5$
  $x = 3$, $y = 7$
- You can complete a table of values and write the **coordinates** of points.

x	0	1	2	3
y	1	3	5	7

- The coordinates are (0, 1), (1, 3), (2, 5) and (3, 7).
- You can plot the points on **axes** to draw a **graph**.

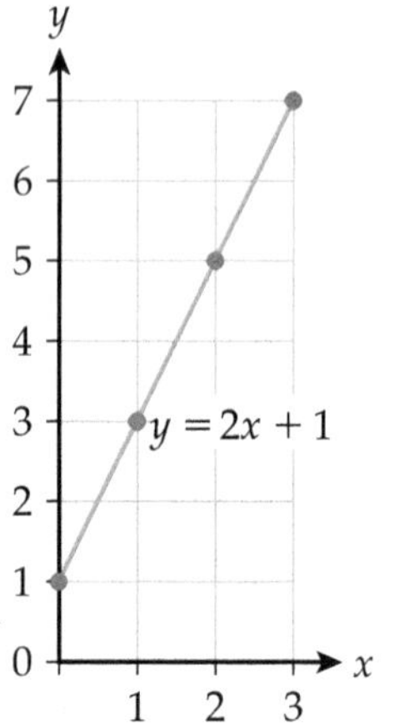

Example

Draw the graph of $y = 12 - 2x$ by constructing a table of values with values of x as 0, 2, 4, 6.

When $x = 0$, $y = 12 - 2 \times 0 = 12 - 0 = 12$
$x = 2$, $y = 12 - 2 \times 2 = 12 - 4 = 8$
$x = 4$, $y = 12 - 8 = 4$
$x = 6$, $y = 12 - 12 = 0$

x	0	2	4	6
y	12	8	4	0

The coordinates are (0, 12), (2, 8), (4, 4) and (6, 0).

Draw the graph on axes using these points.

You need at least three points to draw a straight-line graph. Two points give you the line. The third point is a check.

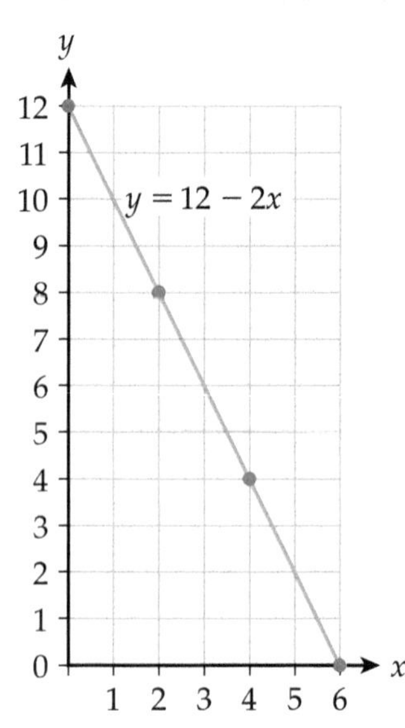

Exercise 6a

1 Use the function machine to complete this table.

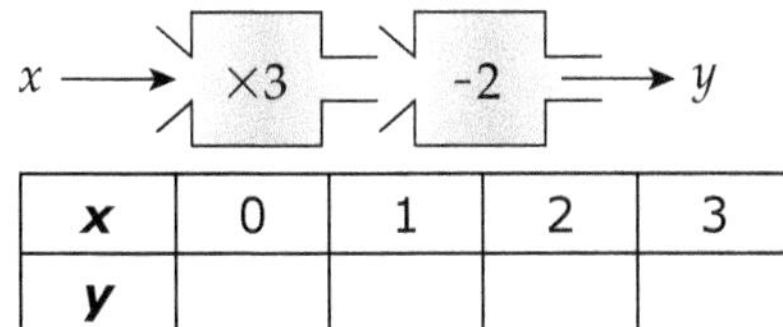

x	0	1	2	3
y				

Plot the points on a graph. The x-axis should run from 0 to 5, and the y-axis from -2 to 12.
Draw the straight-line graph and write its equation.

2 Copy and complete this table for each of the equations.

x	0	1	2	3	4
y					

Draw the graph of each equation on a copy of the axes in **1**.

a $y = x + 2$ **b** $y = x - 2$
c $y = 2x + 3$ **d** $y = 2x - 2$
e $y = 10 - x$ **f** $y = 4 - x$

3 Decide whether each point is on the given line. You do not need to draw any graphs.

a (2, 10) and $y = x + 8$
b (5, 17) and $y = 2x + 7$
c (3, 15) and $y = 3x - 6$
d (4, 2) and $y = 8 - 2x$

4 Match the equation of the graph to its description.

a $y = x + 2$ **b** $y = 2x$
c $y = x$ **d** $y = x - 2$
e $y = \frac{1}{2}x$

The y-coordinate:

1 is always double the x-coordinate
2 is always equal to the x-coordinate
3 is always half the x-coordinate
4 is always 2 more than the x-coordinate
5 is always 2 less than the x-coordinate.

Problem solving

5 The graphs of $y = 2x$ and $y = 9 - x$ and the x-axis are the three sides of a triangle.
Draw the triangle by drawing its sides on axes labelled from 0 to 9.
Find the height and the area of the triangle.

6 A youth club hires a hall for a disco. The cost of electricity, £C, depends on the number of hours, x, that the hall is needed. Copy and complete this table using the formula $C = 2x + 5$.
Draw the graph of C against x.
For how many hours does the club hire the hall if the charge for electricity is

a £12 **b** £21?

x	1	2	3	4	5
C					

7 Use a computer spreadsheet to create a table of values for the equations $y = 3x - 4$ and $y = 2x + 12$.
Extend the spreadsheet downwards to find the coordinates of the point where the graphs of these two equations intersect.

	A	B	C
1	x	y	y
2	0	=3*A2–4	=2*A2+12
3	=A2+1	=3*A3–4	=2*A3+12
4	=A3+1	=3*A4–4	=2*A4+12
5	=A4+1	=3*A5–4	=2*A5+12

6b Drawing straight-line graphs

Straight lines can be vertical, horizontal or diagonal.
You can tell what a straight-line graph looks like from its equation.

- Horizontal lines have equations x = a number. They are **parallel** to the y-axis.
- Vertical lines have equations y = a number. They are parallel to the x-axis.
- Diagonal lines have both x and y in their equations, the line slopes up or down.

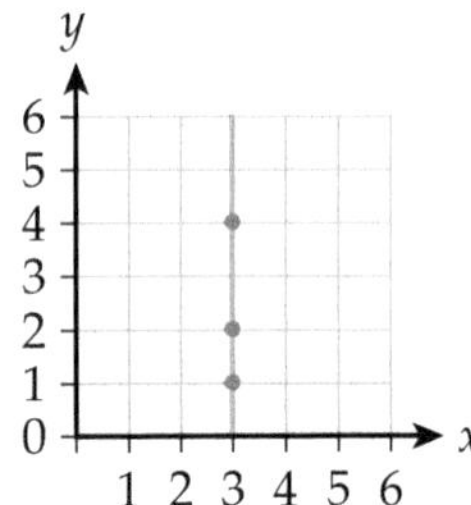

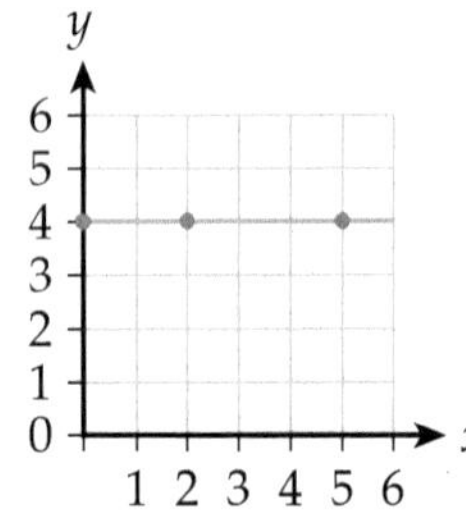

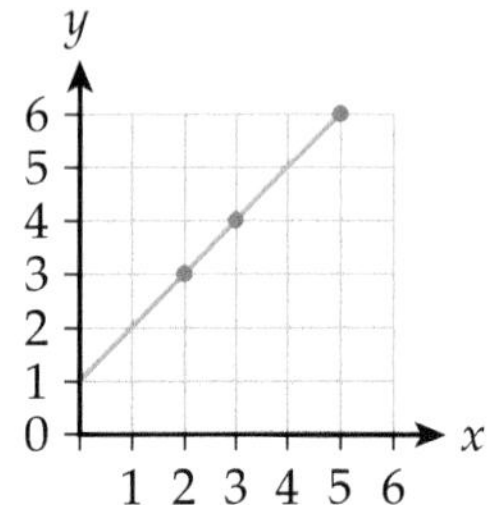

y = 4 contains the points (0, 4), (2, 4) and (5, 4).

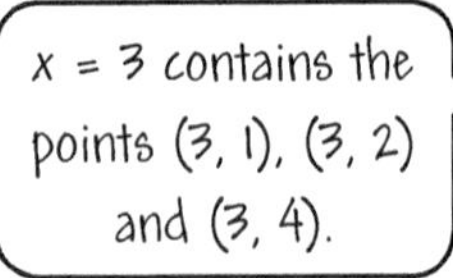

y = x + 1 contains the points (2, 3), (3, 4) and (5, 6).

You can describe shapes using equations of straight lines.

Example

A triangle is enclosed by the straight lines
$x = 6$, $y = 2$ and $y = \frac{1}{2}x + 1$.
Draw the triangle and find its area.

The line $x = 6$ has the points (6, 0), (6, 2), (6, 5), …
and is parallel to the y-axis.
The line $y = 2$ has the points (0, 2), (3, 2), (4, 2), …
and is parallel to the x-axis.
The line $y = \frac{1}{2}x + 1$ has the points (0, 1), (4, 3), (6, 4)
and slopes diagonally.
The triangle has a base of 4 units and a height of 2 units.
Its area is $\frac{1}{2} \times 4 \times 2 = 4$ square units.

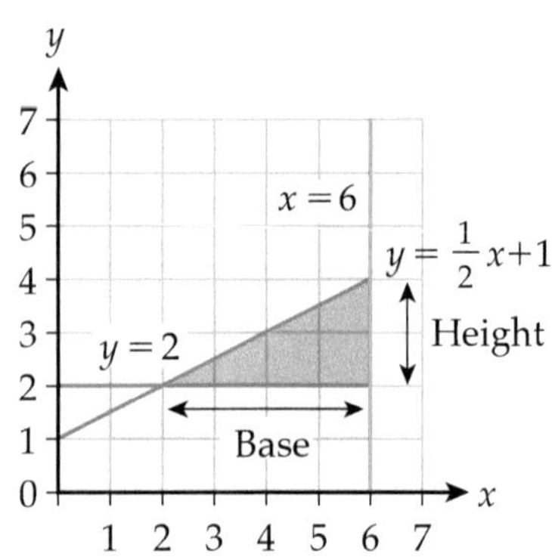

Exercise 6b

You could use the graphical package on a computer to draw some of the graphs in this exercise and so check your answers.

1 Match the equations in the box with the lettered lines in the diagram.

$y = x + 3$	$x = 2$	$x = 5$
$y = 2$	$y = 4$	

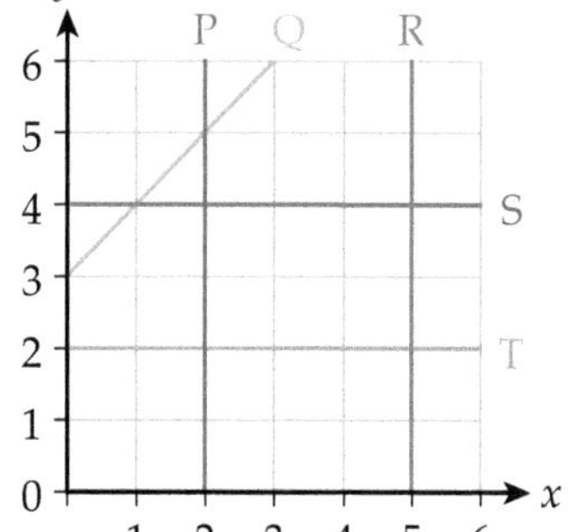

2 For each set of equations

i draw the four lines on axes from 0 to 7.

ii shade the rectangle that you make and find its area.

a $x = 3, x = 5, y = 4, y = 6$

b $x = 4, x = 5, y = 1, y = 4$

c $x = 1, x = 6, y = 3, y = 5$

3 Each of these sets of points are the corners of a square.

i On axes from -6 to 6, draw each square.

ii Find the equations of the diagonals of each square.

a (3, 2), (5, 4), (3, 6), (1, 4) **b** (2, -2), (4, -4), (6, -2), (4, 0)

c (-5, -3), (-2, -6), (1, -3), (-2, 0) **d** (-5, 3), (-4, 4), (-3, 3), (-4, 2)

Problem solving

4 For each pair of equations,

i copy and complete two tables of values.

x	0	2	4	6
y				

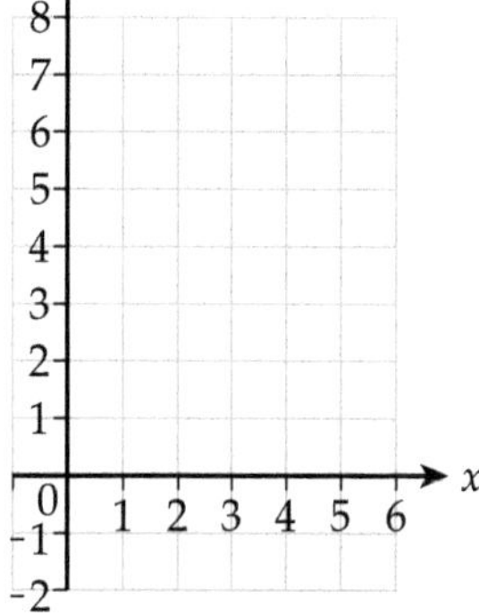

ii draw the graphs of both lines on a copy of these axes.

iii find the coordinates of the point where the two lines intersect.

a $y = x + 2, y = 2x - 1$ **b** $y = x + 3, y = 3x - 1$

c $y = x + 1, y = \frac{1}{2}x + 3$ **d** $y = x - 1, y = 7 - x$

e $y = 4, y = 5 - x$ **f** $y = 8 - 2x, x = 2$

5 On axes from 0 to 8, draw triangles whose sides are the lines with these equations. Find the area of each triangle.

a $y = 2, y = x + 2, y = 6 - x$ **b** $x = 2, y = 7 - x, y = x$

c $x = 6, y = 8 - x, y = \frac{1}{2}x + 2$

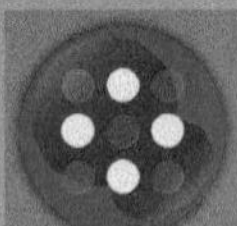

6c Gradient of a straight-line graph

- You measure the steepness of a sloping line by finding its **gradient**.

Draw a staircase on the line with horizontal steps of 1 square. The gradient is the number of squares that each step goes up or down.

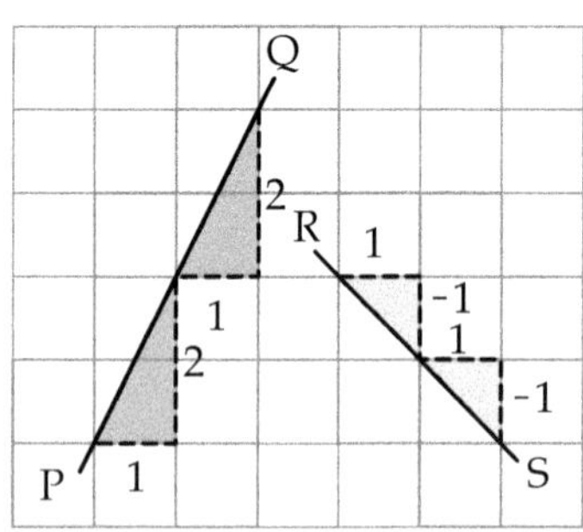

- A rising line has a positive gradient.
  A falling line has a negative gradient.

The gradient of line PQ is 2. The gradient of line RS is -1.

Example

Find the gradients of the lines $y = 2x$ and $y = \frac{1}{2}x$.

Each right-angled triangle is part of a staircase.

The line $y = 2x$ has a gradient of 2.

The line $y = \frac{1}{2}x$ has a gradient of $\frac{1}{2}$.

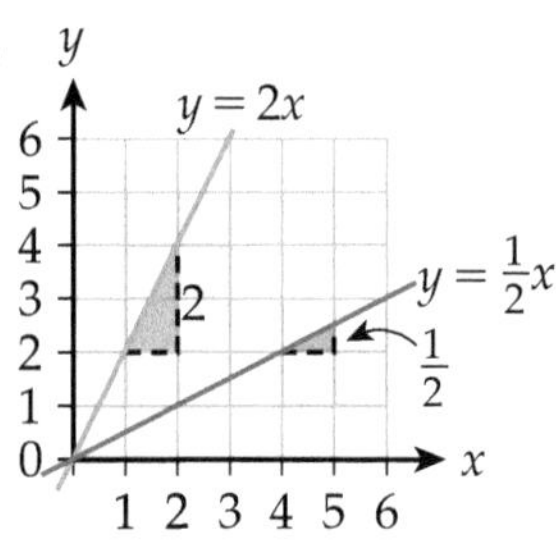

- The line $y = mx$ has a gradient of m.

Example

Find the gradients of the lines $y = 2x + 1$ and $y = -x + 6$.
State if each line is a rising or falling line.

Each right-angled triangle gives the gradient.

The line $y = 2x + 1$ has a gradient of 2.
It is a rising line.
The line $y = -x + 6$ has a gradient of -1.
It is a falling line.

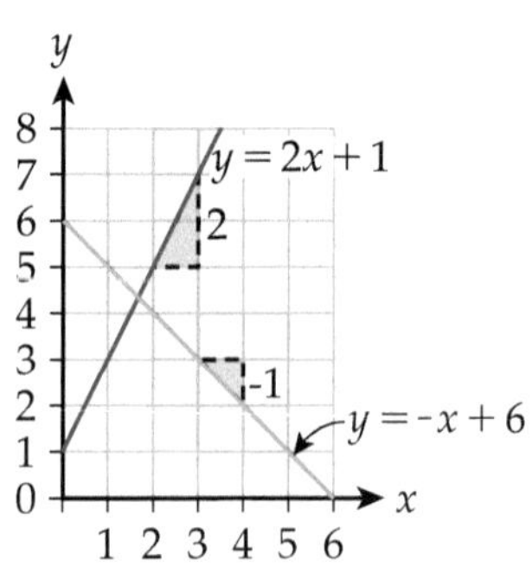

You can write y = x + 4 as y = 1x + 4, giving a gradient of 1.

- The line $y = mx + c$ has a gradient of m.

Exercise 6c

1 Find the gradients of the straight lines A to G.

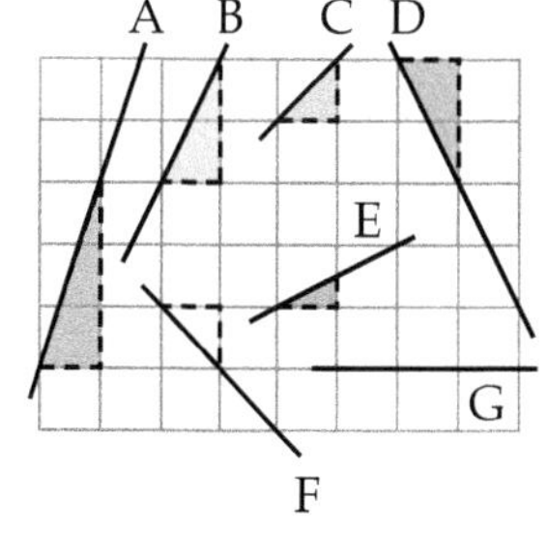

2 Draw and label axes from 0 to 8.
Plot each pair of points and join them with a straight line.
Find the gradient of each line.

a (1, 4) and (3, 8) **b** (1, 4) and (2, 7)
c (1, 4) and (7, 7) **d** (1, 4) and (6, 4)
e (1, 4) and (5, 0) **f** (1, 4) and (3, 0)

3 Find the gradients of the straight lines with these equations.
Do not draw any graphs.

a $y = 5x + 2$ **b** $y = 4x - 7$ **c** $y = x + 3$
d $y = \frac{1}{2}x + 6$ **e** $y = -6x + 4$ **f** $y = -3x + 1$

4 Find the gradients of the straight lines with these equations.

a $y = 8x + 3$ **b** $y = -8x + 3$ **c** $y = 3 - 8x$
d $y = 2 - 4x$ **e** $y = 5 - x$ **f** $y = 1 - \frac{1}{2}x$

Problem solving

5 Copy and complete this table of values for the equations
$y = 2x - 1$ and $y = \frac{1}{2}x + 3$.

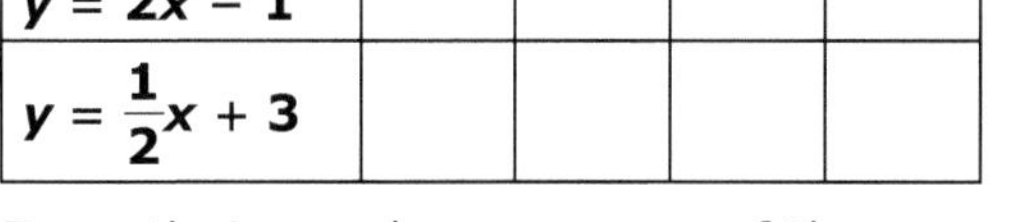

x	0	2	4	6
$y = 2x - 1$				
$y = \frac{1}{2}x + 3$				

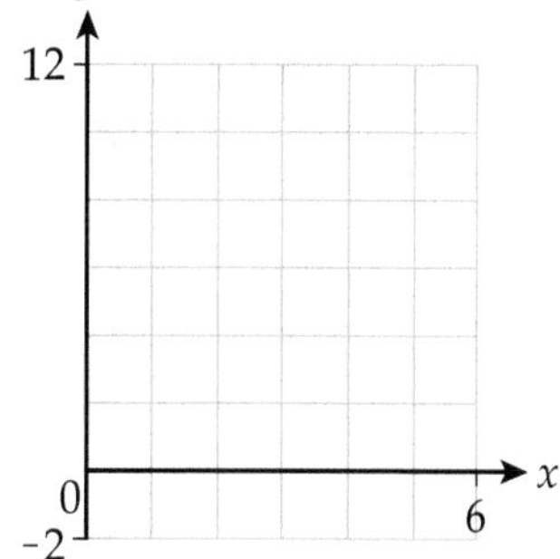

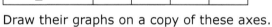

Draw their graphs on a copy of these axes.
Find the gradient of each line.

6 The temperature, T°C, in a science experiment rises over time x minutes so that $T = 3x + 2$.
Draw the graph of T for $x = 0$ to $x = 5$.
How fast is the temperature rising in degrees per minute?

7 Use the graphical package on a computer to draw the graphs of $y = mx + 3$ where m has

a whole-number values from 1 to 5
b whole-number values from -1 to -5
c the value 0
d any value greater than 100.

Explain your answers to parts **c** and **d**.

6d y-intercept of a straight-line graph

- When a straight line cuts the y-axis, the value of y at the point of **intersection** is called the **y-intercept**.

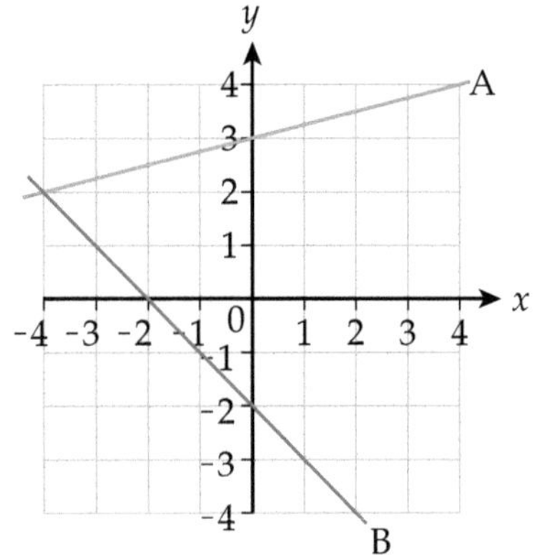

Line A cuts the y-axis at the point (0, 3)
Its y-intercept is 3

Line B cuts the y-axis at the point (0, -2)
Its y-intercept is -2

Example

This diagram shows the graphs of $y = 2x + 3$, $y = 2x + 1$, $y = 2x$, $y = 2x - 2$ and $y = 2x - 4$.
Describe the similarities and differences of these lines.
Find the y-intercept of each line.

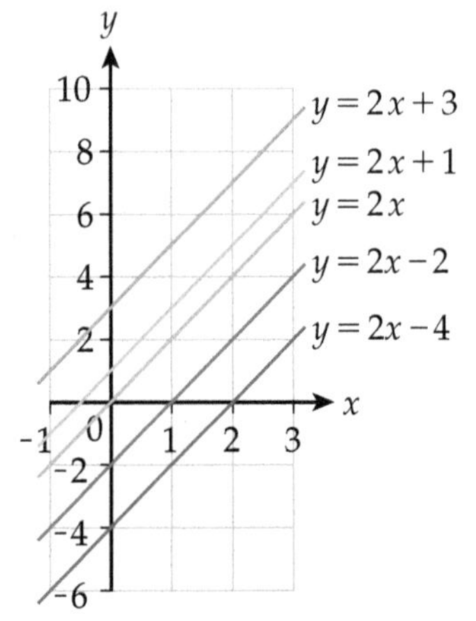

All the lines are parallel because they all have a gradient of 2.
The lines cut the y-axis at different points and so they all have different y-intercepts.

Equation	y-intercept
$y = 2x + 3$	3
$y = 2x + 1$	1
$y = 2x$	0
$y = 2x - 2$	-2
$y = 2x - 4$	-4

- The line $y = mx + c$ has a y-intercept of c. Its gradient is m.

Example

Without drawing any graphs, find the y-intercepts of these lines.

a $y = 4x$ **b** $y + 3 = 4x$

a Compare $y = mx + c$ with $y = 4x + 0$.
The y-intercept is 0.

b Re-arrange $y + 3 = 4x$ by subtracting 3 from both sides
$y = 4x - 3$.
Compare $y = mx + c$ with $y = 4x - 3$.
The y-intercept is -3.

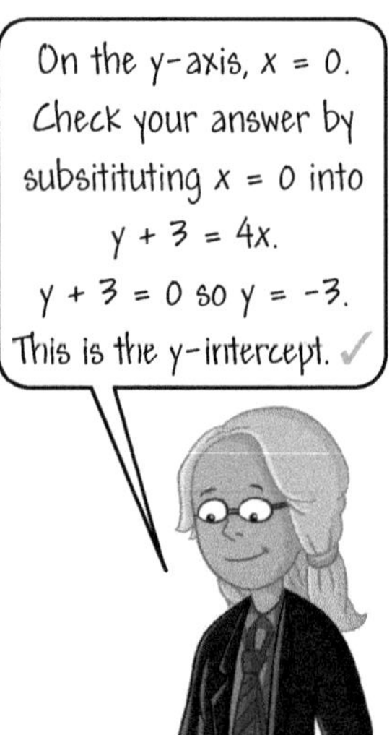

On the y-axis, x = 0.
Check your answer by
subsitituting x = 0 into
y + 3 = 4x.
y + 3 = 0 so y = -3.
This is the y-intercept. ✓

Exercise 6d

1 Find the y-intercepts of the lines A to D.

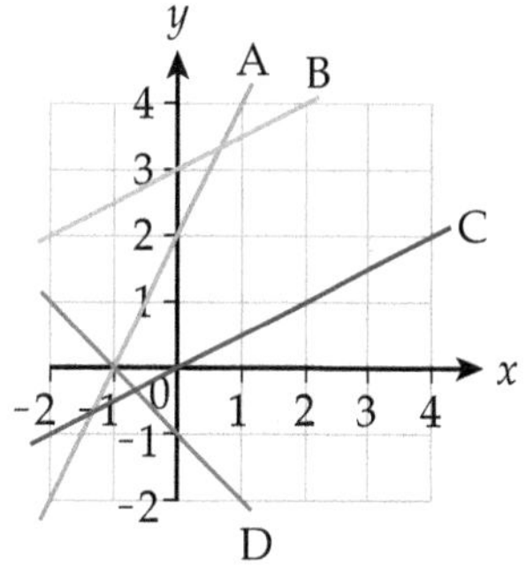

2 Draw and label both axes from -5 to 5.
Plot each pair of points and join them with a straight line.
Find the y-intercept of each line.

a (-2, 4) and (2, 2) **b** (-1, 1) and (2, 4)
c (-1, -2) and (4, -2) **d** (-4, -2) and (2, 1)
e (-2, -2) and (4, -5) **f** (-3, -4) and (3, -5)

3 Find the y-intercept of the straight lines with these equations.
Do not draw any graphs.

a $y = 3x + 6$ **b** $y = 4x + 1$ **c** $y = 2x - 5$
d $y = \frac{1}{2}x - 2$ **e** $y = 6x$ **f** $y = x + 1$

4 Find the y-intercept of the straight lines with these equations.

a $y = 8x + 5$ **b** $y = 3 + 2x$ **c** $y = 3 - 2x$
d $y = 6 - 2x$ **e** $y = 9 - 4x$ **f** $y = 8 + \frac{1}{2}x$

Problem solving

5 Copy and complete this table of values for the equations $y = 2x - 3$ and $y = \frac{1}{2}x + 3$.

x	-2	0	2	4	6
$y = 2x - 3$					
$y = \frac{1}{2}x + 3$					

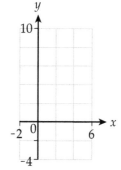

Draw their graphs on a copy of these axes.
Find the y-intercept of each line.

6 A resistor increases a voltage, V, over a time x seconds using the equation $V = 4x + 2$.

a Draw the graph of V for $x = 0$ to $x = 4$.
b What is the initial voltage when $x = 0$?

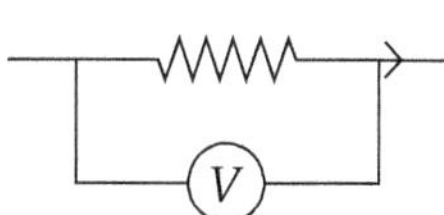

7 Use the graphical package on a computer to draw the graphs of $y = 2x + c$ where c has

a whole-number values from 1 to 5
b whole-number values from -1 to -5
c the value 0.

If you repeat for the graphs of $y = 3x + c$, using the same values of c, what will be different about your graphs?

6e The equation $y = mx + c$

- The graph of the equation $y = mx + c$ is a straight line which has a gradient of m and a y-intercept of c.

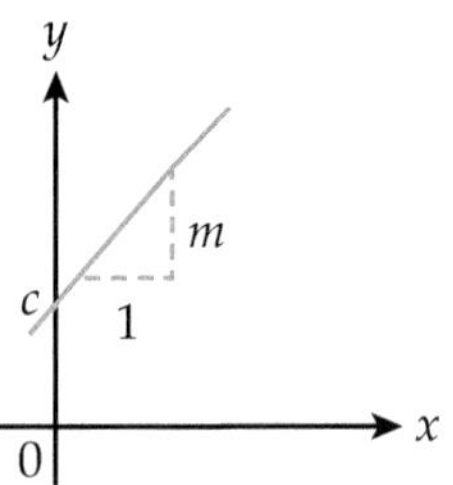

Example

This line passes through points A(-1, 1) and B(2, 7).

a Find the gradient and the y-intercept of the line.

b Find its equation.

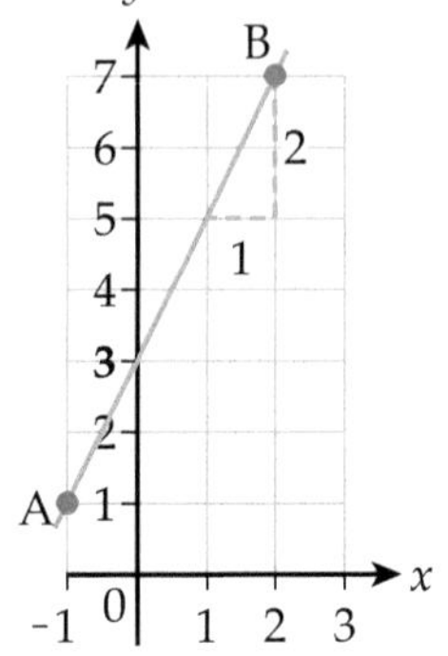

The graph shows the line through points A and B.

a Its gradient is 2.

Its y-intercept is 3.

b Its equation is $y = 2x + 3$.

- You can draw a graph of a straight line using the y-intercept and the gradient.

Example

Find the y-intercept and the gradient of the line $y = 3 - \frac{1}{2}x$.
Use your answers to draw its graph.

Re-arrange the equation: $y = -\frac{1}{2}x + 3$

Compare with $y = mx + c$.

The y-intercept is 3 and the gradient is $-\frac{1}{2}$.

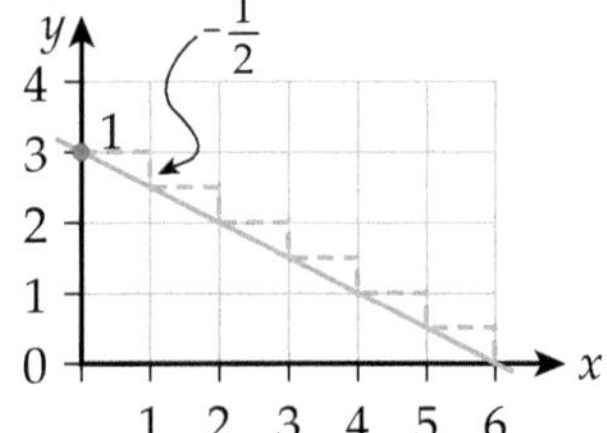

To draw the graph

- mark the point (0, 3)
- draw a line with a gradient of $-\frac{1}{2}$
- then draw the line $y = 3 - \frac{1}{2}x$.

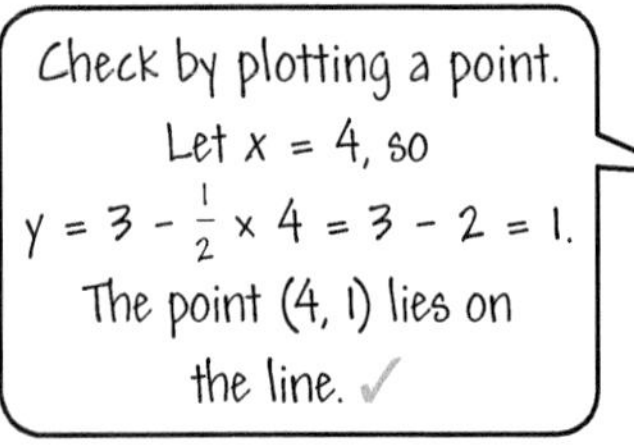

Check by plotting a point.
Let $x = 4$, so
$y = 3 - \frac{1}{2} \times 4 = 3 - 2 = 1$.
The point (4, 1) lies on the line. ✓

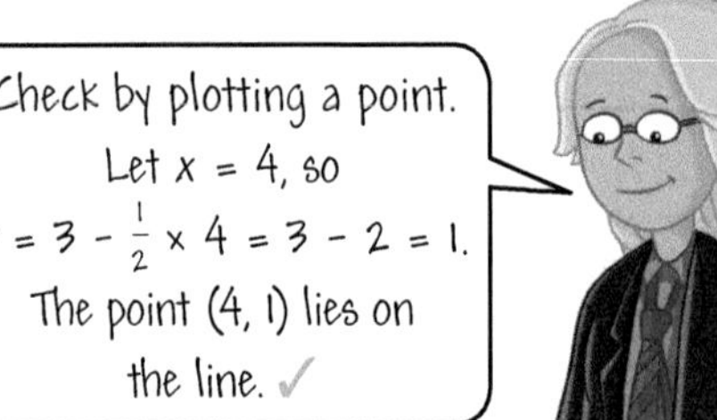

Exercise 6e

1 Copy and complete this table.

Equation	$y = 3x + 1$	$y = 4x - 5$	$y = \frac{1}{2}x + 2$	$y = 4 - 2x$
Gradient				
***y*-intercept**				

2 For each of these straight lines A to E, find

a the gradient

b the y-intercept

c the equation of the line.

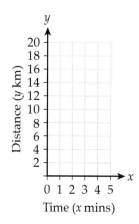

3 Draw and label axes from -6 to 6.

Plot each pair of points and join them with a straight line.

Find the gradient, the y-intercept and the equation of each line.

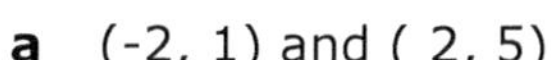

a (-2, 1) and (2, 5) **b** (-2, -3) and (1, 3)

c (0, 5) and (4, 1) **d** (-1, -5) and (1, 1)

e (-2, 0) and (6, -4) **f** (-3, -4) and (3, -4)

4 Find the gradient and the y-intercept of the straight lines with these equations. Do not draw any graphs.

a $y = 6x - 4$ **b** $y = 7x + 2$

c $y = 4x - 2$ **d** $y = 9 - 4x$

e $y = 7 - \frac{1}{2}x$ **f** $y = 3 - x$

Problem solving

5 A train travels 10 km from a station, then passes a signal box B.

It then travels 2 km each minute for the next 5 minutes.

a Copy these axes and plot (0, 10) to show B.

b Plot points to show the position of the train for each of the next 5 minutes.

c Draw a line to show the distance of the train from the station during this time and find its equation.

d What is the speed of the train, in km per minute?

6 Here are the equations of five straight lines.

$y = 3x - 1$, $y = 2x + 1$, $y = 4 - 2x$, $y = 3x + 4$, $y = 1 - 2x$

By looking at the equations, find lines which

a are parallel to each other

b have the same y-intercept.

Check your answers using the graphical package on a computer.

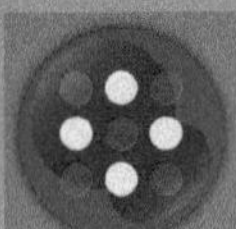

6f Equations given implicitly

$2x + y = 6$ and
$3x - 4y = 5$ are both
straight lines.

- Some equations have x and y on the same side of the equals sign. They are often called **implicit** equations.

- You can draw the graph of the line $ax + by = c$ by finding the intercepts on both axes.

Example

Find the y-intercept of the straight line with the equation $3y + 4x = 12$.
Draw the graph of the straight line.

All points on the y-axis have x-coordinate 0.
Substitute $x = 0$ into the equation. $3y + 4 \times 0 = 12$

$3y = 12$

Divide by 3 $\quad y = 4$

The point (0, 4) lies on the line, so the y-intercept is 4.

All points on the x-axis have y-coordinate 0.
Substitute $y = 0$ into the equation. $0 + 4x = 12$

$x = 3$

The point (3, 0) lies on the line.
Draw the graph using the two points (0, 4) and (3, 0).

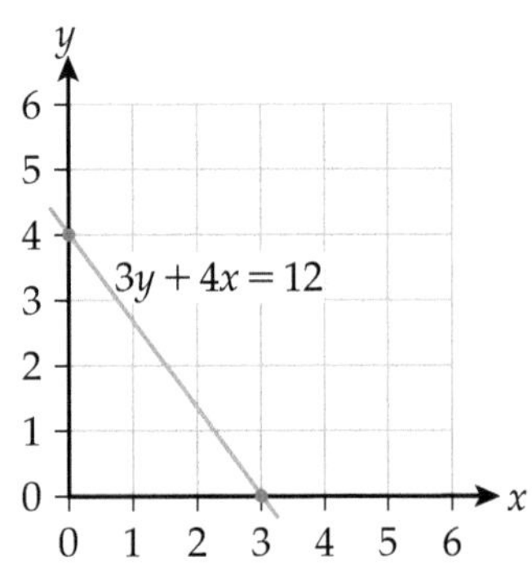

- You can find the gradient of the line $ax + by = c$ by drawing the graph.

Example

Find the gradient of the straight line with the equation $2y - 3x = 12$.

Find the intercepts on the x- and y-axes.
When $y = 0$, $0 - 3x = 12$

$x = -4$

When $x = 0$, $2y - 0 = 12$

$y = 6$

The points (−4, 0) and (0, 6) lie on the line.
Use these two points to draw the line.
From the graph, the gradient of the line is $\frac{6}{4} = 1\frac{1}{2}$

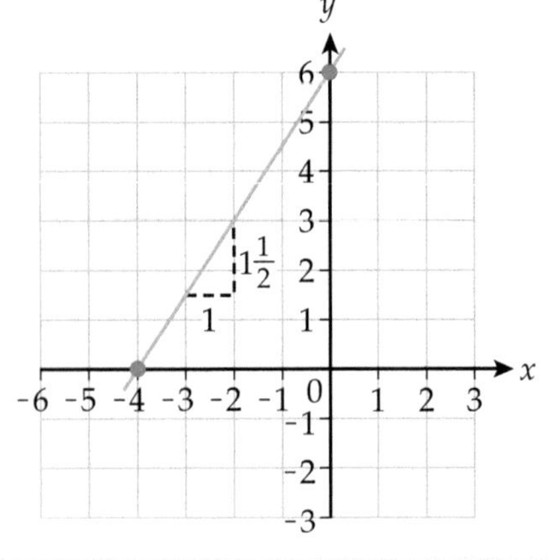

Exercise 6f

1 Find the intercepts on both axes for the lines with these equations. Draw the lines on a copy of these axes.

a $2x + 3y = 12$ **b** $5x + 2y = 10$
c $3x + 5y = 15$ **d** $4x + 3y = 12$
e $2x + 3y = 9$ **f** $x + 3y - 6 = 0$

2 Find the intercepts on both axes for the lines with these equations. Draw the lines on axes labelled from -6 to 6.

a $2x - 4y = 8$ **b** $6x - 5y = 30$ **c** $3x + 4y = -12$

3 Find the intercepts on both axes for the lines with these equations.
Draw the lines on axes labelled from 0 to 8.
Use your graphs to find the gradient of each line.

a $2x + y = 8$ **b** $3x + y = 6$ **c** $x + 2y = 4$

Problem solving

4 Draw axes labelled from -6 to 6.
On your axes, draw the graphs of the lines with these equations.
Find the gradient of each line from your graph.

a $3x - y = 3$ **b** $6x - 2y = 12$ **c** $x + 2y = -4$
d $x - y = 6$ **e** $x - 2y = 6$ **f** $2x + y = -2$

5 A shopkeeper buys x boxes of apples and y boxes of oranges for £24 where $2x + 4y = 24$.

a Draw the graph of $2x + 4y = 24$ on axes from 0 to 12.
b Use your graph to find the five different possible pairs of values for x and y. Remember that they must be whole numbers as she buys at least one box of each.
c If x and y are equal, how many of each does she buy?

6 A market gardener plants two kinds of apple tree.
He plants x Coxes and y Bramleys.
Each Cox needs $4\,m^2$ of space and each Bramley needs $8\,m^2$. He plants a total area of $84\,m^2$.
Write an equation involving x and y for the total area that he uses.
Draw a graph of your equation.
Find all possible values of x and y from your graph.
He decides to plant equal numbers of Coxes and Bramleys. Find how many.

6g Real-life graphs

- You can use graphs and equations to help you work out **real-life** problems.

Example

Mark needs to arrive at the airport two hours before his flight. The total time of his journey, T hours, depends on the distance, x miles, that he flies.
It can be calculated using this formula.

$$T = \frac{x}{500} + 2$$

Copy and complete this table of values.

x (miles)	500	1000	2000	3000
***T* (hours)**				

Draw a graph of the results.
How far does he travel if the journey takes 7 hours?

When $x = 500$, $T = \frac{500}{500} + 2 = 1 + 2 = 3$

When $x = 1000$, $T = \frac{1000}{500} + 2 = 2 + 2 = 4$

x (miles)	500	1000	2000	3000
***T* (hours)**	3	4	6	8

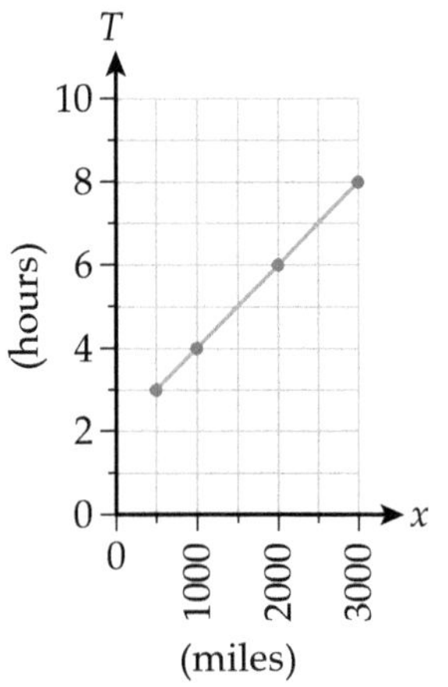

From the graph, when $T = 7$, $x = 2500$.
So Mark travels 2500 miles if his journey lasts 7 hours.

Example

The number of New Zealand dollars, y, that Mark gets when he changes x British pounds is given by $y = \frac{5x}{2} - 3$.
He has to change at least £5.
Draw a graph of y against x for values of x from 5 to 30.
Explain why the graph stops at a certain point.

Construct a table of values.

When $x = 5$, $y = \frac{5 \times 5}{2} - 3 = 12.5 - 3 = 9.5$

When $x = 10$, $y = \frac{5 \times 10}{2} - 3 = 25 - 3 = 22, \ldots$

x (pounds)	5	10	20	30
y (dollars)	9.5	22	47	72

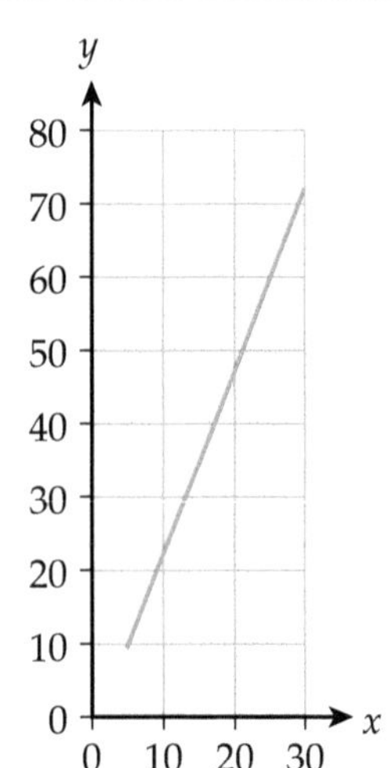

The graph stops at (5, 9.5) as the bank won't change less than £5.

Exercise 6g

1 Triangle ABC is isosceles.

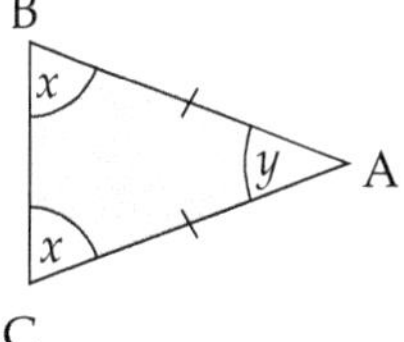

a Calculate y for different values of x.
Copy and complete this table and draw a graph of your results.

b What happens when

i $x = 45°$ **ii** $x = 90°$?

x	10	20	30	40	60	80	90
y							

2 A hire company charges £20 plus 2 pence for every mile you travel in their van.
If you travel x miles the cost, £C, is given by $C = \frac{2x}{100} + 20$.

a Copy and complete this table and draw a graph of your results on a copy of these axes.

x (miles)	50	100	200	300
C (£)				

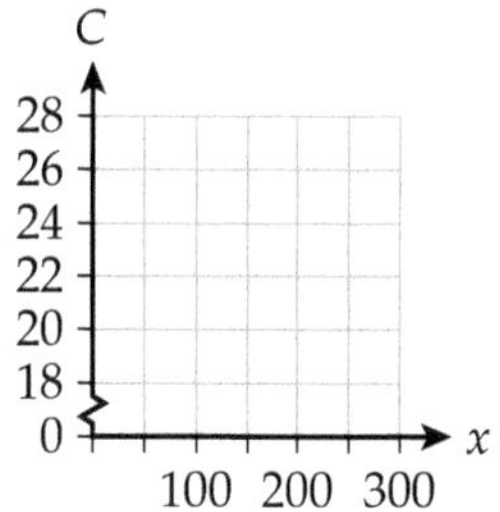

b If you use the van for 250 miles, how much are you charged?

3 A car starts its journey with a full tank of petrol.
After travelling x km it has y litres of petrol left in the tank, where $y = 40 - \frac{x}{20}$.

a Copy and complete this table and draw a graph of your results.

x (km)	0	100	200	400	600	800
y (litres)						

b How many litres are in the full tank?

c How far can the car travel before running out of petrol?

4 You drop a stone from a tall building.
It falls a distance x metres in a time t seconds where $x = 5 \times t^2$.

a Copy and complete this table and draw a graph of your results.

t (secs)	1	2	3	4	5
x (metres)					

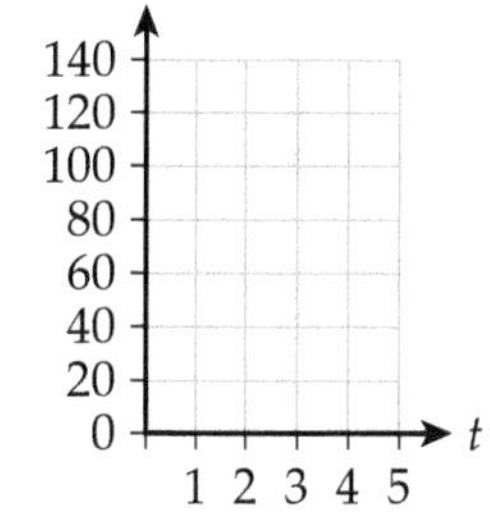

b What symbol in the equation tells you that the graph will not be a straight line?

c If the stone hits the ground after 4.5 seconds, estimate the height of the building.

5 A farmer makes a rectangular pen for his sheep so that it always has a perimeter of 24 metres.

a Construct a table of possible values of x and y and draw a graph of your results.

b Find the equation which links x and y.

c Which values of x and y give the maximum possible value of the area of the sheep-pen? What kind of rectangle is it in this case?

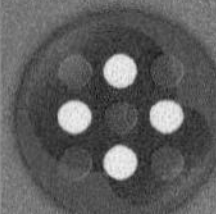

6h Distance–time graphs

- You can show a journey on a **distance–time** graph.
- The speed is the gradient = $\frac{\text{distance travelled}}{\text{time taken}}$

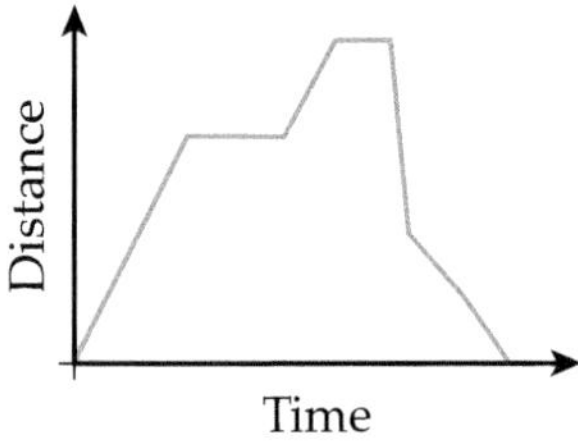

Example

This graph shows the height of a balloon after a child lets it go.
Find its speed

a in the first 5 minutes

b in the next 10 minutes.

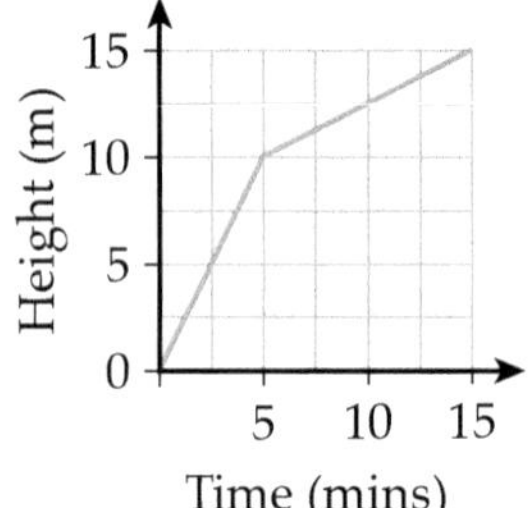

a In the first 5 minutes it rises 10 metres.

Its speed is $\frac{10}{5}$ = 2 metres per minute.

b In the next 10 minutes it rises a distance of 15 − 10 = 5 metres.

Its speed is $\frac{5}{10} = \frac{1}{2}$ metre per minute.

Example

Sara goes on her bike to post a letter.
She leaves home, stops at a junction on the way to the post office, posts the letter and returns home.
The graph shows her journey.

a Find her speed from home to the junction.

b How long does she stop at the post office?

c How far does she cycle altogether?

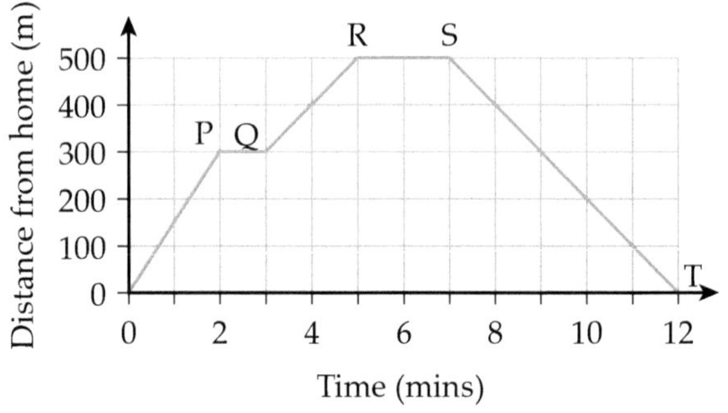

a The line OP shows Sara's journey from home to the junction.

Her speed for this stage is $\frac{300}{2}$ = 150 metres per minute.

b The line RS shows her stay at the post office.

She stopped for 7 − 5 = 2 minutes at the post office.

c She cycles 500 + 500 = 1000 metres altogether.

A horizontal line means that Sara stayed in one place.

Exercise 6h

1 This graph shows Harry taking his dog for a walk.

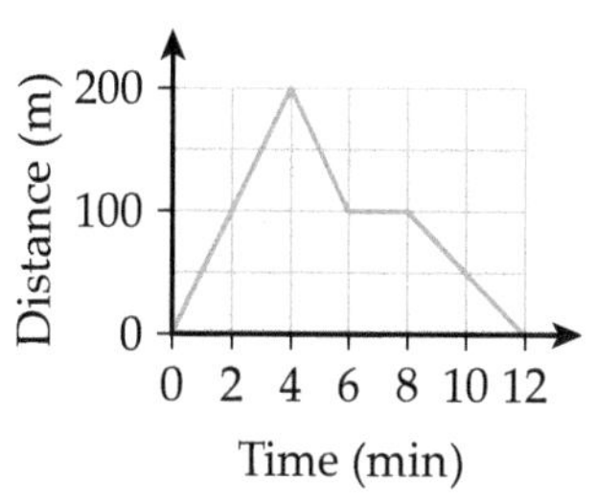

- **a** What is their furthest distance from home?
- **b** How long does it take to get this far?
- **c** For how long do they stop on the way back?
- **d** How far from home are they when they stop?
- **e** How long in total do they take to get back home?
- **f** How long does the whole walk take?

2 You are waiting at a bus stop and you see your bus 800 m away. This graph shows its journey.

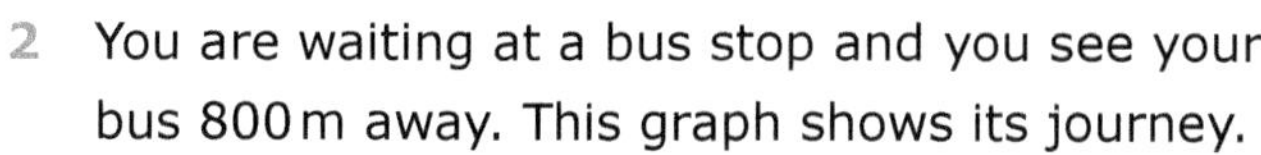

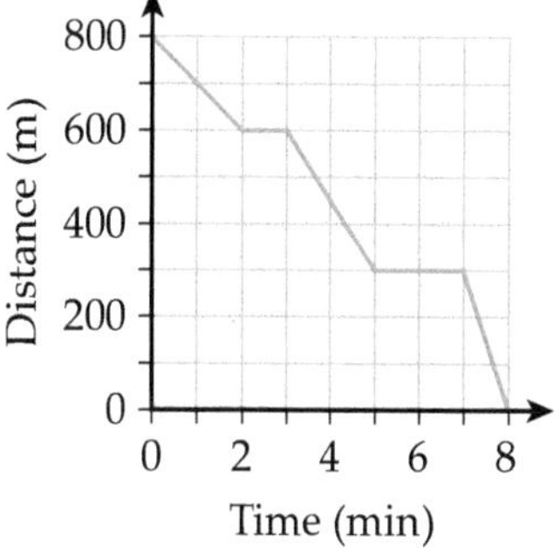

- **a** How many times does the bus stop before it reaches you?
- **b** How long does it take to reach its first stop?
- **c** How far apart are the first and second stops?
- **d** How long does it spend at its second stop?

3 Match the graphs with the descriptions of a car

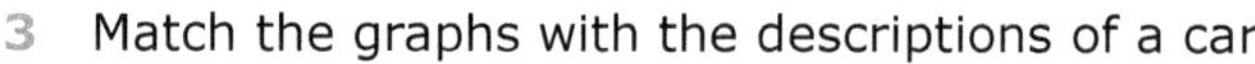

- **a** moving away from you at a speed of 4 m/s
- **b** moving towards you at a speed of 4 m/s
- **c** stopped at a distance of 20 m from you.

m/s means metres per second.

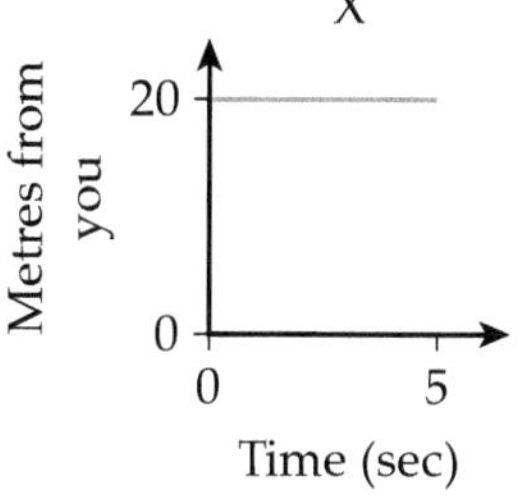

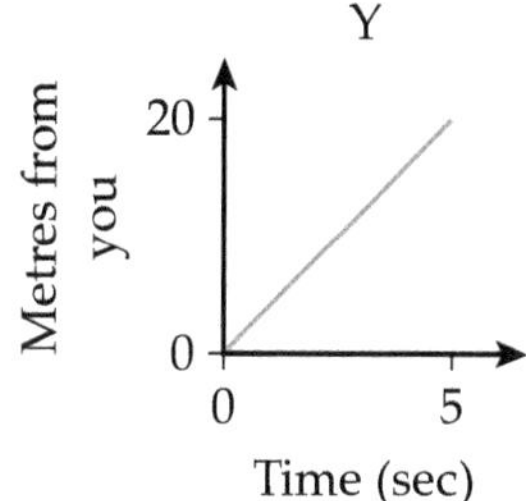

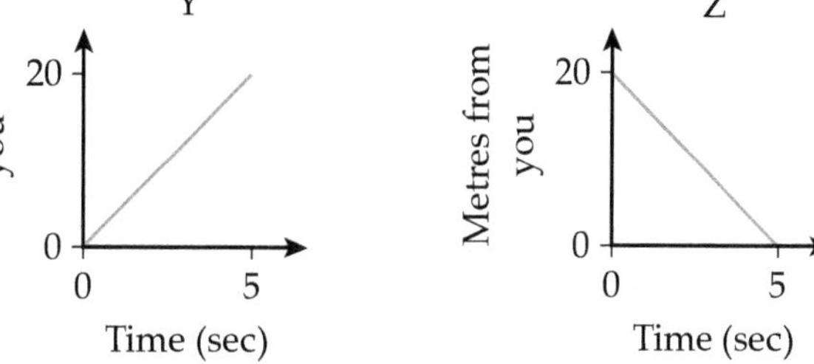

4 Mei-Ling and Shara cycle on the same road in opposite directions, as shown on this graph.

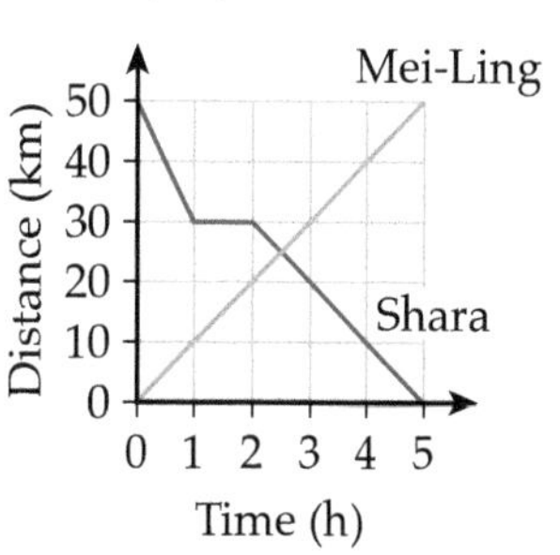

- **a** Who has a rest on the way? How long is the rest?
- **b** How long is it before they pass each other?
- **c** How far does Mei-Ling cycle and what is her speed?
- **d** What is Shara's speed after she has rested?

Problem solving

5 Draw a graph for your journey to school in the morning.
Include any times when you stop, such as when you are waiting for a bus.
Show how far you travel and how long each part of your journey takes.

6i Time series

- A **time series** shows how a quantity changes over time.

Example

This table and graph show the monthly profit (in millions of £) made by a company in 6 months.

	Jan	Feb	Mar	Apr	May	June
Profit (£M)	2	1	4	5	4	4

a In which month did the company make the most profit?

b Calculate the average profit in the first four months.

c Is the **trend** in the profit rising, falling or level?

a The company made the most profit in April.

b The average profit from January to April is

$$\frac{2+1+4+5}{4} = \frac{12}{4}$$

$= £3$ million.

c There is a rising trend.

- You can sometimes **sketch** a graph of a time series rather than drawing it accurately.

Example

Water is poured into three containers of different shapes.
The graphs show how the depth of water, D, increases with time, t.
Match the containers to the graphs. Explain your match.

a

b

c

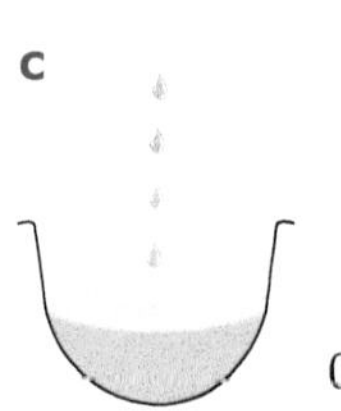

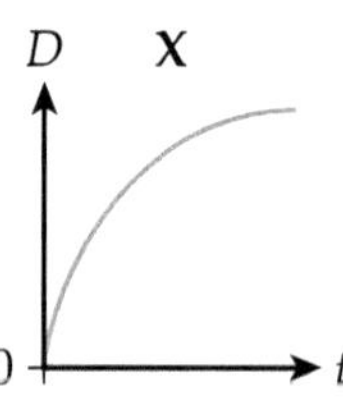

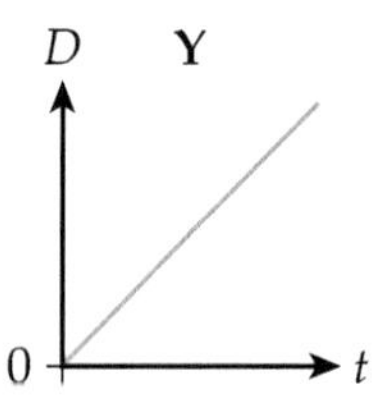

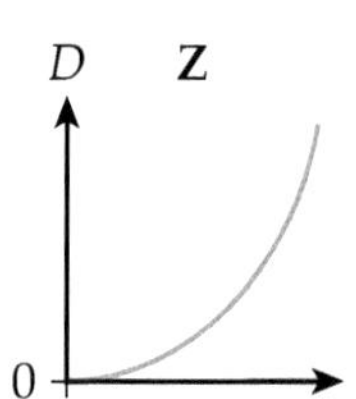

Y matches **a**. The level rises steadily.
The graph is straight because the beaker has constant width.

Z matches **b**. The level rises slowly at first because the flask has a wide base. As it narrows, the level rises more quickly.

X matches **c**. The container is narrow at the bottom so the level will initially rise quickly. As it widens, the level rises more slowly.

Exercise 6i

1 This graph shows the number of births in a hospital over a period of five weeks.

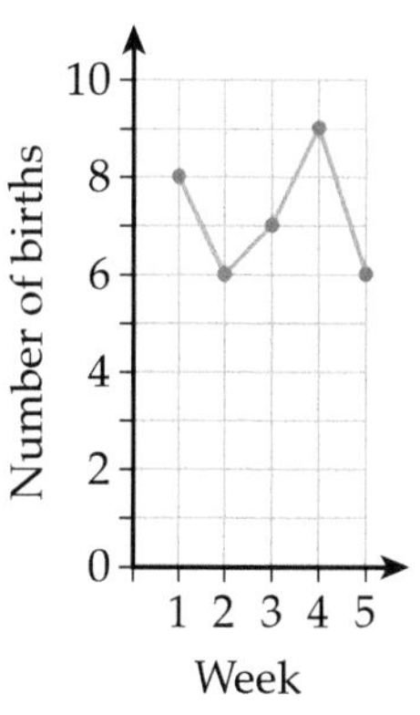

a Copy this table and complete it using the graph.

Week	1	2	3	4	5
No. of births					

b In which weeks were there fewest births?

c Calculate the mean number of births in the first three weeks.

d Is the trend in the number of births rising, falling or level?

2 This table show the number of accidents at a road junction over a period of six months.

Month	Jan	Feb	March	April	May	June
No. of accidents	16	14	15	10	8	9

a Draw a time-series graph for this data.

b What is the largest monthly fall in the number of accidents?

c Calculate the mean number of accidents over the 6 months.

d Is the trend in the number of accidents rising, falling or level?

3 The volume of tea in a cup changes as you drink it.
Match the descriptions **a** to **d** with the graphs.

a The tea is drunk all at one go.

b The tea is drunk in two gulps, half a cup each time.

c The tea is drunk sip by sip.

d The tea is not drunk at all.

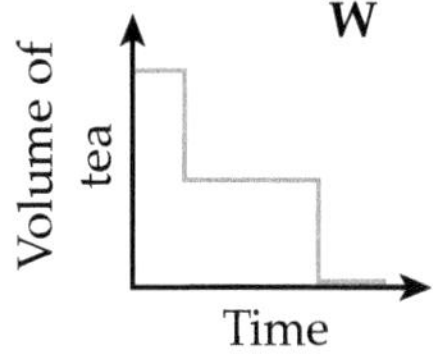

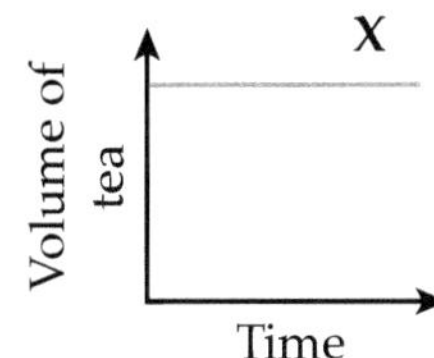

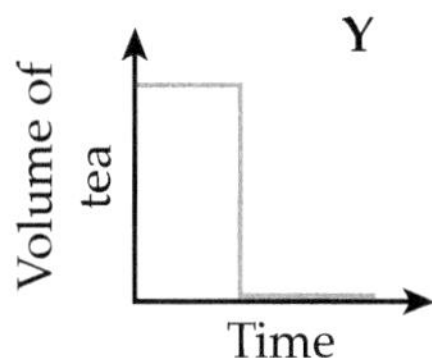

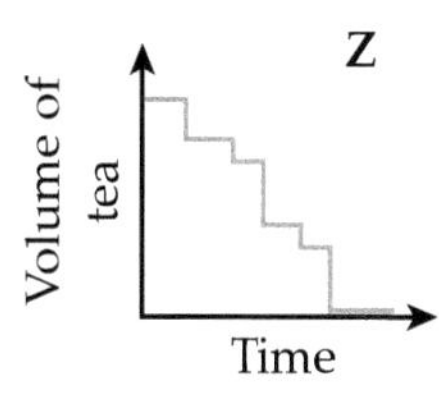

4 A cook uses olive oil from a 1-litre bottle.
This graph shows the amount of oil in the bottle over a week.
Give an explanation for the shape of the graph.

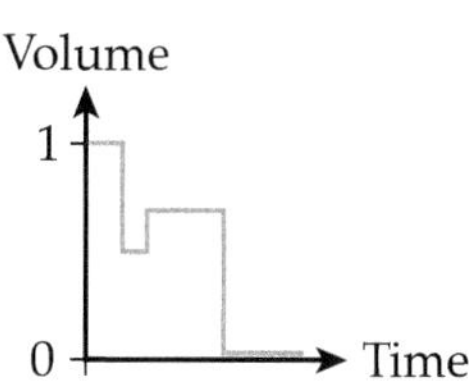

Problem solving

5 Sketch graphs to illustrate these situations.

a The selling price of a car, bought new, over its lifetime.

b The annual repair costs of a car, bought new, until it is scrapped.

c The annual mileage of a car with several different owners over its lifetime.

Explain why the graphs have their shapes and describe any trends.

6 MySummary

Check out

You should now be able to ...		Questions
✓ Use a table of values to draw a straight-line graph.	6	1
✓ Recognise the equations of simple straight-line graphs.	6	2 – 4
✓ Relate gradient and y-intercept to the general equation $y = mx + c$.	6	5 – 6
✓ Draw and interpret real-life graphs.	6	7 – 9

Language	Meaning	Example
Equation	A statement of mathematical equality.	$y = 2x + 1$
Table of values	A table giving the coordinates of the points on a given line.	x: 0, 1, 2, 3; y: 1, 3, 5, 7
Constant	A number in an expression or equation. It does not change.	$y = 2x + 1$ 1 is a constant
Gradient	A number that describes the steepness of a line defined as $\frac{\text{change in } y}{\text{change in } x}$.	A line through (0, 0) and (4, 2) has gradient $\frac{2-0}{4-0} = \frac{2}{4} = \frac{1}{2}$.
Intercept	The point at which a line crosses an axis.	The line $y = 2x + 1$ has a y-intercept (0, 1).

6 MyReview

1 For the equation $y = 12 - 4x$

a copy and complete the table

x	1	2	3
y			

b plot the graph of the equation

c on the same axes draw the graph of $y = \frac{1}{2}x + 3$

d find the coordinates of the point where the lines intersect.

2 Does the line $y = 11 - 3x$ pass through the point (2, 5)?

3 Find the equations of each of these straight lines.

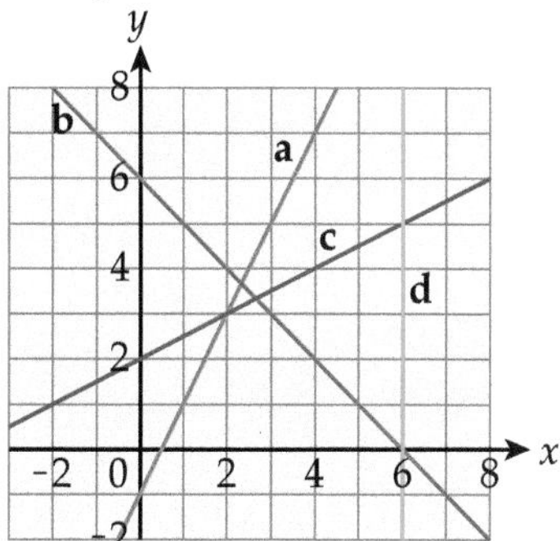

4 Where does the graph of $4x + 3y = 24$ intersect the coordinate axes?

5 Find the gradients of the straight lines with these equations.

a $y = \frac{x}{2} - 4$ **b** $y = -7(3 - 2x)$

6 Find the y-intercepts of the straight lines with these equations.

a $y = 11 - 7x$ **b** $y = 5x$

7 **a** Calculate the area of this triangle when $x = 4$ cm.

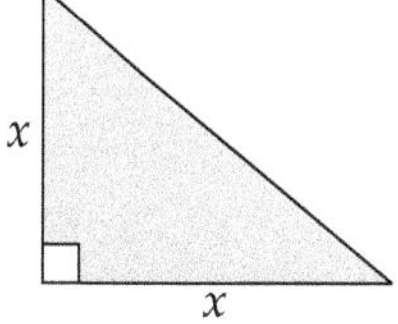

b Copy and complete the table of values to show A for different values of x.

x	1	2	3	4	5	6	7
A							

c Draw a graph of your results.

8 Kate leaves her school which is 6 km from her home at 15:10. She takes 40 minutes to walk 4 km towards her home. She stops at her friend's house for 30 minutes.
She cycles the rest of the way home at a speed of 12 km per hour.
Draw this journey on a distance-time graph.

9 The money in Geoff's bank account on Monday morning each week for a month is shown on the time-series graph.

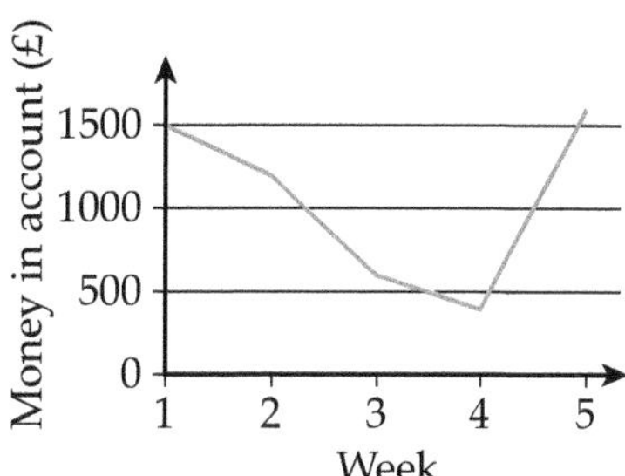

During which week do you think

a Geoff was paid

b Geoff had to pay his rent?

What next?

Score		
0 – 4		Your knowledge of this topic is still developing. To improve look at Formative test: 3B-6; MyMaths: 1059, 1153, 1312, 1322, 1395, 1396 and 1939
5 – 7		You are gaining a secure knowledge of this topic. To improve look at InvisiPen: 262, 263, 264, 265, 273, 274, 275 and 276
8, 9		You have mastered this topic. Well done, you are ready to progress!

6 MyPractice

6a

1 Copy and complete this table for each of the equations.

x	0	2	4	6
y				

Draw the graph of each equation on appropriate axes.

a $y = 2x - 3$ **b** $y = 9 - x$ **c** $y = 10 - 2x$

6b

2 Match the equations in the box with lines A, B, C or D.

$y = x + 6$ $y = 6 - x$ $x = 3$ $y = 3$

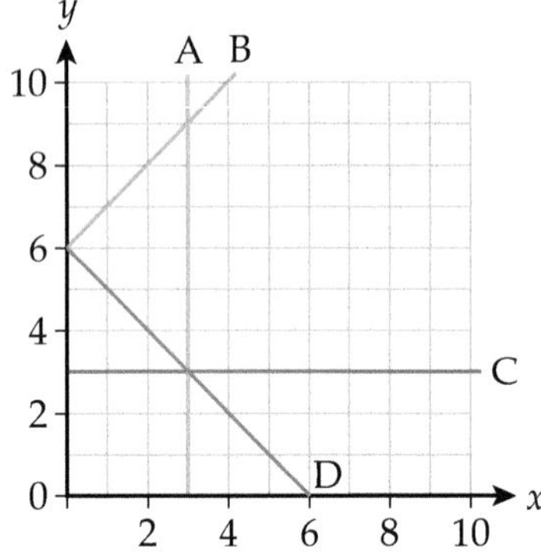

6c

3 Draw and label axes from 0 to 6. Plot each pair of points and join them with a straight line. Find the gradient of each line.

a (1, 2) and (3, 6) **b** (3, 5) and (6, 2) **c** (0, 1) and (4, 3)

6d

4 Find the y-intercepts of the lines A to C in the graph.

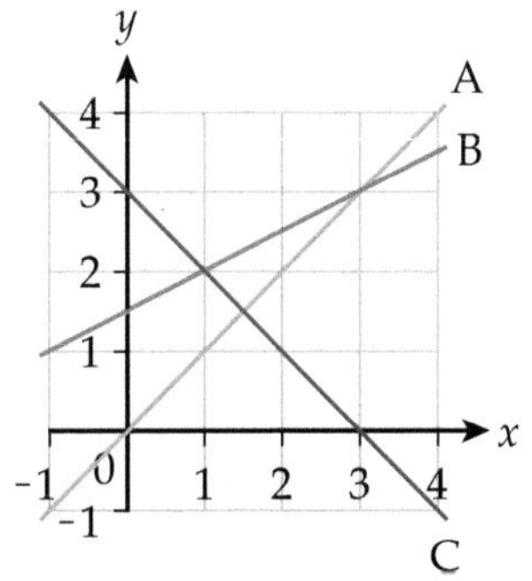

6e

5 Find the gradient and the y-intercept of the straight lines with these equations. Do not draw any graphs.

a $y = 5x - 2$ **b** $y = \frac{1}{2}x + 9$

c $y = -3x + 4$ **d** $y = 6 - 2x$

6 For the straight lines P, Q, R and S, find

a the gradient **b** the y-intercept **c** the equation.

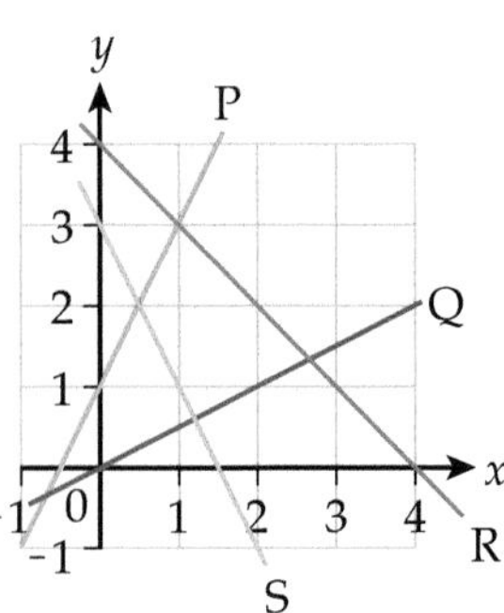

6f

7 Find the points where these lines cut the x-axis and y-axis.
Draw their graphs on axes labelled from -6 to 6.
Use your graphs to find the gradient of each line.

a $2x + y = 6$ **b** $2x + 4y = 12$ **c** $2x - 2y = 9$

6g

8 A car has a full tank of petrol. It uses p litres. It can now travel a further distance of d km before it needs more petrol.

a If $d = 800 - 20p$, copy and complete this table and draw a graph of your results on a copy of these axes.

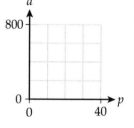

p	0	10	20	30	40
d					

b What is the furthest distance the car can go on a full tank?

c How many litres does a full tank hold?

d What is the gradient of the graph?
What does the gradient tell you about the fuel consumption?

6h

9 The graph shows the distance travelled by a railway truck over a period of 40 seconds.
Find its speed during

a the first 10 seconds

b the next 10 seconds

c the last stage of its journey.

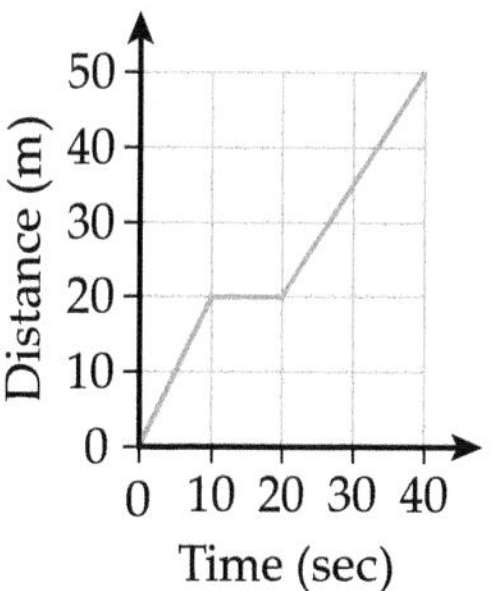

6i

10 These four graphs show changes over time t.
Match the graphs to these descriptions of the variable, y.

a The distance travelled by a train moving at a steady speed

b The temperature of a cup of coffee left undrunk

c The outdoor temperature on a cloudy day

d The amount of pocket money still to be spent during a holiday.

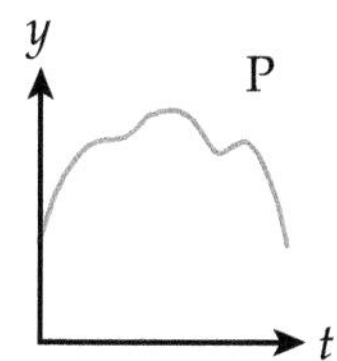

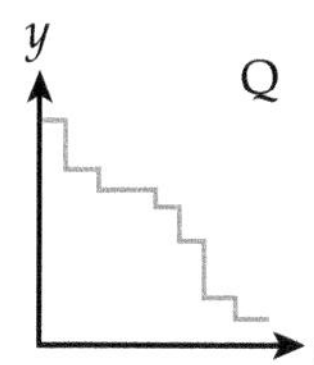

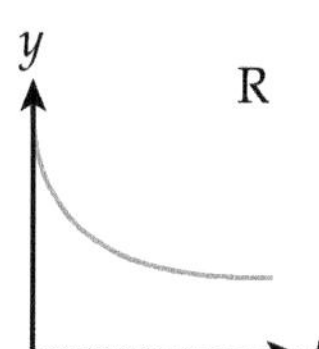

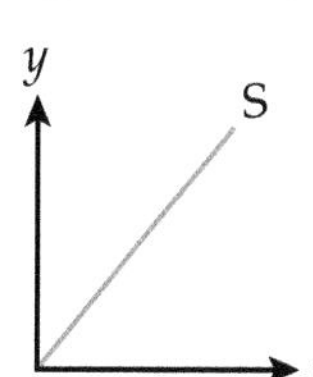

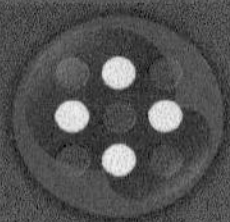

Case study 2: Jewellery business

Katie and Jess are going to make bracelets and necklaces to sell on an online auction site. They need to ensure that they keep their costs down, to help them run a profitable business.

Katie and Jess have found out the cost of materials from two suppliers.

Each supplier quotes prices for two types of bead—long ones or round ones.

They also quote prices for waxed cord or leather thread.

diameter x length
8mm x 16mm beads

diameter x length
12mm x 9mm beads

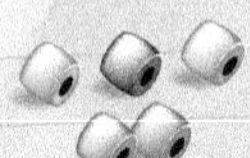

1 NATURAL BEAD COMPANY

Postage and packing: £3.50 for any size of order

8 x 16mm beads	12 x 9mm beads
8p per bead	5p per bead
£1.30p per 20	80p per 20
£2.90 per 50	£1.80 per 50
£4.80 per 100	£3.00 per 100
£8.00 per 250	£5.00 per 250

Leather thread	Waxed cord
50p per metre	10p per metre
£11.95 per 50m	£4.95 per 100m

Task 1

a Katie and Jess want 2000 beads of each size. Which supplier should they use? Show your workings out.

b They also want 50m of leather thread, as well as 50m of waxed cord. Again, decide which supplier they should use, showing clearly your workings out.

2 BEAD-E-IZE

Free postage and packing. Minimum order charge of £10

8 x 16mm beads	12 x 9mm beads
7p per bead	4p per bead
£1.50p per 25	85p per 25
£6.75 per 150	£3.75 per 150
£19.00 per 500	£10.75 per 500

Waxed cord

Leather thread	Waxed cord
45p per metre	11p per metre
£19.00 per 80m	£1.95 per 20m
	£9.50 per 200m

Leather thread

Task 2

Katie and Jess want their bracelets to be 16cm long, with an adjustable tie. Only ¾ of this length can be used for beads.

a How many long beads would fit on a bracelet?

b How many round beads would fit on a bracelet?

c If they just make bracelets, how many bracelets could they make?

Task 3

Katie and Jess want their necklaces to 30cm long. Only ⅔ of this length can used for beads.

a How many long beads would fit on a necklace?

b How many round beads would fit o necklace?

c If they just made necklaces, how n necklaces could the girls make?

d (Harder) Research shows that the sell twice as many bracelets as necklaces. How many of each wou you recommend that the girls m

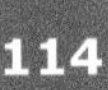

http://www.onlineauction.co.uk/

online auction

Task 4

In an online auction, Katie and Jess will have to pay the website:

- for advertising their jewellery (listing fee)
- for selling their jewellery (selling fee)

The fees for selling the items in the online auction are:

Auction listing fee:

starting price	fee
£0.01 – £0.99	0p
£1.00 – £4.99	15p
£5.00 – £14.99	25p
£15.00 – £29.99	50p

Auction selling fee:

not sold	0p
sold	10% of selling price

a What are the benefits of starting an auction at 99p?
b What are the risks?

Task 5

If they want to, they can sell the items at a set price rather than an auction. The fees for this are:

Fixed price sales

Listing fee	40p
Selling fee	8.5% of selling price

a If they sell bracelets for £4.99, are they better off starting an auction at £4.99 or using the fixed price option?
b What is the lowest selling price at which fixed price fees would be less than auction fees?

Task 6

Your challenge!

Decide what you would do if you were setting up an online jewellery business. Think about things such as:

- What designs you would make
- How many of each item you would make (Making more can save money on materials but lose more if the items don't sell)
- What the items would cost to make
- How much you would sell them for
- Whether you would sell as an auction or at a fixed price (don't forget to include postage and packing costs – you can look these up on popular websites like eBay)
- How much profit you would hope to make
- How much you would initially spend to get started (you might want to limit the amount so that you don't lose too much money if your items don't sell)

Present your decisions as a business plan, setting out all the details and the reasons for the decisions you make.

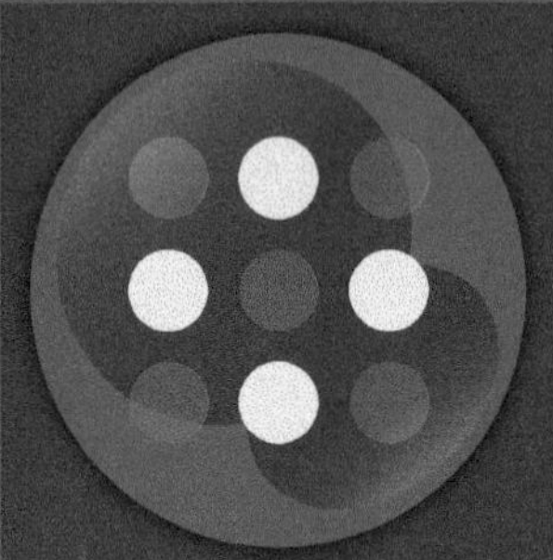

7 Decimal calculations

Introduction

Have you ever wondered how a computer manages to calculate so quickly? Computers are essentially a set of switches which can either be 'on' or 'off'. For that reason they read numbers in **binary code**. This uses just two symbols '1' and '0', so you can write the number 5 as 101. So, the computer 'sees' the number 5 as two switches turned 'on' (1) and one switch turned 'off' (0).

When the computer needs to calculate, it converts the numbers into binary and then uses patterns of logic gates (which can be either OR, NOT or AND) to add, multiply and perform other types of calculation.

What's the point?

Computers are very useful devices because they can perform lots of calculations very quickly. This enables them to do highly complex tasks in seconds that it could take humans millions of years to do!

Objectives

By the end of this chapter, you will have learned how to ...

- Consolidate a range of mental and written strategies for addition and subtraction of decimals.
- Consolidate a range of mental and written strategies for multiplication of decimals.
- Consolidate a range of mental and written strategies for division of decimals.
- Know and use the correct order of operations.
- Use the function keys on a calculator and interpret the calculator display.

Check in

1. Calculate
   a 2.9×100 b $38.6 \div 10$ c $42 \div 0.1$ d 42×0.1
2. Round each of these numbers to the nearest **i** 100 **ii** 10 **iii** 1 dp.
   a 2456.78 b 928.2735
3. Calculate these using an appropriate method.
   a $5.6 + 3.9$ b $9.3 - 2.9$ c $13.8 + 4.9$ d $18.3 - 9.4$
   e 13×11 f 43×25 g 322×23 h 11×2.8
4. Calculate these using an appropriate method.
   Give your answer to 1 dp as appropriate.
   a $126 \div 8$ b $240 \div 15$ c $170 \div 9$ d $500 \div 17$
5. Work out these calculations using the order of operations.
   a $(3^2 + 5) \times 2$ b $\dfrac{4^2 \times (7 - 2)}{10}$

Starter problem

Here is a scientific calculator.

Unfortunately only the number 4 is working on the calculator.

However, all the operation and function keys are working.

Can you make all of the numbers from 1 to 20?

7a Adding and subtracting decimals

Try to work out simple additions and subtractions in your head.

- The **partitioning** method splits the numbers you are adding into easier parts.
- The **compensation** method rounds one of the numbers and then adds or subtracts the extra amount.

Both methods change the calculation to two smaller steps which are easier to work out.

Example

Work out these calculations mentally.

a $5.7 + 6.6$ **b** $9.8 - 2.98$

a Use partitioning:

Split 6.6 into 6 + 0.6

Add the parts to 5.7

$5.7 + 6.6 = 5.7 + 6 + 0.6$

$= 11.7 + 0.6$

$= 12.3$

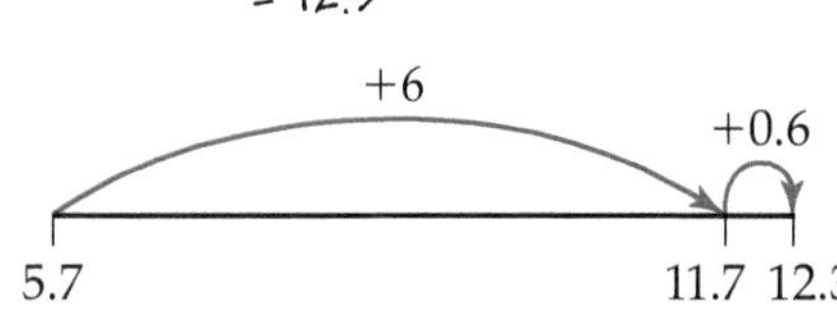

b Use compensation:

Subtract 3 and add 0.02

$9.8 - 2.98 = 9.8 - 3 + 0.02$

$= 6.8 + 0.02$

$= 6.82$

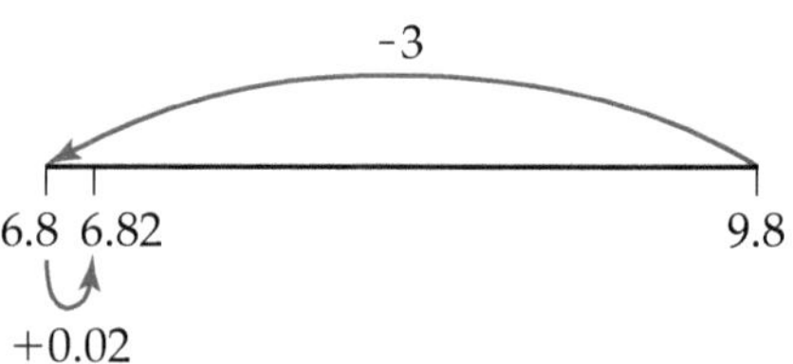

- When numbers are too difficult to add or subtract in your head use a written method.

Example

Work out these using a written method.

a $372 + 29.06 + 0.078$ **b** $751.3 - 16.4 - 0.7$

a

```
   372.000
    29.060
 +   0.078
   401.138
```

Line up the decimal points. Fill in with zeros so that all the numbers have the same number of decimal places.

$372 + 29.06 + 0.078 = 401.138$

b

```
   751.3   (5 crossed out, 4 written above)
 −  17.1
   734.2
```

$751.3 - 16.4 - 0.7 = 734.2$

16.4 + 0.7 = 17.1. It's easier to subtract 17.1 in one step.

Exercise 7a

1 Work out these using a mental method.

a	8.8 + 5.6	**b**	13.4 − 4.9
c	13.6 + 4.7	**d**	12.8 + 6.7
e	15.6 − 7.9	**f**	12.2 − 3.8
g	4.7 + 6.5	**h**	11.4 − 6.95

2 Choose an appropriate method to work out these.

a	15.4 + 6.8	**b**	3.57 + 5.9
c	8.9 + 4.35	**d**	8.2 + 7.95
e	13.4 − 2.9	**f**	9.86 − 7.9
g	4.85 − 7.5	**h**	7.1 + 6.8 + 5.3

3 Copy and complete these number sentences.

a	4.15 + □ = 6	**b**	3.8 + □ = 20
c	□ + 9.3 = 15	**d**	6.95 + □ = 30

4 Work out these using a written method.

a	534.8 + 95.1	**b**	357.42 + 43
c	28.45 + 52.6	**d**	171.2 − 95.6
e	423.9 − 38.64	**f**	758.93 − 409.6

5 Work out these using an appropriate method.

a 5.83 + 635.4 + 9
b 84.6 + 216.8 + 52.38
c 9.14 + 0.6 + 4 + 0.86
d 624.5 + 38.36 + 0.089
e 45.3 + 279.6 − 28.7
f 1456.3 + 42.36 − 7.9
g 146.3 − 37 − 45.8
h 58.6 + 284.6 − 36.46

Problem solving

6 Here are the masses of some items on the planet Pewn.

Fuzz 785.8 kg

Burper 1.25 kg

Slurp 0.057 kg

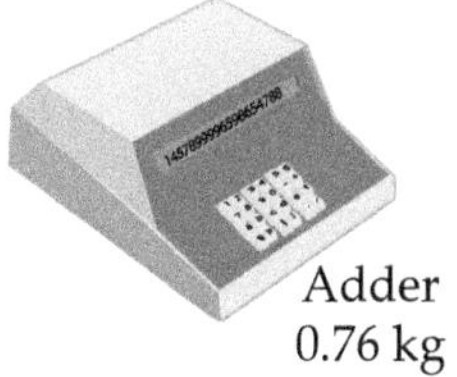
Adder 0.76 kg

Pewnen 67.8 kg

a Calculate the total mass of these.
- **i** A Pewnen in a Flyer
- **ii** A Pewnen consuming two Burpers and a Slurp
- **iii** A Fuzz with two Pewnens and a Flyer with three Pewnens
- **iv** A Fuzz with a Pewnen and an Adder

b How much greater is the mass of a Fuzz than the combined mass of a Flyer with two Pewnens?

7 Here are six numbers.

6.4 12.75 3.9 4.56 7.85 5.6

You can use each number only once in each question.

a Which four numbers have a total of 30.9?
b Which three numbers can be subtracted from 28 to make 1?
c How can you add and subtract all six numbers to make 12.94?
d By adding and subtracting the six numbers, what is the closest number to zero that you can make?

7b Multiplying decimals

Try to work out multiplications in your head.

- You could rewrite a number as a pair of **factors** and do two simpler multiplications.
- You could use **partitioning** to split the number into parts which are easier to multiply.

A **product** is the result of a multiplication.

Example

Work out these **products**.

a 35×0.04 **b** 4.2×22

a Using factors:

$35 \times 0.04 = 35 \times 0.01 \times 4$
$= 0.35 \times 4$
$= 1.4$

b Partitioning:

$4.2 \times 22 = (4.2 \times 20) + (4.2 \times 2)$
$= 84 + 8.4$
$= 92.4$

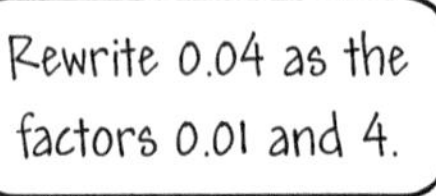

Rewrite 0.04 as the factors 0.01 and 4.

Split 22 into two parts: 20 and 2.

- Use a standard written method when you cannot do the calculation in your head.

Example

Kenny is making some shelves.
He buys 4.8 m of wood. The wood costs £1.23 per metre.
How much does Kenny pay for the wood?

Estimate the answer first.

$4.8 \times 1.23 \approx 5 \times 1 \approx £5$

Change into an equivalent whole number calculation.

$4.8 \times 10 = 48$
$1.23 \times 100 = 123$
Work out 48×123
Using the standard method
$48 \times 123 = 5904$
$5904 \div 1000 = 5.904$
The total cost of the wood
$= 4.8 \times £1.23$
$= £5.904$
$= £5.90$ (rounded to 2 dp)

	123
	× 48
40 × 123 =	4920
8 × 123 =	984
	5904

Altogether you have multiplied by $10 \times 100 = 1000$. So you need to divide 5904 by 1000 to find 4.8×1.23.

Exercise 7b

1 Work out these using a mental method.

a 6.4×3.1 **b** 3.4×0.05
c 3.6×1.2 **d** 4.5×0.03
e 4.2×7.5 **f** 45×0.04
g 3.1×27 **h** 83×0.02

2 Work out these using a written method.

a 17×52 **b** 43×82
c 315×6 **d** 623×4
e 143×24 **f** 13×625
g 516×32 **h** 44×444

3 Work out these using an appropriate method.

a 21×4.2 **b** 14×0.2
c 15×1.44 **d** 29×12.1
e 4.1×23 **f** 3.5×1.21
g 28×2.1 **h** 5.1×16.4

4 Latifa works out $28 \times 139 = 3892$.

a Use her answer to work out these calculations.

i 28×1.39 **ii** 0.28×13.9
iii 280×1390 **iv** $28\,000 \times 0.0139$

b What other multiplications could you do?
Can you work out any divisions?

5 Work out these using a written method.
Remember to do a mental estimate first.

a 5×4.13 **b** 6×4.52
c 13×6.2 **d** 27×5.3
e 18×0.35 **f** 26×0.62
g 38×4.13 **h** 19×12.7
i 27×5.23 **j** 33×6.84
k 69×8.35 **l** 3.6×17.4
m 4.3×16.8 **n** 4.7×2.85
o 3.8×1.54 **p** 6.3×5.24

Problem solving

6 a Hanif is a baker.
He buys a large 7.5 kg jar of jam.
The jam costs £1.88 per kilogram.
How much does the jar of jam cost?

b Ismail buys a big piece of cheese with a mass of 1.6 kg.
The cheese costs £7.69 per kilogram.
How much does Ismail pay for the piece of cheese?

c Cat food costs £0.32 per 100 g pouch.
Karen's cat eats 2.5 pouches per day.

i How much does Karen need to spend on cat food each week?
ii How much will Karen spend on cat food in a year?

7 Connor is given these digits: 3 4 5 6 7

He is asked to find a way of multiplying these digits together to make the smallest possible product. Connor starts with $34 \times 56 \times 7$.

a Work out $34 \times 56 \times 7$. Explain and justify your answer.
b Find the smallest product possible.
c Find the largest product possible.
d Try using a different set of five numbers.

7c Dividing decimals

- Try to work out divisions in your head. You could use factors or partitioning.

Example

Work out these divisions mentally.

a 390 ÷ 15 **b** 388 ÷ 12

a Using factors:

$390 \div 15 = 390 \div 3 \div 5$
$= 130 \div 5$
$= 26$

b Partitioning:

$388 \div 12 = (360 \div 12) + (28 \div 12)$
$= 30 + 2\text{ r}4$
$= 32\text{ r}4$

Rewrite 15 as the factors 3 and 5.
Split 388 into two parts which are easier to divide by 12, e.g. 360 and 28.

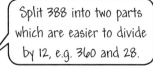

- When you are dividing a number by a decimal, change to an equivalent calculation with a whole number **divisor**.

Example

Work out 470 ÷ 3.4 giving your answer to 1 dp.

Estimate first

$470 \div 3.4 \approx 450 \div 3 \approx 150$

Rewrite with a non-decimal divisor

$$\frac{470}{3.4} \overset{\times 10}{\underset{\times 10}{=}} \frac{4700}{34}$$

$470 \div 3.4 = 4700 \div 34$

Work out 4700 ÷ 34 using a standard **written method**.

```
       138.23
34 ) 4700.00
    -3400        34 × 100 = 3400
     1300
    -1020        34 × 30 = 1020
      280
     -272        34 × 8 = 272
        8.0
       -6.8      34 × 0.2 = 6.8
        1.20
       -1.02     34 × 0.03 = 1.02
        0.18
```

$470 \div 3.4 = 138.2$ (1 dp)

You don't need to divide by 10 at the end because 4700 ÷ 34 is **equivalent**.

Exercise 7c

1 Work out these using an appropriate mental method.

- a 102 ÷ 6
- b 117 ÷ 9
- c 192 ÷ 12
- d 345 ÷ 15
- e 504 ÷ 12
- f 360 ÷ 15
- g 451 ÷ 11
- h 368 ÷ 16
- i 322 ÷ 14
- j 403 ÷ 13
- k 352 ÷ 16
- l 357 ÷ 17

2 Work out these using an appropriate mental method. Give your answer with a remainder where appropriate.

- a 250 ÷ 12
- b 300 ÷ 13
- c 350 ÷ 14
- d 500 ÷ 15
- e 495 ÷ 16
- f 230 ÷ 19
- g 221 ÷ 17
- h 700 ÷ 12
- i 228 ÷ 6
- j 352 ÷ 8
- k 408 ÷ 17
- l 608 ÷ 19

3 Work out these using an appropriate method. Give your answers to 1 dp where appropriate.

- a 16.8 ÷ 7
- b 57.6 ÷ 9
- c 43.2 ÷ 16
- d 97.2 ÷ 18
- e 55 ÷ 8
- f 152 ÷ 7
- g 225 ÷ 16
- h 433 ÷ 18
- i 36.5 ÷ 6
- j 48.7 ÷ 9
- k 74.5 ÷ 17
- l 39.6 ÷ 19

4 Work out these using an appropriate method. Give your answer to 1 dp where appropriate.

- a 792 ÷ 3.6
- b 952 ÷ 2.8
- c 646 ÷ 1.9
- d 697 ÷ 4.1
- e 500 ÷ 3.7
- f 580 ÷ 2.5
- g 470 ÷ 1.4
- h 506 ÷ 2.2
- i 473 ÷ 3.8
- j 323 ÷ 0.7
- k 517 ÷ 2.3
- l 963 ÷ 0.9

Problem solving

5 Give your answers either with a remainder or as a decimal to 1 decimal place, depending upon the problem.

- a Usman runs 100 m in 9.7 seconds.
  What is his speed in metres per second?
- b Victor drives his car from Ayton to Betaville.
  He travels a distance of 140 km and uses 8.8 litres of petrol.
  How many kilometres does his car travel on each litre of petrol?
- c Winnie buys eight pots of honey.
  The total mass of the honey is 7.6 kg.
  The total cost of the honey is £24.32.
  - i How much does 1 kg of honey cost?
  - ii How much honey is there in 1 pot?

How many metres does he travel in each second?

6 Penny says that multiplying always makes things bigger and dividing always makes things smaller.

- a Start with the number 360.
  - i Multiply 360 by 1.4
  - ii Multiply 360 by 0.8
  - iii Divide 360 by 1.4
  - iv Divide 360 by 0.8

  Write what you notice.
- b Repeat for a different starting number.

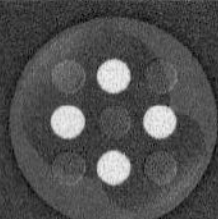

7d Using a calculator

- You must follow the **order of operations** to do calculations.
  - Brackets first — B
  - Then powers (indices) or square roots — I
  - Then divisions and multiplications — DM
  - Then additions and subtractions. — AS

Brackets
Indices
Divide | Multiply
Add | Subtract

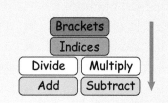

- Scientific calculators understand the order of operations.

However you must type in the calculation correctly.

Example

Calculate $\frac{7 + 4^2}{\sqrt{2 \times 8}}$

$\frac{7 + 4^2}{\sqrt{2 \times 8}} = (7 + 4^2) \div \sqrt{(2 \times 8)}$

$= (7 + 4^2) \div (\sqrt{(16)})$ inner brackets

$= (7 + 16) \div (4)$ powers inside brackets

$= 23 \div 4$ division

$= 5.75$

You can rewrite the calculations as a division using brackets.

You should know these keys on your calculator.

Example

Fraction key

Calculate $\frac{2}{3} + \frac{4}{5}$

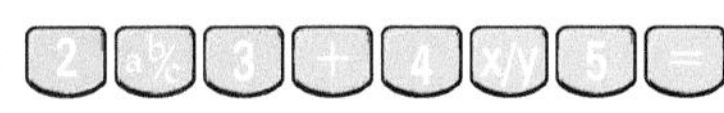

The answer is $\frac{22}{15}$.

Example

Power key

Calculate $(1.5)^4$

The answer is 5.0625.

Example

Sign change key

Calculate 5.6×-3.4^2

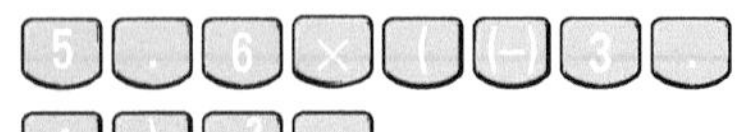

Put -3.4 inside an extra pair of brackets to work out $(-3.4)^2$, and not 3.4^2 with a negative sign in front of it.

The answer is 64.736.

Example

Square root key

Calculate $\sqrt{5 \times 9}$

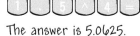

Use brackets to find the square root of the product.

The answer is 6.708 (to 3 dp).

Exercise 7d

1 **i** Two possible answers are given for each calculation. Choose the correct answer.

Calculation	Answer X	Answer Y
a $(5 + 3^2) \times 2$	28	128
b $(10 + 3)^2 - 1$	18	168
c $8 - 5^2$	9	-17
d $(-5)^2 + 8$	33	-17
e $160 \div (8 \times 5) - (2 \times 3)^2$	40	-32
f $(2 \times 3^2) \div 3 \times 2$	12	3

ii Explain your method and reasoning for each answer.

iii Explain the mistake made for each incorrect answer.

iv Check your answers using a calculator.
Be careful to type in the operations correctly.

2 Calculate these, giving your answer to 1 dp where appropriate.

a $\dfrac{(7-2)^2}{\sqrt{4-1}}$ **b** $\dfrac{(4^2-2)(7-3)^2}{(11-7)^2}$ **c** $\dfrac{(8-5)^2\sqrt{30-5}}{(6-3)^3}$

3 Calculate these, giving your answer to 2 dp where appropriate.

a $\left(\dfrac{2}{5}+\dfrac{3}{8}\right)^2$ **b** $\sqrt{120-3.8^2}+11.7$ **c** $17 \times (6.5-5.6)^4$

Problem solving

4 Erik is trying to solve two puzzles.
He must use each of the numbers 2, 3, 4, 5 and 6 only once to make each mathematical calculation correct.

$\dfrac{\sqrt{\square + \square\square}}{\square} + \square = 6$ $\dfrac{\square^4 \times \square \times \square}{\square \times \square} = 10$

Copy and complete each calculation so that it is correct.
Use your calculator to help you.

5 Nina is trying to make all the whole numbers from 1 to 10 using exactly four 4s.
So far she has only got one answer.

$4(4 \div 4) + 4 = 8$

a Find the other numbers using exactly four 4s.
You must use all four 4s in each calculation.
You may use any of the operations including powers and square roots.
Write all calculations using the correct order of operations.

b Investigate numbers bigger than 10.

7e Interpreting the calculator display

- When you use a calculator for a division you may have a **remainder**. It can be written as a whole number, a fraction or a decimal.

Example

At the local supermarket giant baked beans are on special offer.
You can buy a six-pack of tins for £8.
Xin buys a six-pack.
How much did she pay for each tin of beans?

Estimate first: $8 \div 6 \simeq 8 \div 4 = 2$
Using a calculator: $8 \div 6 = 1.3333...$
Each tin cost £1.33

Decide how to interpret the answer in the context of the problem. As the answer is money, round to 2 dp

- You can convert decimal remainders into whole numbers by multiplying by the divisor.

Example

Convert 5000 seconds into minutes and seconds.

Estimate first: $5000 \div 60 \simeq 5000 \div 50 = 100$
Using a calculator, convert the seconds into minutes.

$5000 \div 60 = 83.333...$

Multiply the remainder by the divisor.

0.333... minutes = 0.333... × 60 seconds
= 20 seconds
5000 seconds = 83 minutes and 20 seconds

Divide by 60 to change seconds to minutes.

Example

Ciara and Celine convert $\frac{6}{7}$ into a percentage, giving their answer to 1 dp.

Ciara		Celine	
$6 \div 7$	= 0.857 14...	$6 \div 7$	= 0.857 14...
	= 0.9		= 85.714...%
	= 90.0%		= 85.7%

Explain why their answers are different.

Ciara has rounded her answer to 1 decimal place **during** the calculation.
Celine has rounded **at the end of** the calculation.
Celine's answer is more accurate.

Exercise 7e

1 Without using a calculator choose the most likely answer for each question by doing a mental estimate.

a $(38)^2 =$ 54872 or 1444 or 76

b $130 \div 0.45 =$ 58.5 or 244.2 or 288.9

In each case explain the reasoning behind your choice.

2 Do these divisions using your calculator.
Give the answer in the form stated.

a £30 ÷ 7 (a decimal to 2 dp)

b 30 cakes ÷ 7 (with a whole number remainder)

c 30 pies ÷ 7 (a fraction)

3 Convert these measurements to the units in brackets.

a 2458 cm (into m and cm)

b 3876 seconds (into minutes and seconds)

c 43 155 mm (into m, cm and mm)

Did you know?

The first hand-held calculators were released in the late 1960s. They could perform addition, subtraction, multiplication and division, and could display 12-digit numbers.

Problem solving

4 Solve these problems.
Give your answer in a form appropriate to the question.

a Dale sells free range eggs.
She has 155 eggs. She packs them into boxes of 12.
How many boxes of eggs does she need to pack the eggs?

b At a charity event, 12 competitors eat a total of 155 pizzas.
Each competitor eats exactly the same amount of pizza.
How much pizza did each person eat?

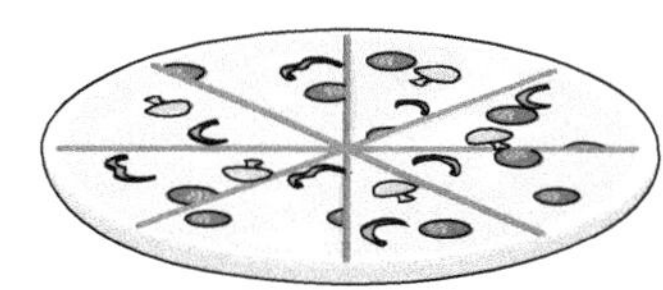

5 Solve these problems.
Give your answer in a form appropriate to the question.

a Igor buys 7 kg of sugar.
He wants to put the sugar into 1.5 kg jars.
How many jars will he need?
How much sugar will there be in the last jar?

b The Year 9 students at Oxford Sports College are going on a trip to a theme park.
There are 189 students and 16 staff going on the trip.
Each coach can hold 45 people.
How many coaches should be ordered?

6 Convert 99 999 999 seconds into years, weeks, days, hours, minutes and seconds.

7 MySummary

Check out

You should now be able to ...

	Test it ➡ Questions
✓ Consolidate mental and written strategies for addition and subtraction of decimals.	(6) 1 – 2
✓ Consolidate mental and written strategies for multiplication and division of decimals.	(6) 3 – 6
✓ Know and use the correct order of operations.	(6) 7
✓ Use the function keys on a calculator and interpret the calculator display.	(7) 8 – 9

Language	Meaning	Example
Partitioning	Splitting a number into parts to make a mental calculation easier.	$5.7 \cdot \mathbf{6.6} = 5.7 \cdot \mathbf{6} \cdot \mathbf{0.6}$
Factor	Factors of a number divide into it exactly.	The factors of 6 are 1, 2, 3 and 6
Divisor	The number you divide by.	In $10 \div 5 = 2$, 5 is the divisor
Order of operations	A standard order of doing operations in a calculation: **B** brackets **I** powers/indices **D** division **M** multiplication **A** addition **S** subtraction.	$3 + (\mathbf{4^2 - 7 \times 2})$ $= 3 + (\mathbf{16 - 14})$ $= 5$
Rounding errors	Errors that occur by rounding an intermediate answer in a calculation.	
Remainder	The number left after a division.	$26 \div 5 = 5$ remainder 1
Estimate	Work out an approximate answer.	An estimate of £7.56 shared between 9 people would be: $8 \div 10 = 0.8$ or 80 p.

7 MyReview

1 Work out these without using a calculator.

a $0.383 + 5.48 + 89.1$

b $103.2 + 25.11 + 1.57$

c $9.56 - 0.892 + 0.09$

d $44.42 - 0.147 - 0.0319$

2 Three adults in a lift have a combined weight of 195.4 kg.
The weights of two of the adults are 65.03 kg and 77 kg. What is the weight of the third adult?

3 Work these out using a written method.

a 3.1×4.5

b 0.4×57.4

c 31.8×0.28

d 816×1.58

4 Carrots cost 1.32 per kg and come in 750 g bags. What is the cost of six bags?

5 Work out these, give your answer with a remainder.

a $39 \div 7$

b $437 \div 8$

c $699 \div 9$

d $626 \div 12$

6 Work out these, give your answer to 1 dp where appropriate.

a $836 \div 3.8$

b $741 \div 3.5$

c $509 \div 0.8$

d $767 \div 1.9$

7 Calculate these, giving your answer to 2 dp where appropriate.

a $(47 - 2^5) \times 3$

b $\dfrac{\sqrt{130 + 2 \times 9}}{25 - 17.1}$

c $14 \times (7.3 - 2.4)^3$

d $\dfrac{(8.1 - 9.9)^2}{\sqrt{19.3 + 7.8}}$

8 Convert these measurements.

a 2095 cm to m and cm

b 1678 s to minutes and seconds

c 5243 mm to m, cm and mm

d 49088 minutes to weeks, days, hours and minutes

9 Terrence has eight 1.35 l bottles of orange juice. He fills 250 ml glasses with the juice.

a How many glasses can he fill completely?

b How much orange juice is left over?

What next?

Score	
0 – 4	Your knowledge of this topic is still developing. To improve look at Formative test: 3B-7; MyMaths: 1007, 1008, 1010, 1011, 1167, 1932 and 1933
5 – 7	You are gaining a secure knowledge of this topic. To improve look at InvisiPen: 128, 129, 131, 132, 133 and 134
8 – 9	You have mastered this topic. Well done, you are ready to progress!

7 MyPractice

7a

1 Work out these calculations using a written method.

a 452.7 + 86.6 b 753.68 + 67 c 82.65 + 58.4

d 939.8 − 45.9 e 687.1 − 72.46 f 852.17 − 690.4

2 Work out these calculations using an appropriate method.

a 4.27 + 475.6 + 3 b 26.4 + 894.2 + 58.72

c 65.7 + 831.4 − 82.3 d 4567.4 + 68.74 − 23.8

e 364.3 − 73 − 54.4 f 42.4 + 526.4 − 74.69

7b

3 Work out these products using a written method.
Remember to do a mental estimate first.

a 6×3.97 b 4×6.58 c 24×4.8

d 43×5.7 e 38×0.75 f 44×0.48

g 53×6.97 h 32×18.3 i 35×7.87

j 61×4.26 k 73×2.78 l 7.4×13.6

m 6.7×14.2 n 6.3×8.25 o 7.2×1.66

p 4.7×6.86

4 Nigella buys 3.2 kg of olives.
The olives cost £4.78 per kilogram.
How much do the olives cost Nigella?

7c

5 Work out these divisions using an appropriate method.
Give your answer to 1 dp where appropriate.

a $756 \div 4.2$ b $756 \div 3.8$ c $756 \div 2.1$

d $754 \div 5.8$ e $754 \div 5.9$ f $754 \div 6$

g $414 \div 1.8$ h $414 \div 1.9$ i $414 \div 2$

j $386 \div 0.6$ k $386 \div 0.5$ l $406 \div 0.7$

6 Boris runs 60 m in 5.9 seconds.

a What is his speed in metres per second?

b How long would it take Boris to run 100 m at this speed?

How many metres does he travel in each second?

7d

7 Calculate these giving your answer to 1 dp where appropriate.

a $\dfrac{(5+6)^3}{\sqrt{35+41}}$ **b** $\dfrac{(4+3^2)(2-5)^2}{(18-3)^2}$

c $\dfrac{(12-3.5)^2\sqrt{28-4.5}}{(7-2.5)^2}$

8 Calculate these giving your answer to 2 dp where appropriate.

a $\left(\dfrac{4}{15}+\dfrac{5}{3}\right)^2$ **b** $\sqrt{45-4.8^2+13.2}$

c $14 \times (2.4-0.63)^3$

7e

9 Calculate these divisions using your calculator.
Give the answer in the form specified.

a 48 kg ÷ 9 (a decimal to 2 dp)

b 48 sheep ÷ 9 (a whole number remainder)

c 48 pizzas ÷ 9 (a fraction)

10 Convert these measurements to the units in brackets

a 3867 seconds (into minutes and seconds)

b 4126.7 m (into km, m and cm)

c 3675 ml (into litres and ml)

d 7395 minutes (into days, hours and minutes)

11 Use your calculator to solve these problems.

a Sezer has 110.5 hours of music downloaded on her computer.
She accidentally deletes 80.15 hours of her music (luckily she has a back-up)!
How much music does Sezer have remaining on her computer?
Give your answer

i in hours and minutes

ii in minutes.

b Véronique puts carpet in her bedroom.
The bedroom is rectangular with length 4.23 m and width 3.6 m.
The carpet cost £6.79 per m^2 and can only be bought by the square metre.

i Calculate the floor area of the bedroom.

ii Calculate the cost of the carpet that is needed to cover the floor.

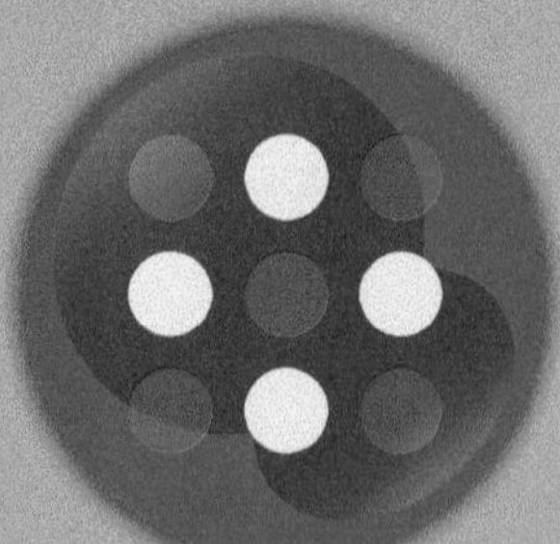

8 Statistics

Introduction

> Watching TV is as bad for you as smoking cigarettes—every 30 minutes of watching TV shaves 11 minutes off the rest of your life!

This frightening headline certainly makes you think twice about watching TV, but statistics are not always what they seem. Politicians, advertisers and businesses often use techniques like this to represent statistics in order to support the ideas they want you to believe. Watching TV does not really shave 11 minutes off the rest of your life, but people who watch TV for most of their waking day tend to be less active and it is this lack of exercise which is unhealthy.

What's the point?

An appreciation of statistics enables you to critically analyse the sheer wealth of advertising and messaging that you receive every day, and work out what it really all means.

Objectives

By the end of this chapter, you will have learned how to ...

- Organise data into frequency tables.
- Plot and analyse time-series graphs.
- Plot scatter graphs and describe correlation.
- Calculate the mean, median and mode averages and decide on the most appropriate to use in different situations.
- Estimate averages for data presented in tables.
- Make comparisons between sets of data.

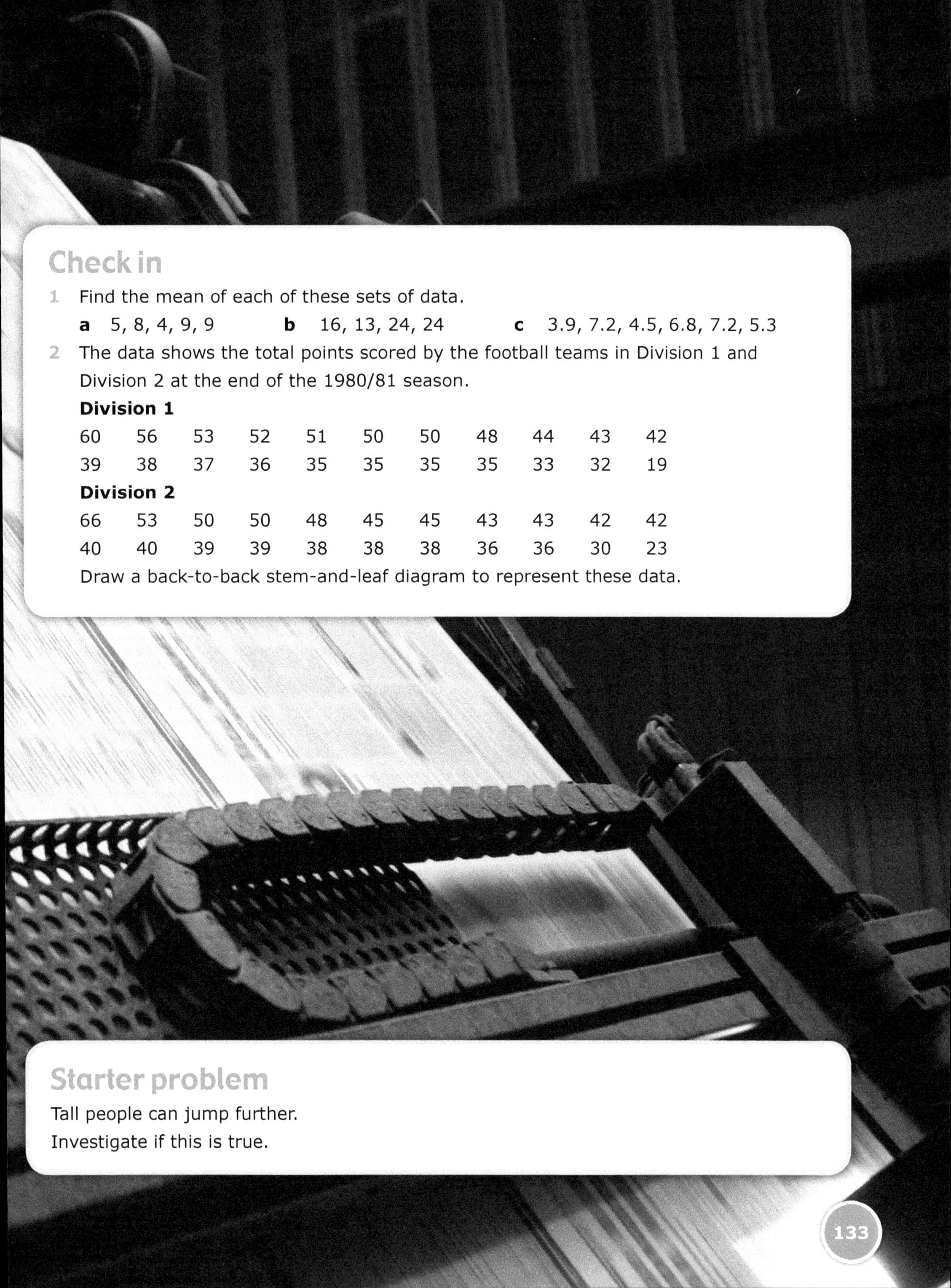

Check in

1 Find the mean of each of these sets of data.

a 5, 8, 4, 9, 9 **b** 16, 13, 24, 24 **c** 3.9, 7.2, 4.5, 6.8, 7.2, 5.3

2 The data shows the total points scored by the football teams in Division 1 and Division 2 at the end of the 1980/81 season.

Division 1

60	56	53	52	51	50	50	48	44	43	42
39	38	37	36	35	35	35	35	33	32	19

Division 2

66	53	50	50	48	45	45	43	43	42	42
40	40	39	39	38	38	38	36	36	30	23

Draw a back-to-back stem-and-leaf diagram to represent these data.

Starter problem

Tall people can jump further.

Investigate if this is true.

8a Planning a project

Carla wins the long jump on her school sports day. She is quite tall and wonders if taller students tend to jump further in the long jump than shorter students. She decides to investigate this.

Carla plans her project using these stages.		
Make a **conjecture**.	Carla's conjecture is that taller people tend to jump further.	
Identify the information needed.	Carla needs the height *and* the distance jumped for a set of people. The information Carla collects is called the **data**.	
Decide whether to use **primary** or **secondary data**.	If Carla collects data by getting information from students at her school, this will be primary data. If Carla looks up the heights and distances of long jumpers on the Internet, this will be secondary data.	
Think about **sample size**.	If Carla only collects data on two or three people, the sample size will be too small. If Carla looks up the data of athletes around the world at every sporting event for the last 20 years, the sample size will be too big as she won't have time to complete the investigation.	
Make sure the sample is **representative**.	If Carla only collects data on the *winners* of the long jump at her school sports day, her data will not be representative as it will not represent a range of competitors.	

- **Categorical data** is data that is not numerical. For example, *gender* is categorical data.
- **Discrete data** has values that are fixed. For example, shoe sizes in the UK are discrete because they have fixed sizes 1, $1\frac{1}{2}$, 2, $2\frac{1}{2}$, 3, $3\frac{1}{2}$, etc.
- **Continuous data** can have any value in a certain range. All measurements are continuous data and you have to decide on the **degree of accuracy**. For example, in the Olympics the distance in metres in a long jump is given to 2 decimal places.

Categorical data is often called **qualitative**.

Exercise 8a

1 Students in class 9A planned a project at their school sports day. Here are some of the conjectures they suggested.

a This year's results will be better than last year's.

b The weather has a big effect on sports results.

c Some people are better at sport than others.

For each one, explain why it is not a good conjecture and suggest improvements.

Did you know?

A census is a survey of all the people living in a country. The earliest complete UK census is for England and Wales in 1841.

2 Students in class 9B were asked to choose their own topics for a data-handling project.
These are some of their conjectures.

The number of children taken to school by car is increasing.	Year 9 students spend more time on homework than Year 7 students.
Girls send and receive more text messages than boys.	Teenagers smoke more now than they did 10 years ago.

For each of these conjectures, suggest one source of primary or secondary data that could be used.
Explain your choices.

Most data that you find on the Internet is reliable. Do you agree?

3 Rebecca and Jason are measuring people's heights for a science project.
Rebecca says, 'We need accurate results so we should measure people to the nearest millimetre.'
Jason says, 'That will be too fiddly and take too much time. Let's just measure people to the nearest 10 cm.'
What do you think? Explain your answer.

Problem solving

4 This claim appeared in an advertisement for a new type of cat food.
Do you think this claim is fair?
What questions would you want to ask the advertisers?
Suggest how the cat food manufacturers could collect primary data to check the claims that appear in the advertisement.

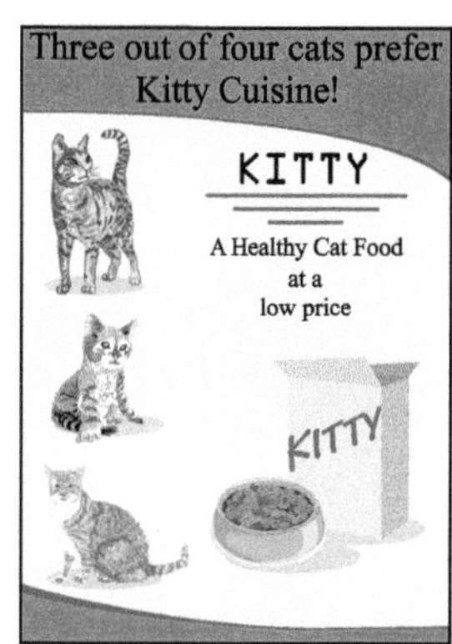

Three out of four cats prefer Kitty Cuisine!

A Healthy Cat Food at a low price

8b Data collection

A **data-collection sheet** is important when you are carrying out a **survey** or recording the results of an experiment.

You should know these types of **data:**

Categorical **data can be described.**	Discrete **data can have only certain values.**	Continuous **data can have any value in a range.**
Eye colour, gender	Number of houses, shoe size	Height, length, volume

Example

Carla now wants to find out how a jumper's height, age and gender is **related** to the distance jumped.
Design a suitable data-collection sheet.

Name	M/F	DoB	Height	Distance

When each person fills in a sheet of their own it is a **questionnaire**. When you fill in answers for several people on each page it is a data-collection sheet.

Example

Carla went to a practice session to try out her data-collection sheet but ...

- each jumper had three attempts and there wasn't enough space on the form
- they tried to measure people's heights after each jump and record their date of birth but did not have enough time.

What changes could she make?

Record the school year instead of the date of birth for each person.

Name	M/F	Year	Height	Dist 1	Dist 2	Dist 3

Add space to record three distances and circle the best one for each jumper.
Get the names of the competitors in advance.
Measure and record the heights in advance, perhaps as competitors arrive for the event.

It's important to test data-collection sheets beforehand. You may need to make changes!

Exercise 8b

1 Mei-ling is carrying out a survey and needs to collect this information from each person she interviews.

- First name, second name, post code
- Gender, date of birth
- How they travel to work, journey distance and duration

Design a data collection sheet that she could use.

Make the form easy to use by giving options to choose from.

2 These questions were included in a questionnaire.
There is a problem with each of them.

a Suggest what the problems might be with each question.

b Design an improved version of this section of the questionnaire.

> How old are you? (Tick one box) ☐ Young ☐ Middle-aged ☐ Old
>
> Do you watch a lot of television? ☐ Yes ☐ No
>
> How many people live in your house? (Tick one box)
> ☐ 0 ☐ 1–2 ☐ 2–3 ☐ 3+

3 Alisdair is collecting information about driving habits.
He wants to see if men and women tend to drive different types of vehicle.
Here is part of his data-collection sheet.

	Tally	**Frequency**
Male drivers		
Female drivers		
Large cars		

a Suggest why this data-collection sheet might not work properly.

b Design an improved version.

4 Klara wants to know how people feel about this statement:
'Being vegetarian is good for your health'.
Which of these two methods of collecting data would be better in your opinion, and why?

> **A** Mark a cross on this scale to show your opinion.
> Disagree ◄──────────────► Agree

> **B** Tick one of these boxes.

Strongly disagree	Disagree	Cannot decide or no opinion	Agree	Strongly agree

Problem solving

5 You are asked to investigate the amount of time that students in your school spend on homework in different subjects. Design a data-collection sheet and compare it with another student.
Describe your choices to each other.

- A **two-way table** can be useful for displaying discrete data.

This table shows how many boys and girls participated in the long jump on two different sports days.

	Day 1	**Day 2**
Boys	26	54
Girls	55	32

- You can use a **frequency table** to organise your data.

Example

These are the ages (in years) of 20 long-jump competitors.

15 14 15 15 16 16 16 14 15 15
16 15 16 14 15 15 16 16 16 15

Draw a frequency table for this set of data.

This is **discrete numerical** data.
You can use a **tally** to produce a simple frequency table.

Age	Tally	Frequency
14	|||	3
15	卌 ||||	9
16	卌 |||	8

You can organise a set of **categorical** data in the same simple way.

- For **continuous** data, you need to pick suitable **class intervals**.

Example

These are the heights, in centimetres, of 30 athletes.

174 174 173 178 168 171 172 178 176 179
172 179 177 178 173 182 170 174 175 176
180 173 179 176 177 170 182 174 182 174

Draw a frequency table for this set of data.

Height (cm)	Tally	Frequency
$165 \le h < 170$	|	1
$170 \le h < 175$	卌 卌 |||	13
$175 \le h < 180$	卌 卌 ||	12
$180 \le h < 185$	||||	4

This is just one way of defining the class intervals.

The $\le$ and $<$ symbols show that this is continuous data. $165 \le h < 170$ means 'from 165 cm to 170 cm but not including 170 cm.'

Exercise 8c

1 Letty asked boys and girls in her class which sport they had chosen.
She recorded either: B (boy) or G (girl) and H (hockey) or B (basketball).

BH	BB	BB	GH	GH	BB	GB	GH	GB	BB
GH	BB	BB	GB	GB	GH	GB	BH	BB	BB
GB	GH	GH	BB	BH	BB	BB	GH	BH	GB

BB means a boy who chose basketball.

Draw a two-way table for this data set.

Use a tally to make sure you include all of the data.

2 Here are the shoe sizes of 60 Year 9 boys.

8	4	7	7	9	7	6	4	8	6
5	7	4	6	6	8	6	5	5	9
6	5	7	7	6	5	7	7	4	5
9	6	6	8	8	4	5	6	7	5
5	6	6	4	6	8	7	6	6	5
7	4	6	6	7	8	4	5	7	5

Construct a tally and frequency table for this set of data.

3 32 students measured their height in centimetres to the nearest 0.1 cm.

169.1	161.0	167.1	169.1	164.7	164.5	176.1	165.9
176.0	157.7	165.9	180.0	161.0	164.3	183.0	165.2
160.7	170.5	159.9	168.0	169.7	169.0	171.6	160.8
177.0	180.4	168.2	176.6	164.5	172.6	163.2	174.4

Construct a frequency table for this set of data using class intervals for the height (h cm) of $155 \leqslant h < 160$, $160 \leqslant h < 165$, ...

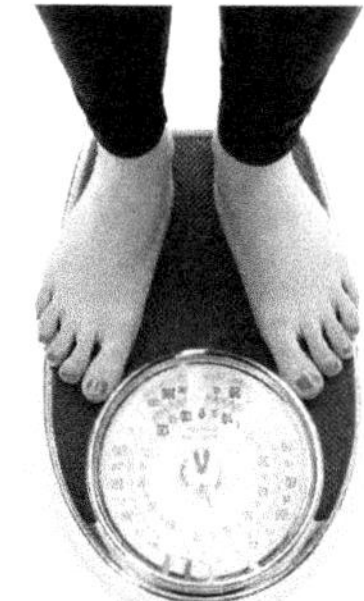

4 32 people were weighed, in kilograms, to the nearest 0.1 kg.

72.6	67.3	58.2	59.2	67.4	63.6	71.7	61.8
78.5	80.9	53.5	44.7	52.8	58.9	58.0	53.8
59.2	51.5	69.8	47.0	56.6	58.7	70.2	60.3
63.1	63.0	67.9	55.7	74.0	67.1	53.1	75.4

Construct a frequency table for this set of data using suitable class intervals.

Problem solving

5 The shoe sizes and heights, in centimetres, of 32 people were measured and recorded in the form (shoe size, height).

(4, 161)	(4, 160)	(7, 166)	(5, 161)	(4, 155)	(8, 167)
(3, 158)	(5, 161)	(4, 157)	(6, 162)	(5, 158)	(7, 165)
(4, 159)	(7, 168)	(6, 166)	(5, 164)	(5, 160)	(3, 159)
(5, 160)	(3, 155)	(9, 169)	(8, 169)	(3, 154)	(6, 163)
(6, 165)	(5, 159)	(5, 164)	(7, 164)	(6, 162)	(8, 171)
(9, 170)	(3, 154)				

Show how to organise this data into a two-way table.
Explain your choices.

8d Statistical diagrams 1

- You can show data using **pictograms, bar charts, pie charts** for discrete data and **frequency diagrams** for continuous data.

Graphs can make data easier to understand. Different graphs highlight different features of the data.

Example

Marsha surveys the eye colour of students in her class.
Draw a pie chart for her data.

Eye colour	Frequency
Blue	7
Green	14
Brown	8

To find the angles for the pie chart:
first, find the total frequency: $7 + 14 + 8 = 29$
then calculate the angles.

Blue: $\frac{7}{29} \times 360° = 87°$

Green: $\frac{14}{29} \times 360° = 174°$

Brown: $\frac{8}{29} \times 360° = 99°$

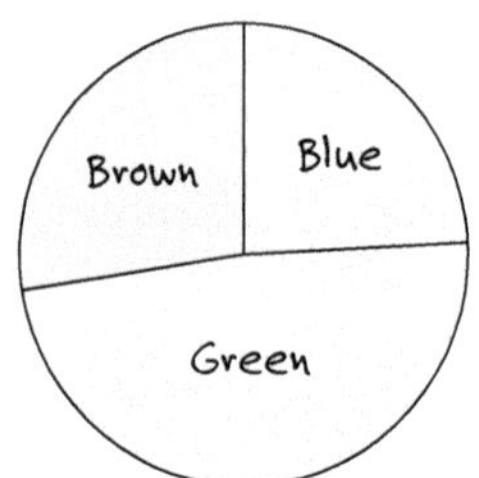

Calculate and draw the angles to the nearest degree.
Check: $87 + 174 + 99 = 360$

Example

Marsha then measures the heights of 25 friends.
Draw a frequency diagram for her data.

Height, h cm	Frequency
$150 \leqslant h < 160$	5
$160 \leqslant h < 170$	12
$170 \leqslant h < 180$	8

There are no gaps between the bars in this frequency diagram because the data is continuous.

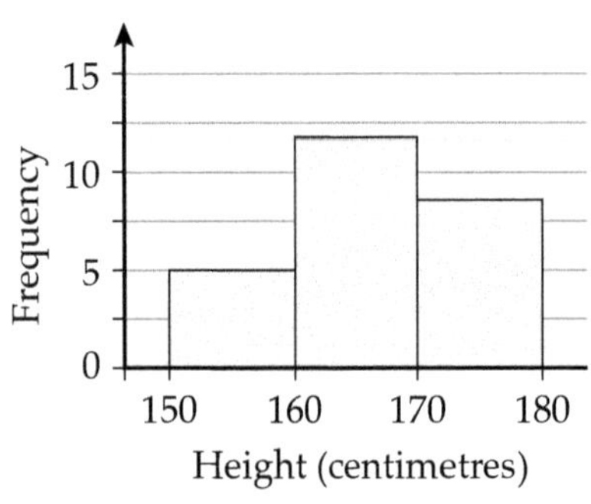

A **bar chart** for **discrete** data would have gaps between the bars.

Exercise 8d

1 This pictogram shows the number of cars in Aspen School car park on three consecutive mornings.

Day	
Monday	🚗 🚗 🚗 🚗 🚗
Tuesday	🚗 🚗 🚗
Wednesday	🚗 🚗 🚗 ◖

Key: 🚗 = 10 vehicles

Draw a **horizontal bar chart** for this set of data.

Horizontal bar charts have the scale across the page and the bars horizontal.

2 This table shows the colours of the cars in Aspen School car park on Thursday morning.

Colour	Frequency
Silver/Grey	18
Red	8
Blue	11
White	9

Draw a pie chart to represent this set of data.
What was the most common colour?

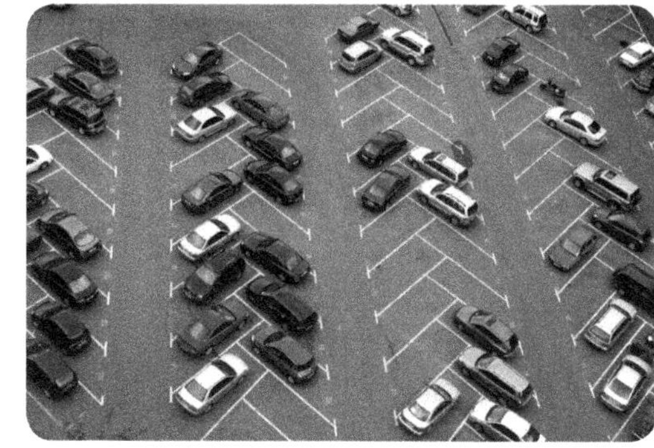

3 These are average temperatures for Glasgow in one year.
Draw a **vertical bar chart** for this set of data.

Month	Jan	Feb	Mar	Apr	May	Jun	Jul	Aug	Sep	Oct	Nov	Dec
Average max temp (°C)	5	11	14	18	19	21	23	25	19	14	11	6

Describe the pattern of the chart.

4 These are the weights of some gym members.
Draw a frequency diagram for this set of data.

Weight, w kg	Frequency
$60 \leqslant w < 65$	2
$65 \leqslant w < 70$	19
$70 \leqslant w < 75$	24
$75 \leqslant w < 80$	9

Problem solving

5 This table shows the favourite subjects of students in class 9X.

Subject	Maths	English	Science	Art	PE
Frequency	6	8	7	6	4

Represent this set of data as

a a bar chart **b** a pie chart.

Explain the advantages and disadvantages of each chart.

Which chart was easiest to draw?
What features are easiest to see with each chart?

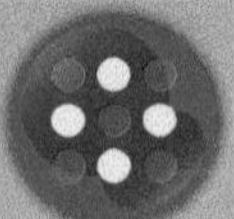

8e Statistical diagrams 2

Displaying information in a graph can help you to see connections in large sets of data.

- To find the **mean**, add up all the values, and then divide by the number of items.

Example

This table shows how the population, in thousands, of the city of Austin, Texas has grown since 1860.
Represent this set of data as a **time series** graph.

Year	1860	1880	1900	1920	1940	1960	1980	2000
Pop. (1000s)	3	11	22	35	88	187	346	657

p.144 ›

Describe the key features of the graph.

On a time-series graph, each point shows the value of the data at a particular time. You can join the points to show a **trend**.

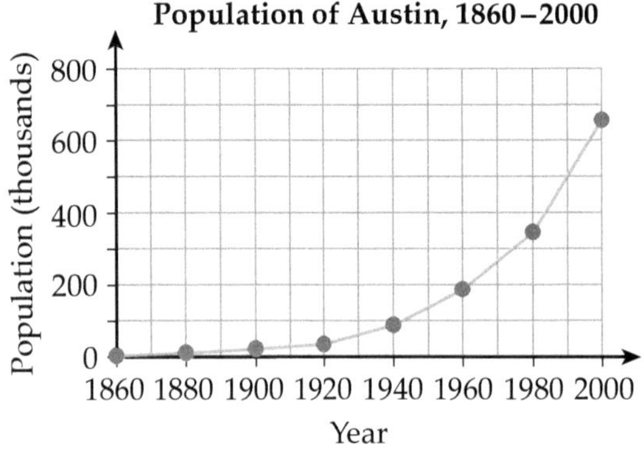

The graph shows that the population increased slowly until the second half of the 20th century, when it increased at a greater rate.

Sarah is considering a career in computer programming.
She is wondering how her salary might change as she gains experience.
She finds the number of years' experience and the salary for 10 programmers.

Experience (years)	1	3	5	2	12	10	7	2	15	11
Salary (£K)	18	24	28	22	52	38	36	19	50	47

Sarah draws a **scatter graph**.

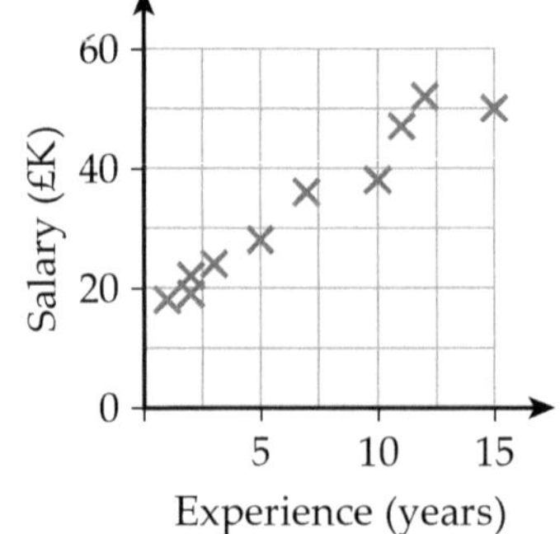

Each cross shows the salary and the number of years' experience for a person.

The scatter graph shows that there is an increase in salary as the number of years' experience increases.

Exercise 8e

1 Draw a time series graph for this set of data.

Aspen High School: Year 9 students achieving Level 5 or above in mathematics	
Year	**%**
2002	68%
2003	73%
2004	75%
2005	79%
2006	78%
2007	82%
2008	85%
2009	87%

Describe the trend in the results.

2 Draw a time series graph for this set of data about smoking in Britain.

Percentages of adults (aged 16 or over) smoking.		
Year	**Men**	**Women**
1974	51	41
1978	45	37
1982	38	33
1986	35	31
1990	31	29
1994	28	26
1998	30	26
2002	27	25

Describe the trend shown in the graph.

3 Draw a scatter graph for this set of data. Plot both sets of data on the same graph but use a different symbol to plot each data set, for example, dots and crosses.

Mathematics and science test scores for 12 students		
Student	**Maths**	**Science**
A	29	20
B	28	33
C	47	38
D	17	12
E	48	50
F	41	34
G	29	34
H	19	31
I	24	28
J	27	19
K	31	23
L	43	44

Do students do equally well in both Maths and Science?

Plot the data on the same graph but with different symbols.

Problem solving

4 This table shows the median heights for boys aged 4 to 18 years.

Age	4	6	8	10	12	14	16	18
Height (cm)	102	115	128	138	149	164	174	176

a Plot this set of data as a time series graph.

b Plot these boys' heights as points on the same graph.

Are any of the boys particularly tall or short for their age? Explain your answer.

Name	Ben	Theo	Neil	Mike
Age	13	8	15	7
Height (cm)	180	126	155	118

8f Calculating averages

- Averages are used to summarise a set of data.
  - **Mode**: the most common value
  - **Median**: the middle value when the data is put in order
  - **Mean**: add all the values and divide by number of items

Example

The table shows the gender, age and amount of money spent by 12 customers in a coffee shop.
Calculate a suitable average for each type of data recorded.

Gender	F	F	F	M	F	M
Age (years)	15	15	14	21	23	18
Spend	£1.85	£1.45	£1.85	£2.75	£3.05	£1.85

Gender	F	F	M	M	F	M
Age (years)	14	11	42	14	16	16
Spend	£1.45	0	£8.45	0	£2.75	£3.05

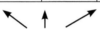

It is possible that one father paid the bill for himself and two children.

Gender: The mode is Female.
This is the only average that can be found.

Age: Any average is possible but the median is a good choice because it often gives a whole number.
11 14 14 14 15 15
16 16 18 21 23 42
Median age is $(15 + 16) \div 2 = 15.5$ years.

Money spent: The mean is a good choice.
Total spend = £28.50
Mean spend = £28.50 ÷ 12 = £2.38

The mean of the ages would be affected by the one large value (42). Try working it out and see what you get. Is the mean **representative** of the data?

- To work out what is a suitable average, think about
  - how easy it is to calculate
  - how well it summarises all the data
  - if it would be affected by one very large or small value.

- You can also use the **range** of values to help you summarise the data.
  Range = maximum value − minimum value
  For the data in the example,
  the range of ages is 42 − 11 = 31

Exercise 8f

1 Find the mean, median and mode of each of these sets of data.

a 8, 5, 5, 7, 9 **b** 6, 7, 24, 9, 14, 9 **c** 4, 3, 2, 8, 6, 5, 8, 5

d 1.4, 1.8, 1.7, 1.6, 1.5 **e** -2, 4, 0, 4, -3, 2, 0

2 A volunteer working at a charity television event took these donations over the telephone.

£5	£15	£10	£7	£5	£5
£12	£15	£5	£500	£20	£10

a Find the mode, mean and median of this set of data.

b Are each of the averages you calculated representative of the whole data?
Explain your answer and say which average you would use in this case.

3 This table shows the number of words on each of the first eight pages of a book.

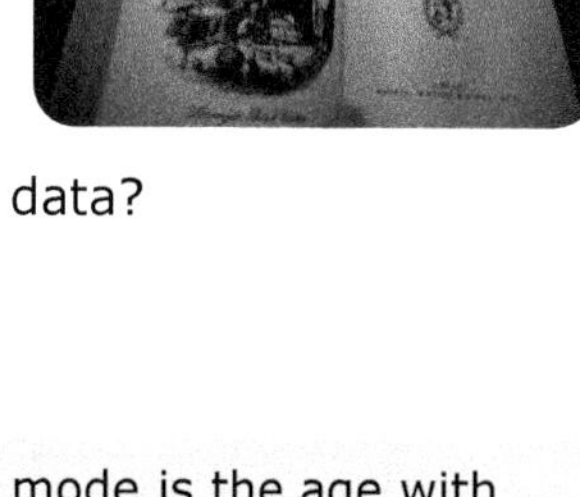

Page	1	2	3	4	5	6	7	8
No. of words	30	125	159	133	121	147	128	133

a Find the mode, mean and median of this set of data.

b Are each of the averages you found representative of the whole data?
Explain your answer.

c Find the range of this set of data.

d Which average would you use to represent the data?
Explain why.

4 This frequency table shows the ages of people attending a youth club.

Age (years)	14	15	16
Frequency	8	11	4

a Find the mode of this set of data.

b Find the median age of the people attending the club.

c Find the mean of the ages.

The mode is the age with the greatest frequency.
The median is the value in the middle position.
To find the mean, calculate the total of all the ages (14×8, ...) and divide by the total of all the frequencies.

Problem solving

5 This bar chart shows the number of points awarded to some students in a yodelling competition.
Calculate the mode, median and mean of this set of data.
Show all of your working.

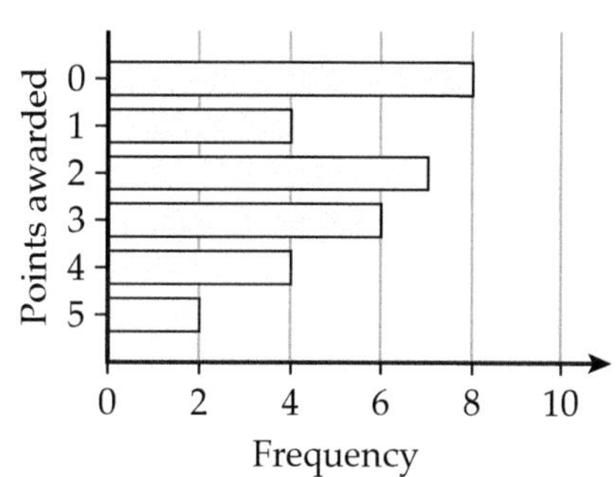

8g Interpreting graphs

Statistical diagrams can help you **interpret data** and answer statistical questions.

Example

The Arcott family are going on holiday. They look at a chart that summarises the climate where they are going. What mistakes have they made in reading this chart?

Monthly rainfall (mm)
70 65 60 55 50 45 40 35 30 25 20
Av. max. daily temperature (°C)
25 20 15 10 5 0
Jan Feb Mar Apr May Jun Jul Aug Sep Oct Nov Dec
Rain (mm) Av. max. daily temp.

'The average maximum daily temperature in January was 32°C'.

'You won't need a jumper in July because the temperature will never drop below 20°C'.

'There was more than twice as much rain in October as in September'.

- Dad has used the wrong scale. The correct answer is 6°C.
- Mum has used the right scale but read the values incorrectly.
- Liz has interpreted the data wrongly. The chart gives average temperature.

Be careful when interpreting graphs and charts!

Some charts can be vague, misleading or difficult to read.

If there is a **scale**, read it carefully. Take care with scales that don't start at zero.

Think carefully about the data. Don't assume that trends will continue. Be aware of gaps.

Exercise 8g

1 This chart and table of data shows the telephone votes for four finalists A, B, C and D in a TV singing competition by country.

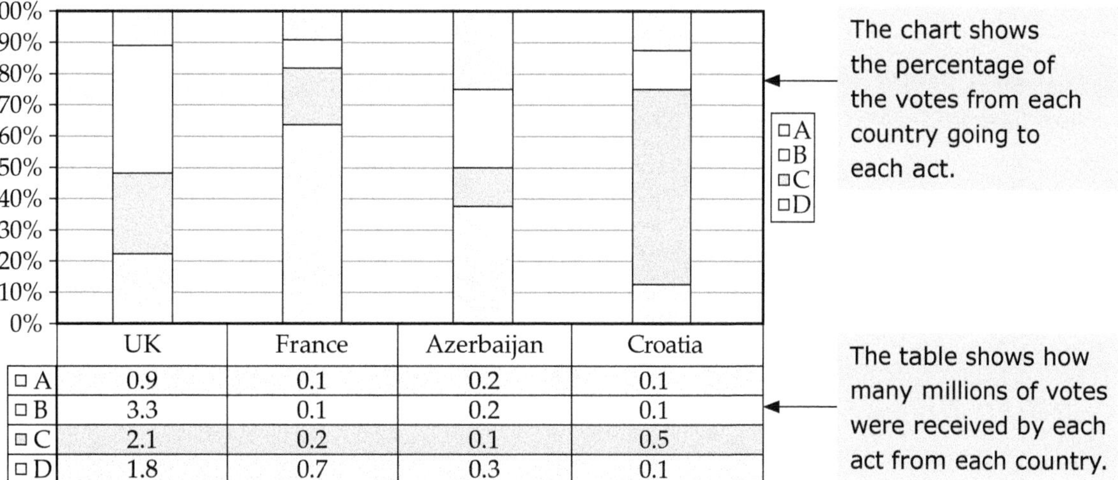

	UK	France	Azerbaijan	Croatia
A	0.9	0.1	0.2	0.1
B	3.3	0.1	0.2	0.1
C	2.1	0.2	0.1	0.5
D	1.8	0.7	0.3	0.1

The chart shows the percentage of the votes from each country going to each act.

The table shows how many millions of votes were received by each act from each country.

a Which act (A, B, C or D) won the competition?

b Can you suggest which countries some of the acts came from?

Can you be sure?

c Redraw the chart as a series of stacked bars showing the **actual** numbers of votes received (rather than the percentages).

d Draw a pie chart for each act to show the total number of votes cast for them by each country.

e Which of the three charts gives the fairest impression of the votes cast? Explain your answer.

2 The table shows the speed of a river, measured every hour.

T	1	2	3	4	5	6	7	8	9
v	5.9	1.6	4.8	0.8	3.2	0.4	2.6	0.3	1.5

T = Time (hours), v = speed (metres per second)

a Plot a time-series graph for this set of data.

b 'When T = 12 hours, the graph shows that the speed will be about 6 metres per second.'

i Explain how somebody could make this prediction.

ii Do you think this is a sensible prediction? Can you make another suggestion? Explain your answer.

Draw lines on your graph to illustrate your answer.

Problem solving

3 The table shows the average number of copies sold for two daily newspapers. Produce a bar chart for the Daily News that makes it look as if they sold twice as many copies as the Gazette.

Daily News	Gazette
485000	446000

8h Correlation

Some sets of **data** are made up of pairs of **variables**.

A **scatter graph** will show up any **correlation** between the variables.

Correlation is a measure of how two or more things are connected.

A variable is something you can count or measure.

Example

Describe the correlation shown in these scatter graphs.

a Age and price of 14 cars **b** Heights and weights of 20 people

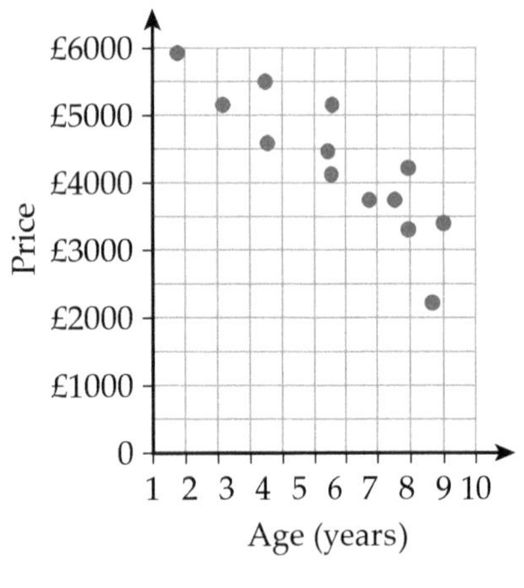

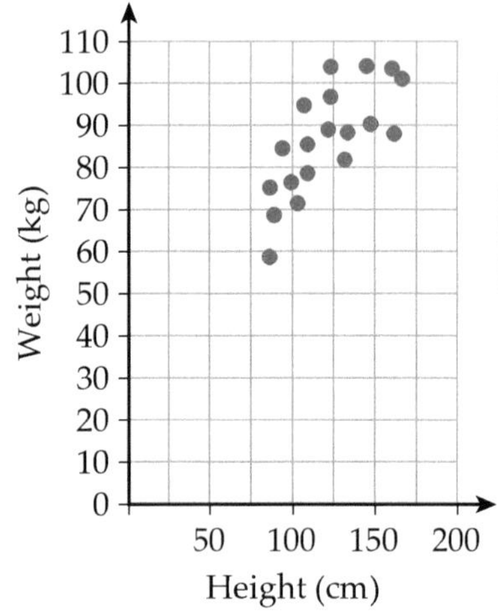

a The graph shows that taller people tend to weigh more. This is a **positive** correlation.

b The graph shows that as the age increases, the price generally decreases. This is a **negative** correlation.

If there was no clear pattern, there would be no correlation between the variables.

You should be able to identify these different types of correlation.

Positive correlation

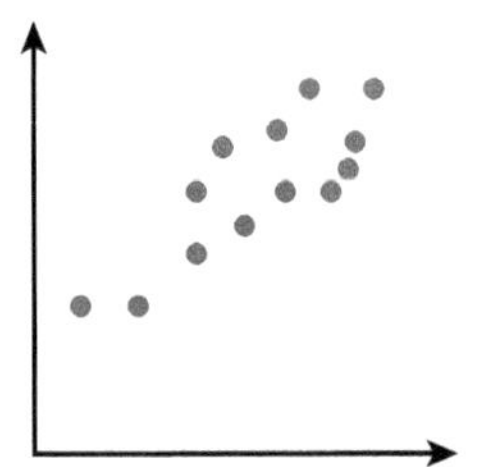

As one variable increases so does the other.

Negative correlation

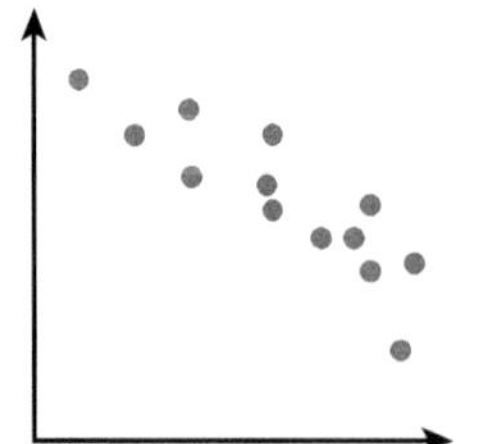

As one variable increases, the other decreases.

No correlation

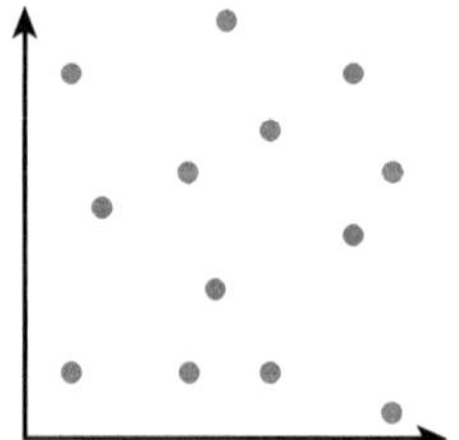

No clear connection between the variables.

Exercise 8h

1 Choose the type of correlation for each situation: positive, negative or zero.

   a Height and eye colour of year 9 students.

   b Children get taller as they get older.

   c As you eat a cake, there are fewer slices left.

   d Sales of fish and chips, and outdoor temperature.

   e Size of televison and average weekly time spent watching.

2 **a** Use the data in the table to plot a scatter graph.

   b Describe the correlation shown in the graph.

Region	Number of burglaries per 10 000 households	Number of car thefts per 10 000 people
North East	99	28
North West	137	34
Yorks & Humber	167	38
East Midlands	135	30
West Midlands	129	32
East of England	95	26
London	193	45
South East	89	24
South West	87	23

Source: British Crime Survey 2007–2008

3 **a** This table shows the GDP and the average fertility rate (number of children born per woman) for selected countries. Plot a scatter graph for this set of data.

   b Describe the correlation between the variables.

Country	Fertility rate	GDP US$ per head
Italy	1.26	26 700
Hong Kong	1.32	28 800
Switzerland	1.48	32 700
Cuba	1.61	2900
Finland	1.70	27 400
Croatia	1.93	10 600
Indonesia	2.50	3200
Malaysia	3.13	9000
Turkmenistan	3.50	5800
Zimbabwe	3.66	1900
Gabon	4.83	5500
Laos	4.94	1700
Nigeria	5.40	900
Somalia	6.98	500

Problem solving

4 GDP (Gross Domestic Product – a measure of a country's income per head) is a useful measure of how wealthy the inhabitants of a country are.
What would you expect the relationship between GDP and life expectancy to be?
Investigate the GDP and life expectancy for various countries.

8i Averages from grouped data

Data can be put into groups and shown in a table to make it easier to understand.

Example

The table shows the marks of 31 students who took a fitness test.

For this data, estimate

a the mean **b** the median

c the mode **d** the range for the data.

Marks	0 – 4	5 – 9	10 – 14	15 – 19
Frequency	3	6	20	2

a You do not have the original data so you have to **estimate** the mean.

Use the **midpoint** of each group.

The mark at the middle of the first group (the midpoint) is **(0 + 4)** ÷ 2 = **2.**

Marks	**0 – 4**	5 – 9	10 – 14	15 – 19
Frequency	3	6	20	2
Midpoint	**2**	7	12	17
Total marks	3 × 2 = 6	6 × 7 = 42	20 × 12 = 240	2 × 17 = 34

3 students scoring 2 marks each = 2 × 3 = 6 marks.

The mark at the middle of the last group is $\frac{15 + 19}{2} = 17$.

Estimated mean = estimated total marks ÷ number of students.

Total number of marks for all the students is

6 + 42 + 240 + 34 = 322

Estimated mean = 322 ÷ 31

= 10.4 marks (1 dp)

b The median is the middle value out of 31, the 16th score.

The first two groups contain the first 9 scores, so the median falls in the 10–14 group.

c You can only give the **modal class**, which is the group with the highest frequency.

The modal class is 10–14 marks.

d The range is the difference between the biggest and smallest possible values.

Range = 19 − 0

= 19.

Exercise 8i

1 A group of students took part in a survey and recorded the number of text messages they sent one day.

Messages sent	Frequency
0 – 4	6
5 – 9	5
10 – 14	4

a How many students took part in the survey?

b Find the modal class for this set of data.

c Estimate the mean and range of the data.

2 20 teenagers recorded the number of portions of fruit and vegetables they ate in a week.

Portions	Frequency
0 – 9	2
10 – 19	4
20 – 29	6
30 – 39	4
40 – 49	3
50 – 59	1

a Estimate the range of the number of portions.

b Explain why the range is an estimate and not an exact answer.

2 **c** Find the modal class of the data.

d Explain why the modal class is not an estimate.

e Estimate the mean of the data.

f Find the class in which the median lies.

3 In a science experiment, Gemma planted batches of 100 azalea seeds into trays. After a week, she counted the number of seedlings that had germinated in each tray.

Number of seedlings	Frequency
0 – 24	7
25 – 49	9
50 – 74	14
75 – 99	3

a How many trays of seeds were there altogether?

b What was the modal class for these results?

c Estimate the mean and range of the data.

Problem solving

4 A researcher measured the lengths, in centimetres, of a sample of fish.

119.9	137.1	129.8	116.9	104.3	136.0	126.7	112.7
110.6	108.2	125.3	128.4	119.7	117.3	137.6	120.8
112.8	114.2	130.4	138.4	127.6	115.4	105.0	130.5
123.5	118.9	118.0	128.8	124.5	129.3	123.7	

This is **continuous** data. You can use groups like 100–109, 110–119 and so on, but make sure you know where 109.4 or 109.6 would go.

a Use a tally chart to organise the data into groups.

b Use the grouped data to estimate the mean length.

c Use the original data to calculate the exact mean.

d Compare the estimated and exact results. Explain any differences.

8j Comparing distributions

- To compare **distributions** you can use
  - an **average** (**mean**, **median**, **mode** or **modal class**) to compare typical values
  - the **range** to show how widely spread the values are.

Example

Jez says, *'United had the best season by far'*.
Pete says, *'Rovers had some fantastic matches – they did much better.'*
The table shows data on the numbers of goals scored.
Can you say which team had the better season?

Team	Mean	Range
Rovers	2.8	7
United	1.6	4

Mean: on average, Rovers scored more goals per match than United.
Range: Rovers had more variation in the number of goals scored.
Rovers could have scored seven goals in one (or more) matches and no goals in some of their matches.
There is not enough information to say which team won most games. You also know nothing about the number of goals scored **against** each team.

Sometimes you can make comments from someone else's data; other times you need to **explain why** conclusions cannot be made.

- You can compare the **distributions** of two sets of data using statistical diagrams such as **frequency** diagrams.

Example

A scientist placed 20 insect traps at location A and 20 at location B.
She left the traps overnight and in the morning counted the number of insects in each trap.

Number of insects	3	4	5	6	7
Frequency at location A	2	5	6	4	3
Frequency at location B	8	4	4	3	1

Use a pair of frequency diagrams to compare these sets of data.

There were more traps containing three insects at B than at A. However, there were more traps containing higher numbers of insects at A than at B.
Overall, there were more insects trapped at A than at B.

The modal number of insects per trap was five at location A and three at location B.
The range of both distributions was the same.

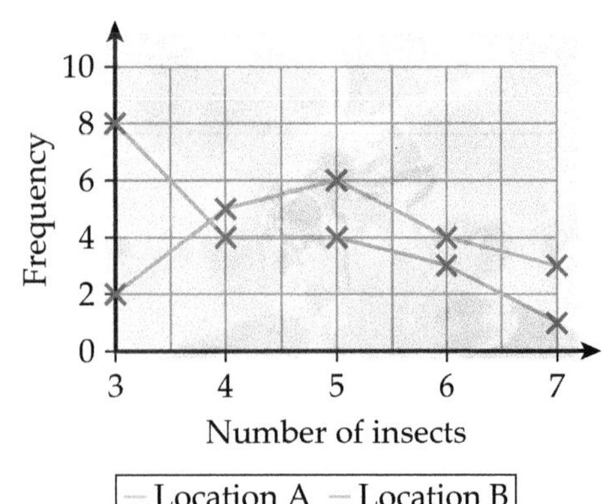

Exercise 8j

1 This comparative bar chart shows the numbers of people in the cars using a road between 9 a.m. and 10 a.m. on two days.

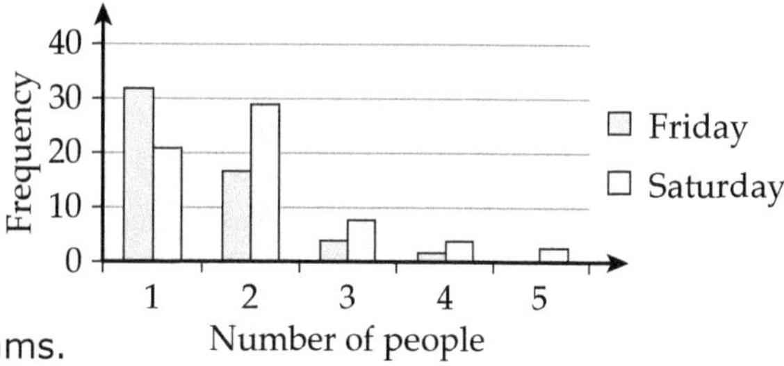

a Use the chart to compare the distributions of the data sets.

b Redraw the chart as a pair of frequency diagrams.

2 The table shows the grades awarded to students in two classes who took part in a recycling project.

	A	B	C	D
9A	18	5	4	3
9B	10	16	4	0

This is categorical data. A is the best possible grade and D is the lowest.

Do you know how to produce both sorts of diagrams by hand and using a spreadsheet?

a Draw a pair of pie charts to represent this data.

b Now draw a diagram showing the data as a pair of frequency diagrams.

c Use the diagrams to describe the differences between the distributions of grades for the two classes.

d Explain which diagram makes it easier to compare the distributions and why.

3 Two groups of students took a French test marked out of 100. The table shows their marks.

Group	French test marks
A	45 50 41 60 56 90 68 63 82 74 83 47 66 52 35 73 81 71 52 75 46 63 74 84 42 62 60 90 58 82 50 87 94 47 92 66 60 58 54 68 64 74
B	36 31 29 52 58 54 13 62 19 41 14 45 56 61 59 43 36 15 25 22 16 15 15 53 46 28 13 50 17 13 24 51 34 54 14 32 33 33 20 13 36 15

a Draw a **back-to-back stem-and-leaf diagram** for this data.

b Find the median and the range of each set of data.

c Use the statistics you calculated to compare the performance of the two groups.

d The teacher said 'The students in Group A did more preparation for the test than those in Group B'.

Do you agree? Explain your answer.

Problem solving

4 For a science project, Carla and Dan measured the height, in centimetres, of dandelions in two portions of a field. Compare the two distributions.

Carla's data				
20.7	19.0	20.3	20.1	23.0
24.4	15.4	17.6	21.6	17.1
18.8	21.2	19.8	18.7	18.4
19.2	18.8	16.2	18.8	28.8
20.4	18.9	14.9	16.3	25.2
19.7	20.5	25.4	20.7	16.1

Dan's data				
22.5	19.7	19.6	23.4	21.8
19.4	18.5	20.7	21.6	22.0
16.9	19.3	21.4	21.3	21.8
17.1	18.4	22.1	20.0	20.5
23.7	21.8	20.0	23.3	18.6
19.6	18.9	21.0	17.1	21.0

This is continuous data and you will need to organise it into suitable groups.

8k Communicating the results of an enquiry

The final stage of a statistical enquiry is to **present** and make sense of your findings. Answer your initial questions where possible, using statistical calculations and diagrams to support your **conclusions**.

The whole point of statistics is to be able to draw useful conclusions from data.

Jenny did some research for a geography project about health and poverty. She made comparisons between the G8 group of industrialised countries, South American countries (SAM) and countries in sub-Saharan Africa (SSA). She collected this data from the World Heath Organization.

Country	Group	Income[1]	Population (1000s)	Population growth (%)	Number of doctors[2]	Adult mortality[3]	Life expectancy[4]
Angola	SSA	3890	16557	2.8	1165	493	41
Brazil	SAM	8700	189323	1.3	198153	176	72
Canada	G8	36280	32577	0.9	62307	72	81
Chad	SSA	1170	10468	3.1	345	445	46
Chile	SAM	11300	16465	1	17250	91	78
Colombia	SAM	6130	45558	1.4	58761	131	74
Ecuador	SAM	6810	13202	1.1	18335	166	73
Ethiopia	SSA	630	81021	2.5	1936	326	56
France	G8	32240	61330	0.6	207277	91	81
Germany	G8	32680	82641	0	284427	81	80
Italy	G8	28970	58779	0.2	215000	64	81
Japan	G8	32840	127953	0	270371	67	83
Kenya	SSA	1470	36553	2.6	4506	416	53
Liberia	SSA	260	3579	3.9	103	457	44
Mozambique	SSA	660	20971	2.1	514	477	50
Paraguay	SAM	4040	6016	1.9	6355	132	75
Peru	SAM	6490	27589	1.1	29799	136	73
Russia	G8	12740	143221	-0.5	614183	300	66
Senegal	SSA	1560	12072	2.5	594	271	59
S. Africa	SSA	8900	48282	0.7	34829	564	51
UK	G8	33650	60512	0.4	133641	80	79
USA	G8	44070	302841	1	730801	109	78
Uruguay	SAM	9940	3331	0.2	12384	125	75
Venezuela	SAM	10970	27191	1.7	48000	142	74

[1]Mean annual income per person, US Dollars http://www.who.int/whosis/en/

[2]Number of doctors per 1000 population

[3]Mean number of deaths per 1000 population, between ages of 15 and 60 years

[4]Life expectancy at birth, years

Exercise 8k

Jenny could use her data to answer many questions.
Here are some questions and some techniques that you could use to produce statistics and diagrams.
There could be different interpretations for some of the data so you should explain your evidence and reasoning carefully!

1 How do the average incomes of people in the three groups of countries (G8, SAM and SSA) compare?
Find the median of the incomes for each group of countries.
Write a short conclusion and present the statistics you calculated in a table.

The median is a more meaningful average than the mean here. Why?

2 How many doctors are there per 1000 people in each group of countries?
For each country, divide the 'Doctors' figure by the population size.
Find the median of the calculated values for each group of countries.

You can use different symbols for the countries in each group to provide additional information to readers.

3 What connection is there between average income and life expectancy?
Draw a scatter diagram using income and life expectancy as your variables.
Explain any patterns in the data.

4 You might expect the last two variables in the table (adult mortality and life expectancy) to be related.
What sort of correlation would you expect for these variables?
Draw a scatter diagram to check your suggestion.

Did you know?

The WHO is part of the United Nations system. It provides leadership, research and support for health issues around the world.

5 How do the annual population growth rates for each group of countries compare?
Is there any connection between population growth rates and average incomes?

6 What are the overall conclusions that Jenny could reach about the connections between health and poverty in different countries of the world?

7 Devise some other questions about health, international development and poverty.
(Alternatively, you may prefer to investigate the questions raised here in more depth, for example, by looking at data for more countries.)
Visit the WHO website www.who.int/en/ to find any information you need to answer your questions. Present statistical evidence to support the conclusions that you reach.

8 MySummary

Check out

You should now be able to ...

		Test it ➡ Questions
✓ Organise data into frequency tables.	6	1 – 2
✓ Interpret statistical diagrams.	6	3
✓ Plot and analyse time-series graphs.	6	4
✓ Estimate averages from grouped tables.	6	5 – 6
✓ Make comparisons between sets of data.	6	7

Language	Meaning	Example
Categorical data	Data that can be described in words and may not have any numerical values.	Hair colour and gender are examples of categorical data.
Discrete data	Data that can only take certain values.	Number of people in a classroom and shoe size are examples of discrete data.
Continuous data	Data that can take any value in a range.	Height and weight are examples of continuous data.
Average	One number that represents a set of numbers.	Mean, median and mode are different types of averages.
Correlation	A relationship between two variables, such as number of ice creams sold and temperature.	There is a positive correlation between the number of ice creams sold and the temperature. As the temperature increases, so does the number of ice creams sold.
Mean	An average value found by adding the data and dividing by the number of data items.	9, 9, 9, 15, 2, 3, 5 This mean is: $\frac{9+9+9+15+2+3+5}{7} = \frac{49}{7} = 7$
Median	The middle value in order of size.	2, 3, 5, (9), 9, 9, 15 The median is 9.
Mode	The value that occurs most often	The mode is 9.
Range	The difference between the largest and smallest data values.	$15 - 2 = 13$ The range is 13.

8 MyReview

1 Phil is going to record how many of each type of bird he sees in the morning, afternoon and evening. The birds he thinks he will see are chaffinch, sparrow, starling and wood pigeon. Design a data-collection sheet for him to use.

2 The weights of 3 month old babies were recorded (kg).

5.8	5.7	4.9	6.1	6.7	5.4
5.0	4.5	6.2	6.2	7.2	7.4
6.8	4.9	5.5	5.8		

Construct a frequency table for this data.

3 The pie chart shows the flavours of ice cream sold.

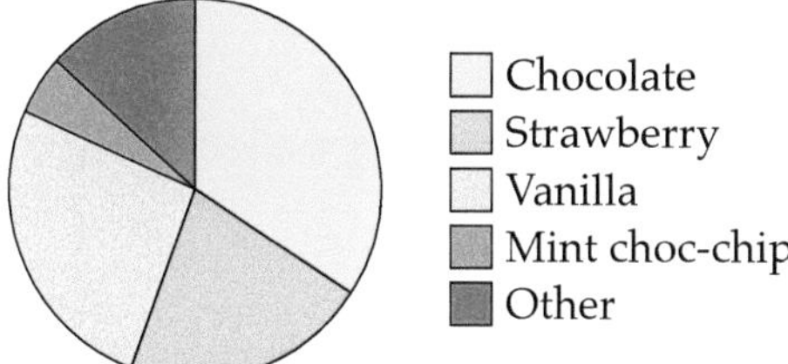

38 people were asked in total. How many preferred each flavour?

4 The graph shows the approximate population of a town over 60 years.

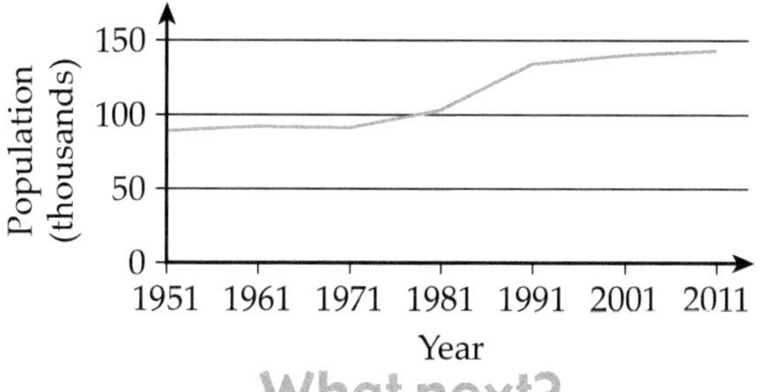

4 **a** Describe the trend.

b A large factory employing thousands of people opened in the town. In which ten-year period do you think this happened?

5 The table shows the class sizes in a school.

Size	26	27	28	29	30
Frequency	1	2	1	2	6

Find

a the mode **b** the mean (to 1 dp)

c the median **d** the range.

6 A group of students recorded how many pieces of homework they were set in a week.

Homework	0–4	5–9	10–14	15–19
Frequency	2	12	13	6

a Estimate the range.

b Find the modal class.

c Estimate the mean (1 dp).

d Estimate the median.

7 The score of boys and girls in a spelling test was recorded.

Score	0	1	2	3	4	5
Boys	1	4	7	8	3	2
Girls	0	2	13	8	1	1

a Draw frequency diagrams on the same axes for the boys and the girls.

b Compare these sets of data.

What next?

Score	
0 – 3	Your knowledge of this topic is still developing. To improve look at Formative test: 3B-8; MyMaths: 1192, 1196, 1201, 1202, 1205, 1207, 1213, 1215, 1248, 1249, 1254, 1936 and 1939
4, 5	You are gaining a secure knowledge of this topic. To improve look at InvisiPen: 411, 413, 414, 421 – 424, 426, 427, 441 – 444, 446 – 448
6, 7	You have mastered this topic. Well done, you are ready to progress!

8 MyPractice

8a

1 Students in class 9B were given a choice of topics for a statistics project.
For each of the topics, suggest one conjecture that could be made and tested.

a Healthy lifestyles **b** Travel to school **c** Leisure and recreation

8b

2 This question was included in a questionnaire.

How much television do you watch?

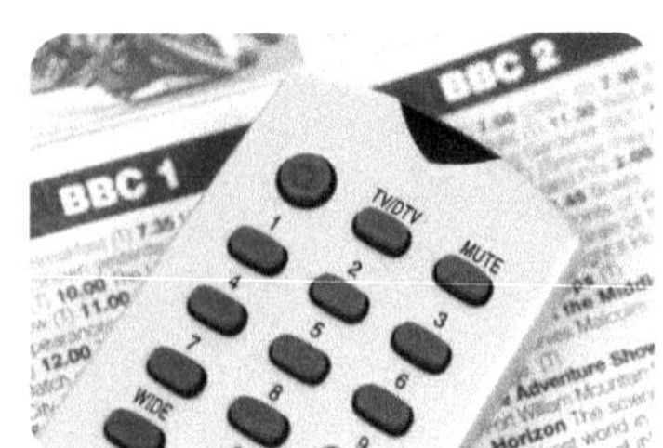

a Explain why the answers to this question might not be easy to analyse.

b Write a better version of this question.

8c

3 Jack measures the heights, in cm, of 40 seedlings in an experiment.

13.5	13.6	13.7	12.9	14.0	13.6	13.2	12.6	13.5	13.8
13.2	13.7	13.7	13.2	13.1	13.1	14.2	13.2	13.8	13.2
14.5	13.7	13.9	13.8	14.4	13.9	13.5	13.3	13.0	13.4
13.5	14.1	13.5	13.5	13.7	12.9	14.0	13.6	14.1	12.7

Construct a frequency table for this set of data.

8d

4 This table shows the sports options chosen by students in class 9Y.

Option	Football	Hockey	Rounders	Tennis
Frequency	9	11	7	4

Draw **a** a bar chart **b** a pie chart for this set of data.

8e

5 The table shows the growth of the population of New York City.
Draw a time-series graph for this set of data.

Year	1800	1850	1900	1950	2000
Population (thousands)	79	696	3437	7891	8008

8f

6 This frequency table shows the number of points awarded to competitors in an athletics competition.

Points	0	1	2	3	4	5
Frequency	13	28	41	39	21	7

Find the mean, median and mode of this set of data.

8g

7 This chart shows the number of sofas sold one weekend in three different branches of a furniture store.

a Explain why this chart is misleading.

b Draw a new version of the chart to give a fairer impression of the data.

Number of sofas sold

45
40
35
30
25

Ayton Beaton Seaton

8h

8 Students on a PE course did a fitness test at the beginning of the course and repeated the same test at the end.

Student	A	B	C	D	E	F	G	H	I	J
Test 1	24	37	16	23	29	42	31	22	21	29
Test 2	39	42	34	35	30	44	40	33	35	39

a Plot a scatter graph for this set of data.

b What does the graph tell you about the course?

8i

9 This frequency table shows the number of points awarded to competitors in a skating competition.

a Find the range of this set of data.

b Find the mean, median and mode of the number of points awarded.

Points	1	2	3	4	5
Frequency	2	9	18	12	3

8j

10 The table shows the number of parking tickets issued to vehicles parked on two streets each day during one week.

Day	Mon	Tue	Wed	Thu	Fri	Sat	Sun
King Street	8	7	6	6	3	8	0
Queen Street	4	3	5	2	4	11	0

a Find the mean, median, mode and range of the number of tickets issued each day in each street.

b Use the statistics you calculated in part **a** to compare the two distributions.

8k

11 Gather information similar to that shown in the table on page 152 for a selection of countries in Asia. Investigate any link between health and poverty in these countries, and report your findings.

MyAssessment 2

These questions will test you on your knowledge of the topics in chapters 5 to 8. They give you practice in the questions that you may see in your GCSE exams. There are 85 marks in total.

1 Calculate the values of

a angles p and q and $(p + q)$ (2 marks)

b angle r. (1 mark)

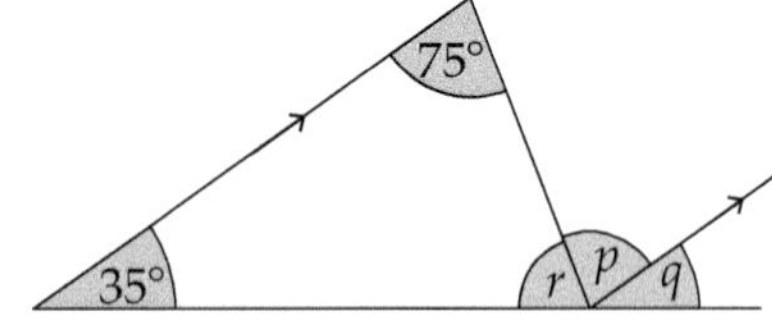

2 Name the quadrilateral that has these properties: Rotational symmetry of order 2, two lines of reflection symmetry and four equal sides (2 marks)

3 **a** Calculate the angles marked with letters. (3 marks)

b Determine $a + b + c + d$ and state what property it shows. (2 marks)

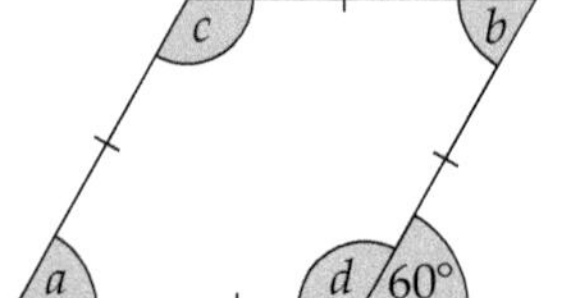

4 This is a regular nonagon. Calculate

a the angle at the centre a (2 marks)

b the angle marked b in the isosceles triangle (2 marks)

c the interior and exterior angles of a regular nonagon (3 marks)

d the sum of all the interior and exterior angles of a regular nonagon. (4 marks)

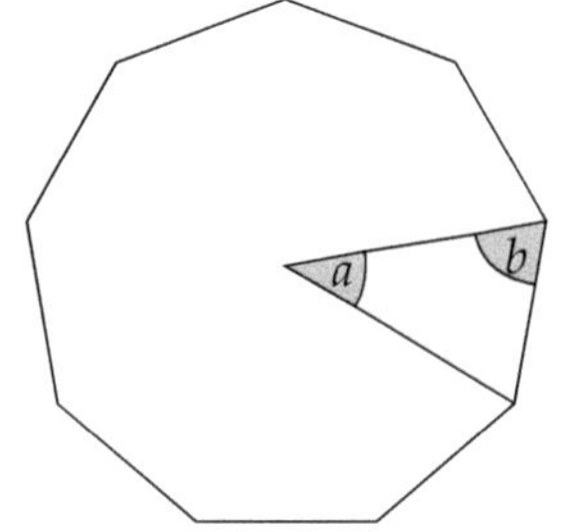

5 The diagonals of two pentagons joined together are drawn to form a set of triangles.

a Which triangles are congruent to triangle A? (give your reasons) (2 marks)

b Which triangles are congruent to triangle B? (give your reasons) (2 marks)

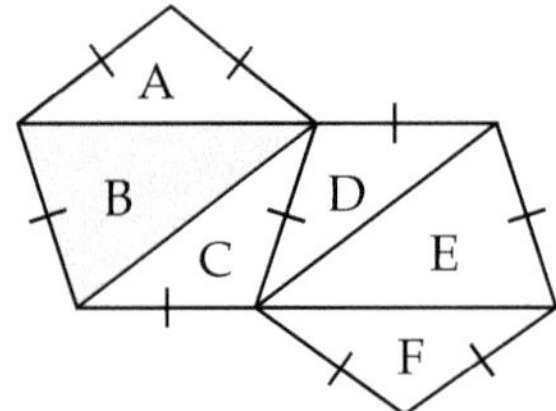

6 **a** On square grid paper draw an x-axis from -3 to +4 and a y-axis between ± 10. (2 marks)

b Copy and complete this table of values for the equations $y = 2x + 2$ and $y = 4x - 2$ (4 marks)

x	-2	-1	0	1	2	3
$y = 2x + 2$						
$y = 4x - 4$						

c What is the gradient of the graph $y = 4x - 2$? (1 mark)

d What is the y-intercept of the equation $y = 2x + 2$? (1 mark)

e Plot both graphs and give the coordinate point where both lines meet. (4 marks)

7 **a** Find the gradient and the y-intercept of the straight lines with these equations. Do not draw any of the graphs.

i $y = -2x - 5$ (2 marks) **ii** $2y = -10 - 4x$ (2 marks)

iii $y = \frac{2}{3}x + 6$ (2 marks) **iv** $12 + 9x = 3y$ (2 marks)

b Rewrite each of these equations in the form $ax + by = c$ (5 marks)

8 Work out these using an appropriate method.

a $7.49 + 87.12 - 34.5$ (1 mark) **b** $2391 - 678.9 + 38.48$ (1 mark)

c 76×13.95 (2 marks) **d** $738 \div 6.3$ (2 marks)

9 **a** Convert 63 400 seconds into hours minutes and seconds. (3 marks)

b Calculate these expressions giving your answer to 1 dp.

i $\frac{(9 - 2^3)\sqrt{(65 - 27)}}{(3 + 3^2)}$ (3 marks) **ii** $\frac{(-6)^2 + (-2^3)}{(-3^4)}$ (3 marks)

10 The amounts of money collected during a schools' charity week were

£2.34 £1.98 £2.89 £3.03 £0.95 £1.64 £3.32 £1.12 £1.78 £2.18
£3.15 £0.78 £1.98 £1.76 £2.36 £2.71 £1.73 £0.90 £3.16 £2.07

a Construct a frequency table using class intervals £0 $\le m <$ £0.50, £0.50 $\le m <$ £1.00, ... (4 marks)

b Draw a bar chart to represent this information. (4 marks)

c What was the mean amount of money collected per form group? (3 marks)

11 This table shows the journey time to work for 50 people. The times are recorded to the nearest minute

Time (minutes)	1–5	6–10	11–15	16–20	21–25	26–30	31–35	36–40
Number of people (f)	3	7	5	11	14	5	2	3

a For this data, estimate

i the mean (3 marks) **ii** the median (2 marks)

iii the mode (1 mark) **iv** the range for the data. (1 mark)

b What conclusions can you draw about the journey to work? (2 marks)

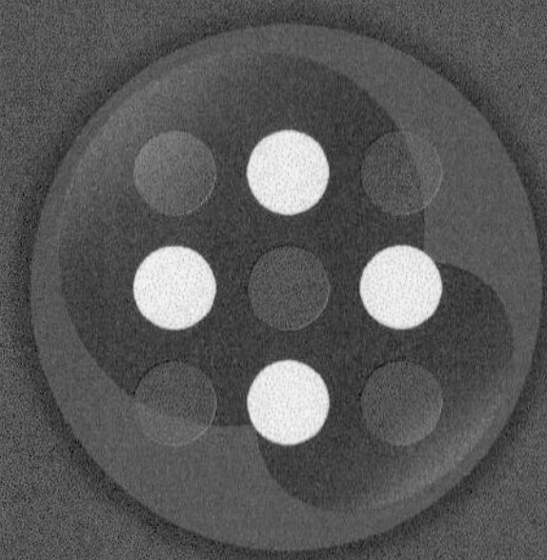

9 Transformations and scale

Introduction

Since the 15th century artists have used the ideas of perspective to draw pictures of 3D objects and images. The use of constructional lines which meet at a 'vanishing point' allows the artist to accurately draw and position smaller objects so that they appear to be in the distance and therefore give the illusion of depth to the picture.

What's the point?

The construction lines and vanishing points used by artists are based upon the mathematics used to construct enlargements.

Objectives

By the end of this chapter, you will have learned how to ...

- Reflect, rotate and translate 2D shapes.
- Enlarge a 2D shape using a given centre of enlargement.
- Use combinations of transformations.
- Use and interpret maps and scale drawings.
- Use bearings to specify direction.

Check in

1 Copy this diagram. Draw the flag after a translation of 4 units to the right and 2 units down.

2 Draw the enlargement of this kite with a scale factor of 3 on squared paper.

3 Convert these metric measurements to the units in brackets.

a 230 cm (m) **b** 400 000 cm (km)

c 5.5 km (m) **d** 4.5 km (cm)

4 Use a protractor to measure the marked angles.

a

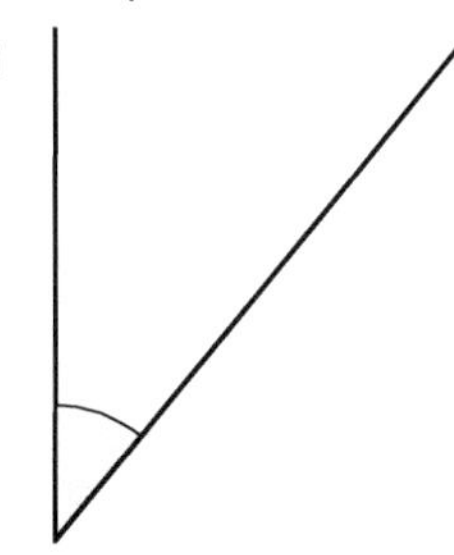

b **c**

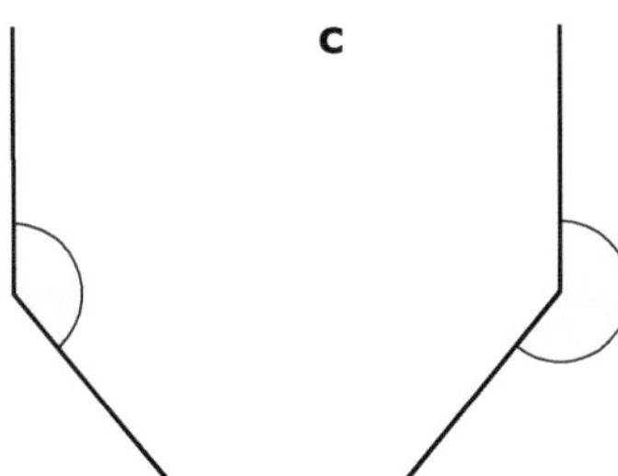

d

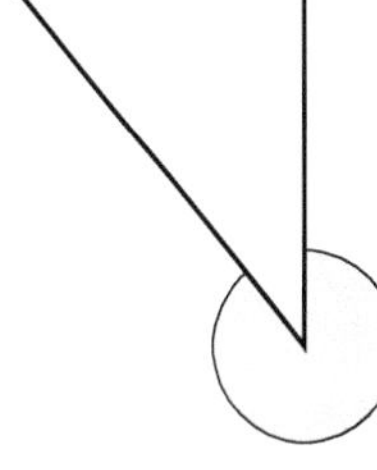

Starter problem

Look at the photograph below. You can see some lines which are parallel and some which seem to converge at a point called the vanishing point. Investigate the heights of the 'objects in the photograph' and their distances from the vanishing point.

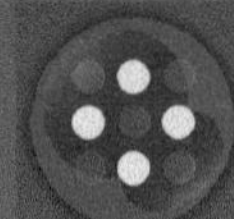

9a Transformations

- A **transformation maps** an **object** to its **image**.

- A **reflection** flips the object over a mirror line. You describe a reflection by describing the mirror line.

A reflection in the line $x = 2$

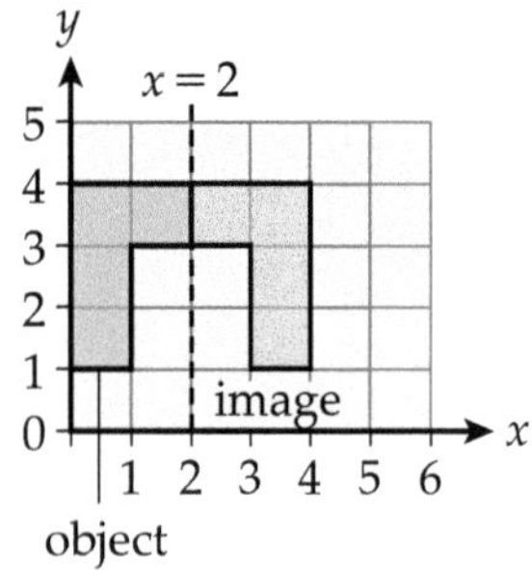

- A **rotation** turns the object about a point, called the centre of rotation. You describe a rotation by giving
  - the centre of rotation
  - the angle of rotation
  - the direction of turn (clockwise or anticlockwise)

An anticlockwise rotation of 90° about (3, 3)

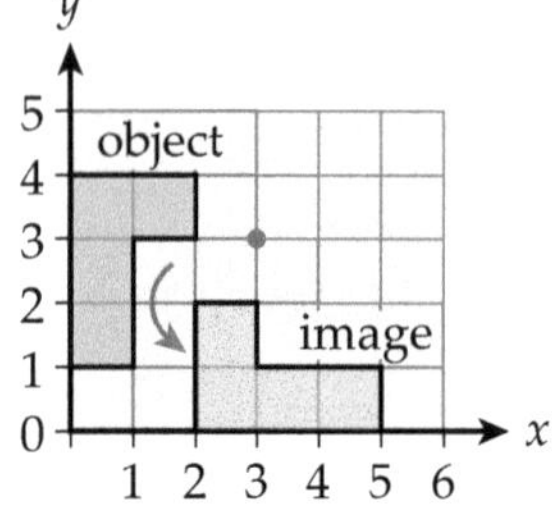

- A **translation** slides the object. You describe a translation by giving
  - the distance moved right or left
  - the distance moved up or down.

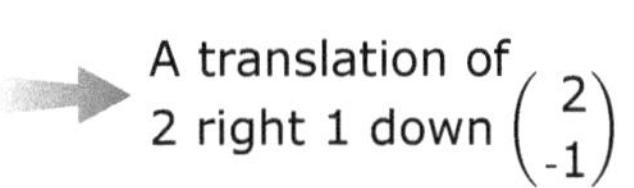

A translation of
2 right 1 down $\begin{pmatrix} 2 \\ -1 \end{pmatrix}$

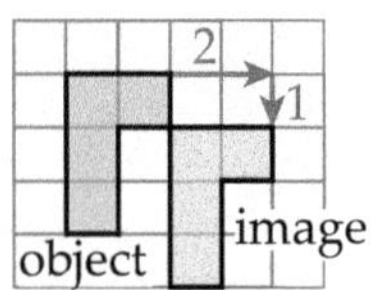

- The object and the image are **congruent** for reflections, rotations and translations. Congruent shapes are the same shape and the same size.

These two trapezia are congruent.

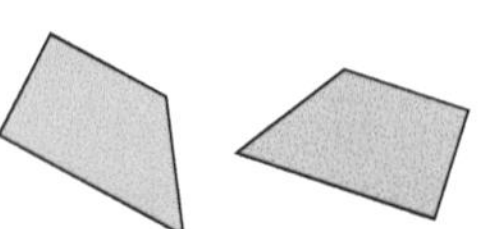

Example

The blue hexagon is mapped to the green hexagon.
Find the centre of rotation and the angle of rotation.

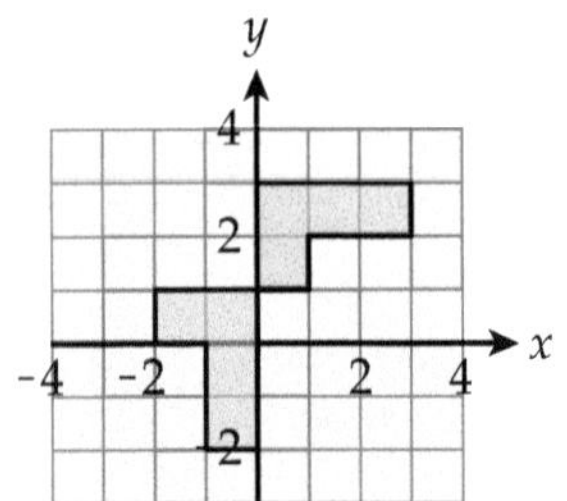

The transformation is a clockwise rotation of 90° (or anticlockwise 270°) about the point (-1, 2)

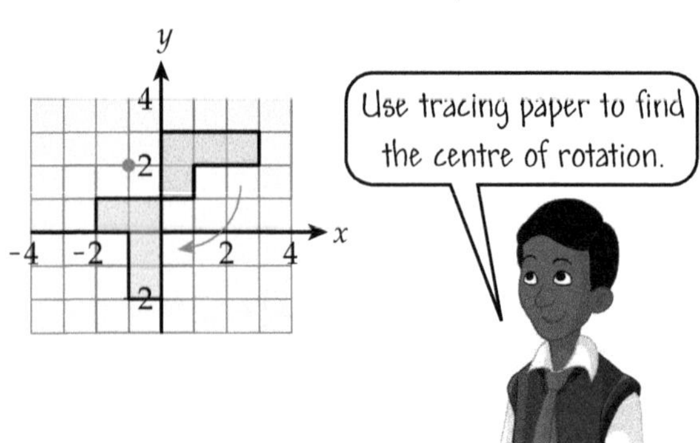

Exercise 9a

1 Rotate each triangle through 180° about the dot.
Write the mathematical name of the quadrilateral formed by the object and the image and explain your reasoning.

a 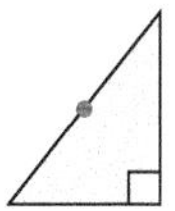 **b** 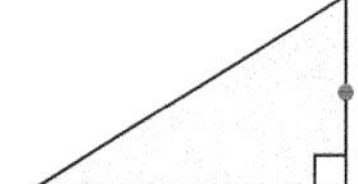 **c** 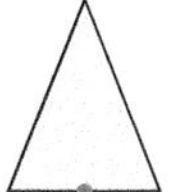 **d** 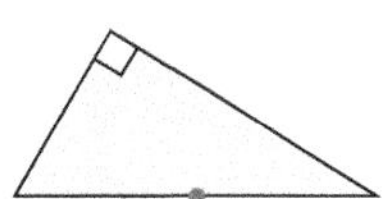 **e** 

2 Describe the translation on this grid that maps
- **a** shape A to shape B
- **b** shape B to shape C
- **c** shape A to shape C.

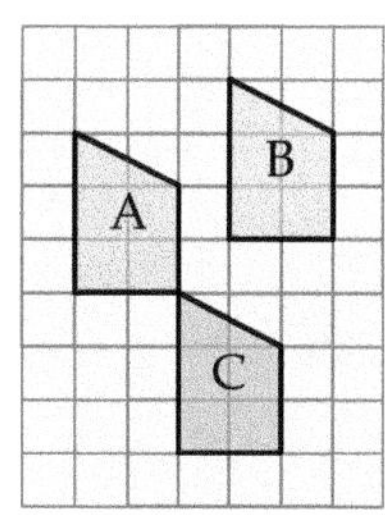

Problem solving

3 **a** Draw the blue triangle and its reflection in the y-axis.
b Reflect both triangles in the x-axis.
c What is the mathematical name of the shape formed by the blue triangle and its images? Explain your reasoning.

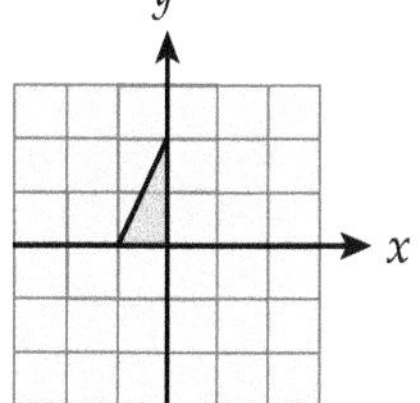

4 **a** Draw the quadrilateral ABCD on square grid paper and reflect it in the x-axis. Mark the equal angles and the equal sides on your diagram.
b Repeat part **a** but this time reflect the quadrilateral in the y-axis.

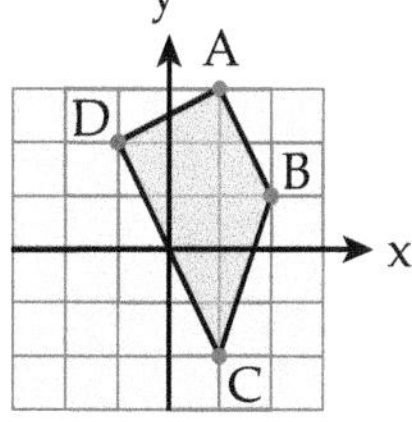

5 **a** On square grid paper, draw a triangle with vertices (0, 0), (0, 2), (1, 2).
b After a rotation the coordinates of the vertices of the image are (1, -1), (-1, -1), (-1, 0).
Find the centre of rotation and the angle of rotation.

6 Transform the tile ◤ to create three different patterns.

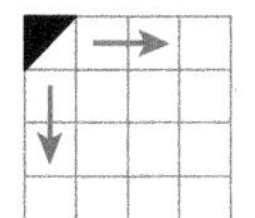
Translations by either one square across or down.

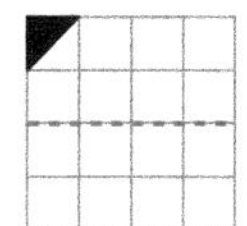
Reflections in a horizontal or a vertical line.

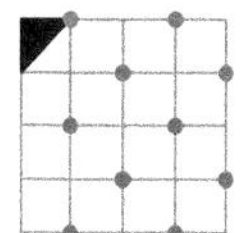
Anticlockwise rotations of 90° about the dots.

9b Enlargements

An **enlargement** is a type of transformation that alters the size of a shape. You multiply the lengths of the shape by a **scale factor**.

The object and the image are **similar** as they are the same shape but a different size.

The position of the image is fixed if you use a **centre of enlargement**.

Draw lines from the centre of enlargement through the vertices of the object.

Multiply the distance from the centre to the object by the scale factor. This gives the distance to the image along the same extended line.

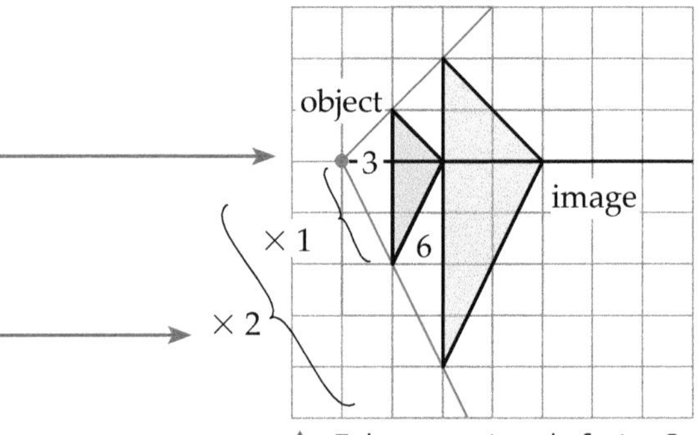

object
3
image
× 1
6
× 2

▲ Enlargement scale factor 2

Example

Enlarge the pink rectangle by scale factor 2 using (0, 1) as the centre of enlargement.

Draw lines from (0, 1) through the vertices of the rectangle.
Multiply the distance from (0, 1) to each vertex by 2 to find the vertices of the image.
The image and the pink rectangle are similar.

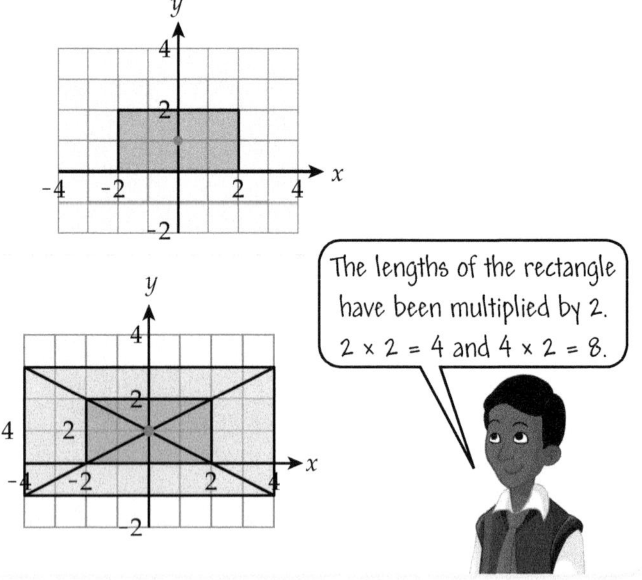

y
x
4
2
-4
-2
The lengths of the rectangle have been multiplied by 2.
2 × 2 = 4 and 4 × 2 = 8.

Exercise 9b

1 Each blue shape is an enlargement of the pink shape.
Copy each diagram onto square grid paper.
Calculate the scale factor and find the coordinates of the centre of enlargement.

a

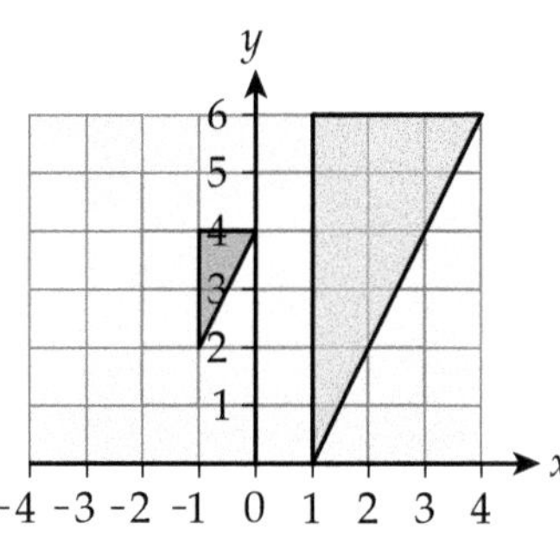

b

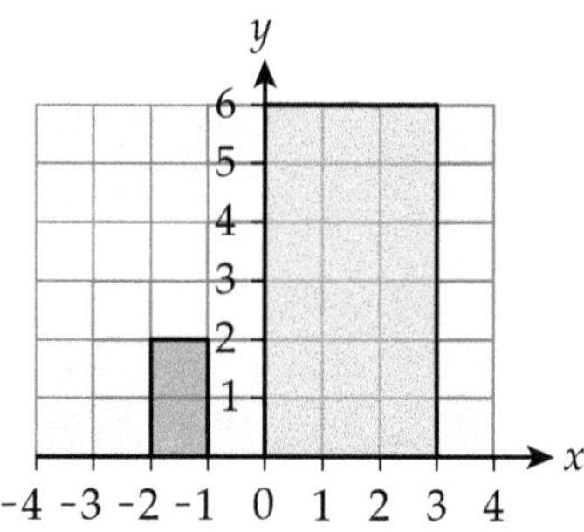

c

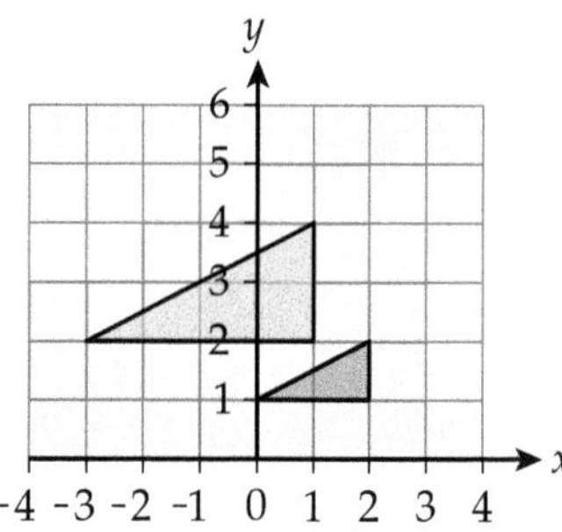

2 Copy each shape onto square grid paper.
Draw the enlargement of the shape using the dot as the centre of enlargement and the scale factor given.

a

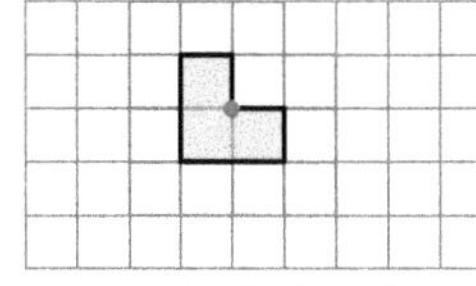

scale factor 4

b

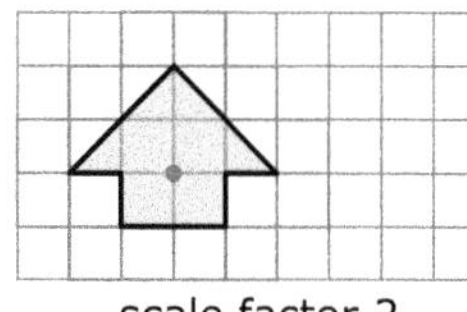

scale factor 2

c

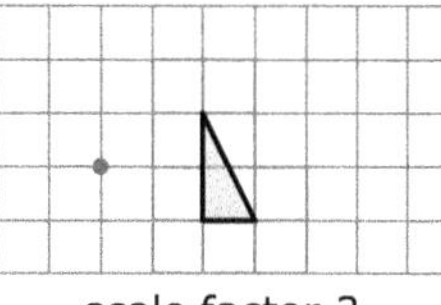

scale factor 3

Problem solving

3 **a** Draw triangle ABC on a coordinate grid.
b Enlarge the triangle by scale factor 2 using (0, 0) as the centre of enlargement.
c What are the coordinates of the vertices of the enlarged triangle?
d What do you notice about the coordinates of the object and the image?

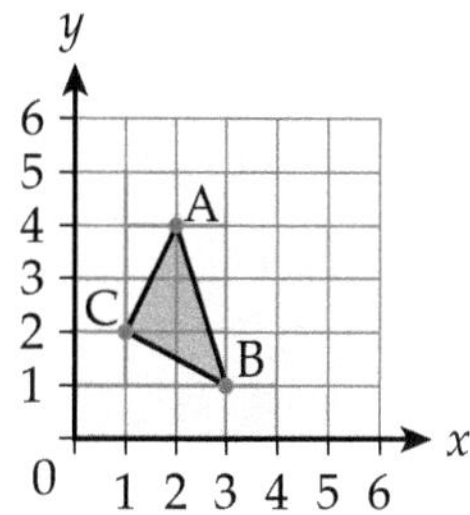

4 The green rectangle is an enlargement of the blue rectangle.
The blue rectangle measures 3 cm by 2 cm.
One side of the green rectangle measures 12 cm.
a What are the two possible scale factors of the enlargement?
b Calculate the unknown length of the green rectangle in each case.

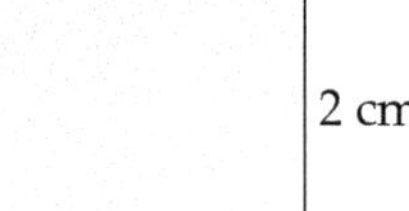

5 **a** Enlarge the shape by scale factor 2.
b Divide the enlargement into four congruent shapes.

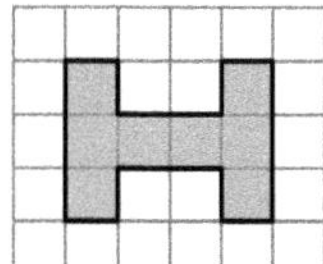

Congruent shapes are exactly the same size and the same shape.

9c Combinations of transformations

The object and image are **congruent** in reflections, rotations and translations.

Congruent means the same size and the same shape.

- You can transform 2D shapes using a combination of transformations.

Example

The blue hexagon is reflected in the y-axis to give the red hexagon.
The red hexagon is reflected in the line $x = 5$ to give the green hexagon.
What single transformation maps the blue hexagon onto the green hexagon?

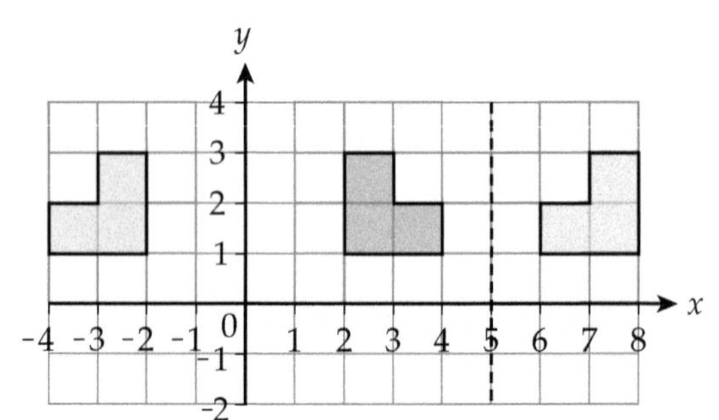

A translation of $\begin{pmatrix} 10 \\ 0 \end{pmatrix}$ or 10 right, 0 up.

Example

a Reflect triangle A in the y-axis.
Call the image B.

b Reflect triangle B in the line $y = x$
Call the image C.

c Describe the single transformation that maps triangle A to triangle C.

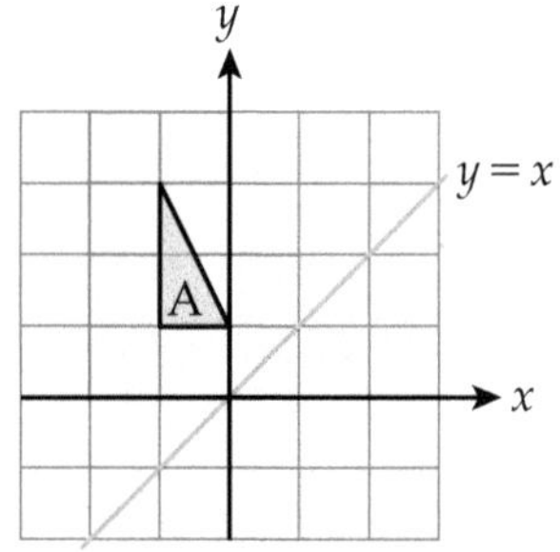

a Reflection in the y-axis.

b Reflection in the line $y = x$.

c A clockwise rotation of 90° about (0, 0).

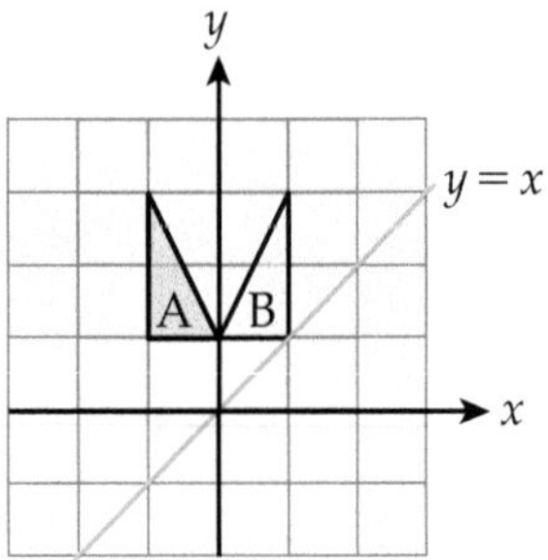

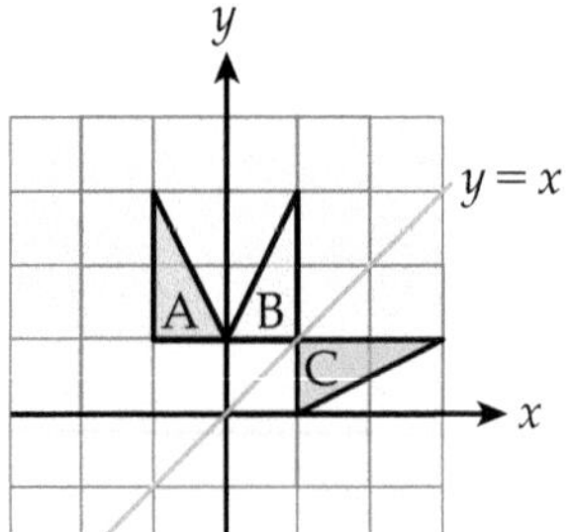

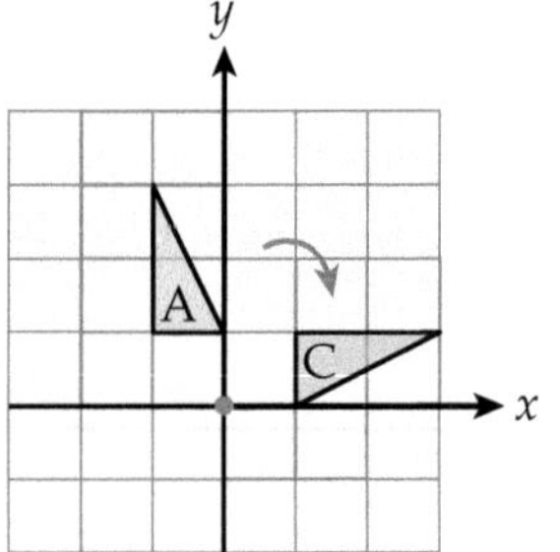

Use tracing paper to find the centre of rotation.

Exercise 9c

1 The right-angled triangle ABC is reflected in the line AB. The triangle and the image are then reflected in the line CB extended to the right.

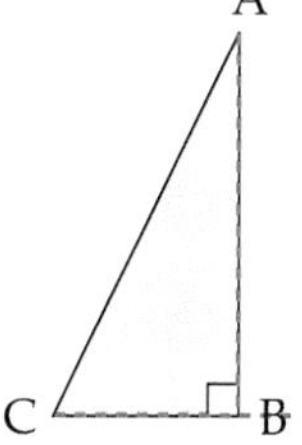

a What is the mathematical name of the shape formed by the object and the image?

b Give reasons to explain your answer.

2 A shape is translated by $\begin{pmatrix} \text{5 right} \\ \text{1 up} \end{pmatrix}$.

The image is translated by $\begin{pmatrix} \text{4 left} \\ \text{3 down} \end{pmatrix}$.

Write a single transformation that is equivalent to the two translations.

3 The pink triangle is reflected in the line $y = x$.

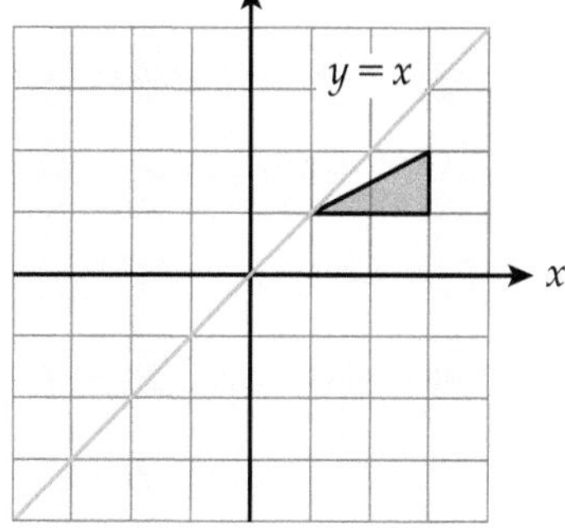

a Draw the image and label it I_1.

b The triangle I_1 is reflected in the x-axis. Draw the new image and label it I_2.

c Describe the single transformation that maps the pink triangle to triangle I_2.

4 **a** Describe the single transformation that maps hexagon A to hexagon C.

b Find a combination of rotations that maps hexagon A to hexagon C through hexagon B.

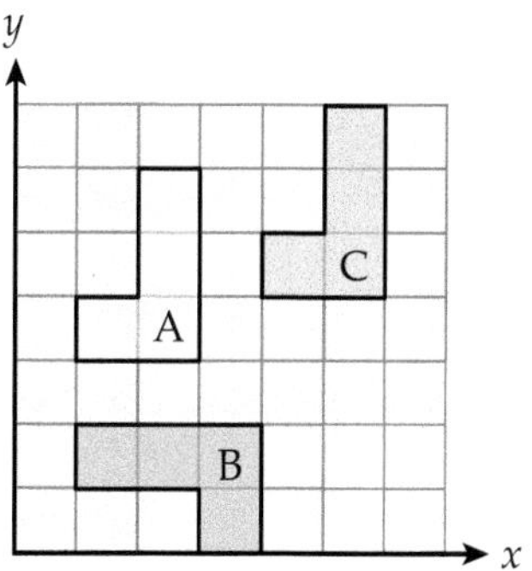

Problem solving

5 Draw a 2 by 2 square.

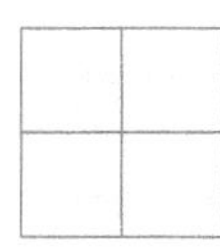

Translate and rotate the triangles as shown.

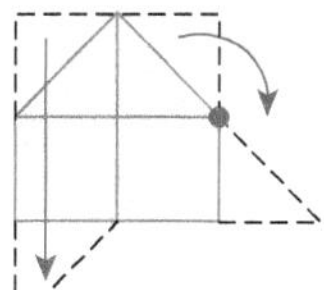

Show that this shape **tessellates** using a combination of rotations and translations.

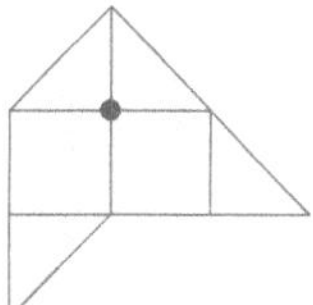

9d Maps and scale drawings

Real-life distances can be reduced or enlarged in **proportion** using a **scale**. The angles stay the same. The scale means you can interpret a **map** or **scale drawing**.

The height of the elephant is 350 cm.

Scale 1 : 100
1 cm represents 100 cm

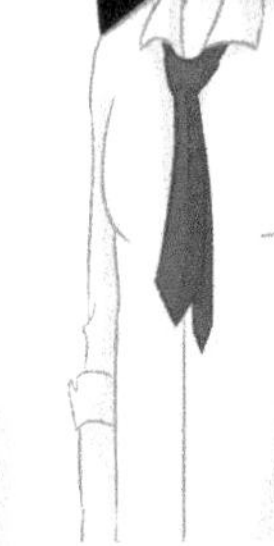

The lengths in the scale drawing are 100 times smaller then in real life.
The real-life lengths are an enlargement, scale factor 100, of the scale drawing.

- The scale on a map or scale drawing can be written as a **ratio.** Corresponding lengths are in the same ratio.

Example

The scale on the map is 1 : 50 000.

a The distance between Calver and Stoney Middleton on the map is 2 cm. Calculate the distance between the villages in real life.

b The distance between Baslow and Stoney Middleton in real life is 4.25 km. Find the distance between the villages on the map.

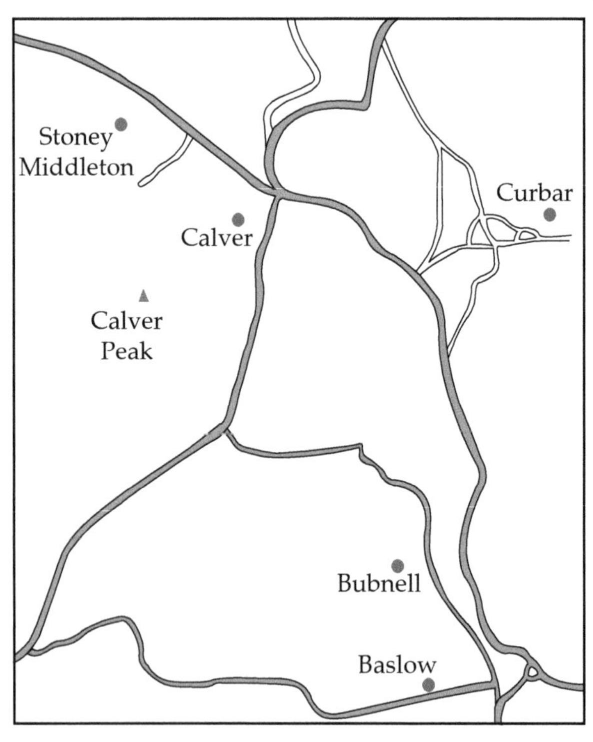

a The real-life distances are 50 000 times larger.

$2\,\text{cm} \times 50\,000 = 100\,000\,\text{cm}$
$= 1000\,\text{m}$
$= 1\,\text{km}$

b The distances on the map are 50 000 times smaller.

$4.25\,\text{km} \div 50\,000 = 4250\,\text{m} \div 50\,000$
$= 425\,000\,\text{cm} \div 50\,000$
$= 8.5\,\text{cm}$

Exercise 9d

1 A map has a scale of 1 cm represents 5 km.

a Calculate the real-life distance represented by these lengths.

i 8 cm   ii 15 cm   iii 6.5 cm
iv 3.4 cm   v 30 mm

b Calculate the distance on the map for these real-life distances.

i 15 km   ii 60 km   iii 125 km
iv 12.5 km   v 2.5 km

Did you know?

A 1 : 16 scale model of the Angel of the North was valued at £1 000 000.

Problem solving

2 A scale drawing uses a scale of 1 cm represents 5 metres. The height of the lighthouse in the scale drawing is 4.5 cm. What is the height of the lighthouse in real life?

The angles remain the same.

3 Cath walks in a straight line for 75 metres. She turns through 90° and walks for a further 45 metres.

a Draw a scale drawing of her journey using a scale of 1 cm represents 10 metres.

b How far is she from her starting point?

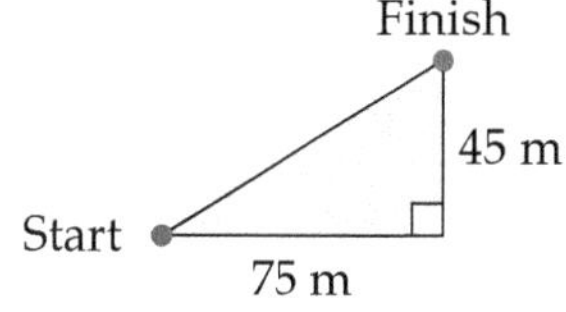

Scale: 1 cm represents 5 m

4 A lorry has these dimensions:

Length:	16.5 m
Height:	4.4 m
Width:	2.5 m

A scale model is made using a scale of 1 : 20. Calculate the length, height and width of the model in centimetres.

5 Use a scale of 1 : 100 to draw a scale drawing to represent the heights and lengths of these animals.

	Height	**Length** (shoulder to tail)
Brachiosaurus	1500 cm	1400 cm
Tyrannosaurus	600 cm	300 cm
Giraffe	500 cm	200 cm
Hippopotamus	160 cm	350 cm

Now make a drawing of yourself on the same scale.

9e Bearings

This photograph is taken looking east from Kala Patthar (5545 m) in Nepal. Mount Everest (8848 m) is in the background.

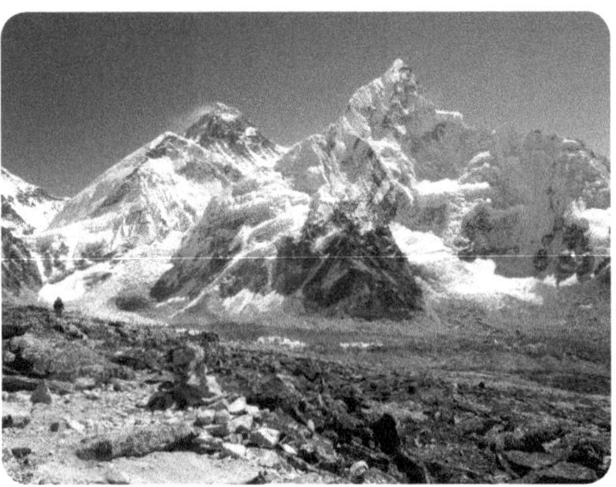

The direction of Everest from Kala Patthar is 090°.
This angle is called the **bearing**.

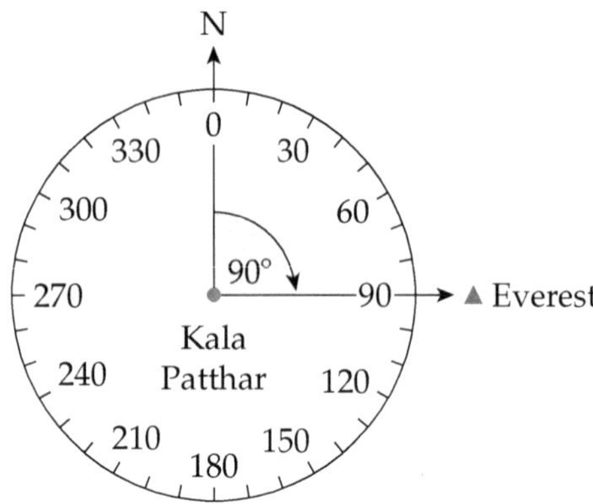

- When you give a **three-figure bearing**
  - measure from North
  - measure in a clockwise direction
  - use three digits.

Example

Work out the bearing of

a the oil rig from the lighthouse

b the lighthouse from the oil rig.

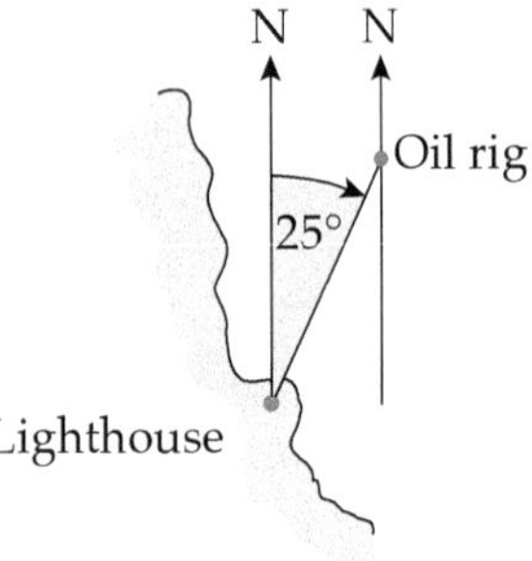

Not drawn accurately

a Imagine you are at the lighthouse. Measure clockwise from North.

The bearing is 025°

b Imagine you are at the oil rig. Measure clockwise from North.

The bearing is 180° + 25° = 205°

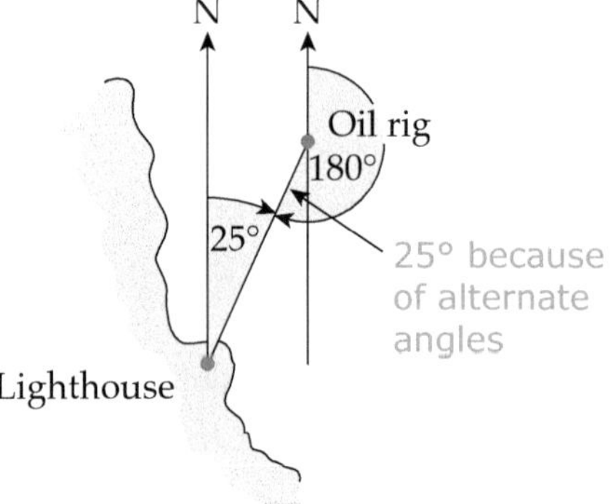

Notice that 25° + 180° = 205° and 205° − 180° = 25°.

- You either add or subtract 180° to find the **reverse bearing**. This is also called the **back bearing**.

Exercise 9e

1 Measure the bearings of these points from the point O.

a Abbey b Barn
c Church d Dentist
e Estate f Field
g Gate h House
i Ice rink j Jetty

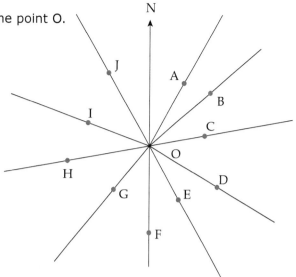

2 Draw accurate diagrams to show these bearings from a point O.
Remember to mark the direction of North.

a 045° b 190° c 300°
d 120° e 240°

Problem solving

3 Put a cross in the middle of your page.
Plot these sets of points and join them in order to form a shape.
Give the mathematical name of the shape and draw any lines of symmetry.

a

Bearing from the cross	045°	135°	225°	315°
Distance from the cross	5 cm	5 cm	5 cm	5 cm

b

Bearing from the cross	000°	090°	180°	270°
Distance from the cross	3 cm	5 cm	3 cm	5 cm

4 a Give the bearing of B from A.
b Calculate the bearing of A from B.
c Give the bearing of D from C.
d Calculate the bearing of C from D.

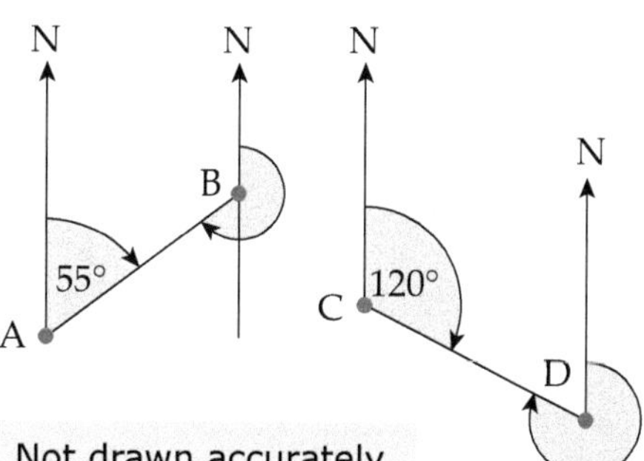

Not drawn accurately

Did you know?

You need to make an adjustment when you use a compass as true North and magnetic North are different. Magnetic North varies slightly with place and time. This difference is printed on every OS map.

5 A yacht sails on a bearing of 040° for 10 sea miles, then on a bearing of 160° for a further 7.5 sea miles.
a Construct a scale drawing to show the voyage.
b What is the yacht's distance and bearing from the starting point?
c What bearing should the yacht take to return to the starting point?

Not drawn accurately

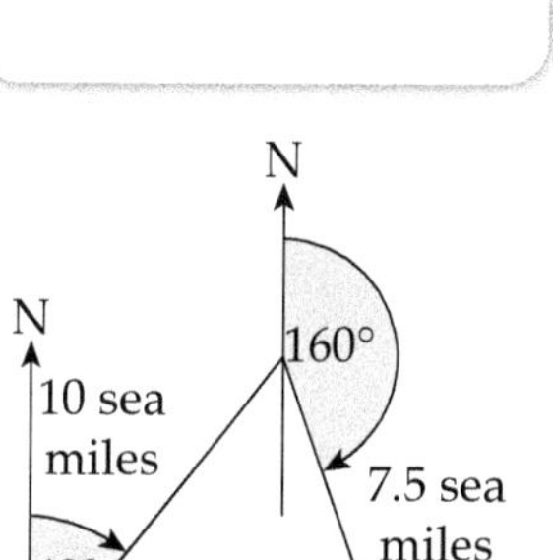

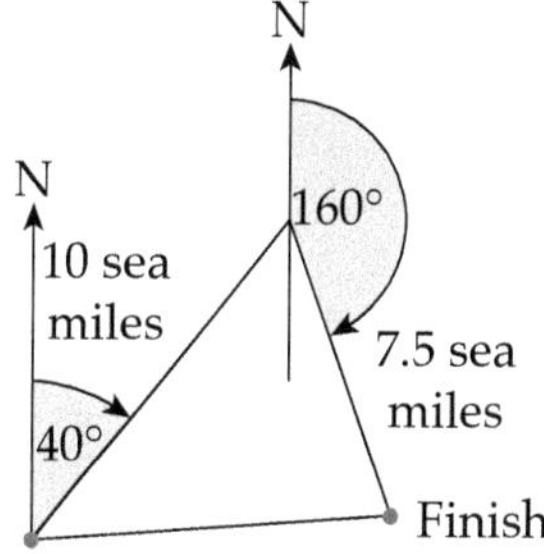

Check out

You should now be able to ...

	Test it ➡ Questions
✓ Reflect, rotate and translate 2D shapes.	 1 – 3
✓ Enlarge a 2D shape using a given centre of enlargement.	 4 – 5
✓ Use maps and scale drawings.	6
✓ Use bearings to specify direction.	7

Language	Meaning	Example
Object	The 2D shape to be transformed.	
Image	The 2D shape after transformation.	
Reflection	The object is flipped over a given mirror line.	A reflection in the line $x = 2$
Rotation	The object is turned through a given angle and direction about a fixed point.	An anticlockwise rotation of 90° about (3, 3)
Translation	The object is slid across the plane using a vector.	
Enlargement	A transformation that can change the size of the image.	
Centre of enlargement	Point used to set the position of the image in an enlargement.	
Scale (factor)	The number of times lengths are enlarged.	

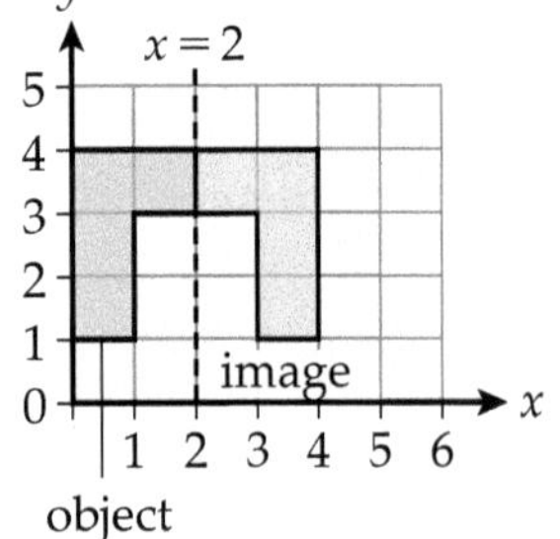

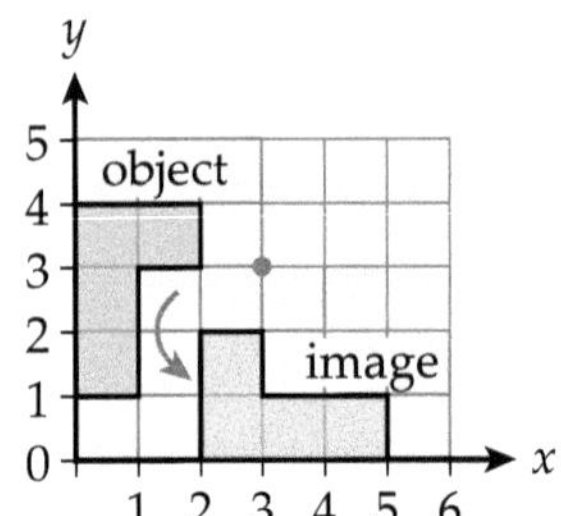

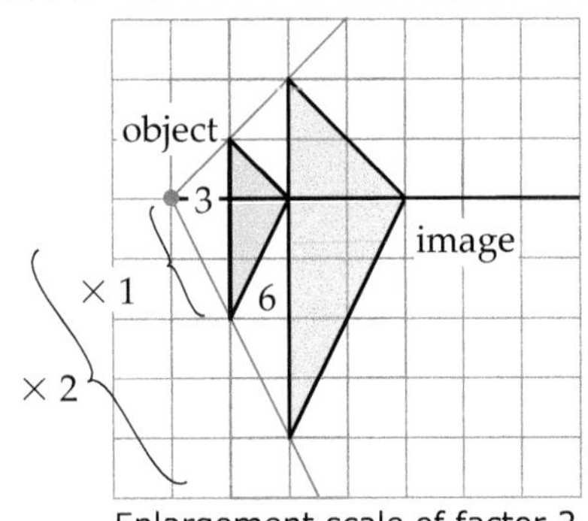

Enlargement scale of factor 2

9 MyReview

1 Describe fully the transformation that moves.

a triangle A to B

b triangle A to C

c triangle B to D.

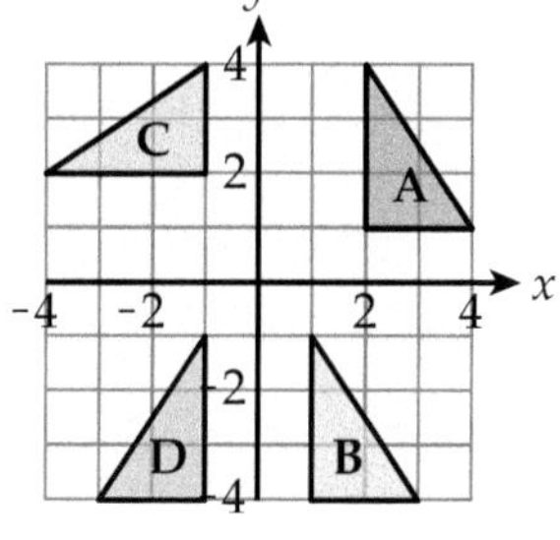

2 Copy the shape on squared paper. Reflect the shape in the mirror line.

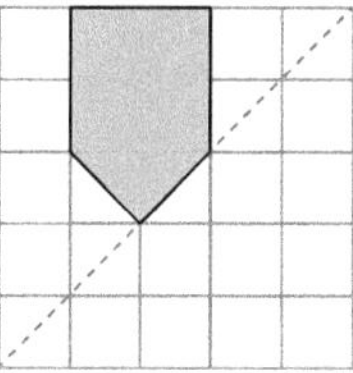

3

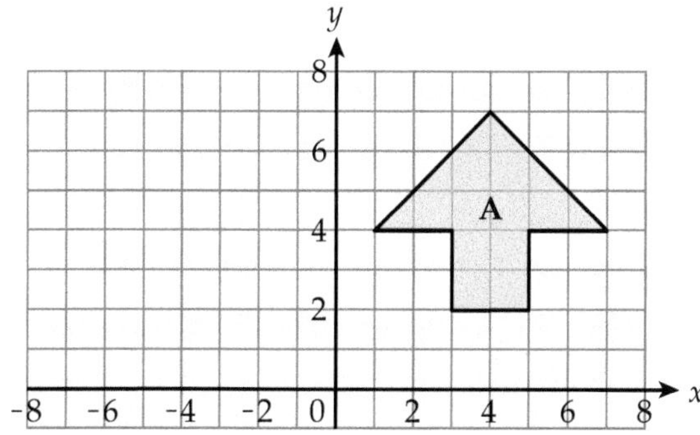

Copy the diagram and extend it downwards to -8.

a Rotate the shape 90° clockwise about (0,0) and label the image B.

b Reflect B in the line $x = 0$ and label the image C.

c Translate C by $\begin{pmatrix} 8 \text{ up} \\ 0 \text{ across} \end{pmatrix}$ and label the image D.

3 **d** Describe fully the single transformation that moves A to D.

4 B is enlarged to give B′. Calculate the scale factor and find the coordinates of the centre of enlargement.

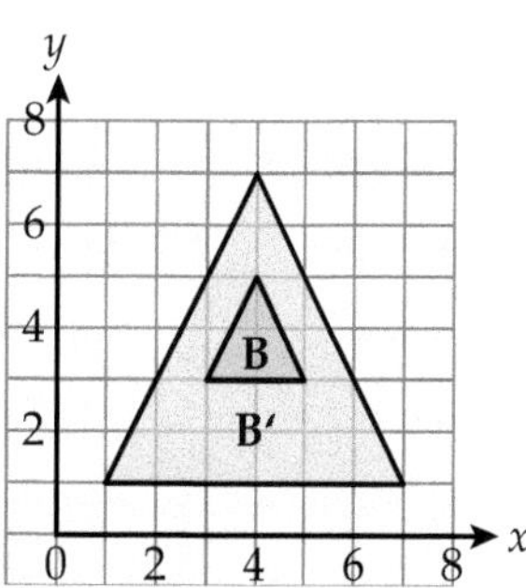

5 Copy the shape onto squared grid paper and enlarge it by scale factor $\frac{1}{2}$ using the dot as the centre of enlargement.

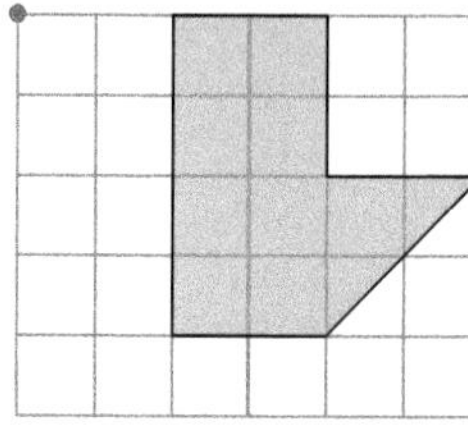

6 John starts at A, walks due north for 6 m then west for 9 m and arrives at B.

a Draw a scale drawing of his journey using a scale of 1:300

b How far is John from his starting point?

7 Calculate the bearing of

a B from A

b A from B

c C from A

d A from C.

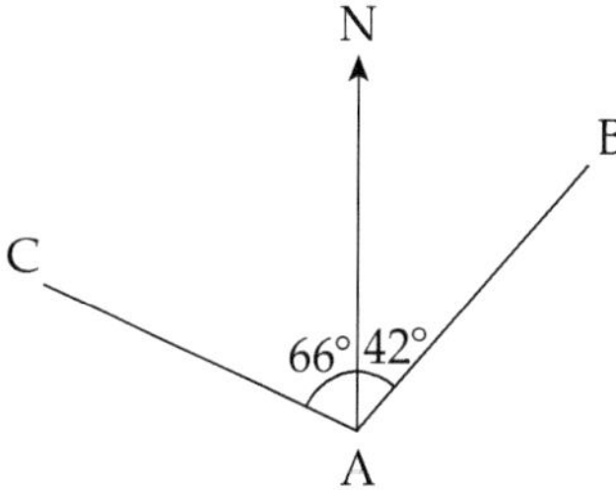

What next?

Score

0 – 2	Your knowledge of this topic is still developing. To improve look at Formative test: 3B-9; MyMaths: 1086, 1099, 1103, 1113, 1115, 1117, 1125 and 1127
3 – 5	You are gaining a secure knowledge of this topic. To improve look at InvisiPen: 362, 363, 364, 366, 368, 372 and 374
6	You have mastered this topic. Well done, you are ready to progress!

9 MyPractice

9a

1 A shape is rotated three times through a right angle about the point O.
Write the mathematical name of the shape formed by the object and its images when the rotated shape is

a a right-angled isosceles triangle

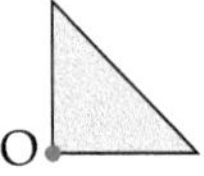

b a square.

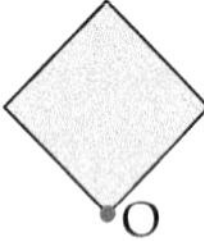

9b

2 **a** Draw an enlargement of the grey trapezium by scale factor 2.

b Show how four congruent grey trapeziums tessellate to make the image.

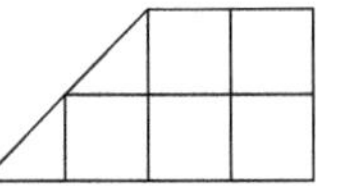

3 Draw coordinate axes from 0 to 10 on square grid paper.
Plot and join the points (2, 1), (3, 2), (3, 3) and (2, 4) to form a quadrilateral.

a What is the mathematical name of the quadrilateral?

b Enlarge the quadrilateral by scale factor 3 using (0, 1) as the centre of enlargement.

c Write the coordinates of the vertices of the enlargement.

9c

4 Two mirrors M_1 and M_2 are 4 units apart.

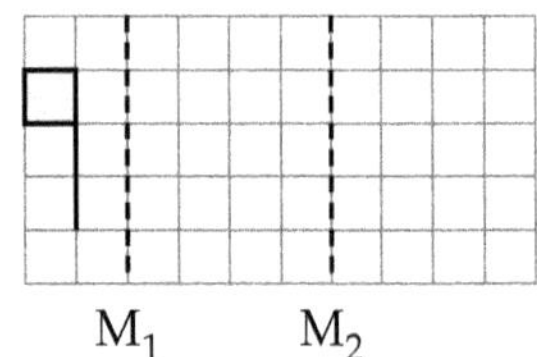

a Reflect the green flag in the mirror M_1.
Label the image I_1.

b Draw the reflection of I_1 using the mirror M_2.
Label the image I_2.

c Describe the single transformation that maps the green flag to I_2.

9d

5 The scale on a map is 1 : 25 000.

a Calculate the real-life distance represented by

i 7 cm ii 8.5 cm iii 4.5 cm iv 24 cm.

b Calculate the distance on the map for these real-life distances.

i 1200 m ii 850 m iii 8 km iv 4.5 km.

6 The diagram shows the positions of four trees drawn to scale. Calculate the real-life distances between these trees.

a Ash to Beech
b Ash to Cherry
c Ash to Oak
d Beech to Cherry
e Beech to Oak
f Cherry to Oak

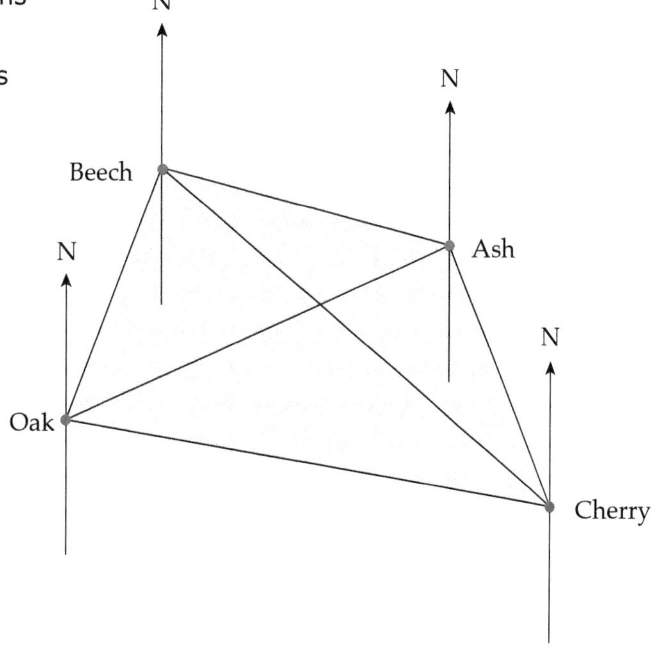

Scale: 1 cm represents 0.5 km

9e

7 Use the diagram in question **6**.
Measure the bearing of

a Ash from Oak
b Beech from Oak
c Beech from Ash
d Cherry from Ash
e Oak from Ash
f Cherry from Beech
g Oak from Beech
h Ash from Beech
i Ash from Cherry
j Beech from Cherry.

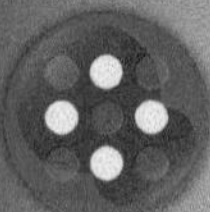

Case study 3: Climate change

The Earth's climate has always changed due to natural causes such as change of orbit, volcanic eruptions and changes in the sun's energy, but now there is real concern that human activity is upsetting the balance by adding to 'greenhouse gases'.

Greenhouse gases

This diagram shows some of the main factors behind global warming.

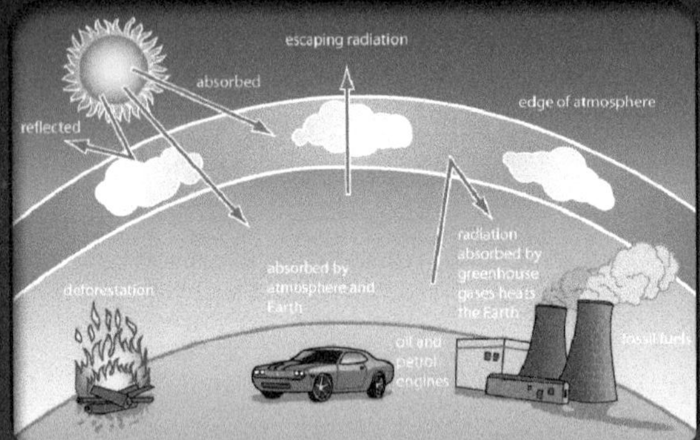

Task 1

The pie chart shows the contribution made to the warming effect by the main greenhouse gases

carbon dioxide
methane
nitrous oxide
others

a Which greenhouse gas causes about ¼ of the warming effect?

b Roughly what fraction of the warming effect is caused by carbon dioxide (CO_2)?

Task 2

THE DAILY NEWS

What's News

GREENHOUSE GASES UP BY 25%

A recent report says that in the last 60 years, CO_2 concentrations have increased by around 25%.

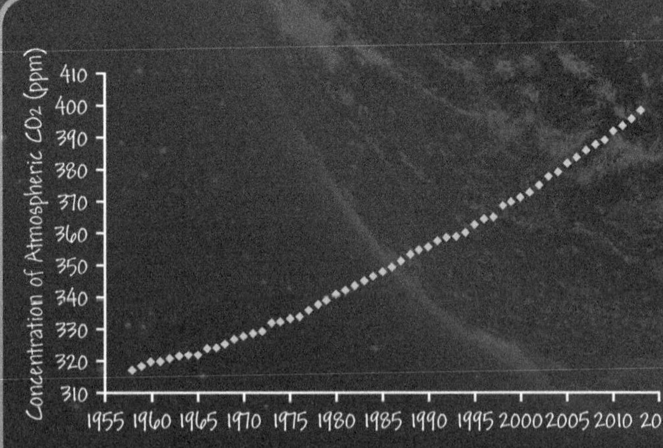

a Does the graph show the same increase in CO_2 levels as the report? Show your workings out.

b In the year 1000 AD, CO_2 concentration was around 280 ppm (parts per million). By what percentage has it increased?

c (Harder) If CO_2 concentrations continue at their current rate, in what year would you predict the CO_2 concentration to reach 500 ppm?

Global temperature change

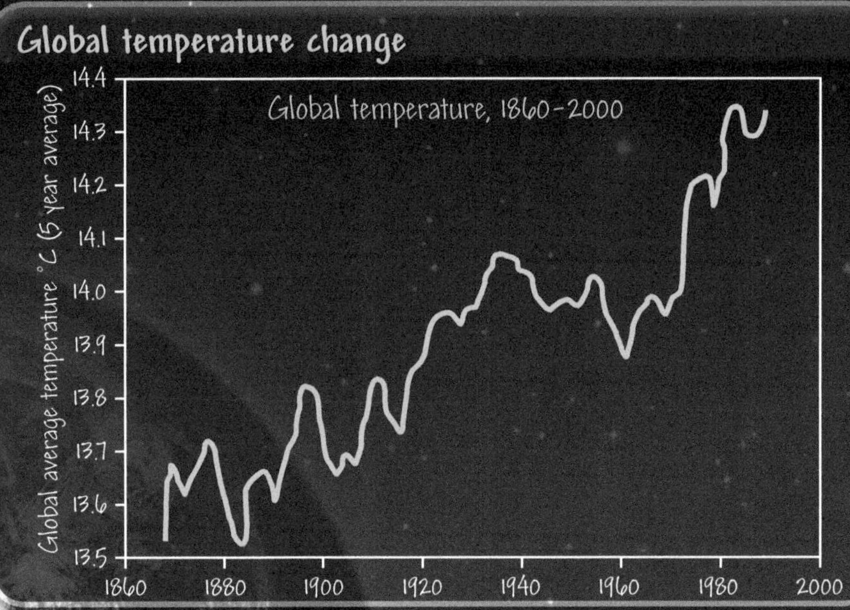

Task 3

a Describe in words what the graph shows.

b Estimate the global temperature in

i 1880

ii 1980

c Calculate the percentage change in temperature, giving the answer on your calculator display to 1 decimal place.

Task 4

Here are the monthly temperatures for Oxford in 1908 and 2008.

1908	Jan	Feb	Mar	Apr	May	June	July	Aug	Sep	Oct	Nov	Dec
max °C	5.5	8.6	8.3	10.4	17.6	20.5	21.5	20	17	16.1	11.1	6.5
min °C	-0.4	2.7	1.5	2.4	9	9.8	12.2	10.7	9.4	8.1	5	1.6

2008	Jan	Feb	Mar	Apr	May	June	July	Aug	Sep	Oct	Nov	Dec
max °C	10.3	10.5	10.6	13.1	18.7	20.1	21.7	20.8	17.6	14.3	9.9	6.5
min °C	4.7	1.7	3.5	4.7	9.5	11.1	12.8	13.9	10	6.3	4.6	1.3

a Write down the range in **i** maximum temperatures, **ii** minimum temperatures, for each year.

b Calculate the mean of

i maximum temperatures,

ii minimum temperatures, for each year.

c Use your results from **a** and **b** to compare the temperatures in Oxford in 1908 and 2008. Are your findings in agreement with the graph in Task 3?

d Why might using data for just two year in a single city not be adequate to make any firm conclusions about global warming?

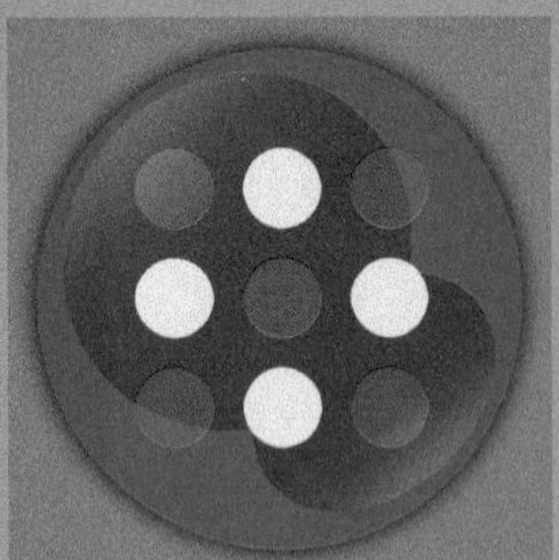

10 Equations

Introduction

You might think that equations only exist in maths textbooks, but ...

Astronomers use equations to describe the movements of planets and the paths of asteroids. Nuclear physicists use equations to calculate the half – lives of dangerous radioactive isotopes. Biologists use equations to predict the likely growth or decline of populations of endangered animals. The police force use equations to determine the cause of accidents by calculating speeds and braking distances of the vehicles involved.

What's the point?

Equations are used in all walks of life to model complex real-life situations.

Objectives

By the end of this chapter, you will have learned how to ...

- Solve equations by using inverse operations.
- Solve equations that have brackets.
- Solve equations that have fractions.
- Solve equations with unknowns on both sides.
- Create your own equations and solve them.
- Use trial and improvement to solve equations.

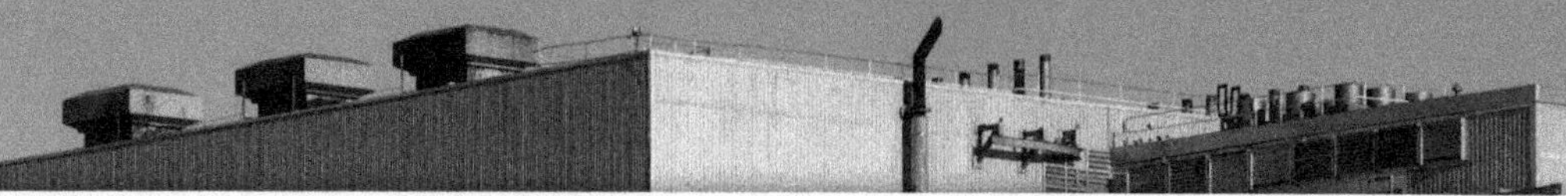

Check in

1 Copy and complete these calculations.

Use the same number in all three boxes in **a**.

a $\square \times \square \times \square = 27$ **b** $\square^2 = 9$

2 Use inverse operations to find the numbers that go in the boxes.

a $\square + 4 = 12$ **b** $\square - 4 = 12$

c $4 \times \square = 12$ **d** $\square \div 4 = 12$

3 Simplify these expressions by collecting 'like terms'.

a $3x + 2y + 4x + 5y + x$ **b** $9x + 3y - x + 6y - 2x$

4 **a** Work out $3(6 - 5) + 2(8 - 3)$ **b** Simplify $2(3x + 5) + 5(x + 3)$

Starter problem

Hans sells two types of housing pods: Blauhaus and Gelbhaus.

The pods are built on top of each other to make blocks.

Use the information to work out the height of each of the housing pods.

Gelbhaus

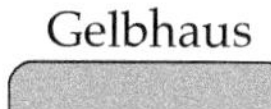

Blauhaus

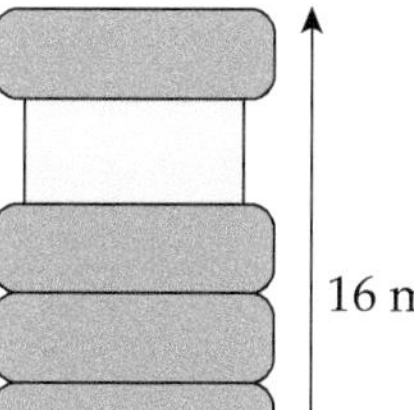

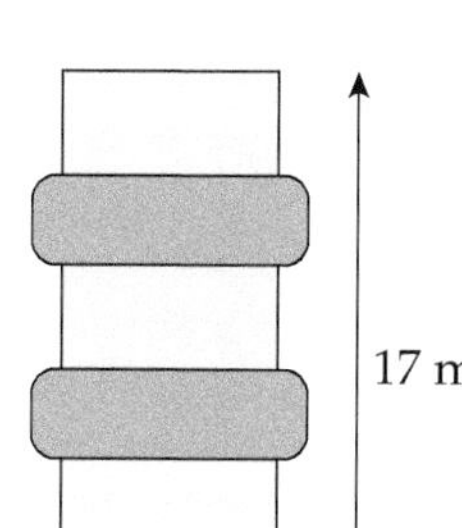

10a Solving equations

- Each of the four operations (+, −, × and ÷) has an **inverse operation**. You use inverses to **solve equations**.

Example

Solve the equations.

a $x - 9 = 23$

a The inverse of − is +,
So add 9 to both sides
$x - 9 + 9 = 23 + 9$
$x = 32$

b $4x = 52$

b The inverse of × is ÷,
So divide both sides by 4
$\frac{4x}{4} = \frac{52}{4}$
$x = 13$

Think of an inverse as undoing what's already been done.

- To solve some equations you use more than one inverse operation.

Example

Solve the equation $3x + 8 = 2$

Subtract 8 from both sides.
Divide both sides by 3.

$3x + 8 = 2$
$3x = -6$
$x = -2$

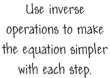

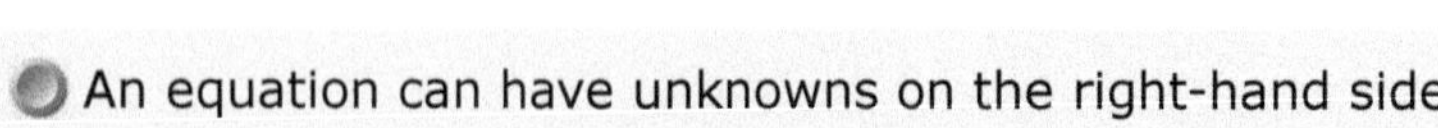

- An equation can have unknowns on the right-hand side.

Example

Solve the equation $23 = 5x - 7$

Rewrite the equation.
Add 7 to both sides.
Divide both sides by 5.

$5x - 7 = 23$
$5x = 30$
$x = 6$

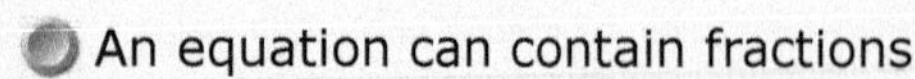

- An equation can contain fractions.

Example

Solve the equation $\frac{x}{2} - 5 = 3$

Add 5 to both sides.
× both sides by 2.

$\frac{x}{2} - 5 = 3$
$\frac{x}{2} = 8$
$x = 16$

Exercise 10a

1 Solve these equations using inverse operations.

a $x + 4 = 9$ **b** $x - 4 = 9$ **c** $x + 3 = 4$

d $2x = 10$ **e** $\frac{x}{2} = 10$ **f** $3x = 15$

g $\frac{x}{3} = 2$ **h** $x - 7 = 1$ **i** $x + 4 = 1$

2 Find the value of x in each of these balances.

a

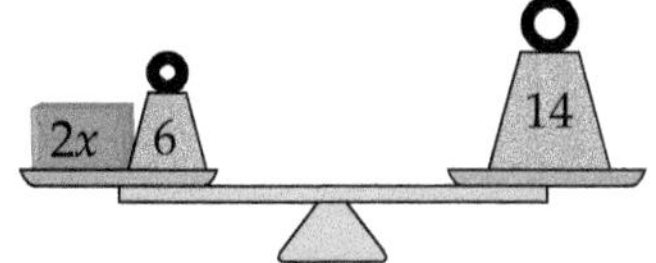

b

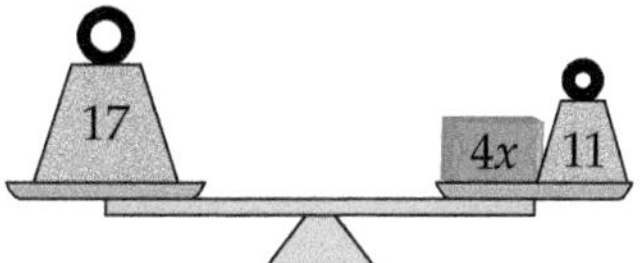

3 Solve these equations. Each **solution** takes two steps.

a $2x + 1 = 15$ **b** $2x - 1 = 15$ **c** $3x + 6 = 21$

d $3x - 6 = 21$ **e** $4x + 5 = 17$ **f** $6x + 7 = 7$

g $2x + 5 = 8$ **h** $2x - 1 = 10$ **i** $6 = 4x - 3$

j $40 = 7x + 5$ **k** $2 = 4x + 8$ **l** $1 = 6x + 4$

4 Solve these equations. Some solutions are negative.

a $5x - 2 = 33$ **b** $2x + 6 = 2$ **c** $4x + 10 = 2$

d $3x - 9 = 0$ **e** $16 = 3x + 1$ **f** $13 = 2x + 15$

g $12 = 2x + 11$ **h** $3 = 4x + 9$ **i** $2x - 1 = -5$

j $3x - 2 = -5$ **k** $2x + 7 = -1$ **l** $4x + 3 = -6$

5 Solve these equations. You need to use a mixture of methods.

a $6x + 5 = 5$ **b** $2x - 16 = 1$ **c** $4x - 3 = 7$

d $\frac{x}{2} + 3 = 8$ **e** $\frac{x + 3}{2} = 8$ **f** $\frac{x}{4} - 1 = 2$

g $\frac{x - 1}{4} = 2$ **h** $10 = 3x + 2$ **i** $5 = 9 + 2x$

j $5x - 1 = -11$ **k** $4 = 12 + 2x$ **l** $3 - x = 2$

Did you know?

The Ahmes (Rhind) papyrus shows how Egyptian students learned to solve linear equations such as $x + \frac{x}{7} = 19$, almost 4000 years ago!

6 Jon has 5 books of stamps with x stamps in each. Sari has 3 books of stamps and another 12 single stamps. Find the value of x if Jon and Sari have equal numbers of stamps.

Problem solving

7 **a** The rectangle R has width x cm. Its length is three times its width. Its perimeter is 40 cm. Find the value of x and the area of the rectangle.

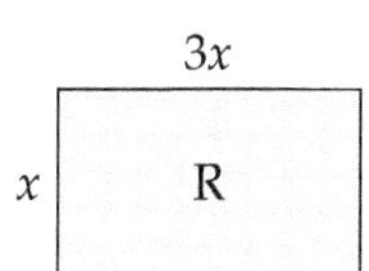

b The rectangle S has the lengths shown here. Find the value of y.

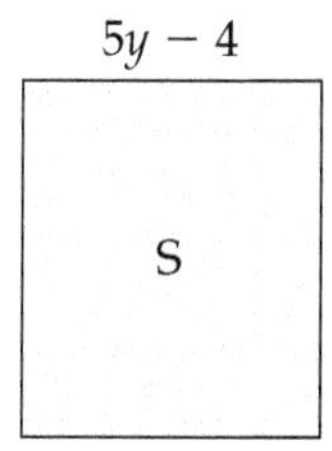

p.96

10b Equations with brackets

- Equations can have **brackets**.

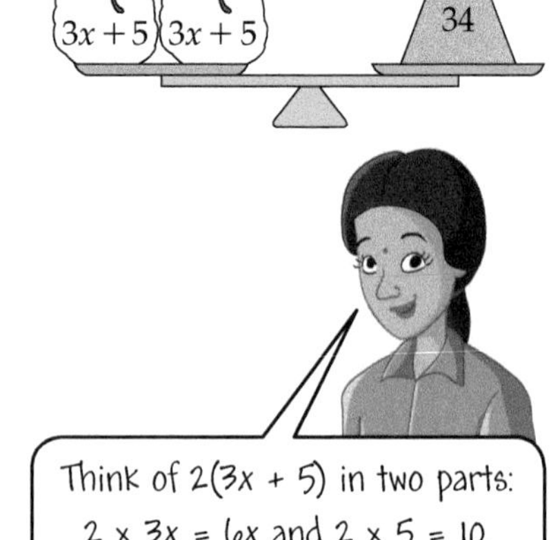

The diagram on the right shows a balance.

The equation of the balance is $2(3x + 5) = 34$.

	$2(3x + 5) = 34$
Expand the brackets.	$6x + 10 = 34$
Subtract 10 from both sides.	$6x = 24$
Divide both sides by 6.	$x = 4$

Think of $2(3x + 5)$ in two parts: $2 \times 3x = 6x$ and $2 \times 5 = 10$.

- Equations can have more than one pair of brackets.

Example

Solve $3(5x + 2) - 2(4x - 3) = 26$.

Expand the brackets.	$3(5x + 2) - 2(4x - 3) = 26$
Collect **like terms**.	$15x + 6 - 8x + 6 = 26$
Subtract 12 from both sides.	$7x + 12 = 26$
Divide both sides by 7.	$7x = 14$
	$x = 2$

Think $-2 \times 4x = -8x$ and $-2 \times -3 = +6$.

Collect like terms.
$15x - 8x = 7x$
$6 + 6 = 12$

- You can solve problems using equations and brackets.

Example

John starts with £x and he earns £3 more.
His mum doubles his money.
He then spends £x and has £20 left.
How much did he have to start with?

He earns an extra £3.	$x + 3$
His mum doubles his money.	$2(x + 3)$
He then spends £x and has £20 left.	$2(x + 3) - x = 20$
Expand the brackets.	$2x + 6 - x = 20$
Collect like terms.	$x + 6 = 20$
Subtract 6 from both sides.	$x = 14$
He had £14 to start with.	

Check:
$14 + 3 = 17$
$2 \times 17 = 34$
$34 - 14 = 20$
There is £20 left. ✓

Exercise 10b

1 Find the value of x in each balance.

a

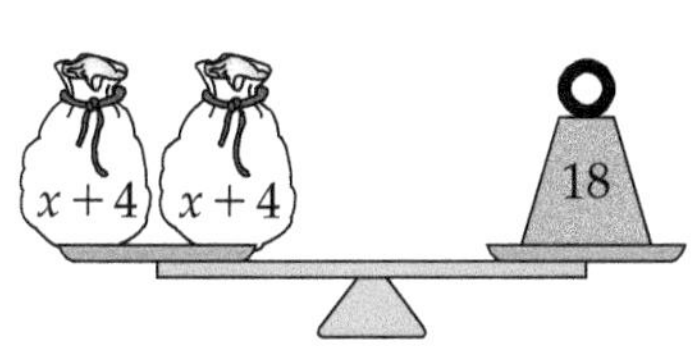

b

2 Solve these equations.

a $2(3x + 2) = 16$ **b** $4(2x + 3) = 28$ **c** $3(2x - 3) = 15$

d $5(x - 2) = 30$ **e** $2(6x - 7) = 10$ **f** $\frac{1}{2}(4x + 6) = 13$

g $20 = 4(2x + 3)$ **h** $12 = 3(5x - 6)$ **i** $7 = \frac{1}{4}(8x - 12)$

3 Solve these equations. You will need to collect like terms.

a $4(2x + 1) + 3(3x + 2) = 44$ **b** $2(5x + 2) + 5(x + 2) = 29$

c $3(4x + 3) + 4(2x - 2) = 1$ **d** $6(2 + x) + 2(1 - 2x) = 20$

e $5(2x - 3) + 4(5 - 2x) = 9$ **f** $4(3 - 2x) + 9x - 15 = 0$

g $(8x - 6) + 7 - 2x = 12$ **h** $(9x + 12) - 2(x + 3) = 6$

Remember:
+ times − is −
− times − is +

4 Solve these equations. Some answers are negative.

a $2(2x - 4) = 4$ **b** $2(2x + 4) = 4$

c $3(3x - 5) = 12$ **d** $4(3x + 6) = 12$

e $5(2x + 3) - 8x = 11$ **f** $2(7 + 5x) - 6x = 2$

g $5x + 3(2x - 9) = 17$ **h** $9x + 4(2 - 2x) = 5$

i $4(1 - x) + 7x = 4$ **j** $5(1 - 2x) - 2x = -7$

5 Solve these equations.

a $3(3x + 2) + 4(2x + 2) = 48$ **b** $4(2x + 3) + 3(2x - 3) = 17$

c $5(2x - 1) + 2(3x + 4) = 51$ **d** $4(3x - 5) + 3(2 - 3x) = 1$

e $3(5x + 2) - 2(3x - 2) = 19$ **f** $6(3x - 2) - 2(2x - 5) = 26$

g $8(3 - 2x) + 20x - 9 = 31$ **h** $5x - 2 - 3(6 - 2x) = 2$

i $2(2x - 5) - 3(4 + 6x) = 6$ **j** $\frac{1}{2}(4 - 6x) - 2(\frac{1}{2}x - 4) = 26$

Problem solving

6 Mayah has £x and she spends £5.
She trebles how much she has left with
a gift from her grandma.
She then spends another £5 and has £13 left.
Write an equation and find the value of x.
How much did her grandma give her?

10c Unknowns on both sides

Equations can have unknowns on both sides.

There's more than one way to solve an equation. Some ways are quicker than others!

Here is an equation:	$8x + 2 = 3x + 12.$
Subtract $3x$ from both sides.	$5x + 2 = 12$
Subtract 2 from both sides.	$5x = 10$
Divide both sides by 5.	$x = 2$

Equations can also involve fractions.

Example

Solve these equations.

a $\frac{1}{3}(7x - 1) = 2x + 3$ **b** $\frac{4x - 3}{5} = x - 2$

a $\frac{1}{3}(7x - 1) = 2x + 3$

Multiply both sides by 3.	$7x - 1 = 6x + 9$
Subtract $6x$ from both sides.	$x - 1 = 9$
Add 1 to both sides.	$x = 10$

b $\frac{4x - 3}{5} = x - 2$

Multiply both sides by 5.	$4x - 3 = 5x - 10$
Subtract $4x$ from both sides.	$-3 = x - 10$
Add 10 to both sides.	$7 = x$
Rearrange.	$x = 7$

You can solve word problems by writing them as equations.

Example

Sanjeev is x years old.
His father is 27 years older than him.
Sanjeev's age is a quarter of his father's age.
How old is Sanjeev?

Sanjeev's father is $x + 27$ years old.	$x = \frac{x + 27}{4}$
Multiply both sides by 4.	$4x = x + 27$
Subtract x from both sides.	$3x = 27$
Divide both sides by 3.	$x = 9$

Sanjeev is 9 years old.

$\frac{x + 27}{4} = \frac{1}{4}(x + 27)$

Check:
$x + 27 = 9 + 27 = 36$
$\frac{1}{4}$ of $36 = 9$ ✓

Exercise 10c

1 Solve these equations.

a $7x + 3 = 4x + 18$
b $6x + 2 = 4x + 9$
c $8x - 2 = 6x + 1$
d $4x - 6 = x + 1$
e $9x - 8 = 5x + 4$
f $7x - 6 = 5x - 2$
g $9x - 8 = 5x - 3$
h $5x - 1 = 3x + 6$
i $3(2x + 5) = 2x + 20$
j $8x - 7 = 2(3x - 1)$

2 Solve these equations. Take care with negative signs.

a $8x + 4 = 34 + 2x$
b $8x + 4 = 34 - 2x$
c $5x + 6 = 18 + x$
d $5x + 6 = 18 - x$
e $3x - 2 = 8 - x$
f $7 + 3x = 12 - x$
g $9 + x = 3(3 - x)$
h $x + 2 = 2(4 - x)$
i $2x + 5 = 10 - 3x$
j $3 + x = 8 - x$

3 Solve these equations.

a $\frac{6x + 1}{2} = 2x + 3$
b $\frac{7x - 2}{2} = 3x + 4$
c $\frac{5x + 4}{3} = x + 2$
d $\frac{8x - 1}{3} = 2x + 1$
e $3x - 2 = \frac{10x + 1}{4}$
f $4x + 1 = \frac{8x + 23}{5}$
g $3 + x = \frac{15 - x}{2}$
h $5 + 2x = \frac{29 - x}{3}$
i $5 + 2x = \frac{1}{3}(29 - x)$

4 Use a range of methods to solve this mixture of equations.

a $8x + 3 = 6x + 17$
b $8x - 3 = 6x + 17$
c $8x + 3 = 17 - 6x$
d $\frac{11x - 3}{2} = 4x + 3$
e $\frac{1}{2}(9x - 3) = 5x - 4$
f $\frac{7x - 2}{3} = 4x - 6$

Problem solving

5 a Harry is x years old. His mother is 26 years older than him. Harry's age is a third of his mother's age. How old is Harry?

b Jo has £30 and buys two shirts at £x each. Sue has £40 and buys shoes for £$3x$. They have the same amount left over. Find the cost of the shoes.

6 The number in a square is the sum of the two numbers in the circles on either side of the square.

a Find expressions in terms of x for the values inside circles B and C.

b Write an equation in x and then solve it to find the value of x.

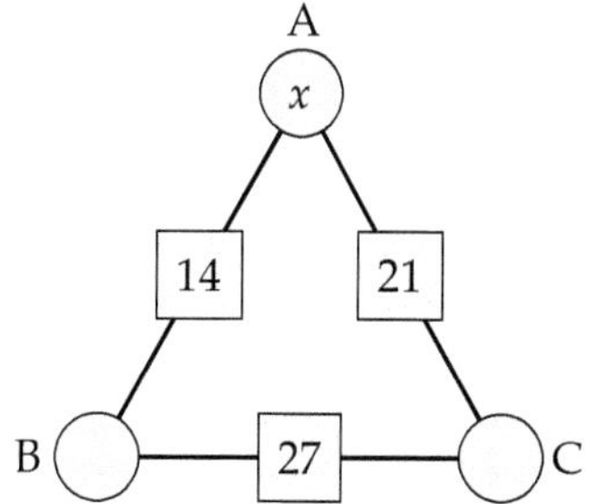

10d Constructing equations

You can often make word problems easier to solve by writing them as equations.

Example

Hassim thinks of a number, x, trebles it, subtracts 4 and then doubles the result. His final answer is four times his original number, x. Find the value of x.

		Now write the equation.	$2(3x - 4) = 4x$
Start with	x	Expand the brackets.	$6x - 8 = 4x$
Treble it.	$3x$	Add 8 to both sides.	$6x = 4x + 8$
Subtract 4.	$3x - 4$	Subtract $4x$ from both sides.	$2x = 8$
Double it.	$2(3x - 4)$	Divide both sides by 2.	$x = 4$

Setting up your equation is just as important as solving it, so don't rush through it!

You can often solve shape problems by using equations.

Example

This quadrilateral has one right angle.
It has two equal angles of $x°$ each.
The fourth angle is 60° bigger than $x°$.
Find the value of x.

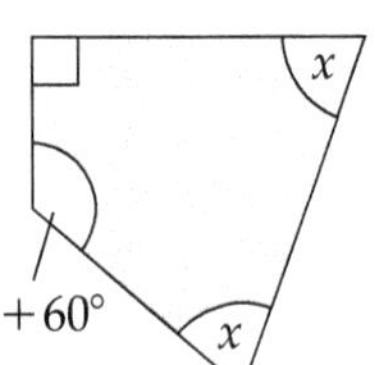

The four angles of any quadrilateral add up to 360°.

$$x + x + 90 + (x + 60) = 360$$

Simplify. $3x + 150 = 360$

Subtract 150 from both sides. $3x = 210$

Divide both sides by 3. $x = 70°$

Check:
The four angles are 70°, 70°, 90° and (70° + 60°) = 130°.
The sum of the angles is 70° + 70° + 90° + 130° = 360° ✓

Example

Each brick is the sum of the two bricks below.
If the value of brick P is six times that of brick Q, find x.

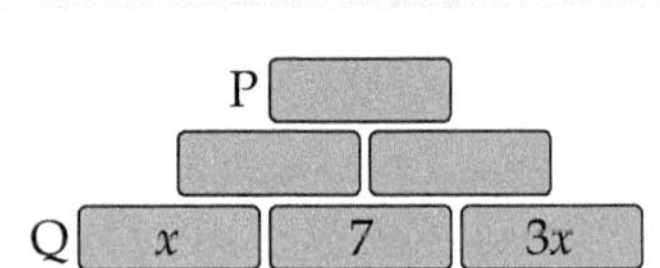

Add pairs of bricks.

Write an equation using bricks P and Q.

$$4x + 14 = 6x$$

Subtract $4x$ from both sides. $14 = 2x$

Divide both sides by 2. $7 = x$

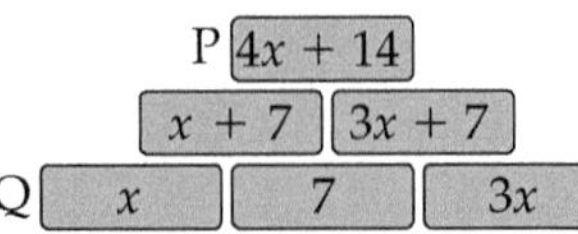

Check using $x = 7$.
$4x + 14 = 4 \times 7 + 14 = 28 + 14 = 42$ and
$6x = 6 \times 7 = 42$ ✓

Exercise 10d

1 Find the value of x in each diagram.

a

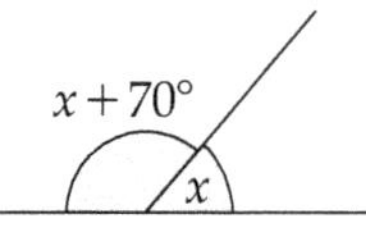

b

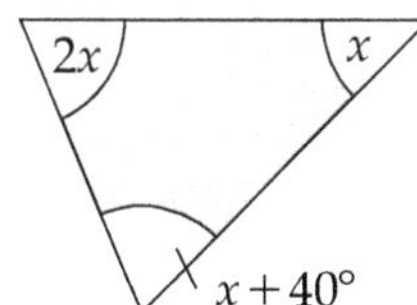

c

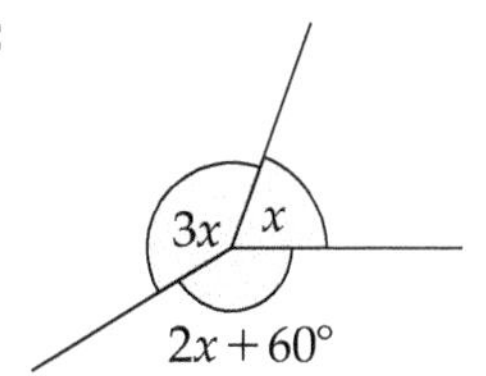

d

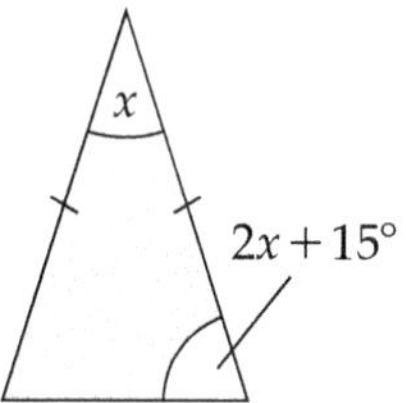

2 Find the value of x in each shape.

a

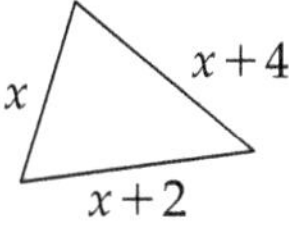

Perimeter = 21 cm

b

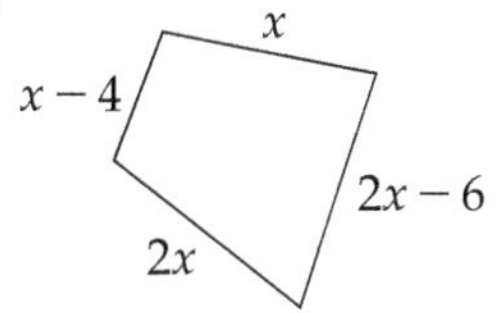

Perimeter = 14 cm

c

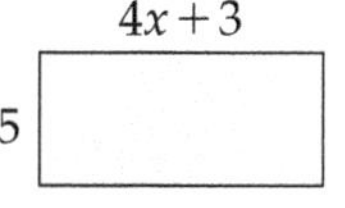

Area = 65 cm²

d

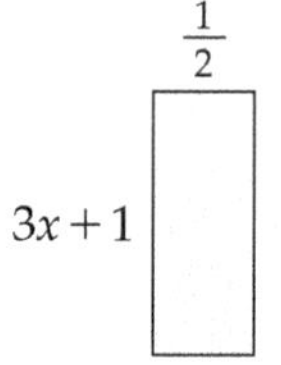

Area = 8 cm²

e

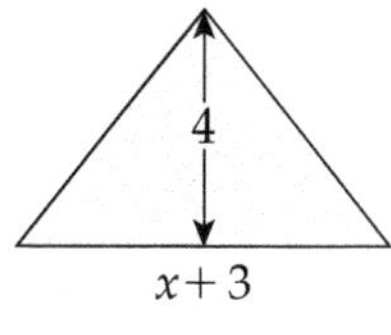

Area = 20 cm²

f

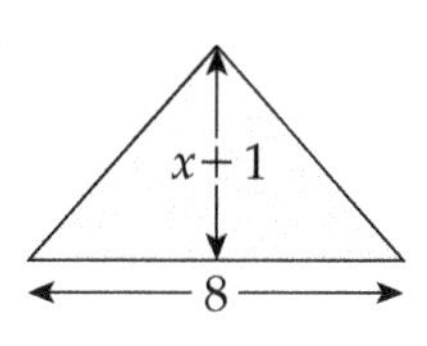

Area = 12 cm²

3 Write an equation and find the number x in each of these cases.

a You think of a number, multiply it by 3 and add 5.
Your answer is four times the original number.

b When you double a number and add 7, you get the same answer as when you add 29 to the number and divide by 2.

4 A patio is x metres wide. Its length is 5 m longer than its width. The perimeter is $6x$ metres.

a Find the width of the patio.

b Find the area of the patio.

5 Jane has £40 and Kate has £50.
Kate gives Jane £x. Jane now has twice as much as Kate.
How much did Kate give Jane?

6 Melissa has £x. Antoinette has 5 times more than Melissa. Antoinette gives Melissa £30. Antoinette now has three times more than Melissa.
How much did Melissa have originally?

Problem solving

7 There are two routes from Start to Finish.
The starting number, x, must give the same end number for the two routes.
Find the value of x.

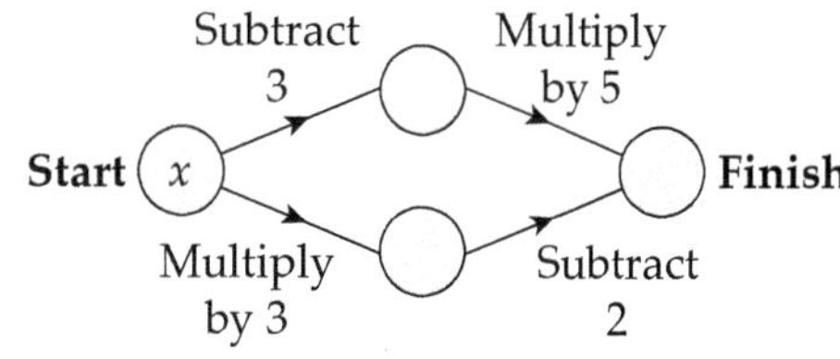

10e Trial and improvement

Some equation are very difficult to solve using algebra.
You can often solve these using **trial and improvement**.

Ben knows that the cube and the square of a number add together to give 576.
He uses trial and improvement to find the number.

The equation to solve is $x^3 + x^2 = 576$.

He makes a guess (or trial) and then improves on it.

This example involves an exact answer, but trial and improvement often involves rounding.

Try	x^3	x^2	$x^3 + x^2$	Comment
$x = 2$	8	4	12	$12 < 576$, far too low
$x = 10$	1000	100	1100	$1100 > 576$, too high
$x = 7$	343	49	392	$392 < 576$, too low
$x = 8$	512	64	576	Spot on!

The solution is $x = 8$.

- Trial and improvement often gives a decimal solution.

Example

Solve the equation $x^2 + x = 50$.
Give your answer correct to 1 dp.

Take $x = 6$ as your first trial and then improve on it.

Try	x^2	x	$x^2 + x$	Comment
$x = 6$	36	6	42	$42 < 50$, too low
$x = 7$	49	7	56	$56 > 50$, too high
$x = 6.5$	42.25	6.5	48.75	$48.75 < 50$, too low
$x = 6.6$	43.56	6.6	50.16	$50.16 > 50$, too high
$x = 6.55$	42.9025	6.55	49.4525	$49.4525 < 50$, too low

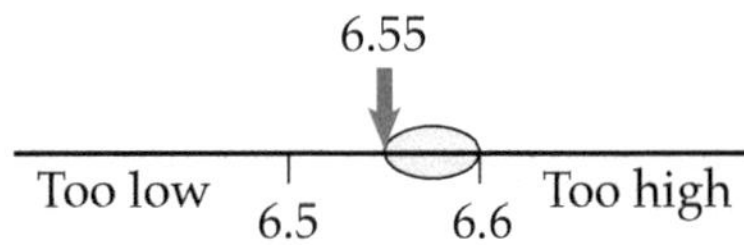
6.55
Too low
6.5
6.6
Too high

The solution must be between 6.5 and 6.6.
The solution is greater than 6.55.
The solution is $x = 6.6$ correct to 1 dp.

- You can use a computer spreadsheet instead of a calculator to construct your table of values.

	A	B	C	D
1	Try	x^2	x	$x^2 + x$
2	6	= A2*A2	= A2	= B2 + C2
3	7	= A3*A3	= A3	= B3 + C3
4	8	= A4*A4	= A4	= B4 + C4

Exercise 10e

1 Use this table to solve the equation $x^3 - x^2 = 294$.
Use $x = 5$ as your first trial.

Try	x^3	x^2	$x^3 - x^2$	Comment
$x = 5$				

2 Make your own tables to solve these equations.

a $x^2 - x = 272$ (Try $x = 10$) **b** $x^3 + x = 738$ (Try $x = 5$)

c $x^3 + x^2 = 1872$ (Try $x = 10$) **d** $x^2 + 5x = 176$

e $x^3 - 8x = 287$ **f** $x^4 - 3x^2 = 1188$

g $(x - 3)(x + 1) = 256$

h $2x^2 - x = 1035$

i $x + \sqrt{x} = 182$

j $x^2 - 6x = 112$

3 Use this table to solve the equation $x^3 - x = 150$.
Give your answer correct to 1 dp.

Try	x^3	x	$x^3 - x$	Comment
$x = 5$				

4 Make your own tables to solve these equations correct to 1 dp.

a $x^3 + x = 100$ (Try $x = 4$) **b** $x^2 - x = 50$ (Try $x = 7$)

c $x + x^2 = 80$ (Try $x = 8$) **d** $x^2 = 30$

e $x^3 = 30$ **f** $x^2 - 2x = 30$

g $x^4 + 4x = 700$ **h** $(x + 1)(x + 2) = 60$

i $x + \sqrt{x} = 25$ **j** $x^3 - x = 100$

5 **a** When a number, n, its square and its cube are all added together the total is 584. Find the number n.

b If the total of n, n^2 and n^3 is 600, find the value of n correct to 1 dp.

6 This rectangle is 4 cm longer than it is wide. Its area is 70 cm^2. Find its width, z, by solving the equation $z(z + 4) = 70$.

$z + 4$

z

Use this table to help you with a first try of $z = 6$.

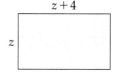

Try	z	$z + 4$	$z(z + 4)$	Comment
$z = 6$				

Problem solving

7 A plant pot has a square base of side x cm and four rectangular sides of height 10 cm.
Find the value of x if the total area of these five shapes is

a 500 cm^2 **b** 400 cm^2.

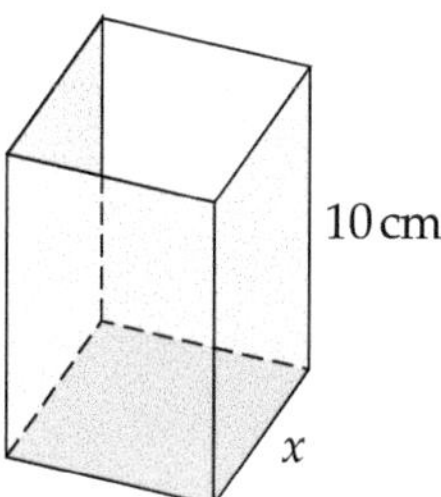

8 n is an odd number.
The next odd number after n is $n + 2$.

a Write down the next odd number after $n + 2$.

b These three odd numbers are multiplied together to give 117 453.
Find their values.
Use a calculator or computer spreadsheet to help you.

10 MySummary

Check out

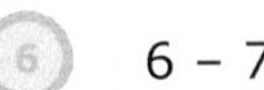

You should now be able to ... **Questions**

You should now be able to ...		Questions
✓ Solve equations, including with brackets and fractions.	6	1 – 3
✓ Create your own equations and solve them.	6	4 – 5
✓ Use trial and improvement to solve equations.	6	6 – 7

Language	Meaning	Example
Equation	A statement using letters and numbers that contains an equals symbol and an unknown.	$6x - 2 = 28$
Unknown	The letter in the equation that you are trying to find the value of.	In the equation $6x - 2 = 28$ x is the unknown.
Inverse operation	The mathematical operation that undoes an operation.	Multiplying and dividing are inverse operations. When you multiply by 5, you can undo this by dividing by 5.
Expand brackets	Remove brackets by multiplying by the value outside the bracket.	Expand the brackets: $6(4x - 3)$ becomes $24x - 18$.
Trial and improvement	A method for solving complex equations by making a guess, then improving on that guess until you are very close to the correct answer.	The equation $x^3 + x = 245$ can be solved by trial and improvement.

1 Solve these equations.

a $7x - 5 = 58$

b $4x + 9 = 11$

c $8x + 20 = 4$

d $-25 = 14x - 4$

e $\frac{3x - 1}{4} = 2$

f $\frac{x}{2} + 13 = 19$

g $14 - 2x = -6$

2 Solve these equations.

a $24 = 6(3x + 16)$

b $6(3b - 4) + 8(2b - 5) = 140$

c $3(5c + 7) - 2(9c - 3) = -6$

d $2(4x - 1) + 3x = -13$

3 Solve these equations.

a $6g + 14 = 28 - g$

b $21 - 3h = 69 + h$

c $8(6i - 15) = 12(38 - 2i)$

d $12 - 5j = -66 - 11j$

e $\frac{1}{2}(11x - 3) = 8x + 6$

f $\frac{12x - 7}{5} = 2x + 5$

4 Find the value of x in each diagram.

a

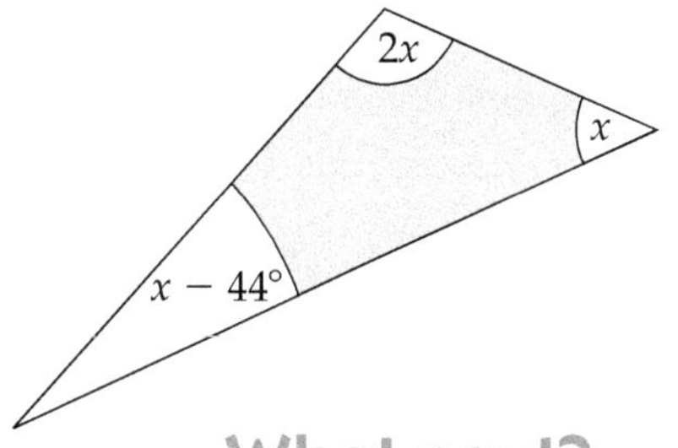

b

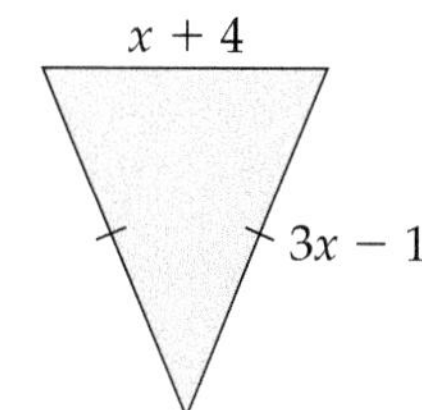

c

$x + 4$

$3x - 1$

Perimeter = 37 cm

5 Copy and complete this table to find a solution of $x^3 + x = 200$.

x	x^3	$x^3 + x$	Result
5	125	130	low

6 Use a trial and improvement method to find a positive solution of the following equations. Give your answers correct to 1 dp.

a $x^4 = 35$

b $3^x = 18$

c $x^3 + x^2 = 100$

7 A cuboid has side lengths p, p and $p + 2$. The volume of the cuboid is 70 cm³. Find p correct to 1 dp.

What next?

Score	
0 – 2	Your knowledge of this topic is still developing. To improve look at Formative test: 3B-10; MyMaths: 1057, 1154, 1182 and 1928
3 – 5	You are gaining a secure knowledge of this topic. To improve look at InvisiPen: 214, 231, 234, 235, 236, 237, 238 and 242
6	You have mastered this topic. Well done, you are ready to progress!

10 MyPractice

10a

1 Use inverse operations to solve these equations.

a $x + 5 = 7$ b $x - 8 = 2$ c $3x = 18$ d $\frac{x}{2} = 5$

2 Solve these equations. Each solution takes two steps.

a $2x + 3 = 11$ b $2x - 3 = 11$ c $6x + 1 = 19$

d $\frac{x}{2} + 1 = 4$ e $\frac{x}{2} - 1 = 4$ f $\frac{x}{3} + 2 = 7$

3 Solve these equations. Take care with the signs and fractions.

a $2x + 7 = 3$ b $3x - 8 = -2$ c $2x + 1 = 6$

d $4x - 2 = 7$ e $-1 = 5x + 8$ f $4 = \frac{x}{4} - 1$

10b

4 Solve these equations.

a $2(3x + 5) = 22$ b $5(2x + 4) = 30$ c $7(3x - 2) = 28$

d $3(2x - 1) = 12$ e $16 = 2(4x + 3)$ f $18 = 6(2 + 3x)$

5 Solve these equations. You will need to collect like terms.

a $2(3x + 1) + 3(4x + 2) = 44$ b $5(3x - 2) + 2(x + 7) = 55$

c $4(4x + 1) + 3(5 - x) = 32$ d $2(x + 3) + 3(4 - 2x) = 16$

e $2(x - 1) + 8(x + 3) = 2$ f $5(2x + 7) + 6(2 - x) = 43$

6 Solve these equations. Remember how to multiply positive and negative numbers.

a $5(2x + 3) - 3(2x + 4) = 15$ b $3(6x + 1) - 2(7x - 4) = 43$

c $3(3x + 4) - 2(2x + 1) = 30$ d $9(2x + 1) - 3(5x - 3) = 18$

e $3(2 + 4x) + 3(5 - x) = 30$ f $7(2 + 5x) + 4(8 - 7x) = 60$

10c

7 Solve these equations which have unknowns on both sides.

a $5x + 7 = 3x + 15$ b $4x - 1 = 2x + 13$ c $2(3x + 2) = 5(x + 3)$

d $3(3x + 2) = 8x + 5$ e $4(2x - 1) = 6x + 8$ f $4(2x - 1) = 6x - 8$

g $x + 4 = 13 - 2x$ h $2x + 6 = 9 - x$ i $2x - 6 = 9 - x$

j $8x - 4 = 6x + 1$ k $x + 5 = 12 - x$ l $2(2x - 1) = 3x - 7$

8 Solve these equations.

a $\frac{5x + 1}{2} = 2x + 3$ b $\frac{5x - 1}{2} = 2x + 3$ c $\frac{7x + 2}{4} = x + 2$

d $2x - 3 = \frac{8x + 2}{5}$ e $3x - 1 = \frac{7x - 2}{3}$ f $\frac{1}{2}(3x - 1) = 2x - 1$

10d

9 Cerys thinks of a number.
She doubles it, subtracts 5 and then trebles the result.
Her final answer is four times her original number.
What number did Cerys think of?

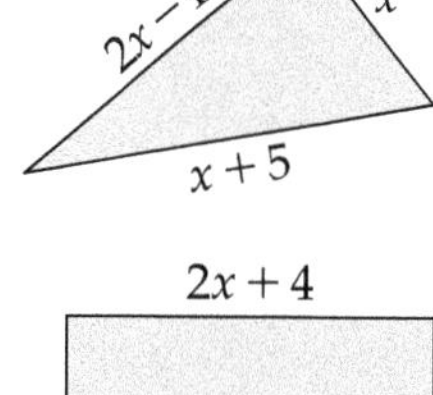

10 **a** The triangle has a perimeter of $6x$.
Find the value of x.

b For this rectangle

i find the value of x

ii work out the perimeter.

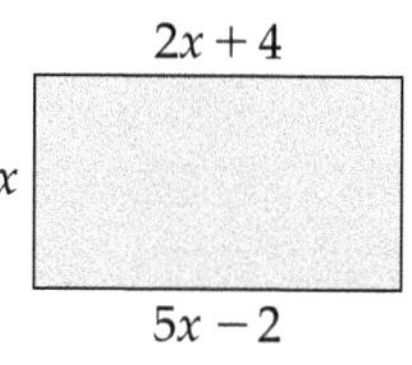

11 **a** Ethan has £x. He earns £30.
He now has three times his original sum.
How much did Ethan have to start with?

b April has £x and June has £20.
They add what they have and then share it out equally.
April now has £4 more than she started with.
How much did April have to start with?

12 A rectangular sheet of metal has a rectangular hole cut in it.
This diagram gives the dimensions in metres.
The area which is left is $11x\,\text{m}^2$.
Find the value of x and the area of the original sheet.

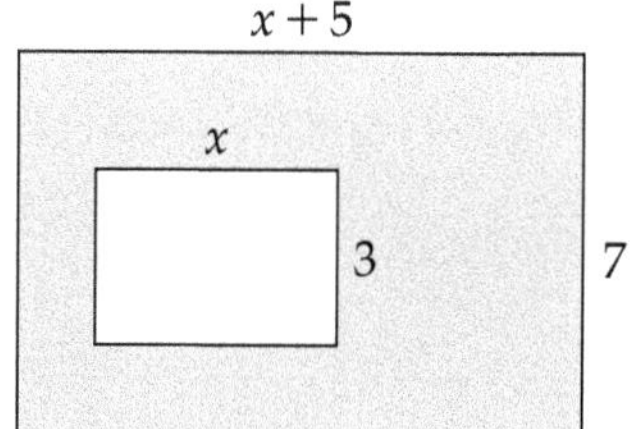

10e

13 Use this table to solve $x^2 + x = 48$.
Give your answer correct to 1 dp.
Try $x = 6$ as your first trial.

Try	x^2	x	$x^2 + x$	Comment
$x = 6$				

14 Use your own table to solve $2x + \sqrt{x} = 100$.
Give your answer correct to 1dp.
Try $x = 49$ as your first trial.

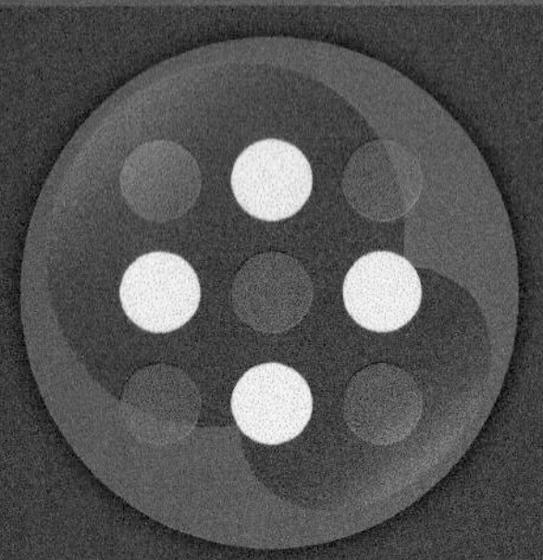

11 Powers and roots

Introduction

When you look up at the night sky you might see the M31 Galaxy, more commonly known as the Andromeda Galaxy. It is about 24 000 000 000 000 000 000 km from the Earth. Astronomers write the distance of the galaxy in **standard index form** as 2.4×10^{19} km. The light from the M31 galaxy has taken about 2.3 million years to reach the earth, so you are effectively looking back in time!

What's the point?

Scientists and astronomers have to work with very large numbers. Standard index form was invented so that a number like the distance of the M31 galaxy can be written down in a much easier and clearer way than writing lots of zeros.

Objectives

By the end of this chapter, you will have learned how to ...

- Find square and cube roots by trial and improvement or with a calculator.
- Use some of the rules of indices to simplify powers.
- Simplify expressions written in surd form.
- Change between ordinary numbers and standard form numbers.

Check in

1 Copy and complete these statements.

a $3 + 3 + 3 + 3 + 3$ is written as $5 \times \square$.

b $3 \times 3 \times 3 \times 3 \times 3$ is written as $3^{\square}$.

2 Work out the value of

a $2^2 \times 2^8$ **b** $2^4 \times 2^6$ **c** $2^7 \times 2^3$

Explain in words why your answers are the same.

3 Which of these numbers are square numbers?

14 16 25 49 30 100

4 Which of these numbers are cube numbers?

6 8 25 27 450 1000

Starter problem

Distance of Earth to Moon: 384 000 km

Length of 1 stride: 80 cm

How many steps would you need to take to walk to the moon?

How long would it take you?

What if you had to walk to the Sun, the nearest star, the nearest galaxy...

Investigate.

11a Square roots and cube roots

- Finding a **square root** or **cube root** is the **inverse** of finding a square or a cube.

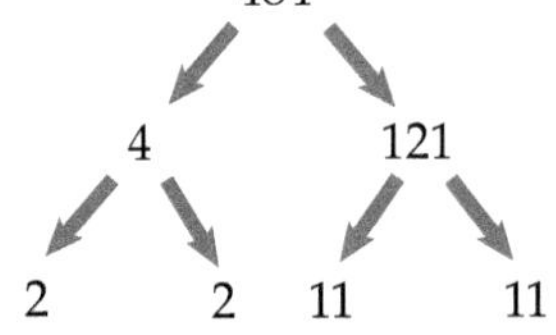
484
4
121
2
2
11
11

$5^2 = 25 \longleftrightarrow \sqrt{25} = 5 \qquad 2^3 = 8 \longleftrightarrow \sqrt[3]{8} = 2$

- You can find some roots using **factors**.

$\sqrt{900} = \sqrt{9 \times 100} = 3 \times 10 = 30$

$\sqrt{484} = \sqrt{2 \times 2 \times 11 \times 11} = 2 \times 11 = 22$

You can use your calculator if it has these keys.  

To find $\sqrt[3]{60}$ press 

The display will show 3.914 867 641.

So $\sqrt[3]{60} = 3.91$ to 2 dp.

Check by working out 3.91^3 on your calculator. The answer should be close to 60.

- You can use **trial and improvement** to find a root.

Example

Use trial and improvement to find $\sqrt[3]{80}$ to 1 dp.

x	x^3	Comment
4.2	74.09	too low
4.3	79.51	too low
4.4	85.18	too high
4.35	82.31	too high

Because $64 < 80 < 125$, $4 < \sqrt[3]{80} < 5$

So take $x = 4.2$ as the first trial.

$\sqrt[3]{80}$ lies between 4.3 and 4.4, so try the midpoint 4.35

So $\sqrt[3]{80}$ lies between 4.3 and 4.35

$\sqrt[3]{80} = 4.3$ to 1 dp.

Example

A circle has an area of 100 cm².

Use the formula $A = \pi r^2$ to find its radius to 1 dp.

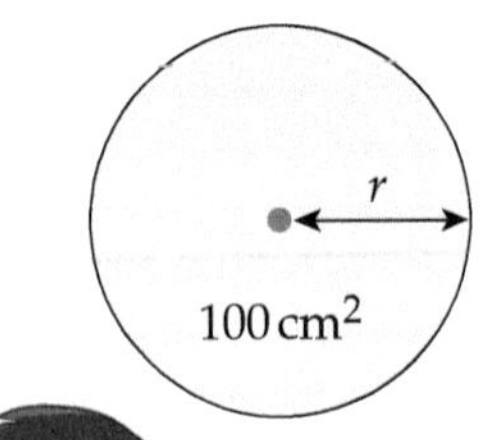
r
100 cm²

Substitute $A = 100$ and $\pi = 3.14$ into the formula.

$100 = 3.14 \times r^2$

Divide both sides by 3.14 $\quad r^2 = \frac{100}{3.14} = 31.847...$

Square root both sides. $\quad r = \sqrt{31.847...}$

$= 5.643$

Use a calculator to work it out.

So the radius, r, is 5.6 cm to 1 dp.

Check by working out $\pi \times 5.6^2$. The answer should be close to 100.

Exercise 11a

1 Work out these square roots without using a calculator.

a $\sqrt{400}$ **b** $\sqrt{1600}$ **c** $\sqrt{2500}$ **d** $\sqrt{10000}$ **e** $\sqrt{\frac{9}{100}}$ **f** $\sqrt{\frac{4}{100}}$

2 Find the prime factors of these numbers and then find their square roots.

a $\sqrt{196}$ **b** $\sqrt{225}$ **c** $\sqrt{1089}$ **d** $\sqrt{3025}$ **e** $\sqrt{1764}$

3 Use trial and improvement to find these roots to 1 dp.
Use this table of squares and cubes to help you choose your starting values.
You could use tables like those on the right.

x	1	2	3	4	5	6	7	8
x^2	1	4	9	16	25	36	49	64
x^3	1	8	27	64	125			

x	x^2	Comment

x	x^3	Comment

a $\sqrt{30}$ **b** $\sqrt{46}$ **c** $\sqrt{62}$ **d** $\sqrt{85}$ **e** $\sqrt{105}$

f $\sqrt[3]{30}$ **g** $\sqrt[3]{10}$ **h** $\sqrt[3]{55}$ **i** $\sqrt[3]{100}$ **j** $\sqrt[3]{120}$

Check your answers.

Problem solving

4 The area A of a circle of radius r is given by the formula $A = \pi r^2$.
Find the radius, to 2 decimal places, of circles with these areas.

a 24 cm² **b** 50 cm² **c** 75 cm² **d** 120 cm² **e** 240 cm²

5 The area of one side of a £2 coin is 6.33 cm².
What is its radius, to 1 dp?

6 A circular helipad has an area of 725 m².
Find its radius and its diameter, to the nearest whole metre.

7 A light bulb with a wattage W and resistance R needs an electrical current I given by $I = \sqrt{\frac{W}{R}}$. Calculate I for

a an old-style light bulb with $W = 60$ and $R = 960$

b a modern low-energy light bulb with $W = 12$ and $R = 4800$.

8 A sphere of radius r has a surface area A given by $A = 4\pi r^2$.

a If the surface area of a standard football is 1550 cm², calculate its radius.

b Use the Internet to find the dimensions of a standard (size 5) football and an indoor (size 4) football.

c Who would use the even smaller size 3 football?

11b Indices

- An **index** or **power** is used when a number or letter is multiplied by itself.
  $3^4 = 3 \times 3 \times 3 \times 3 \qquad y^5 = y \times y \times y \times y \times y$

You say '3 to the power 4' and 'y to the power 5'

Example

Simplify these expressions giving your answers as a power.

a $2^4 \times 2^3$ **b** $\frac{5^7}{5^4}$ **c** $(4^2)^3$

a $2^4 \times 2^3 = (2 \times 2 \times 2 \times 2) \times (2 \times 2 \times 2)$
$= 2^7$

b $\frac{5^7}{5^4} = \frac{5 \times 5 \times 5 \times 5 \times 5 \times 5 \times 5}{5 \times 5 \times 5 \times 5}$
$= 5 \times 5 \times 5$
$= 5^3$

c $(4^2)^3 = 4^2 \times 4^2 \times 4^2$
$= (4 \times 4) \times (4 \times 4) \times (4 \times 4)$
$= 4^6$

In part a, 3 + 4 = 7
In part b, 7 - 4 = 3
In part c, 2 × 3 = 6

There are three **rules** that you should know about indices.

- Rule 1: $x^a \times x^b = x^{a+b}$
- Rule 2: $\frac{x^a}{x^b} = x^{a-b}$
- Rule 3: $(x^a)^b = x^{a \times b}$

To use the rules, the base number must be the same.

You can apply the rules of indices to letters as well as numbers.

Example

Simplify **a** $\frac{z^4 \times z^6}{z^8}$ **b** $\frac{8(y^4)^3}{2y^2 \times y^7}$

a $\frac{z^4 \times z^6}{z^8} = \frac{z^{10}}{z^8}$
$= z^2$ using rule 1 and then rule 2.

b $\frac{8(y^4)^3}{2y^2 \times y^7} = \frac{8y^{12}}{2y^2 \times y^7}$
$= \frac{8y^{12}}{2y^9}$
$= 4y^3$ using rules 3, 1 and then 2.

Exercise 11b

You can only use the rules to simplify indices of the same letter.

1 Simplify these expressions, using indices in your answers.

a $a \times a \times a \times a$ **b** $y \times y \times y \times y \times y$

c $a \times a \times a \times a \times z \times z \times z$ **d** $r \times s \times s \times r \times r \times r \times s$

e $2 \times 2 \times p \times p \times 2 \times p$ **f** $3 \times a \times 3 \times y \times a \times a \times y$

2 Use the rule $x^a \times x^b = x^{a+b}$ to simplify these expressions.

a $x^4 \times x^5$ **b** $y^6 \times y^4$ **c** $z^7 \times z$ **d** $p \times p^5$

e $k^3 \times k^2 \times k$ **f** $a^4 \times a^2 \times a^3$ **g** $b^2 \times b^5 \times y^3 \times y^2$ **h** $q^2 \times q^4 \times r^6 \times r^3$

i $m^2 \times t^3 \times m^5 \times t^2$ **j** $a^2 \times b^3 \times a \times b^4$ **k** $x^2y^3 \times x^4y$ **l** $a^3b^4 \times a^3b^5$

3 Use the rule $\frac{x^a}{x^b} = x^{a-b}$ to simplify these expressions.

a $\frac{x^7}{x^3}$ **b** $\frac{y^8}{y^2}$ **c** $\frac{z^4}{z^3}$ **d** $\frac{a^7}{a^5}$ **e** $\frac{m^9}{m^4}$

f $\frac{a^8b^5}{a^2b^2}$ **g** $\frac{p^7q^6}{p^5q}$ **h** $\frac{x^3y^4}{xy^3}$ **i** $\frac{s^4t^3}{s^3t^2}$ **j** $\frac{y^4z^2}{y^4z}$

4 Use the rule $(x^a)^b = x^{a \times b}$ to simplify these expressions.

a $(x^2)^3$ **b** $(y^3)^2$ **c** $(z^5)^3$ **d** $(m^3)^5$ **e** $(n^4)^2$

f $(x^3y^4)^2$ **g** $(a^4b^2)^3$ **h** $(m^2n)^5$ **i** $(s^2t^4)^3$ **j** $(p^3q^4)^5$

5 Simplify these expressions.

a $2x^3 \times 4x^5$ **b** $6y^7 \times 3y^2$ **c** $\frac{8z^6}{4z^2}$ **d** $\frac{p^4 \times p^6}{p^7}$

e $\frac{q^6 \times q^4}{q^2 \times q^3}$ **f** $\frac{r^2 \times r^5}{r^4 \times r^2}$ **g** $\frac{8a^5 \times a^6}{2a^7}$ **h** $\frac{3c^5 \times 4c^6}{6c^8}$

i $\frac{5x^6 \times 4x^3}{10x^8}$ **j** $\frac{6(x^4)^3}{3x^2}$ **k** $\frac{12(y^5)^3}{4y^7 \times y^3}$ **l** $3(y^3)^2 \times 5y^4$

Problem solving

6 A billion in the USA is a thousand million = $10^3 \times 10^6$.

A billion in the UK can also mean a million million = $10^6 \times 10^6$.

A US trillion is (a million)^2

A UK trillion is (a million)^3

Write these four numbers in the form 10^a.

Did you know?

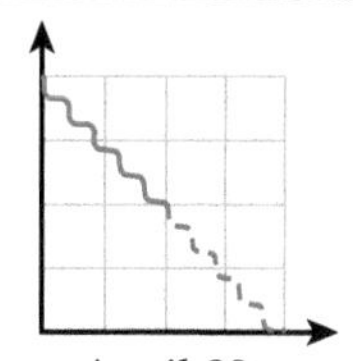

In April 2009, the International Monetary Fund warned that 'credit crunch' losses could reach \$4 trillion.

7 **a** Work out the value of $\frac{2^3}{2^3}$

i using $\frac{2 \times 2 \times 2}{2 \times 2 \times 2}$ **ii** using rule 2.

What can you say about the value of 2^0 and x^0?

b Work out the value of

i $9^{\frac{1}{2}} \times 9^{\frac{1}{2}}$ **ii** $\sqrt{9} \times \sqrt{9}$

What can you say about the value of $9^{\frac{1}{2}}$ and $x^{\frac{1}{2}}$?

11c Indices and surds

Most square roots cannot be written as exact decimals.

$\sqrt{9} = 3$ but $\sqrt{10} = 3.1622776 \ldots$

It is more accurate to leave these numbers in **surd** form.

You can carry out calculations with surds without converting to decimals.

- A **surd** is a square root that cannot be expressed accurately as a decimal.

- You can multiply numbers written in surd form.
  $\sqrt{a} \times \sqrt{b} = \sqrt{a \times b} = \sqrt{ab}$

$\sqrt{5} \times \sqrt{2} = \sqrt{5 \times 2} = \sqrt{10}$ and $\sqrt{5} \times \sqrt{5} = \sqrt{5 \times 5} = \sqrt{25} = 5$

- You can use the multiplication rule to **simplify** surds.

Example

Write these surds in their simplest form.

a $\sqrt{27}$ b $\sqrt{32}$

a $\sqrt{27} = \sqrt{9 \times 3} = \sqrt{9} \times \sqrt{3} = 3 \times \sqrt{3} = 3\sqrt{3}$

b $\sqrt{32} = \sqrt{16 \times 2} = \sqrt{16} \times \sqrt{2} = 4 \times \sqrt{2} = 4\sqrt{2}$

- You can multiply numbers written in simplified surd form.

Example

Calculate

a $2\sqrt{5} \times 3\sqrt{5}$ b $2\sqrt{5} \times 3\sqrt{2}$

a $2\sqrt{5} \times 3\sqrt{5} = (2 \times 3) \times (\sqrt{5} \times \sqrt{5}) = 6 \times 5 = 30$

b $2\sqrt{5} \times 3\sqrt{2} = (2 \times 3) \times \sqrt{5 \times 2} = 6 \times \sqrt{10} = 6\sqrt{10}$

- A square root is a number raised to the power $\frac{1}{2}$.
- A cube root is a number raised to the power $\frac{1}{3}$.

You can use a calculator to evaluate indices.

Example

Write these square roots and cube roots in index notation.

a $\sqrt{4}$ b $\sqrt{10}$ c $\sqrt[3]{8}$ d $\sqrt[3]{10}$

a $\sqrt{4} = 4^{\frac{1}{2}}$ b $\sqrt{10} = 10^{\frac{1}{2}}$

c $\sqrt[3]{8} = 8^{\frac{1}{3}}$ d $\sqrt[3]{10} = 10^{\frac{1}{3}}$

Exercise 11c

1 Use the x^2 and $\sqrt{\ }$ buttons on your calculator to evaluate these amounts.

a **i** 1.73^2 **ii** $\sqrt{3}$

b **i** 2.24^2 **ii** $\sqrt{5}$

c **i** 2.65^2 **ii** $\sqrt{7}$

d **i** 3.32^2 **ii** $\sqrt{11}$

Explain why your answers to part **i** and **ii** are different.

Did you know?

$\sqrt{2} = 1.41421356237...$

Around **500 BC** Hippasus of Metapontum proved that $\sqrt{2}$ could not be written as a fraction. According to legend, this so upset his fellow Pythagoreans that they drowned him!

2 Calculate the following leaving your answers in surd form.

a $\sqrt{3} \times \sqrt{3}$ **b** $\sqrt{4} \times \sqrt{4}$ **c** $\sqrt{5} \times \sqrt{3}$ **d** $\sqrt{6} \times \sqrt{2}$

e $\sqrt{7} \times \sqrt{3}$ **f** $\sqrt{2} \times \sqrt{18}$ **g** $\sqrt{2} \times \sqrt{32}$ **h** $\sqrt{5} \times \sqrt{20}$

i $\sqrt{27} \times \sqrt{3}$ **j** $\sqrt{8} \times \sqrt{18}$ **k** $\sqrt{8} \times \sqrt{7}$ **l** $\sqrt{8} \times \sqrt{50}$

m $\sqrt{20} \times \sqrt{45}$ **n** $\sqrt{6} \times \sqrt{24}$ **o** $\sqrt{12} \times \sqrt{5}$ **p** $\sqrt{5} \times \sqrt{45}$

3 Write these numbers in their simplest form.

a $\sqrt{12}$ **b** $\sqrt{8}$ **c** $\sqrt{18}$ **d** $\sqrt{24}$ **e** $\sqrt{40}$

f $\sqrt{48}$ **g** $\sqrt{32}$ **h** $\sqrt{50}$ **i** $\sqrt{72}$ **j** $\sqrt{98}$

4 Calculate the following leaving your answers in surd form.

a $2\sqrt{3} \times 3\sqrt{3}$ **b** $3\sqrt{2} \times \sqrt{2}$ **c** $4\sqrt{5} \times 2\sqrt{3}$ **d** $3\sqrt{6} \times 2\sqrt{2}$

e $4\sqrt{7} \times 2\sqrt{3}$ **f** $3\sqrt{2} \times 4\sqrt{5}$ **g** $\sqrt{2} \times 2\sqrt{3}$ **h** $\sqrt{5} \times 3\sqrt{20}$

i $3\sqrt{5} \times 4\sqrt{5}$ **j** $4\sqrt{3} \times \sqrt{27}$ **k** $2\sqrt{2} \times \sqrt{32}$ **l** $3\sqrt{8} \times 4\sqrt{18}$

5 Write these numbers using index notation.

a $\sqrt{8}$ **b** $\sqrt[3]{8}$ **c** $\sqrt{18}$ **d** $\sqrt[3]{24}$ **e** $\sqrt[3]{40}$

6 Work out the value of each of these expressions.

a 3^2 **b** $9^{\frac{1}{2}}$ **c** $8^{\frac{1}{3}}$ **d** $16^{\frac{1}{2}}$

e $64^{\frac{1}{3}}$ **f** $27^{\frac{1}{3}}$ **g** $25^{\frac{1}{2}}$ **h** $125^{\frac{1}{3}}$

i $144^{\frac{1}{2}}$ **j** $64^{\frac{1}{2}}$ **k** $1000^{\frac{1}{3}}$ **l** $81^{\frac{1}{2}}$

Problem solving

7 **a** Calculate the area of this triangle.

b Calculate the length of the missing side, leaving your answer as a surd in its simplest form.

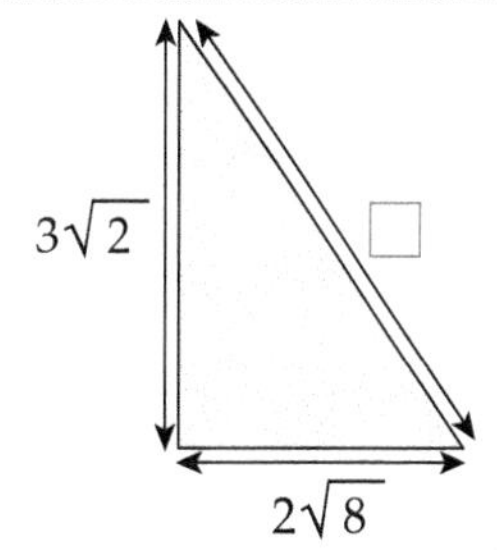

11d Standard form for large numbers

- The decimal system is based upon **powers** of 10. You can write all powers of ten using **index notation**.

The power is also called the index.

1 million (mega)	= 1 000 000	= 10 × 10 × 10 × 10 × 10 × 10	= 10^6
1 thousand (kilo)	= 1000	= 10 × 10 × 10	= 10^3
1 hundred	= 100	= 10 × 10	= 10^2
1 ten	= 10	= 10	= 10^1
1 unit	= 1		= 10^0
1 tenth	= $\frac{1}{10}$ = 0.1	= $\frac{1}{10^1}$	= 10^{-1}
1 hundredth (centi)	= $\frac{1}{100}$ = 0.01	= $\frac{1}{10^2}$	= 10^{-2}
1 thousandth (milli)	= $\frac{1}{1000}$ = 0.001	= $\frac{1}{10^3}$	= 10^{-3}

Any number to the power of zero is equal to 1.

- To multiply by a positive power of ten, 10^n, move the digits n places to the left of the decimal point.

Example

Write out in full

a 3.3×10^3 **b** 2.75×10^5.

a $3.3 \times 10^3 = 3.3 \times 1000$
$= 3300$

Th	H	T	U	•	$\frac{1}{10}$
			3	•	3
3	3	0	0		

b $2.75 \times 10^5 = 2.75 \times 100\,000$
$= 275\,000$

The digits move to the left of the decimal point.

3.3×10^3 and 2.75×10^5 are in **standard index form**.

You can use powers of 10 to write very large numbers.

- In **standard index form**, a number is written as $A \times 10^n$.
  - A is a number between 1 and 10 (but not including 10).
  - n is an integer.

Example

Write these numbers in standard index form

a 6700 **b** 26 000 000.

Divide the number by a power of 10 so that it becomes a decimal between 1 and 10.

a $6700 \div 1000 = 6.7$
$6700 = 6.7 \times 1000$
$= 6.7 \times 10^3$

b $26\,000\,000 \div 10\,000\,000 = 2.6$
$26\,000\,000 = 2.6 \times 10\,000\,000$
$= 2.6 \times 10^7$

The digits move to the right of the decimal point.

Exercise 11d

1 Each of these numbers is in standard index form.
Write out each number in full.

a 3.7×10^2 b 4.7×10^3 c 1.23×10^6 d 4.02×10^7
e 3.01×10^6 f 4.9×10^9 g 7.37×10^{11} h 1.004×10^6

2 Write each of these numbers in standard index form.

a 230 b 4870 c 340000 d 78000000
e 4100000000 f 2380000 g 238.3 h 3878.8

3 Calculate the following, giving your answers in standard form.

a $3.6 \times 10^4 + 2.2 \times 10^4$ b $3.8 \times 10^4 - 1.2 \times 10^4$

4 Write each of these numbers in standard index form.

a 27×10^1 b 573×10^2 c 0.53×10^4 d 34.2×10^3
e 3010×10^4 f 0.492×10^6 g 0.048×10^5 h 0.000378×10^8

Problem solving

5 Round each of these numbers to the nearest thousand.
Give your answers in standard form.

a 5.3×10^3 b 2.85×10^4 c 4.1365×10^5 d 3.5072×10^4

6 Write each of these numbers in standard index form.

a The population of Maryport is 35600.
b The population of the UK in 1990 was 59 million.
c The speed of light is 186000 miles per second.
d The nearest star is 24790000000000 miles away.

7 Put these numbers in order from smallest to largest.

a 2.6×10^3, 2.5×10^4, 270, 2.55×10^4, 2.58×10^3
b 3×10^{12}, 2.8×10^{14}, 2.9×10^{13}, 2980000000000000

8 a Carla flies 3.6×10^3 miles in 6 hours. What is the average speed of the plane?
b Keiley wins €1.3×10^7 in a lottery. She spends €3.85×10^5 on a new house and €32500 on a new car. How much money does she have left?

Did you know?

As of 2007, the amount of data stored worldwide was 295 exabytes, that's the same as over a billion hard drives!

9 Complete these statements; the first one is done for you.

a $5 \times 10^n = 50 \times 10^{\square} = 50 \times 10^{n-1}$ b $0.5 \times 10^n = 5000 \times 10^{\square}$
c $500 \times 10^n = 5 \times 10^{\square}$ d $500000 \times 10^n = 50 \times 10^{\square}$

11e Standard form for small numbers

- Negative **powers** can be thought of as '1 divided by':
  $10^{-4} = \frac{1}{10^4} = \frac{1}{10000}$.

You can multiply or divide by a negative power of 10.

Multiplying by $\frac{1}{1000}$ is the same as dividing by 1000.
Dividing by $\frac{1}{100}$ is the same as multiplying by 100.

Example

Calculate

a 330×10^{-3} **b** $27.5 \div 10^{-2}$

a $330 \times 10^{-3} = 330 \times \frac{1}{1000}$
$= 330 \div 1000$
$= 0.33$

H	T	U	•	$\frac{1}{10}$	$\frac{1}{100}$
3	3	0			
		0	•	3	3

b $27.5 \div 10^{-2} = 27.5 \div \frac{1}{100}$
$= 27.5 \times 100$
$= 2750$

Th	H	T	U	•	$\frac{1}{10}$
		2	7	•	5
2	7	5	0		

- To write a small number in **standard index form** write it as a number between 1 and 10 multiplied by a negative power of 10.

Example

Write these numbers in standard index form.

a 0.67 **b** 0.000026

Rewrite the number as a decimal between 1 and 10 divided by a power of 10.

a $0.67 = 6.7 \div 10$
$= 6.7 \div 10^1$

b $0.000026 = 2.6 \div 100000$
$= 2.6 \div 10^5$

Write the number in standard form using a negative power of 10.

$= 6.7 \times \frac{1}{10^1} = 6.7 \times 10^{-1}$

$= 2.6 \times \frac{1}{10^5} = 2.6 \times 10^{-5}$

Dividing by 10^5 is the same as multiplying by $\frac{1}{10^5} = 10^{-5}$.

- You can use a calculator to work with numbers written in standard form by using the exp button.

Your calculator might have a different key.

Example

Calculate $(3.2 \times 10^4) \times (2.5 \times 10^3)$.

Enter the numbers on the calculator using the exp button

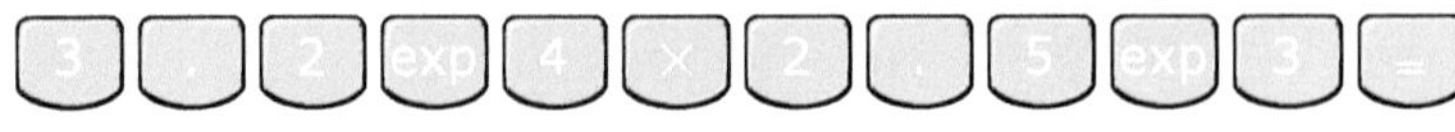

The calculator display will show

You can interpret this answer as 8×10^7.

Exercise 11e

1 Calculate the following.

a	$47 \div 10^2$	**b**	$2900 \div 10^3$	**c**	$123 \div 10^4$	**d**	$4 \div 10^5$
e	31.8×10^{-4}	**f**	$39\,000 \times 10^{-2}$	**g**	0.3×10^{-3}	**h**	2.4×10^{-2}

2 Each of these numbers is in standard index form. Write each number as a decimal.

a	2.8×10^{-2}	**b**	3.6×10^{-3}	**c**	9.34×10^{-4}	**d**	5.13×10^{-3}
e	4.92×10^{-5}	**f**	3.8×10^{-6}	**g**	6.25×10^{-8}	**h**	1.234×10^{-10}

3 Write each of these numbers in standard index form.

a	0.3	**b**	0.48	**c**	0.034	**d**	0.00078
e	0.000 003	**f**	0.0067	**g**	0.00 000 456	**h**	0.000 000 000 024

4 Put these numbers in order from smallest to largest.

2×10^{-8}, 1.8×10^{-7}, 2.3×10^{-8}, 2.2×10^{-7}

5 Use your calculator to evaluate the following, giving your answers in standard form.

a $(6.5 \times 10^3) \times (2.4 \times 10^5)$ **b** $(6.5 \times 10^3) + (2.4 \times 10^5)$

c $(6.5 \times 10^{-3}) \div (2.4 \times 10^{-5})$ **d** $(6.5 \times 10^{-3}) - (2.4 \times 10^{-5})$

Problem solving

6 Write each of these numbers in standard index form.

a A millipede is 0.094 inches long.

b The diameter of a human blood cell is 0.000 000 68 m.

7 Write these measurements in standard form.

a One hundredth of a kilometre

b Three thousandths of a gram

c Five millionths of a litre

d 11 thousandths of a metre

8 Calculate the following, giving your answers in standard form.

a A light year is 9.43×10^{12} km. A star is 12.4 light years from Earth. How far away is the star in km?

b The population of India is 1.05×10^9 and India has a land area of 3.3×10^6 km^2.
On average how many people live in each square kilometre of India?

Did you know?

The most densely populated country on Earth is Monaco with 1.7×10^4 people/km^2. The average population density of Earth is 45 people/km^2.

11 MySummary

Check out

You should now be able to ...

Test it ➡

Questions

	Level	Questions
✓ Find square roots.	6	1
✓ Find cube roots.	6	2
✓ Use the rules of indices.	7	3
✓ Simplify surds.	8	4 – 8
✓ Convert to and from standard index form.	7	9 – 10

Language	Meaning	Example
Square root	The square root of any number is the number which, when multiplied by itself, gives the starting number.	The square root of 81 is 9 because 9×9 is 81.
Cube root	The cube root of any number is the number which, when multiplied by itself and then multiplied by itself again, gives the starting number.	The cube root of 27 is 3 because $3 \times 3 \times 3$ is 27.
Index / power	The index or power tells you how many times to multiply a number by itself.	In 4^3, the index or power is 3. This represents $4 \times 4 \times 4$.
Surds	A root that cannot be written as a fraction, or as a terminating or recurring decimal.	$\sqrt{2}$ is in surd form – the decimal value cannot be given completely.
Standard index form	A short way of writing very large or very small numbers. A standard index form number is a number between 1 and 10 multiplied by a power of 10: $A \times 10^n$	42 000 can be written as 4.2×10^4 in standard form. 0.000 42 can be written as 4.2×10^{-4} in standard form.

11 MyReview

1 Use prime factors to find these square roots.

a $\sqrt{576}$ **b** $\sqrt{1225}$

2 Use trial and improvement to find these roots to 1 dp.

a $\sqrt{700}$ **b** $\sqrt[3]{200}$

3 Simplify these expressions, using indices in your answers.

a $a \times a \times 3$

b $b \times 2 \times b \times 3 \times c \times c \times b$

c $d^2 \times 4 \times d^3 \times d$

d $e^4 \times e^6 \times f^2 \times f$

e $g^3h^2 \times h^4g$

f $\frac{i^6}{i^5}$

g $\frac{j^4k^7}{j^2k}$

h $(m^2)^4$

i $(n^3p^2)^5$

j $\frac{4q^3 \times 7q^6}{14q^4}$

k $\frac{8(sr^3)^2}{2r^4s}$

4 Calculate the following.

a $\sqrt{5} \times \sqrt{5}$ **b** $\sqrt{9} \times \sqrt{4}$

c $\sqrt{6} \times \sqrt{24}$ **d** $\sqrt{8} \times \sqrt{50}$

5 Write these numbers in their simplest form.

a $\sqrt{28}$ **b** $\sqrt{72}$

c $\sqrt{125}$ **d** $\sqrt{363}$

6 Calculate the following leaving your answers in surd form.

a $\sqrt{3} \times \sqrt{6}$ **b** $2\sqrt{5} \times \sqrt{3}$

c $3\sqrt{7} \times 2\sqrt{21}$ **d** $5\sqrt{2} \times 3\sqrt{24}$

7 Write these numbers using index notation.

a $\sqrt{3}$ **b** $\sqrt[3]{4}$

c $\sqrt{7}$ **d** $\sqrt[3]{10}$

8 Work out the value of each of these expressions.

a $25^{\frac{1}{2}}$ **b** $1000^{\frac{1}{3}}$

c $121^{\frac{1}{2}}$ **d** $64^{\frac{1}{3}}$

9 Write each of the numbers out in full.

a 8.2×10^7 **b** 5.42×10^3

c 3.1×10^{-4} **d** 6.09×10^{-6}

10 Write each number in standard form.

a 5600 **b** 873000

c 0.062 **d** 0.000107

e 24.5×10^5 **f** 0.42×10^{-1}

What next?

Score	
0 – 4	Your knowledge of this topic is still developing. To improve look at Formative test: 3B-11; MyMaths: 1033, 1049, 1050, 1051, 1053, 1057 and 1064
5 – 8	You are gaining a secure knowledge of this topic. To improve look at InvisiPen: 181, 182, 183, 184, 185, and 186
9, 10	You have mastered this topic. Well done, you are ready to progress!

11 MyPractice

1 Work out these square roots.

a $\sqrt{1600}$ b $\sqrt{4900}$

c $\sqrt{14400}$ d $\sqrt{\frac{81}{100}}$

2 Use trial and improvement to find these roots to 1 dp.
You could use tables like the ones on the right.

a $\sqrt{38}$ b $\sqrt{62}$

c $\sqrt[3]{38}$ d $\sqrt[3]{250}$

Check your answers by finding squares or cubes.

x	x^2	Comment

x	x^3	Comment

3 A circle of radius r has an area $A = \pi r^2$.

a Find A to 1 decimal place when $r = 6$ cm.

b Find r to 1 decimal place when $A = 240\,\text{cm}^2$.

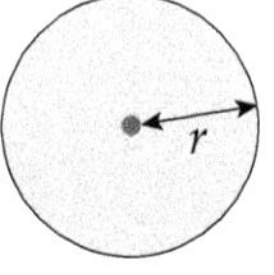

4 An ice cube has a volume of $10\,\text{cm}^3$.
Find the length x of its edges, to 1 dp.

5 Simplify these expressions using indices in your answers.

a $y \times y \times y \times y \times y$ b $a \times a \times a \times a \times a \times a$

c $x \times x \times z \times z \times x$ d $m \times n \times m \times m \times n \times n$

e $n \times 4 \times n \times n \times 4$ f $3 \times c \times c \times 3 \times 3 \times c$

6 Use the rules of indices to simplify these expressions.

a $x^6 \times x^7$ b $3a^3 \times a^5$ c $2x^6 \times 4x^7$

d $a^2 \times b^4 \times a^3 \times b^2$ e $s^3t^2 \times s^4t$ f $x^3y^4 \times x^2y^3$

g $\frac{x^8}{x^2}$ h $\frac{m^6n^2}{m^3}$ i $\frac{x^8y^5}{x^2y^3}$

j $(x^4)^2$ k $(2y^5)^3$ l $(m^3n^4)^4$

11c

7 Use the x^2 and $\sqrt{\ }$ keys on your calculator to work out these amounts.
Give answers to 2 dp where appropriate.

a 2.25^2 b 3.14^2 c 6.01^2
d $\sqrt{10}$ e $\sqrt{20}$ f $\sqrt{62}$

8 Calculate the following, leaving your answers in surd form.

a $\sqrt{3} \times \sqrt{4}$ b $\sqrt{5} \times \sqrt{2}$ c $\sqrt{6} \times \sqrt{3}$
d $2\sqrt{3} \times \sqrt{8}$ e $\sqrt{7} \times 3\sqrt{3}$ f $2\sqrt{7} \times \sqrt{4}$

9 Write these amounts using index notation.

a $\sqrt{10}$ b $\sqrt{12}$ c $\sqrt[3]{5}$ d $\sqrt[3]{50}$

11d

10 Each of these numbers is in standard index form.
Write out each number in full.

a 4.2×10^2 b 5.1×10^3
c 4.38×10^5 d 3.09×10^6
e 2.001×10^7 f 7.281×10^8

11 Write each number in standard index form.

a 270 b 3190
c 42 875 d 38 291
e 491 500 f 2 810 000

11e

12 Each of these numbers is in standard index form.
Write each number as a decimal.

a 3.1×10^{-1} b 2.9×10^{-2}
c 9.25×10^{-4} d 6.19×10^{-6}
e 3.25×10^{-8} f 1.9871×10^{-9}

13 Write each number in standard index form.

a 0.2 b 0.58
c 0.075 d 0.00089
e 0.000 009 f 0.0078
g 0.00 000 567 h 0.000 000 000 037

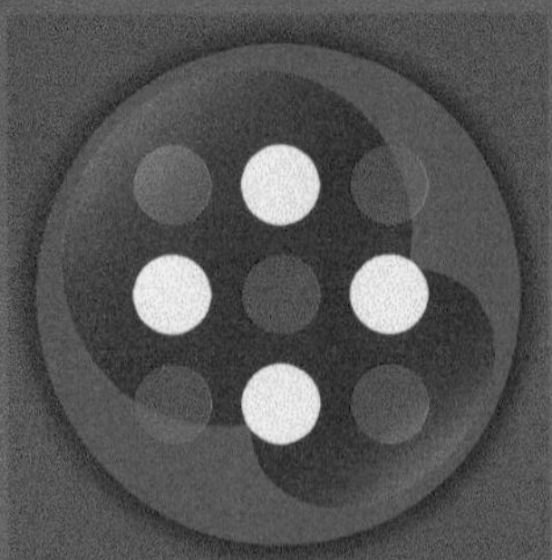

12 Constructions and Pythagoras

Introduction

How do you build a pyramid? The Great Pyramid of Giza is one of the seven wonders of the ancient world. It was completed in approximately 2560 BC and took about 20 years to build. At its time and for the next 3000 years it was the tallest building in the world!

What's the point?

To construct any complex building requires accurate scale drawings and mathematical calculations for all the dimensions.

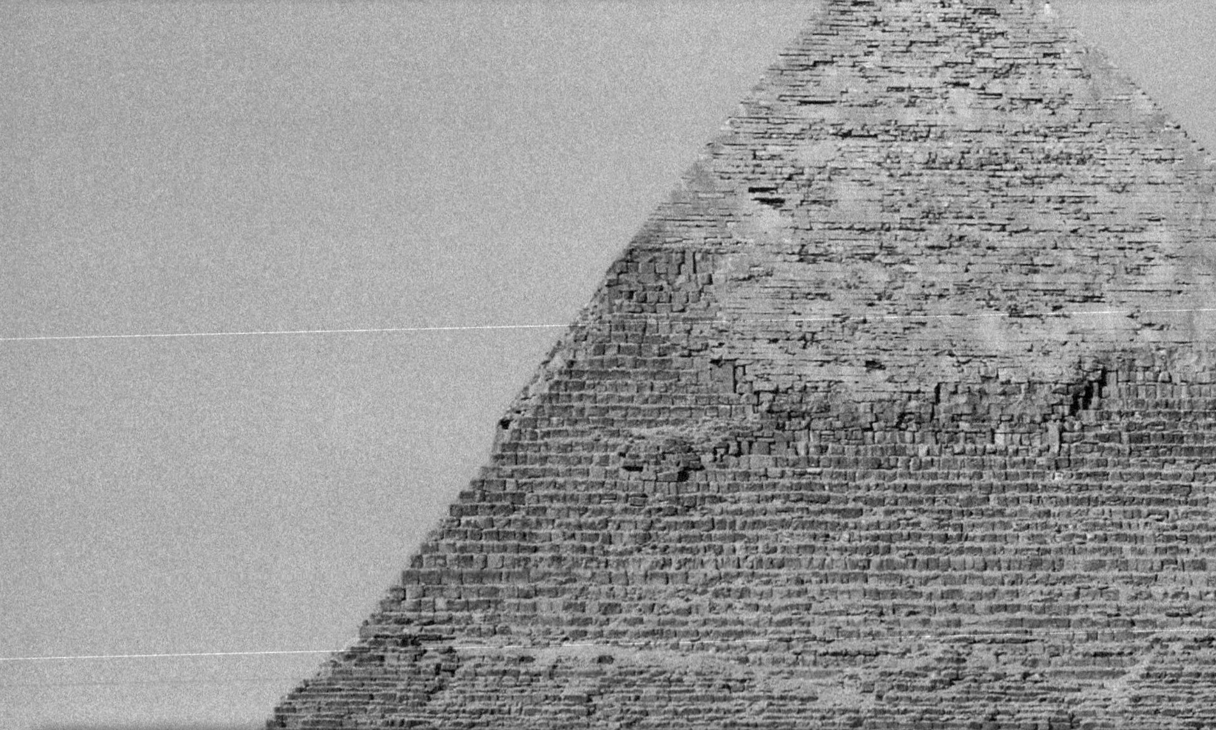

Objectives

By the end of this chapter, you will have learned how to …

- Construct triangles and line and angle bisectors.
- Find loci.

Check in

1 Draw angles of these sizes.

a 40° **b** 72° **c** 139° **d** 253° **e** 312°

2 Work out:

a 3^2 **b** 12^2 **c** $\sqrt{81}$ **d** $\sqrt{196}$

3 Plot these points on a grid:

a (2, 3) **b** (-2, 1) **c** (-1, -2) **d** (3, -2)

Starter problem

The Great Pyramid of Giza was built to a height of 146.5 m and has a square base of side 230.4 m.

Design and build an accurate scale model of the pyramid.

12a Constructing a triangle 1

In order to **construct** a **unique** triangle using a ruler and **protractor**, you need to be given the right information.

- You will always construct a unique triangle if you are given
  - two sides and the **included** angle (SAS) or
  - two angles and the included side (ASA).

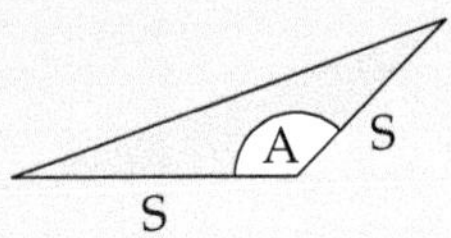

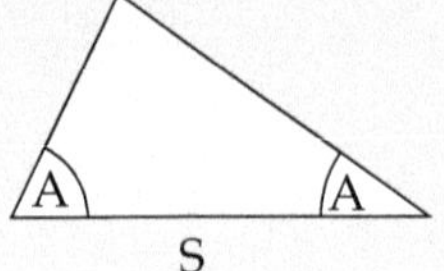

Example

Construct triangles ABC and PQR where

a AB = 6 cm, angle A = 60° and AC = 3 cm

b angle Q = 45°, angle R = 30° and QR = 5 cm.

a

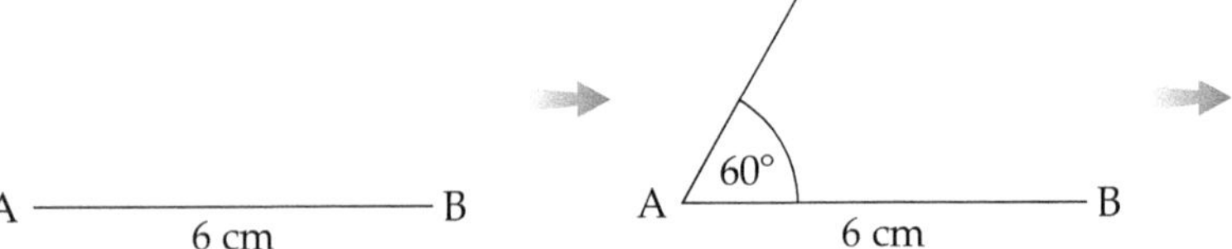

Draw a base line of 6 cm with your ruler.

Draw an angle of 60° at A with your protractor.

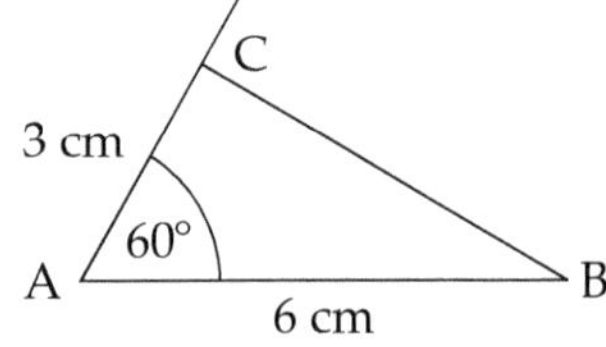

Measure 3 cm along the line and label it C.
Join B and C.

b

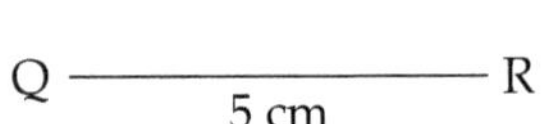

Draw a base line of 5 cm with your ruler.

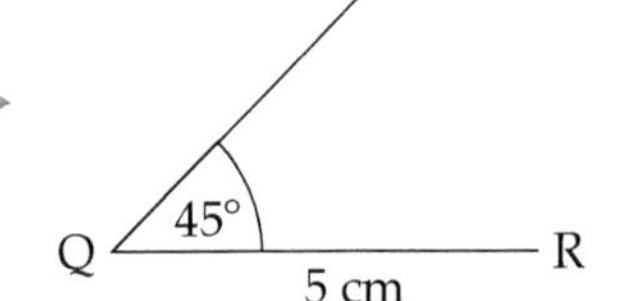

Draw an angle of 45° at Q with your protractor.

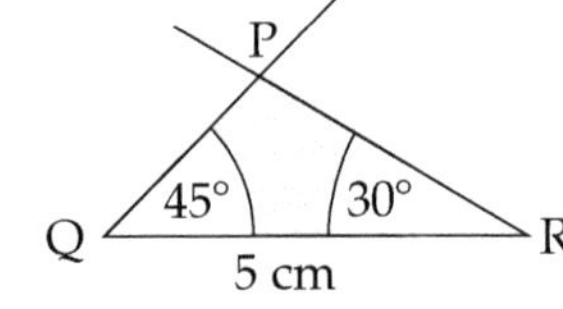

Draw an angle of 30° at R and mark where the lines cross P.

Gillian and Chris both constructed triangle PQR. Gillian's answer is shown in the example above but Chris's triangle looks different – what happened?
They both used the same ASA information so the triangles are congruent – identical in size and shape.

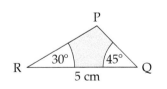

One is a reflection of the other!

Exercise 12a

1 Using a ruler and protractor, construct each triangle and give its mathematical name.

a 6 cm, 40°, 4 cm
b 45°, 5.5 cm
c 50 mm, 60°, 50 mm
d 75°, 25°, 6 cm
e 40°, 45°, 7.5 cm
f 72°, 48°, 4.2 cm

2 Draw a sketch and then construct these triangles.
Measure and calculate the perimeter of each triangle.

a AB = 6.5 cm, angle A = 40°, angle B = 45°
b QR = 6 cm, PR = 5 cm, angle R = 50°
c XY = 5 cm, angle X = 35°, angle Y = 55°

3 Construct these quadrilaterals using a ruler and protractor. Give the mathematical name of the quadrilateral and measure the length of the unknown diagonal.

a

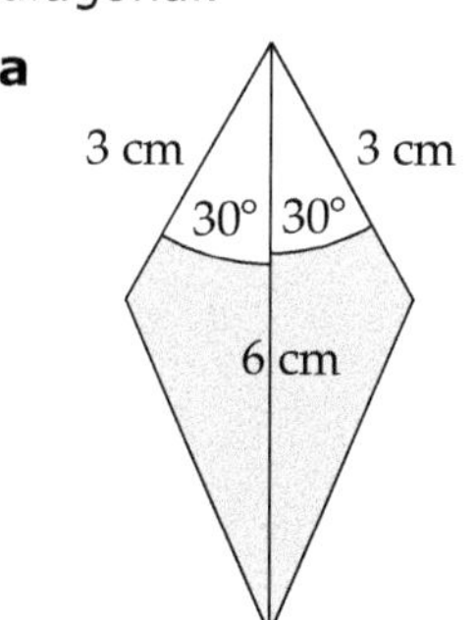

b

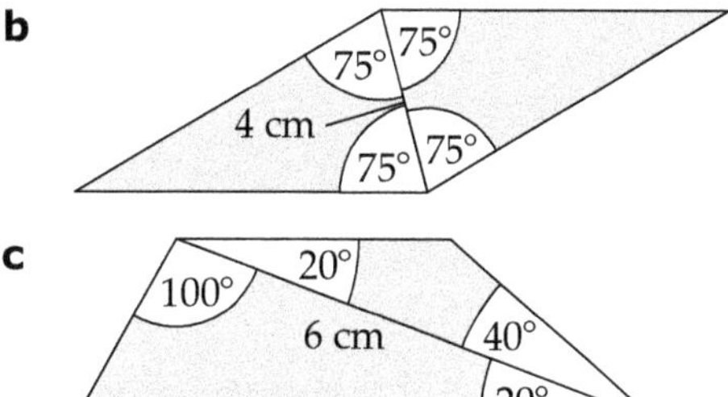

c 100°, 20°, 6 cm, 40°, 20°

Problem solving

4 The diagonal of a square lawn measures 8 metres.

a Construct a scale drawing of the lawn using a scale of 1 centimetre representing 1 metre.
b What is the perimeter of the lawn?

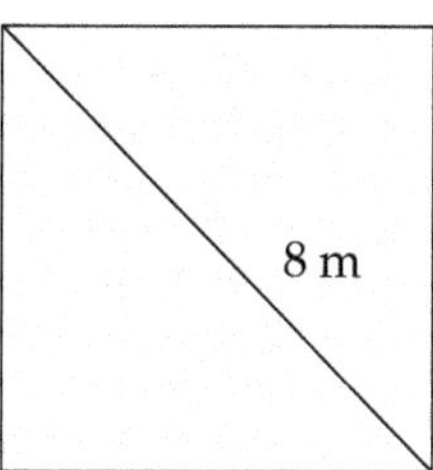

5 **a** Use four of these congruent right-angled triangles to accurately construct these shapes.

- **i** a square
- **ii** a rectangle
- **iii** a right-angled triangle
- **iv** an isosceles trapezium
- **v** a different isosceles trapezium.

b Measure the perimeter of each shape.

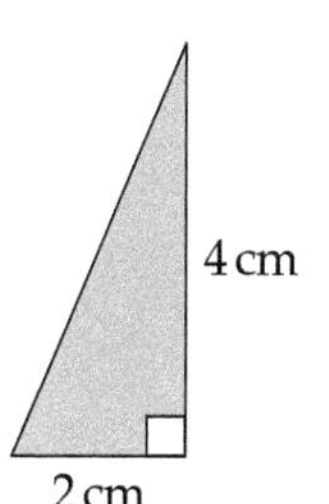

Did you know?

The impossible triangle was first drawn by the graphic artist Oscar Reutersvärd. It was popularised by father and son Lionel and Roger Penrose in 1958.

12b Constructing a triangle 2

There are two other ways, beside SAS and ASA, to uniquely specify a triangle.

- You will always **construct** a unique triangle if you are given
  - ▶ three sides (SSS) **or** ▶ a right angle, the **hypotenuse** and a side (RHS).

S S S

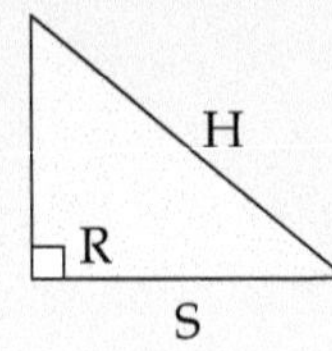

The hypotenuse is the longest side in a right-angled triangle.

Example

Construct these triangles.

a

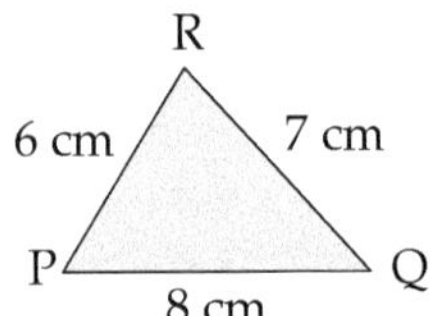

b

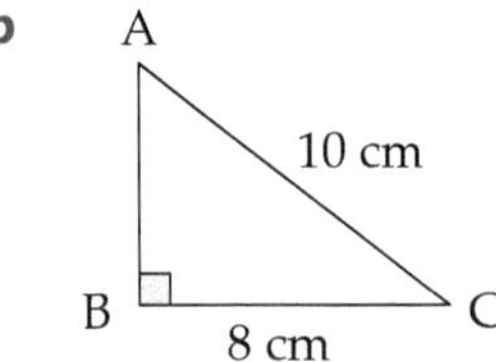

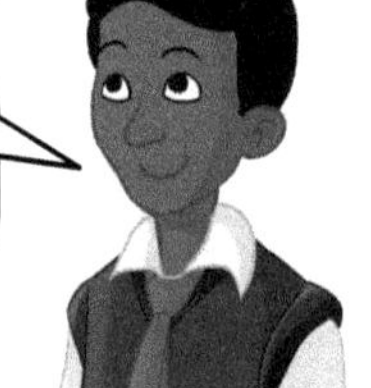

Part **a** is SSS.
Part **b** is RHS.

a

Draw a base line of 8 cm with your ruler.

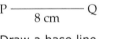

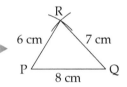

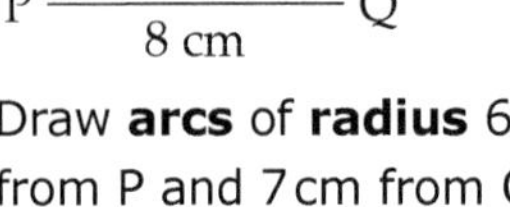

Draw **arcs** of **radius** 6 cm from P and 7 cm from Q with your compasses.

Label the point where the arcs cross R. Add lines RP and RQ.

b

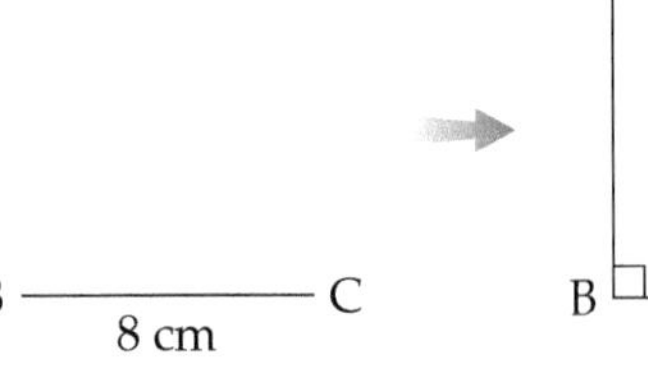

Draw a base line of 8 cm with your ruler.

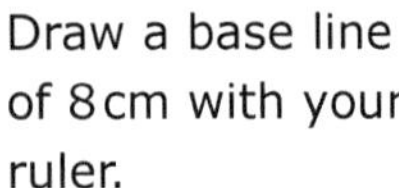

Draw an angle of 90° at B with your protractor.

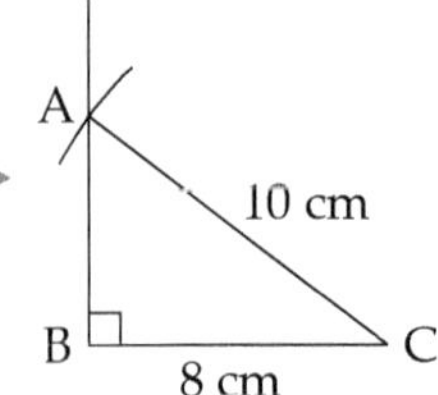

Draw an arc 10 cm from C. Label the point where the arc cuts the **perpendicular** A. Add lines AB and AC.

Do not rub out the construction lines.

Exercise 12b

1 Construct these isosceles triangles.
Measure each angle in the triangles.

a

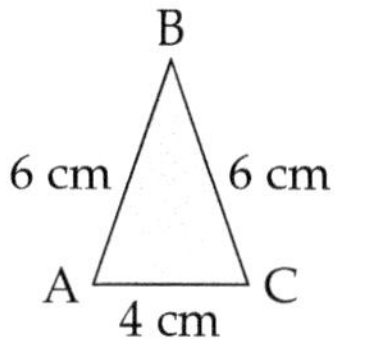

b

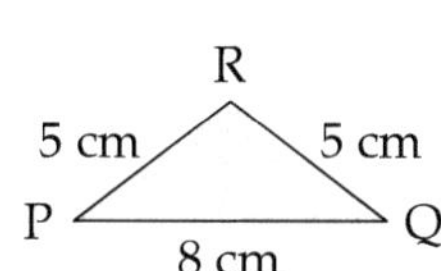

c **d**

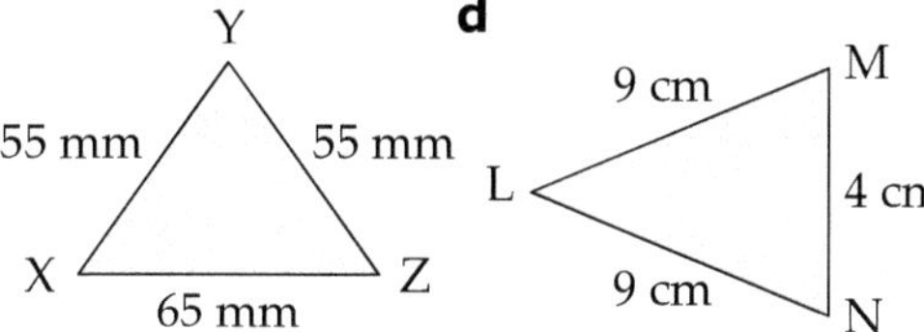

2 Construct these right-angled triangles.
Measure the perimeter of each triangle.

a **b**

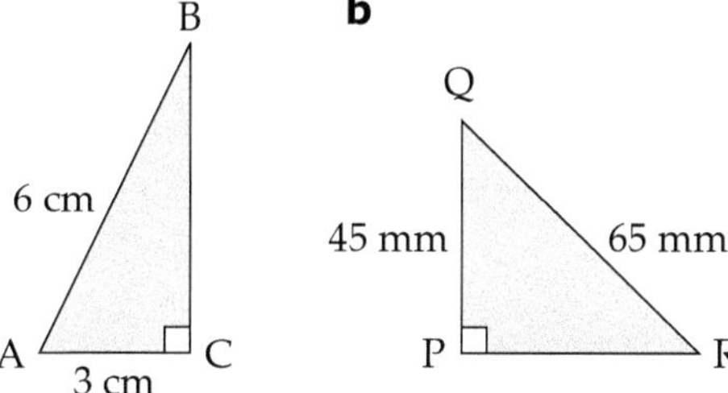

c

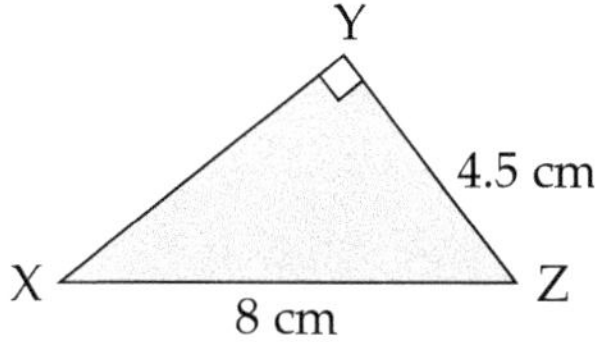

3 Two equilateral triangles of side 4 cm are joined together to form a rhombus.

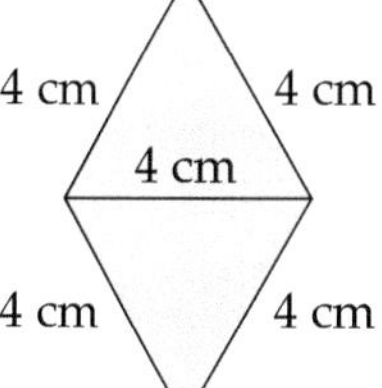

a Using ruler and compasses, construct the rhombus.

b Measure the long diagonal.

c Use a protractor and ruler to check that the diagonals of a rhombus are perpendicular and **bisect** each other.

4 A 5-metre ladder is put against a wall. The foot of the ladder is 2 metres from the wall.

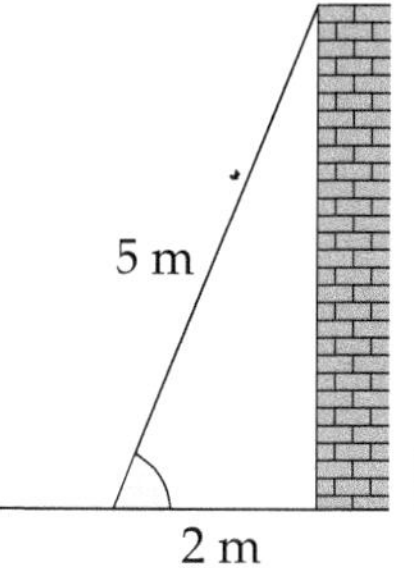

a Construct a scale drawing of the ladder using a scale of 1 centimetre representing 1 metre.

b Measure the angle between the ladder and the ground.

p.172 ›

Problem solving

5 Construct a triangle with sides of length 3 cm, 3.5 cm and 4 cm.
Construct **congruent** triangles to form a **tessellation**.
Use three different colours to show the angles that are equal in the tessellation.

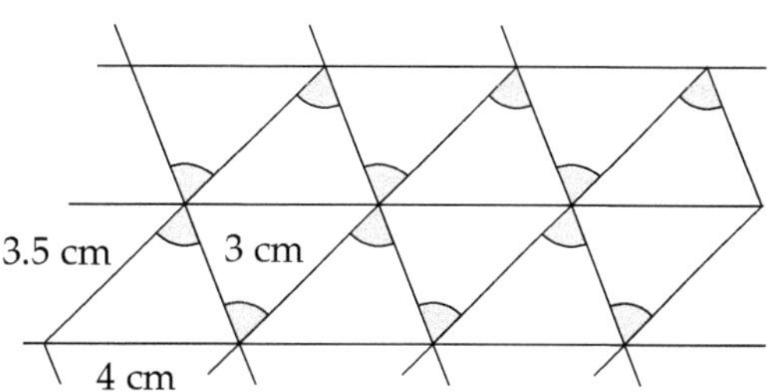

6 Is it possible to construct a triangle with lengths 9 cm, 3 cm and 3 cm?
Explain your answer.

12c Loci and constructions

You can **construct perpendiculars** and **bisectors** using compasses.
Do not adjust your compasses between drawing the arcs.

A perpendicular from a point to a line

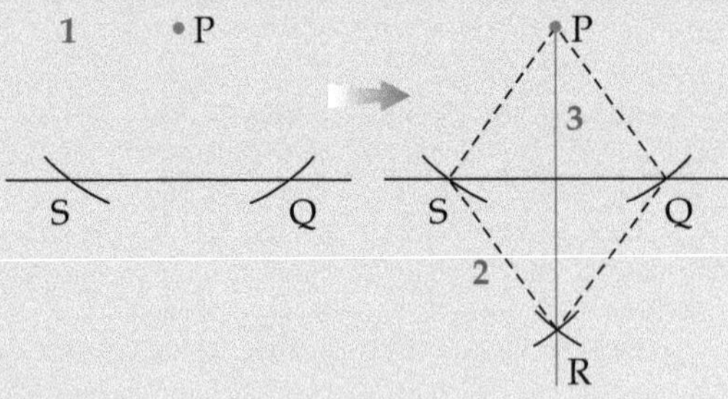

1. Draw arcs equidistant from P cutting the line at Q and S.
2. Using Q and S as centres, draw arcs below the line that cross at R.
3. Draw the line PR.

A perpendicular from a point on a line

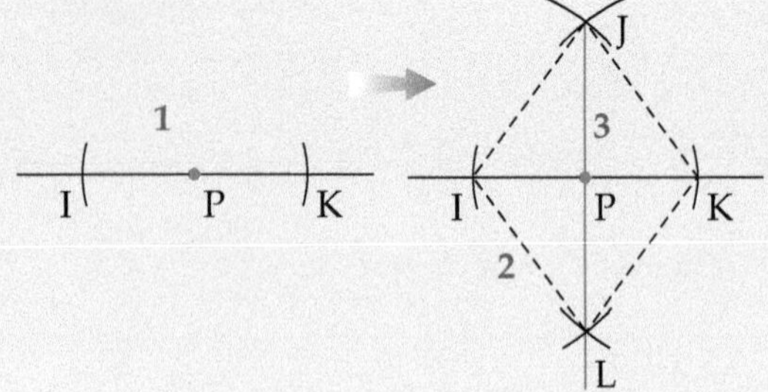

1. Draw arcs equidistant from P cutting the line at I and K.
2. Using I and K as centres, draw arcs above and below the line that cross at J and L.
3. Draw the line JL.

An angle bisector

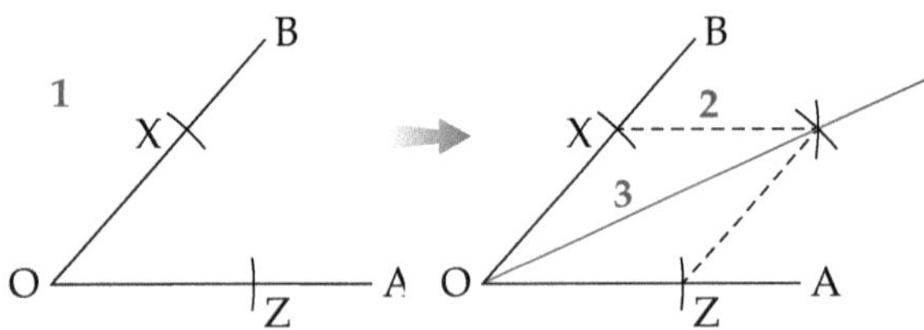

1. Draw arcs equidistant from O cutting OA and OB at Z and X.
2. Using X and Z as centres, draw arcs that cross at Y.
3. Draw the line OY.

A perpendicular bisector of a line

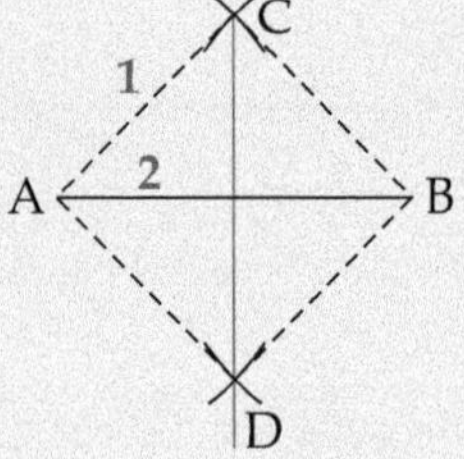

1. Using A and B as centres, draw arcs above and below the line that cross at C and D.
2. Draw the line CD.

Any point on the angle bisector is equidistant from OA and OB.

Any point on the perpendicular bisector is equidistant from A and B.

You can use these techniques to construct **loci**.

A **locus** is a set of points, often forming a curve, that satisfy a given rule. The path of an object can form a locus.

The plural of locus is **loci**.

The locus of the tip of the blade on a wind turbine is a circle.

Exercise 12c

1 Draw a line AB of length 5 cm.
Construct the locus of a point that is equidistant from the points A and B.

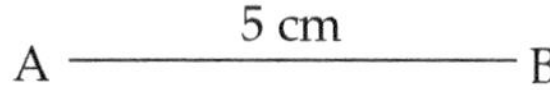

2 Draw the locus of a point that is equidistant from two parallel lines 4 cm apart.

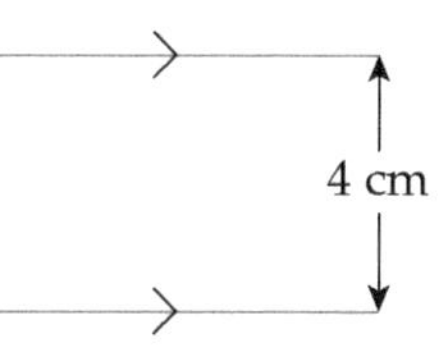

3 Copy the diagrams and draw the locus of all points which are the same distance from both lines.

a

b

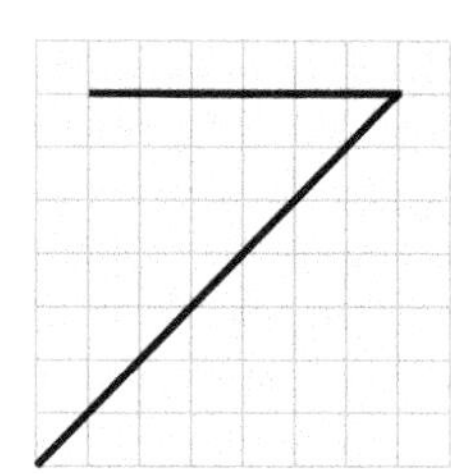

4 Construct the locus of a point that is 30 mm from a fixed point O.
What is your locus called?

5 Use compasses to construct angles of

a 60° **b** 30° **c** 120° **d** 90°.

6 **a** Copy this diagram.

Construct the perpendicular

i from point P to line AB

ii from point Q on line AB.

b Write a property of the two perpendicular lines you have constructed.

7 **a** An equilateral triangle is rolled along a straight line.
Describe the locus of the point P.

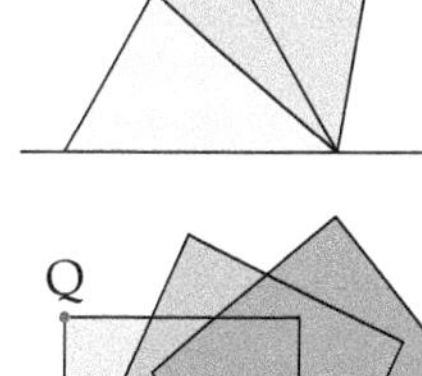

b A square is rolled along a straight line.
Describe the locus of the point Q.

Q

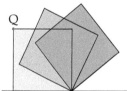

Problem solving

8 **a** Draw two circles with the same radius.

b Draw a line AC joining their centres.

c Draw the line BD.

d BD intersects AC at X.
Are triangles ABX and CBX congruent?

e Use this information to show that BD is the perpendicular bisector of AC.

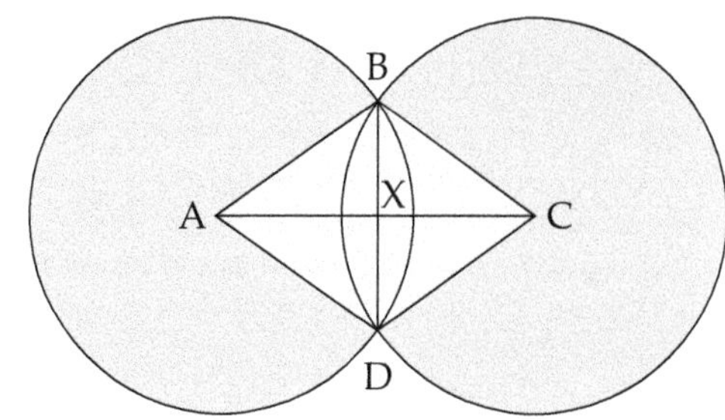

Did you know?

If you pick a point on a circle and trace its path as the circle rolls along a straight line the locus is a **cycloid**. The three arches in this bridge are cycloids.

12d Pythagoras' theorem 1

The longest side of a **right-angled triangle** is called the **hypotenuse**.

You can draw squares on each side of a right-angled triangle.

The yellow area + the blue area = the green area

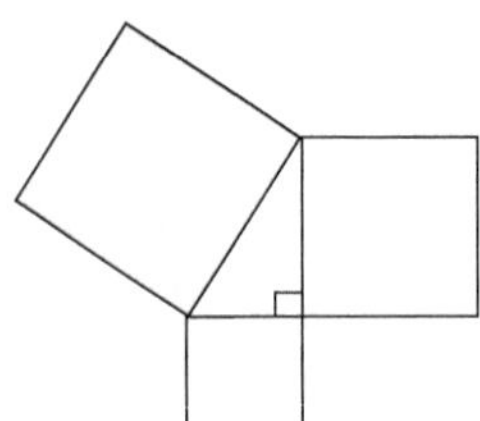

+ =

Pythagoras' theorem states that, for a right-angled triangle,

the area of the square on the hypotenuse = sum of the areas of the squares on the other two sides.

$c^2 = a^2 + b^2$ where c is the hypotenuse.

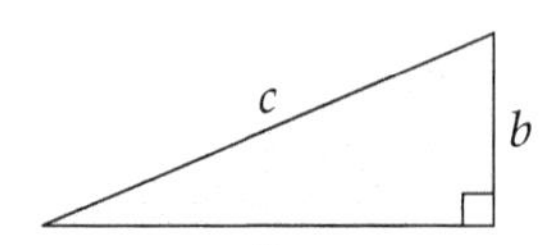

Example

a Calculate the value of c.

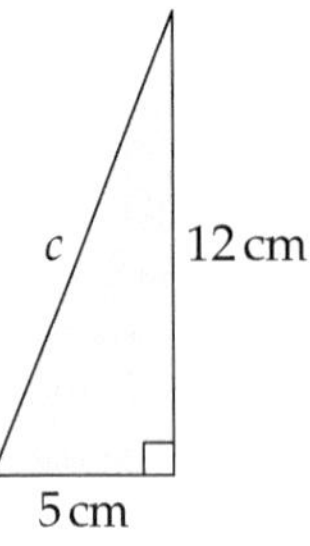

b Calculate the value of a.

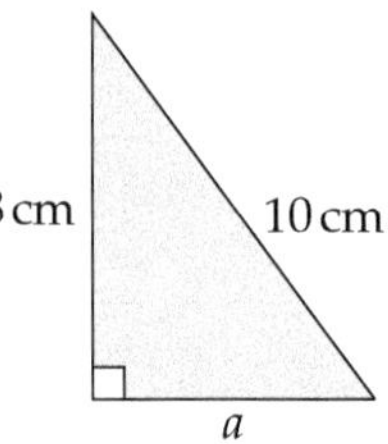

a c is larger than 12 cm and 5 cm.

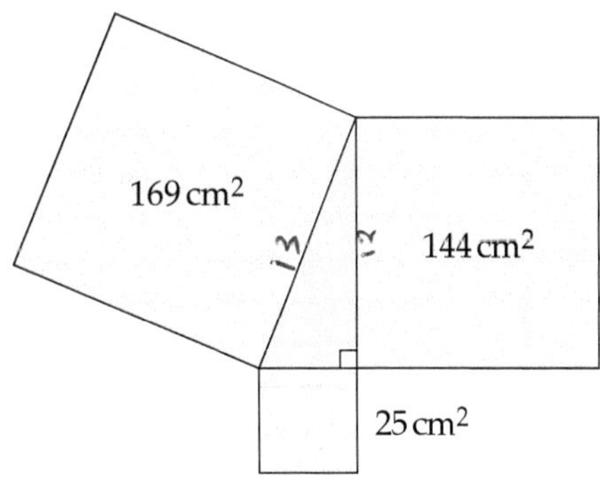

$c^2 = 12^2 + 5^2$ You add the areas.

$= 144 + 25$

$= 169$

$c = \sqrt{169}$ $\sqrt{}$ means **square root**.

$= 13$ cm

b a is smaller than 10 cm.

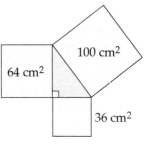

64 cm²
100 cm²
36 cm²

$a^2 = 10^2 - 8^2$ You subtract the areas.

$= 100 - 64$

$= 36$

$a = \sqrt{36}$

$= 6$ cm

Exercise 12d

1 To check that a triangle with sides of length 3, 4 and 5 is right-angled:

- ▶ Put $a = 3$, $b = 4$ and $c = 5$ into $a^2 + b^2 = c^2$.
- ▶ Work out the left-hand side of the equation: $a^2 + b^2 = 3^2 + 4^2 = 9 + 16 = 25$
- ▶ Work out the right-hand side of the equation: $c^2 = 5^2 = 25$ ✓
- ▶ The two sides of the equation are equal so the triangle must be right angled.

Follow the steps to check whether these lengths give right-angled triangles:

a $a = 4, b = 5, c = 6$

b $a = 6, b = 8, c = 10$

c $a = 5, b = 10, c = 12$

d $a = 5, b = 12, c = 13$

2 Calculate the length of the hypotenuse in each triangle.
State the units of your answer.

a

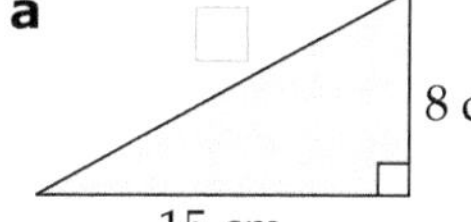

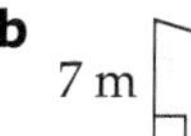

b

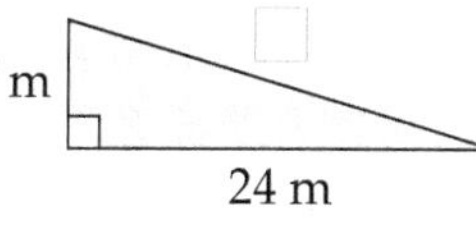

3 Calculate the unknown lengths in these triangles.

a

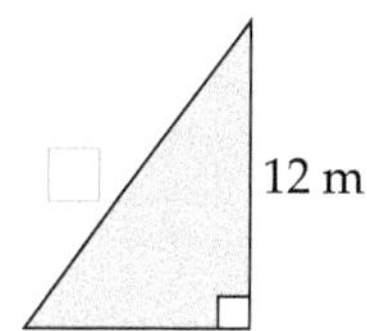

b

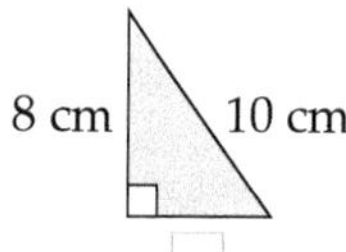

c

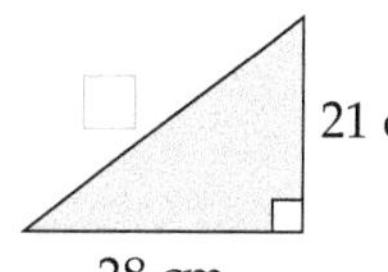

d

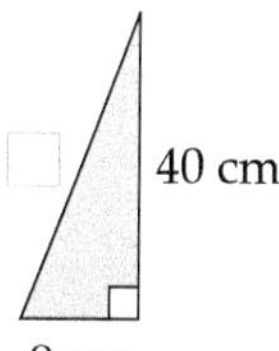

e

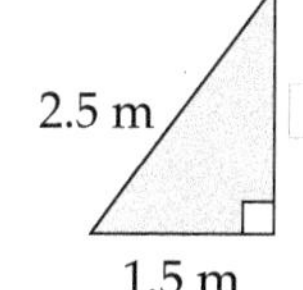

f

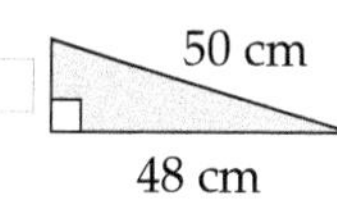

Each answer is an integer.

Did you know?

Pythagoras' theorem has appeared on several stamps. This one is from Suriname in South America.

Problem solving

4 Draw a 3 cm, 4 cm, 5 cm right-angled triangle with a square on each side.

Cut out another 3 cm by 3 cm square.

Cut out another 4 cm by 4 cm square and cut it into four pieces exactly as shown.

Fit these five pieces in the 5 cm by 5 cm square to demonstrate Pythagoras' theorem.

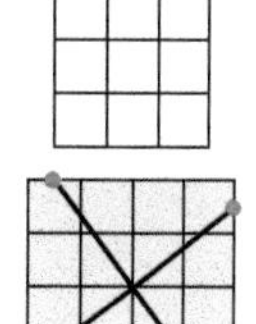

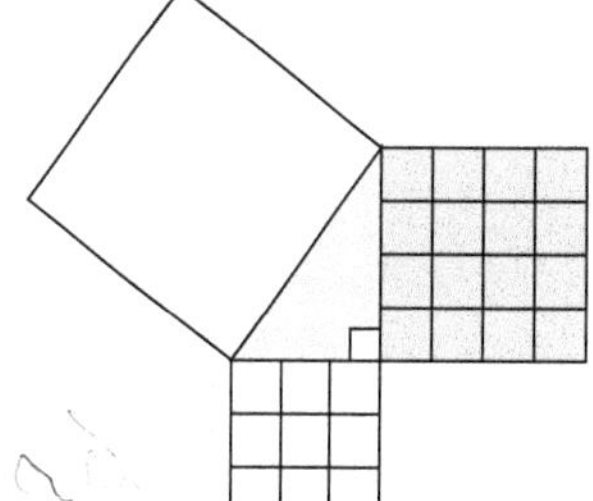

12e Pythagoras' theorem 2

You can use **Pythagoras'** theorem to calculate the length of a side in a **right-angled triangle**.

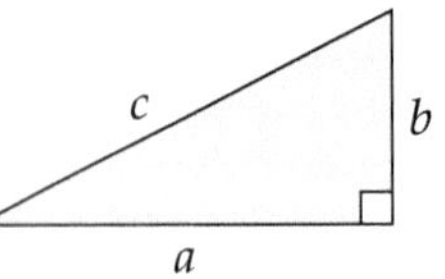

$c^2 = a^2 + b^2$ where c is the hypotenuse.

It must be a right-angled triangle for this theorem to work.

Example

Calculate the distance between the points (-3, 6) and (5, 2).

First draw a right-angled triangle.

The hypotenuse is c.

$c^2 = 4^2 + 8^2$
$= 16 + 64$
$= 80$
$c = \sqrt{80} = 8.9$ units (1 dp)

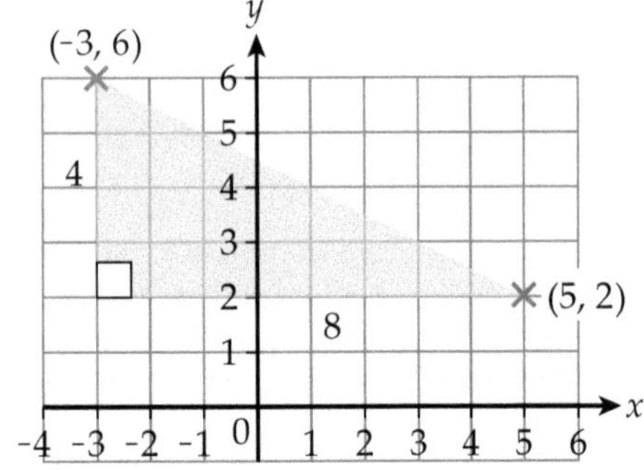

Example

Calculate the area of the equilateral triangle.

Use Pythagoras' theorem in the right-angled triangle.

$h^2 = 10^2 - 5^2$
$= 100 - 25$
$= 75$
$h = \sqrt{75} = 8.660254 \ldots$ cm   Do not round the value of h.

Area of the equilateral triangle
$= \frac{1}{2} \times 10 \times 8.660254 \ldots$
$= 43.30127 \ldots$
$= 43.3$ cm^2 (1 dp)   Now round the answer.

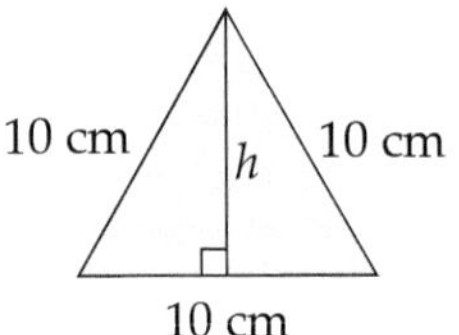

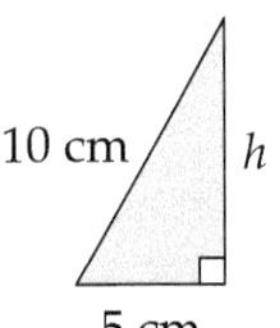

A **Pythagorean triple** consists of three **integers** that could be the lengths of a right-angled triangle.

Another Pythagorean triple is 6, 8, 10 because $6^2 + 8^2 = 10^2$.

Can you find any others?
Remember, all three of the numbers have to be integers.

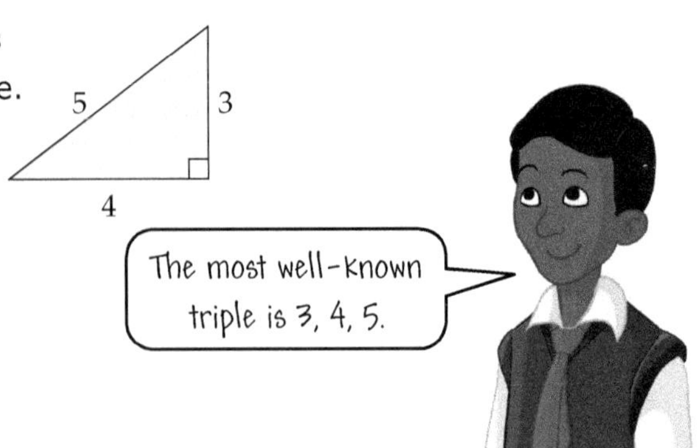

5
3
4
The most well-known triple is 3, 4, 5.

Exercise 12e

1 Use Pythagoras' theorem to decide if these triangles are right-angled.

a

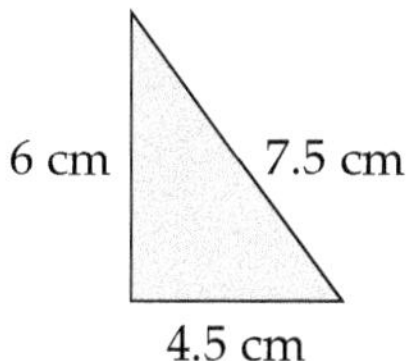

b

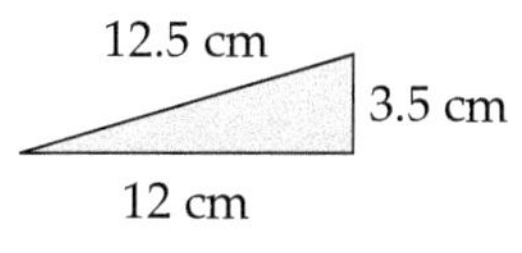

c

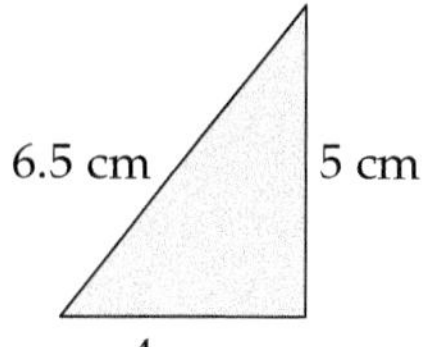

d

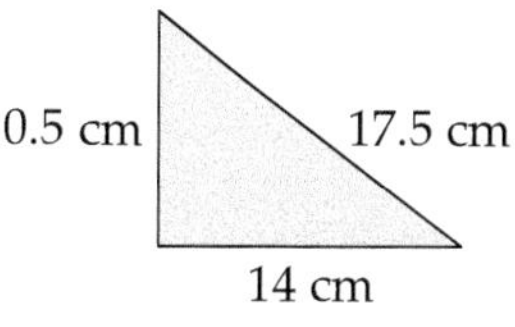

2 Calculate the distances between these pairs of points.

a (1, 2) and (4, 6) **b** (2, -1) and (3, 2) **c** (-2, 5) and (2, 1) **d** (-1, -2) and (1, 0)

Problem solving

3 A 4-metre ladder leans against a wall with its base 1.5 metres from the wall.
How far up the wall does the ladder reach?

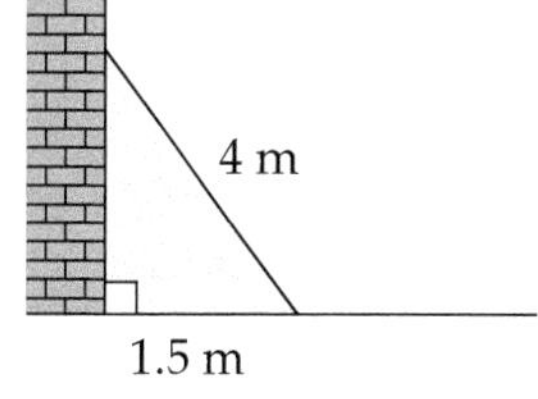

4 Draw a rectangle measuring 4 cm by 6 cm.

a Draw and measure the diagonal of the rectangle.

b Use Pythagoras' theorem to check your answer.

5 Two isosceles triangles have sides of length 24 cm, 20 cm, 20 cm and 32 cm, 20 cm, 20 cm.
For each triangle calculate its

i perpendicular height **ii** area.

a

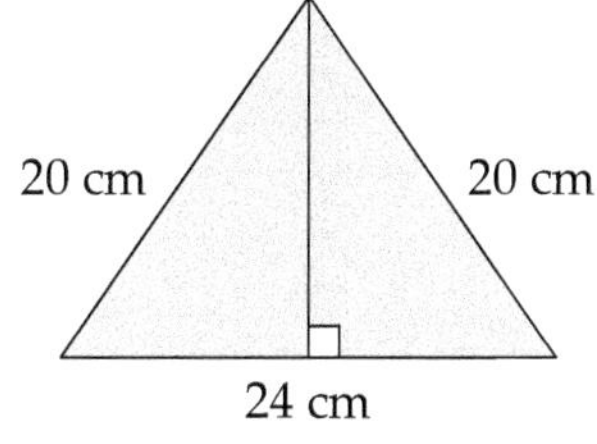

b

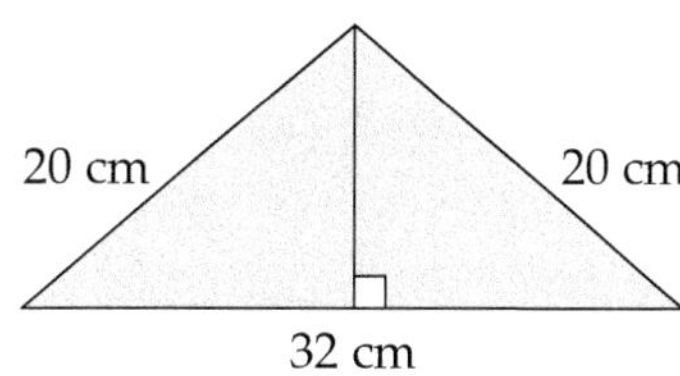

6 PQR and PRS are right-angled triangles.

a Find the length PR.

b Hence find the length PS.

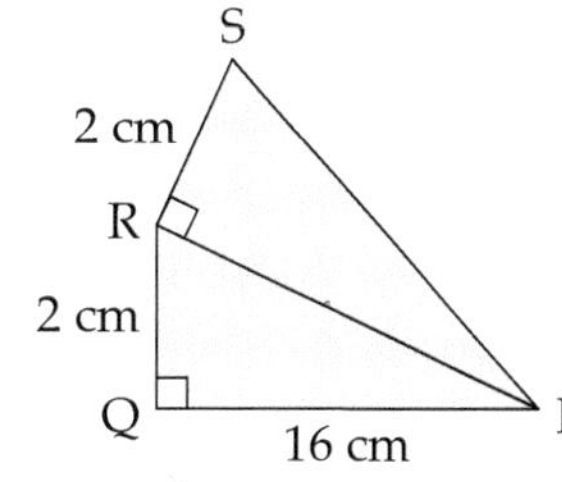

7 ABC and ACD are right-angled triangles.

a Find the length AC.

b Hence find the length AB.

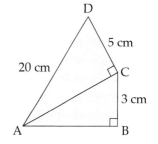

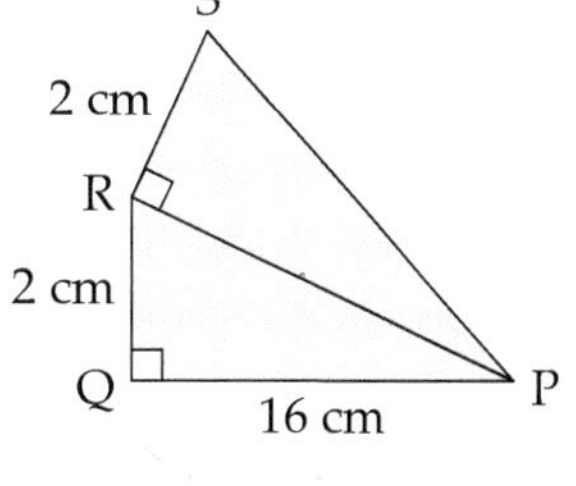

12 MySummary

Check out

You should now be able to ...

Test it ➡

Questions

You should now be able to ...		Questions
✓ Know how to construct ASA, SAS, SSS and RHS triangles, bisectors and perpendiculars.		1 – 2
✓ Find and describe loci.		3 – 4
✓ Use Pythagoras' theorem to solve problems involving right-angled triangles.		5 – 7

Language	Meaning	Example	
Bisector	A line that divides an angle or another line in half.	 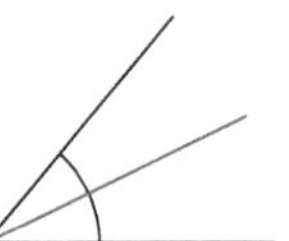	This is an angle bisector.
Locus	A set of points that satisfy a given rule.	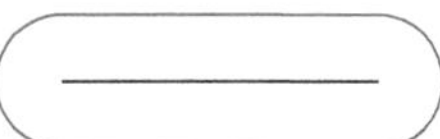	This is the locus of points equidistant from a line.
Construct	To form an angle or shape accurately.	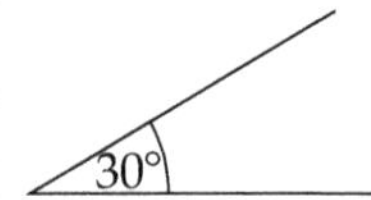	This is a construction of a 30° angle.
Hypotenuse	The longest side in a right-angled triangle.	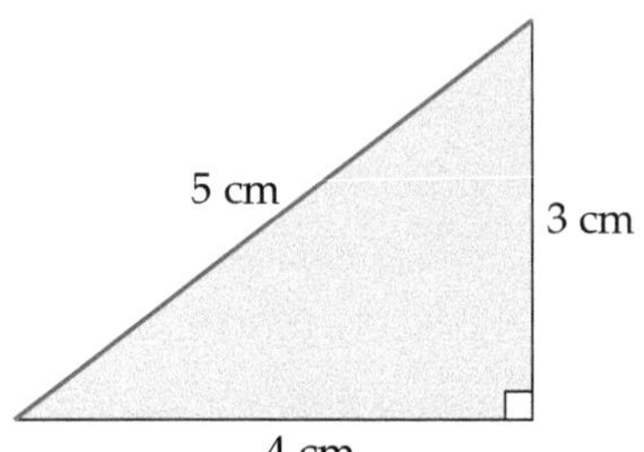 The hypotenuse is the 5 cm length.	
Perpendicular	Two lines are perpendicular to each other if they meet at a right angle.	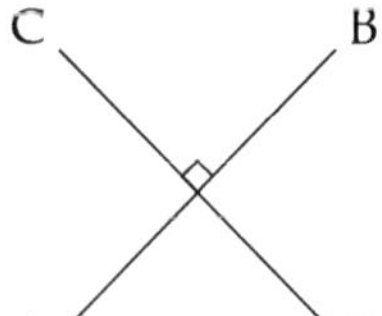	AB and CD are perpendicular.
Pythagoras' theorem	In any right-angled triangle, Pythagoras' theorem gives the relationship between the lengths of the sides.	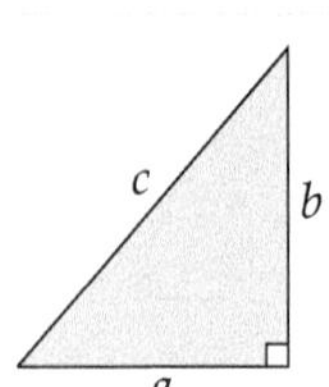	$a^2 + b^2 = c^2$ where c is the hypotenuse.

1 Construct these triangles.

a

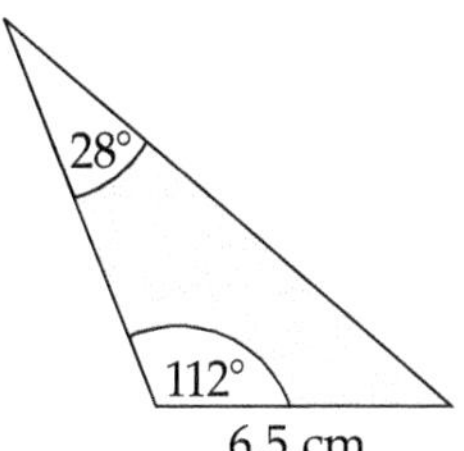

b

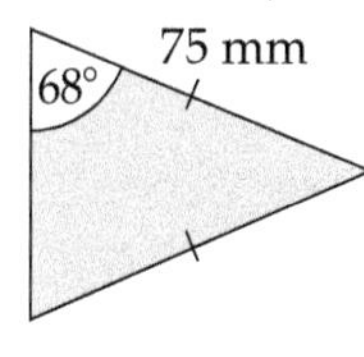

2 a Construct this triangle.

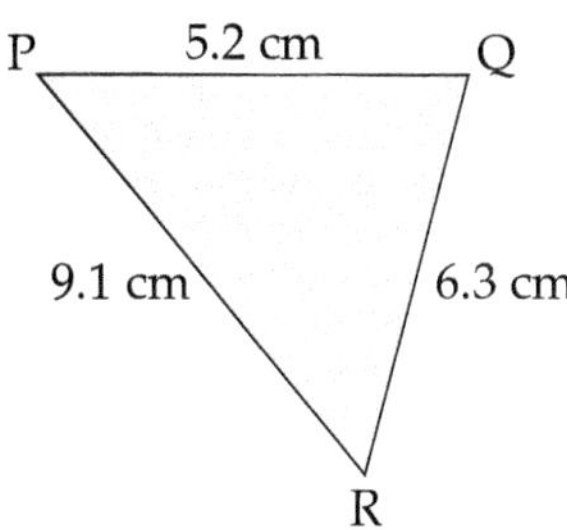

b Construct the perpendicular bisector of PR.

c Construct the angle bisector of Q.

3 a Draw a circle with a radius of 3 cm.

b Draw the locus of the point that is 1 cm from the circumference of the circle.

4 a Use a protractor and ruler to copy the diagram

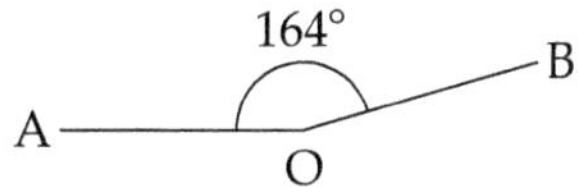

b Use a pair of compasses to construct the locus of a point that is equidistant to OA and OB.

5 Calculate the unknown lengths in these right-angled triangles, and give your answers to 1 dp.

a

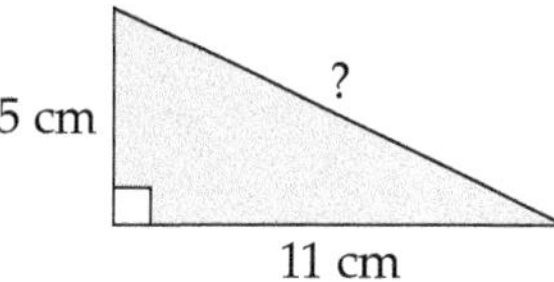

b

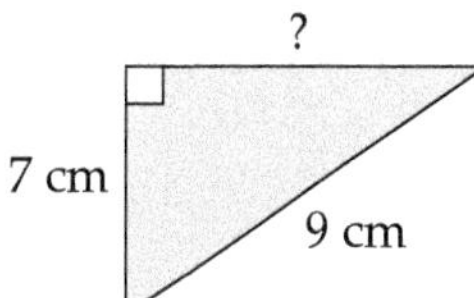

c

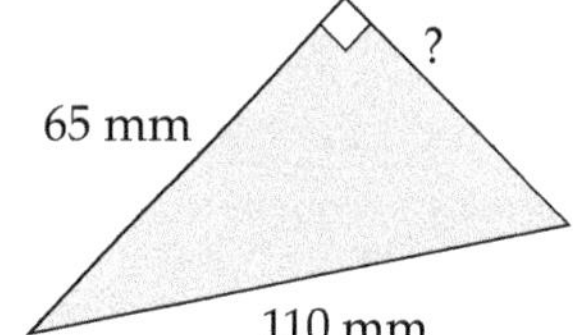

6 Use Pythagoras' theorem to decide if this triangle is right angled.

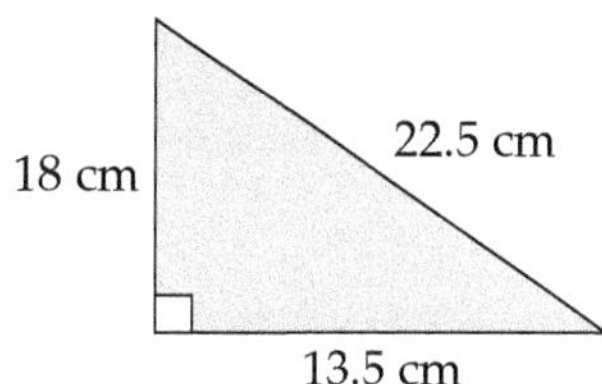

7 Calculate the distances between these pairs of points.

a (4, 7) and (-2, 9)

b (-3, -8) and (-8, 11)

What next?

Score

Score	
0 – 3	Your knowledge of this topic is still developing. To improve look at Formative test: 3B-12; MyMaths: 1089, 1090, 1112 and 1147
4 – 5	You are gaining a secure knowledge of this topic. To improve look at InvisiPen: 371, 373, 375 and 381
6, 7	You have mastered this topic. Well done, you are ready to progress!

12 MyPractice

12a

1 Calculate the unknown angles in these triangles.
Then use a ruler and protractor to construct the triangles.

a

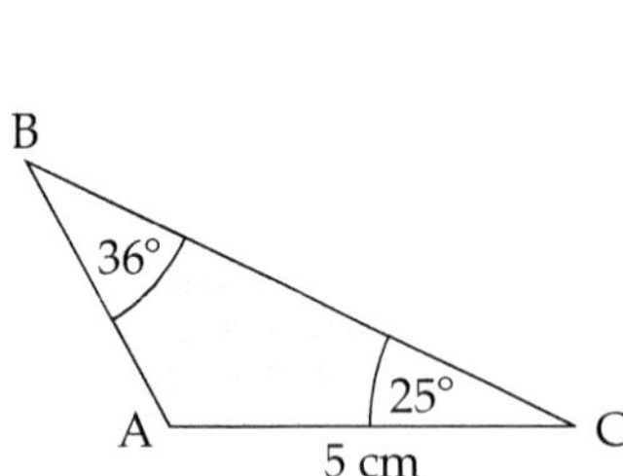

b

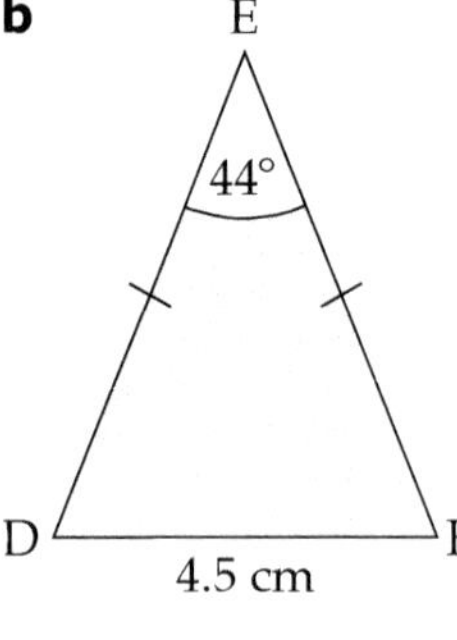

c

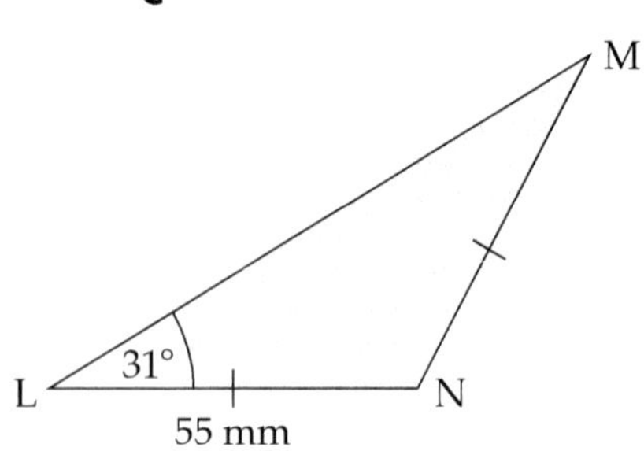

12b

2 Construct these triangles accurately.
Calculate the perimeter of each triangle.

a

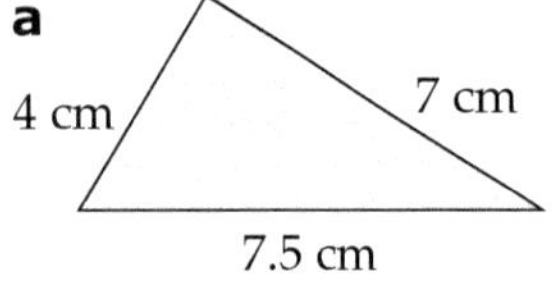

b

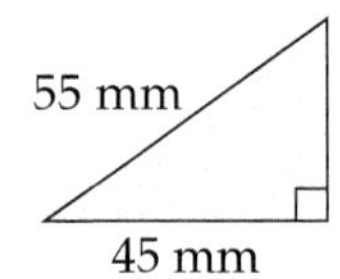

c

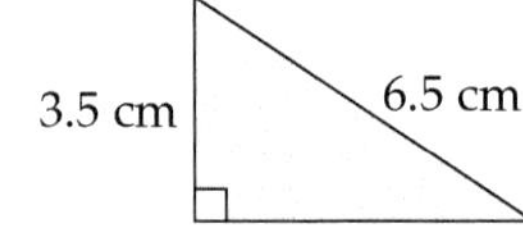

12c

3 You can use these instructions to draw a square.
REPEAT 4
[FORWARD 10 TURN RIGHT 90°]
Devise similar instructions to draw

a an equilateral triangle

b a regular hexagon

c a regular octagon.

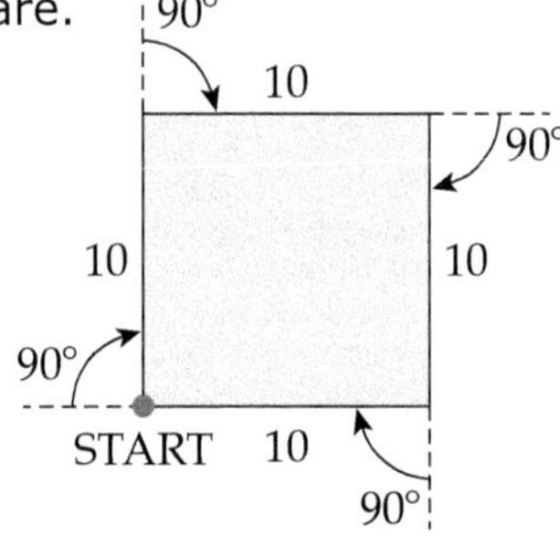

12d

4 Use Pythagoras' theorem to calculate the unknown lengths.

a

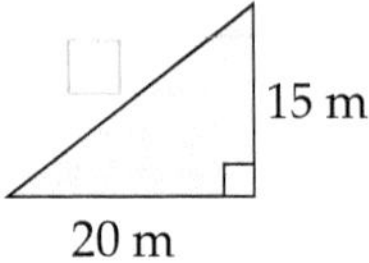

b

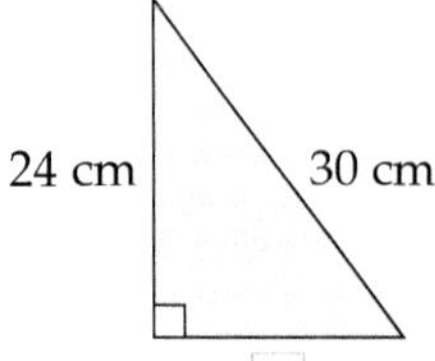

c

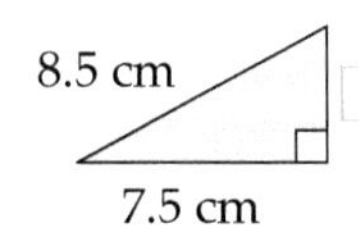

Each answer is an integer.

5 A square is drawn inside a 4 by 4 square. Calculate

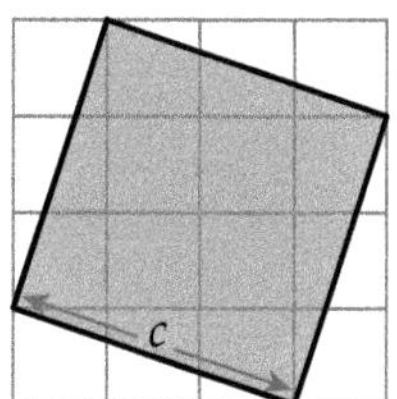

a the length c

b the area of the shaded square.

6 There are two right-angled triangles in the diagram.

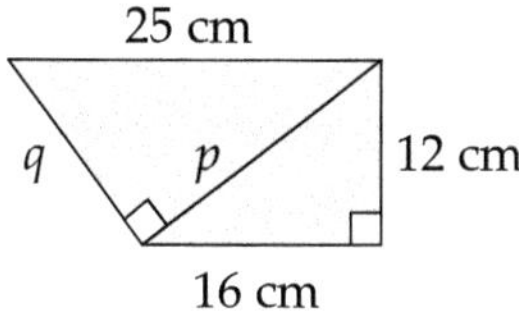

Calculate the value of p and q.

7 Calculate the distance between each pair of points.
Give your answer to 1 dp where appropriate.

a (1, 2) and (5, 6)

b (2, 2) and (6, 5)

c (1, 2) and (2, 5)

d (0, 5) and (4, 1)

e (3, 6) and (6, 0)

f (-2, -1) and (1, 0)

8 A telegraph pole 6 metres tall is held in place by a sloping wire as shown.
Calculate the length, x, of the wire.

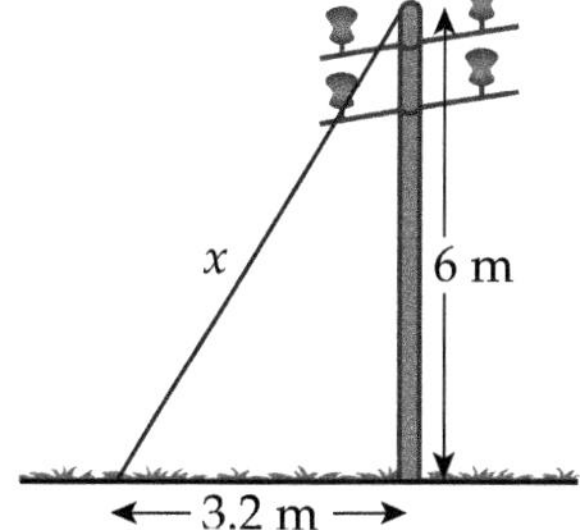

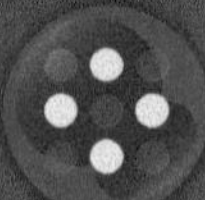

Case study 4: Garden design

Sensory gardens are designed to stimulate the senses - sight, sound, smell, touch and even taste - and are thought to have a beneficial effect on people who visit them. Whilst they must be designed for all users, this case study considers their accessibility for wheelchair users.

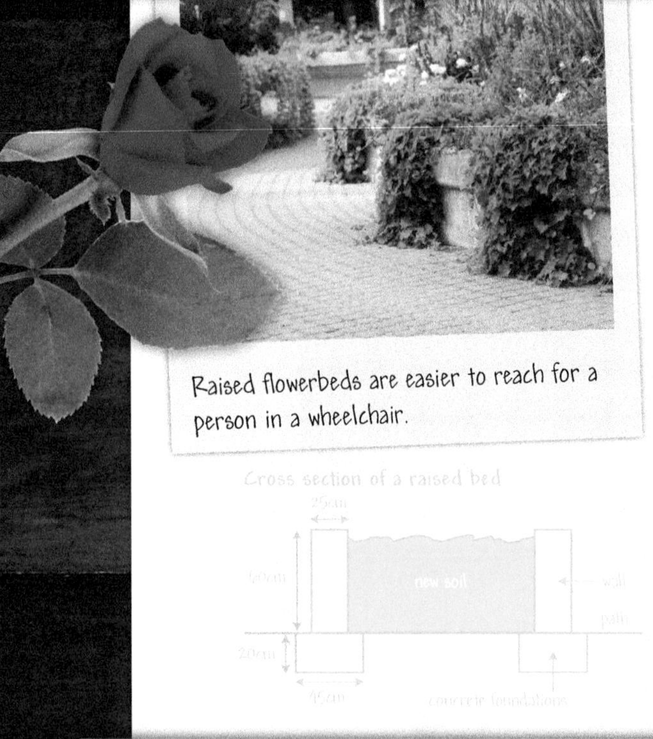

Raised flowerbeds are easier to reach for a person in a wheelchair.

Cross section of a raised bed

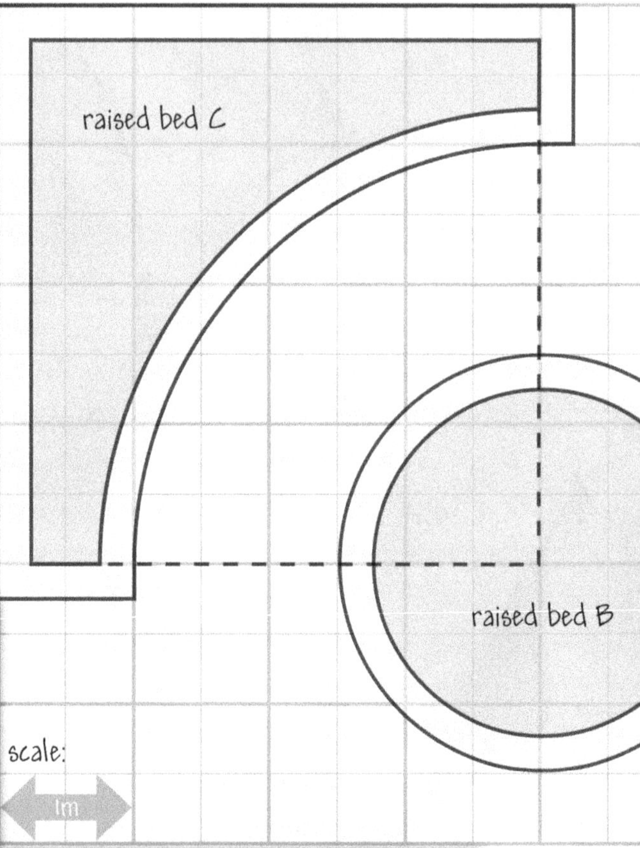

Task 1

Look at the scale drawing of the garden.

Calculate the area in m^2 of

a) bed A b) bed B (to 1 d.p.)

By considering different shapes, calculate the area of

c) bed C (to 1 d.p.) d) bed D (to 1 d.p.)

Wide paths and few sharp corners make it easier to get around.

Task 2

Look at the cross-section diagram of a raised bed. Each bed is to be filled with soil to 5cm from the top of the wall. Calculate the volume of soil needed to fill

a) bed A b) bed B c) bed C
d) bed D

Give your answers in m^3 to 1 d.p. where appropriate.

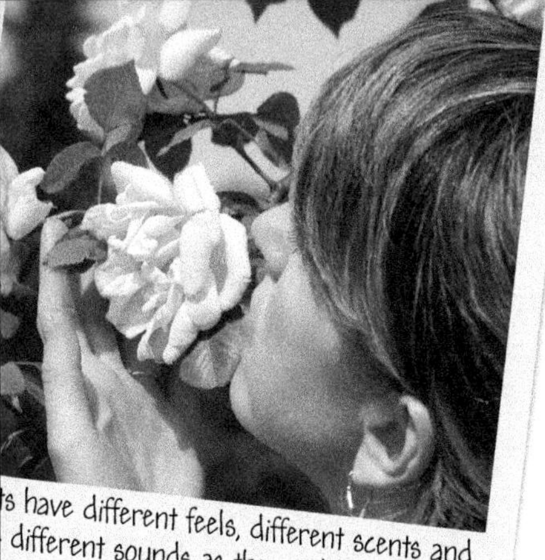

...s have different feels, different scents and ... different sounds as the wind blows. They ...ttract insects which add to the sounds.

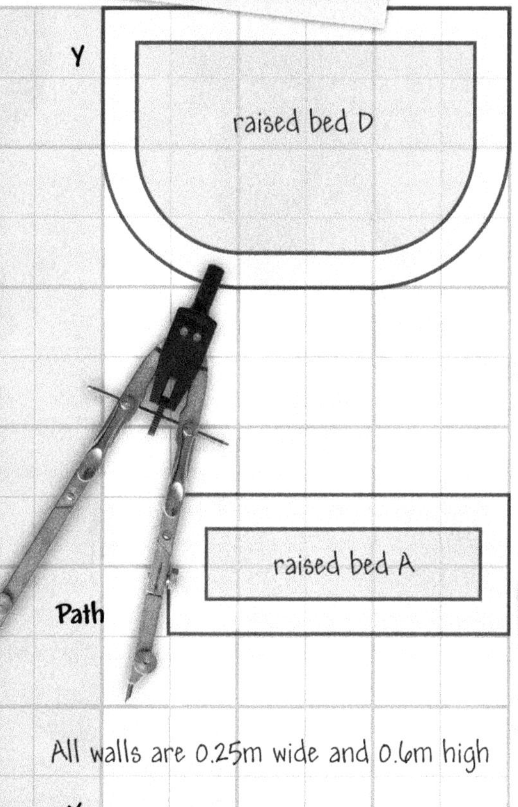

Task 4

The area surrounding the beds and the path will be paved. Calculate the area that is to be paved, giving your answer in m^2 to 1 d.p.

Task 5

The path is made extra wide to fit a wheelchair comfortably.

a) Looking at the scale drawing, how wide is the path?

b) The path is to be sloped to provide access for wheelchair users.

It will have a gradient of 1:20, starting at X and rising up to Y.

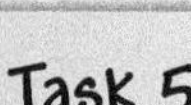

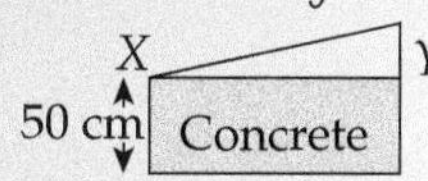

i) At what height above bed B will the path be, at the point where the path meets the bed?

ii) At what height above bed D will the path be, at the end of the path Y?

Water features add sound and touch to a garden.

c) (challenge) Find the total volume of concrete needed for the path, giving your answer in m^3 to 1 d.p.

Task 3 (challenge)

Look again at the cross-section diagram of a raised bed.

Calculate the volume of concrete needed to make the **foundations** of

a) bed A b) bed B

Calculate the volume of concrete needed to make the **walls** of

c) bed C d) bed D

Give your answers in m^3 to 1 d.p. where appropriate.

MyAssessment 3

These questions will test you on your knowledge of the topics in chapters 9 to 12.
They give you practice in the questions that you may see in your GCSE exams.
There are 100 marks in total.

1 **a** Copy this diagram on square grid paper. (2 marks)

b Reflect the shape about the y-axis as a mirror line. (2 marks)

c Translate this reflection four squares down. (1 mark)

d Rotate this translated shape 180° anticlockwise about the point X. (3 marks)

e What is the name of the quadrilateral formed at the centre of the pattern? (1 mark)

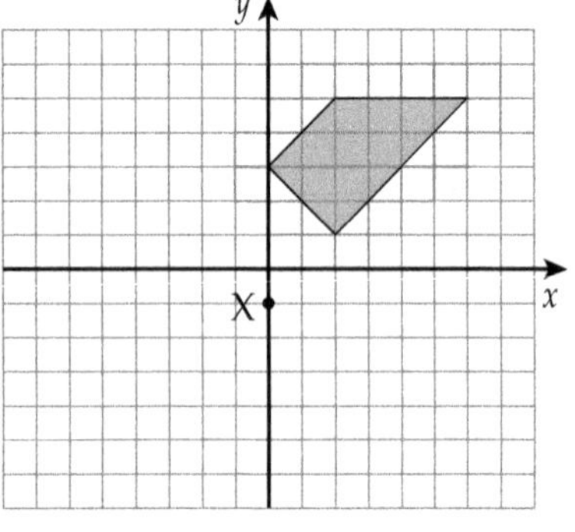

2 **a** Draw the triangle ABC on a coordinate grid. (2 marks)

b Enlarge the triangle by scale factor 2 using (0, 0) as the centre of enlargement. (3 marks)

c What are the coordinates of the vertices of the enlarged triangle? (2 marks)

d What do you notice about the coordinates of the object and the image? (1 mark)

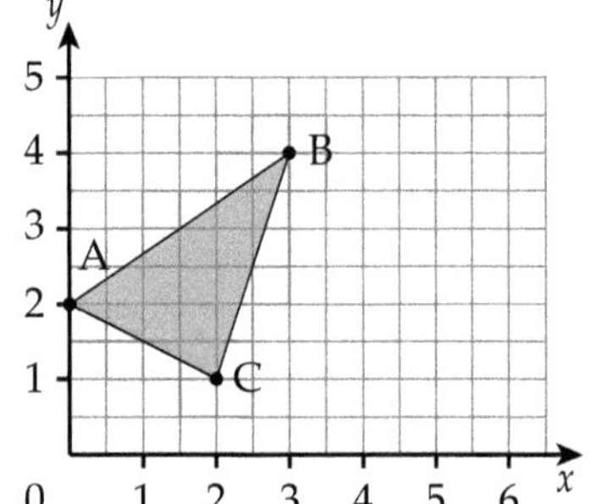

3 The city of Leeds is 58 km away from Manchester on a bearing of 050°.
The city of Sheffield is 52 km away from Manchester on a bearing of 103°.

a Draw a scale drawing showing these three cities (use 1 cm = 10 km). (3 marks)

b What is the distance between Leeds and Sheffield? (1 mark)

c What is the bearing of Sheffield from Leeds? (2 marks)

4 Solve these equations. Some answers are negative.

a $5x - 7 = 13$ (1 mark) **b** $\frac{4x}{3} - 2 = 2$ (2 marks)

c $3(5x - 22) = 24$ (2 marks) **d** $6(2x + 13) = 54$ (2 marks)

e $4(2x + 2) = 2(5x + 7)$ (3 marks) **f** $\frac{5x - 4}{3} = \frac{10 + 4x}{9}$ (3 marks)

5 Find the value of x in each diagram. (4 marks)

a

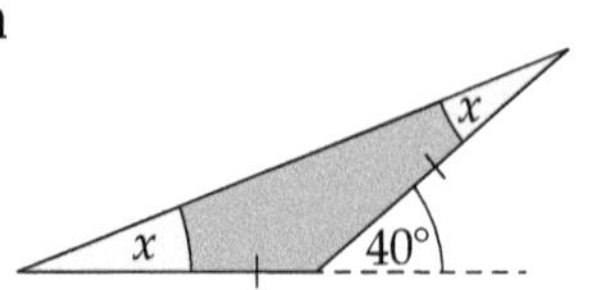

b

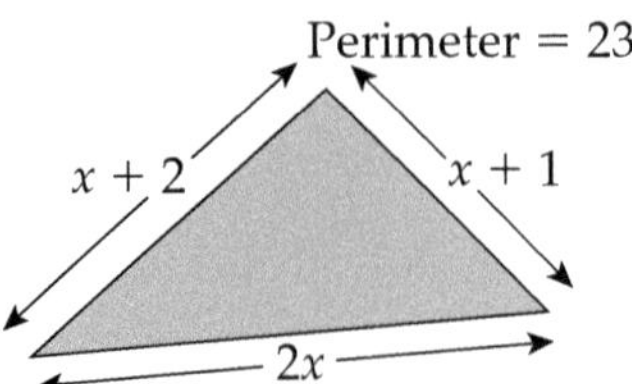

6 A rectangular playing field has an area of $3000\,m^2$. It is 20 m longer than it is wide. If its width is w, solve the equation $w(w + 20) = 3000$ to find the length and width of the field to 1 dp. Initially try $w = 40$. (4 marks)

7 Solve these equations giving your answer correct to 2 dp.

a $x^3 + 3x = 200$ (4 marks) **b** $2x + \sqrt{x} = 24$ (4 marks)

8 **a** The velocity of an object is related to its energy by $v = \sqrt{\frac{2E}{m}}$.
Calculate v when $E = 2000$ and $m = 12$ to 2 dp. (2 marks)

b The time period for a simple pendulum is $T = 2\pi\sqrt{\frac{L}{g}}$
Calculate the time period when $L = 0.6$ and $g = 10$. (2 marks)

c The volume of a sphere is $V = \frac{4}{3}\pi r^3$.
Rearrange the equation to find the value of r when $V = 125$. (4 marks)

9 Simplify these expressions

a $\frac{4(m^3)^2 \times 6m^4}{8m^5}$ (3 marks) **b** $(10^8 \times 10^2)^2$ (2 marks)

10 Give these numbers in standard index form.

a 0.034×10^4 (1 mark) **b** 300 million km per second (2 marks)

c $6.3 \times 10^5 - 2.7 \times 10^4$ (2 marks) **d** 29 800 000 000 000 000 (2 marks)

e $7.2 \times 10^{-8} - 5.8 \times 10^{-7}$ (2 marks) **f** 0.000 000 000 000 035 (2 marks)

11 Write these numbers in their simplest form.

a $\sqrt{72}$ (2 marks) **b** $3\sqrt{2} \times 2\sqrt{8}$ (2 marks)

12 **a** Construct a triangle PQR with side lengths PR = 5 cm, PQ = 7 cm and RQ = 8 cm using a ruler and compasses as accurately as possible. (4 marks)

b Measure the angle PQR with a protractor. (1 mark)

13 Two mobile phone masts A and B are 20 km apart. Mast A has a radius of 15 km and mast B has a radius of 9 km.

a Draw the locus of points covered by these two masts. (3 marks)

b Label the points where the two circles meet as C and D and draw lines AC, BC, AD and BD. (2 marks)

c What is the name given to the quadrilateral ACBD? (1 mark)

d Shade in the locus of points that is covered by both masts. (1 mark)

14 PQRS is a right-angled trapezium with PQ = 5.5 cm, SR = 10.5 cm and PS = 7.5 cm. Angles at Q and R are right angles.

a Draw the right-angled trapezium. (2 marks)

b Work out the length of QR. (3 marks)

c Work out the length of PR. (3 marks)

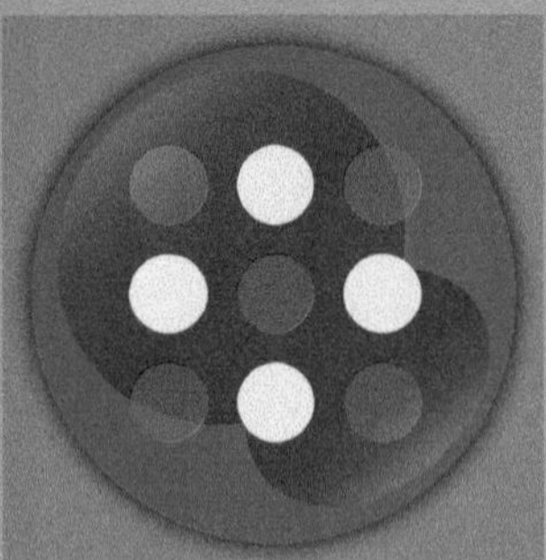

13 Sequences

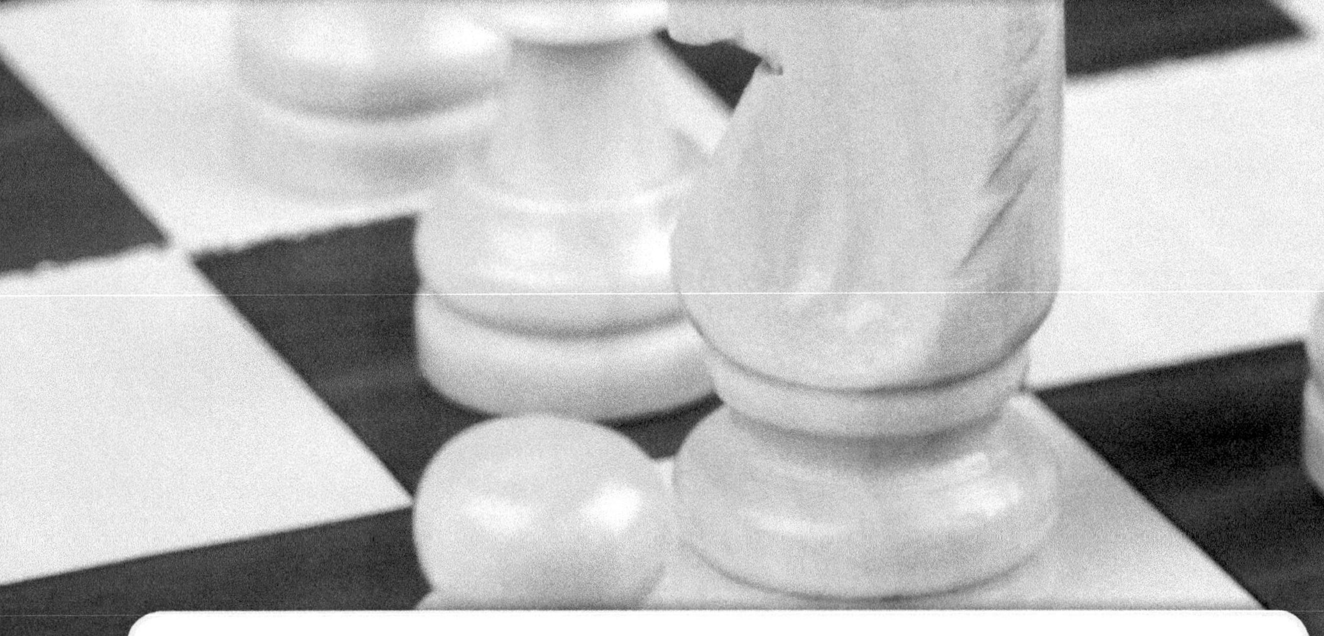

Introduction

There is a famous story told across many cultures of a wise man and a king. The wise man serves the king over many years and is rewarded with any prize he wishes to name. The man asks only for a chessboard and for one grain of rice to be placed on the first square, double this amount on the second square, double this amount on the third square and so on...
The king agrees to this prize.
Was this a good prize to choose?

What's the point?

If the king had known a bit about sequences he would not have agreed to the prize!

Objectives

By the end of this chapter, you will have learned how to ...

- Find the term-to-term rule for a sequence.
- Find the position-to-term rule for a sequence.
- Write the general term using algebra.
- Solve problems involving sequences.

Check in

1 The total cost £C of buying n shirts by mail order is given by this rule:
Multiply by 15 and then add 3.
Find C when
a $n = 4$ **b** $n = 10$.

2 A rule is given as '*divide by 5 and then subtract 4*'.
Find the output when the input is
a 30 **b** 200.

Starter problem

An intelligent girl receives £3 a week in pocket money.
She decides to renegotiate her pocket money with her father.
'Dad could I just have 50 p pocket money this week?'
'Of course', says her father.
'And next week can I have 20 p more?'
'I don't see why not' replies her dad.
'And maybe just 20 p more each week from then on?'
'OK – sounds like I'm getting a good deal here – are you sure?'
Investigate ...

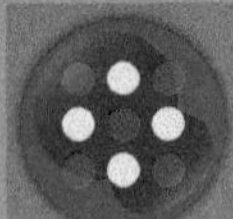

13a Sequences and terms

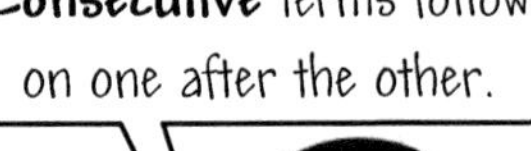

Consecutive terms follow on one after the other.

- A **sequence** is a set of numbers, or **terms**.
  Each term can be found using a **rule** e.g. 3, 5, 7, 9, 11, ...

To generate a sequence you need a starting number and a rule.

- The **term-to-term rule** of a sequence gives the first term and tells you how to find each **consecutive** term from the previous one.

Emma plants a flower bed.
She starts with four plants and keeps adding two more plants.

The sequence for the **total** number of flowers begins 4, 6, 8, ...
The rule is '*start with 4 and add 2 each time*'.
The next two terms are 10 and 12.

Example

The first term of a sequence is 5.
The term-to-term rule is given by this function machine.

Term → [×3] → [−9] → Next term

Generate the first four consecutive terms of the sequence.

The first term of the sequence is 5.
The second term is $5 \times 3 - 9 = 15 - 9 = 6$.
The third term is $6 \times 3 - 9 = 18 - 9 = 9$.
The fourth term is $9 \times 3 - 9 = 27 - 9 = 18$.

The first four consecutive terms are 5, 6, 9, 18.

Example

Here is a sequence:
2, 3, 5, 9, □, 33
Find the missing term.

The first term is 2.
The term-to-term rule is: '× 2 then −1'
The missing term is $9 \times 2 - 1 = 18 - 1$
$= 17$.

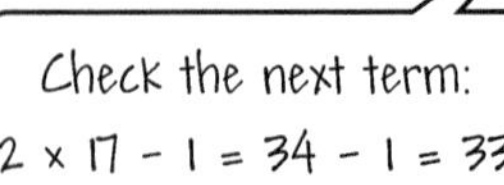

Check the next term:
2 × 17 − 1 = 34 − 1 = 33

Exercise 13a

1 You can use straws to make this sequence of patterns.

a Draw the next pattern of the sequence.

b Write the first four terms to give the sequence of the number of straws.

c Find the term-to-term rule.

d Write the next three consecutive terms.

2 Two sequences both start with a first term of 7.
Use these two function machines to generate the first five consecutive terms of each sequence.

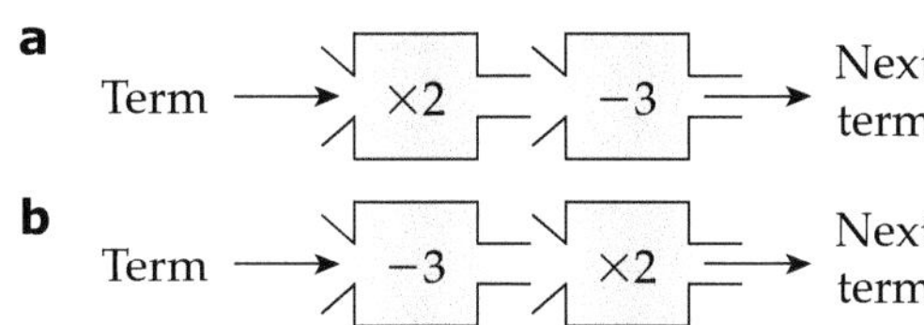

3 Generate the first five terms of the sequences with these rules.

a *First term 4, rule double and subtract 2.*

b *First term 600, rule halve and subtract 20.*

c *First term 0, rule treble and add 1.*

d *First term 0, rule add 1 and treble.*

e *First term $\frac{1}{4}$, rule double and add 1.*

f *First term 4, rule multiply by 3 and subtract 8.*

Problem solving

4 Use this flow diagram to generate consecutive terms of the sequence when **a** $x = 2$ **b** $x = 50$ **c** $x = -30$.

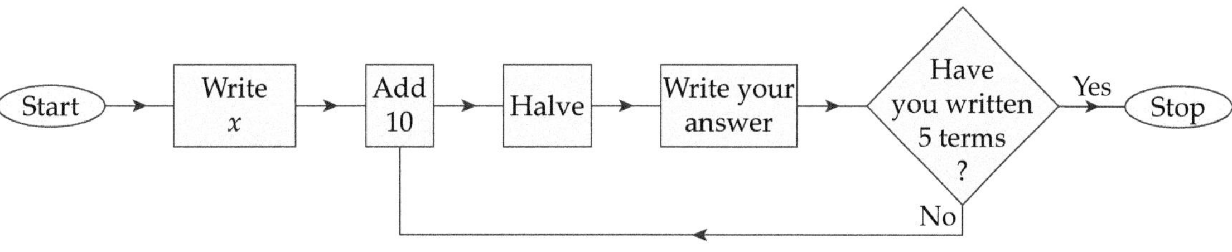

5 For each of these sequences, describe the term-to-term rule in words and find the next three consecutive terms.

a 7, 10, 13, 16, …

b 20, 17, 14, 11, …

c 3, 7, 15, 31, …

d 3, 5, 9, 17, …

e 1, 4, 13, 40, …

f 1, 2, 5, 14, …

g 200, 100, 50, 25, …

h $\frac{1}{2}$, 3, 8, 18, …

i 3, 4, 6, 10, …

6 Use a spreadsheet to generate a sequence with *first term 3, rule double and add 4*.
Invent some sequences of your own.
Write the rule you use in each case.

	A	B	C	D
1	3	=2*A1+4	=2*B1+4	=2*C1+4
2				

13b Position-to-term rules

A **position-to-term rule** gives you the value of any term if you know its position in the **sequence**.

Anwar makes a sequence of patterns using hexagonal tiles.
He adds three extra tiles each time to make the next pattern.

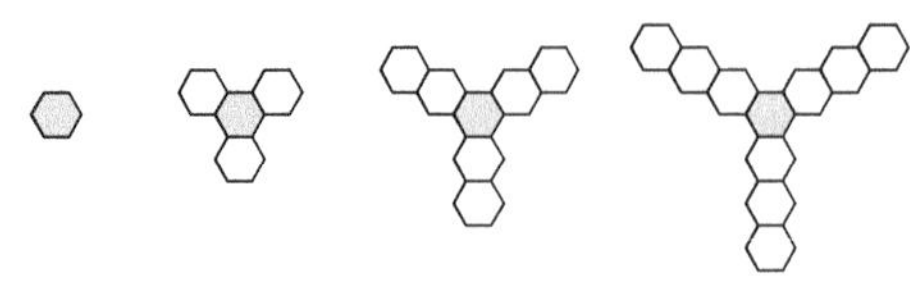

Position	1	2	3	4
Number of tiles	1	4	7	10

+3 +3 +3

The difference between each term is 3, so compare the terms in the sequence with the three times table.

Position	1	2	3	4
3· table	3	6	9	12
Number of tiles (term)	1	4	7	10

×3, −2

Position → ×3 → −2 → Term

Anwar's position-to-term rule is *'multiply the position by 3 and then subtract 2'*.
The 100th position needs $100 \times 3 - 2 = 300 - 2 = 298$ tiles.

Example

The first four terms of a sequence are 5, 9, 13, 17.
Find

a the next term

b the 60th term.

a The sequence grows by adding 4 to each term.

5 9 13 17

+4 +4 +4

The next term is $17 + 4 = 21$.

You can check the 5th term, as calculated in part **a**, with the position-to-term rule.
$5 \times 4 + 1 = 20 + 1 = 21$ ✓

b Draw a table of values.
Include the 4 times table.

Position	1	2	3	4
4× table	4	8	12	16
Term	5	9	13	17

×4, +1

The position-to-term rule is *'multiply the position by 4 and add 1'*.
So, the 60th term is $60 \times 4 + 1 = 240 + 1$
$= 241$.

Exercise 13b

1 This sequence of parallelograms is made using short sticks.

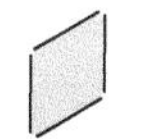 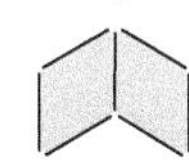 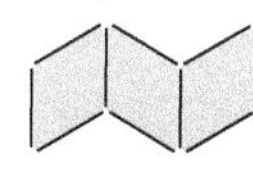 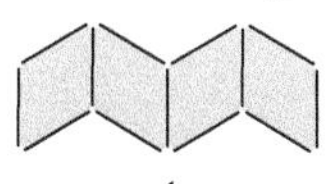

Position 1 2 3 4

a How many extra sticks are needed to make the next position?

b Draw the diagram for position 5.

c Write the term-to-term rule in words.

d Copy and complete this table and use it to find the position-to-term rule.

e How many sticks are needed to make the 50th position?

Position	1	2	3	4	5
...× table					
Term	4				

2 For each of these sequences,

i draw the diagram for position 4

ii make a table of values for the number of sticks in positions 1 to 4

iii use the table to find the position-to-term rule

iv find how many sticks are needed for the 100th position.

a   

b   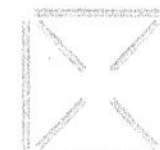 

3 For each of these sequences,

i use a table of values to find the position-to-term rule

ii find the next two terms and the 100th term.

a 2, 6, 10, 14, 18, ... **b** 5, 8, 11, 14, 17, ...

c 1, 7, 13, 19, 25, ... **d** 9, 11, 13, 15, 17, ...

e 2, 11, 20, 29, 38, ... **f** 2, 10, 18, 26, 34, ...

g $3\frac{1}{2}$, 4, $4\frac{1}{2}$, 5, $5\frac{1}{2}$, ... **h** 6, 4, 2, 0, -2, ...

Problem solving

4 Find the missing terms and the 50th term of each of these sequences.

a 5, 11, ☐, 23, 29, ☐ ... **b** $3\frac{1}{2}$, ☐, $6\frac{1}{2}$, 8, ☐, 11 ...

5 The sequence 0, 1, 1, 2, 3, 5, 8, ... starts with 0, 1. You make further terms by adding together the two previous terms.

a Write the next three terms of the sequence.

This sequence is called the *Fibonacci sequence* after an Italian (born in 1170 AD) who studied with Arab mathematicians.

b Investigate how this sequence relates to the branching of a tree, leaves on a stem and patterns in pineapples and sunflowers.

Did you know?

The number of petals and leaves that a flower has is often a Fibonacci number. Perhaps that is why four-leaf clovers are so rare.

- You can use the **general term** to calculate the value of any term. It is written using n and is often called the ***n*th term**.

The terms increase by 4 each time because the square has four sides and each side increases by one circle.

This sequence of squares is made from coloured circles.

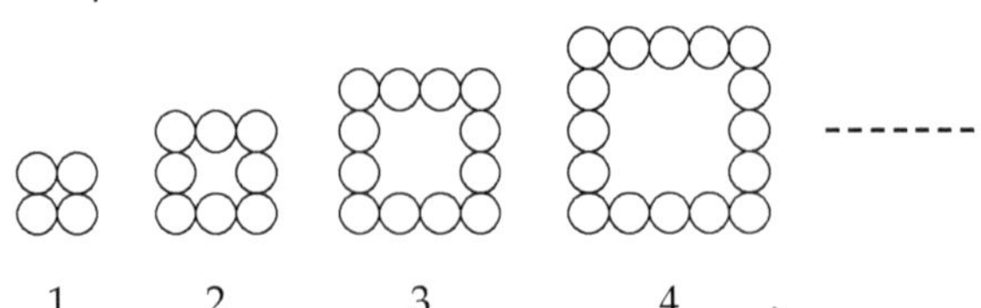

Position	1	2	3	4
Number of circles	4	8	12	16

×4

The position-to-term rule is *'multiply the position by 4'*.

You can continue the sequence to find this table of values.

The 5th term is $4 \times 5 = 20$.

The nth term is $4 \times n = 4n$.

Position	1	2	3	4	5	...	n
Term	4	8	12	16	20	...	$4n$

×4

Example

Find the general term and the 80th term of the sequence 1, 4, 7, 10, ...

1 → 4 → 7 → 10 (+3, +3, +3)

Draw a table of values.

Position	1	2	3	4	...	n
3· table	3	6	9	12	...	$3n$
Term	1	4	7	10	...	$3n - 2$

×3, −2

The general term is $3n - 2$.

The 80th term is $3 \times 80 - 2 = 240 - 2 = 238$.

The sequence increases by 3 each time, so compare the terms with the three times table.

Sequences can also be decreasing.

Example

The nth term of a sequence is $T(n) = 40 - 5n$.

Generate the first three terms of the sequence.

The 1st term has $n = 1$, so $T(1) = 40 - 5 \times 1 = 40 - 5 = 35$.

The 2nd term has $n = 2$, so $T(2) = 40 - 5 \times 2 = 40 - 10 = 30$.

The 3rd term has $n = 3$, so $T(3) = 40 - 5 \times 3 = 40 - 15 = 25$.

So, the sequence begins 35, 30, 25, ...

T stands for term. T(n) stands for nth term. T(1) is the first term, T(2) is the second term, and so on.

Exercise 13c

1 Here is a sequence made from square tiles.

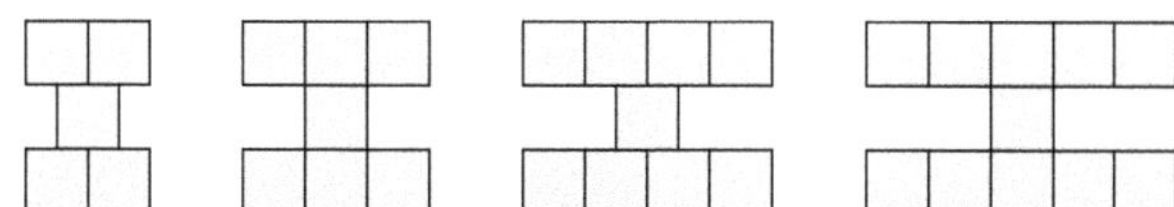

a How many squares are added to get from one term to the next?

b Copy and complete this table of values.

Position	1	2	3	4	5	...	n
...· table							
Term							

↓ ......
↓ ......

c Write the nth term of the sequence.

d Find the 5th term and the 50th term.

Did you know?

Islamic art is famous for its tiling patterns.

2 For each of these sequences,

i construct a table of values
ii write the position-to-term rule in words
iii find the nth term
iv find the 6th term and the 40th term.

a 6, 8, 10, 12, 14, ...
b 0, 2, 4, 6, 8, ...
c 5, 8, 11, 14, 17, ...
d 3, 8, 13, 18, 23, ...
e 7, 13, 19, 25, 31, ...
f 5, 13, 21, 29, 37, ...
g 10, 17, 24, 31, 38, ...
h -1, 3, 7, 11, 15, ...
i -4, -1, 2, 5, 8, ...
j 8, 6, 4, 2, 0, ...

3 Generate the first six terms of the sequences with these general terms.

Substitute $n = 1$ to $n = 6$ into the expression for $T(n)$.

a $T(n) = 2n + 5$
b $T(n) = 3n - 2$
c $T(n) = 4n + 1$
d $T(n) = 10n - 7$
e $T(n) = 6n + 3$
f $T(n) = 2n - 5$
g $T(n) = 2(n + 1)$
h $T(n) = 3(n - 1)$
i $T(n) = 4(2n - 1)$
j $T(n) = \frac{1}{2}n + 2$
k $T(n) = 30 - 2n$
l $T(n) = 6 - 4n$

Problem solving

4 Find the missing term, the next term and the 100th term of each of these sequences.

a 6, 11, 16, ☐, 26, ...
b 12, 22, ☐, 42, 52, ...
c 3, 7, 11, ☐, 19, ...
d 5, 13, 21, ☐, 37, ...

5 A flower bed is surrounded by square slabs.
The surround is always three slabs wide but it can be any length.
Make a table of values for different lengths of the flower bed from 3 to 7 slabs long and the total number of slabs used in each case.
Then find the general term for the sequence of the numbers of slabs.

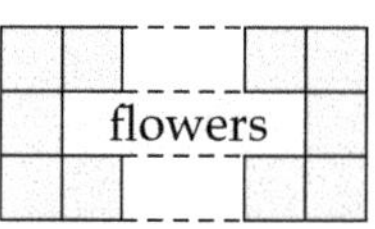

13d Real-life sequences

Kim is given a dog for her birthday.
She has one tin of dog food to start with.
She then buys three tins every day.
She wants to know how many tins she will need to buy in the first 120 days.

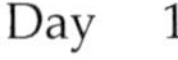

Day 1 2 3

The total number of tins make the sequence 1, 4, 7, 10, ...
The term-to-term rule is *'start with 1 and add 3 each time'*.

Day	1	2	3	4	5	...	n
3× table	3	6	9	12	15	...	$3n$
Tins	1	4	7	10	13	...	$3n - 2$

×3
−2

The difference between the terms is 3, so the nth term will include 3n.

The position-to-term rule is *'multiply by 3 and then subtract 2'*.
The **formula** (nth term) for the total number of tins is $3n - 2$.
In the first 120 days Kim will need to buy:

$3 \times 120 - 2 = 360 - 2$
$= 358$ tins.

Example

In week 1, Stephen has £10 in his bank account.
His grandma adds £6 each week to help him save.
How much is in his account after a year?

BANK STATEMENT			
Date	In	Out	Balance
04/3/09	10.00	–	10.00
11/3/09	6.00	–	16.00

The term-to-term rule is *'start with £10 and then add £6 each week'*.

Week	1	2	3	4	...	n
6× table	6	12	18	24	...	$6n$
Sum (£)	10	16	22	28	...	$6n + 4$

×6
+4

The position-to-term rule is *'multiply by 6 and then add 4'*.
The **sum** in his account after n weeks is £$(6n + 4)$.
A year is 52 weeks.
So, after a year, he will have $6 \times 52 + 4 = 312 + 4 =$ £316.

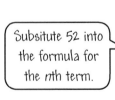

Subsitute 52 into the formula for the nth term.

Exercise 13d

Problem solving

1 Holly covers a wall with square tiles.
She starts with two tiles and then puts four tiles in every column.

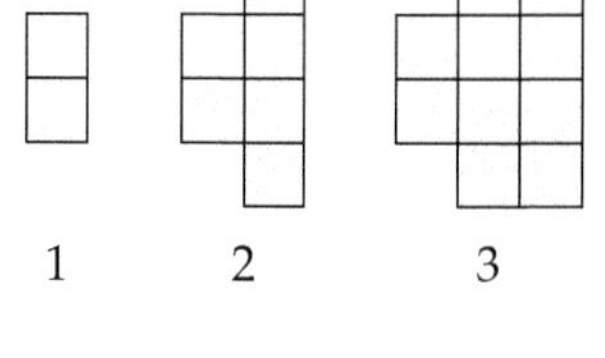

a Write the term-to-term rule and find the next term.

b Construct a table of values and write the position-to-term rule.

c Find an expression for the number of tiles in the nth position.

d How many tiles does Holly need for the 20th position?

2 Safraz buys a new bike. He travels 100 miles on the first day.
He then averages 15 miles every day.

a Generate a sequence for the total miles he has travelled after 1, 2, 3, 4 and 5 days.

b Write the term-to-term rule and find the next two terms.

c Construct a table of values and write the position-to-term rule.

d Find an expression for T(n), the total mileage travelled after n days.

e How far has he travelled in total after 2 weeks?

3 A machine punches holes into a metal sheet.
In the first second it punches 10 holes.
In every further second it punches 4 holes.

a Write the total number of holes punched after 1, 2, 3, 4 and 5 seconds.

b Find the term-to-term rule and the position-to-term rule.

c How many holes has it punched after

i n seconds **ii** 1 minute?

4 In a science experiment, a beaker contains a chemical solution.
The volume of solution, in millilitres, in the beaker after n seconds is $T(n) = 2n + 48$.

a Write a sequence for the volume of solution in the beaker after 1, 2, 3, 4 and 5 seconds.

b How many millilitres are added to the beaker each second?

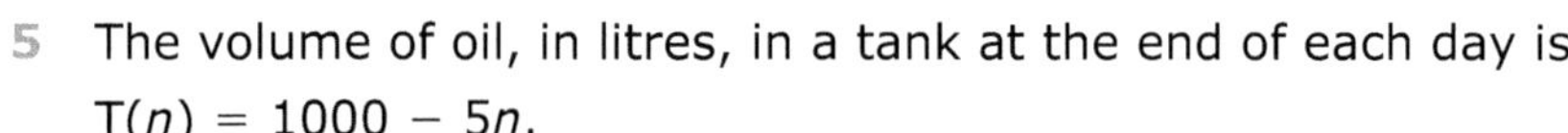

5 The volume of oil, in litres, in a tank at the end of each day is $T(n) = 1000 - 5n$.

a Write a sequence for the volume of oil at the end of each day during the first week.

b How much oil is left in the tank after 3 weeks?

6 Use a spreadsheet to generate the sequence with the general term $T(n) = 5n + 3$.
Invent some sequences of your own.

	A	B	C	D	E
1	Position, n	1	2	3	4
2	Term, T(n)	=5*B1+3			

13e Recursive sequences

Here is a simple **linear sequence**: 7, 13, 19, 25, 31, ...

T(1) means 'the first term', so T(1) = 7, T(2) = 13, T(3) = 19, ...

In a linear sequence, there is a constant difference between terms.

Think of the sequence as a flowchart that feeds back on itself:

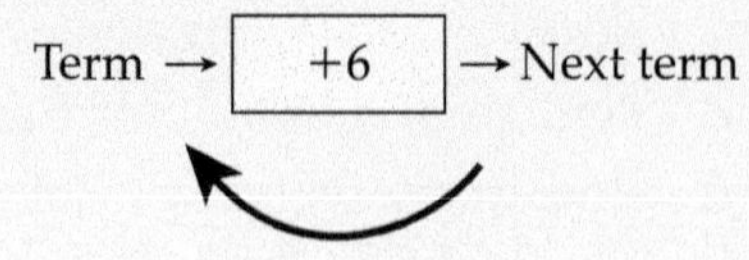

The **term-to-term** rule for this sequence is:

Start from 7 and add 6 to get the next term

You can define this sequence using a **recursive formula**:

$$T(n + 1) = T(n) + 6, \quad T(1) = 7$$

- $T(n + 1)$: The next or $(n + 1)$th term in the sequence
- $T(n)$: Any (nth) term in the sequence
- $T(1) = 7$: This is where you start from

A recursive formula is really just a term-to-term rule!
So T(4) = T(3) + 6 just means 25 = 19 + 6.

Example

Write the first five terms of each of these sequences.

a $T(n + 1) = T(n) + 8$ $T(1) = 3$

b $T(n + 1) = 2T(n)$ $T(1) = 1$

a $T(1) = 3$ then $T(2) = 3 + 8 = 11$ $T(3) = 11 + 8 = 19$, ...

3, 11, 19, 27, 35

b $T(1) = 1$ then $T(2) = 2 \times 1 = 2$ $T(3) = 2 \times 2 = 4$

$T(4) = 2 \times 4 = 8$, $T(5) = 2 \times 8 = 16$

1, 2, 4, 8, 16

$T(n + 1) = 2T(n)$ is a **geometric sequence**.

In the sequence 1, 2, 4, 8, 16, ... you double each time to get the next term.

In a geometric sequence, you multiply each term by a fixed amount to get the next term.

8, 24, 72, 216, 648, ... is a geometric sequence.

Example

A pond contains frogs and lily pads. Each month for a year,

the number of frogs is given by $T(n + 1) = T(n) + 20$

and the number of lily pads is given by $T(n + 1) = 2T(n) - 3$

At the start of the year there are 8 frogs and 4 lily pads.

Write the sequence of the number of

a frogs for the first 6 months

b lily pads for the first 6 months

a $T(2) = 8 + 20 = 28$

8, 28, 48, 68, 88, 108

b $T(2) = 2 \times 4 - 3 = 5$

4, 5, 7, 11, 19, 35

Exercise 13e

1 Write the first five terms of each of these sequences.

a $T(n + 1) = T(n) + 1$, $T(1) = 2$
b $T(n + 1) = T(n) + 2$, $T(1) = 0$
c $T(n + 1) = T(n) + 4$, $T(1) = 3$
d $T(n + 1) = T(n) - 2$, $T(1) = -1$
e $T(n + 1) = T(n) - \frac{1}{2}$, $T(1) = 1$
f $T(n + 1) = T(n) - 0.75$, $T(1) = 0.5$

2 Write the first five terms of each of these sequences.

a $T(n + 1) = 2T(n)$, $T(1) = 2$
b $T(n + 1) = 2T(n) + 1$, $T(1) = 0$
c $T(n + 1) = 2T(n) - 1$, $T(1) = 3$
d $T(n + 1) = 3T(n) - 1$, $T(1) = 1$
e $T(n + 1) = -2T(n) + 4$, $T(1) = 1$
f $T(n + 1) = -2T(n) + 3$, $T(1) = 1$

3 Describe each of these sequences using a recursive formula.

a 2, 4, 6, 8, 10, ...
b 3, 7, 11, 15, 19, ...
c -2, 4, 10, 16, 22, ...
d 4, 1, -2, -5, -8, ...
e -5, -9, -13, -17, -21, ...
f $\frac{1}{2}, \frac{5}{4}, 2, 2\frac{3}{4}, 3\frac{1}{2}, \ldots$

4 Describe each of these sequences using a recursive formula.

a 5, 11, ☐, 23, ☐, 35, ...
b ☐, 15, 23, ☐, 39, 47, ...
c 13, 30, ☐, ☐, 81, 98, ...
d 1, 3, 9, 27, 81, 243, ...
e 1, 4, 16, 64, 256, ...
f 5, 10, 20, 40, 80, ...

Careful: the first 3 are linear and have gaps; the last three are geometric.

Problem solving

5 Zachary starts up a savings account with £300. His bank gives him £3 interest each month. At the end of each month he records the amount in pounds sterling in his account:

303, 306, 309, ...

a Write a rule for this sequence using a recursive formula
b Zadie also starts up a bank account with £300. The total amount including interest increases each month according to this formula:

$T(n + 1) = 1.01\ T(n)$

c Write out the amounts in Zadie's account for the first five months.
d Who has the most money after a year: Zachary or Zadie?

6 Phoebe is a budding musician. She posts a song on the Internet and very soon it has gone viral! In the first week after its release, the number of hits was only 9, but then the weekly number of hits increased by the recursive formula $T(n + 1) = 2T(n) + 6$. Find the number of hits after

a three weeks
b 12 weeks

7 Look back at the example on the opposite page. During the year, will the population of lily pads overtake the population of frogs? If so, after how many months?

13 MySummary

Check out

You should now be able to ...

	Level	Test it ➡ **Questions**
✓ Find the term-to-term rule for a sequence.	5	1
✓ Find the position-to-term rule for a sequence, and write it as the *n*th term.	6	2 – 5
✓ Use sequences to solve problems in practical situations.	6	6
✓ Generate sequences using a recursive formula.	7	7

Language	Meaning	Example
Sequence	A set of numbers that follow a rule.	4, 7, 10, 13, ... is a sequence.
Term	A number in a sequence.	10 is the third term of the sequence 4, 7, 10, 13, ...
Position	The place that a term has in a sequence.	10 is in the third position in the sequence 4, 7, 10, 13, ...
Term-to-term rule	A rule that explains how to get from one term to the next term.	In the sequence 4, 7, 10, 13, ... the rule is 'add 3 each time'.
Position-to-term rule	A rule that uses the position to work out the term.	In this sequence (see table below) the position to term rule is 'Multiply the position by 3 and then add 1'.
***n*th term**	A shorter way to write the position-to-term rule that uses the letter n.	The position-to-term rule 'multiply the position by 3 and then add 1' can be written $3n + 1$.

Position	1	2	3	4
Term	4	7	10	13

13 MyReview

1 Write the term-to-term rule and the next two terms in each case.

a 1, 2, 4, 8, …
b 80, 40, 20, 10, …
c 2, 5, 11, 23, …

2 This sequences is made using short sticks.

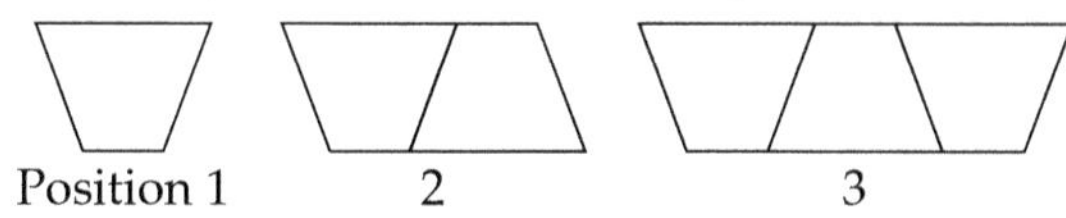

a Write the term-to-term rule in words.
b How many sticks are needed to make position 4?
c Copy and complete the table.

Position	1	2	3	4	5
…x table					
Term	4	7			

d Use the table to find the position-to-term rule.
e How many sticks are needed to make the 20th position?

3 Find the position-to-term rule for each of these sequences.

a 5, 9, 13, 17, …
b 18, 25, 32, 39, …
c 3.5, 4, 4.5, 5, …
d 9, 8, 7, 6, …

4 Generate the first 5 terms of the sequences with these position-to-term rules.

a $T(n) = 6n - 2$
b $T(n) = \frac{1}{2}n - 1$
c $T(n) = 2(n + 3)$
d $T(n) = 12 - 2n$

5 Find the nth term for each of these sequences.

a 3, 5, 7, 9, … **b** 8, 18, 28, 38, …
c -5, 0, 5, 10, … **d** 10, 7, 4, 1, …

6 The volume of diesel (in litres) left in a fuel tank at the end of each day is given by $T(n) = 78 - 5n$.

a Write a sequence for the volume of diesel in the tank at the end of each day for a week.
b How many litres of diesel will be left in the tank after two weeks?
c Day one was a Monday. On which day of the third week will it run out of diesel completely?

7 Describe each sequence using a recursive formula.

a 5, 8, 11, 14, 17, …
b 16, 11, 6, 1, -4, …
c 3, 6, 12, 24, 48, …
d 324, 108, 36, 12, 4, …

What next?

Score	
0 – 3	Your knowledge of this topic is still developing. To improve look at Formative test: 3B-13; MyMaths: 1165, 1173 and 1945
4, 5	You are gaining a secure knowledge of this topic. To improve look at InvisiPen: 281, 282, 283, 285, 286 and 293
6, 7	You have mastered this topic. Well done, you are ready to progress!

1 You can use matches to make this sequence of patterns.

a Draw the next pattern of the sequence.

b Write the first four terms of the sequence that gives the numbers of matches.

c Find the term-to-term rule.

d Write the next three consecutive terms of the sequence.

2 Use this flow diagram to generate the terms of a sequence.

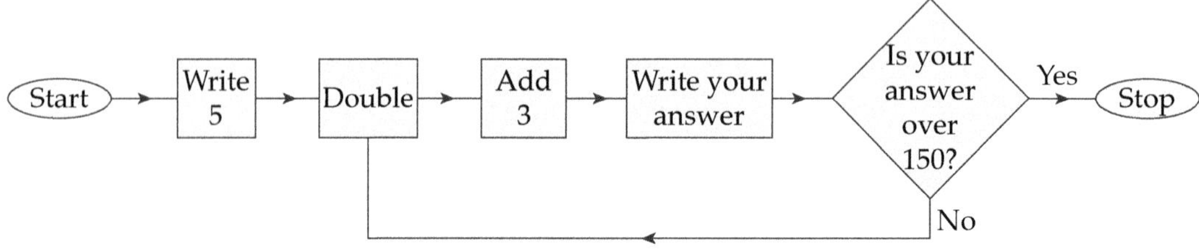

3 For each of these sequences, describe the term-to-term rule in words and find the next three consecutive terms.

a 3, 7, 15, 31, ...　　b 4, 7, 13, 25, ...　　c 30, 27, 24, 21, ...

d $\frac{1}{2}$, 2, 8, 32, ...　　e 400, 200, 100, 50, ...　　f 1, 11, 111, 1111, ...

4 This sequence of crosses is made using square tiles.

a How many extra tiles are added to make the next term in the sequence?

b Draw the diagram for position 4.

c Copy and complete this table and use it to find the position-to-term rule.

Position	1	2	3	4	5	...	*n*
...× table							
Term							

d How many tiles are needed to make the 20th position?

5 For each of these sequences,

i use a table of values to find the position-to-term rule

ii find the next two terms and the 50th term.

a 4, 7, 10, 13, 16, ...　　b 6, 11, 16, 21, 26, ...

c 2, 5, 8, 11, 14, ...　　d 98, 96, 94, 92, 90, ...

6 Find the missing terms and the 100th terms of each of these sequences.

a 5, 8, 11, ☐, 17, 20　　b 1, 4, 7, 10, ☐, 16, ...

13c

7 For each of these sequences,

i construct a table of values

ii write the position-to-term rule in words

iii find the nth term

iv find the value of the 6th term and the 100th term.

a 5, 7, 9, 11, 13, ... **b** 13, 16, 19, 22, 25, ...

c 2, 7, 12, 17, 22, ... **d** 1, 5, 9, 13, 17, ...

8 Generate the first six terms of the sequences with these general terms.

a $T(n) = 2n + 10$ **b** $T(n) = 5n - 5$ **c** $T(n) = 4n + 6$

d $T(n) = 50 - 2n$ **e** $T(n) = 15 - 5n$ **f** $T(n) = 2(3n - 2)$

9 Here is part of a spreadsheet.

Column A gives the position of each term.

Column B gives the actual terms of a sequence.

a Write the position-to-term rule in words.

b Write the nth term.

c Write the first six terms of the sequence.

	A	B
1	Position	Term
2	1	=3*A2−1
3	=A2+1	=3*A3−1
4	=A3+1	=3*A4−1

13d

10 A kitchen wall has three rows of tiles.

The two end columns have tiles with floral patterns.

There are n central columns of plain white tiles.

a Find the total number of tiles used when $n = 3$.

b Find an expression $T(n)$ for the total number of tiles.

c Write the sequence of the values of $T(n)$ for $n = 40$ to $n = 45$.

11 David is saving for his summer holiday.

He starts with £20 and then he saves £8 each week.

a How much has he saved after

i 2 weeks **ii** 5 weeks?

b Find an expression for $T(n)$, the amount, in pounds, he has saved after n weeks.

c How much has he saved after 20 weeks?

13e

12 Describe each sequence using a recursive formula.

a 4, 7, 10, 13, 16, ... **b** 3, 0, -3, -6, -9, ...

c 2, 8, 32, 128, 512, ... **d** 3, 9, 27, 81, 243, ...

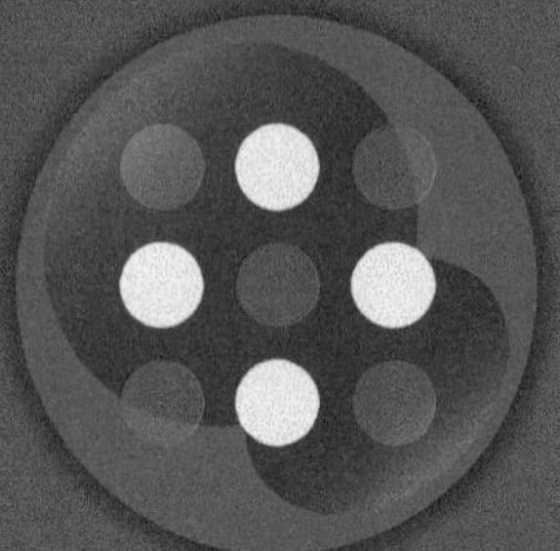

14 3D shapes

Introduction

Small animals such as meerkats only eat a few grams of food a day. However it would only take about a week for a meerkat to eat the equivalent of its own body mass in food. A human on the other hand, eats about 1 kg of food a day but would take nearer two months to eat the equivalent of its own body mass in food. Meerkats have a greater surface area in proportion to their volume than humans, meaning they lose relatively more heat, meaning they need to eat relatively more.

What's the point?

The size and shape of different animals determines their metabolism. Understanding surface area and volume helps us to understand the animal kingdom.

Objectives

By the end of this chapter you will have learned how to ...

- Recognise and name 3D shapes.
- Analyse 3D shapes and deduce some of their properties.
- Draw 3D shapes on isometric paper.
- Analyse 3D shapes through 2D projections.
- Draw the plan and elevations of a 3D shape.
- Recognise reflection symmetry in 3D shapes.
- Identify planes of symmetry.
- Calculate the surface area of a prism.
- Calculate the volume of a prism.

Check in

1 Write the mathematical name of these 2D shapes.

a  b 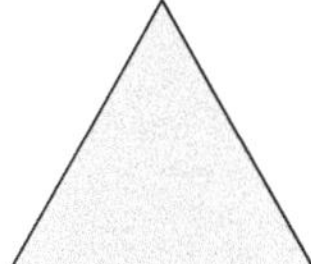 c 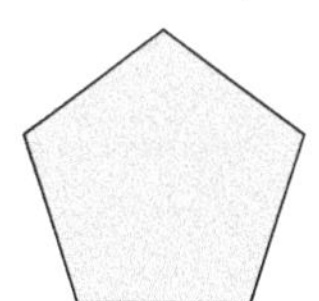 d 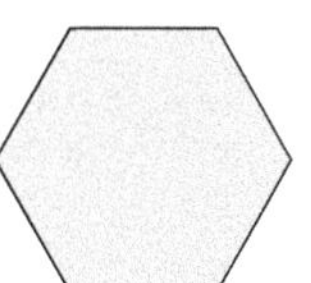 e 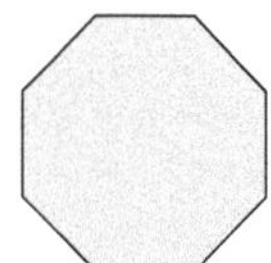

2 Calculate the surface area and volume of these cuboids.

a 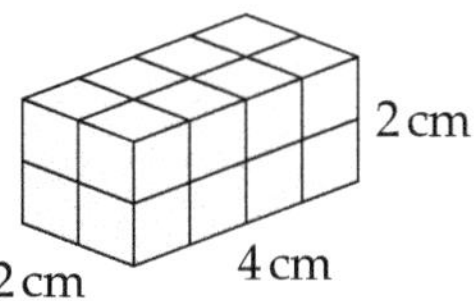

b 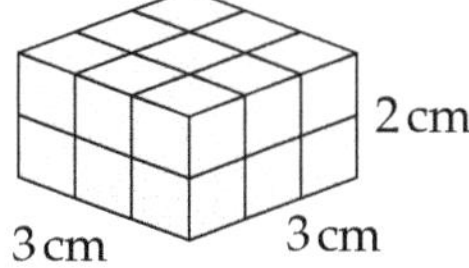

3 Calculate the area of these shapes.

a 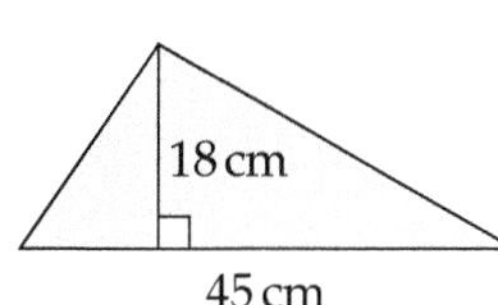

b 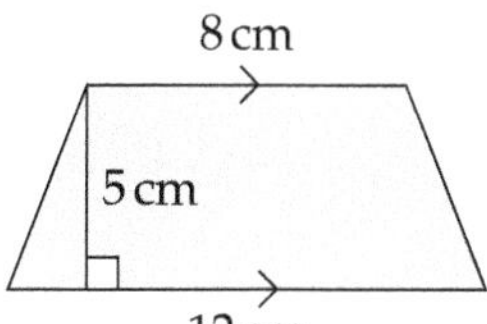

Starter problem

Here is an animal made from cubes.

Calculate the volume and surface area of the animal.

Build an enlargement of the animal which is twice as long, twice as wide and twice as tall.

Calculate the volume and surface area of your new animal.

Investigate.

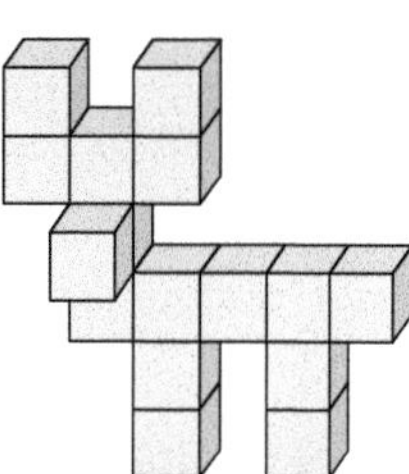

14a 3D shapes

A solid is a three-dimensional (3D) shape.

You should know some of the language associated with 3D shapes.

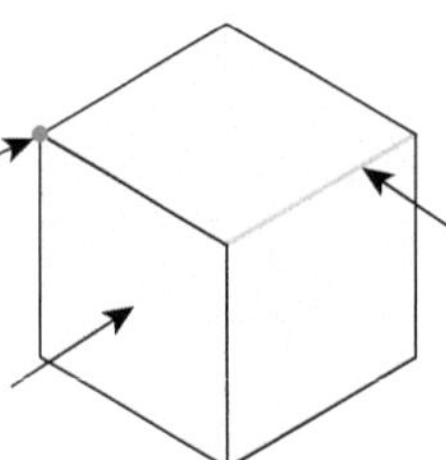

A **vertex** is a point at which three or more edges meet. The plural of vertex is **vertices**.
An **edge** is the line where two faces meet.
A **face** is a flat surface of a solid.

You should also know some different types of 3D shapes.

A **prism** has the same **cross-section** throughout its length.

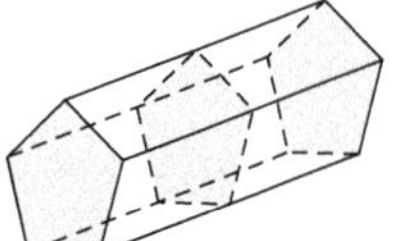

▲ A pentagonal prism

The cross-section is a plane through the solid and decides the name of a prism.
The base decides the name of a pyramid.

A **pyramid** has a base that tapers to a point.

▲ Square-based pyramids.

You can draw some 3D shapes on isometric paper.

Example

a How many faces, edges and vertices does this shape have?

b Draw the solid on isometric paper.

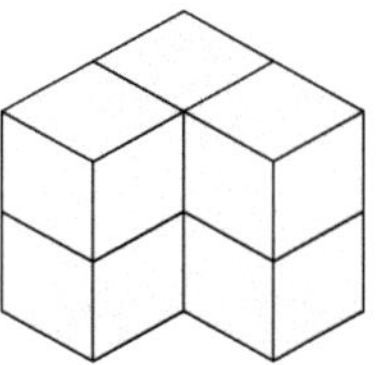

a 8 faces
18 edges
12 vertices

b

You can show lines of equal length on isometric paper. Isometric paper must be orientated this way.

Exercise 14a

1 A triangular prism is made from three blue rectangles and two pink triangles.

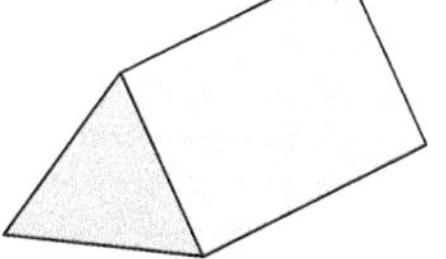

Find the number of edges where

a a blue face meets a blue face

b a blue face meets a pink face

c a pink face meets a pink face.

2 Three cubes are used to make a solid.

a On isometric paper, draw as many different solids as possible using the three cubes.

b Write the number of faces, edges and vertices of each solid.

Problem solving

3 **a** Copy and complete the table. You may need to look up some of these solid shapes.

b Find a rule connecting f, v and e.

Name of solid	Number of faces (f)	Number of vertices (v)	Number of edges (e)
Cube			
Cuboid			
Square-based pyramid			
Tetrahedron			
Triangular prism			
Hexagonal-based pyramid			
Hexagonal prism			
Octagonal-based pyramid			
Octahedron			

Did you know?

Salt crystals are always cubes.

4 The centres of four faces of a cube are marked A, B, C and D. A and C are on opposite faces and B and D are on opposite faces.

a What is the mathematical name of the shape ABCD?

b Explain how you know.

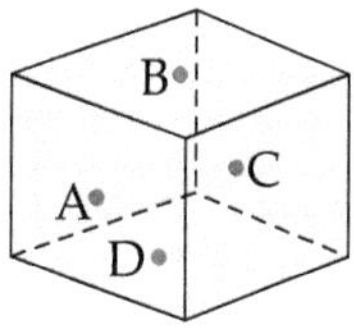

5 **a** Draw these seven solids on isometric paper.

i 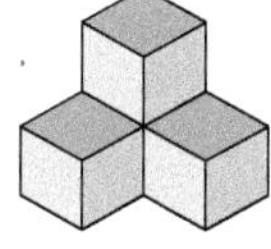

ii 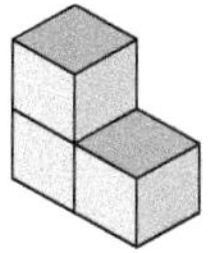

iii 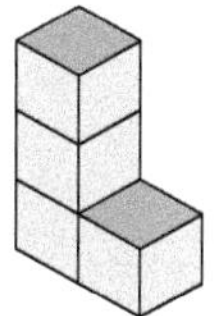

iv 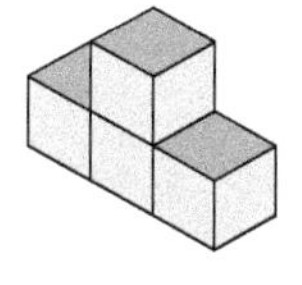

v 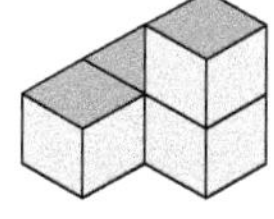

vi 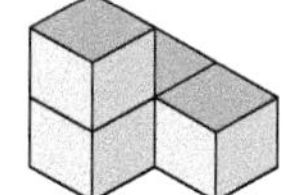

vii 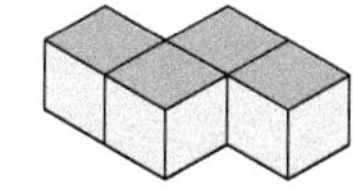

b Calculate the total volume of all the solids.

c Make these shapes using Multilink cubes and fit them together to form a cube.

d What are the dimensions of the cube?

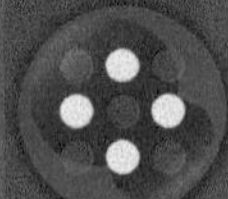

14b Plans and elevations

- Plans and elevations are **projections** of a 3D solid onto a 2D surface.

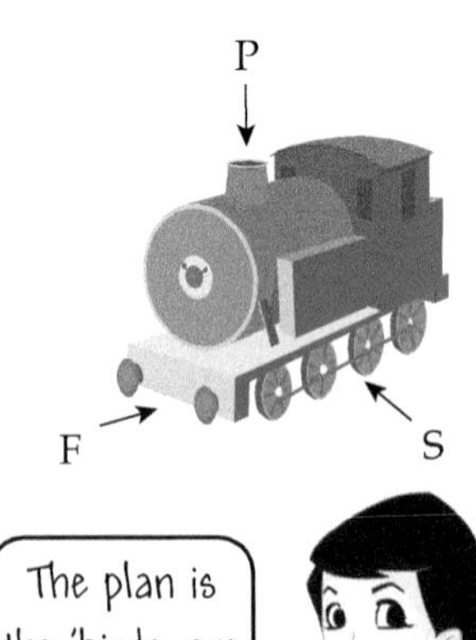

You can look at this toy engine from different directions.

From the front, from the side and from above.

Front elevation (F)

Side elevation (S)

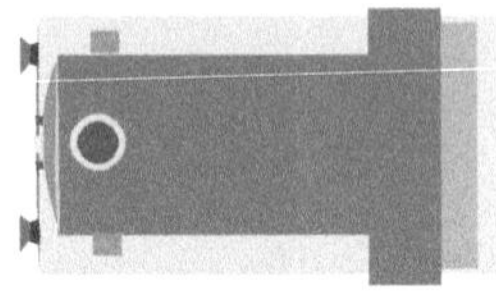

Plan (P)

The plan is the 'birds-eye view'.

Example

Connor draws this prism on isometric paper. Draw the elevations and plan of his solid on square grid paper.

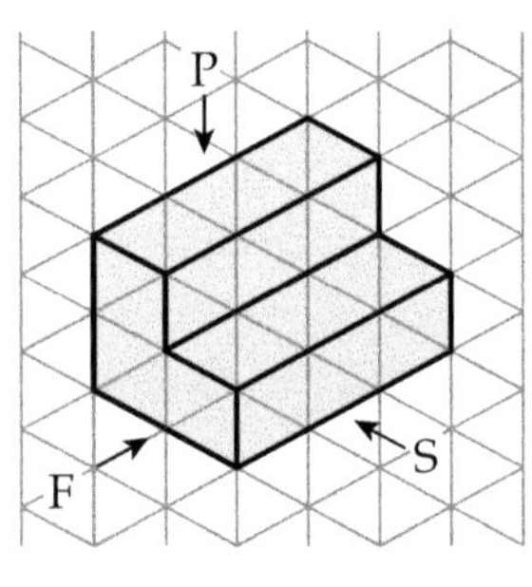

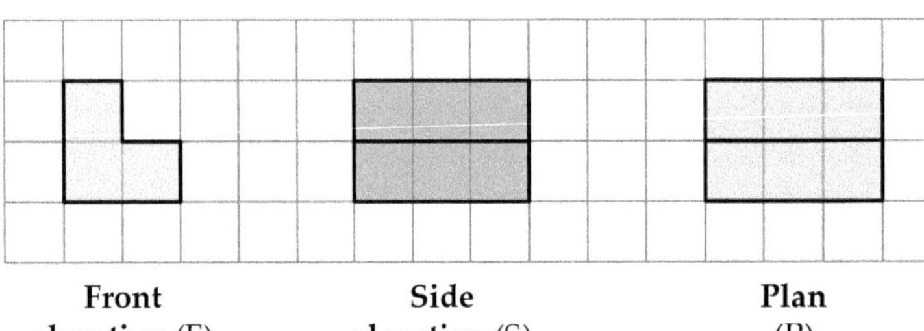

Front elevation (F) **Side elevation** (S) **Plan** (P)

Bold lines are used to show the edges of the solid.

Example

Here are the elevations and plan of a solid.

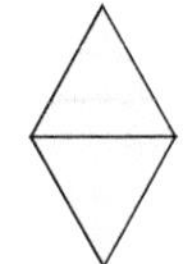

Front elevation (F)

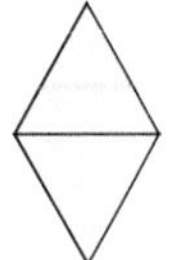

Side elevation (S)

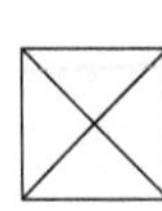

Plan (P)

a What is its mathematical name?

b Draw the solid showing the directions of the elevations and the plan view.

a Octahedron

b

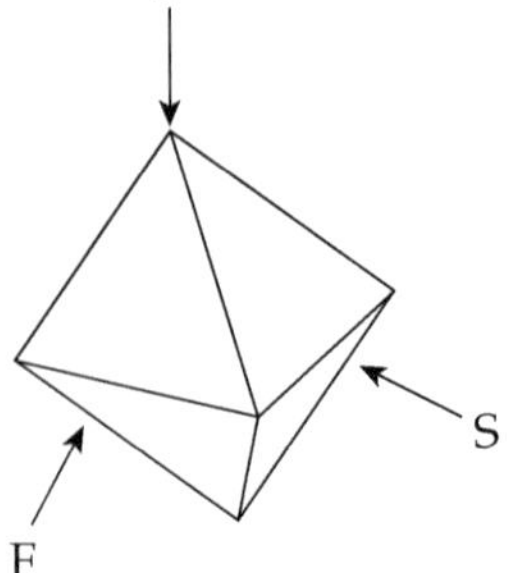

Exercise 14b

1 This solid is made of 12 cubes.
Here are four drawings of the views.
Match each diagram to the correct view.

View D
View C
View A
View B

a 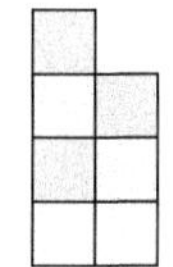
b 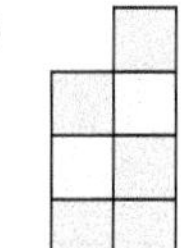
c 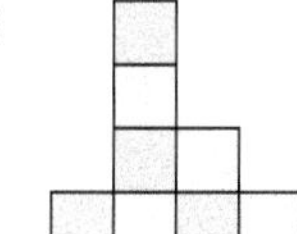
d 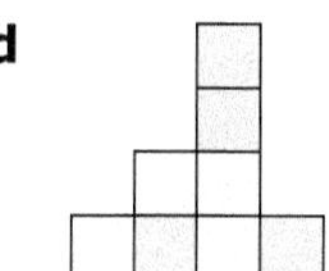

2 Sketch the front elevation (F), the side elevation (S) and the plan (P) of each of these prisms.

a 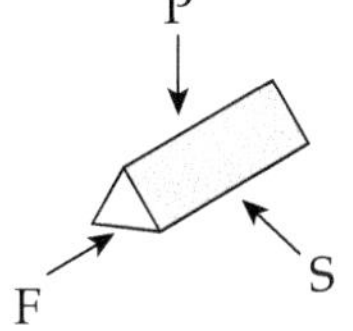

b 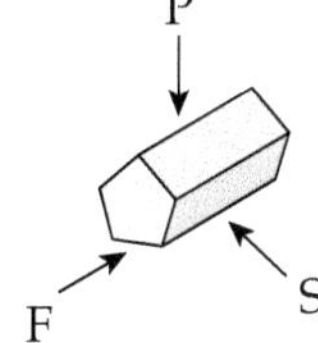

c 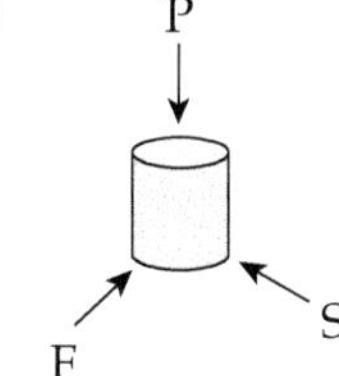

3 Bryony makes a 3D solid from cubes.
Here are the elevations and the plan.

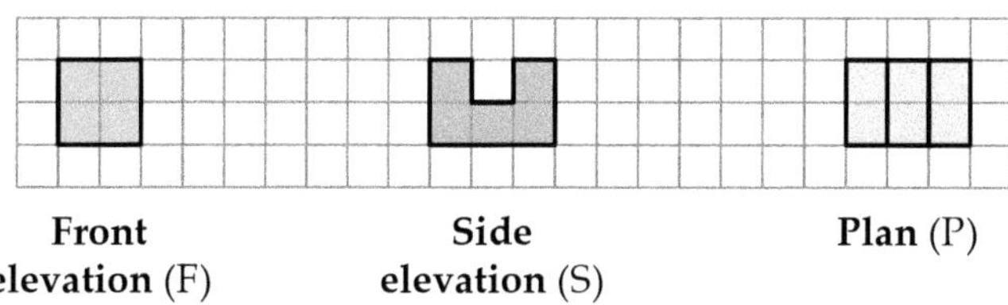

Front elevation (F) **Side elevation** (S) **Plan** (P)

a Draw her solid on isometric paper.
b How many cubes are needed to make the shape?

Problem solving

4 The front elevation of a square-based pyramid is a triangle. Find a 3D solid that has a front elevation of

a a square **b** a rectangle
c a circle **d** a hexagon.

P
F
S

▲ A square-based pyramid

5 Draw an object of your choice. Mark on your drawing the directions of the elevations and the plan view.
Draw the front elevation, the side elevation and the plan of your object.

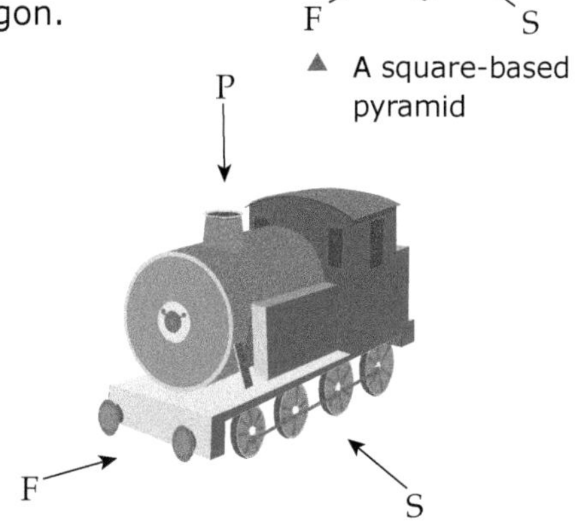

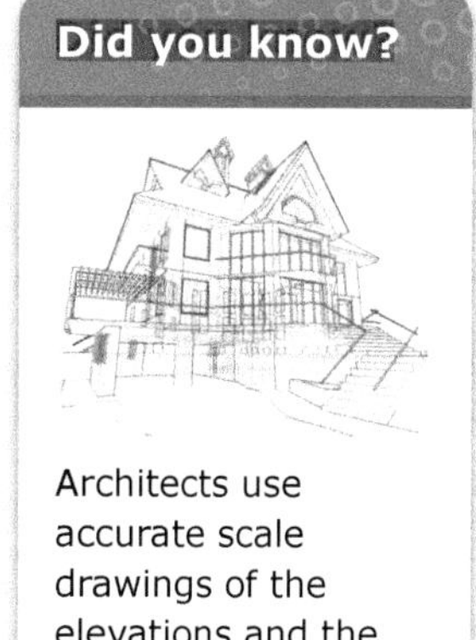

Did you know?
Architects use accurate scale drawings of the elevations and the plan when they design buildings.

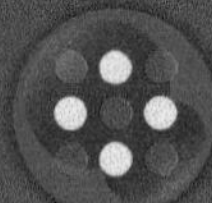

14c Symmetry of a 3D shape

- A **line of symmetry** divides a 2D shape into two identical halves, each of which is the mirror image of the other.

A rectangle has two lines of symmetry.

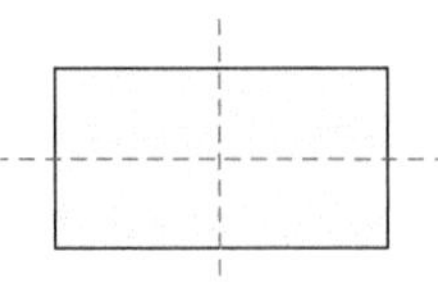

The diagonals of the rectangle are not lines of symmetry.

Some **solids** have **reflection symmetry**.

- A **plane of symmetry** divides a 3D shape into two identical halves. Each is the mirror image of the other.

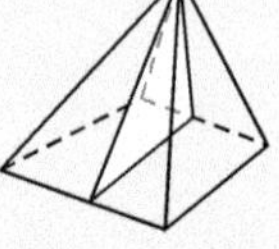

Example

Draw diagrams to show all the planes of symmetry of this cuboid.

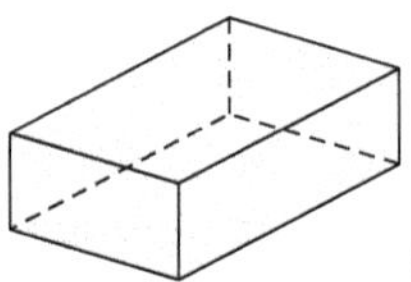

The cuboid has three planes of symmetry.

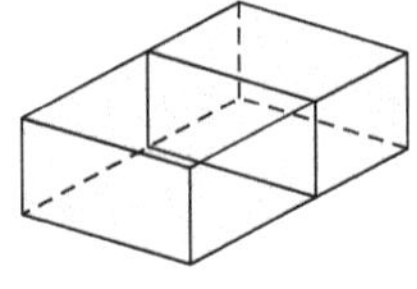

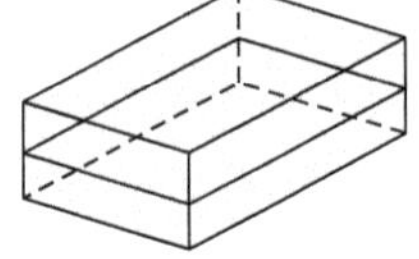

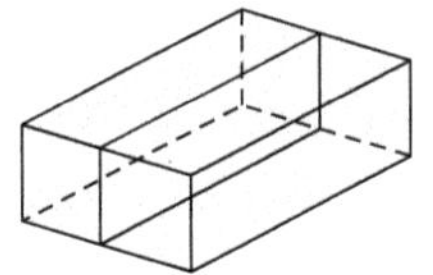

Planes through the diagonals of the rectangular faces are not planes of symmetry.

- A **net** is a 2D shape that folds to form a solid.

Example

Here is the net of a 3D solid.

a Write the name of the solid formed by the net.

b Draw diagrams to show any planes of symmetry.

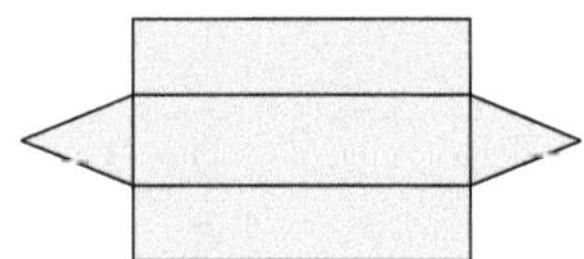

a An isosceles triangular prism.

b

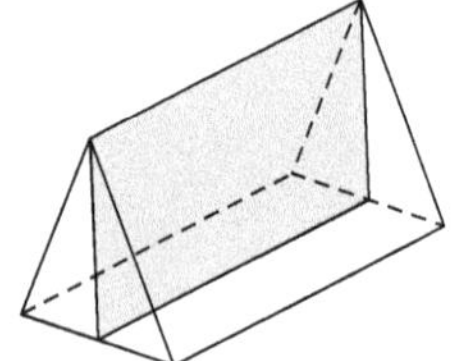

The solid has two planes of symmetry.

Exercise 14c

1 For each of these solids, decide whether the shaded plane is a plane of symmetry. Explain your reasoning.

a

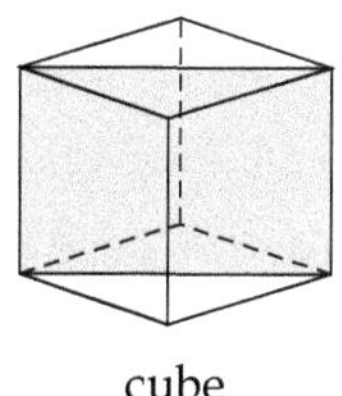

cube

b

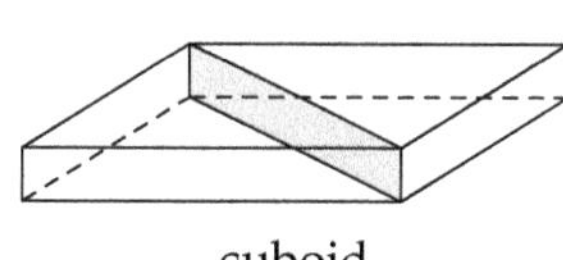

cuboid

c

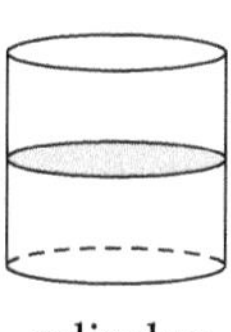

cylinder

2 Draw diagrams to show all the planes of symmetry of these solids.

a

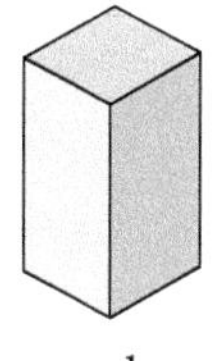

square based cuboid

b

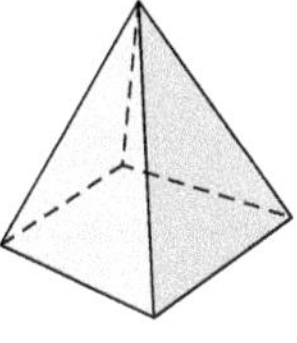

square based pyramid

c

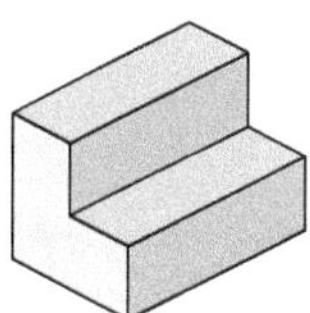

hexagonal prism

Problem solving

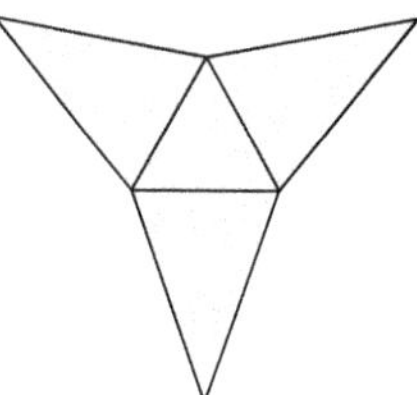

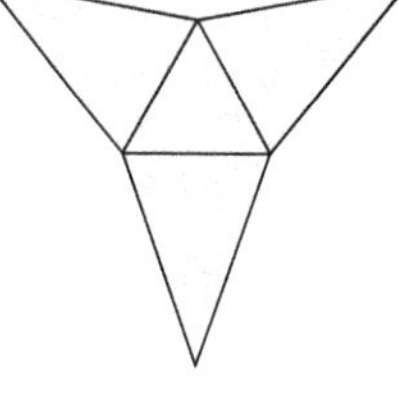

3 The net of a 3D shape consists of three isosceles triangles and one equilateral triangle.

a Give the name of the solid formed by the net.

b How many planes of symmetry does the solid have?

4 You can slice a cube to give a square cross-section. Draw diagrams that show how a cube can be sliced so that the cross-section is

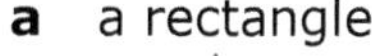

a a rectangle

b a triangle

c a pentagon.

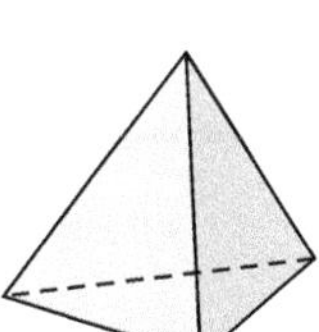

5 **a** Construct a regular tetrahedron of length 5 cm, using materials of your choice.

b How many edges does the solid have?

c How many planes of symmetry does a regular tetrahedron have?

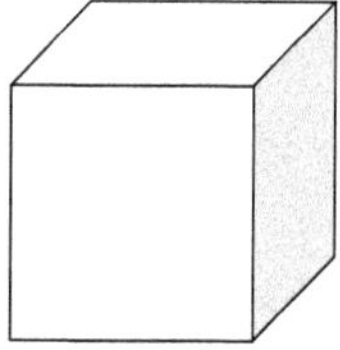

6 **a** Construct a cube.

b Use your solid to decide the number of planes of symmetry of a cube.

14d Surface area of a prism

- A **prism** has the same **cross-section** throughout its length.

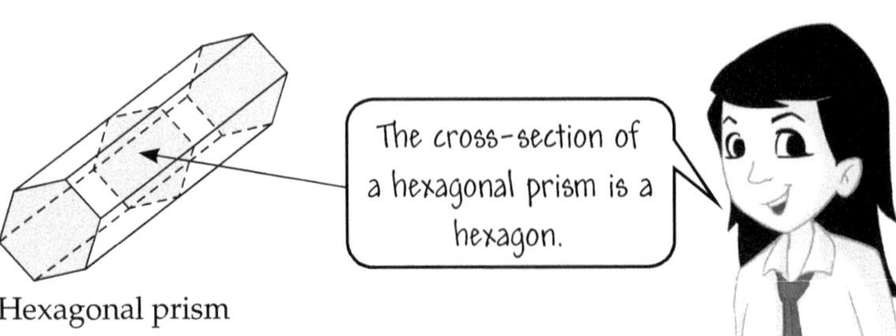

The cross-section of a hexagonal prism is a hexagon.

Hexagonal prism

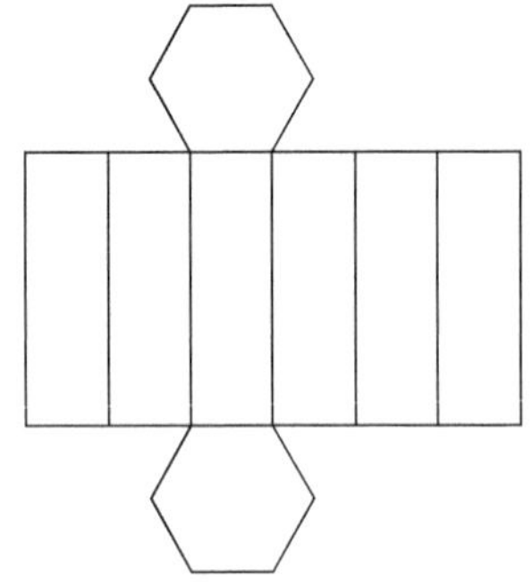

The net of a hexagonal prism

- The surface area of a solid is the total area of its faces. This is the same as the area of the **net** of the solid.

Example

Calculate the surface area of this triangular prism.

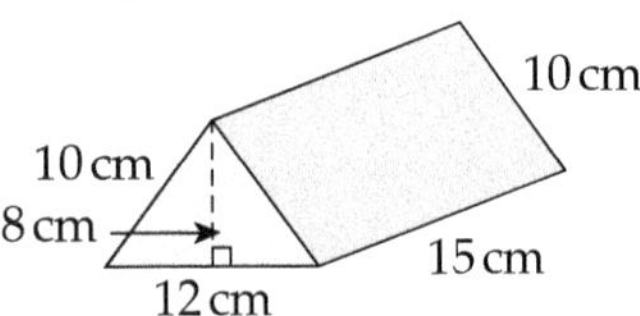

To find the surface area of a prism, calculate the area of each individual face and then sum your answers.

First sketch the net.

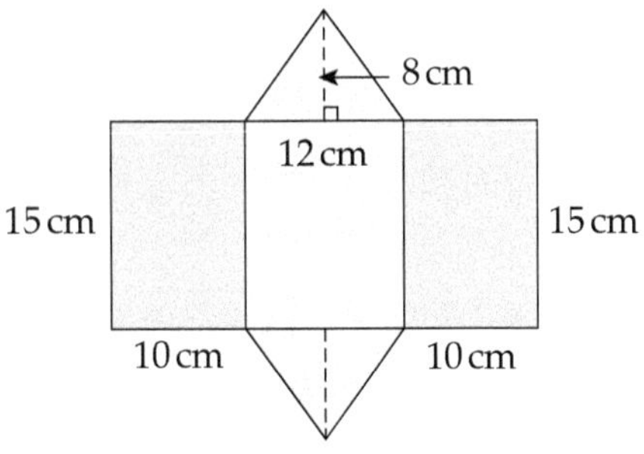

Area of one pink rectangle	$= 15 \times 10$	$= 150\text{ cm}^2$
Area of another pink rectangle	$= 15 \times 10$	$= 150\text{ cm}^2$
Area of the blue rectangle	$= 15 \times 12$	$= 180\text{ cm}^2$
Area of one green triangle	$= \frac{1}{2} \times 12 \times 8$	$= 48\text{ cm}^2$
Area of another green triangle	$= \frac{1}{2} \times 12 \times 8$	$= 48\text{ cm}^2$
Total surface area		$= 576\text{ cm}^2$

Example

The surface area of a cube is 2646 cm^2.
Calculate the length of one edge of the cube.

A cube has six square faces.

The area of one face $= 2646 \div 6 = 441\text{ cm}^2$

Length of one side of the square $= \sqrt{441} = 21\text{ cm}$

Area $= 441\text{ cm}^2$

You can use a calculator to work out the **square root** of 441.

Exercise 14d

1 A prism is made from eight cubes.
Each cube measures 5 metres by 5 metres by 5 metres.
Calculate the surface area of the solid.

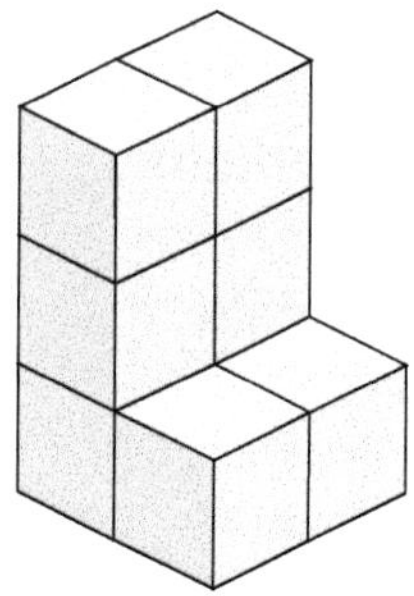

2 Calculate the surface area of this prism.

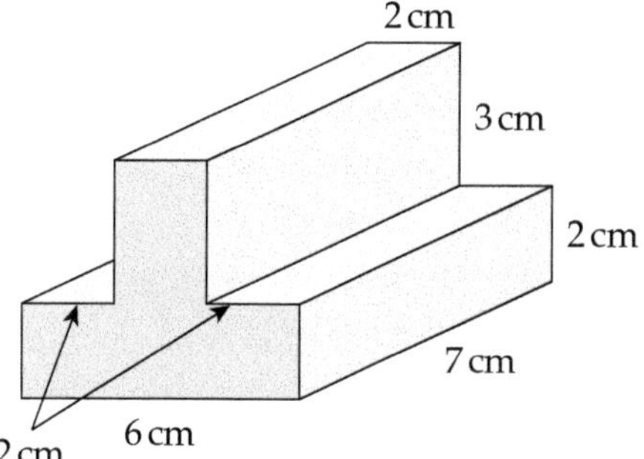

3 Calculate the surface area of these triangular prisms.

a

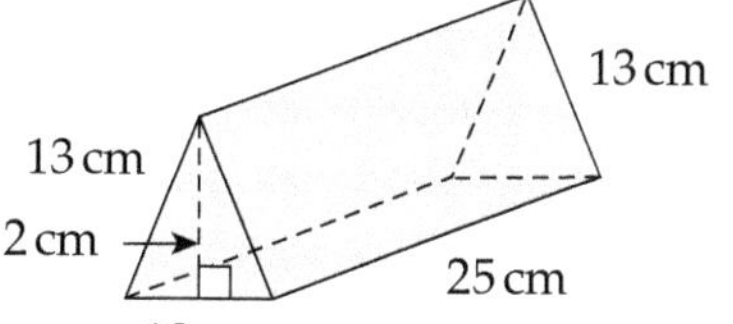

b

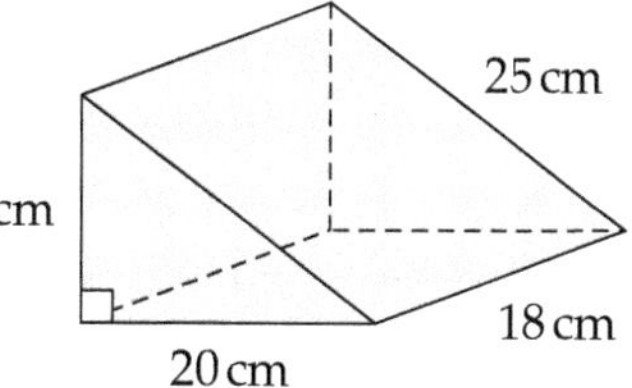

Problem solving

4 Three surfaces of a cuboid have areas of $48\,\text{cm}^2$, $84\,\text{cm}^2$ and $112\,\text{cm}^2$.

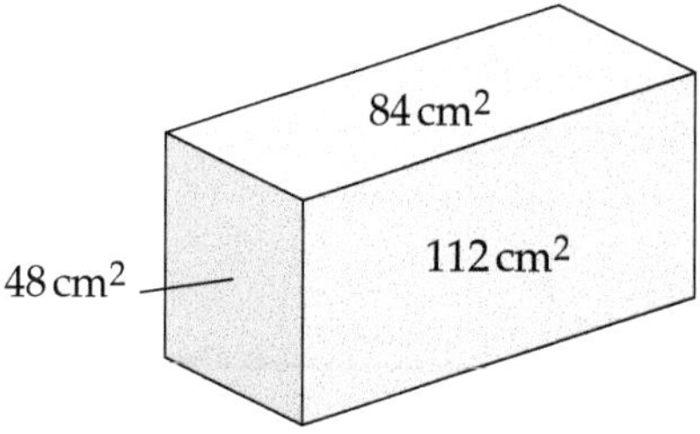

a Calculate the total surface area.
b Find the length, width and height of the cuboid.

5 Calculate the length of one side of a cube if the cube has a surface area of

a $600\,\text{cm}^2$ **b** $1350\,\text{cm}^2$
c $37.5\,\text{cm}^2$ **d** $121.5\,\text{cm}^2$

6 The length of one side of a cube is a.
Calculate the surface area of the cube in terms of a.

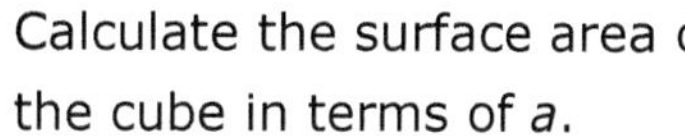

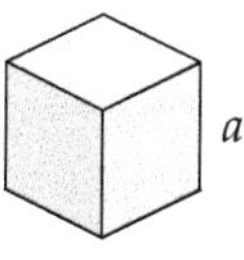

7 Candle Pack makes candles in the shape of a cube.
They want to pack eight candles in a box.

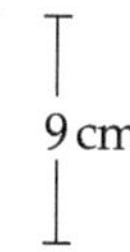

a Write the dimensions of three possible boxes.
b Draw each box on isometric paper.
c Calculate the surface area of each box.
d Describe the boxes that give the smallest and largest surface area. Which would be cheaper to make?
e Extend the investigation by designing a box to pack twelve candles.

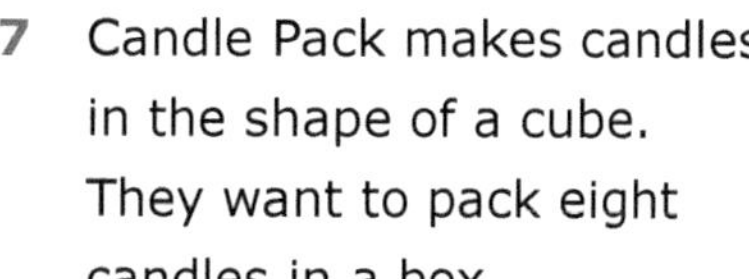

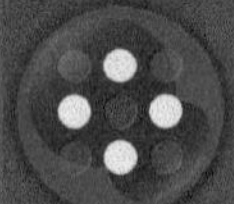

14e Volume of a prism

- The **volume** is the amount of space a 3D solid occupies.

Here is a **cuboid**. It has a rectangular **cross-section**.

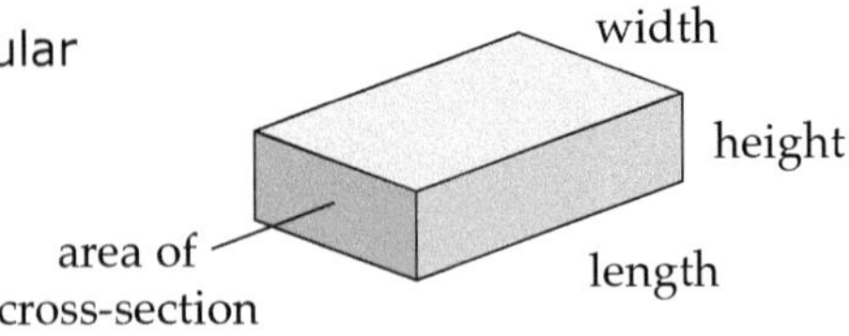

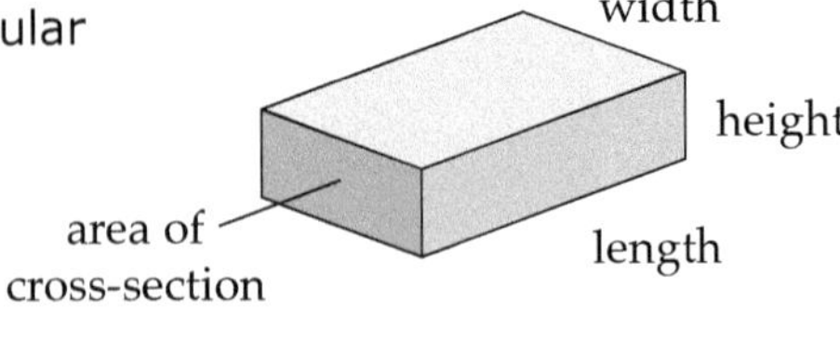

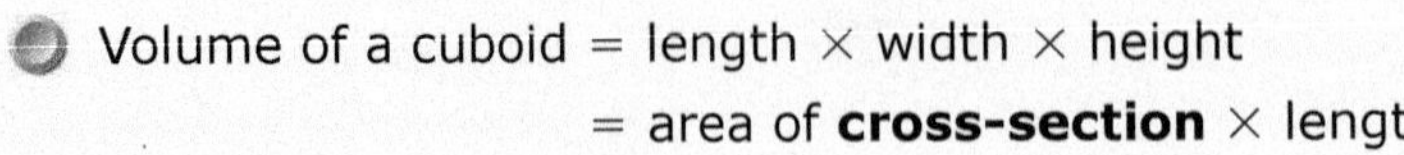

- Volume of a cuboid = length × width × height
  = area of **cross-section** × length

You measure volume in cubic units: cubic millimetres (mm^3), cubic centimetres (cm^3) or cubic metres (m^3).

A cuboid is a type of **prism**.
It has a **uniform** cross-section throughout its length.
Here is a **triangular prism**.

- Volume of a **prism** = area of cross-section × length

Example

a Calculate the area of the cross-section of the prism.
b Hence find its volume.

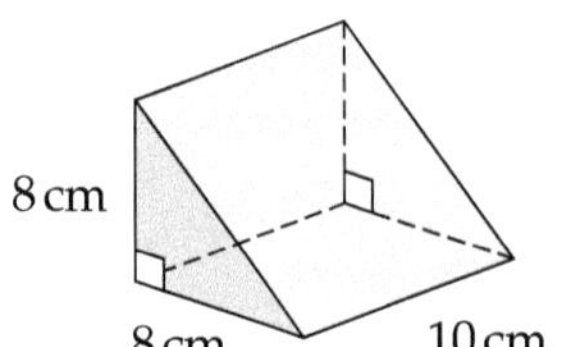

a Area of triangle $= \frac{1}{2} \times 8 \times 8$
$= 32\text{ cm}^2$

b Volume of the prism = area of cross-section × length
$= 32 \times 10$
$= 320\text{ cm}^3$

Example

The volume of a cuboid is 432 cm^3.
The length of the cuboid is 12 cm and its cross-section is square.
a Calculate the area of the cross-section.
b Hence find the length of one side of the square.

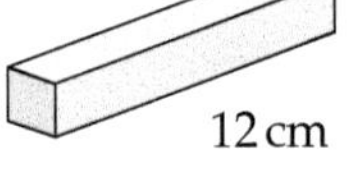

Volume = 432 cm^3

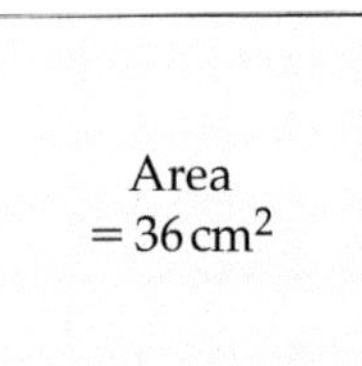

a Volume of the cuboid = area of cross-section × length
432 = area of cross-section × 12
area of cross-section = 432 ÷ 12
$= 36\text{ cm}^2$

b Length of one side of the square $= \sqrt{36}$
= 6 cm

Exercise 14e

1 The trailer of a lorry is a cuboid with length 2 metres, width 2 metres and height 4 metres.
What is the volume of the trailer?

2 The cross-section of a prism of length 5 m is divided into three areas, A_1, A_2 and A_3.
Calculate the volume of the prism when

a $A_1 = 1.5\,m^2$, $A_2 = 5\,m^2$ and $A_3 = 2\,m^2$

b $A_1 = 0.5\,m^2$, $A_2 = 4\,m^2$ and $A_3 = 1\,m^2$

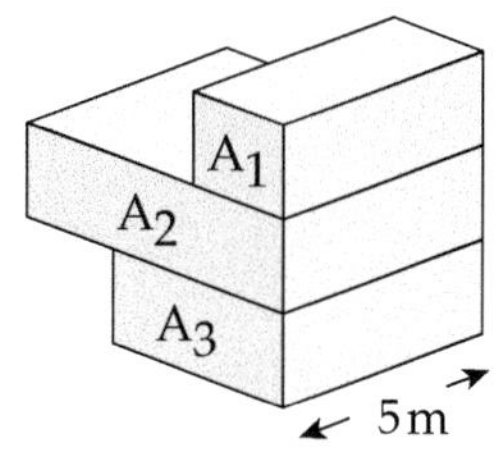

3 The diagram to the right shows a triangular prism.

a Calculate the area of the triangle.

b Hence find the volume of the prism.

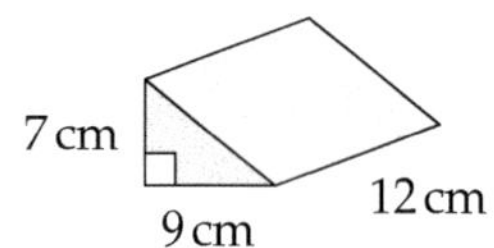

4 A ramp is made in the shape of a prism.
The cross-section is a trapezium.

a Calculate the area of the trapezium.

b Hence find the volume of the ramp.
State the units of your answers.

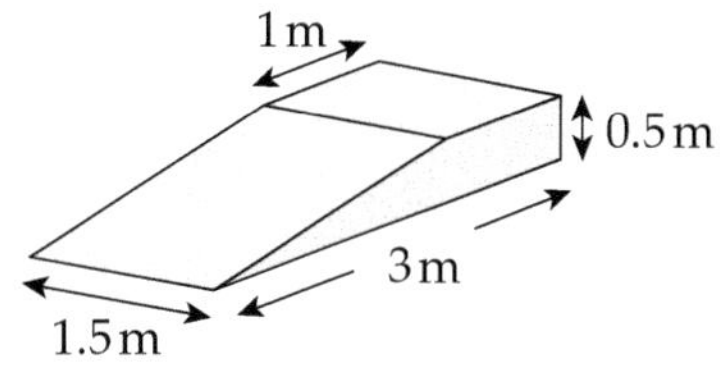

5 The volume of this prism is $127.5\,cm^3$.
The area of the cross-section is $15\,cm^2$.
Calculate the length of the prism.

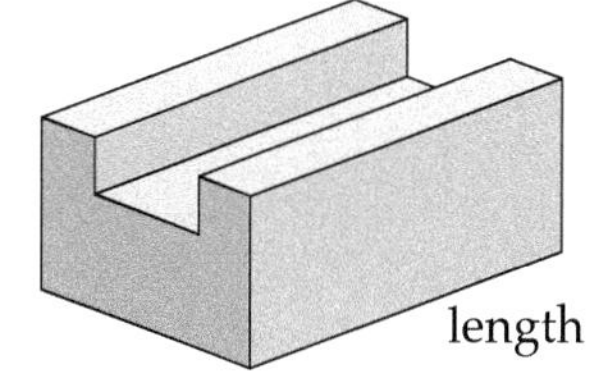

6 The volume of a box with a square cross-section is $540\,cm^3$.
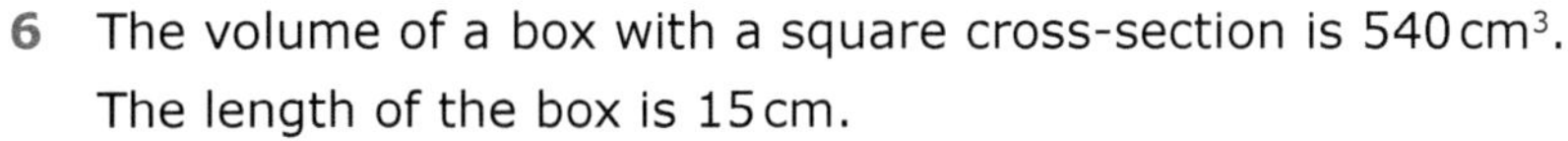
The length of the box is 15 cm.

a Calculate the area of the cross-section.

b Hence find the length of one side of the square.

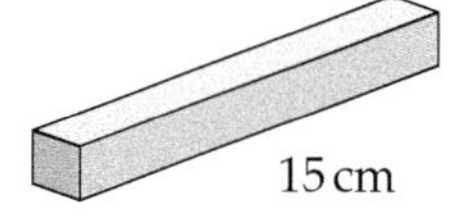

Volume = $540\,cm^3$

Problem solving

7 **a** This cuboid has edges of length of 2 cm, 3 cm and 4 cm.
Calculate the volume of the cuboid.

b The edges of the cuboid are enlarged by scale factor 2.
Calculate the volume of the enlarged cuboid.

c The edges of the original cuboid are enlarged by scale factor 3.
How many times bigger will the volume of the enlarged cuboid be compared to the original cuboid?

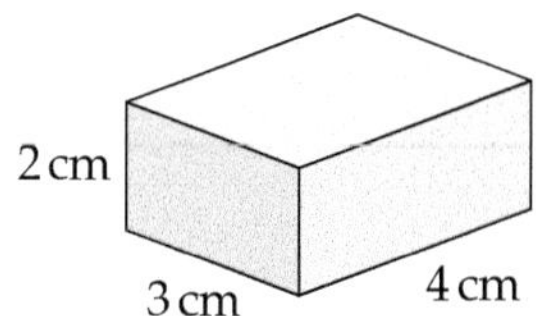

8 **a** Write down the volume of this cube.

b Find other prisms with the same volume.

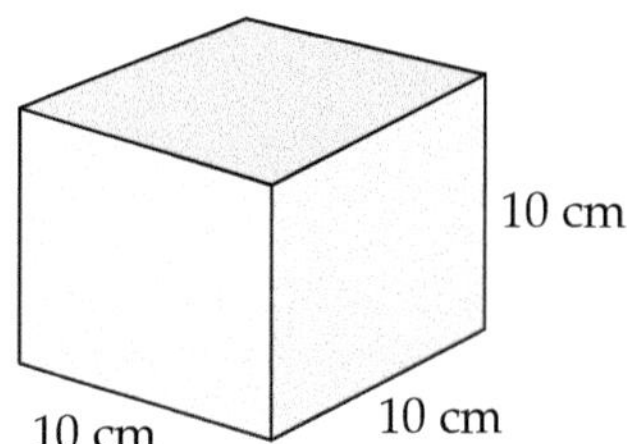

14 MySummary

Check out

You should now be able to ...		**Test it ➡ Questions**
✓ Recognise 3D shapes.	6	1
✓ Draw the plan and elevation of a 3D solid.	6	2 – 3
✓ Identify planes of symmetry.	6	4
✓ Calculate the surface area of a prism, and draw its net.	7	5 – 6
✓ Calculate the volume of a prism.	7	7 – 8

Language	Meaning	Example
Face	A flat surface of a solid.	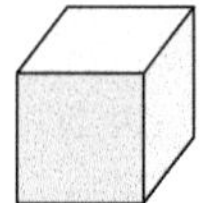
Edge	The line where two faces meet.	
Vertex (plural 'vertices')	A point where three or more edges meet.	A cube has 6 faces, 12 edges and 8 vertices.
Net	A 2D shape that can be folded to form a 3D solid.	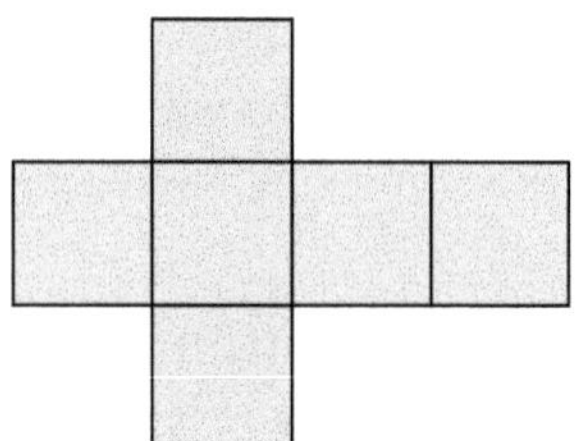 Here is a net of a cube.
Front elevation	The view of a solid from the front.	There are examples of plans and elevations on page 250.
Side elevation	The side view of a solid.	
Plan view	The bird's eye view of the solid (the view from above).	
Prism	A 3D solid with the same cross-section throughout its length.	Here is a triangular prism.

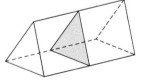

14 MyReview

1 How many

a faces

b edges

c vertices

does the prism have?

2

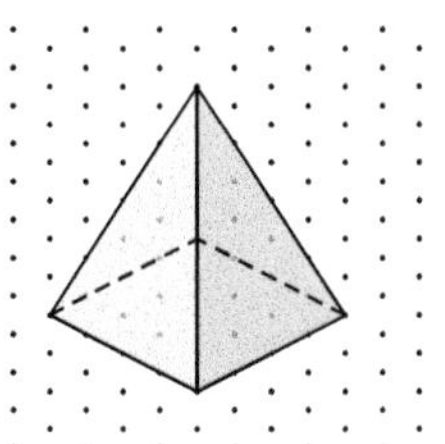

Sketch

a the front elevation

b the side elevation

c the plan view of this solid.

d What is the mathematical name of this solid?

3 A 3D shape is made from cubes. The elevations and the plan view are shown.

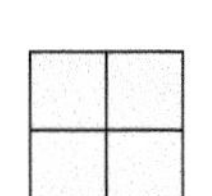

Front elevation

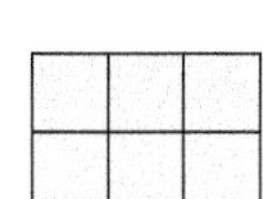

Side elevation

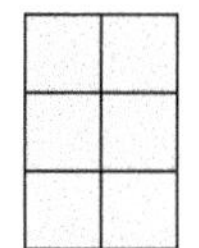

Plan view

a Draw the shape on isometric paper.

b How many cubes are needed to make the shape?

4 How many planes of symmetry does a cuboid have?

5 a Sketch a net of this prism, labelling the dimensions.

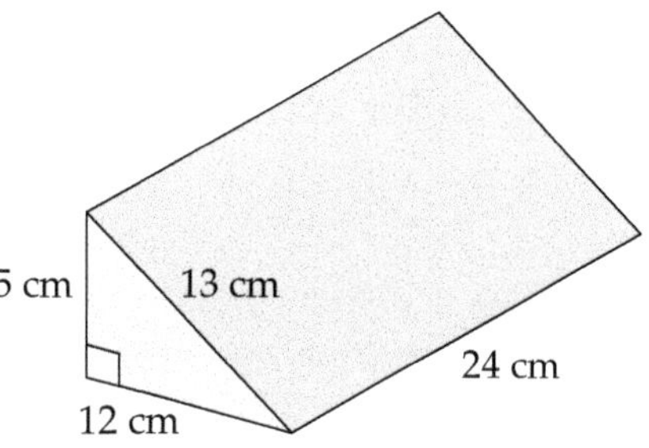

b Calculate the surface area of the prism.

6 Calculate the surface area of a cube with side lengths 7 cm.

7 A cube has a surface area of 864cm^2. What is its volume?

8 Calculate the volume of this prism.

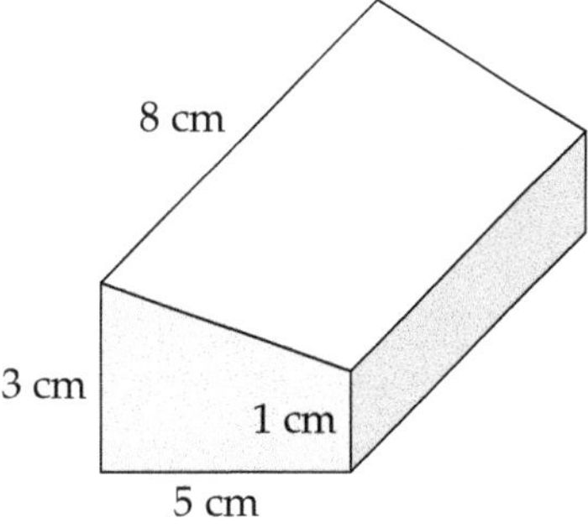

What next?

Score	
0 – 3	Your knowledge of this topic is still developing. To improve look at Formative test: 3B-14; MyMaths: 1078, 1098, 1107, 1137 and 1139
4 – 6	You are gaining a secure knowledge of this topic. To improve look at InvisiPen: 321, 322, 323, 324, 325, 326, 327 and 328
7, 8	You have mastered this topic. Well done, you are ready to progress!

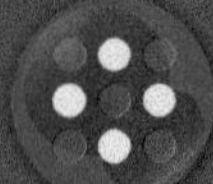

14 MyPractice

1 A regular tetrahedron is made from four equilateral triangles. How many faces, edges and vertices does this solid have?

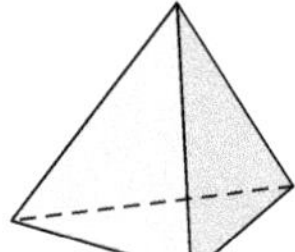

2 A cube is made from 27 identical small cubes.

a Draw the solid on isometric paper.

The centre cube on each face of the solid is now removed.

b Draw the new solid on isometric paper.

3 A square-based pyramid is joined to a cube.
Sketch the front elevation (F), the side elevation (S) and the plan (P) of this solid.

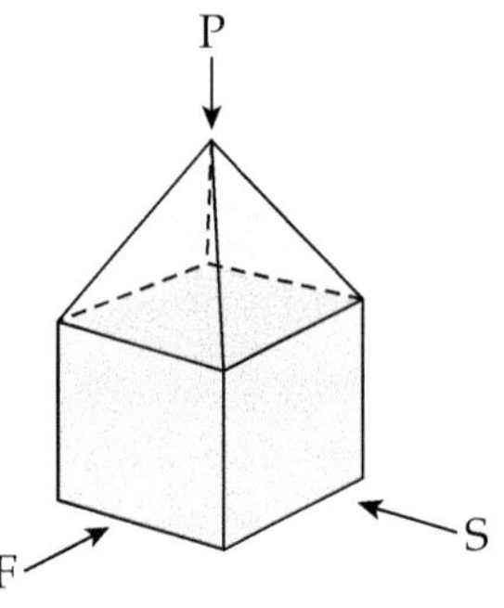

4 The diagram shows the plan of a solid made from cubes.
The number in each square represents the number of cubes in that column.

a Draw the solid on isometric paper.

b Draw the front elevation (F) and the side elevation (S) of the solid.

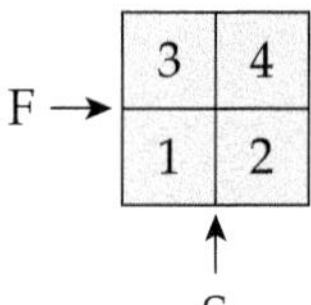

5 A square-based pyramid is sliced horizontally.
Describe the shapes of the cross-section at different heights.

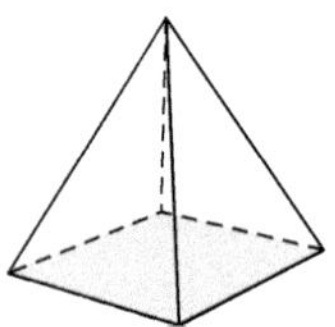

6 A regular octahedron is made from eight equilateral triangles.
Draw diagrams to show all the planes of symmetry of a regular octahedron.

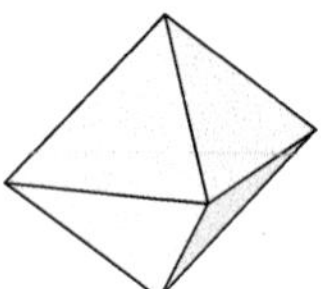

14d

7 Calculate the surface area of this prism.

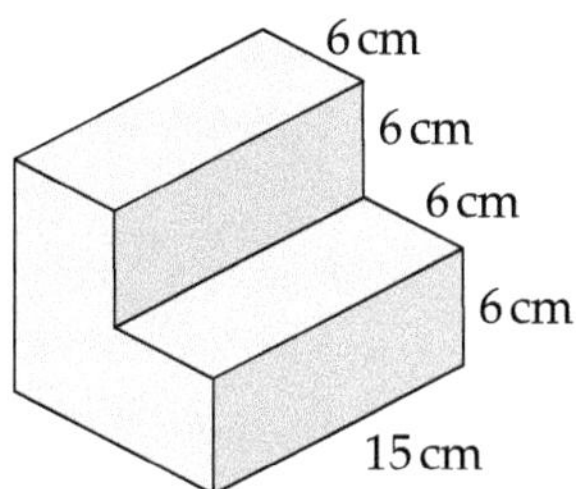

14e

8 A box is made in the shape of a hexagonal prism. The length of the box is 10 cm and the dimensions of the hexagon are shown in the diagram.

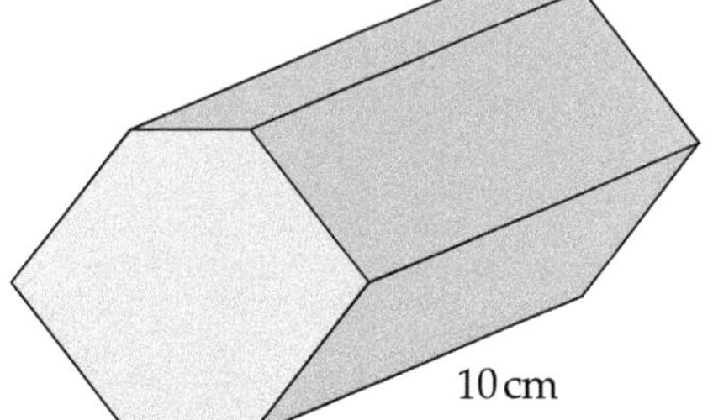

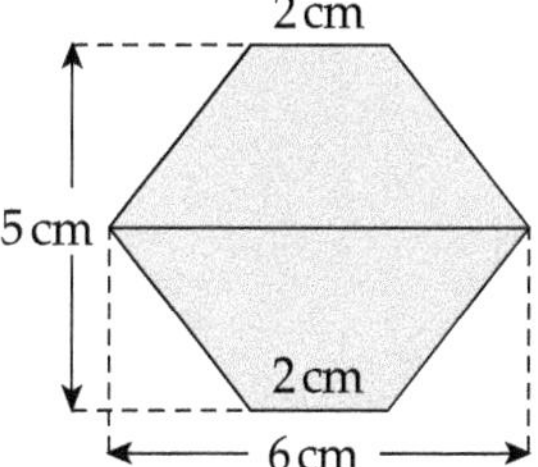

a Calculate the area of the hexagon.

b Hence find the volume of the prism.

9 A tent is in the shape of a triangular prism. The length of the tent is 5 metres.

a Calculate the area of the triangle.

b Hence find the volume of the tent.

State the units of your answers.

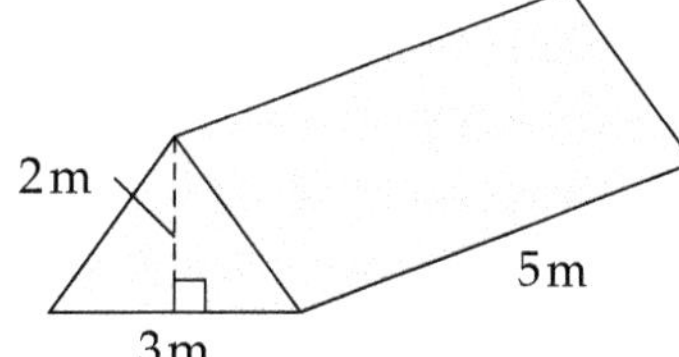

10 A cuboid is made from a rectangular sheet of card 30 cm long and 25 cm wide. The cuboid is 9 cm high. The diagram shows the net of the cuboid.

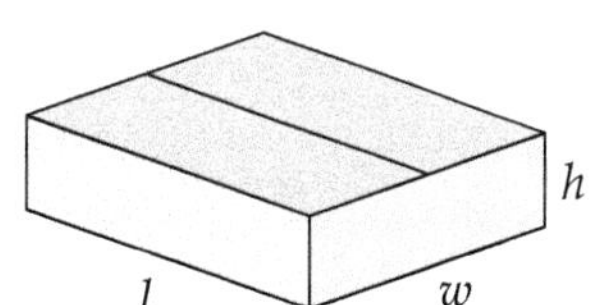

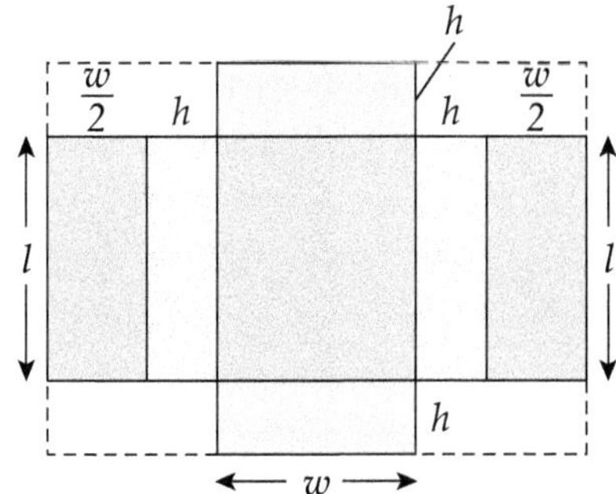

Calculate the volume of the cuboid.

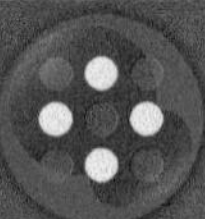

Case study 5: The Golden Rectangle

The golden rectangle has fascinated scholars for over 2000 years. It's a special kind of rectangle, which is often found in art and architecture.

Task 1

Rectangles come in all shapes and sizes, or different **proportions**. Here are six different rectangles. They can be sorted into three pairs of **similar** rectangles.

A: 4 cm × 1 cm
B: 3 cm × 5 cm
C: 15 cm × 9 cm
D: 6 cm × 4 cm
E: 2 cm × 3 cm
F: 8 cm × 2 cm

a Write down which pairs of rectangles are similar.

b For each rectangle, divide the longer side by the shorter side and write down the result.

i What do you notice?

ii What can you say about similar rectangles and the **ratio** of their sides?

Task 2

Here is a square with a narrower rectangle next to it. Together they form a larger rectangle.

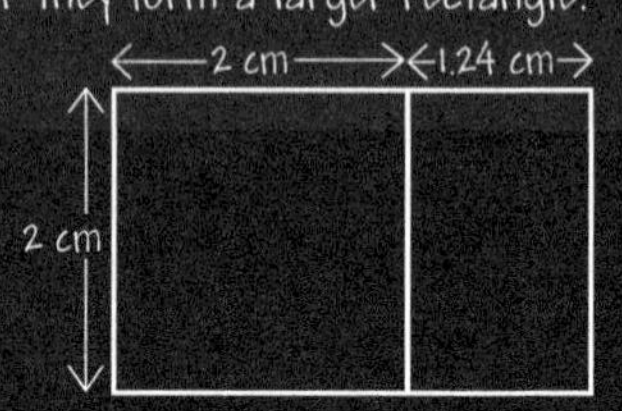

a Look at the larger rectangle. Divide the longer side by the shorter side and write down the result, to 1 d.p.

b Now look at the smaller rectangle and do the same. What do you notice? Describe your findings using the word 'similar' if possible.

Task 3

Here is a **golden rectangle**. The smaller rectangle is similar to the larger rectangle. You can write this as a formula:

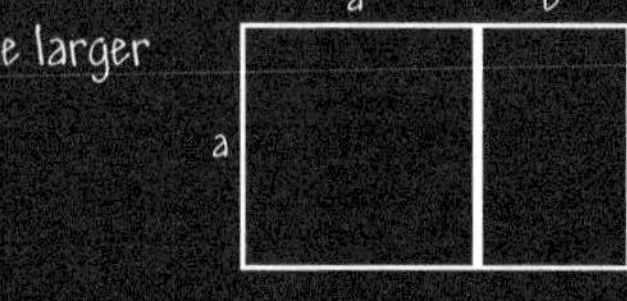

$$\frac{a+b}{a} = \frac{a}{b}$$

a For each rectangle, decide if it is golden or not. Use a calculator to help you, rounding your answers to 1 d.p. If there is a slight difference in your calculator answers, suggest why this might be the case.

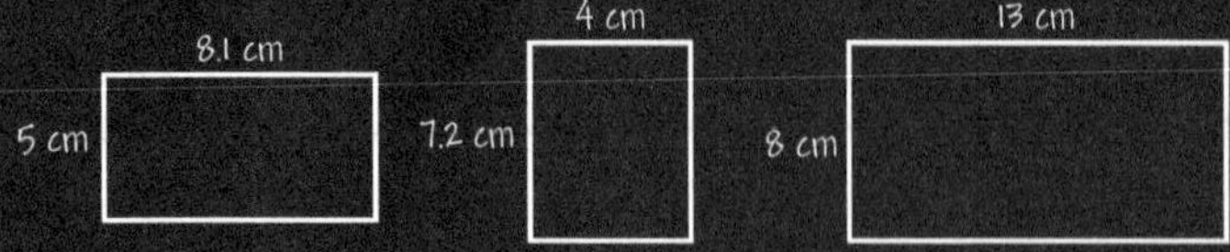

b (challenge) A golden rectangle has shorter length 3 cm.

i See if you can find its longer length to 1 d.p.

ii Construct the rectangle as accurately as you can.

c The number you get when you divide the longer side of a golden rectangle by the shorter side is called the **golden ratio**. Write down its value to 1 d.p.

Leonardo da Vinci, Mona Lisa
The face fits within a golden rectangle. A smaller golden rectangle splits the face at the eye line.

Task 4

Look at the portrait of Mona Lisa, which is shown on this page. By measuring lengths, describe why her face is framed by a golden rectangle.

Task 5

a How to CONSTRUCT A GOLDEN RECTANGLE

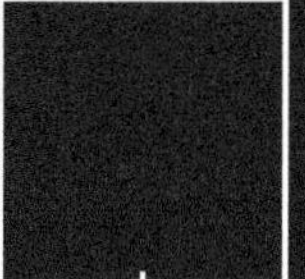

Draw a square. Mark the mid point of the base.

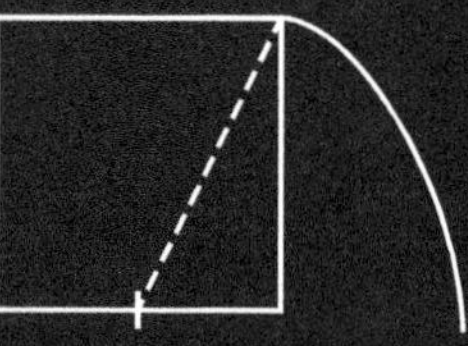

Set a pair of compasses to the distance between the mid point and the top corner and draw an arc.

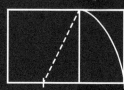

Extend the base of the square to the arc and complete the rectangle.

b Without measuring, find the value of the golden ratio from this construction.

Did you Know

One possible place where the golden ratio occurs is in the ratio of your height to the top of your head, to the height to your navel.

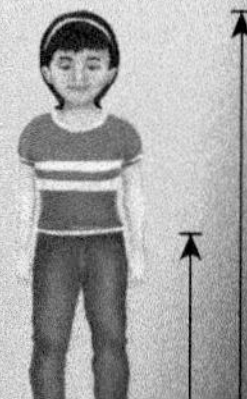

Task 6

In the **Fibonacci series,** each term is generated by adding the previous two terms.

0, 1, 1, 2, 3, 5, 8, 13, . . .

a Find the ratio of any two adjacent numbers from the series, dividing the larger one by the smaller one.

b Try this for several pairs of adjacent numbers, working towards the larger numbers.

What do you notice as you use larger and larger numbers?

The Fibonacci series can be shown as a set of squares.

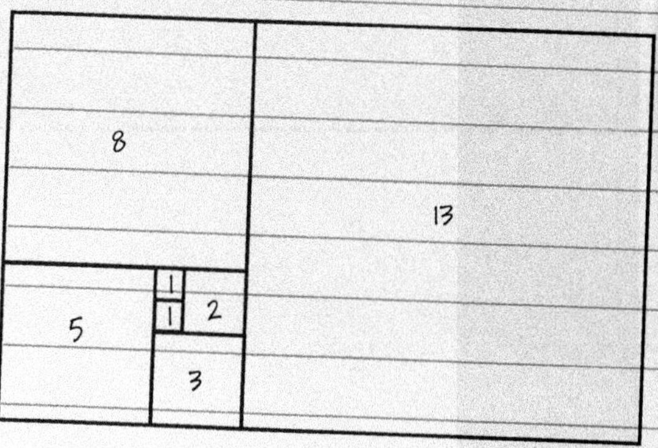

c Draw your own set of squares in this way.

For each new size of rectangle that you produce, find the ratio of its length to its width.

d What do you notice about the ratios?

What does this tell you about the rectangle?

e You can draw arcs in each square to produce a **Fibonacci spiral**.

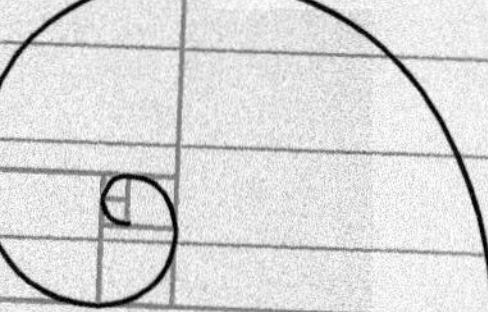

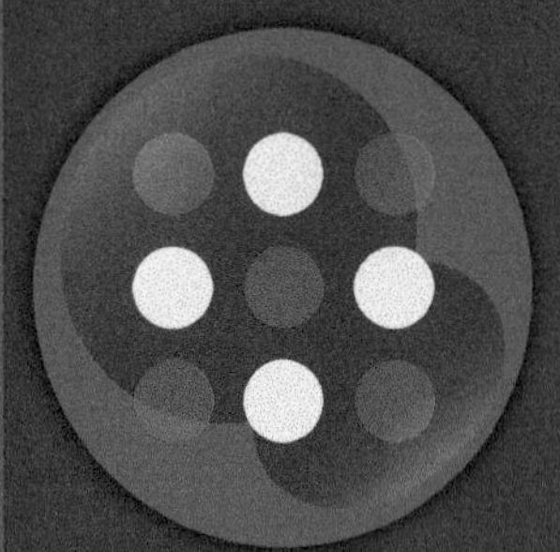

15 Ratio and proportion

Introduction

There are lots of different ways people exercise in the gym. Some people will use weights or go to exercise classes. Other people like to use cardio machines. The more time you spend on a machine, the further the distance you will cover. If you travel at a constant speed, you can say that the distance covered is proportional to the time spent on the machine.

What's the point?

When two quantities are proportional, if one quantity changes by a multiplier, the other quantity changes by the same multiplier. So when you understand proportion, you can work out how one quantity changes when another changes.

Objectives

By the end of this chapter, you will have learned how to ...

- Solve problems that involve direct proportion.
- Calculate percentage increases and decreases.
- Use percentages to compare proportions.
- Simplify ratios.
- Divide quantities in a given ratio.
- Compare ratios.

Check in

1 In each case, **i** simplify the fraction **ii** convert the fraction to a percentage

a $\frac{4}{10}$ **b** $\frac{75}{100}$ **c** $\frac{6}{16}$ **d** $\frac{12}{40}$

2 Write these ratios in their simplest form:

a 3 : 9 **b** 8 : 12 **c** 16 cm : 80 mm **d** 6 kg : 2000 g

Starter problem

If you walk on a treadmill at a constant speed of 3 miles per hour, how long do you need to walk to cover 2 miles?

On an exercise bike you can go much faster, as fast as 20 miles per hour. How long would it take to cover 2 miles on an exercise bike at this speed?

Investigate the speeds travelled doing other types of exercise (for example, running, rowing, and horse riding). How long does it take to cover 2 miles doing these sports?

15a Direct proportion

Lots of real-life problems involve pairs of quantities that are linked by **direct proportion**. Cost and amount is a good example – as the amount goes up, the cost goes up.

Here, the number of text messages is in direct proportion to the cost:

Number of text messages	Cost (£)
10	£0.40
20	£0.80
40	£1.60

($\times 2$ going down, $\times \frac{1}{2}$ going up, on both columns)

If you double the number of messages, you double the cost. If you halve the number of messages, you halve the cost.

- You can use the **unitary method** to solve problems involving direct proportion. You find the value of one unit of a quantity.

Example

5 litres of petrol cost £5.75. What is the cost of 18 litres of petrol?

Find the cost of 1 litre by dividing by 5.

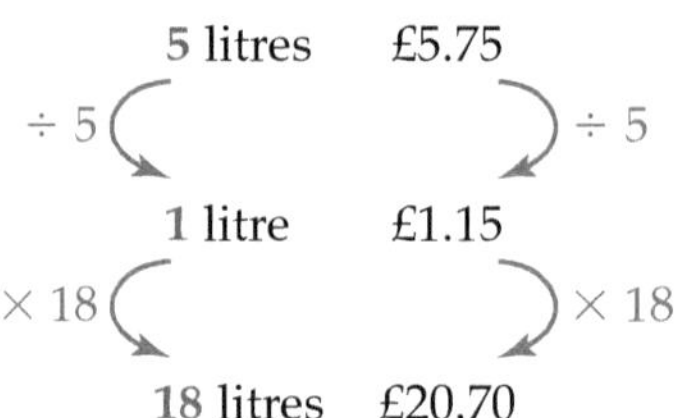

	5 litres	£5.75
$\div 5$		$\div 5$
	1 litre	£1.15
$\times 18$		$\times 18$
	18 litres	£20.70

Multiply the cost of 1 litre by 18 to find the cost of 18 litres.

18 litres cost £20.70.

- You can also use a **scaling** method. You multiply both quantities by the same fraction.

Example

Five litres of water cost 80 p. What is the cost of 18 litres of water?

The number of litres of water has been multiplied by $18 \div 5 = \frac{18}{5}$.

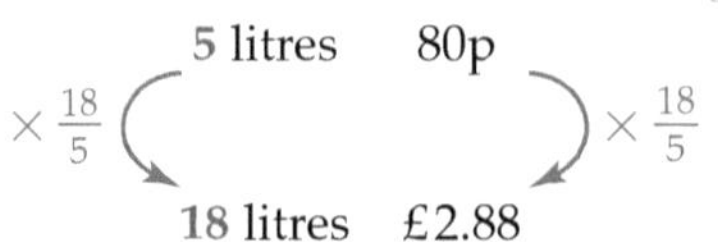

	5 litres	80p
$\times \frac{18}{5}$		$\times \frac{18}{5}$
	18 litres	£2.88

The cost must be multiplied by the same fraction, $\frac{18}{5}$.

18 litres of water cost £2.88.

The unitary method and the scaling method are really the same thing!

Exercise 15a

Problem solving

1 Use direct proportion to solve these problems.

a 4 kg of apples cost £1.20.
What is the cost of 8 kg of apples?

b 50 g of breakfast cereal contain 120 calories.
How many calories are there in 75 g of breakfast cereal?

c A recipe for eight people uses 400 ml of milk.
What amount of milk is needed for six people?

d 250 g of cheese costs £3.80.
What is the cost of 375 g of cheese?

2 Here are two offers for text messages on a mobile phone.
In which of these offers are the numbers in direct proportion?
In each case explain and justify your answers.

Offer A

Number of text messages	Cost (pence)
20	24
50	60
175	210

Offer B

Number of text messages	Cost (pence)
20	26
50	62
175	192

3 Solve these problems using direct proportion.

a 5 litres of oil cost £3.65. What is the cost of 3 litres of oil?

b There are 15 biscuits in a packet. The packet weighs 225 g.
What is the weight of a packet of 20 biscuits?

c 5 miles is approximately 8 km.

i How many kilometres are equal to 35 miles?

ii How many miles are equal to 76 km?

d A 400 g jar of mayonnaise contains 275 g of fat.
How many grams of fat are there in 250 g of mayonnaise?

e A recipe for an apple drink for six people uses 300 g of apples.
Rewrite the recipe for 10 people.

4 Sarah's car can hold 45 litres of petrol when it is full.
On a full tank of petrol she can drive 750 km.

a How far can Sarah's car travel on 20 litres of petrol?

b How much petrol would she need to travel 200 km?

15b Comparing proportions

- You can use **percentages**, fractions and decimals to describe proportions.

Example

Saddique scores 96 out of 150 in his Maths exam.
What proportion of the test did he answer correctly?

The **proportion** can be written as a fraction.

Proportion correct $= \frac{96}{150} \xrightarrow{\div 6} \frac{16}{25}$

The proportion can also be written as a percentage.

Proportion correct $= \frac{96}{150}$

$= 96 \div 150$

$= 0.64$

$= 64\%$

Convert the fraction to a percentage by dividing the numerator by the denominator and multiplying by 100.

Simplify the fraction by dividing by the HCF of 96 and 150.

- You can **compare** proportions by converting them into percentages.

Example

Here are two different chocolate bars.

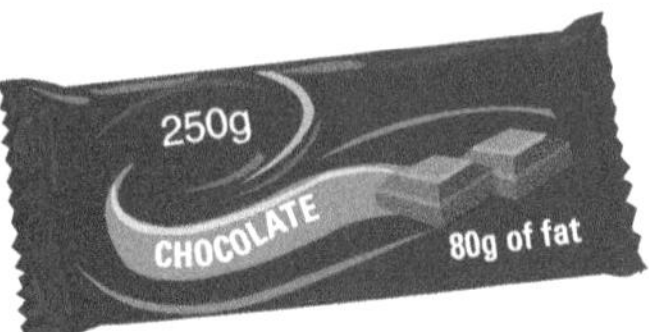

Bar A

Bar B

Which bar contains the higher proportion of fat?

First write the proportion of fat in each bar as a fraction.

Chocolate bar A	Chocolate bar B
$\frac{80}{250}$	$\frac{36}{120}$

Then convert each fraction into a percentage.

$= 80 \div 250$	$= 36 \div 120$
$= 0.32$	$= 0.3$
$= 32\%$	$= 30\%$

Chocolate bar A contains the higher proportion of fat.

Exercise 15b

1 Convert these fractions into percentages using a calculator where appropriate. Round your answers to 2 dp.

a $\frac{17}{20}$ **b** $\frac{13}{25}$ **c** $\frac{28}{40}$ **d** $\frac{5}{7}$ **e** $\frac{38}{45}$

2 Copy and complete these sentences.

a 20 out of ☐ is the same as 40%. **b** ☐ out of ☐ is the same as 15%.

3 **a** Write the proportion of each rectangle that is yellow.

i

ii

iii

b Write each of your answers as a fraction in its simplest form and a percentage (rounded to 1 dp where appropriate).

c Which rectangle has the highest proportion of yellow?

Problem solving

4 For these questions express your answer as a percentage where appropriate. Round to 1 decimal place if necessary. Show your working.

a In John's class there are 16 boys and 14 girls.
In Geoff's class there are 13 boys and 12 girls.
Which class has the higher proportion of girls?

b Hanif scores 25 out of 80 in his History exam and 19 out of 60 in his English exam.
In which exam did Hanif do better?

c In a survey 117 out of 800 women said they were vegetarian.
In the same survey only 39 out of 700 men said they were vegetarian.

i What proportion of the women surveyed were vegetarian?

ii What proportion of the people surveyed were vegetarian?

5 This table shows the number of grams of fat in different snacks.

a Copy and complete the table. Round your answers to 1 dp.

b Which is the least healthy snack? Explain and justify your answer.

c Investigate other snacks to see what percentage of the snack is fat.

Type of food	Mass (grams)	Fat content (grams)	% fat
Crisps	35	11.6	
Olives	28	3.1	
Cereal bar	24	1.7	
Chocolate bar	62	14.9	
French fries	78	9	

15c Ratio

Whether you buy a small can of a fizzy drink, or a large bottle, you expect the flavour to be the same. This is because the ingredients are in the same **ratio** no matter what the size of the container.

- You **simplify** a **ratio** by dividing all parts of the ratio by the same number.

Example

Write these ratios in their simplest form.

a 15 : 12 **b** 18 cm : 60 mm

a

$$15:12 \xrightarrow{\div 3} 5:4$$

b

18 cm : 60 mm

180 mm : 60 mm

$\div 10$

18 : 6

$\div 6$

3 : 1

Change both quantities into the same units. 18 cm is the same as 180 mm.

You can use ratios to divide quantities into unequal sized pieces. This is called **dividing in a given ratio**.

- You can divide a quantity in a given ratio using the unitary method. First find the value of one equal share of the quantity.

The unitary method involves find the value of one unit.

Example

The angles in a triangle, x, y and z, are in the ratio 2 : 3 : 4.
Find the size of each of the three angles.

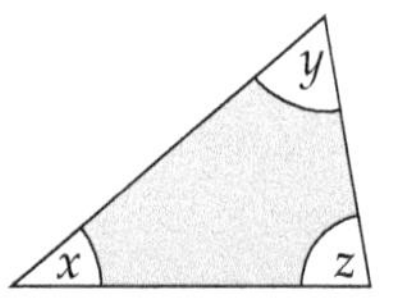

The angles in a triangle add up to 180°.
The ratio 2 : 3 : 4 means that 180° is divided into 2 + 3 + 4 = 9 equal parts.

Each equal part = 180° ÷ 9
= 20°

Angle x is **2** parts = **2** × 20° = 40°
Angle y is **3** parts = **3** × 20° = 60°
Angle z is **4** parts = **4** × 20° = 80°

You can check your answer by adding up all the parts.

40° + 60° + 80° = 180° ✓

You could use the ratio to tell you what proportion each angle is of the total.
Angle $x = \frac{2}{9}$ of 180° = 40°
Angle $y = \frac{3}{9}$ of 180° = 60°
Angle $z = \frac{4}{9}$ of 180° = 80°

Exercise 15c

1 Write these ratios in their simplest form.

a 6 : 10

b 12 : 18

c 25 : 40

d 60 : 36

e 8 : 12 : 20

f 15 : 30 : 40

2 Write these ratios in their simplest form by first changing the quantities into the same units.

a £2 : £6

b £3 : 60p

c 3 cm : 24 mm

d 125 cm : 4 m

e 3 kg : 750 g

f 5 minutes : 50 seconds

3 Work out how many boys and girls there are in each of these classes.

a There are 33 students in total. There are twice as many boys as girls.

b There are 29 students in total. There are three more boys than girls.

c There are 36 students in total. The ratio of boys to girls is 4 : 5.

4 Work out these, giving your answers to 2 decimal places where appropriate.

a Divide 40 apples in the ratio 3 : 5.

b Divide £120 in the ratio 5 : 1.

c Divide 36 kg in the ratio 2 : 7.

d Divide 24 km in the ratio 1 : 2 : 3.

e Divide £72 in the ratio 7 : 3 : 2.

f Divide £65 in the ratio 5 : 4.

Problem solving

5 Solve these problems.

a In a school the ratio of students to teachers is 15 : 1. There are 992 students and teachers at the school. How many teachers are there?

b A cake mixture contains flour, sugar and butter in the ratio 4 : 5 : 3. How much butter is needed to make 900 g of cake mixture?

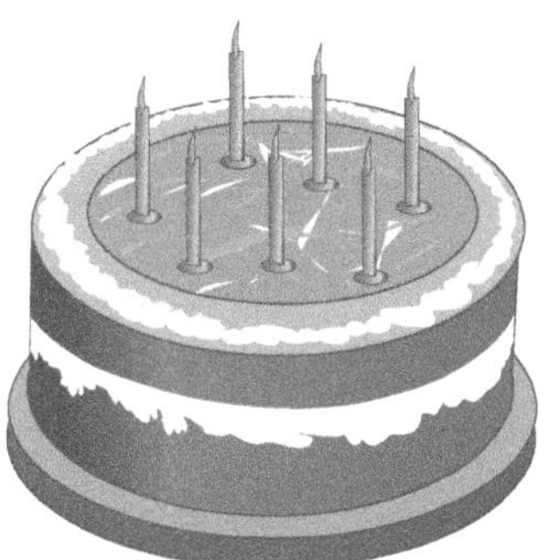

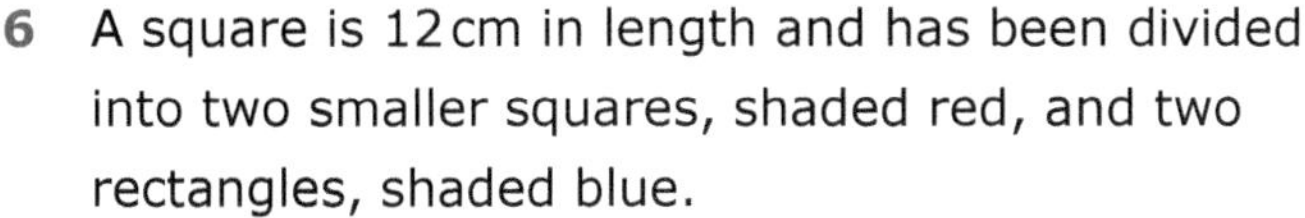

6 A square is 12 cm in length and has been divided into two smaller squares, shaded red, and two rectangles, shaded blue.

a Show that the ratio of red to blue is 13 : 5.

b How would you divide the square into squares and rectangles so that the ratio of red to blue was 5 : 3?

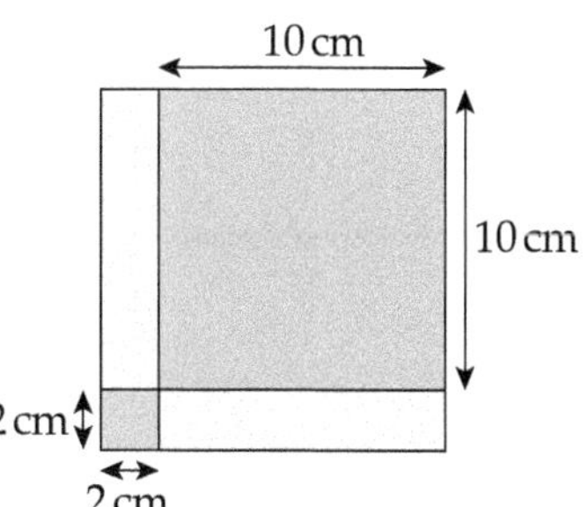

7 The interior angles in a quadrilateral are in the ratio 1 : 2 : 3 : 4. Find the size of each of the four angles. Sketch the quadrilateral.

15d Uses of ratio

- You can **compare ratios** by changing them to the form **1 : *n***.

Example

In class 9A the ratio of boys to girls is 4 : 5.
In class 9B the ratio of boys to girls is 9 : 11.
Which class has the higher proportion of girls?

Write both ratios in the form 1 : *n*.

Class 9A
boys : girls
4 : 5 (÷ 4)
1 : 1.25

Class 9B
boys : girls
9 : 11 (÷ 9)
1 : 1.22 (2 dp)

Class 9A: 1.25 girls for each boy.
Class 9B: 1.22 girls for each boy.
So class 9A has the higher proportion of girls.

Divide both parts of the ratio by the same number, so that one side of the ratio is equal to 1.

- You can solve ratio problems with a unitary method.

Example

Carlos and Belinda share some money in the ratio 3 : 7.
Carlos receives £900. How much in total did they share?

Carlos receives 3 parts = £900
÷ 3: 1 part = £300
So Belinda receives × 7: 7 parts = £2100
Total = £900 + £2100 = £3000

Divide by 3 to find the value of one part.

- You use ratios with maps or drawing to **scale**.

Example

A map has a scale of 1 : 10 000.
What distance does 3.4 cm on the map represent in real life?

map : real life
1 : 10 000
1 cm : 10 000 cm
× 3.4: 3.4 cm : 34 000 cm
= 340 m

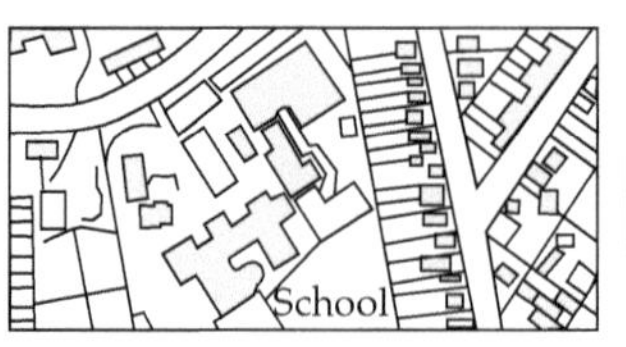

Scale: 1:10000

This scale is a ratio expressed in the form 1 : *n*

Exercise 15d

1 Write each of these ratios in the form $1:n$.

a	4 : 12	**b**	5 : 20	**c**	7 : 35	**d**	2 : 3
e	4 : 9	**f**	5 : 12	**g**	3 : 10	**h**	9 : 16

Problem solving

2 Solve each of these problems.

a At a sports club the ratio of boys to girls is 7 : 9.
There are 117 girls at the club.
How many children are there in the sports club?

b An alloy is made from iron, copper and aluminium in the ratio 4 : 5 : 1.
How much iron is needed to mix with 115 kg of copper?

3 **a** A map has a scale of 1 : 12 000.

i What distance does 7 cm on the map represent in real life?

ii What distance on the map represents a real-life measurement of 900 m?

b A model of a plane is built to a scale of 1 : 16.
The wingspan of the plane is 7.2 m.
What is the wingspan of the model?

4 Simplify the ratios to the form $1:n$ to answer these questions.

a The ratios of nylon to other materials in two T-shirts are 2 : 25 and 3 : 40. Which T-shirt has the greater proportion of nylon?

b The ratio of teachers to students in Oxford School is 3 : 41.
The ratio at Melville Comprehensive is 2 : 29.
Which school has the higher proportion of teachers?

5 Josiah is making rectangular tiles.
The ratio of length : width must always be 5 : 3.

a He makes a tile 15 cm long.
How wide must the tile be?

b He makes a tile 4.5 cm wide.
How long must the tile be?

c He makes a miniature tile in the same ratio, with a length of 2.5 cm. How wide must the tile be?

6 Aftab guessed the masses of some objects.
He wrote the ratio of actual weight : guessed weight in the form $1:n$. He called this his accuracy ratio.
For the bottle of pop his accuracy ratio was 1 : 0.86 (2 dp).

Object	Actual weight	Guess
Bottle of pop	350 g	300 g
Can of pop	240 g	200 g
Loaf of bread	750 g	800 g
Cake	500 g	600 g

a Work out the accuracy ratio for each of the other objects.

b Which guess was the most accurate? Explain your answer.

c Choose some objects, guess their mass and calculate your own accuracy ratios.

15e Ratio and proportion problems

- You can write each part of a ratio as a proportion of the whole.

Example

An alloy is made from copper and iron in the **ratio** 2 : 3.
What proportion of the alloy is iron?

Using fractions

There are 2 + 3 = 5 parts in the alloy.

$\frac{3}{5}$ of the alloy is iron.

$\frac{3}{5} = 3 \div 5 = 0.6 \times 100 = 60\%$

60% of the alloy is iron.

Using unitary method

5 parts ⟶ 100% of the alloy
1 part ⟶ 20% of the alloy
3 parts ⟶ 60% of the alloy.

- You can solve **percentage change** problems using the unitary method. You find the value of 1%.

Example

Alissa buys a laptop in a sale and saves £59.
The label says that this is a '20% reduction'.
What was the original price of the laptop?

20% off!

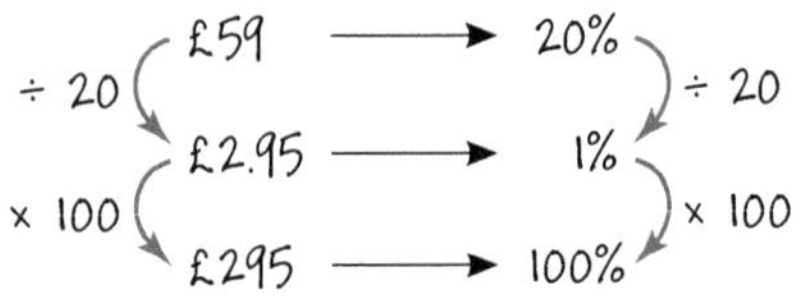

The original price of the laptop was £295.

Divide by 20 to find the value of 1%. Then multiply by 100 to find 100% (the original price).

- You can write the change in an amount as a percentage of the original amount.

Example

A computer is reduced in price from £360 to £306.
What is the percentage reduction?

Reduction in price = £360 − £306 = £54

Percentage reduction = $\frac{54}{360} = 54 \div 360 \times 100\% = 15\%$

The reduction (change) is first written as a fraction of the **original price** (the whole).

Exercise 15e

1 In a bag there are 12 lemon and 18 lime sweets.

  a Write the ratio of lemon : lime sweets in its simplest form.

  b What proportion of the bag is lemon sweets?

2 Different metal alloys are made from iron and zinc in these ratios.

a	2 : 3	**b**	1 : 3	**c**	3 : 7	**d**	5 : 3
e	7 : 13	**f**	7 : 9	**g**	3 : 12	**h**	11 : 14

What proportion of each alloy is iron?

3 In each of these examples calculate the whole (100%).

  a 25% of a quantity is £30. **b** 10% of a quantity is £8.

  c 5% of a quantity is £12. **d** 20% of a quantity is £4.50.

Problem solving

4 **a** Gina bought a DVD in a sale and saved £4.
The label said that it was a 20% reduction.
What was the original price of the DVD?

  b Javid bought a packet of biscuits.
The label said that the packet had 15% extra free.
Javid worked out that he got three extra biscuits free in the packet.
How many biscuits were there in the packet altogether?

5 Calculate the percentage change in price for each of the items in the table on the right.

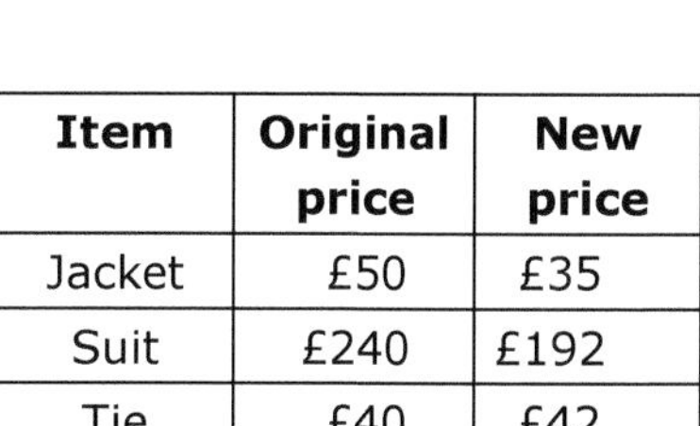

Item	Original price	New price
Jacket	£50	£35
Suit	£240	£192
Tie	£40	£42
Trousers	£45	£39.60

6 **a** A music centre costs £300.
In a sale the price is reduced to £255.
What is the percentage reduction?

  b In one year, the cost of a litre of petrol rises from £1.04 to £1.43.
What is the percentage increase in the cost of a litre of petrol?

7 Solve each of these problems involving ratio and proportion.

  a Pastry is made with fat and flour in the ratio 3 : 5.
How many grams of fat are needed to mix with 300 g of flour?

  b A 370 g packet of coffee costs £2.22.
How much does 100 g of coffee cost?

  c A full box contains identical chocolates with a total mass 495 g.
12 of the chocolates are eaten.
The mass of the chocolates is now 315 g.
How many chocolates were in the box originally?

  d An alloy is made from copper and iron in the ratio 2 : 5.
How much copper needs to be mixed with 65 kg of iron?

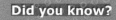

Some foods are made according to very simple ratios - a traditional recipe for short crust pastry uses a ratio of 2 parts flour to 1 part fat.

15f Proportional reasoning

- When two quantities are in **direct proportion**, if one of them increases, the other one increases by the same proportion.

This table shows the amount of flour needed to make different numbers of buns.

Number of buns	Amount of flour
2	80 g
4	160 g
5	200 g
10	400 g

The amount of flour is directly proportional to the number of buns.

If you double the number of buns, you double the amount of flour.

If you halve the number of buns, you halve the amount of flour.

- When two quantities are in direct proportion, you can calculate a proportional change using a unitary method or a single **multiplier**.

Example

Two buns require 80 g of flour. How much flour is needed to make 13 buns?

Using a unitary method

	2 buns	80 g	
÷ 2	1 bun	40 g	÷ 2
× 13	13 buns	520 g	× 13

Find the amount of flour for 1 bun by ÷ 2.

× 13 to calculate the amount of flour for 13 buns.

Using a single multiplier

Number of buns → (× 40) → Amount of flour

13 buns will need $13 \times 40 = 520$ g of flour.

Find the single multiplier by dividing the amount of flour by the number of buns, $80 \div 2 = 40$

Multiply the number of buns required by the single multiplier.

Using a single multiplier is quicker and more **efficient** than the unitary method, but either method is valid for problems involving proportion.

Exercise 15f

Problem solving

1 Here are two offers for memory sticks.
Which offers have the quantities in direct proportion?
In each case explain and justify your answers.

Offer A

Size of memory stick (GB)	Cost
2	£8
4	£14
10	£32

Offer B

Size of memory stick (GB)	Cost
2	£9
5	£22.50
20	£90

2 Vernon has been investigating direct proportion on a spreadsheet. Here are his results.

a Are the numbers in direct proportion?

b What is the single multiplier that connects the number of packets and the cost?

c What formula has Vernon typed into cell B3?

	A	B
1	Number of packets	Cost (£)
2	1	£0.65
3	2	£1.30
4	3	£1.95
5	4	£2.60
6	5	£3.25
7	6	£3.90
8	7	£4.55

3 In these questions the quantities are in direct proportion.
For each question calculate the single multiplier that connects the pair of quantities.

a 5 miles is the same as 8 km.

b 6 pizzas cost £15.

c 10 cm is the same as 100 mm.

d 5 people can eat 350 g of rice.

4 Solve these problems.

a 45 g of breakfast cereal contain 108 calories.
How many calories are there in 150 g of cereal?

b A recipe for eight people uses 1080 ml of stock.
What amount of stock is needed for the same recipe for five people?

c 400 g of cheese costs £6.80.
What is the cost of 1 kg of the cheese?

5 Use **direct proportion** to complete this conversion table for inches and centimetres.

inches	centimetres	inches ÷ centimetres	centimetres ÷ inches
1			
	20		
12	30		
20			

What do you notice?

15g Financial maths 2: Living on a budget

Nicole is a student taking a photography course at university.

Example

Nicole wants to buy a brand new camera, priced at £475. She already has £300 **saved**. She can save £30 per month. After how many months would Nicole have saved up enough money for the camera?

475 − 300 = 175

175 ÷ 30 = 5.833333333 — Use a calculator

It will take Nicole 6 months. — Round up

Nicole needs to **budget** carefully as she has limited money to live on.

Example

Nicole has £900 to live on each month. She plans her monthly **outgoings** on a spreadsheet.

Outgoing	Amount budgeted £
Accommodation	405
Food shopping	180
Household bills	50
Transport	50
Mobile phone	20
Clothes/other	30
Entertainment	75

a How much money does Nicole have left over each month?

b What proportion of Nicole's monthly expenses goes on

i accommodation

ii food shopping?

In each case, give your answer as a fraction in its lowest terms.

a total amount = £810

900 − 810 = 90 — Nicole has £90 left over

b **i** $\frac{405}{810} = \frac{1}{2}$ **ii** $\frac{180}{810} = \frac{2}{9}$

The left-over amount is often referred to as **contingency**, which can be used for unforeseen expenses.

When Nicole goes to the supermarket, she makes choices based on **value for money**.

Example

Nicole is choosing between two similar brands of pasta, A and B. Which brand gives better value for money?

Brand A (2 bags): 1.40 + 0.70 = £2.10 for 1 kg

Brand B (3 bags): 1.50 × 2 = £3.00 for 1.5 kg

To compare value, calculate the price for 1 kg:

A: £2.10 per kg B: £3 ÷ 1.5 kg = £2 per kg

So B is slightly better value for money.

Nicole would need to balance this against option B being more **expensive** in that shopping trip. Which would you choose?

Buy 1 get 1 half price

Buy 2 get the 3rd one free

Exercise 15g

1 Work out how long it would take to be able to afford each of these items, starting from nothing and at the rate of saving given.

- **a** 32 GB tablet, price £320, can save £50 per month
- **b** 18 inch laptop, price £299, can save £40 per month
- **c** Classic designer boots, price £160, can save £45 per month
- **d** 100 watt guitar amp, price £429.95, can save £28 per week.

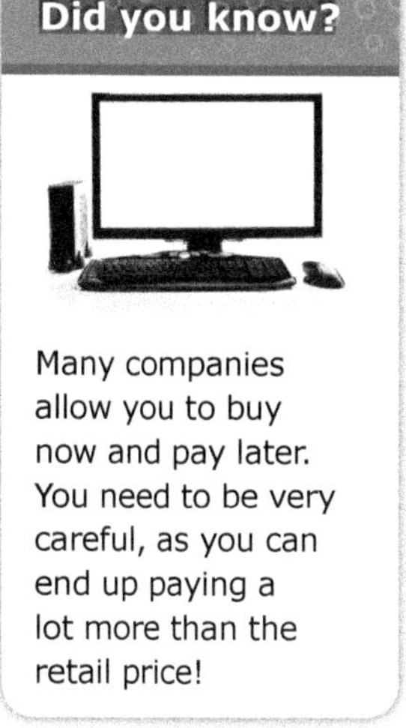

Many companies allow you to buy now and pay later. You need to be very careful, as you can end up paying a lot more than the retail price!

2 Laura has created a budget for her monthly expenses.

Expense type	Amount budgeted £
Accommodation	500
Food shopping	200
Household bills	50
Transport	60
Other essential expenses	90
Amount left over	

- **a** Laura takes home £1200 **salary** each month. How much does she have left over each month for herself?
- **b** Work out the proportion of Laura's salary for each of the six categories in the spreadsheet. In each case, give your answer as a fraction in its lowest terms.
- **c** Draw a pie chart of Laura's monthly spending. Label your diagram clearly.
- **d** Laura's friend Marie says '£1200 per month means you take home £400 per week.' Describe why this is only an **estimate**, and explain whether Laura's weekly pay will be more or less than this.

Problem solving

3 Oscar is deciding which of these two brands of coffee to buy, *Mountain Brand* or *Club Coffee*. He thinks: 'Mountain Brand's got an offer on, but it's a lot smaller.'
Which one would you advise Oscar to buy? Give your reasoning.

£3.99 for 300 g

Buy 1 get 1 free

£2.40 for 100 g

4 Maisie likes houmous! Two competing brands are normally fairly identical, but they now both have offers. Which should Maisie choose, and why?

Brand X
Normally £1.50 for 200 g, now 50% off!

Brand Y
Normally £1.50 for 200 g, now 50% extra free!

5 Look again at Nicole's budget spreadsheet on the opposite page. Due to **price inflation**, the amount she pays for accommodation, food shopping and household bills have all gone up by 10%. She still only has £900 to spend each month. Advise Nicole on where she can make a saving to ensure that she still has £90 left over as contingency.

15 MySummary

Check out

You should now be able to ...

	Grade	Test it ➡ Questions
✓ Solve problems involving direct proportion.	6	1 – 2
✓ Use percentages to compare proportions.	6	3
✓ Calculate with ratios, including dividing quantities in a given ratio.	6	4 – 6
✓ Solve problems involving ratio.	7	7 – 8
✓ Calculate a percentage increase or decrease.	6	9 – 11

Language	Meaning	Example
Direct proportion	Two quantities that are related so that when one is multiplied by a number, the other is multiplied by the same number.	If text messages cost 5 pence each, then the number of text messages is proportional to the cost of the text messages.
Divide in a ratio	To share out a quantity into a number of (usually) unequal parts.	£60 divided in the ratio 2 : 1 is £40 : £20.
Simplify a ratio	To write a ratio in its simplest form by dividing by common factors.	28 : 14 can be simplified to 2 : 1 by dividing both parts by the common factor 14.
1 : *n*	A ratio that has been simplified so that the first number is 1.	4 : 10 can be divided by 4 to give the equivalent ratio 1 : 2.5
Percentage change	The percentage increase or decrease that changes an original amount to a new amount.	A car that cost £20 000 is now worth £15 000. This is a percentage reduction of 25%.

15 MyReview

1 200 g of butter costs £1.28. What is the cost of 250 g of the same butter?

2 A 150 g sharing pack of crisps contains 1.35 g of salt. How much salt is in a single 35 g bag of the same crisps?

3 67 out of 98 students passed test A and 268 out of 400 students passed test B. Which test had the higher percentage of students passing?

4 Write each of these ratios in its simplest form.

a 16 : 32 : 24

b 40 seconds : 3 minutes

5 **a** Divide 600 m in the ratio 7 : 5.

b Divide £117 in the ratio 2 : 8 : 3.

6 Write each of these ratios in the form 1 : *n*.

a 5 : 12

b 150 cm : 2.25 m

7 A map has a scale of 1 : 15000.

a What distance does 4 cm on the map represent in real life?

b What length on the map represents a real-life measurements of 1.2 km?

8 The ratio of strawberry to raspberry yoghurts is 3 : 4.
What proportion of the yoghurts are strawberry?

9 20% of a quantity is £19. Calculate the whole amount.

10 A pair of trainers is reduced from £60 to £45. What was the percentage reduction in price?

11 5 lb is approximately the same is 2.27 kg.

a Calculate the single multiplier that converts pounds (lb) to kg.

b Calculate the single multiplier that converts kg to pounds (lb).

What next?

Score	
0 – 4	Your knowledge of this topic is still developing. To improve look at Formative test: 3B-15; MyMaths: 1036, 1039, 1103, 1245, 1302 and 1934
5 – 9	You are gaining a secure knowledge of this topic. To improve look at InvisiPen: 136, 153, 154, 191, 192, 193, 194 and 195
10, 11	You have mastered this topic. Well done, you are ready to progress!

15 MyPractice

1 Use direct proportion to solve these problems.

- **a** 3 litres of lemonade cost £2.13.
  What is the cost of 5 litres of lemonade?
- **b** There are 21 sweets in a packet.
  The mass of the packet is 336 g.
  What is the mass of a packet of 30 sweets?
- **c** 12 inches is approximately 30 cm.
  - **i** How many centimetres are equal to 20 inches?
  - **ii** How many inches are equal to 100 cm?

2 Statistics are given for three strikers over the course of a football season.
Write the number of goals scored as a proportion of the number of shots taken for each of these strikers.

a	Andrews	12 goals	48 shots
b	Roland	15 goals	40 shots
c	Tonaldo	22 goals	55 shots

Who is the best striker? Explain your answer.

3 At the pony club there are 23 girls and 7 boys.
At the dance club there are 14 girls and 5 boys.
Which club has the higher proportion of boys?
Write your answer as a percentage (rounded to 1 dp where appropriate).

4 Write these ratios in their simplest form.
First change the quantities into the same units.

- **a** £5 : 350 p
- **b** 4 kg : 2500 g
- **c** 12 cm : 50 mm
- **d** 250 ml : 30 cl

5 Work out these quantities, giving your answers to 2 dp where appropriate.

- **a** Divide 60 pears in the ratio 7 : 5.
- **b** Divide £300 in the ratio 2 : 3.

15d

6 At a school the ratio of boys to girls is 4 : 5.
There are 572 boys at the school. How many children are there at the school?

7 A model of a yacht is built to a scale of 1 : 24.
The length of the yacht is 15.6 m.
What is the length of the model yacht?

15e

8 **a** John bought a CD in a sale and saved £5.20.
The label said that it was a 40% reduction.
What was the original price of the CD?

b A mobile phone costs £240. In a sale the price is reduced to £204.
What is the percentage reduction?

15f

9 **a** Kelvin is choosing between two different offers for firewood.
In which of these offers are the numbers in direct proportion?
In each case explain and justify your answers.

Offer A

Mass of wood (kg)	Cost
3	£7.68
5	£12.80
10	£25.60

Offer B

Mass of wood (kg)	Cost
10	£28
50	£135
100	£260

b Kelvin decides to buy 50 kg of firewood.
How much cheaper is offer A?

In part **b** assume the cost is in direct proportion.

10 For each of these problems

i find the single multiplier that connects the quantities

ii solve the problem.

a 75 g of cheese contains 30 g of fat.
How many grams of fat are there in 120 g of cheese?

b A recipe for six people uses 420 g of flour.
How much flour is needed for the same recipe for 11 people?

c 1.5 litres of fruit drink cost 87p.
What is the cost of 5 litres of fruit drink?

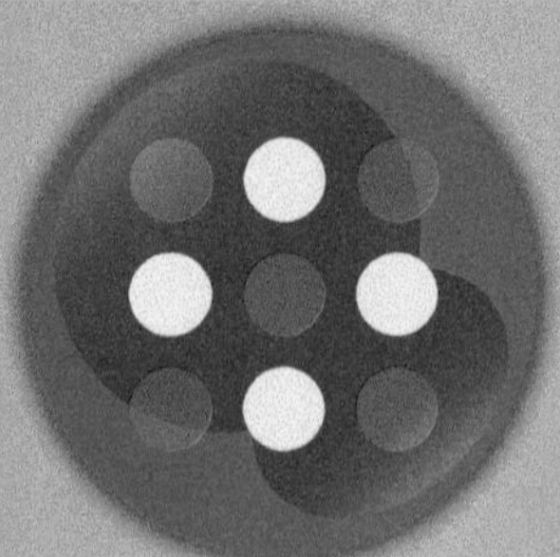

16 Probability

Introduction

Buying a new car or TV is a major purchase for a family. It is important that when you spend a lot of money on an item it is reliable, works well and does not break down. However no product is 100% perfect. Most consumer items have experiments carried out on them to find out their probability of breaking or becoming defective under different conditions.

What's the point?

Understanding probability is vitally important in ensuring the safety levels of cars, planes and trains.

Objectives

By the end of this chapter, you will have learned how to …

- Use the vocabulary of uncertainty and prediction.
- Find and record outcomes of a single trial.
- Understand theoretical probability.
- Calculate probabilities of exclusive events.
- Use sample-space diagrams and tree diagrams.
- Calculate experimental probability and compare with theoretical probability.
- Enumerate sets using Venn diagrams.

Check in

1 Draw a probability scale from 0 to 1.
Show where you might put events that could be described with these words.

- **a** Impossible
- **b** Certain
- **c** An even chance
- **d** Very unlikely

2 An ordinary dice is rolled. What is the probability of the score being a prime number?

3 Convert each of these fractions and percentages to decimals.

- **a** $\frac{3}{5}$
- **b** $\frac{5}{8}$
- **c** $\frac{9}{20}$
- **d** 15%
- **e** 27%
- **f** 3.7%

Starter problem

Inside a bag are three cards with the numbers 1, 2 and 3 written on them.
You are allowed to pick one card from the bag and then replace the card in the bag.
What is the probability you pick the same number twice?

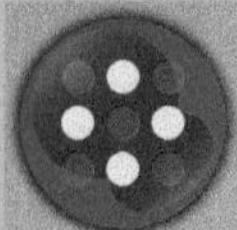

16a Prediction and uncertainty

- You can describe probability in words. For example,
  - a **certain** outcome will always happen.
  - an **impossible** outcome can never happen.

You can also describe probabilities numerically, on a scale of 0 to 1.

Impossible (0) — Unlikely — Even chance — Likely — Certain (1)

Increasing probability →

It is certain that the day after next Tuesday will be Wednesday.

It is impossible that a person in your class will be 200 years old.

- You can use probabilities to explain what you expect to happen in an **experiment**.
  An experiment is a series of **trials**.

The exact results of a particular experiment are usually **unpredictable**.
You might get different results when the experiment is repeated.

Example

In an experiment, a teacher asked students to roll an ordinary dice 60 times.
David produced this set of results.
Should his teacher be suspicious?

Score	1	2	3	4	5	6
Frequency	10	10	10	10	10	10

It is possible that David actually got these results, but his teacher might think he made them up from what he thought the results should be.
Actual results for this experiment would show a lot more **variation**.

The more trials you perform the closer the experimental results will be to the predicted results.

Unpredictability is all around us.

A weather forecast is only a prediction and might be wrong.

People sometimes feel that they are having 'a run of bad luck' when they lose their keys or miss the bus.

Part of the fun of watching a sporting event is that you can't be certain of the result.

A forecast might say, 'a 30% chance of rain by midday'.

This is often simple coincidence.

Some sports and games involve more chance than others.

Exercise 16a

1 A computer is used to select a random whole number between 1 and 100.

Describe these outcomes using probability words.

a The number is not a decimal.

b The number is more than 50.

c The number has three digits.

Explain your answers.

Certain	Even chance
Unlikely	Likely

2 Becky tested a spinner and found that it landed on green 45 times out of 100 spins.

Two other people are also going to test the same spinner 100 times.

Joe says, *'I think I'm going to get green 45 times as well.'*

Rahimah says, *'It's unpredictable, so I've no idea what I'll get.'*

Do you agree with these statements?

Explain your reasoning carefully.

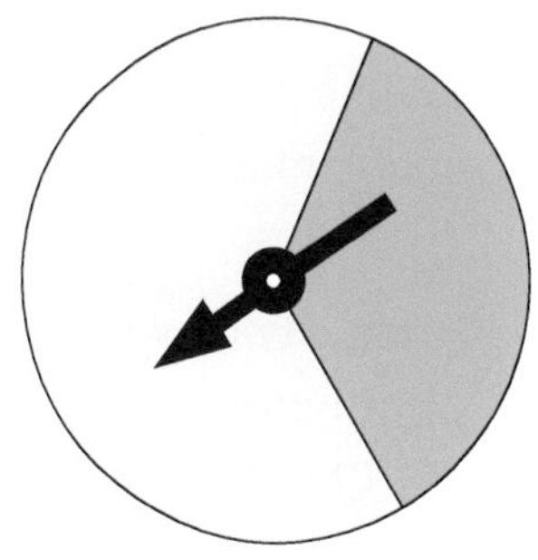

3 Alesha and Sophie are playing a board game using two dice.

Alesha rolls two doubles in a row.

Sophie says, *'You're bound to get doubles again next go.'*

Alesha says, *'No I won't, I've used up all my luck!'*

Explain what you think might happen.

4 Five students were asked to toss a coin 20 times.

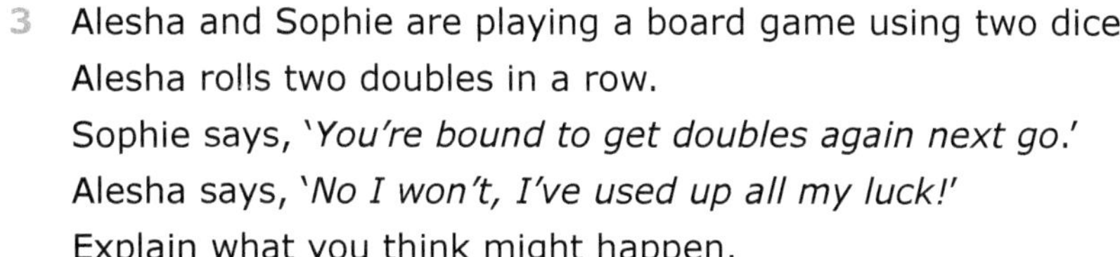

Andy	H T H T H T H T H T H T H T H T H T H T
Beata	T H T T T H T H H H H T T H H H H T T T
Carlo	H H H T T H H T T H T H T T H H T T T T
Dean	H H H H H H H H H H T T T T T T T T T T
Ellie	T H T T T H T H H H H T T H H H H T T T

Their teacher was suspicious about some of the results.

Explain why.

Did you know?

The ancient Romans used to play coin tossing games called *navia aut caput* because the two sides of the coin often showed a ship and the emperor's head.

Problem solving

5 'Dice Race' is a game played with two dice and counters.

Place one counter on each number at the bottom of the board.

Roll the dice and the total shows which counter can move up one square.

The first counter to the top wins!

Does the same counter always win?

What happens if you change the number of moves needed to win?

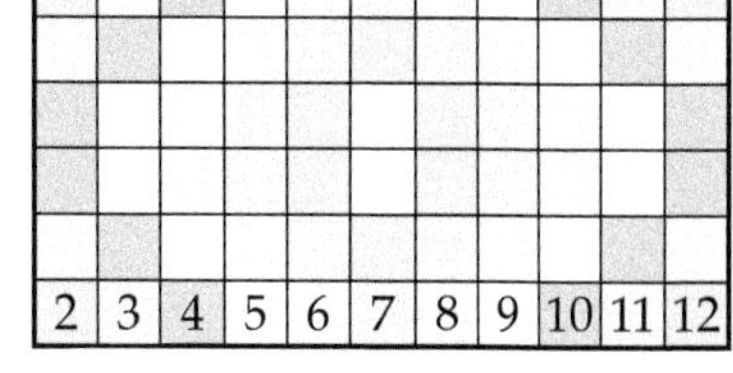

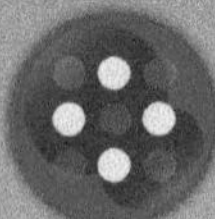

16b Mutually exclusive events

- A **trial** is an action that you can find the result of. A series of one or more trials is an **experiment**.

Rolling a dice is a trial.
Spinning a coin ten times is an experiment.

- The **outcomes** of a trial are the possible results.
- An **event** is a set of outcomes.
- Two events are **mutually exclusive** if they have no outcomes in common. They cannot both happen.
- These two events are mutually exclusive:
  - Choosing an even number from a set of numbers
  - Choosing an odd number from a set of numbers

Example

Keira rolls an ordinary dice.

a List all the outcomes.

b Explain whether these pairs of events are mutually exclusive.

  i An even score and a multiple of 3.

  ii A score less than 4 and a score more than 3.

a The possible outcomes are 1, 2, 3, 4, 5 and 6.

b **i** Outcomes for 'an even score' are {2, 4, 6}.
Outcomes for 'a multiple of 3' are {3, 6}.
The outcome 6 is common to both events.
They are not mutually exclusive.

ii Outcomes for 'a score less than 4' are {1, 2, 3}.
Outcomes for 'a score more than 3' are {4, 5, 6}.
No outcome is common to both sets.
The events are mutually exclusive.

- Outcomes are **exhaustive** if between them they include all the possible outcomes of an event.

Example

Keira rolls a dice again.
Explain whether each pair of events in **b** are exhaustive.

i The outcomes for 'an even score' and 'a multiple of 3' are {2, 4, 6} and {6}. They do not cover all the possible outcomes so they are not exhaustive.

ii The outcomes for 'a score less than 4' and 'a score more than 3' are {1, 2, 3} and {4, 5, 6}. These cover all the possible outcomes, so are exhaustive.

Events that are exhaustive could also be mutually exclusive.

Exercise 16b

1 Alfie rolls an ordinary dice.
X is the event 'the score is even'.
Y is the event 'the score is odd'.

a List all of the outcomes that belong to
 i event X **ii** event Y.

b Are these events mutually exclusive? Explain your answer.

2 A hockey team's result in their next game will be a win, lose or draw.
Explain why

a these three results are mutually exclusive

b these three results are exhaustive.

3 This set of cards is placed in a bag, and a card is picked at random.

a List all the possible outcomes for this experiment.

b The event A is 'the chosen letter is a vowel'.
List the outcomes that belong to event A.

c The event B is 'the chosen letter is a consonant.'
List the outcomes that belong to event B.

d Are events A and B mutually exclusive?
Explain your answer.

e Are events A and B exhaustive?
Explain your answer.

4 Kyle's teacher places this set of cards in a bag and picks a card at random.

1 2 3 4 5 6 7 8 9 10

a List the outcomes that belong to each of these events.
A = 'A prime number' B = 'An odd number'
C = 'An even number' D = 'A factor of 12'

b Explain whether each of these statements is true or false.
 i Events B and C are mutually exclusive.
 ii Events B and C are exhaustive.
 iii Events A and C are mutually exclusive.
 iv Events C and D are exhaustive.

Problem solving

5 Freya says 'If events A and B are both mutually exclusive and exhaustive, then

a either event A will happen or event B will happen

b events A and B cannot both happen.'

Do you agree with her?

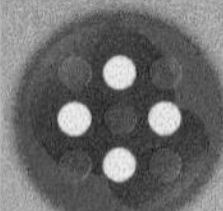

16c Calculating probabilities

- Probabilities can be shown on a probability **scale** from 0 (impossible) to 1 (certain).

Impossible (0) — Unlikely — Even chance — Likely — Certain (1)

Increasing probability →

You can write probabilties as fractions, decimals or percentages.

- You can find the **theoretical probability** of an event when all the outcomes are equally likely.

  Probability of an event =

$$\frac{\text{Number of outcomes belonging to the event}}{\text{Total number of equally likely outcomes}}$$

- You use the notation P(A) to mean 'the probability of event A'.

Example

Sam has a multipack of 24 packets of crisps.
Six are ready salted, six are cheese and onion, six are salt and vinegar and six are barbeque.
Find the probability that he picks a packet of salt and vinegar crisps.

There are 24 equally likely outcomes and six of them are salt and vinegar.

P(salt and vinegar) $= \frac{6}{24} = 0.25 = 25\%$

- If mutually exclusive events are also exhaustive then the total of their probabilities is 1.
  The probability that event A does **not** occur is 1 − P(A).

Example

Find the probability that Sam picks a packet of crisps that are **not** salt and vinegar.

P(salt and vinegar) $= \frac{6}{24} = \frac{1}{4} = 25\%$

P(not salt and vinegar) = 1 − P(salt and vinegar)

$= 1 - \frac{1}{4}$

$= \frac{3}{4} = 0.75 = 75\%$

Always read the question carefully. Words like 'not' are crucial to getting the answer correct!

Exercise 16c

1 Julie rolls an ordinary dice.
Use the formula for theoretical probability to find
a P(2) **b** P(3 or 4) **c** P(a prime number).
Give each answer as a fraction, a decimal and a percentage.

2 Use your answers to question 1 to work out
a P(not 2) **b** P(neither 3 nor 4) **c** P(not a prime number)
Give each answer as a fraction, a decimal and a percentage.

3 Here are the probabilities for three events.
$P(A) = \frac{3}{16}$ P(B) = 0.92 P(C) = 12.5%
Find the probability of each of these events **not** occurring.

4 A set of 20 cards has the numbers 1 to 20 written on them.

Find the probability of each of these events.
a P(even number) **b** P(multiple of 3) **c** P(factor of 18) **d** P(prime number)

5 Use your answers to question **4** to find the probability of each of the events **not** occurring.

6 A computer is used to choose a random whole number from 1 to 100 inclusive.
Find the probability that the chosen number is
a 37 **b** An even number
c A prime number **d** Not prime
e Less than 8 **f** More than 8.

There are 25 prime numbers between 1 and 100.

7 Dave chooses a letter of the alphabet at random.
Find the probability that the chosen letter is
a a vowel **b** not a vowel **c** after T in the alphabet
d not included in the letters of the word 'dog'.
Give each answer as a fraction, a decimal and a percentage.

Problem solving

8 Phil's team are taking part in a baseball tournament.
He says, 'There are three possible outcomes: win, lose or draw.
So, the probability that we will win the tournament is $\frac{1}{3}$.'
Do you agree?

16d The outcomes of two trials

- The set of all the outcomes of an experiment is called the sample space.
- **Sample-space diagrams** can be used to record all the possible outcomes of two trials. These can be **two-way tables** or **tree diagrams.**

Example

Suni tosses a coin twice.

Record all the possible outcomes using

a a two-way table **b** a tree diagram.

a

	H	**T**
H	(H, H)	(H, T)
T	(T, H)	(T, T)

The possible outcomes are {(H, H), (H, T), (T, H), (T, T)}.

b

H → H, T
T → H, T

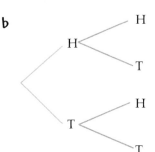

There are four possible outcomes to this experiment on each diagram.

You can match the outcomes to events in different ways.
These are some of the possible events for the example above.

Event A = 'at least one head'	Event B = 'same result on both coins'
Event C = 'first result is tails'	Event D = 'exactly one head'

Example

Marie rolls two dice and calculates the total score.
Show the possible outcomes on a sample-space diagram.

There are 36 separate outcomes.

	1	**2**	**3**	**4**	**5**	**6**
1	2	3	4	5	6	7
2	3	4	5	6	7	8
3	4	5	6	7	8	9
4	5	6	7	8	9	10
5	6	7	8	9	10	11
6	7	8	9	10	11	12

A two-way table is much easier than a tree diagram in this example.
There are many possible events, for example 'doubles' or 'a score greater than 4'.

Exercise 16d

Problem solving

1 Martina plays two games of tennis.
She either wins or loses each game.
a Show the possible outcomes for the two games on a tree diagram.
b Draw a two-way table to show the same information.
c Copy and complete this list of the possible outcomes for the two games: {(win, win), (win, lose), ... }.

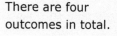

There are four outcomes in total.

2 Zaina's mother drives her to school each day.
On their route they pass two sets of traffic lights.
Each set is either red, amber or green when they reach it.
a Show the possible settings of both sets of lights in a two-way table.
b Draw a tree diagram to show the same information.
c List the possible outcomes.

3 A technician checks a computer by carrying out two tests.
First she tests the monitor and then the hard drive.
The computer either passes or fails each test.
a Draw a tree diagram to show the possible outcomes of this two-stage check.
b List the possible outcomes.

4 In an experiment, a coin is tossed and a random whole number between 1 and 10 is chosen by a computer.
Which sort of diagram would be best to show all the outcomes for this experiment, a two-way table or a tree diagram?
Explain your answer and draw your chosen diagram.

5 A music exam has two parts: a theory test followed by a performance test.
The possible outcomes are {(pass, credit), (pass, pass), (pass, fail), (fail, credit), (fail, pass), (fail, fail)}.
a Draw a tree diagram to show the possible outcomes.
b Show the same information in a two-way table.
c Give an example of an event which includes exactly three of the outcomes given.

6 Draw a suitable sample-space diagram for each of these experiments.
a Two ordinary dice are rolled and the product of the scores is calculated.
b A coin is tossed four times, and the result is recorded each time.
Justify your choice of diagram in each case.

16e Experimental probability

Increasing the number of trials makes the estimated probability more reliable.

- You can calculate **theoretical probabilities** when
  - you know all the possible outcomes of a trial
  - and that all the outcomes are equally likely.

Sometimes you might not know what all the possible outcomes are.

The next bird you see from your window will be a robin.

Or you may not be sure that they are all equally likely.

The next game played by a netball team will end in a draw.

Probability experiments allow you to **estimate** the probability of an event.

- In an experiment you use the **relative frequency** of an event as an **estimate** of its probability.

$$\text{Relative frequency} = \frac{\text{Number of successful trials}}{\text{Total number of trials}}$$

Example

Afzal and Barry tested this spinner.
Here are their results.

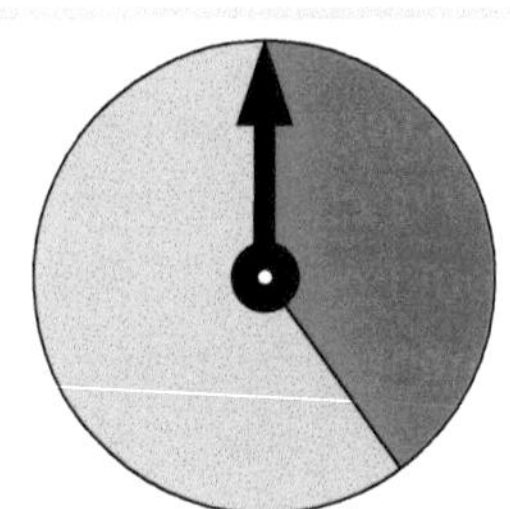

	Afzal	Barry
Red	42	18
Blue	58	32

Use the data to estimate the probability of the spinner landing on red.
Comment on your answers.

In Afzal's experiment there were 42 successful trials out of 100.

$$\text{P(red, Afzal)} = \frac{42}{100} = 0.42$$

In Barry's experiment there were 18 successful trials out of 50.

$$\text{P(red, Barry)} = \frac{18}{50} = 0.36$$

Afzal's results are more reliable as there is a larger number of trials.

You could also combine both sets of data to get a more reliable estimate.
There were 60 successful trials out of 150.

$$\text{P(red)} = \frac{60}{150} = 0.4$$

Exercise 16e

1 Tim practised darts by aiming at the bull's-eye.
He hit the bull's-eye 13 times and missed 47 times.

a How many trials were there in this experiment?

b How many of the trials were successful?

c Estimate the probability of Tim hitting the bull's-eye with a single dart. Show your working.

2 In an experiment, three students threw a drawing pin and recorded the number of times it landed 'point up' and 'point down'.

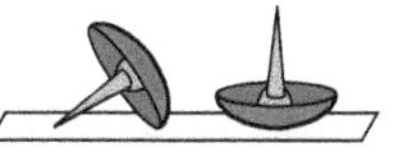

	Up	Down
Dan	63	37
Caz	34	16
Charlie	135	65

a Find the estimated value of P(down) for each student.

b Whose value of P(down) should be most reliable? Explain your answer.

c Combine all three sets of data to calculate a better estimate of the experimental probability. Show all your working.

3 Jenny wrote the letters of the word MATHS on five pieces of paper of various shapes and sizes. She put the pieces in a bag, picked one without looking, recorded the letter and put the paper back. Jenny's experiment had 50 trials. These are her results.

H	M	S	H	H	S	M	M	M	H	A	H	A	T	H	M	H
H	T	H	H	S	M	H	M	H	T	H	H	S	M	S	H	H
M	S	M	S	H	H	T	M	H	M	H	H	S	H	H	S	

a Explain why the five possible outcomes for each trial are not equally likely.

b Estimate the experimental probability of each outcome.

Problem solving

4 The coach of a hockey team is preparing for the first match of the new season.
She looks at the results of their matches last season.
There were 12 wins, 8 losses and 2 draws.
She says, 'We won 12 out of 22 games, so there's a better than even chance that we'll win our first game of the new season.'
Do you think this statement is reasonable?
Explain your answer.

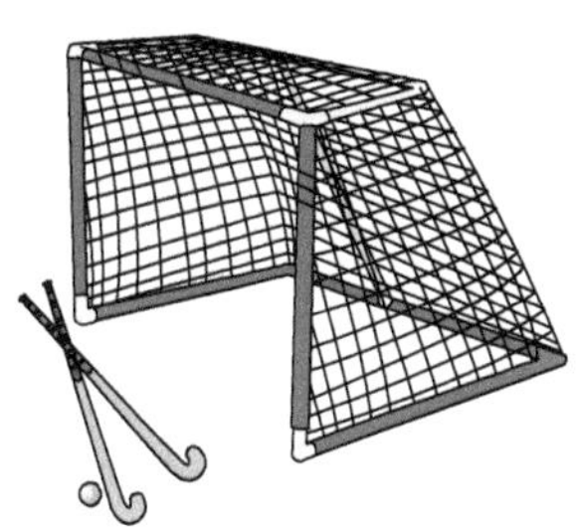

16f Comparing theoretical and experimental probabilities

- You can compare **theoretical** probabilities with estimated **experimental** probabilities.

Example

A fairground game uses a spinner with four regions labelled 1 to 4. In one evening the game is played 150 times. Calculate the experimental probability from the results in the table and compare these to the theoretical probabilities. Comment on your results.

Score	1	2	3	4
Frequency	32	43	35	40

Score	1	2	3	4
Relative frequency	0.21	0.29	0.23	0.27

$$\text{Relative frequency} = \frac{\text{Number of successful trials}}{\text{Total number of trials}}$$

$$\text{Probability of an event} = \frac{\text{Number of outcomes belonging to the event}}{\text{Total number of equally likely outcomes}}$$

For each score, the theoretical probability is $\frac{1}{4} = 0.25$.
The theoretical and experimental probabilities are reasonably close together.

- The relative frequencies should get nearer to the theoretical probabilities as the number of trials increases. If this does not happen, the experiment may be **biased**.

Do not expect the relative frequencies to be exactly the same as the theoretical probabilities, especially if the number of trials in the experiment is small.

Example

George thinks that the same game at a different fairground might be biased.
He records these results from 150 trials.

Score	1	2	3	4
Frequency	60	30	25	35

Is the game biased? Explain your answer.

The relative frequencies are 0.4, 0.2, 0.17 and 0.23.
The theoretical probabilities are all 0.25.
There does seem to be a bias toward the number 1 as it has a higher probability than the theoretical value, but more trials would make the results clearer.

Exercise 16f

1 Jake tested a coin by tossing it.
There were 38 heads and 27 tails.

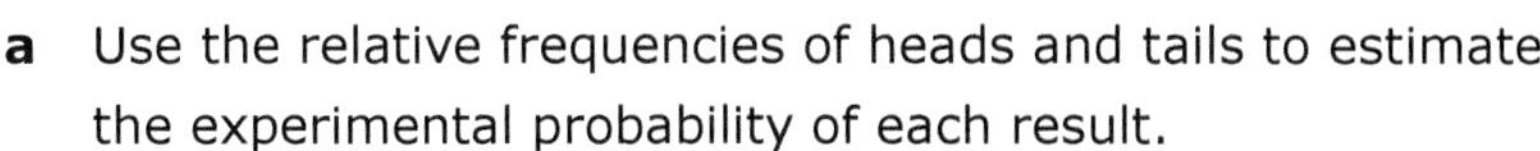

- **a** Use the relative frequencies of heads and tails to estimate the experimental probability of each result.
- **b** Compare the experimental and theoretical probabilities for each result. Is the coin fair? Explain your answer.

2 Kathryn tested a dice by counting the number of sixes after 10, 50, 100 and 200 rolls.

Number of rolls	10	50	100	200
Number of sixes	1	6	14	32

- **a** Calculate the relative frequency of a score of six after 10, 50, 100 and 200 rolls. Give your answers to 2dp.
- **b** Calculate the theoretical probability of getting a score of 6 with a roll of the dice.
- **c** Compare your answers to parts **a** and **b**.

3 In an experiment, Petra shuffles a pack of standard playing cards and picks one at random. She records the card, then returns it to the pack before shuffling and dealing again.
She picks 60 cards altogether. Her results are shown below (7♣ means '7 of Clubs')

7♣	K♦	8♣	A♥	6♠	5♠	9♥	8♥	5♠	5♥
3♣	4♠	4♦	4♦	7♥	9♦	2♥	Q♥	4♥	8♣
K♠	7♠	9♦	10♣	5♣	Q♣	A♥	K♥	Q♠	K♦
5♣	6♣	A♥	10♠	K♣	J♦	Q♣	2♥	3♠	4♥
5♠	Q♥	2♣	10♥	A♥	J♥	3♣	A♦	3♠	J♥
7♦	K♣	7♦	5♣	6♦	6♠	K♣	10♠	5♠	A♦

- **a** From this data, estimate the experimental probability of picking
  i a Club (♣) **ii** a red card (♥ or ♦) **iii** a 2, 3 or 4.
- **b** Compare your answers to the theoretical probabilities and comment on your answers.

An ordinary pack of card contains 52 cards: 26 red (diamonds and hearts) and 26 black (clubs and spades).

Problem solving

4 Darren rolled two ordinary dice and recorded the total 100 times.

Total	2	3	4	5	6	7	8	9	10	11	12
Frequency	1	6	7	17	13	21	9	7	8	8	3

- **a** Draw a sample-space diagram and calculate the probability of each total, giving your answers to 2dp.
- **b** Use the experimental results to calculate the relative frequency of each score.
- **c** Compare the theoretical and experimental probabilities. Do you think the dice are fair? Explain your answer.

16g Venn diagrams

- The **universal set**, which has the symbol Ω, is the set containing all the elements. The empty set, which has the symbol $\varnothing$, contains no elements.

Example

Ω = {1, 2, 3, 4, 5, 6, 7, 8, 9}, E = {even numbers}, F = {odd numbers} and G = {multiples of 4}. Find

a $E \cap G$ **b** $F \cup G$ **c** $E \cap F$

E = {2, 4, 6, 8} F = {1, 3, 5, 7, 9} G = {4, 8}

a $E \cap G$ = {4, 8} **b** $F \cup G$ = {1, 3, 4, 5, 6, 8, 9} **c** $E \cap F$ = {∅}

- Two events are mutually exclusive if $A \cap B = \varnothing$.

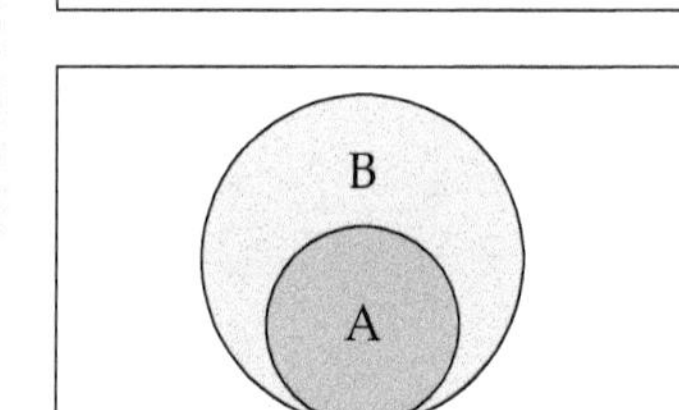

{even numbers} ∩ {odd number} = ∅

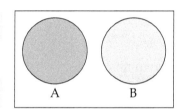

- A is a proper subset of B if:
  - every element in A is also contained in set B
  - set A does not contain every element in B.

  We write $A \subset B$.

{multiples of 4} ⊂ {even numbers}
All multiples of 4 are even numbers, but not all even numbers are multiples of 4.

- You can use Venn diagrams to work out probabilities.

$$P(A) = \frac{\text{number of elements in set A}}{\text{total number of elements}}$$

Example

Jess asked 30 students at her school if they have a laptop or a tablet. She showed her results on a Venn diagram.

a Shade the region $L \cap T'$. **b** Find $P(L \cap T')$.

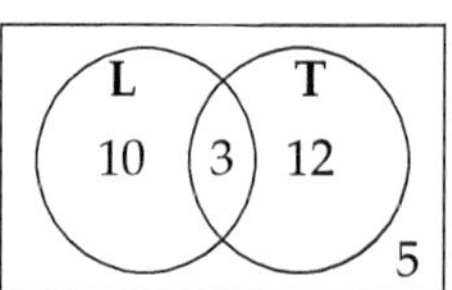

a Shade L using vertical lines.
Shade T′ using horizontal lines.

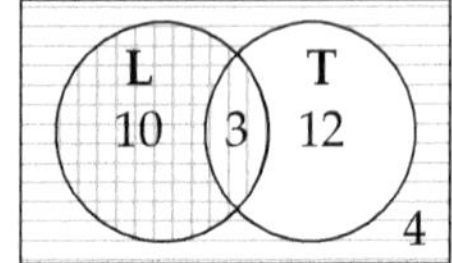

b $P(L \cap T') = \frac{10}{30} = \frac{1}{3}$

The shading overlaps in the intersection. The total shaded region is the union.

Exercise 16g

1 Decide if the following sets are mutually exclusive. If the sets are not mutually exclusive, state an element that is in the intersection.

  a A = {even numbers}, B = {prime numbers}
  b C = {multiples of 3}, D = {factors of 16}
  c E = {1, 2, 3, 5, 8, 13}, F = {square numbers}
  d G = {multiples of 5}, H = {multiples of 7}.

2 Decide if the following sets are a proper subset of Z = {1, 2, 3, 6, 7, 11, 12, 15, 16}. Give a reason for each answer.

  a A = {1, 2, 4}
  b B = {11, 12, 15}
  c C = {factors of 6}
  d D = {factors of 12}

3 Alexa manages a gym. She surveys 30 members to find out which exercise classes they take. She sorts her results into the sets A = {aerobics} and K = {kickboxing}.

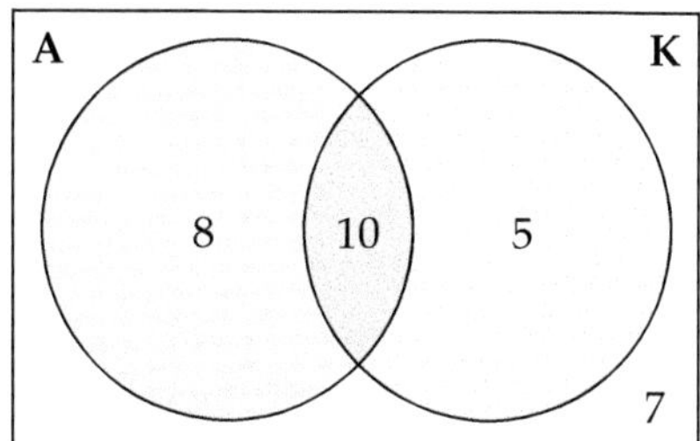

  a Find P(A ∩ K)
  b Shade the region A ∩ K′
  c Find P(A ∩ K′)
  d Shade the region A′ ∪ K′
  e Find P(A′ ∪ K′)

Problem solving

4 Rini sorts a group of objects into the sets A and B. She draws a Venn diagram to show her results.

  a Explain why Rini must have started with 40 objects.
  b Use $x = 2$ to find
    i P(A)
    ii P(B′)
    iii P(A ∪ B)
    iv P(A ∩ B)
  c If A and B are mutually exclusive, find the value of x. Hence find P(A′ ∪ B).
  d If $x = -10$, what can you say about the sets A and B?

5 **a** Cori claims that P(A ∪ B) = P(A) + P(B), if A and B are mutually exclusive. Use a Venn diagram to explain why Cori is right.

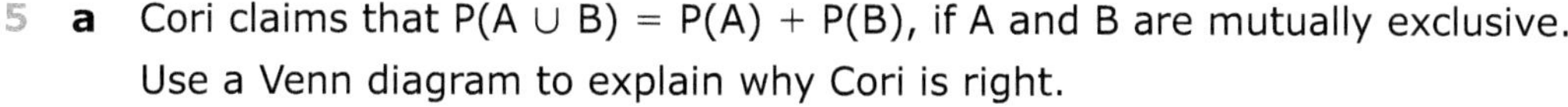

  b Can you write down a formula that would work for any two events?

Hint: the formula is P(A ∪ B) = P(A) + P(B) − something

16 MySummary

Check out

You should now be able to ...

	Level	Test it ➡ Questions
✓ Generate sample spaces for events and use these to calculate probabilities.	6	1 – 4
✓ Understand that the probabilities of all possible outcomes sum to 1.	6	5
✓ Analyse the frequency of outcomes of simple probability experiments.	7	6 – 7
✓ Enumerate sets using Venn diagrams.	7	8

Language	Meaning	Example
Experiment	A series of trials.	Tossing a dice 100 times is an experiment.
Trial	An activity that you can record the result of.	Rolling a dice is a trial.
Outcome	Possible result of a trial.	The possible outcomes of rolling a dice are 1, 2, 3, 4, 5, 6.
Event	A set of outcomes.	'Rolling an even number' on a dice is an event.
Mutually exclusive	Events that cannot both happen together.	Raining and not raining are mutually exclusive events.
Exhaustive	All the possible outcomes of a trial.	'An even score' and 'an odd score' on a dice.
Relative frequency	An estimate of probability from experimental data.	Weather forecasters use patterns to estimate the probability of rain.
Probability	A measure of how likely an event is to occur.	'The probability of rain tomorrow is $\frac{3}{10}$.'

16 MyReview

1 Two dice are thrown. State if these pairs of events are mutually exclusive

a *'one of the dice shows a 3'* and *'the sum of both dice is 7'*

b *'one of the dice shows and even number'* and *'the product of the two dice is even'*

c *'one of the dice shows a 4'* and *'the difference between the dice is 5'*

2 A card is chosen at random from a set of digit cards from 1 to 20. Find the probability of each of these events.

a P(even number) **b** P(odd number)

c P(multiple of 3) **d** P(prime number)

3 A letter from the word SUMMER is chosen at random. Find the probability of each of these events.

a P(R) **b** P(M)

c P(a vowel) **d** P(P)

4 Two fair dice are thrown and the numbers multiplied together.

a Construct a two-way table which shows the sample space.

b Calculate the probability of getting a product of more than 12.

5 A fair dice is thrown twice and each time it is recorded whether it is a 6 or not a 6. Record the outcomes on a tree diagram.

6 Aidan is practising on a putting green. He records how many shots per hole in the table.

Shots	1	2	3+
Frequency	3	11	4

Estimate the probability Aidan takes 3 or more shots.

7 A five-sided spinner is spun 20 times and the results recorded.

1 4 5 3 5
2 4 3 4 3
3 5 4 2 3
4 3 5 1 4

a Calculate the relative frequency of each number.

b Calculate the theoretical probability of each number.

c Do you think the spinner is fair?

8 Ω = {the integers 1 to 10}

A = {multiples of 2}

B = {factors of 18}

a Draw a Venn diagram to show this information.

b Shade the region $A' \cap B$.

c Find $P(A' \cap B)$.

C = {multiples of 4}

d What can you say about the sets A and C?

e What can you say about the sets B and C?

What next?

Score	
0 – 3	Your knowledge of this topic is still developing. To improve look at Formative test: 3B-16; MyMaths: 1199, 1209, 1210, 1211, 1264, 1921 and 1922
4 – 6	You are gaining a secure knowledge of this topic. To improve look at InvisiPen: 451, 452, 453, 454, 461, 462, 463, 464, 472, 474, 475 and 476
7, 8	You have mastered this topic. Well done, you are ready to progress!

16 MyPractice

1 Kate puts cards marked with each whole number from 1 to 100 into a box and then picks a card at random.
Give an example of an outcome that is

a Certain
b Impossible
c Very unlikely
d An even chance.

2 A computer is used to choose a number between 1 and 1000.
Give examples of

a a set of three events that are exhaustive
b a set of four events that are mutually exclusive.

3 Peter rolls a red dice and a blue dice.
The event X is 'The product of the scores on the two dice is odd'.
The event Y is 'The score on the red dice is 4'.

a Explain why the events X and Y are mutually exclusive.
b Explain why the events X and Y are not exhaustive.

16c

4 Two 'Jokers' are added to an ordinary pack of 52 playing cards.
A card is picked at random.

a Find the probability that the card chosen is a Joker.
Give your answer as a fraction in its simplest terms, a decimal and a percentage.
b Use your answers to part **a** to find the probability that the chosen card is not a Joker.
Give your answer in all three forms.

5 James deals these four cards from a pack of 20 cards labelled 1 to 20.

3 16 5 1

What is the probability that the next card dealt from the remaining pack is a prime number?
Give your answer as a percentage.

16d

6 A brown bag contains three cards marked A, B and C.
A white bag contains two cards marked X and Y.
Shayla picks a card at random from each bag.
Show all the possible outcomes using

a a two-way table **b** a tree diagram.

7 This two-way table shows the possible outcomes when Ben chooses cards from two boxes.

	1	2	3
A	(A, 1)	(A, 2)	(A, 3)
B	(B, 1)	(B, 2)	(B, 3)

Draw a tree diagram to show this set of outcomes.

16e

8 Steve was practising his basketball shooting and scored 9 times out of 32 attempts.
Estimate the probability of Steve scoring with his next shot.

9 A radio show played 24 songs one morning.
Nine of these songs were by solo female artists.
Use this information to estimate the probability of the first song played in the next day's programme being by a female solo artist.

10 A technician checked the maintenance records for a computer network.
He found that the server had crashed on 43 days over the past year.

a Use this data to estimate the probability that the server crashes on any day chosen at random.

b He was not told whether the data was for a leap year.
Explain why this does not make much difference.

16f

11 Carol tested a dice and got three 6s out of six rolls.

a Is there enough evidence to suggest that the dice is biased?
Explain your answer.

b Carol carried on testing the dice and ended up with 18 sixes in 60 rolls.
Is there now enough evidence to suggest that the dice is biased?
Explain your answer.

16g

12 Decide whether each set is a proper subset of $\Omega = \{1, 2, 3, 4, 5, 6, 7, 8, 9, 10\}$

a A = {4, 7, 9} **b** B = {0, 3, 8} **c** C = {factors of 10} **d** D = {multiples of 3}

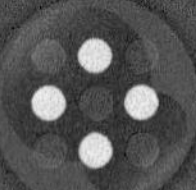

Case study 6: Crime scene investigation

Forensic experts have used mathematical techniques to solve crimes for a long time. Probability, formulae and graphs are three of the topics that they need to be familiar with.

The Weekly Bugle

Following a jewellery shop raid in Park Street, Tooting, on Saturday afternoon, in which shots were fired but nothing was stolen, a getaway car was found abandoned at the junction with Fisher Row. The Ford Fiesta had narrowly missed a cyclist after skidding 53 metres. The driver and passenger of the car were seen running from the scene. A male in his 20s suspected of being the passenger was apprehended by police officers later that day. Police investigating the incident are keen to trace the driver of the car.

Task 1

Detectives searching for clues at the jewellery shop notice that a safe has been tampered with, though not successfully unlocked. The safe has a combination lock consisting of five windows that can be any one of five colours: **Green, Red, Blue, Purple or Yellow.**

Only one combination will open the safe. How many possible combinations are there?

Task 2

Detectives at the jewellery shop notice a bullet hole in a wall, at a height of 4 m from the floor. They calculate that the equation of the path of the bullet is

$$y = x - \tfrac{1}{20}x^2,$$

where y is the height of the bullet above the floor in metres and x is the horizontal distance of the bullet from the gun in metres. It is believed that the person firing the shot was somewhere between 10 and 16 metres away from the wall when they fired the shot. Using trial-and-improvement, try to provide a more accurate estimate. Give your answer in metres to 1 decimal place.

Task 3

A DNA analysis of the abandoned car shows that two samples of DNA match the detained suspect's DNA. It is estimated that there is a one in a billion chance that a single sample of DNA will provide an exact match to another sample of DNA.

a Write the number 1 billion in standard form.

b Calculate the probability of two independent samples of DNA matching, and give your answer in standard form.

c Comment on whether or not the analysis provides evidence to support the theory that the suspect was in the car at the time of the crime.

Task 4

The length of the tyre marks left by a skidding car depends on its speed when it started skidding.
These are typical values for a tarmac road surface and dry weather conditions.

Initial speed	length of tyre marks
10 mph	1.5 metres
15 mph	3.3 metres
20 mph	5.9 metres
25 mph	9.3 metres
30 mph	13.3 metres
35 mph	18.1 metres
40 mph	23.7 metres
45 mph	30 metres

a What happens to the length of the tyre marks as the speed doubles?

b What happens as the speed trebles?

c Is the relationship between the speed and the length of the skid a linear one?

d Use the data to draw a graph of the length of the tyre marks against speed.

e Join the points with a smooth line.

f What type of relationship does the graph show?

g Extend your graph to get an approximate speed for the car in the news article.

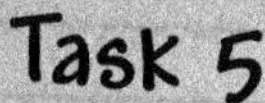

Task 5

The relationship between speed and the length of the skid is given by the equation

$$\text{speed} = \sqrt{90 \times \text{length} \times \text{friction}}$$

where friction is the drag factor of the road

a How far would the car have skidded if it had been on a concrete road surface with a drag factor of 0.9?

b How far would it have skidded if it had been on snow with a drag factor of 0.3?

- The tarmac road has a drag factor of 0.75

c Was the resident right in thinking that the car was doing at least 80 mph?

- You could use the equation to set up a spreadsheet.

d How quickly would it have been travelling if it skidded for 53 metres on a concrete road?

MyAssessment 4

These questions will test you on your knowledge of the topics in chapters 13 to 16.
They give you practice in questions that you may see in your GCSE exams.
There are 95 marks in total.

1 **a** Find the term-to-term rule of each of these linear sequences. (4 marks)

i 27, 31, 35, 39, 43, … **ii** 77, 67, 57, 47, 37, …

b For each sequence in **a**, find the position-to-term rule in words and hence give the equation for the general term. (6 marks)

c Use the general term to find the value of the 20th term of each sequence. (2 marks)

2 The amount of fuel left (in litres) in a car after n days $T(n) = 45 - 4n$.

a Write a sequence for the amount of fuel during the first week. (2 marks)

b How much fuel is left after 11 days? (2 marks)

3 A group of walkers are dropped off 50 km from their home base and walk back at an average pace of 5 km per hour.

a Generate a sequence for the number of km they are from their home base. (2 marks)

b Write a term-to-term rule and hence find the position-to-term rule. (3 marks)

c Find an expression for $T(n)$, the total number of km travelled after n hours. (3 marks)

d How long does it take the group to reach the home base? (1 mark)

4 **a** For each of these shapes determine the number of faces, vertices and edges. (3 marks)

i

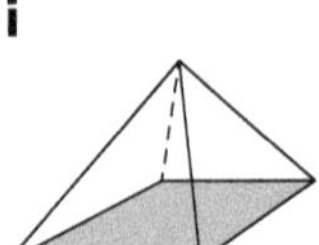

ii

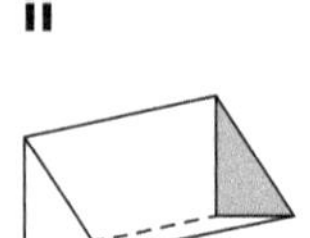

iii

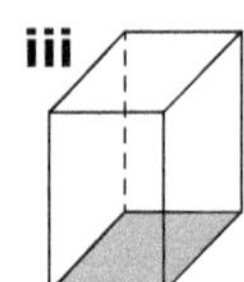

b What names are associated with each of these shapes? (3 marks)

5 **a** Copy this 8-cube shape onto squared grid paper. (2 marks)

b Draw the elevations and plan views of this solid on squared grid paper. (6 marks)

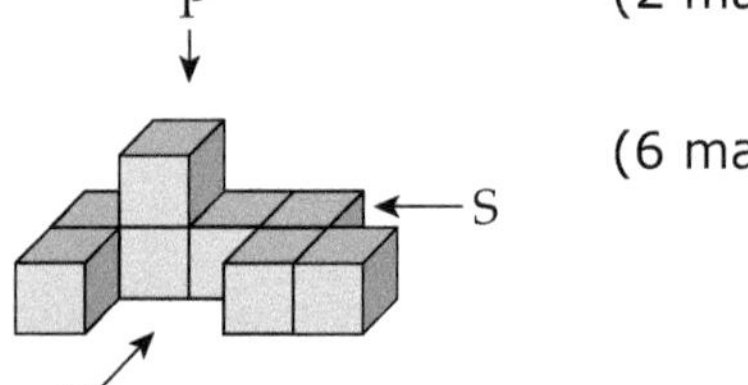

6 **a** For the shapes shown in question **4** give the number of planes of reflection symmetry. (3 marks)

b For the shapes in question **4** draw the net of each shape. (6 marks)

7 For each of these triangular prisms calculate

a the surface area (8 marks) **b** the volume. (4 marks)

i

10 cm
8 cm
15 cm
12 cm

ii

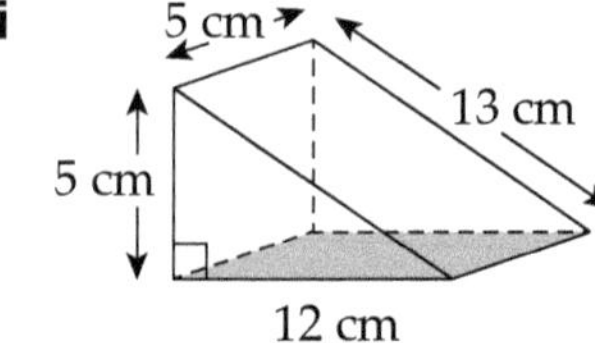

8 **a** 250 g of butter is used to make a Queen Victoria Sponge.
How much butter is needed to make 5 sponges? (2 marks)

b 18 litres of diesel costs £25.00.
How much diesel can you get for £40? (2 marks)

9 The World's land area is about 150 million km^2. Europe's land area is approximately 10 million km^2. What proportion of the World's land area is occupied by Europe? Give your answer to 1 dp. (2 marks)

10 The area occupied by the World's oceans is 360 million km^2 and that of the land is 150 million km^2. Write this as a ratio in its simplest form. (2 marks)

11 **a** A map has a scale of 1 : 10 000.
What distance does 4.6 cm on the map represent? (2 marks)

b A model plane has a wingspan of 22 cm.
If the scale is 1 : 32 what is the actual length of the wing? (2 marks)

c In a bag there are 10 red sweets and 16 yellow sweets.

i Write the ratio of yellow to red sweets. (1 mark)

ii What proportion of sweets are red? (2 marks)

12 **a** An ordinary dice is rolled. List all the outcomes. (1 mark)

b Calculate the probability of these events.
Give your answer as a fraction and as a percentage (1 dp).

i 'a prime number is rolled' (2 marks)

ii 'a score more than 3 but less than 5 is rolled'. (2 marks)

13 A three-sided coloured spinner, with equal colour areas of red, blue and green is spun twice.

a Record all the possible outcomes in a two-way table and a tree diagram. (6 marks)

b Calculate the probability of the event 'red–green' in that order. (2 marks)

c What is the probability of 'red–green' or 'green–red'? (3 marks)

14 An ordinary drawing pin is tossed 100 times and the results for pin-up and pin-down are recorded, as shown; the experiment is repeated.

	Pin-up	**Pin-down**
Experiment A	65	35
Experiment B	71	29

a Find the relative frequency for 'pin-up' in both experiments (to 1 dp). (2 marks)

b Find the relative frequency for both experiments combined. (1 mark)

c What would you do to provide a better value for the relative frequency? (1 mark)

17 Everyday maths

You are about to meet six students who have volunteered to go to Kangera in East Africa to work with a charity helping to rebuild a school. There is a lot of work to be done and your mathematical skills will be put to good use helping them.

Solving real life problems often requires you to think for yourself and to use several pieces of mathematics at once. If you are going to be successful you will need to practice your basic skills.

- **Fluency** – Can you confidently work with numbers, graphs and formulae?
- **Reasoning** – Can you use algebra to describe a situation?
- **Problem solving** – Can you cope if a problem doesn't look familiar?

Fluency

Being good at mathematics doesn't just mean being able to do sums and solve equations.

It can also mean how you think about things. Can you look at a 2D drawing and see the 3D shape?

Scale drawings, based on careful measurement and 3D reasoning, are used in architecture and engineering to plan projects. Many of the same ideas are used to produce the graphics in computer games.

Reasoning

It is often said that we are living in the information age. Newspapers, television, the internet... they are all bombarding us with statistics and they are not always right.

To make sense of all this information you need to understand the mathematics and be able to reflect on what the statements might mean.

Perhaps you will be asked to produce a report yourself explaining some statistics.

Problem solving

Scientists use mathematics to describe the world around us. By understanding how forces change on a scale model, engineers can investigate the drag on a real car.

They can then use real and mathematical models to ensure that cars are more fuel efficient.

17a The AfriLinks project

The AfriLinks project links schools in Europe with schools in Africa.

Six British students travel to Kangera in East Africa.

Greg

Ella

Imran

Maxine

Josh

Wah Wah

The local school has been destroyed in a mudslide. The students will help build a new school.

Before they depart, the students find out about the Kangera region.

1 The population is 9953.
The table shows the population by age.

Age group	0–20	21–40	41–60	60+
Number	3490	2988	2450	1025

a Round these numbers to the nearest 100.

b Draw a pie chart to display the rounded data values.
Make sure you provide a key.

2 The graph shows average temperature and rainfall over a 30-year period in the Kangera region.

a What is the range of temperatures?

b What is the range of rainfall measurements?

c What is the median average rainfall for a year?

d What is the mean average temperature for a year?

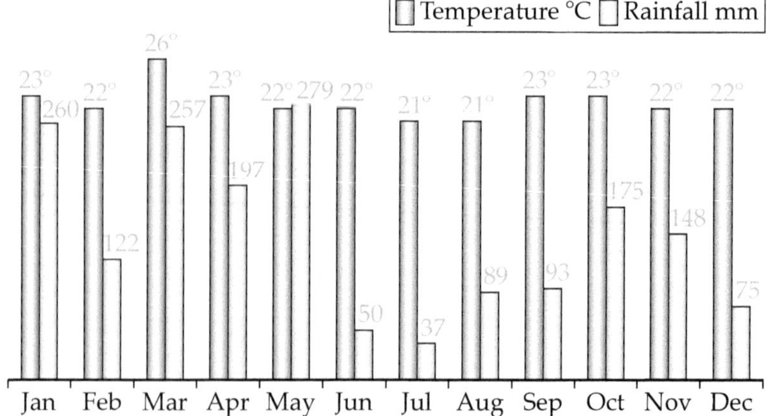

3 The table shows rainfall measurements for the first five months of this year.

Month	Jan	Feb	Mar	Apr	May
Rainfall (mm)	180	242	368	492	481

a What do you notice when you compare these figures with the average rainfall?

b Suggest why you think the school building was destroyed.

Most pupils walk to school in Kangera.
The map shows some of the pupils' journeys.

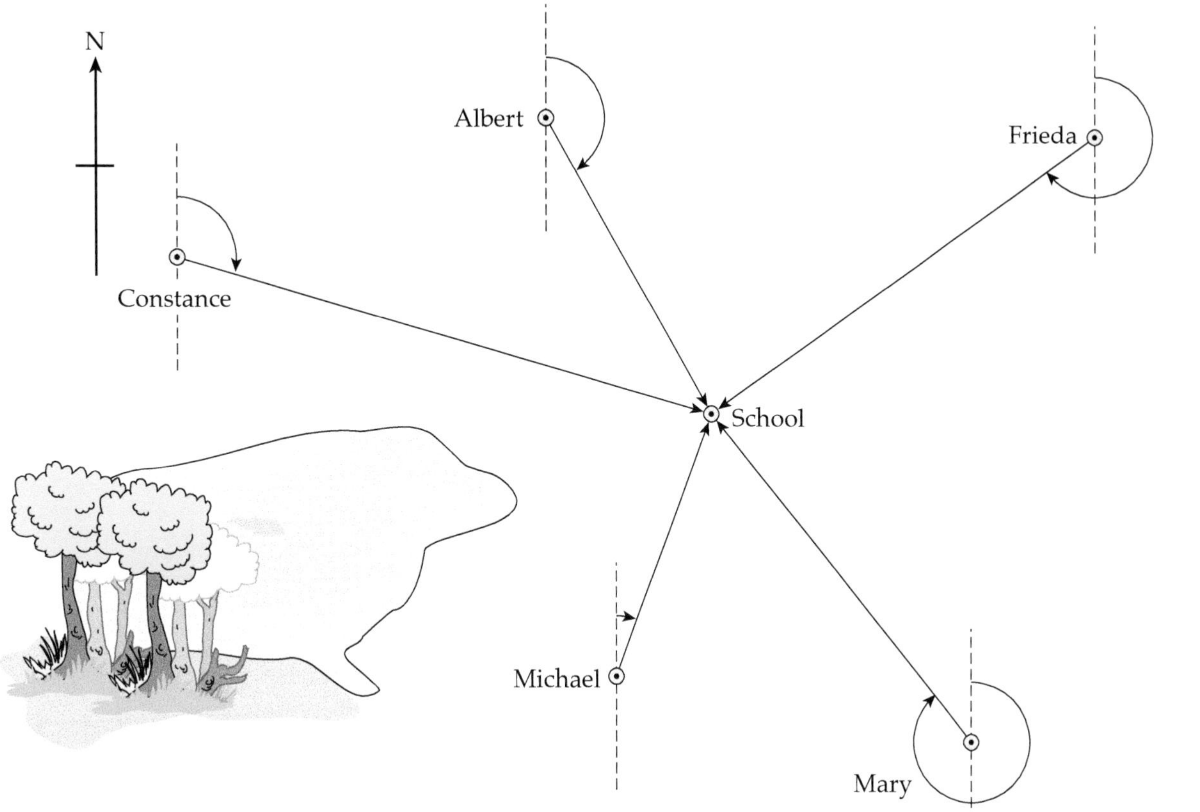

scale 2 cm : 1 km
(1 : 5000)

4 Work with a partner to copy and complete this table.

Name	Distance (km)	Bearing in ° from school to home	Bearing in ° from home to school
Albert			
Constance			
Michael			
Mary			
Frieda			

Give the directions as three-figure bearings.

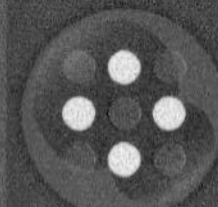

17b Building the schoolhouse

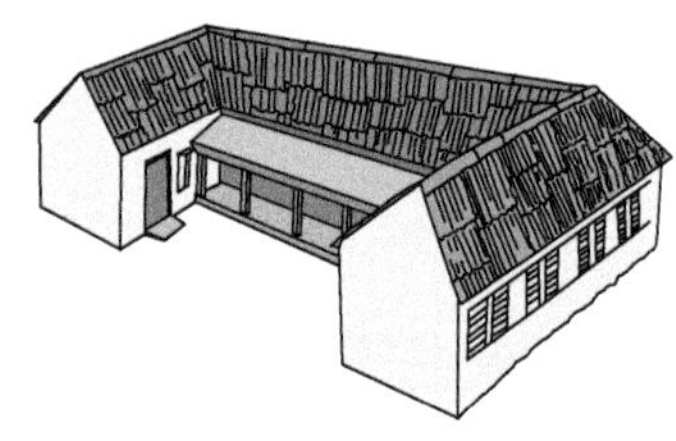

Josh and Maxine are making draft plans for the schoolhouse.

They make a rough sketch of the building and the floor space that it will need.

1 Redraw the plan neatly to a scale of 1 : 200.

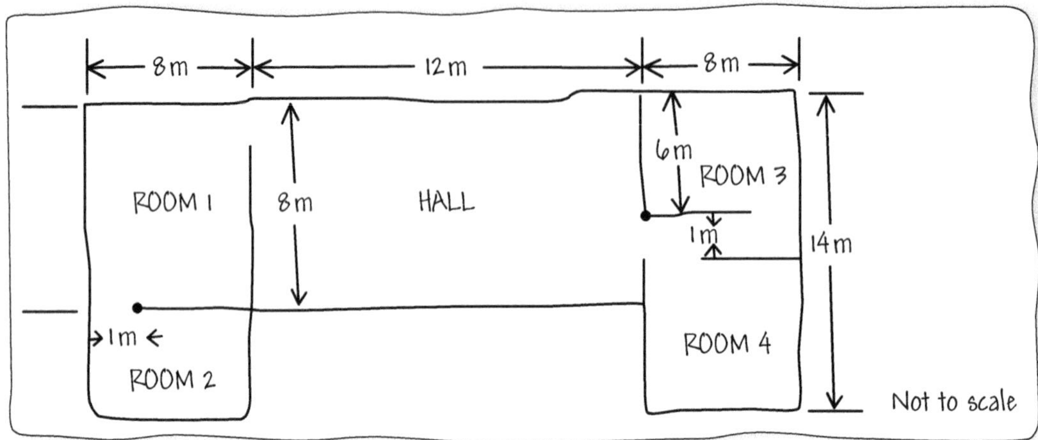

2 **a** Use your plan to calculate the total area of the floor space.

b The headteacher wants the classroom areas to have 1 m^2 for each pupil. If there are 210 pupils in the school, will there be enough floor space for them?

c As an estimate, to the nearest 10% what percentage of the total floor space is the classroom space?

3 To make sure that the building is strong, they dig foundations for all of the outer walls.
They dig trenches 80 cm deep and 40 cm wide.

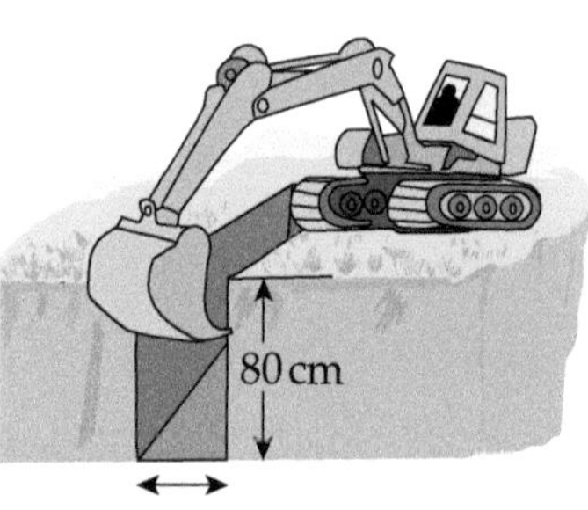

a What is the volume of soil removed from the ground? Give your answer to the nearest whole m^2.

b To make the foundations strong, concrete is poured into the trench.
The concrete costs \$45 per cubic metre plus \$15 delivery cost.
How much will the foundations cost?

4 To cope with the rain during tropical storms Josh says that the roof has to slope at an angle of 35°.

a Make a scale drawing of the roof section using a scale 1 cm : 1 m.

b Use your drawing to measure

i the height, h, of the triangular roof section (write your answer to the nearest 1 dp)

ii the length, s, of the slope.

c Use the drawing to calculate the total area of this gable wall.

The wall is made from 'Breeze-blocks' like this.

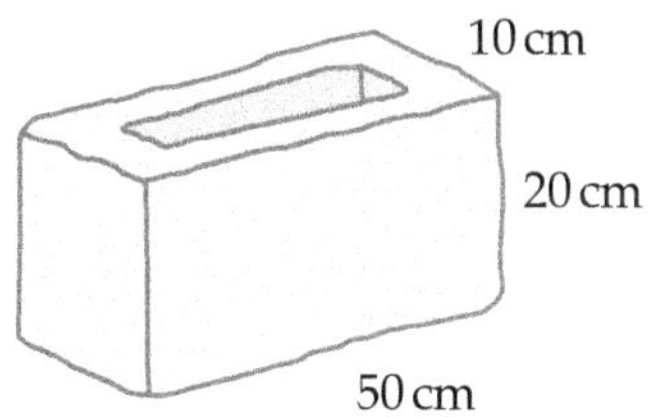

They measure 10 cm × 20 cm × 50 cm.

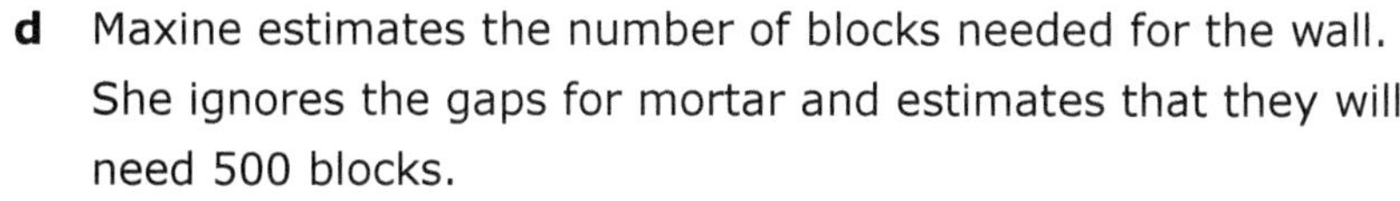

d Maxine estimates the number of blocks needed for the wall. She ignores the gaps for mortar and estimates that they will need 500 blocks.
Use your answer to part **c** to say exactly by how many blocks she is wrong. Has she overestimated or underestimated?

The blocks are held together by a cement mortar. The mortar is made by mixing sand, cement and water. Stronger mortar uses more cement, weaker mixtures use more sand.

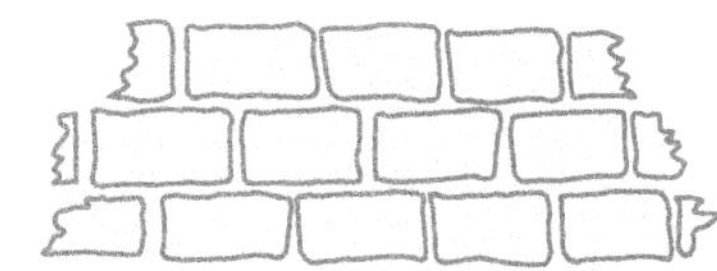

The label shows the ratio of three mixes.

5 **a** What strength of mix are each of these?

i 28 parts of sand and 8 parts of cement.

ii 24 parts of sand and 9 parts of cement.

iii 4 parts of cement and 20 parts of sand.

Mix	Sand	Cement
Strong	8	3
Medium	7	2
Weak	5	1

b Maxine uses 16 parts of sand to make a strong mix.
How many parts of cement will she need to use?

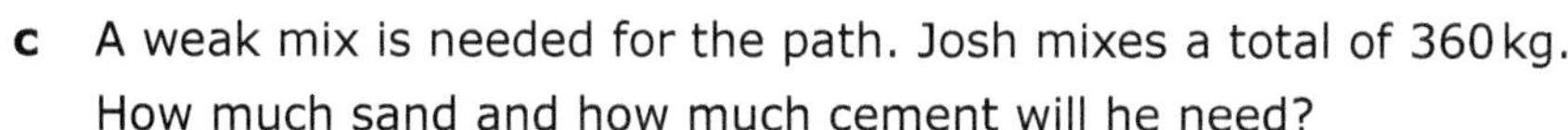

c A weak mix is needed for the path. Josh mixes a total of 360 kg.
How much sand and how much cement will he need?

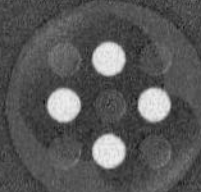

17c Laying the path

Greg and Wah Wah are laying the path.

1 a From the picture, what is the ratio of yellow to red tiles?

b They need to use 24 yellow tiles. Imran has ordered 142 red tiles.

i Will they be able to complete the path?

ii If they have not ordered enough red tiles, how many more will they need?

2 The red tiles are packed on pallets.

a Make an equation from the information below.

3 pallets and 16 tiles weigh the same as 1 pallet and 166 tiles.

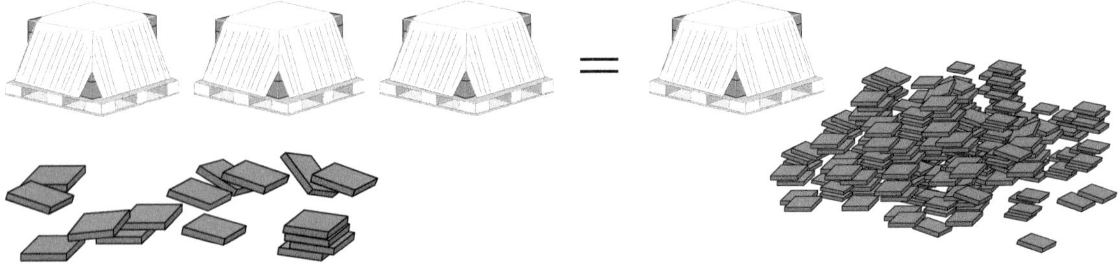

b Solve the equation to calculate the number of tiles on a pallet.

c The total weight of a full pallet and tiles is 126.5 kg.

An empty pallet weighs 14 kg. How much does each tile weigh?

3 A collection of red blocks and green slabs are laid in a pattern like this.

a How many green slabs will be laid before the pattern begins to repeat itself?

b What will be the ratio of slabs to blocks in the pattern?

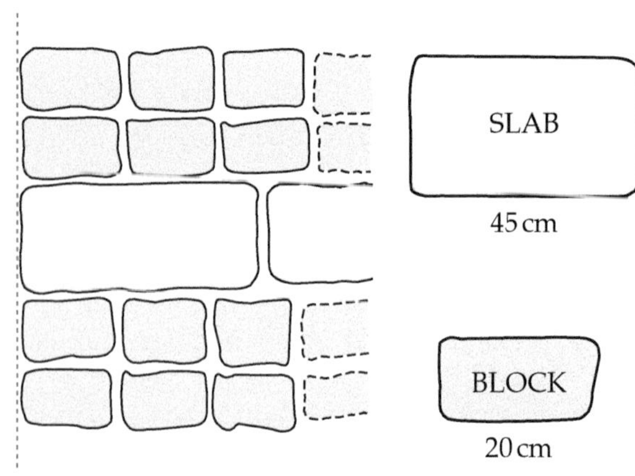

4 Wah Wah wants to make a circular flowerbed.
The flowerbed is surrounded by a path.
The outer radius of the path is 4.5 metres and the inner radius is 1.2 metres.

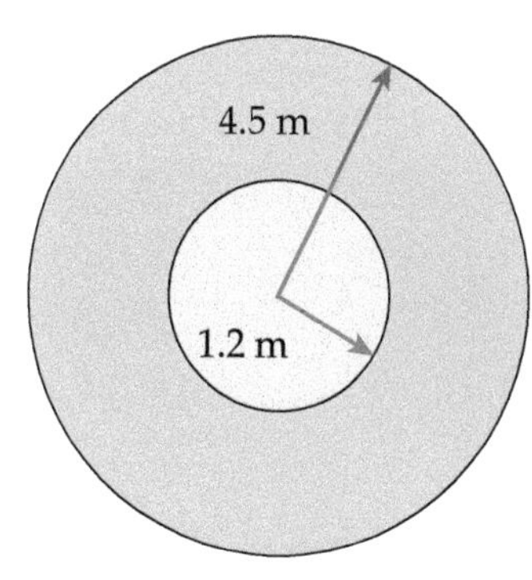

The outside and inside of the path have a plastic border.
The border is sold in 5-metre rolls.

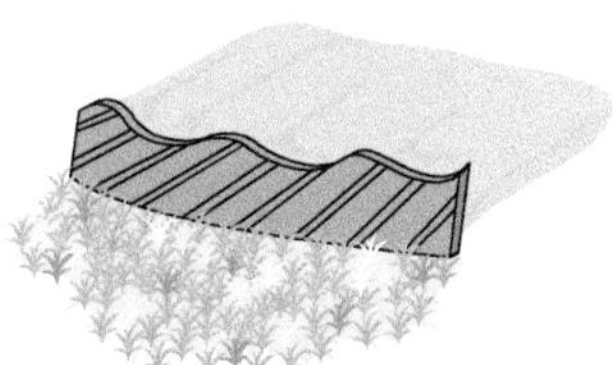

a How many rolls should Wah Wah buy?

b To the nearest 10 cm, how much border will be wasted? (use $\pi = 3.14$)

c What is the area of the path?

5 Greg wants to use different patterns in the play areas. He tries different shaped slabs to see if they will tessellate.

Here is an example of Greg's first tessellation made from rectangles in a 'herring-bone' pattern.

a Sketch two other ways of tessellating using rectangles that are twice as long as they are wide.

b Make a sketch for these shapes to show that Greg will be able to tessellate them.
Repeat the shape at least eight times for each sketch.

i 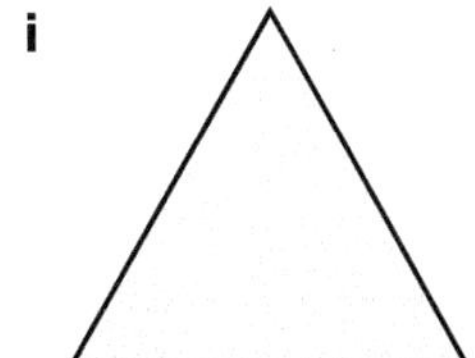

ii 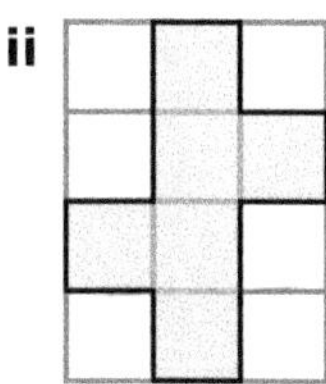

iii 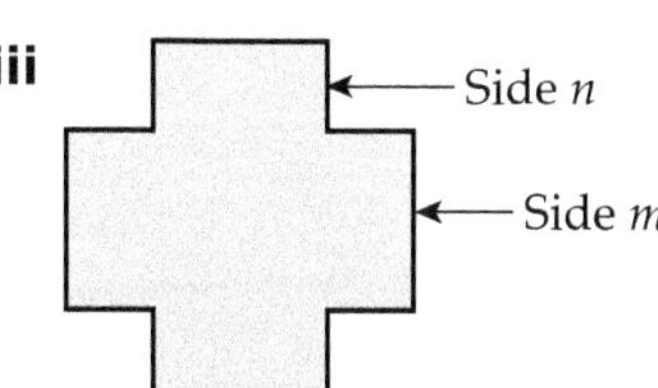

c Wah Wah starts to make a scale drawing of the cross-shaped slab. The shape will only tessellate if the sides n and m are designed in a certain ratio. What is the ratio?

d If side n is 8 cm, calculate the perimeter of the whole shape.

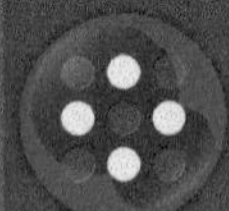

17d The basketball court

Ella, Imran and Greg are going to mark out a basketball court. Imran can only find a piece of rope, two sticks and a tape measure.

1 Write a description to explain how they should use these items to mark the circles and semicircles on the court.

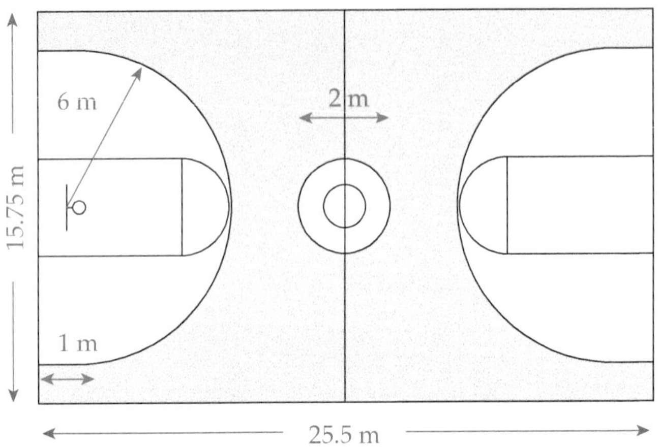

2 **a** What is the area of the court?

b There is a 'D' shape at each end of the court. The semicircle has a radius of 6 m and the straight lines are 1 m long. What is the area of the 'D' shape?

Use $\pi = 3.14$ and give the answer to three significant figures.

3 Ella marks the boundary of the court with tape. If the tape is sold in 20 m rolls, how many rolls will she need to buy? Allow an extra 10% for wastage.

4 The students have a school team. They are asked to choose their own kit from these colours.

      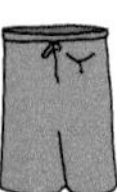

a Greg says that there are 13 different combinations of kit using these colours. Draw a probability table and hence explain why he is wrong.

b What is the probability that the kit will be all the same colour?

To celebrate the opening of the court the students arrange a basketball tournament with the locals.

The score keeper records the performance of each competitor.

Here are the statistics for six players.
The table records the number of baskets scored during their games.

Baskets scored in a game	Number of games					
	Isaac	Imran	Veronica	Jacob	Oilolay	Maxine
0	0	0	0	0	2	0
1	1	0	2	0	1	0
2	0	0	3	2	0	1
3	6	0	1	0	1	0
4	3	12	3	4	4	1
5	1	0	2	0	0	0
6	4	4	0	3	0	3
7	0	4	0	1	0	6

5 **a** Which player scored the most baskets?

b What is the modal number of baskets scored in a game?

6 **a** Which of the three averages – mode, median or mean – gives you the best idea of the players' performances? Explain your choice.

Discuss your ideas with a partner before answering this question.

b Using the mean, rank the players from strongest to weakest.

7 Based on his current average, if Isaac plays three more games predict his new total score.

8 From the table above choose a set of data which, in your opinion, can be best displayed as a pie chart.

This pie chart shows how Isaac performed.
Draw a pie chart showing your own data.

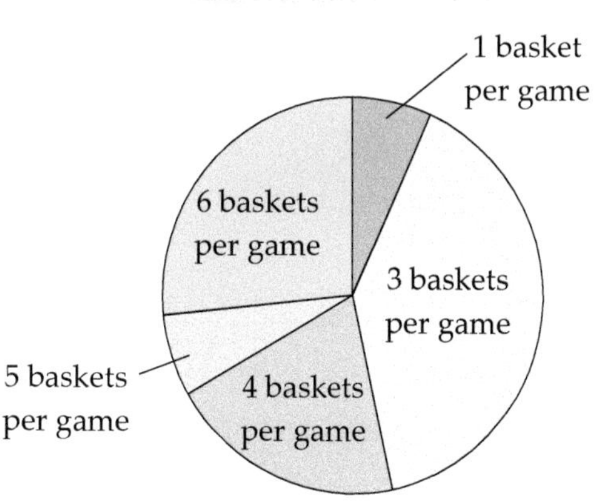

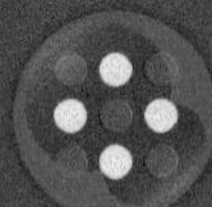

17e The school garden

The students are working in the school's garden.

They find some old gardening items in a shed.

A ruler that measures inches

A watering can that measures pints and gallons

A weighing scale that measures pounds and ounces

Some useful conversions:
1 inch ≈ 2.5 cm
1 ounce ≈ 30 g
1 pint ≈ 0.6 litres
1 lb (pound) ≈ 0.45 kg

All their instructions are in metric measures; they will have to convert units into imperial measures to complete the task!

Mix 7 kg of compost with 3 kg of sharp sand.

Mix 600 g of fertiliser with 4.5 litres of water.

Dig a trench 15 cm deep and 70 cm long.

1 **a** How many pounds of compost will be needed?

b How many pounds of sharp sand will be needed?

c How many ounces of fertiliser will be needed?

d Imran says that he needs 3.5 pints of water. Show that his answer is not right.

e Ella dug the trench 6 inches deep. Will it be the right depth?

f How many inches long is the trench?

2 Imran puts 3 bags of soil and 2 bags of compost onto the weighing scales. The total weight is 79 kg.

Imran puts 1 bag of soil and 3 bags of compost onto the weighing scales. The total weight is 52 kg.

Imran puts 2 bags of soil and 4 bags of compost onto the weighing scales. He then sits on top of the bags. The total weight is 135 kg.

a What is the weight of each bag of soil?

b What is the weight of each bag of compost?

c How much does Imran weigh?

3 Josh has some seeds to plant from a packet.

8 onion seeds	10 tomato seeds
6 pepper seeds	12 chilli seeds

Work with a partner to solve these problems.

Josh sneezes and the seeds are mixed up.
He picks up one seed at random. What is the probability it will be

a a pepper seed

b not a chilli seed?

Josh decides to plant seeds from a bigger packet instead.
The mix of seeds is in the same proportion as the smaller packet.
He plants a seed in each of 90 flowerpots.

c Estimate the likely numbers of each of the four types of plants.

4 The school is to have a goat in the garden.
Ella, Wah Wah and Maxine have to build a pen for the goat.
They have these 10 fence panels to make the four walls of the rectangular pen.

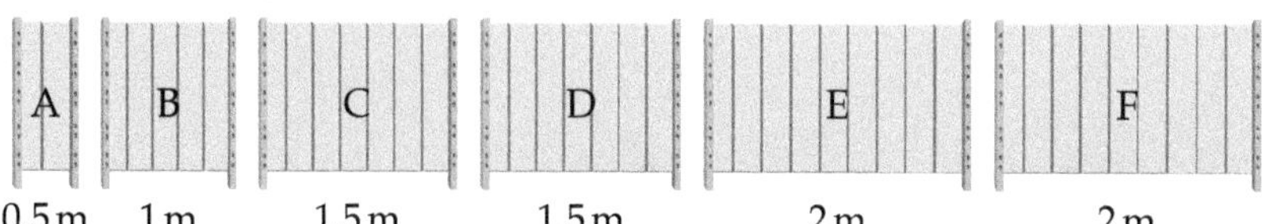

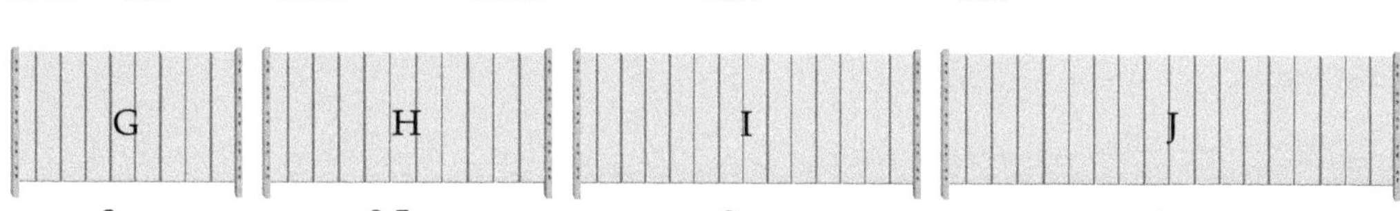

Find the biggest area that can be enclosed with these panels.
Draw a sketch to show how the panels should be fitted together.

5 Greg goes to collect the goat. He meets the three Makale brothers who are arguing about how to divide up the 11 goats given to them by their family.

- The eldest brother is given $\frac{1}{2}$ of them.
- The middle brother is given $\frac{1}{3}$ of them.
- The youngest brother is given $\frac{1}{12}$ of them.

Greg has a great idea. He lends them his goat.

a Calculate how many goats each brother receives.

b Show that Greg has his goat returned to him.

c Explain how Greg's great idea works.

Check in 1

1 **a** 20 **b** 4 **c** 7 **d** 7.5

2 3.085, 3.8, 3.825, 3.83, 3.9

MyReview 1

1 **a** 0.076 **b** 4510 **c** 1520
d 920 **e** 2.168 **f** 3.6

2 **a** 7200 **b** 8290000
c 0.041 **d** 0.000308

3 **a** 10^7 **b** 10^7 **c** 10^{16}
d 10 **e** 10^3 **f** 10^4

4 **a** 300 **b** 270 **c** 271
d 271.1 **e** 271.10 **f** 271.099

5 **a** 500 **b** 30000 **c** 6
d 0.3 **e** 0.09 **f** 1

6 **a** $2^3 \times 3^3 \times 11$ **b** $2 \times 3 \times 7 \times 13$
c $2^3 \times 5 \times 17$

7 **a**

180 240
3 5 2^2 3 2^2

b 60 **c** 720

8 **a** 800 **b** 4 **c** 30
d 320000 **e** 0.9 **f** 70

9 **a** £16
b £1.48 × 36 ≈ £1.50 × 40 ≈ £60. This is an underestimate, £60 will be enough.

Check in 2

1 **a** 30 cm, 50 cm^2 **b** 24 cm, 36 cm^2
c 36 cm, 48 cm^2

2 36 m^3

3 **a** 5500 **b** 40

MyReview 2

1 **a** 4900 mm **b** 0.87 l **c** 470 g
d 90 mm^2 **e** 30000 cm^2 **f** 3000 cm^3

2 **a** 1.8 l **b** 10.9 kg
c 144 km **d** 0.975 m

3 28 cm^2

4 8 cm

5 42.5 m^2

6 **a** 153.9 cm^2 **b** 44.0 cm

7 **a** 153.9 cm^2 **b** 50 cm

8 **a** 40 miles per hour **b** 11.3375 g/cm^3

Check in 3

1 **a** **i** $3n + 4$ **ii** 22
b **i** $3(n + 4)$ **ii** 30

2 **a** 32 **b** $13x + 7$

MyReview 3

1 **a** $3(5x - 1)$ **b** $8(a + 3b)$
c $24p(q + 2)$ **d** $7(3 - 4v)$

2 **a** $x(x + 8)$ **b** $3x(x + 3y)$
c $z(z^2 + 3z - 1)$ **d** $4y^2(4y - 3)$

3 **a** $2r$ **b** $\frac{pq}{5}$
c $3ab$ **d** $\frac{3x}{4yz}$

4 **a** $\frac{x}{52}$ **b** $\frac{a}{14}$
c $\frac{19y}{24}$ **d** $\frac{11b}{24}$

5 72

6 **a** $x = 2a + 3b$ **b** $x = \frac{y - 15}{2}$
c $x = \sqrt{\frac{5z - 4y}{3}}$

7 **a** $v = \sqrt{\frac{2E}{m}}$ **b** 7.56 **c** 22.2

8 **a** $A = 48p$ **b** 6 cm

9 **a** $A = 66 - 10x$

b

x(cm)	1	2	3	4	5	6
***A*(cm²)**	56	46	36	26	16	6

c

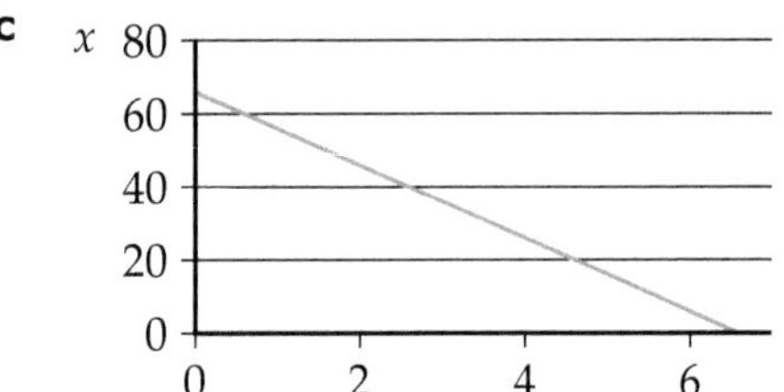

Check in 4

1 **a** 12 **b** 35 **c** 5

2 **a** £4.50 **b** 22 km **c** £23.04

3

Fraction	Decimal	Percentage
$\frac{13}{20}$	0.65	65%
$\frac{5}{8}$	0.625	62.5%
$\frac{2}{25}$	0.08	8%

4 **a** 35 **b** 24 **c** 30 **d** 48

5 **a** 5 **b** 14 **c** 126

MyReview 4

1 **a** $\frac{17}{32}$ **b** $\frac{9}{20}$ **c** $\frac{15}{28}$ **d** $\frac{61}{84}$

2 **a** $\frac{109}{28}$ **b** $\frac{23}{18}$ **c** $\frac{151}{24}$ **d** $\frac{23}{12}$

3 **a** £16.36 **b** 17.78 kg
c 14.67 m **d** 571.43 m

4 **a** $\frac{12}{7}$ **b** $\frac{21}{4}$ **c** $\frac{9}{110}$ **d** $\frac{3}{14}$

5 **a** $\frac{56}{3}$ **b** $\frac{4}{3}$

6 **a** 0.15 **b** 0.2
c 1.1 **d** 0.225

7 **a** 92 **b** 148.8

8 £928.80

9 16%

10 9.3%

11 B

Check in 5

1 **a** 63° **b** 54° **c** 49°

2 A rectangle, B rhombus,
C isosceles trapezium, D arrowhead,
E parallelogram, F kite, G square

MyReview 5

1 a = 97°, corresponding angles are equal
b = 21°, angles in triangle add up 180°
c = 114°, other two angles in triangle are 66 since it is isosceles, angles on a straight line add up 180°
d = 88° angles at top of triangle are both 46° (angles straight line, isosceles triangle)

2 a = 109° b = 144° c = 36°

3 **a** 8 **b** 8 **c** 135° **d** 45°

4 **a** yes **b** yes **c** no **d** yes

5 **a** 9 cm **b** 132° **c** 48°

6 Check student's drawings

Check in 6

1 **a** $y = 2$ **b** $y = 0$ **c** $y = 8$

2 **a** Check students' drawings
b D(3, -2)
c 48 square units

MyReview 6

1 **a**

x	0	1	2	3
y	12	8	4	0

b,c

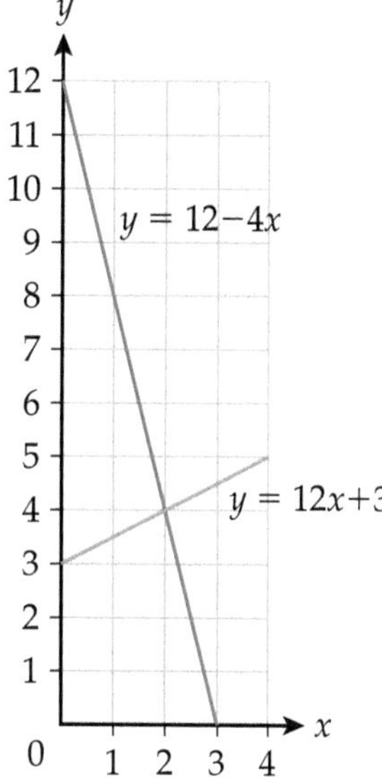

d (2, 4)

2 yes

3 **a** $y = 2x - 1$ **b** $y = 6 - x$
c $y = \frac{1}{2}x + 2$ **d** $x = 6$

4 (0, 8), (6, 0)

5 **a** $\frac{1}{2}$ **b** 14

6 **a** 11 **b** 0

7 **a** $\frac{1}{2}x^2 = \frac{1}{2} \times 4^2 = 8\text{cm}^2$

b

x	1	2	3	4	5	6	7
A	0.5	2	4.5	8	12.5	18	24.5

c

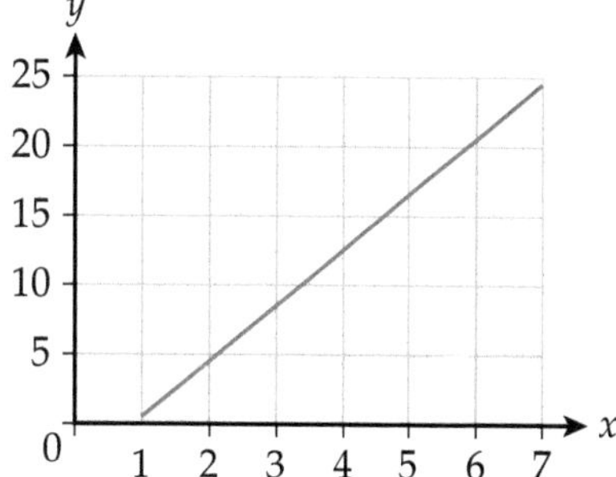

8

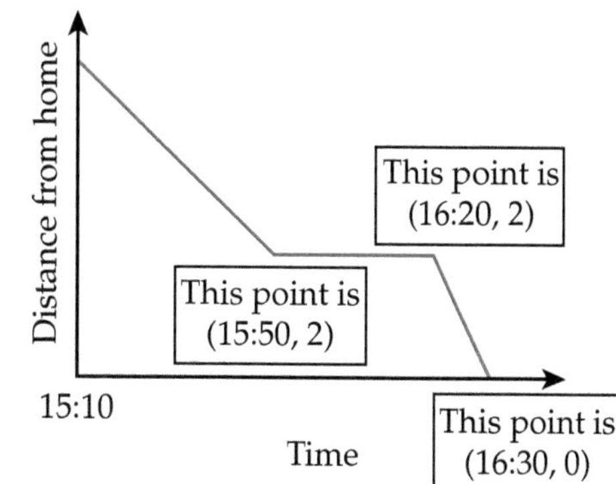

9 **a** week 4 **b** week 2

Check in 7

1 **a** 290 **b** 3.86 **c** 420 **d** 4.2

2 **a** **i** 2500 **ii** 2460 **iii** 2456.8

b **i** 900 **ii** 930 **iii** 928.3

3 **a** 9.5 **b** 6.4 **c** 18.7 **d** 8.9

e 143 **f** 1075 **g** 7406 **h** 30.8

4 **a** 15.8 **b** 16 **c** 18.9 **d** 29.4

5 **a** 28 **b** 8

MyReview 7

1 **a** 94.963 **b** 129.88

c 8.758 **d** 44.2411

2 53.37 kg

3 **a** 13.95 **b** 22.96

c 8.904 **d** 1289.28

4 £5.94

5 **a** 5 r4 **b** 54 r5

c 77 r6 **d** 52 r2

6 **a** 220 **b** 211.7

c 636.3 **d** 403.7

7 **a** 45 **b** 1.54

c 1647.09 **d** 0.62

8 **a** 20 m, 95 cm **b** 27 min, 58 s

c 5 m, 24 cm, 3 mm

d 4 weeks, 6 days, 2 hr, 8 min

9 **a** 43 **b** 50 ml

Check in 8

1 **a** 7 **b** 19.25 **c** 5.82

2

Division 1		Division 2
0	**6**	6
6 3 2 1 0 0	**5**	0 0 3
8 4 3 2	**4**	0 0 2 2 3 3 5 5 8
9 8 7 6 5 5 5 3 2	**3**	0 6 6 8 8 8 9 9
	2	3
9	**1**	

MyReview 8

1

Time	Chaffinch	Sparrow	Starling	Wood Pigeon
Morning				
Afternoon				
Evening				

2

Weight, w	Frequency
$4.5 \le w < 5$	3
$5 \le w < 5.5$	2
$5.5 \le w < 6$	4
$6 \le w < 6.5$	3
$6.5 \le w < 7$	2
$7 \le w < 7.5$	2

3 chocolate 13

strawberry 8

vanilla 10

mint choc-chip 2

other 5

4 **a** increasing **b** 1981~1991

5 **a** 30 **b** 28.9

c 29.5 **d** 4

6 **a** 19 **b** 10-14

c 10.5 **d** 10.9

7 **a**

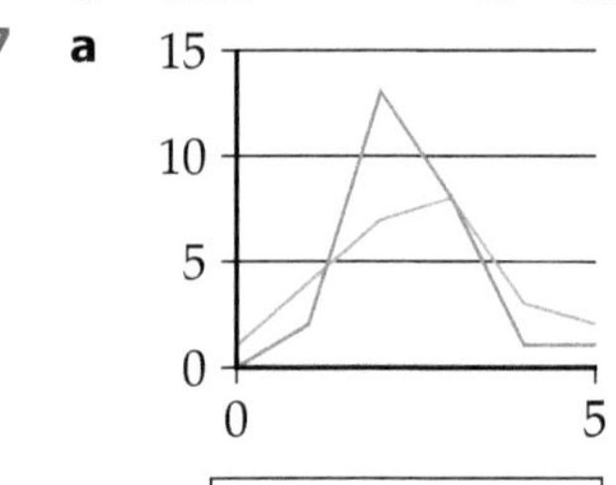

b e.g. mode for boys higher than girls, boys have bigger range

Check in 9

1

2

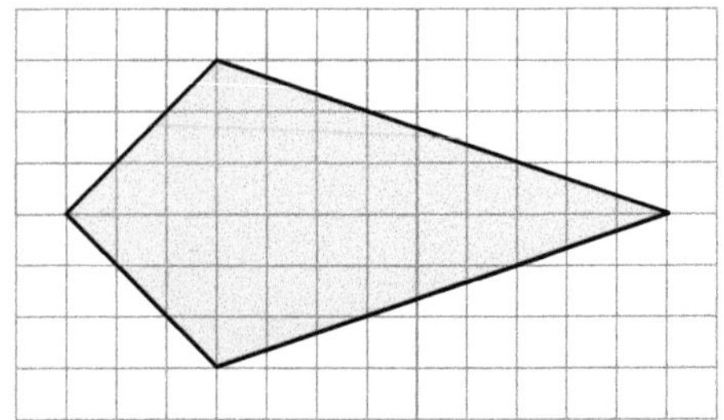

3 **a** 2.3 m **b** 4 km
c 5500 m **d** 450 000 cm
4 **a** 40° **b** 140°
c 220° **d** 320°

MyReview 9

1 **a** translation of 1 unit left and 5 units down
b rotation of 90° anti-clockwise about (0, 0)
c reflection in the y-axis / line $x = 0$

2

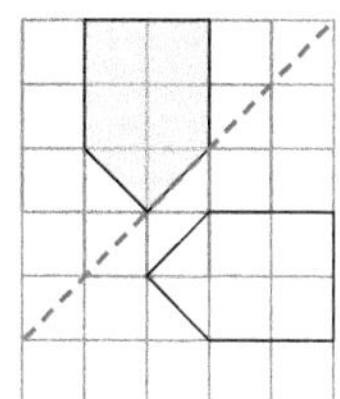

3 **a,b,c**

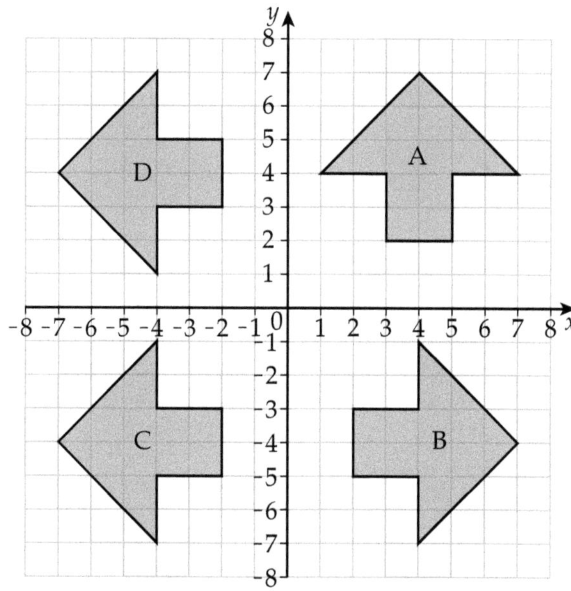

d rotation 90° anticlockwise about (0, 0)

4 scale factor 3, centre of enlargement (4, 4)

5

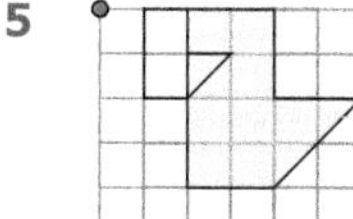

6 **a**

3 cm
2 cm
A

b 10.8 m

7 **a** 042° **b** 222°
c 294° **d** 114°

Check in 10

1 **a** $3 \times 3 \times 3 = 27$ **b** $3^2 = 9$
2 **a** 8 **b** 16 **c** 3 **d** 48
4 **a** $8x + 7y$ **b** $6x + 9y$
5 **a** 13 **b** $11x + 25$

MyReview 10

1 **a** 9 **b** $\frac{1}{2}$ **c** −2
d $-\frac{3}{2}$ **e** 3 **f** 12
g 10
2 **a** −4 **b** 6 **c** 11
d −1
3 **a** 2 **b** −12 **c** 24
d −13 **e** −3 **f** 16
4 **a** 56 **b** 4 **c** 5
5 5.8
6 **a** 2.4 **b** 2.6 **c** 4.3
7 3.6

Check in 11

1 **a** 3 **b** 5
2 **a** 1024 **b** 1024 **c** 1024
All answers $= 2^{10} = 1024$
3 16, 25, 49, 100
4 8, 27, 1000

MyReview 11

1 **a** 24 **b** 35
2 **a** 26.5 **b** 5.8
3 **a** $3a^2$ **b** $6b^3c^2$ **c** $4d^6$
d $e^{10}f^3$ **e** g^4h^6 **f** i
g j^2k^6 **h** m^8 **i** $n^{15}p^{10}$
j $2q^5$ **k** $4r^2s$
4 **a** 5 **b** 6
c 12 **d** 20
5 **a** $2\sqrt{7}$ **b** $6\sqrt{2}$
c $5\sqrt{5}$ **d** $11\sqrt{3}$
6 **a** $3\sqrt{2}$ **b** $2\sqrt{15}$
c $42\sqrt{3}$ **d** $60\sqrt{3}$
7 **a** $3^{\frac{1}{2}}$ **b** $4^{\frac{1}{3}}$
c $7^{\frac{1}{2}}$ **d** $10^{\frac{1}{3}}$
8 **a** 5 **b** 10
c 11 **d** 4
9 **a** 82000000 **b** 5420
c 0.00031 **d** 0.00000609

10 **a** 5.6×10^3 **b** 8.73×10^5
c 6.2×10^{-2} **d** 1.07×10^{-4}
e 2.45×10^6 **f** 4.2×10^{-2}

Check in 12

1 Check students' drawings
2 **a** 9 **b** 144 **c** 9 **d** 14
3 Check students' drawings

MyReview 12

1 **a** check ASA: 112°, 6.5 cm, 40°
b check SAS: 75 mm, 44°, 75 mm
or ASA: 68°, 75 mm, 44°
2 check SSS: 5.2 cm, 6.3 cm, 9.1 cm
3 **a** check circle radius of 3 cm
b check circle radius of 4 cm with the same centre as circle in part a
4 check angle of 164° bisected to two 82° angles
5 **a** 12.1 cm **b** 5.7 cm **c** 88.7 mm
6 yes
7 **a** 6.32 **b** 19.6

Check in 13

1 **a** £63 **b** £153
2 **a** 2 **b** 36

MyReview 13

1 **a** double (the previous term); 16, 32
b halve; 5, 2.5
c double then add 1; 47, 95
2 **a** add 3 **b** 13
c

Position	1	2	3	4
..3... times table	3	6	9	12
term	4	7	10	13

d multiply (the position) by 3 then add 1
e 61
3 **a** multiply (the position) by 4 then add 1
b multiply by 7 then add 11
c multiply by 0.5 then add 3
d subtract the position from 10
4 **a** 4, 10, 16, 22, 28
b -0.5, 0, 0.5, 1, 1.5
c 8, 10, 12, 14, 16
d 10, 8, 6, 4, 2
5 **a** $2n + 1$ **b** $10n - 2$
c $5n - 10$ **d** $13 - 3n$
6 **a** 73, 68, 63, 58, 53, 48, 43
b 8 **c** Tuesday
7 **a** $T(1) = 5, T(n + 1) = T(n) + 3$
b $T(1) = 16, T(n + 1) = T(n) - 5$
c $T(1) = 3, T(n + 1) = 2T(n)$
d $T(1) = 324, T(n + 1) = \frac{1}{3}T(n)$

Check in 14

1 **a** Square
b Equilateral triangle
c Regular pentagon
d Regular hexagon
e Regular octagon
2 **a** 40 cm², 16 cm³ **b** 42 cm², 18 cm³
3 **a** 405 cm² **b** 50 cm²

MyReview 14

1 **a** 8 **b** 18 **c** 12
2 **a** **b**

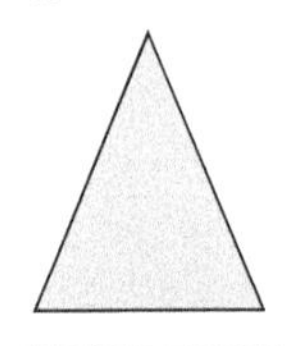

c

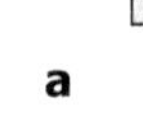

d square-based pyramid

3 **a**

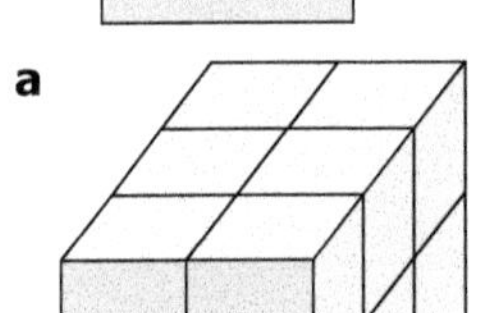

b 12

4 3
5 **a**

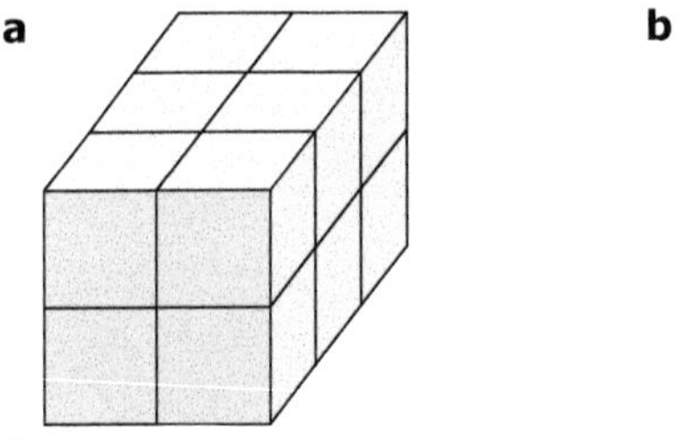

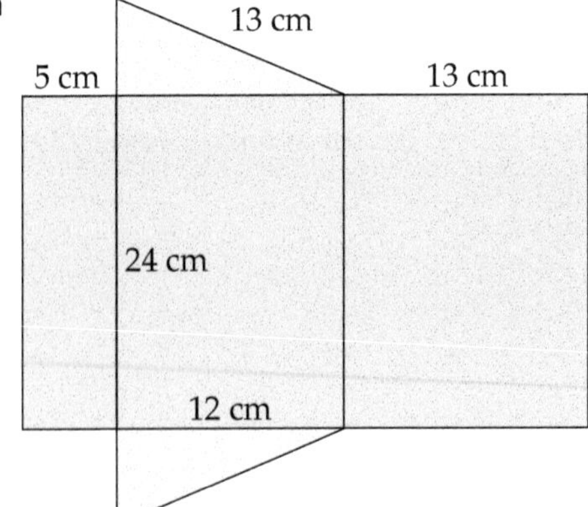

b 780 cm²
6 294 cm²
7 1728 cm³
8 80 cm³

Check in 15

1 a i $\frac{2}{5}$ ii 40%

b i $\frac{3}{4}$ ii 75%

c i $\frac{3}{8}$ ii 37.5%

d i $\frac{3}{10}$ ii 30%

2 a 1:3 b 2:3 c 1:5 d 3:1

MyReview 15

1 £1.60
2 0.315 g
3 A
4 a 2:4:3 b 2:9
5 a 350 m, 250 m b £18, £72, £27
6 a 1:2.4 b 1:1.5
7 a 600 m b 8 cm
8 $\frac{3}{7}$ or 42.9%
9 £95
10 25%
11 a 0.454 b 2.20 (2 dp)

Check in 16

1 Impossible

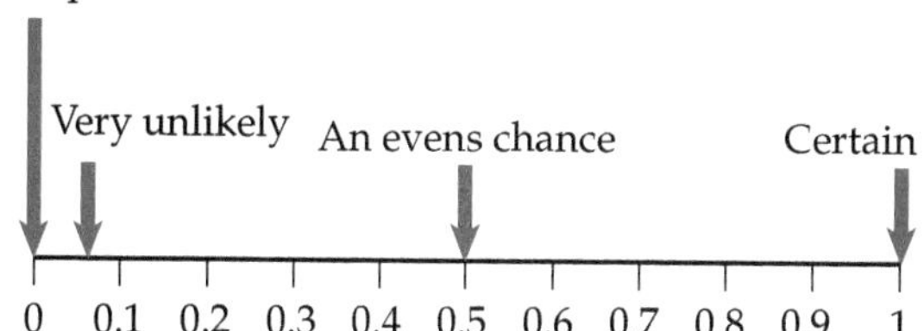

2 The probability of getting a prime number

$= \frac{\text{Number of prime scores}}{\text{Total number of scores}} = \frac{3}{6} = \frac{1}{2}$

3 a 0.6 b 0.625 c 0.45
d 0.15 e 0.27 f 0.037

MyReview 16

1 a no b no c yes

2 a $\frac{1}{2}$ b $\frac{1}{2}$ c $\frac{3}{10}$ d $\frac{2}{5}$

3 a $\frac{1}{6}$ b $\frac{1}{3}$ c $\frac{1}{3}$ d 0

4 a

×	**1**	**2**	**3**	**4**	**5**	**6**
1	1	2	3	4	5	6
2	2	4	6	8	10	12
3	3	6	9	12	15	18
4	4	8	12	16	20	24
5	5	10	15	20	25	30
6	6	12	18	24	30	36

b $\frac{13}{36}$

5

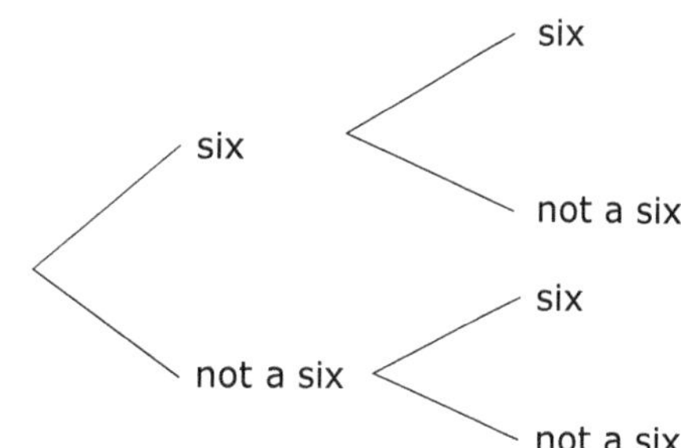

6 0.22
7 a 0.1, 0.1, 0.3, 0.3, 0.2 b all 0.2
c could be fair, results not unreasonable, not enough evidence
8 a,b

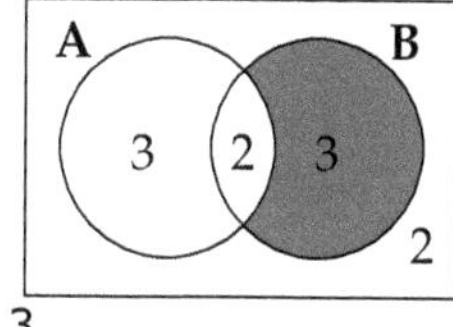

c $\frac{3}{10}$

d C is a proper subset of A.

e B and C are mutually exclusive.